HOMELAND

HOMELAND

The War on Terror in American Life

RICHARD BECK

CROWN
NEW YORK

Published in the United States by Crown, an imprint of the Crown Publishing Group, a division of Penguin Random House LLC, New York.

crownpublishing.com

CROWN and the Crown colophon are registered trademarks of Penguin Random House LLC.

Portions of this work were originally published in *n+1*.

Library of Congress Cataloging-in-Publication Data
Names: Beck, Richard, 1986– author.
Title: Homeland: the war on terror in American life / by Richard Beck.
Description: First edition. | New York: Crown, [2024] | Includes bibliographical references and index.
Identifiers: LCCN 2023058923 (print) | LCCN 2023058924 (ebook) |
ISBN 9780593240229 (hardback) | ISBN 9780593240236 (ebook)
Subjects: LCSH: War on Terrorism, 2001–2009. | United States—Social life and customs—21st century.
Classification: LCC HV6432.7 .B385 2024 (print) | LCC HV6432.7 (ebook) |
DDC 973.931—dc23/eng/20240416
LC record available at https://lccn.loc.gov/2023058923
LC ebook record available at https://lccn.loc.gov/2023058924

Hardcover ISBN: 978-0-593-24022-9
Ebook ISBN: 978-0-593-24023-6

Printed in the United States of America on acid-free paper

Editor: Kevin Doughten
Editorial assistant: Amy Li
Production editor: Liana Faughnan
Production manager: Dustin Amick
Proofreader: Carol McKenna
Indexer: Eldes Tran
Publicist: Stacey Stein
Marketer: Mason Eng

9 8 7 6 5 4 3 2 1

First Edition

Book design by Andrea Lau
Jacket design by Tyler Comrie

For Kelley Deane

Remembering at once gives way to acting out. . . . The patient brings out of the armory of the past the weapons with which he defends himself.
      —Sigmund Freud, "Remembering, Repeating, and
                                                Working-Through"

Never forget.
      —popular injunction regarding September 11

CONTENTS

Introduction   For the Beauty of the Earth   *xi*

PART I   A Sense of War

Chapter 1   No Time Zones   3
Chapter 2   Iron Men   42
Chapter 3   I Think Security Is Very Tight, but I'm Still
             Concerned   79

PART II   Islam Is Peace

Chapter 4   Keep Quiet and Stay in Your Home   125
Chapter 5   I Do Break Regulations   160
Chapter 6   Geronimo   198

PART III   Growth, Stagnation, Surplus

Chapter 7   Our Little, Imaginary World   237
Chapter 8   The Sign of Autumn   265
Chapter 9   Borders, Squares, Real Estate, Streets   300

PART IV   Impunity Culture

Chapter 10   The Iraq War Debate Did Not Take Place   343
Chapter 11   Mom, Can You Not Read over My Shoulder?   381
Chapter 12   They Do This All the Time   418

Epilogue   Reality Principle   462

             Acknowledgments   501
             Notes   503
             Index   547

For the Beauty of the Earth

The stars above give thanks to thee; / All praise to those who live in peace.
—Paul Winter, "Canticle of Brother Sun," *Missa Gaia*

I was fourteen years old on September 11, and for most of that day I knew very little about what was going on. I saw the second plane hit the World Trade Center on live TV at 9:03 a.m., at the end of a first-period high school class with a lazy teacher who sometimes liked to give up on the day's lesson plan and turn on *SportsCenter* highlights instead. The bell rang for second period a few minutes later, and shortly after that the school's administrators decided that the TVs would stay off and the teachers remain silent about what was happening. Lessons, tests, presentations, and readings all went on as normal. Left to their own devices, students spent the rest of the day trading rumors in between classes and at lunch. By the time I walked through the front door of my family's home in a Philadelphia suburb that afternoon, I thought the Pentagon, White House, Capitol Building, and Washington Monument had all been destroyed.

A few minutes watching ABC News clarified things, but I had

trouble knowing how I was supposed to feel. We had one family friend who worked at the World Trade Center. My parents were quite scared for him during the morning, but it turned out he had been sent to California on a last-minute business trip the day before—he was safe. It was a dramatic story, but I had never met him, so I couldn't connect the memory of a face or voice to his close call. As for the images on the screen, they looked unreal. They looked like scenes from a disaster movie, not something that could actually be happening in the world I inhabited. I don't believe that seeing fake violence on screens desensitizes people to experiencing real violence in life, but I know for certain that seeing fake violence on screens desensitizes people to seeing real violence on screens.

My family and I watched until about midnight. I remember that at one point my dad got excited when it seemed as though retaliatory strikes were already under way somewhere, but those turned out to be part of an ongoing civil war that none of us knew anything about. We spent a lot of time looking at aerial shots of the dust cloud that had swallowed up lower Manhattan. Then, after the sun went down, we watched ABC News correspondents talk among themselves while footage from earlier in the day played in an endless loop. Then we all went to sleep.

A week or so later, teachers and parents began to discuss whether we would still make our planned trip to New York in early October. I was a tenor in my suburban high school's audition choir, and each year the choir sang in the Earth Mass at St. John the Divine, an Episcopal cathedral in the Morningside Heights neighborhood of upper Manhattan. St. John the Divine is made of granite and limestone, and its design, a mix of Gothic Revival and Romanesque, effectively communicates the heaviness of its materials. It is one of the largest cathedrals in the world. Inside, it is gray and dim, overwhelming, a little inelegant. The nave's thick pillars stretch up into the cathedral's cool, damp air, and if the sun comes out in the afternoon, it shines through the stained-glass rose window that sits over the main entrance, turning the air inside the color of violets. It sits far uptown, seven miles away from Ground Zero, but parents worried about allowing their kids to make the trip—who could be certain the city was safe? The weekend's plans would have us trekking through Penn Station, riding on the subway, and seeing a show near Times Square, all plausible targets for another attack. The choir director and a group of parents met a few times and made a decision: The trip would go on as planned, with the caveat that any parents who wanted to keep their child at home that weekend should feel free to do so. Mom and Dad told me I could go, so long as I didn't try to get near Ground Zero. This instruction confused me. It hadn't quite occurred to me that Ground Zero was an actual place, nor that I could just walk up to it if I wanted to. I promised that I would stay uptown.

We left early on a Saturday morning, the students and the choir director and half a dozen parent-chaperones all meeting at the modest commuter rail station in Swarthmore, a fieldstone building with a canopy over the platform and a liberal arts college sitting up the hill. The clattering little SEPTA train that shuttled us into Philadelphia's 30th St. Station was familiar to me, but I had never been on the Amtrak before. The seats were cushioned, the lights were soft, and whatever noise the train made churning out of Philadelphia and into New Jersey barely penetrated the hushed interior. I heard there was a dining car toward the front of the train and got out of my seat. On my way, I paused in the vestibules that separated the cars, listening to the racket and feeling cool air fly in through the gaps. My parents were getting farther away with each rhythmic thump of the tracks. I bought a muffin and ate it standing up before heading back to my seat.

There were about sixty of us in the choir. Heading uptown on the subway, we hugged our sleeping bags and swayed back and forth, reached out too late for poles as the train lurched forward or shuddered to a halt, stumbled and fell into one another, annoyed the locals with our hysterics. We got out at 110th Street and walked east, passing within a few blocks of a Greek restaurant where I'd often come for lunch as a freelancer fifteen years later. We filed back along the south side of the cathedral until a small stairway led us down underneath an enormous, crude flying buttress. The basement looked just like a school, with linoleum flooring, clanking radiators, and tumbling mats in the gymnasium for us to sleep on. We piled our things into a storage closet. It was eleven in the morning. The choir director told us to be back upstairs for rehearsal at three in the afternoon. We could spend the next few hours however we liked, and the chaperones would not be coming with us; the adults needed a break.

I had never been so unsupervised in my life. I was aware of this at the time, and the feeling was exhilarating. Adults think that children want to be left alone so that they can get away with doing things they aren't supposed to, but that's not unique to children—adults like large crowds and business trips and late nights for the same reason. Teenagers also want to be left alone so that they can move through the world without an intermediary guiding and interpreting and nudging them at every turn. I left the cathedral with three friends. We hadn't known this time would be given to us. What would we do with it, and where would we go? We would decide for ourselves.

We walked down Broadway—twenty, thirty blocks. We bought lunch at a corner deli and ate our bagel sandwiches while sitting on a bench. We saw the diner from *Seinfeld.* I loved the people who walked by and didn't stop to notice the diner, didn't find it amazing to share the neighborhood with a building that appeared in reruns on every television in the country five nights a week. We came across a bookstore that wasn't part of a national chain. It doubled as a campus bookstore for students at Columbia University, and the whole sprawling second floor had been organized by college course. Here were the books you read in a course on the eighteenth-century novel. Here were books on computer science. Here were books explaining something called existentialism. I had never seen anything like them. Their covers were plain. They looked meant to be read rather than displayed on a shelf. With half an hour left before rehearsal, we walked over to Riverside Drive. Looking west, we could see Riverside Park and the West Side Highway below, with the Hudson River flowing by in the background, though I didn't know the names of the highway or the river at the time. Turning around and looking east, we admired an apartment building with wrought-iron gates over the first-floor windows and stone carvings of vines and flowers ornamenting the entrance. We didn't know anything about architecture, either. We didn't know what we were admiring. We were admiring our own independence.

In Henry James's *The Ambassadors,* Strether, the editor of a small magazine in Massachusetts, leaves America for the first time. He goes to Paris to help a widow with her delinquent son, and once he arrives, he has a few days to kill before he needs to get down to work. One morning after breakfast, he and an acquaintance decide to see the city on foot. "They walked, wandered, wondered and, a little, lost themselves," James writes. "Strether hadn't had for years so rich a consciousness of time—a bag of gold into which he constantly dipped for a handful." That's what the afternoon felt like for me. It was my first conscious experience of freedom.

In a cathedral, the choir goes in a part of the church that is also called the choir: two long, multitiered rows of seats that face each other and sit between the transept (the arms of the cross shape) and the altar. The Earth Mass required more singers than could fit in the choir, so half of them filled up the space in between the seats. From back to front, sopranos and altos sat on sloping risers, singing straight out into the nave. The musicians were in front of them, a group of about a dozen, with a cello, oboe, guitar, piano, bass, and percussion instruments of all kinds. Tenor and bass singers sat in the choir. The choir singers were amateurs, groups from different colleges and high schools, but the soloists and the musicians who played instruments were all hired professionals. I had never played with pros before, and all through rehearsal I watched them with a hungry fascination. At school rehearsals, any attempt to make music had to be preceded by the director's efforts to make us quiet down. But these musicians were attentive and relaxed. They used pencils to annotate their scores in between takes. They were neither visibly impressed by the venue nor eager for rehearsal to end. They all had different postures, different ways of holding themselves and their instruments, that suited them. I wondered about where they went after rehearsal, where they lived and what that was like.

After rehearsal, we had greasy, delicious pizza across the street, yanking slices from pies that left little room on the table for our plates and elbows, drinking soda out of big cups made of clear red textured plastic. We took the subway to midtown and saw a show (I think it involved puppets). We returned to our basement gymnasium and got into our sleeping bags, the girls at one end of the basketball court and the boys at the other, with adults arrayed across the middle of the room to prevent any commingling. I lay on my tumbling mat and looked at the ceiling, listening to chaperones shush my friends.

The next morning, with an hour to go before the Mass began, I ran around to the cathedral's front and crossed the street to a bakery that sat on the opposite corner. Hundreds of people were queued up along Amsterdam Avenue waiting for the church doors to open, with vendors walking up and down the line selling flowers. Dogs tugged at their leashes, and pet birds flapped their wings inside cages; the Earth Mass celebrates the Feast Day of St. Francis, and people are invited to bring their animals into the church, where they receive a blessing at the end of the service. Steam rose out of paper coffee cups and bits of pastry tumbled to the ground, giving the dogs something else to sniff. The air was clear and a little cool. I wore a yellow shirt, khaki pants, and a tie, as though I were dressed for a homecoming dance.

Missa Gaia, the music that accompanies the service, is a work of hippie spiritualism composed by Paul Winter. Some of its themes and motifs are based on the sounds of the natural world. The "Kyrie" takes its melody from the howl of an Alaskan tundra wolf, a high, keening tone that descends just a bit more than an octave over four notes. Inside the cathedral, the "Kyrie" is introduced by a recording of an actual wolf's cry that plays over the PA system. Every year, dozens of dogs start barking when they hear the wolf. Other parts of the Mass take inspiration from different kinds of church music—Renaissance polyphony, gospel, stately hymns from the Anglican songbook—and then embellish those source materials with "world music" flourishes (especially West African drumming). It is an endearing and possibly naive ode to the peaceful coexistence of living things, well suited to its occasion, and performing it with so many other musicians felt incredible. I didn't feel like a performer, someone trying to get a certain reaction out of people. I felt like someone helping out at a nineteenth-century barn raising, like I was helping to build a large and beautiful sound. The sound we made hovered and rippled around us, like sunlight seen from the bottom of a pool.

The Mass reached its climax after Communion, with a procession meant to enact the peaceful coexistence that our music had been praising for more than an hour. Congregants were told to refrain from flash photography, and then a line of animal handlers in robes began to walk down the aisle toward the altar. This was the "Procession of the Animals," and the creatures were ordered from "small" to "great." The man at the head of the silent parade held aloft a small tank with green water sloshing around inside: algae. He was followed by someone with a mouse on a pillow, then chickens, geese, a turkey, a pig, a macaw on a woman's shoulder, a miniature pony, a kangaroo, a camel, and a tortoise being pushed along on a wheeled platform, its shell garlanded with flowers. Finally, to everyone's astonishment, an elephant came through the doors and walked up the aisle. People did not refrain from flash photography. The elephant was curious about its new environment, turning its head back and forth to consider all the people staring back at it. Each animal received a blessing as it arrived at the altar, and then all the handlers and their creatures turned around and faced the congregants.

The Mass was almost over. Soon we would sing a reprise of "Canticle of Brother Sun," which included woo-woo choreography (reaching out, swaying back and forth, holding hands). Then we would follow the clergy and the animals back up the aisle and outside, singing the whole way as parents jockeyed for position with their cameras. Before the music could begin, however, some priest or church official came to the microphone and said there was an important announcement. They had received news that earlier today—certainly within the past couple of hours, and potentially while the Mass itself was taking place—America had launched its first air strikes in Afghanistan. Bombing had been reported in Kabul (the country's capital), Kandahar, and Jalalabad. President Bush hadn't yet gone on television to give a speech, but a ground invasion was clearly soon to follow. I don't remember the specific wording of the announcement, whether there was any injunction to pray for the safety of our troops or the wisdom of our leaders. The priest or church official stepped away from the microphone, and the concluding prayers resumed.

I didn't have much of a reaction to the news. It didn't make me scared for the people close to me. I was from a reasonably affluent suburb, and the adults in my life were white-collar professionals, people with college and graduate degrees. They were not going to Afghanistan to hunt for Osama bin Laden. Nor did the news surprise me. As soon as the government identified bin Laden as the man behind the attacks, it was obvious that the military would be sent to get him. My parents didn't like George W. Bush, but they didn't have a problem with going after bin Laden, and it would be several years before I had a politics of my own. But as we began to sing the concluding hymn, I saw that people around me were having a different reaction. Some older members of the choir had been overcome with emotion. Two women in the alto section weren't singing at all. They were wrapped up in a hug and appeared to be holding on tight, their faces buried in each other's shoulders. A baritone standing in the choir that faced mine across the aisle, a man who had sung the whole Mass to that point without any visible display of feeling, was now singing with his eyes shut and a look of grief on his face. He threw his whole body into the choreography. He sang, "For the beauty of the Earth, / sing, oh sing today," and he raised and lowered his arms with devoted concentration. He sang, "Nature human and divine, / all around us lies," and swayed back and forth, his hands grasping those of the people on either side of him.

What was going on? What were these people feeling, and why couldn't I feel it, too? There was now something other than the shimmering pool of sound hovering above us, and I couldn't see or touch or understand it. I wanted to stop singing, for reasons I could not explain to myself. Looking back now, I think I wanted to stop singing so that I could walk down to the two embracing women and ask them what was happening, what it was I didn't know. But I didn't ask anyone anything, and I didn't stop singing. The clergy gathered up their various accessories and descended from the altar, and the choir shuffled out behind them. I ran into two alto friends as the lines of singers merged at the bottom of the altar steps, and we made our way up the aisle. An older woman walked nearby. She looked up at the rose window over the main entrance, and tears streamed down her face as she sang. I slowed my pace to match hers. I watched her intently, all the way up the aisle and out of the cathedral, where she disappeared into a swirling crowd of people and animals. Proud parents called for their children and posed for photographs, and dogs went cheerfully insane as they made dozens of new friends at once. It was a cool October afternoon. The sun was out, and a street fair was under way.

· · ·

The war on terror began with the most visually spectacular attack in the history of armed conflict. There is a good chance that anyone who is reading this book can close their eyes and immediately summon images of the flaming towers, the blue sky behind them, and the smoldering pile of steel and ash that remained after they fell. In the years that followed, however, the war became difficult to see.

What is the war on terror, anyway? Is "war" the right word? (For several years, its official government name was "overseas contingency operations.") It is a strange war that can dominate politics for more than fifteen years without ever being formally declared. The closest the Bush administration got was Proclamation 7463, issued on September 14, 2001, in which the president announced that "a national emergency" was in effect, "by reason of the terrorist attacks" at the World Trade Center and the Pentagon.[1] The U.S. Department of Defense says that it will stop awarding its Global War on Terrorism Service Medal, a gold medallion dangling from a blue, yellow, and red ribbon, once this national emergency comes to its official end.[2] As of this writing in 2023, it is still in effect.

Where is the war on terror? The closest Congress got to a formal declaration of hostilities was its Authorization for Use of Military Force (AUMF), passed exactly one week after September 11. The

AUMF gave the president permission to strike against "those nations, organizations, or persons" that had "planned, authorized, committed, or aided" the attacks on New York and Washington, but it did not specify who or what any of those nations, organizations, or persons were. Instead, Congress said that the president could determine who was responsible, and who would have to be punished, all on his own.[3] Since the passage of the AUMF, the U.S. military has engaged in combat in twelve countries. It has also conducted special operations in four, drone strikes in seven, counterterrorism training exercises in forty-one, and other forms of police and border force training in nearly eighty.[4] A war launched to avenge an attack committed by a couple dozen people with less than half a million dollars in funding quickly came to span much of the globe.

Who is the enemy? What is a terrorist? It isn't just Osama bin Laden and al-Qaeda. Osama bin Laden was at the top of the FBI's Ten Most Wanted Fugitives list for almost a decade (the wanted poster helpfully specified that he was to be "considered armed and extremely dangerous"), but the U.S. military did not call its troops and drones back to the homeland after killing him in May 2011.[5] It isn't Muslims, either, at least not exactly. Though it was Muslim extremists who attacked the United States, President Bush was quick to assure the world that America's quarrel was only with *some* of the world's 1.3 billion practitioners of Islam. In the midst of launching a series of military campaigns that would result in some 900,000 deaths by 2021, including the deaths of nearly 400,000 civilians, the overwhelming majority of whom were Muslim,[6] Bush made the time to give a speech at the Islamic Center of Washington, D.C., in which he told American Muslims that he bore them nothing but goodwill. He said, "Islam is peace."[7] Defining the enemy in terms of particular extremist groups doesn't clarify matters, either. Since 2001, the U.S. military has engaged in combat with an estimated twenty affiliates of al-Qaeda, nineteen affiliates of ISIL, the Taliban in Afghanistan and Pakistan, more than fifty other extremist groups that still exist as of 2023, and dozens more that don't. And that's not to mention the "lone wolf" or "homegrown" extremists who have occasionally carried out attacks in the United States and other parts of the affluent West. They're the enemy, too.

Who fought for America in the war on terror? Not soldiers as one traditionally understands the term, or not only soldiers. Along with enlisted men and women, members of the National Guard, Special Forces operating under the authority of the CIA, mobilized reservists, and handfuls of soldiers from dozens of other countries (some of whom weren't allowed to actually engage in combat), thousands of private contractors took to the global battlefield. For a majority of America's occupations of Iraq and Afghanistan, private contractors outnumbered the American troops stationed there, helping defense companies to outperform the rest of the stock market by more than 50 percent between 2001 and 2021.[8] This made it harder to know who, exactly, was doing the fighting, and it also made it harder to know whose lives were being extinguished to protect the homeland. When enlisted troops started dying in Afghanistan and Iraq, a ban first instituted by George H. W. Bush in 1991 made it illegal for news organizations to photograph their flag-draped coffins returning home.[9] When contractors started dying in those same countries, the Department of Defense simply declined to count the bodies; the government does not track casualty numbers for contractors. It wasn't until 2020 that researchers at Brown and Boston Universities announced that America's wars in the Middle East had killed more contractors than troops, a finding that had no effect on public policy.[10] "You don't see yellow ribbons around trees for contractors," one researcher said.[11]

The war's steady drumbeat of drone strikes, special ops raids, and security alerts has also been punctuated by regular presidential assurances that the whole project was on the verge of winding down. The first of these was delivered in May 2003, when President Bush stood on the deck of the USS *Abraham Lincoln* in front of a banner reading MISSION ACCOMPLISHED. "Major combat operations in Iraq have ended," he said. Over the next four years, Iraq collapsed into a civil war, and Bush had to send in an additional 20,000 troops to supplement the 130,000 who were already stationed there. Bush was then replaced in 2008 by a president who won election in no small part thanks to his promises to end what even then were being called the "forever wars," to wind down the occupation of Iraq and win the war in Afghanistan. President Barack Obama brought most of America's soldiers home from Iraq, but he replicated Bush's Iraq surge with a surge of his own in Afghanistan and then broke a 2012 campaign pledge to end that occupation by the middle of his second term. Obama also carried out ten times as many drone strikes as his predecessor. Under the war on terror's second commander in chief, drones bombed Yemen, Somalia, and Pakistan more than 550 times, killing as many as eight hundred civilians.[12] Donald Trump followed Obama, assuring Americans that "the stupid endless wars, for us, are ending!" even as he slightly increased the total number of American soldiers deployed abroad.[13] In 2021, President Joe Biden finally removed U.S. troops from Afghanistan as the Taliban seized Kabul, sealing America's defeat. Nevertheless, Biden renewed the state of emergency for yet another year in September 2023. Just as the government never formally declared the war's beginning, it is possible and even likely that it will never declare the war's end.

The complexities involved in fixing the war on terror in time and space also make it harder to define the war's effects on those who live in the country that has waged it. Floating in and out of awareness, with all of the military violence occurring overseas even as the threat of sudden mass death permeated life at home, the war on terror was simultaneously everywhere and nowhere, a kind of water that people noticed just every so often even though they spent their lives swimming in it. On the morning of September 12, 2001, Americans woke up to the message, delivered by news anchors, politicians, celebrities, pundits, professional athletes, signs in storefront windows, and homemade banners strung across porches and fire escapes, that September 11 had "changed everything." At the same time, however, Americans heard a different message, one delivered by the same people as the first: Don't worry, September 11 won't change anything at all. "We must stand against terror by going back to work," Bush said just a few weeks after September 11. He also thought Americans should stand against terror by going on vacation: "Get down to Disney World in Florida. Take your families and enjoy life the way we want it to be enjoyed."[14] Vigilance was required to prevent the terrorists from "winning" by carrying out another successful attack, but too much vigilance could also let the terrorists win. "We cannot give them the victory," Obama said at a 2015 press conference, "of changing how we go about living our lives."[15] Maybe the only healthy response to this kind of self-contradictory public messaging is to tune out the whole situation and hope for the best. A lot of people did just that.

Life in America did change, though. The war changed people's sense of themselves and the communities in which they lived. It changed how they felt about their neighbors, their co-workers, and the strangers they sat next to on airplanes. It changed what they watched, read, and listened to. It changed how they traveled from place to place, and it changed how they inhabited public space, how they decided what was safe and what wasn't worth the risk. Most of all, it changed people's experiences of citizenship. Was the United States a place where citizens had a say in how their government behaved? Was it a place where decisions about military force, domestic surveillance, and the proper role of law enforcement were genuinely open to public opinion? Was it a place where religion could be practiced freely, or that would give minority views a fighting chance to make themselves heard? Did Americans—all of them—get to decide what their government did? Many people who would have answered those questions one way in the summer of 2001 found themselves with a very different set of answers fifteen years later.

A crude but useful way to gauge the depth and significance of these changes is to remember that on November 8, 2016, Donald Trump was elected president. This book starts out from two propositions. The first is that if September 11 had not occurred, Donald Trump could never have become president. On the campaign trail in 2000 and in office thereafter, George W. Bush was so notorious for his malapropisms—he once told the members of a New Hampshire chamber of commerce that he knew they were "working hard to put food on your family"—that comedians such as Jon Stewart made whole careers out of mocking them. But Bush's campaign could never have survived his being caught on tape bragging that he liked to grab women "by the pussy," nor could it have survived multiple credible allegations of sexual assault. Trump's campaign did, and his election threw many aspects of American politics and society into crisis.

The second proposition is that crises do not come out of nowhere. Since 2016, much has been made of the damage Trump did to the American political system: to the trust people place in government, to respect for law as the final arbiter of public conduct, to norms of civility, to the expectation that public servants conduct themselves with decency, and to the idea that government functions should be transparent to citizens whenever possible. But it cannot be the case that Trump set all of this in motion by himself in 2016. No one like him had ever become the leader of a wealthy democracy. With his lack of political experience, contempt for the customs and traditions of government, indifference to being caught in lies, disinterest in policy issues, and openly avowed reputation for predatory sexual behavior, Trump was perhaps the least likely and least qualified candidate to attain high office in the history of modern democracy. His presidency came to pass because the United States was *already* beset by crises well before 2016, and all of them were either triggered or exacerbated by the fifteen years of war that preceded him.

In some respects, the task of this book is to explain how those crises made Trump's presidency possible. I use the qualifier "*some* respects" for two reasons. The first is that it would be wrong to assume that Trump's election will always appear to be the most important consequence of the war on terror. In fifty, twenty-five, or even ten years, Trump may look more like a precursor to larger social and political fractures. The second is that I would rather not gratify Trump's narcissism by making a multi-decade, global war entirely about him. The war's impact stretches far beyond the political career of a single mediagenic New York City realtor and socialite. The war changed life for Muslim and Arab Americans, people who serve in the military, political activists, teenagers, and students, as well as anyone who spends time in public spaces, travels by plane, attends professional sporting events, or uses the internet—in short, nearly everybody. At the risk of giving too much away right at the beginning, the war on terror made it clear to millions of people that they exerted far less control over the government that claimed to represent them than they had previously thought. This book is a history of what it felt like to live through those changes as they took place.

In order to tell that story, I've organized my argument around four crises that the war helped to fuel over the past two decades. First, I'll argue that the militarism that consumed American politics after September 11 changed much more than the country's foreign policy. It transformed everything from the kinds of heroes Americans wanted to see on television to the vehicles they drove to the grocery store and the city streets on which they walked. And while American troops never fought a battle against al-Qaeda on American soil, militarism nevertheless made much of the country, especially its public spaces, feel like a place where war could break out at any moment. This militarism was controversial at times, but in the aggregate Americans embraced it. September 11 was an unprecedented experience of national humiliation. Not even Vietnam could really compete with the trauma of watching three thousand Americans die, live on television, over the course of a single gorgeous morning. Many people found the experience unbearable. A couple weeks after the attacks, one anguished commentator wrote that the "seeming passivity" of the passengers on the planes reminded him of Jews being led to the gas chambers during World War II.[16] Militarism held out a seductive promise: You will never have to feel that way again.

Second, I'll describe how the war sparked an explosion of racism and xenophobia that accelerated all the way through the end of Obama's second term. Both Obama and his predecessor gave many speeches about tolerance and inclusion, and both disputed the idea that there was any irreconcilable enmity between the United States and the world's Muslim population. But each also devoted much of his time in office to fighting wars that killed Muslims almost exclusively, and that sent a message that easily drowned out their occasional monologues in praise of racial harmony. Obviously, it was Muslims outside of the United States who bore the brunt of America's racist violence during the war, but Muslim and Arab Americans also suffered enormously at home. Government agencies decimated communities with mass arrests, suspicious airport security agents turned commercial air travel into a grueling ordeal, and the mass media—from news networks to public intellectuals to action dramas like *24*—fixated relentlessly on the idea that any Muslim was a potential threat. This climate of fear and hostility helped to energize the right wing of a Republican Party that was otherwise somewhat adrift in the latter years of the Bush presidency, and that energy exploded into organization and action once voters put an African American in the White House for the first time. The racism and bigotry of the war on terror also transformed how the country weighed the benefits of immigration against its supposed dangers, particularly after America's invasion of Iraq and the Arab Spring revolutions of 2011 produced refugee crises that destabilized governments in both Europe and the United States.

Third, I'll try to illuminate the economic rationale behind the war on terror, which remains mysterious to most people. I'll argue that the war itself was a product of the same long-simmering economic problems that produced catastrophes like the global financial crisis in 2007–8. Income and wealth inequality constitutes one of the defining crises of the past twenty years, but in the United States the popular press and even many activist groups have not done a good job of making connections between economic inequality and America's foreign policy. Politicians themselves have little reason to clarify the subject, partly because acknowledging the economic benefits of America's military adventures abroad would require also acknowledging that America's relationship to much of the rest of the world is an imperial one. Although nearly everybody understands that countries do not choose to go to war unless they believe it to be in their economic self-interest, the specifics of that self-interest—what the interests are, how waging war against another country will serve them, and who will make money as a result—are in many ways unspeakable. Leaders of wealthy democracies do not give speeches about how their bombs and fighter jets and Special Forces will keep the prices of important natural resources at acceptable levels or help a domestic auto manufacturer consolidate market share.

Insofar as critics have tried to explain the war on terror in economic terms, they have usually done so by describing the invasion of Iraq as a play for that country's oil reserves. That's not the half of it. The economic motivations for the war on terror, and the roots of our new Gilded Age, go back to at least the end of World War II, and possibly five or six hundred years earlier than that. Finding those roots and tracing their winding path into the present will require the book's third section to be somewhat different from the first two. In addition to tracking changes in the daily lives of ordinary people, it will zoom out to the level of global (or "macro") economics. It will look at the history of how America's economic power turned it into the world's most powerful nation, and it will look at how the slow but steady decline of that power, which started in the 1970s but began to have more serious consequences in the twenty-first century, forced the U.S. government to adapt as it tried to maintain global supremacy.

Charting that decline and tracing its fallout for Americans who lived through the war on terror will involve discussing subjects and terms that often don't appear in books like this one: growth rates, balance of payments, currency depreciation, surplus industrial capacity, and the problems of global debt. These topics are not difficult to understand, yet many Americans who correctly think of themselves as well informed are unfamiliar with even the basics of economic policy. As the novelist and essayist John Lanchester once wrote, "On the radio or the TV or in the papers, a voice is going on about fiscal and monetary this or that, or marginal rates of such-and-such, or yields or equity prices, and we sorta-kinda know what they mean, but not really."[17] I am not someone who believes that economics explains everything, nor do I believe that the economic explanation for an event is the *fundamental* explanation, with cultural or social factors teetering somehow less fundamentally on top of the economic bedrock. But I do believe that in order to understand why the war on terror happened, what it did to the United States, and what its consequences might be in the future, one has to be able to follow the economic argument in real time. In their book on the history of Israel, Jonathan Nitzan and Shimshon Bichler point out that until the early part of the twentieth century, politics and economics "were studied not separately, but rather as a unified discipline of 'political economy,'" the idea being that one could understand the full extent of how societies change only by taking politics and economics as subject to the same historical process.[18] This third section will attempt a return to that older tradition of political economy. This is the part of the book I most enjoyed writing, and I hope it's just as enjoyable to read.

Finally, I'll talk about the crisis that only comes into view once you survey the damage caused by the first three and then ask yourself, "Why wasn't anybody held accountable for any of this?" By almost any metric, the war on terror has been a failure. Iraq's democracy is fragile and weak, the Taliban defeated the United States in Afghanistan, Syria lies in ruins, and Yemen has been devastated by civil war. The United States alienated many of its closest allies, and its adversaries are mostly stronger than they were on September 10, 2001. At home, things do not look any better. If Americans can agree on anything, it is that the last quarter century has been bad for the United States. The last time more than half of Americans thought the country was headed in the right direction was December 2003, shortly before Iraq began to spiral into chaos.[19] Despite the United States spending as much as a trillion dollars on homeland security, Americans feel less safe than they did before. More than a third of Americans said in 2017 that terrorism made them less likely to attend crowded public events, and nearly half said they were less willing to travel overseas.[20] Political polarization is up, and trust in the news media, government institutions, and fellow citizens is down. In January 2022, more than 60 percent of Americans said they thought democracy was "in crisis and at risk of failing."[21] The Trump presidency worsened these trends, but the trends themselves were in place well before Trump took the stage.

Despite all of this, examples of government officials being held accountable for the failures of the last twenty years are few and far between. International law has proved to be utterly toothless with respect to the many crimes committed by American soldiers and politicians since 2001. Just a month after the invasion of Iraq, one preeminent expert found it "inescapable that an objective observer would reach the conclusion that this Iraq War is a war of aggression, and as such, that it amounts to a Crime against Peace of the sort for which surviving German leaders were indicted, prosecuted and punished at the Nuremberg trials."[22] Nevertheless, Bush served two terms, and no one from his administration ever faced charges for using false intelligence to justify the invasion, nor for establishing a program of illegal detention and torture. No one from the Obama administration has been held accountable for the civilian casualties caused by drones, nor for the assassination of two American citizens, one of whom was a child. No one at the National Security Agency (NSA) has faced criminal charges for illegally spying on millions of Americans for years (although the people who brought those crimes to public attention have been driven into exile and prison). The FBI has never been held to account for its harassment of Muslim Americans after September 11.

It has become a kind of reflex, a government-wide inability or refusal to face consequences for any of the outrages of the past two decades. The term for this reflex is "impunity culture," and it has transformed how the U.S. government relates to the people it governs. This final section will look at how the erosion of free speech, the elimination of public space, the rise of mass surveillance, and the violent suppression of protest have evacuated citizenship of much of its content since 2001. When Barack Obama was asked in the early days of his presidency about the possibility of investigating Bush administration officials for war crimes, he said, "We need to look forward as opposed to looking backward," meaning that he wouldn't be opening investigations of any kind.[23] But looking forward without seeking any kind of accountability for past failures and crimes is a delusion. Without looking into the past, without taking stock of what has happened and working out how the available materials might be assembled into something new, we will find it impossible to look forward in a way that means anything. What you get instead is what the great Mike

Davis called "the victory of pathological presentism," in which progress and reform must always be sacrificed on the altar of an existential threat that has to be addressed today.[24] Under impunity culture, you get an unbearable "today" that never seems to end.

I began this introduction with a story from my adolescence because I believe that the timing of my birth has a lot to do with my interest in the war on terror. I am part of a generation of Americans who became adults while the war was already under way. Born too late to have any memory of the Soviet Union as something other than a historical relic, I was taught in high school that history, for all intents and purposes, was over. The American model had triumphed, and all that remained was for the rest of the world to gradually, fitfully, but inevitably join the United States on the march to freedom. Born too early to think that permanent global war was normal, I could feel how much had been destabilized by September 11 and America's response. I came of age as a decade-long interregnum of confidence and relative stability came to an end, as history lurched out of its grave and began to stagger across the landscape once again.

It wasn't just the television footage and the thousands of deaths that made September 11 traumatic. September 11 announced that history was back, and it forced that realization on everyone, even people who didn't usually pay attention to such things. That is traumatic in its own right. It may sound obnoxious for a relatively comfortable citizen of the world's richest country to describe having a basic awareness of history as traumatic, but traumas don't really respect privilege; they can happen whenever one of the beliefs that anchors your life and your understanding of the world suddenly turns out to be false. For my younger self, and for most other Americans, "history is over" was one of those beliefs, and it was all the more fundamental for being a belief you almost never had to think about. To have that assumption overturned in a single day was destabilizing for Americans regardless of their politics, and today it is not clear that any of America's political factions has been more or less successful than the others at coming to terms with our new state of affairs.

The war on terror demands of us the recognition that major social and political questions remain open, and it also forces us to come to terms with a world in which certain cherished possible futures are no longer viable. Finally, it requires us to make peace with the fact that history is something you have to try to understand even as you live through it. I have been struggling with the meaning of that realization ever since I spent a beautiful Sunday morning in the choir at St. John the Divine. My hope for this book is that its readers will find those struggles faithfully reflected and, to whatever extent possible, overcome.

PART I

A Sense of War

CHAPTER 1

No Time Zones

*We got to South Street Seaport pretty quickly. We went to a
bar, which was full. We got some juice and some water. As
we were watching it on CNN, we could actually see the
Towers through the glass window. The TV was right in front
of us, and we could see the Towers to our left. We could see
the second one starting to fall. You saw the whole bar turn
their heads to look through the window. As the second tower
fell past the point where you couldn't see it anymore,
everyone turned back to the TV and watched it fall all
the way.*

—Ian Oldaker, staff, Ellis Island[1]

A little before 8:00 p.m. on September 11, the ABC News anchor
Peter Jennings, who by that point had been on the air for
nearly eleven hours, said, "There are no time zones in the
country today."[2] He meant that everyone was watching television.
Around the world, as many as two billion people either watched the
attacks live or watched TV news coverage of the day's events.[3] In Don
DeLillo's novel *Underworld*, a man remembers when Bobby Thomson's

ninth-inning home run won the pennant for the New York Giants in 1951. "People rushed outside," he says. "People wanted to be together. Maybe it was the last time people spontaneously went out of their houses for something. Some wonder, some amazement. Like a footnote to the end of the war." Then he remembers how things changed over the next twelve years. "When JFK was shot," he says, "people went inside. We watched TV in dark rooms and talked on the phone with friends and relatives. We were all separate and alone."[4] September 11 marked the end of the era that began with Kennedy's death. It was the last time Americans learned about the history unfolding around them by watching it happen on a tiny handful of major television stations. The war America launched in response to the attacks would increasingly be followed and debated on the internet and an expanding list of cable news networks that catered to a politically fractured society. But it started on network TV. People spent the whole day watching.

The morning news program was invented just three months after Thomson's home run. In January 1952, an NBC news anchor began the inaugural broadcast of the *Today* show by reading out the time and the date from the network's New York City headquarters. "We are in touch with the world," the anchor said. "We will tell you what's happening today." The new format provided an easygoing alternative to the weightier news programming that went on the air each evening: a quick tour of the headlines, brief reports from international correspondents, personal banter among the hosts, and a weather report. Pat Weaver, who produced the *Today* show's first incarnation, wanted the broadcast to give people something agreeable that could fill the morning silence as they made their coffee and prepared for the day. "We cannot and should not try to build a show that will make people sit down in front of their set and divert their attention to the screen," Weaver wrote in a memo. "We want America to shave, to eat, to dress, to get to work on time."[5] The morning news was never designed to be something you had to watch, start to finish. If you found yourself unable to look away, that meant something had gone wrong.

On September 11, ABC's *Good Morning America* program opened with exactly this mix of the somewhat substantive and the somewhat frivolous. Co-host Charlie Gibson began by announcing that jury selection was about to begin in the trial of a woman charged with drowning her five children (tragic, frightening, serious—something that might cause one to throw a concerned glance at the screen), but right away he switched to the news that Michael Jordan seemed to be on the verge of returning to the NBA (exciting or tiresome, depending on your view of Jordan, but background noise either way). Gibson, dressed in a gray suit and a blue tie, sat next to Diane Sawyer, who wore a tan knee-length skirt and a pink short-sleeved turtleneck. Sawyer previewed a story about the Senate Aging Committee cracking down on a scam involving supplements that promised to "reverse aging" and "restore sexual power." The pair sat on a couch with notes and papers scattered in front of them. Gibson held a pen, and the studio lights glinted off the gold bracelet around Sawyer's wrist. The tableau created a pleasing impression of informality, warmth, and relaxed, unselfconscious glamour. In the background, a selection of houseplants overlooked the streets of New York. Cars still had their headlights turned on, but it was getting lighter.

The show's energy picked up as the traffic increased down in Times Square. "Don't you kind of like our song?" Sawyer asked Gibson with a grin as the *Good Morning America* jingle brought the show back from a commercial break. "Don't you kind of bounce into the morning? I do." She really was bouncing. "And I've heard it only twenty-six thousand times so far," Gibson replied, playing the good-hearted grump. Each new correspondent and guest who called in was like another colleague coming out of the elevator, holding take-out coffee in one hand and waving a friendly hello before settling down at their desk. Sawyer delivered a report on a man whose cellphone had continued to work even though his kayak had overturned, leaving him to bob around in the ocean for about an hour. "Can you believe this?" Sawyer said. "Mine doesn't work on dry land!" A small crowd stood behind the *Good Morning America* weatherman and cheered as he talked about rain in the Southeast. The show's consumer correspondent reported on faulty GE kitchen appliances that caught fire. "I

looked over, to where I saw flames," said a man named Richard Westfal, "and it was clearly, literally coming out of my dishwasher." A chy-
ron at the bottom of the screen identified Westfal as "dishwasher fire
victim." Gibson and the ABC News reporter John Miller sat in arm-
chairs and discussed whether Jimmy Hoffa's murder would ever be
solved. There were ads for breakfast cereal, prescription drugs, Toy-
otas, and soap. Sawyer talked about a medical "breakthrough" involving "free radicals" that could increase the life span of dogs, and she
also interviewed the creator of a TV series designed to be a straight
male version of *Sex and the City*. "An ad for the new HBO TV series
The Mind of the Married Man says, 'In marriage, no one can hear you
scream,'" Sawyer said. "Ha ha ha! Why am I laughing?!"

The show returned from what would have been its final commercial break at 8:51 a.m. Gibson and Sawyer were sitting in the arm-
chairs now, and they exchanged a quick, concerned look before
Sawyer started to talk:

> We want to tell you what we know, as we know it, but we just
> got a report in that there's been some sort of explosion at the
> World Trade Center in New York City. One report said—and
> we can't confirm any of this—that a plane may have hit one of
> the towers of the World Trade Center, but again, you're seeing
> the live pictures here. We have no further details than that. We
> don't know anything about what they have concluded hap-
> pened there this morning, but we're going to find out and of
> course make sure that everybody knows on the air.

As she said this, the screen filled with the first of the images that
would consume the world's television airwaves for the rest of the
day. A helicopter camera showed a live shot of the top third of
the towers. One of them (the North Tower) had a large black gash in
its side. Smoke poured out of the gash, as it did from the back of the
tower as well. New Jersey, the Hudson River, and the rest of New York
all glittered in the sunshine below. The first correspondent to call in
to the studio was Don Dahler, who had found himself just several

blocks from the World Trade Center when he heard a loud sound overhead. "I can only describe as it sounded like a missile," he said, "not an airplane. Then there was a loud explosion and immediately lots of screaming out on the streets." Dahler didn't want to cause "any undue speculation," but he had grown up on military bases and was quite familiar with the sounds of prop planes, jets, and weaponry. "If it was an airplane," he said, "it had to be huge." For several minutes, Gibson, Sawyer, and Dahler all looked at the towers and wondered what was going on. It's not often that television news reporters aren't afforded at least a few minutes to package the news they report, but here they were trying to broadcast events that were happening in real time, and one can tell it made them uncomfortable. As the helicopter camera zoomed in, one could see not just smoke but flames coming out of the building. The smoke was getting thicker and blacker. By 8:58, the helicopter camera was capturing other news helicopters hovering around the towers. At 9:01, the ABC anchors learned that the Associated Press had reported that an aircraft was the cause of the explosion. And at 9:03, they all watched as a second plane came in from the right side of the helicopter shot and crashed into the South Tower. A fireball exploded out of the building's opposite side. Don Dahler cut himself off and said, "Oh my God." In the ABC studio, off camera, a man's voice yelled, "Oh my God!" Under her breath, Sawyer said, "Oh my *God.*"

Gibson and Dahler spent a moment discussing what had just happened. Dahler had been on the wrong side of the towers to see the second plane; all he saw was the fireball. "So this looks like it is some sort of a concerted effort to attack the World Trade Center that is under way in downtown New York," Gibson said. Then nobody talked for four seconds, which is a long time for television. Sawyer was the first to interrupt the silence. Her voice was shaking. "We will see that scene again just to make sure we saw what we thought we saw," she said. They replayed the shot of the plane coming in from the right side and crashing into the other tower. Then they played it a third time, in slow motion. "To watch, powerless," Sawyer said, "is a horror." For hours afterward, there was nothing to do but watch.

Of course, that was the purpose of the attack. Al-Qaeda got lucky in two ways that morning. First, the two impacts were separated by seventeen minutes. After the first plane hit, all the news camera operators in New York City rushed to lower Manhattan, took up their positions, trained their lenses on the towers, and started rolling. They understood themselves to be reporting the news, but at 9:03 they learned that they had been unwittingly pressed into service as publicists for terrorism—the second plane's impact aired live on ABC, CBS, NBC, Fox, and CNN. Second, the time of day at which the attacks occurred meant that most of the people on earth were awake to see them. "It's probably the only period in a day when the whole world *could* actually watch the same event at the same time," one photo agency executive told a journalist. "Between nine and ten in the morning [eastern daylight time], it's still not yet nighttime in Europe, Africa, and Asia. It never happens with the Olympics or the World Cup. It never happens when wars start because they usually start under cover of night. . . . This could be seen at once, anywhere, in both hemispheres, any latitude, any culture, throughout the world, live."[6]

On ABC, *Good Morning America* gave way to Peter Jennings, who anchored the network's main news desk. For about an hour, however, there wasn't much that he could add to the images that kept looping across the TV screen. Those images *were* the news, in its entirety. At 9:37, American Airlines Flight 77 crashed into the western side of the Pentagon, but the Pentagon is a low, squat building, and the attack in Washington could not compete visually so long as the Twin Towers were still vomiting smoke into the sunshine. Crazy rumors flew around. At various points, ABC reported the detonation of a car bomb outside the State Department, a plane ominously "circling the White House," and an explosion at the Capitol, none of which had actually happened. And in addition to the threat of further attacks that might still be to come, there was a vague but foreboding sense that watching itself could be dangerous. At regular intervals, ABC's national broadcast would hand things over to its local affiliates, one of which was based in Washington. That station took a call from a woman who had seen the plane crash into the Pentagon from the window of her high-rise apartment building. She said she had been "glued to the television" all morning, watching the news from New York, when suddenly the news had started happening right outside. The anchors, getting a little panicky, asked the caller, "Are you in a safe place right now?" She laughed nervously: "Uh, as far as I know." Nobody knew where it was safe to be, in other words, and for a period people seemed to freeze in place as they watched and wondered what was going to happen next. "All of lower Manhattan," Jennings said about an hour into the attack, "is just standing in the street on this sunny morning looking at this unrealistic sight."[7]

At 9:59, the South Tower collapsed, folding down onto itself like an accordion and producing apocalyptic thunderheads of ash and debris that filled the streets. The images of the collapse proved to be quite literally unbelievable. On ABC, Jennings noticed that something was happening on the screen and interrupted an interview: "Because we now have—what do we have? . . . Now it may be that something fell off the building." Don Dahler, reporting from the scene via telephone, interjected:

DAHLER: The second building that was hit by the plane has just completely collapsed. The entire building has just collapsed as if a demolition team . . . It folded down on itself and it is not there anymore.

JENNINGS: The whole side has collapsed?

DAHLER: The whole *building* has collapsed.

JENNINGS: The whole *building* has collapsed?

DAHLER: The building has collapsed.

Dahler's report was perfectly audible, and he emphasized three times—"completely collapsed . . . entire building has just collapsed . . . it is not there anymore"—that the tower was gone. He said nothing about the "side" of the building. Jennings asked whether the "whole side" had collapsed because he could not believe what he had seen and heard. On other networks, it took even longer for the anchors and re-porters to realize what had happened. On CNN, six minutes passed before viewers were told that the building had fallen. On NBC, it was seven minutes. About half an hour later, the North Tower went down as well. "It's hard to put it into words," Jennings said, "and maybe one doesn't need to." After a long pause, John Miller, who had spent the earlier part of his morning in an armchair talking about Jimmy Hoffa, mentioned the "constant" intelligence reports he'd heard about sug-gesting that Osama bin Laden wanted to attack the United States. Then he had a thought: "It's also interesting to say there is no type of security"—and now Jennings cut in and finished the thought for him—"which would have prevented against this today." Jennings caught himself immediately ("that may not altogether be true," he said), but it was Miller's original thought, one Jennings had been able to finish on his own, that expressed the situation's emotional truth. It was a feeling of total helplessness, that there was nothing anyone could do.[8]

• • •

That feeling of helplessness—of finding oneself unprepared for the worst, of being made to watch as the disaster unfolds, of failing to comprehend what you're seeing, and of being unable to do anything to stop it—was the core American experience of September 11. It is very hard for an individual to feel that way for long without disap-pearing into themselves or losing their mind. For an entire society to feel that way, all at the same time, is totally unbearable, even for a single day. What makes the experience so awful when it happens on such a large scale is that it becomes impossible to grab on to anything tangible that might pull you out of the current and back to safety. Where do you turn for reassurance when everyone needs reassuring? How do you avoid falling into despair when everyone around you has the same stunned look on their face?

In moments of universal social disaster, the usual means of coping with life's trials suddenly become inadequate, and people are forced to draw on the deep recesses of their shared memory and wisdom. In the United States, September 11 was one of these moments, and from the very beginning the trauma of the attacks on New York and Washington activated a specific set of fears that are expressed in parts of America's national mythology and constitute a core part of what it means to be an American. Cowboys are part of this national mythology, as are the Pilgrims, Paul Revere, George Washington's unwillingness to lie, Abraham Lincoln's pragmatic decency, GIs storming the beaches at Normandy, and the civil rights movement. Americans repeat these stories and pass them down to their descendants because they are reminders of their own national identity and purpose. They let Americans know what they should expect from life, how they should inhabit the world, and what they should do when the enemy (especially a nonwhite enemy) shows up at the front door. In the days, months, and years after September 11, Americans reached back even further than cowboys to the myths that emerged out of the European settlers' very first experiences on the continent. These stories, which focused on the dangers faced by white settlers at the hands of Native Americans, made up the original foundation of the national mythology. They emerged out of experiences of vulnerability, helplessness, and terror, and they recommended that colonists respond with unlimited, righteous violence. They began to structure a stunned country's response to September 11 from the moment the first plane hit the North Tower.

In 2007, the great feminist journalist Susan Faludi published an elegant and unsentimental book about September 11 called *The Terror Dream*. It is not very well known today, perhaps because some people still find it provocative to discuss the attacks as anything other than a violation of national innocence. September 11, Faludi wrote, "was not, in fact, an inconceivable event; it was *the* characteristic and formative American ordeal, the primal injury of which we could not speak, the shard of memory stuck in our throats. Our ancestors had already fought a war on terror, a very long war, and we have lived with its scars ever since."[9]

The ordeal to which Faludi referred was the taking of English captives, usually women, by Native Americans during the series of wars that pitted Puritan colonists against the continent's original peoples during the seventeenth century. These wars lasted for decades. They nearly destroyed the colonies as functioning political entities, and for the Puritans who fought them, they dramatized in the most vivid terms the violent opposition between their own civilizational project and the pagan wilderness that menaced them at every turn. In Faludi's book, the Indian Wars are the key to understanding how Americans in the twenty-first century tried to process the horrors of terrorism. Yes, Americans took pleasure in violence. Only a country with a long-standing "relish for the kill," as Faludi put it, could have invented the Western or the Hollywood action movie. But Faludi noted that Americans had an "even longer sense of disgrace on the receiving end of assault," assaults on both "our women in our own settlements and in our own homes." "What if the deepest psychological legacy of our original war on terror," she wrote, "wasn't the pleasure we now take in dominance but the original shame that domination seeks desperately to conceal?"[10]

That strikes me as a usefully provocative way of characterizing the country's national identity. Throughout the postwar period, Americans have largely understood that national identity to be rooted in a more positive set of emotions: optimism, confidence, a can-do spirit, and expansionary zeal. From the Puritan John Winthrop's description of "a city on a hill," to the civilizing westward gaze of "manifest destiny," to Martin Luther King's belief that the "arc of the moral universe . . . bends toward justice," Americans have preferred to think of themselves as a band of good-hearted and ingenious dreamers, a people both insightful enough to build a just society and powerful enough to remake the rest of the world in their own image. That self-image has a lot to recommend it, but what if the bright-eyed optimism and moral certitude is also serving as a cover for something that is harder to talk about? Shame is a difficult emotion to experience, but as any competent therapist knows, it is even harder to discuss. People go to extraordinary lengths to avoid it. They deflect, lash out, rationalize, or lose themselves in hysterics. They start fights they can't win, search desperately for hidden enemies in their midst, and see the world that surrounds them as filled with potential threats. Americans did a lot of starting fights and searching for enemies after September 11, and it was Faludi's insight to perceive, lurking behind her country's increasingly erratic behavior, the colonists' original experiences of shame. It was shame that forged the original national mythology, and it was the Indian Wars that made such myths necessary for survival.

Some three decades before September 11, another American historian, also writing during wartime, described the Indian Wars as "the distinctive event of American history, the unique national experience."[11] Richard Slotkin spent thirty years tracing the development of America's national mythology from the colonial period through the late twentieth century. The power he credited to myths was immense. He saw them as the means by which "the psychology and world view of our cultural ancestors are transmitted to modern descendants, in such a way and with such power that our perception of contemporary reality and our ability to function in the world are directly, often tragically affected."[12] He thought that myths allowed people to gather up the disparate matter of their experiences and turn them into a kind of symbol, or drama—something that made sense. Myths tell people what their ancestors went through, impart the lessons learned from those earlier experiences, and provide guidance to understanding a present that always seems at least somewhat bewildering to those living through it. Their influence becomes more important at moments of particular anxiety or stress.

For Faludi and Slotkin, the mythological chain winding its way through more than three hundred years of Euro-American history finds its deepest roots in the captivity narrative, which Slotkin called "the first coherent myth-literature developed in America for American audiences."[13] Between 1680 and 1720, captivity narratives constituted most of the frontier stories published in America and accounted for three of the period's four bestsellers.[14] According to Faludi, the captivity narrative is the *only* genre that is indigenous to American literature.[15] In these stories, Native Americans symbolize all the dangers of the unexplored continent, while an innocent white woman symbolizes the colonists. In the standard captivity narrative, this woman is kidnapped by Native American raiders, taken from her co-lonial settlement, and forced into the wilderness. Held prisoner, she is then subjected to a spiritual ordeal, physical trials, and sexual danger. The woods are filled with terrors and snares, and while the heroine always survives, her children, who are sometimes kidnapped as well, may not be so lucky. She prays to her Christian God, but trapped as she is among the godless, she does not know whether her prayers will be heard. Making matters worse, her virtue will be tested as well. She knows she cannot expect or deserve God's mercy if she allows herself to fall into sin, and Native American men are always looking for new wives. She is helpless and alone. There is no band of colonists follow-ing her trail through the woods in the hope of effecting a rescue. That element of the story would be added later, but in the seventeenth cen-tury the colonies were too weak, undeveloped, and small to imagine themselves dominating the continent and its original inhabitants. Survival was the best one could hope for, and even that seemed un-likely. If the captive wanted to return from the woods to her home, she needed to throw herself on the mercy of the divine. Only through submissive piety could she hope for deliverance.

The first and most popular of these captivity narratives was Mary Rowlandson's *The Sovereignty and Goodness of God*. Published in 1682 and reprinted many times, it told the true story of Rowlandson's cap-ture during King Philip's War in 1676, when Native Americans led by the Nashaway Nipmuc leader Monoco attacked Lancaster in the Mas-sachusetts Bay Colony. "On the tenth of February," Rowlandson wrote, "Came the *Indians* with great numbers upon *Lancaster:* Their first coming was about Sun-rising."[16] What followed was excruciating. First, Rowlandson had to watch helplessly as the raiders murdered her neighbors:

> When we are in prosperity, Oh the little that we think of such dreadfull sights, and to see our dear friends, and Relations ly bleeding out their heart-blood upon the ground. There was one who was chopt into the head with a Hatchet, and stripped

naked, and yet was crawling up and down. It is a solemn sight to see so many Christians lying in their blood, some here, and some there, like a company of Sheep torn by Wolves.[17]

Then she was captured and taken into the wilderness. For eleven weeks, her captors marched her through the woods, with occasional stops at Native American settlements, as they continued to raid English villages. She was separated from her oldest daughter, and her youngest, a six-year-old named Sarah, died a week after her kidnapping. "About two houres in the night, my sweet Babe, like a lamb departed this life," she wrote. "I cannot but take notice, how at another time I could not bear to be in the room where any dead person was, but now the case is changed; I must and could ly down by my dead Babe, side by side all the night after."[18] A group of English soldiers tried to pursue and retrieve Rowlandson, at one point getting close enough to see the smoke from the Indians' wigwams, but they were unable to ford the Baquaug River, and the Indians got away. This amused Rowlandson's captors. "*I cannot but remember how the* Indians *derided the slowness, and dullness of the* English *Army, in its setting out,*" she wrote. "They asked me when I thought the *English Army* would come after them? I told them I could not tell: It may be they will come in *May,* said they. Thus did they scoffe at us, as if the *English* would be a quarter of a year getting ready."[19] In order to fend off despair, she read a Bible her kidnappers gave to her, sewed clothing in exchange for food, and quit smoking. When she met the Native American leader King Philip, he offered her a tobacco pipe, "but this in no way suited me," she wrote. "For though I had formerly used Tobacco, yet I had left it ever since I was first taken."[20] Finally, she was ransomed for £20 and reunited with her family, and the Rowlandsons settled in Boston. But just as New Yorkers who lived through September 11 suffered from sleeplessness and vicious nightmares for months and years afterward, Mary Rowlandson found that her return to white civilization could not restore her inner peace. "*I can remember the time, when I used to sleep quietly without workings in my thoughts, whole nights together, but now it is other wayes with me,*" she wrote. "When all are fast about me, and no eye open, but his who ever waketh, my thoughts are upon things past, upon the awfull dispensation of the Lord towards us."[21]

The archetype for many similar narratives to follow, Rowlandson's account gave the Puritan colonists a way to understand the terrors, insecurity, and spiritual difficulties of their migration out of civilized England and into the untamed American landscape. That the narrators of the captivity stories were always taken *unwillingly* into the wilderness also helped to assuage the Puritans' feelings of guilt over having *chosen* to leave their European communities behind. Captivity narratives converted real, traumatic experiences into parables of trial and redemption. They could not dispel the colonists' feelings of terror and helplessness—in some ways, they amplified them. But by converting the colonists' experiences of absolute vulnerability and seemingly random violence into parables of God's mercy and lessons on the importance of submissive piety, the captivity narratives could lend those experiences meaning. It was a similar need for meaning, for a way of understanding the attacks as something other than a spectacle of brutality and victimization, that reactivated those myths on September 11.

• • •

For several hours after the towers collapsed, ABC struggled and failed to give the attacks meaning. The worst was over in reality— unbeknownst to news organizations, the fourth and final hijacked plane had already crashed in central Pennsylvania—but on television the horrors were multiplying. New images of the attacks, sometimes accompanied by a label reading "earlier today," trickled out over the airwaves as ABC's camera crews sent the footage they had recorded that morning back to headquarters. Viewers saw a section of a wall at the Pentagon crumble as firefighters tried to tame the blaze. They saw people standing down in Times Square with their heads tilted up toward the big screens on the side of the ABC studios, watching television just like hundreds of millions of their countrymen. They saw a zoomed-in shot of someone leaning out of the gash in one of the towers, peering down at the ground and wondering what to do, and they saw a man-on-the-street interview get interrupted by the second tower's collapse. There were not yet any hard figures attached to the morning's devastation, and so the rules of journalism required Jennings and other reporters to say that there were no confirmed casualties even though all of their viewers had just watched thousands of people die on the screens in front of them. "There is an intensity in the air," Jennings said, "a fear, a trauma in the air." There were periods where he seemed to have trouble keeping it together, where he misspoke several times in quick succession, referring to the "second tower of the Pentagon" and saying that President Bush had canceled his education trip to Washington before correcting himself; he meant to say Florida. As the network replayed a shot of the second tower coming down, he said, "Good Lord, it just . . ." and never finished his thought. On ABC's affiliate in Washington, reporters weren't doing much better. They leaned hard on the favorite topic of local news broadcasts everywhere: the traffic. One said, of the exodus of people fleeing the city, that he hadn't seen the District clear out this quickly since the blizzard of 1996.[22]

Each attempt to bring the event under control, to turn it into something that could be contained within a news program, seemed to undermine itself. Around two in the afternoon, Senator Joe Biden, brimming with sober determination, said, "We've come face to face with a new reality. . . . If in fact in order to respond to that reality we have to alter our civil liberties, change the way we function, then we have truly lost the war." (Notice how quickly all of the clichés and catchphrases of the war on terror debate established themselves.) Biden also said that "the way to conduct the war is to demonstrate that our institutions are functioning."[23]

But as ABC was reporting in detail, America's institutions were doing the opposite. The stock market was closed, and it would not reopen for six days. The PGA Tour announced that its golf tournaments were postponed, Major League Soccer canceled its upcoming games, the Emmy Awards were postponed, and the Latin Grammy

Awards were canceled. Minor League Baseball decided that its playoff games would be put off, and Major League Baseball soon followed up by announcing the postponement of all regular season action (this was the first time since D-day that all of baseball had been put on hold, a detail the news broadcasters would repeat constantly, neurotically, throughout the rest of the day). "There are no planes taking off in the United States at the moment," Jennings said. "You can feel across the country that aircraft that were in flight are beginning to settle down." The local news was listing school closures and public transit lines that had been paused or rerouted. Shortly after 1:00 p.m., Jennings spent several minutes simply listing all of the different ways in which the country was grinding to a halt:

> As you watch this on the East Coast of the United States, think about that in California all airports were closed. Places like Knott's Berry Farm were closed today, the Museum of Tolerance in Los Angeles was closed, the Library Tower—all closed! . . . In Florida, you know what happened, Walt Disney World was evacuated, closed its parks and shopping and entertainment complex. You talk about the effect that this incident has all across the country. Airports were closed everywhere across the country as we know, including in Georgia and Illinois, where the Sears Tower was also shut down in Chicago. And all state government buildings in Chicago and in Springfield, the capital, were closed down. In Indiana all the federal offices were put on alert. In Kentucky, where the southern governors were about to have the full scope of their annual fall conference, it was canceled. And obviously the governors of Tennessee, Kentucky, West Virginia, Louisiana, and Mississippi all went home to their respective capitals because of this. In Louisiana, where the president has just left, the upper floors of the capitol building were closed. The offshore oil port which handles the supertankers in the Gulf of Mexico suspended operations. . . . In Michigan, the tunnel between Detroit and Windsor, Ontario, was closed to car traffic, and we do know

from other reporting that security was increased at all of the border crossings between the U.S. and Canada, and between the U.S. and Mexico.[24]

This was a moving piece of broadcasting. In the space of a single spoken paragraph, Jennings covered every region of the United States, encompassing activities from amusement parks and museums to heavy industry in the Gulf. As one watches it today, it becomes easier to understand the idea that now-marginal cultural institutions like network news used to help the country think of itself as a unified whole. So many people, spread out over an enormous continent and engaged in an impossible variety of work and activity, all stopped what they were doing for the same reason. This is why, despite everything that followed over the next twenty years, it is not *completely* fatuous to say that September 11 was a unifying experience for the United States. What makes it *somewhat* fatuous to say that, however, is that what unified people was feeling helpless, angry, and afraid.

In the days and weeks following the attacks, the media and the wider public tried to keep those feelings at bay by latching on to New York's firefighters as symbols of heroism in a time of crisis. Every firefighter in the city had been summoned to lower Manhattan after the planes hit, and by the end of the day 343 of them had died, including 60 who were off duty when the attacks occurred.[25] Here were the men who, to use the phrasing employed countless times in the fall of 2001, had run toward the danger while everyone else ran away. Here were the men who had not been paralyzed by helpless terror, who knew they might not make it out of the towers but went in anyway in search of people to save, who stared unblinking into the face of death even as death came crashing down around them. "America has witnessed heroism on a Homeric scale," wrote the editorial board of *The Wall Street Journal*, which went on to outline a hierarchy of valor in which firefighters came out on top:

A soldier may spend an entire career without ever having a single shot directed at him. A police officer's family prays

mightily for the same. But from the smallest hamlet to the biggest metropolis, firefighters, volunteer and professional alike,
routinely face a life-taking enemy that always enjoys the advantage of surprise and unpredictability.[26]

No praise was too much to lavish on them. Similarly, no criticism
of the firefighters' behavior on September 11 could be mild or qualified enough to merit anything less than an overwhelming rebuttal.
Too much depended, psychologically, on the story of the firefighters'
heroism to allow anyone to chisel away at it. In the second half of
2002, William Langewiesche, an award-winning journalist at *The Atlantic Monthly,* published a series of articles based on months spent
reporting from the Ground Zero cleanup site. Though he did not engage in the same kind of hagiography that characterized much of the
media's coverage of New York's emergency workers, it was a wholly
admiring portrait of their courage, ingenuity, and determination to
help put the city back on its feet. Included as part of this portrait,
however, was the allegation that rescue workers had found one fire
truck buried in the rubble that had stacks of brand-new Gap jeans,
with the tags still attached, inside the cab; at least some of the firefighters, it seemed, had looted the stores on the concourse underneath
the towers.[27] This became the only part of Langewiesche's series that
anyone wanted to discuss, so outraging people that another journalist
even went so far as to produce a fifty-page reconstruction purporting
to demonstrate that such looting wouldn't even have been possible.[28]
No story that contradicted the national ballad of the FDNY's sacrifice
could be allowed to stand. As New York's mayor, Rudy Giuliani, put it,
"Our firefighters helped save more than twenty-five thousand lives
that day—the greatest single rescue mission in America's history."[29]

Many of the firefighters themselves, as well as other emergency
workers, felt quite differently. In a sense, they were victimized twice—
first by al-Qaeda and its hijacked planes, and then by the myths the
news media spent the rest of the year piling on their already overburdened shoulders. Giuliani's claim about the FDNY saving twenty-five
thousand lives was nonsense. Almost none of the firefighters made it

anywhere close to where the planes had hit the towers. American Airlines Flight 11 crashed into the North Tower between the ninety-third and the ninety-ninth floors, followed by United Airlines Flight 175, which hit the South Tower between the seventy-seventh and the eighty-fifth floors. The impacts rendered the elevators in both buildings largely useless, and the dark clouds of smoke made it impossible to attempt any kind of helicopter rescue on the towers' rooftops. This left the firefighters with no choice but to take the stairs, a process that was further slowed by their heavy equipment and the thousands of office workers coming down the stairs as they tried to escape. Only one team, led by Battalion Chief Orio Palmer, made it to the impact zone in the South Tower, and that was due to their good luck in finding the one elevator that still worked (which then got stuck on the way back down). No one who went up to the seventy-eighth floor with Palmer survived. These facts do not diminish their courage in any way, but the idea that firefighters saved large numbers of people in the towers is fantasy. Almost all of the workers who did make it out of the World Trade Center did so by walking down the stairs under their own power or with the help of their colleagues. In a documentary made about one lower Manhattan fire company that responded to the attacks, one firefighter remembered these workers wondering why he was climbing the stairs at all. "People pretty much said, 'Why are you going up there? Get out,'" he said.[30] "The grim truth," as Susan Faludi wrote, "is that the human toll would have been significantly lower had the firefighters never entered the buildings."[31]

In the fall and winter of 2001, the city assembled a task force to conduct interviews with every emergency worker who had been called in as part of the response. It then spent years, however, working to prevent those interviews from being released to the public, perhaps because they confirmed that many of the first responders spent September 11 feeling just as helpless as anyone else.[32] Like millions of Americans, some of them felt as though they were watching television or a Hollywood blockbuster that day, even though they were there in person. "I remember seeing, it looked like sparkling around one specific layer of the building," a deputy fire commissioner said.

I assume now that that was either windows starting to collapse like tinsel or something. Then the building started to come down. My initial reaction was that this was exactly the way it looks when they show you those implosions on TV. I would have to say for three or four seconds anyway, maybe longer, I was just watching. It was interesting to watch, but the thing that woke everybody up was the cloud of black material. It reminded me of *The Ten Commandments,* when the green clouds come down on the street.[33]

An EMT also thought of the movies. "It was coming—the force—you see like the—shit, the whole top of the building go off and just the junk that was coming out of there," he said, "and the explosion was—I thought it was Hollywood."[34] "I could see the tower," another EMT said, "and the tower was starting to break off. . . . We sat there like for a split second and we just watched it in amazement that this building was coming down, the second building was coming down. The building was hitting other buildings. It was hitting buildings over here. It was crazy."[35] This is one of the main themes of these interviews, the moments when people became so overwhelmed by the spectacle unfolding in front of them that there was nothing they could do but watch. "I was in shock," one firefighter said. "I was standing there, standing on the roof, not watching the TV, standing on the roof watching."[36]

Those who were able to tear their eyes away from the spectacle found themselves with another problem: Sometimes the enormity of the tasks that confronted them was overwhelming, but sometimes (and this was worse) there wasn't anything to do at all. Forget saving others; it was hard enough simply to survive, to maintain one's composure. "There were body parts on the street," one EMT said. "I saw something that looked like a helmet, but it wasn't a helmet. It was a head." How does someone keep their mind intact when presented with a human head lying in the street? "At one point I couldn't take it," the EMT said. "I would keep yelling, 'Can we go help them, can we go help them.' But he is like, 'You can't,' because the scene wasn't safe. So there was nothing we could do."[37] Sometimes the carnage was right there in front of you. A firefighter named Bobby Senn remembered watching a man in a brown suit fall to the earth. "When I got to him he was in a circle probably about eight feet in diameter," he said. "Everything that used to be inside of him was now outside of him."[38] Sometimes it snuck up on the edge of your field of vision. "I noticed people jumping off the building," another EMT said. "I caught this one guy over there. My eye caught him. It was just one of those things. My eye caught him. I was watching."[39] And sometimes you didn't see it at all until it had already happened. One FDNY captain was walking toward the South Tower with several others when someone who had jumped to escape the fire hit and killed one of the firefighters, a Brooklyn native named Daniel Suhr. According to one of his colleagues, Suhr's last words were "Look out for the people jumping. If one of them hits us, we are dead."[40] "He was right to my right and behind me," the captain said. "It was as if he exploded. It wasn't like you heard something falling and you could jump out of the way. He gets hit."[41]

Injured people could have been helped to safety and received treatment, but September 11 didn't injure people so much as it obliterated them. Nearly a year after the attacks, the Medical Examiner's Office had identified the remains of 1,209 victims. Fewer than 300 of those victims were found more or less intact, and the remaining 900 were identified out of a mass of nearly 20,000 individual bits of human remains.[42] More than half of those who died in the Twin Towers had still not been found or identified when the recovery effort ended—the collapse of the buildings, and the fires that burned both before and after they came down, ground or burned them up into dust.[43] One paramedic walked down to the ferry terminal at the very southern tip of Manhattan. "We started to get ready for mass casualties to see how many people were coming and who we could try to help," he said. "But there were no patients. Nobody was coming."[44] "There wasn't really much for us to do," an EMT said. "You had four hundred ambulances there, just idling their engines. Not really doing anything. It was a shame."[45] As late as 8:00 that evening, the ambulances were still idling, because the fires at Ground Zero were burning too hot to attempt any coordinated rescue operation. The operation that was eventually attempted didn't turn up much. "Our first shift was twenty-four hours," one firefighter said, "and in all that time, there was one person pulled out alive. One. It was beyond discouraging—it was even hard to understand."[46] Emergency workers train obsessively for mass casualty events, but September 11 was not something one could train for. "It was really organized," an EMT named Jody Bell said. "I mean, in the middle of a disaster, we were really prepared and we wanted to treat a lot of people, but unfortunately we kind of knew there wasn't going to be a lot of patients. We knew, but we were in denial." Bell kept it together for a couple of days, and then she didn't. "I woke up Friday morning and I fell apart. That's when I fell apart. It really hit me. I was in shambles. I was in bad shape."[47]

Early in the afternoon, after reporting that Yasser Arafat had given a statement conveying his condolences, ABC aired video of Palestinians celebrating the attacks on the streets of the West Bank. This video was quite striking, though not for the incendiary politics of its contents. It was one of the only times on September 11 that ABC showed what was happening anywhere outside the United States. For most of the day, it was as though the rest of the world had temporarily ceased to exist. Nothing much happened during the afternoon, at least as far as the images on television were concerned. Instead, the news repeated itself as the reporters and correspondents waited for something to happen, and this added to the dreamlike atmosphere. "For over two hours now, we've been looking at this plume of smoke," said one reporter of the Pentagon.[48] New footage of the attacks would find its way to the airwaves—producers seemed to be putting it on the screen just as fast as it came in—and Jennings would cut off the correspondent sitting next to him so that everyone could watch it. One became able, over time, to catalog these different shots, to notice which ones aired again and again, and which ones fell out of the rotation. In a perverse way, one even began to get impatient for new images. *Why are they showing me this dust-covered man holding a Sprite for the third time? He just stands there. Are they ever going to find footage of the first plane hitting the tower?*

To feel this kind of morbid impatience for new images of death is humiliating in its own right. Viewers needed to see a rescue operation under way, to see people being carried to safety, to see victims on stretchers being ministered to by the expert hands of doctors and EMTs. At the very least, they needed to see leadership from elected officials. They needed to see Americans on television who weren't just terrified victims. But this, too, was in frustratingly short supply during the morning and afternoon. Although the incident didn't become famous until it was included in Michael Moore's 2004 documentary *Fahrenheit 9/11,* one of the most emblematic pieces of September 11 footage that wasn't made in New York or Washington was taken by the cameramen who had followed President Bush to Florida for his education event. Bush was sitting in front of a classroom of second graders in Sarasota when his chief of staff interrupted and whispered to him, "A second plane hit the second tower. America is under attack." Rather than leaving right away, Bush sat where he was and followed along as the teacher led her students through a reading exercise focused on words that ended with the letter *e* (the exercise, "The Pet Goat," has been largely misremembered as "My Pet Goat," including in Moore's film). He sat there for six or seven minutes. While leaping out of his seat right away wouldn't have changed anything about what happened over the rest of the day, the classroom footage was seriously damaging to the image of a president who spent most of his vacation time literally dressed as a cowboy on his Texas ranch. Twenty minutes after wrapping up "The Pet Goat," Bush made his first public statement about the attacks: "Ladies and gentlemen . . . difficult moment for America . . . two airplanes . . . apparent terrorist attack," etc. Then he left Sarasota and spent much of the day flying from place to place in an attempt to elude any potential threats to his own life, on the advice of the Secret Service. These evasive maneuvers made it impossible for Bush to keep himself in front of TV cameras, and on ABC the mystery surrounding Bush's whereabouts became a topic of increasing annoyance and frustration to Peter Jennings. "I don't mean to say this in melodramatic terms, [but] where is the president of the United States?" Jennings asked. "I know we don't know where he is, but pretty soon the country needs to know where he is, and it seems to, I think, *me*, anyway"—here Jennings let out a small, self-deprecating laugh. "I apologize," he said. "The president needs to talk to us."

Bush was on his way to Barksdale Air Force Base in Louisiana, and soon after his arrival the press received word that he would deliver his second statement on the attacks. Jennings smirked a little as he relayed the update to his viewers. "The president is not coming back to Washington at the moment," he said, and Bush then delivered prepared remarks for about two minutes.[49] As Bush prepared to leave Louisiana following his remarks, Jennings returned again to the subject of the president's leadership. "We have no idea where he's going," he said. "You have to assume he's going back to Washington. The president cannot be seen to be running around the country."[50] Around 3:30 in the afternoon, one of ABC's correspondents phoned in from Offutt Air Force Base in Nebraska. "President Bush is here at the home of the Strategic Command," she said. He had "disappeared down the rabbit hole" and would be chairing a meeting of the National Security Council from an underground bunker.[51] That was all America would see of its president until after 6:00 p.m.

As Jennings eventually acknowledged, Bush's peripatetic Tuesday wasn't hard to justify. The two largest buildings in the country's biggest city had been destroyed. The country's secretary of defense, Donald Rumsfeld, had been inside the Pentagon when terrorists crashed a plane into it. Nobody knew where the fourth plane, which had gone down in a field in central Pennsylvania, had been headed, but the Capitol and the White House were at the top of the list of likely targets. The details of Bush's trip to Florida had been public knowledge for weeks, and why wouldn't the terrorists target the president as well? As soon as the gravity of the day's events became clear, getting Bush on the move to somewhere safe, and as quickly as possible, became a top priority. A White House stenographer who was traveling with the president that morning remembered that once Air Force One took off from Florida, it climbed so high and so fast that she thought they might need to put on oxygen masks.[52] People watching the news on television, however, weren't going to be reassured by what was reasonable, nor were the people broadcasting the news. The day's television had looked like the first act of a Hollywood disaster movie, and in the second and third acts of a Hollywood disaster movie, viewers get to see the heroes fight back and win. Nine hours after the first plane hit, those images were nowhere to be found.

Nine hours is an extremely long time to spend watching television even under the best of circumstances. When those nine hours comprise an unremitting barrage of violence, and when the news stations have all done away with commercial breaks for the day, the experience is particularly grueling. To watch September 11 on television, with its repetitive circuit of images—shot of the crash, shot of the towers collapsing, shot of the smoking Pentagon, shot of the anchor at his desk, shot of people on the street covered in ash—was to feel trapped in a bad dream that refused to end. One of the only ways to verify that it *would* eventually end, that time had in fact continued to pass, was to notice how the light changed in the aerial shots of New York. On ABC, one became very familiar with what looked like a helicopter panorama of lower Manhattan, though it could also have been taken by a camera mounted on the roof of a tall building in New Jersey. The first time it appeared, after both towers fell, it looked as though the entirety of downtown was on fire. The office towers and apartment buildings were wreathed in a haze of smoke and ash, which slowly spilled out onto the Hudson like dry-ice fog in a theater production drifting over the lip of the stage and down into the orchestra pit. Throughout the afternoon, ABC returned to this shot, a great cloud condensing out of the ruins of the towers and slowly diffusing itself out of the city. Bit by bit, the sky overhead changed color several times. Then it went dark.

• • •

Myths are not static. If they want to hold on to their place in a culture, they can't afford to be. The colonial women who were held captive by seventeenth-century Native Americans and then lived to publish their stories became mythical figures because their experiences condensed and expressed something about what the new Puritan society of New England was experiencing as a whole. The Indian Wars, and especially King Philip's War, which began in 1675, left no part of the colonies untouched. The Puritans' fight against the Wampanoag leader Metacom, whom they had called King Philip in an earlier period of friendship, remains the deadliest war in American history when ranked by the percentage of the population that was killed. One in sixteen men of military age died by the war's end, out of a total population of sixty thousand, and half of the towns they lived in were damaged as well.[53] The original captivity narratives, with their heroines able to do little more than pray for deliverance, reflected both the helplessness of being menaced from all sides and the steadfast piety that was required to endure.

By the end of the eighteenth century, however, those stories no longer fit the American situation. It was clear by then that although the struggle to colonize Native American land remained perilous, it was now the Indians themselves, and not the settlers, who faced displacement and extermination. The colonists were more confident and secure than had seemed possible a century earlier, and that meant the myths they relied on to understand the world around them would have to change. "The psychology of the early colonial wars," wrote Richard Slotkin, "with its sense of total endangerment, was culturally preserved in order to justify the project of dispossessing the Indians," but the pious, helpless, female captive no longer worked as a protagonist.[54] A different hero was needed, someone in whom Americans could recognize their growing ambitions. A new generation of writers invented the figure who would serve as the template for all the myth heroes to follow, from the cowboys and outlaws of the American West all the way down to Batman. That figure was the hunter.

Daniel Boone was the first of these hunter legends. He was a real person, born into a family of Pennsylvania Quakers in 1734. As a young man, he participated in a number of the Indian Wars and supported his family as a hunter and trapper. In 1769, he set out on a two-year hunting expedition into the wilds of Kentucky, which were reputed to be filled with game as well as fertile land. It was as a Kentucky pioneer that Boone made his name, thanks in large part to a historian named John Filson. In 1784, when Boone was fifty years old, Filson published *The Discovery, Settlement, and Present State of Kentucke.* The book ended with an appendix—much longer than the main text itself—chronicling Boone's exploits, which included constant battles with Native Americans trying to prevent the whites from taking their land, the founding of one of the first European settlements west of the Appalachians, the rescue of three young white girls from Native American kidnappers, and his own escape from captivity at the hands of the Shawnee. Filson's aim in writing his book was to persuade new settlers to pull up stakes and head for a new life, and to that end his version of Boone, though largely faithful to the biographical details of the man's life, featured long disquisitions in which Boone would extol the natural wonders of the new territory as well as the morally fortifying effects of building a new civilization from scratch, far from the decadent metropolis. *Kentucke* turned Boone into a celebrity on both sides of the Atlantic, and his story was soon being told and retold by writers who were more comfortable exaggerating his feats of daring and strength (one famous account had him escape from a band of Native Americans by swinging away on vines, like Tarzan).[55] In 1853, a large marble sculpture by Horatio Greenough was put on display at the Capitol, where it would stay for more than a hundred years. The sculpture depicted an enormous white man, towering over and restraining an ax-wielding Native American warrior, as a faithful dog looked on and a white woman and her baby cowered in the rear. Greenough titled his sculpture *The Rescue,* and while he never named the heroic figure at its center, everyone knew who it was. The name the wider public gave to the sculpture leaves no doubt as to the strength of the mythological chain connecting Boone to all of Hollywood's twenty-first-century action heroes: *Daniel Boone Protects His Family.*[56]

Various heroes popped out of the mold first cast by Filson's Daniel Boone, each with his own defining characteristics. In a series of five novels published between 1823 and 1841, the most famous being *The Last of the Mohicans,* James Fenimore Cooper told the life story of the frontiersman Natty Bumppo (a.k.a. Leatherstocking, Hawkeye,

Deerslayer, Pathfinder, and, to some of his French and Native American enemies, *La Longue Carabine*).[57] Where Boone was a fully pragmatic hunter-colonist, a contemplative man looking to reconcile the wanderer's impulse and the thrill of the chase with the stabilizing imperatives of family and civilization, Natty Bumppo was something of an autodidact mystic. Many of his adventures centered on lakes or other bodies of water, dreamlike, rippling expanses evoking the view that the wilderness itself was a kind of ocean into which one could plunge in search of truth and renewal. Bumppo is a white man who spends much of his life among Native Americans, one of whom, the Mohican chief Chingachgook, is his best friend. No other white man is better equipped to admire what is admirable in Native American civilization, but as Natty is quick to remind those around him, he *is* white—in his phrasing, he is a "man without a cross." He knows which side he is on, and he will fight the Native Americans whenever they kidnap some white woman or commit any other outrage, a task for which, again, because of the time he spends learning their ways, no other white man is more qualified. It is because of his regular contact with the very people the European settlers have to exterminate to secure their own civilization that Bumppo becomes the embodiment of everything the settler civilization values about itself. He knows the Indians well. He respects their customs, gifts, talents, and tactics, but he will not become one of them. That white people are different—superior, in fact—can never be forgotten, and Bumppo uses what he learns to help his white brethren push the Native Americans out of the way as the colonists surge west. Thus is the new American society continually renewed and replenished through its violent encounters with the people it steadily dispossesses. Of Bumppo's various names, the one he values most is Hawkeye, which is the name a fallen Huron enemy bestowed on him with his dying breaths, in admiration of the white man's superhuman marksmanship.

One can follow the emergence of new variations on the type, each suited to his own historical moment, all the way up to the present day. Boone, the philosopher-king of the woods, and Bumppo, the warrior-mystic living in the halfway place between white civilization and Native "savagery," were accompanied by Davy Crockett, the high-spirited idiot who simply loved killing for its own sake. At moments of uncertainty and defeat in the late nineteenth century, the country could turn to George Armstrong Custer, whose heroic "last stand" at the hands of Lakota Sioux, Northern Cheyenne, and Arapaho fighters in the Battle of the Little Bighorn became America's most famous tale of sacrifice and redemption, one that still provides inspiration to recent Hollywood films such as *300* and *Lone Survivor*. In the twentieth century, Hollywood served as the most important temple dedicated to the preservation and refinement of the national mythology, embodied above all in Westerns and the figure at the center of many of them, John Wayne.

It is beyond my expertise to specify the degree to which these figures are *uniquely* American—many cultures have myths in which a hero defends society against barbarians—but there is no questioning their power and influence over the American identity. These characters were all distinct in their own ways, but their personalities and stories share certain traits that have held constant for nearly four hundred years. First, they are white men, exclusively. The female heroine of the original Puritan captivity narratives was not completely discarded by the hunter myths that succeeded her, but she was relegated to a supporting role as the hero's daughter or wife, the one whose kidnapping sets the main story, the rescue narrative, in motion. If real-life women played too large or too active a role in the lives of the frontier heroes, the writers who turned those heroes into mythological figures made the necessary adjustments. That's how Daniel Boone's wife, Rebecca, who kept Boone's large family together and moved it around the country multiple times, by herself, when the Indian Wars were at their fiercest, appeared in Filson's account as only an unnamed "wife" whose activities were not discussed at all.[58] Second, the hunter heroes are preternaturally skilled in combat, capable of precision shooting at hundreds of yards, unflappable calm under fire, comprehensive knowledge of the terrain, and unmatched feats of strength and endurance. They favor solitude, or, at most, the company of a good woman and one or two trusted friends, but they have a gift for leading others that will make itself known if that's what the situation requires. They prefer action to chitchat and individual initiative to the useless planning of bureaucrats, and they know—this is crucial—that while rules are a crucial part of the order that makes civilization possible, there are also times when one must be willing to go beyond what's allowed. Poised on the frontier, the edge of the wilderness, they help to define the contours of American civilization by exploring its outer limits. They are not like Kurtz in *Heart of Darkness,* plunging into savagery and losing himself to madness in the process. They learn just enough about the savages to know how to fight them, and this knowledge allows them to understand better than anyone why it is that America is the world's great beacon of hope. No sacrifice could be too much if made to protect America from barbarism, and the hunter heroes are ready to make it. Above all, they are willing to fight. In these stories, violence is the only remedy for humiliation, fear, and trauma, and it will be administered in whatever quantities are required to wipe the enemy off the face of the earth. As afternoon turned to evening on September 11, the ghosts of these myth figures floated among the clouds of smoke and ash that emanated from lower Manhattan.

• • •

The Italian writer and academic Umberto Eco once wrote an essay about *Casablanca.* He'd seen the film screened for students at American universities, and he'd watched the students "greet each scene and canonical line of dialogue ('Round up the usual suspects,' 'Was that cannon fire, or is it my heart pounding?'—or even every time that Bogey says 'kid') with ovations usually reserved for football games." He wondered why audiences responded with such enthusiasm, because he thought that *Casablanca,* "aesthetically speaking," was "mediocre." "It is a comic strip," he wrote, "a hotch-potch, low on psychological credibility, and with little continuity in its dramatic effects." He didn't think the movie's fans were dupes—quite the opposite, in fact. There could be no doubting that *Casablanca* was an amazing success. But he wanted to identify what it was that made the film so successful, because it wasn't the things that made most great films successful.

The secret, Eco thought, was to be found in the fact that the film was made up as it was shot. The script was only half-written when shooting began, which meant that no one on set, not even the director himself, could know with certainty what the characters would say or which of her two lovers Ingrid Bergman would choose. Forced to improvise, the director, cast, and crew drew on the various storytelling and filmmaking clichés they had at hand, one after another. Crucially, they didn't just choose a few of them. "When the choice of the tried and true is limited," Eco wrote, "the result is a trite or mass-produced film, or simply kitsch. But when the tried and true repertoire is used wholesale, the result is . . . a sense of dizziness, a stroke of brilliance." *Casablanca* used *all* of the clichés, all at once, and this was the key to its genius. Eco cataloged them: the location, Morocco ("the Exotic"), "Unhappy Love," a "Passage to the Promised Land," the "Magic Key" (the visa every character chases), the "Fatal Game" (roulette), the "magic circle" (Rick's Place) where "everything can (and does) happen," the "Last Outpost on the Edge of the Desert," and the "Triumph of Purity" at the end (only those whose intentions are pure can have what they want). To an extent unmatched by any previous film, *Casablanca* piled every storytelling cliché in the book on top of one another, and it was rewarded with a place in film history that remains unassailable today. "When all the archetypes burst in shamelessly, we reach Homeric depths," Eco wrote. "Two cliches make us laugh. A hundred cliches move us."[59]

Though it would take weeks to unfold, something similar started to happen on television and in the media more generally around 6:00 p.m. on September 11. That's when President Bush arrived back in Washington, D.C. After a day that produced many Hollywood-style images of destruction and mayhem but refused to follow anything like a Hollywood script, here, finally, was a scene that could make people feel good. The president's frightening, improvised odyssey around the country was over, and here he was exiting the helicopter, saluting the Marine at the bottom of the staircase, and striding toward the White House, just as so many presidents before him had done so many times. Other officials had prepared the ground and set the tone for his arrival. "There is a pervasive sense of anger among the military officers I've talked to today," a reporter told Peter Jennings. "They have mentioned, again and again, Pearl Harbor. . . . They are ready to go to war, there is a sense of war here at the Pentagon."[60] William Webster, the former director of both the FBI and the CIA, phoned in to urge that America's intelligence agencies not be weighed down with oversight as they went hunting for the perpetrators. "Professionals are very willing to do their job under court orders and the appropriate procedures," he said. "All that they ask is that they not be unduly burdened by restrictions that in times like this get in the way of finding the culprits and bringing them to justice."[61] The chairman of the Joint Chiefs came on the air. "Make no mistake about it," he said, breaking the fourth wall to address Americans directly, "your armed forces are ready." He was followed by Senator Carl Levin, who said that terrorists "are the common enemy of the civilized world." Levin, in turn, was followed by Senator John Warner, a Republican, who said that "Congress stands behind our president, and the president speaks with one voice for this entire nation." As for Bush himself, an ABC reporter described him as "agitated and angry." Bush's press secretary added that "the president is very eager to make plain tonight that his mood is retaliatory. . . . We will find these people and they will suffer the consequences of taking on this nation."[62]

For an exciting moment, it even seemed that the terrorists were already on the receiving end of America's anger. Just before 6:00 p.m., CNN reported that explosions were going off in Kabul, Afghanistan. The network's international correspondent had heard perhaps a dozen blasts around the city's perimeter, as well as aircraft overhead, and he had seen tracer fire shooting up from the ground. Based on his experiences reporting in Belgrade and Baghdad—in other words, based on his intimate knowledge of the savage wilderness outside America's borders—the correspondent judged that the detonations sounded more than anything like "large missiles." It was the middle of the night in Kabul, and so CNN could only report what its correspondent could see and hear from the roof of the Kabul Intercontinental Hotel, but it certainly appeared to him that the Afghan defense forces had detected a "threat in the air." There was a fire on the horizon. It had begun as a "faint yellow" but was now a "bright orange blazing." Detonations were going off in "multiple areas," reverberating off the mountains that surrounded Kabul, and rockets were being launched into the sky. By this point, it was widely known that American officials suspected that Osama bin Laden was behind the attacks in the United States, and it was also known that bin Laden had established his base of operations in Afghanistan. In addition to the fire burning on the horizon and the explosions pounding the area near Kabul's airport, CNN's reporter could see other flashes reflecting off the underside of clouds farther out. He allowed that those flashes could just be lightning, but one couldn't discount the possibility that the bombardment was occurring across a wider area.

CNN then shifted over to one of its political correspondents, who was on the line with the former secretary of defense William Cohen. She finally put into words the suspicion—the hope, rather—that had prompted CNN to pay attention to Kabul in the first place: "Is this something that is likely to be the United States retaliating, which I think is what immediately comes to people's minds?" Cohen threw cold water on the idea, correctly pointing out that the U.S. was most likely still in the intelligence gathering stage of formulating its response and further noting that Afghanistan had been in the grip of a civil war for some time. The simplest explanation for the fighting was that it was just part of that ongoing war (as it would turn out, that was also the correct explanation). This did not satisfy CNN, whose reporter pressed Cohen. She had just got off the phone with George H. W. Bush's secretary of state, a man with the magnificently American name Lawrence Eagleburger, and he had told her that what the country needed to do "was strike against countries like Afghanistan that are harboring terrorists, and not wait to find out exactly who was responsible for today's atrocities." Cohen rejected that idea as well, but CNN pushed on, speaking next to the Republican senator Orrin

Hatch. "Again," she began, "we're stressing that we have no idea who is behind these attacks in Kabul," when what she was really stressing was the opposite, the possibility that America's missiles had already started to fly. "But if this were the West," she continued, enlarging the aggrieved party from a single country to an entire civilization, "if this were the United States, would it be appropriate to retaliate so quickly?" Hatch replied, more or less, that it would. He'd tried to warn people about bin Laden all the way back in 1996, after all, when he went on *Meet the Press*.[63]

The skirmish in Kabul, being totally unrelated to what was happening in the United States, did not actually satisfy the hunter myth's requirement for swift and violent retribution, but that did not stop the television networks from pretending that it did. That kind of thing happened a lot over the following weeks. In *The Terror Dream*, Susan Faludi pointed out that in its September 13 issue, *Newsweek* ran a photograph of a firefighter carrying a little girl to safety with the caption, "Horror at home." But the photograph wasn't taken on September 11—it was from the aftermath of the Oklahoma City bombing in 1995.[64] It wasn't as though *Newsweek* lacked for actual photographs of September 11 to choose from, but contemporary images didn't tell the kind of story that Americans had been conditioned by their own mythology to want: a story about women and children being rescued by men. September 11 couldn't provide images of firefighters pulling little girls out of the flames, though, because in addition to the fact that very few people survived to be pulled out of the rubble, a majority of the workers at the financial firms that dominated the upper floors at the Twin Towers, as well as those working for the military at the Pentagon, were men, and almost all of the victims of September 11 were adults. Men accounted for 75 percent of the dead, and just eight children, all of whom were aboard the hijacked planes, were killed in the attacks. *Newsweek*'s publication of a six-year-old photograph of a totally different event was a kind of work-around, a way to give the people what they wanted even if reality refused to cooperate.

Faludi went on to observe that the mythological tableau of a pious mother tending to her cabin hearth while a husband stood guard with a rifle in hand also seemed to govern the kinds of lifestyle pieces that the media churned out after the attacks. Virginia Heffernan, a writer for *The New York Times Magazine,* believed the attacks had sent women rushing to the altar, casting off whatever ambivalence they might previously have felt toward holy matrimony. "The old indecisiveness comes to seem out of sync with the country's renewed sense of purpose," Heffernan wrote. "It seems somehow unpatriotic."[65] Another story from the newspaper's style section observed that while single women might previously have understood themselves to be happy adults with rewarding careers and rich social lives, the attacks had demonstrated that what they really felt was loneliness. If these reformed women wanted to settle down, they were truly going to need to settle, or, in the article's words, "reprioritize the rigid criteria they apply to selecting a mate."[66] Men weren't exempt from this kind of patronizing advice, either. *The Washington Post* observed that the "touchy-feely sensitive male" was out. America might have had its fun demonizing alpha males as antisocial and violent, but metrosexuals weren't going to win the war against al-Qaeda and the Taliban. It was time to find a new appreciation for those strong men who had been "psychopathologized by howling fems."[67]

But just as *Newsweek*'s Oklahoma City photograph didn't reflect the reality of what took place on September 11, this flurry of articles about women's new desire to marry did not reflect any concrete change in Americans' romantic practices. Divorce rates briefly dropped after the attacks, which makes sense: People confronted with a destabilizing catastrophe like September 11 are unlikely to want to add more instability to their lives, even if those lives are unsatisfying. But marriage rates didn't spike; in fact, they didn't change at all.[68] Heffernan's friends might well have bemoaned their solitude for a period of time, but there was no wider rush to the altar.

September 11 also prompted an immediate discussion on television about how many rules America would be willing to break in its pursuit of revenge. This is one of the most important traits of Indian fighters like Daniel Boone, Davy Crockett, and General Custer, the willingness to go beyond what polite society permits so as to ensure that polite society survives. Civilized war, after all, is for civilized people. If you want to win a war against barbarians, you have to be willing to behave like one. Just after 6:15 p.m., ABC's local affiliate in Washington interviewed Eric Holder, who had previously served as deputy attorney general for the Justice Department and would go on to become attorney general under President Obama. "It has long been a belief," the anchor said, "that this nation will not assassinate a foreign leader or a target. Is there a different set of circumstances that come into play as a result of today's terrorist attacks?"

It is worth pausing here for a moment to observe just how strange this question was, especially because it is such an instinctive and natural question for Americans to ask. Bin Laden, by that point the day's prime suspect, was an international pariah, a man forced to shelter in one of the world's poorest countries. Meanwhile, the United States had at its disposal the strongest military in world history, plus the unadulterated goodwill of the international community. Pressuring the Taliban to hand over bin Laden in exchange for its continued survival was not likely to be difficult. Indeed, the Taliban made exactly that offer in October 2001; the United States turned it down.[69] At the very least, it would have been no more difficult for the United States to formally declare war on Afghanistan and then use the overwhelming might of its conventional military to capture or kill al-Qaeda's leader. Both of those options would have been well within the boundaries of American law, and there was no reason to think that either option would fail.

What's strange, then, is that Holder's interviewer jumped immediately to an unnecessary third option, in which America would mete out justice beyond the boundaries of its own laws. Holder, one of the most powerful lawyers in the country, took up this third option with enthusiasm. "Federal law prohibits the assassination of individuals or leaders of countries," he began, "but federal law *does* permit us to go after people for defensive purposes, and a person like bin Laden, given what has happened today and what he has done to this country in the past, I think certainly would fall outside that prohibition of assassination." Legal semantics aside, the most obvious interpretation of Holder's words was that despite America's legal prohibition on assassination, the gravity of bin Laden's actions justified killing him. That's certainly what Holder's interviewer understood him to be saying. "So if President Bush gives the order," the anchor said, "Osama bin Laden can be assassinated legally within the parameters of United States law?" "Yeah," Holder said, before engaging in one last bit of hairsplitting. "I wouldn't use the term 'assassination.'"[70] He might as well have winked.

Another strange aspect of the Holder interview was that no government official had yet confirmed that bin Laden was the architect of the attacks, though anonymous intelligence and Bush administration figures had voiced their suspicions throughout the day. The public knew almost nothing concrete about the attacks beyond what they had been able to see on their television screens; hard facts about who had carried out the plan, or where they came from, or how they did it remained obscure.

The simple version of the story that would be pieced together in the following weeks and months goes like this: At some point in the mid-1990s, a Pakistani extremist named Khalid Sheikh Mohammed began to think about using commercial aircraft to attack the United States. Though he was not a formal member of al-Qaeda, he hoped that Osama bin Laden's group could supply the money and operatives needed to carry out the operation. Bin Laden, born to an aristocratic Saudi family in 1957, had founded al-Qaeda in 1988, and by 1996 he was living in Afghanistan and raising money to train mujahideen fighters. KSM met bin Laden in Afghanistan and proposed what would come to be known as the "planes operation," and bin Laden decided to support it in April 1999.

After selecting the targets in collaboration with KSM and deciding it would be a suicide mission, bin Laden began choosing people who would put the plan into action. Some of the operatives trained in Afghanistan and then received instruction about the United States in Karachi, Pakistan. From there, the operatives made their way to America via Kuala Lumpur, and another group of aspiring jihadists based in Hamburg joined up as well. By early 2000, members of the plot were arriving in the United States and undertaking flight training in Oklahoma, Florida, Minneapolis, and Arizona. Bin Laden and

KSM also recruited operatives who would serve as the "muscle," that is, carry out the hijacking and keep passengers at bay while the pilots took control of the plane. These operatives began to arrive in the United States in April 2001. By July, all nineteen operatives were inside the country. Fifteen came from Saudi Arabia, one from Lebanon, one from Egypt, and two from the United Arab Emirates. On the morning of September 11, they boarded four separate flights, two departing from Boston, one from Newark, and one from Washington, D.C. All four planes were headed for California. Armed with knives, box cutters, and pepper spray, they hijacked their flights shortly after takeoff and then diverted the planes to their final destinations.

The time required to compile this information, however, could not be allowed to delay America's response, and heading into the evening, different parts of the federal government began to present themselves to television cameras in formal tableaux of mourning, unity, determination, and resolve. Speaker of the House Dennis Hastert spoke on the steps of the Capitol, with members of Congress behind him, and glowered, really glowered, while saying that "those who brought forth this evil deed will pay the price," his rhetoric simultaneously recalling old Westerns and the Bible. The camera pulled back as he spoke, and by the time it had finished zooming out, one could see thirty-one different people on the screen. At least twenty-nine of them were men, and all of them appeared to be white. Hastert asked for a moment of silence, after which the assembled legislators began to disperse until someone broke out with the opening strains of "God Bless America." At the end of the song, Congress applauded itself.[71]

Around 8:30 p.m., President Bush arrived on the screen to speak from the Oval Office. His travels were finally over. Here was the president as he was meant to be seen, seated at his gleaming oak desk in the room that symbolized his power, with an American flag behind one shoulder and a flag bearing the country's seal behind the other. Peter Jennings introduced the speech as a kind of political climax to the day's events, summarizing Bush's travels and then emphasizing the significance of what he was about to say. "The president is back in Washington now," he said, "and there has been no time in his presidency, and there may never be a time like this again, when it has been so important what he says to the country, because I think we all know at moments like this the country looks to the president of the United States for understanding, for knitting the country together. Some presidents do it brilliantly, and some do not. Here is Mr. Bush."

The feed switched over to the White House, and for three or four seconds Bush sat there in silence, staring into the television lights with his brow furrowed. "Okay, this was a—well . . ." Jennings trailed off, audibly irritated. "The president isn't sitting there trying to think about what to say, I can assure you. The president is sitting there because someone in network television has sat him down and said, 'We'll cue you in thirty seconds, Mr. Bush.' And so as awkward as it looks to him, this is what we'd expect him to do." For nearly twelve hours now, Jennings had been trying to narrate, interpret, and contain a set of images that simply overwhelmed anything one could say about them, and here was another. He and ABC's viewers had expected Bush to launch straight into an address that would finally take some measure of governmental control over the day's events, and instead the president was just sitting there with his hands folded. Finally, the studio producers and the network people at the White House synced up. "And now here he is," Jennings said. The president began to speak.

Toward the end of his remarks, Bush said, "We will make no distinction between the terrorists who committed these acts and those who harbor them." This was the line that the ABC News correspondent George Stephanopoulos seized on when discussing the speech on the air afterward. "The words that the president used were so expansive, Peter. It wasn't just 'supported' or 'funded.' It was, 'any who harbor them,' who may have given them sanctuary at any time. That is a very open-ended commitment."[72]

CHAPTER 2

Iron Men

My rifle is human, even as I am human, because it is my life.
—The Creed of a United States Marine

About an hour before President Bush gave his Oval Office address on September 11, ABC ran a segment it had filmed earlier in the day at a high school. Students were following the news on television, and ABC wanted to know what they thought. "I always thought America was my superhero," one girl said. "I mean, nothing could harm America. America is everyone's defender."[1] Four years later, the Hollywood director Christopher Nolan, who to that point had directed two knotty psychological thrillers about guilt, truth, and the unreliability of memory, started making Batman movies.

The first, *Batman Begins*, was released in 2005, at the height of the Iraq War. It is about Batman's struggle to save a city that is tearing itself apart because of fear (terrorists have slipped a panic-inducing neurotoxin into Gotham's water supply).[2] In *The Dark Knight*, from 2008, Batman confronts the Joker, a lone-wolf terrorist whose crimes are motivated solely by his desire to "watch the world burn," mirroring the standard account of al-Qaeda's irrational hatred of freedom that prevailed in the early years of the war on terror. Batman only catches the Joker by inventing a machine that turns every cellphone in Gotham into a surveillance device, a necessary move that he knows is morally indefensible.[3] In the trilogy's final installment, *The Dark Knight Rises*, the villain Bane promises to redistribute Gotham's wealth and holds show trials for the city's elites, but his master plan, which he thinks will snuff out "hope" once and for all, is simply to destroy the city with a nuclear bomb.[4] The trauma of September 11 echoes through all three of these movies. Toward the end of *The Dark Knight*, Batman surveys the wreckage of one of the Joker's attacks, with twisted metal, smoldering fires, and the arcing jets of the firefighters' hoses intentionally recalling images of Ground Zero in the fading light of that first evening. The film's poster, with a flaming Batman logo cutting across the side of an office building, replicates the gashes left in the sides of the Twin Towers before they came down.[5] The third film introduces Bane with a plane hijacking, and then he announces his arrival in Gotham by bombing a football field while a game is in progress. Tens of thousands of spectators watch in horror, like people looking across the river to Manhattan from their rooftops, as the earth opens up and swallows their team.

Nolan said in 2012 that his Batman movies "genuinely aren't intended to be political." When his interviewer pressed him on the subject, noting that "a lot of people would argue that all art is political," Nolan said, without elaborating, "But what's politics?"[6] The way to understand inanities like this is to take them at face value: Nolan doesn't have any specific understanding of what politics is, and professionally he doesn't need one. He is not a polemicist, nor do his movies advocate for causes. As a Hollywood director, he simply needs to convince viewers that the money they spent purchasing a ticket wasn't wasted. That requires its own kind of genius, though, and Nolan has it. He is like a weather station, picking up on things in the atmosphere—stories in the news, images that stick in people's minds, consumer goods or turns of phrase that are completely new one day and ubiquitous the next—and then using hundreds of millions of dollars to put them into movies. It would be overstating things to say that *The Dark Knight*

Rises is a movie *about* Occupy Wall Street or the Tea Party. It's too incoherent for that, and Nolan doesn't have a party line he is trying to push. *The Dark Knight Rises* is just a normal Batman movie that was made specifically for audiences that had spent the past several years hearing about Occupy Wall Street and the Tea Party all the time. What makes it effective is that Nolan's atmospheric pressure readings are more sensitive and detailed than those of most other Hollywood directors. Taken as a set, his three Batman movies constitute a vision of the first ten years of the war on terror as seen through the fever dreams of a teenage comics fan. Americans of all ages found Nolan's dream compelling. The Batman movies made $1.2 billion at the domestic box office, and they were nominated for nine Academy Awards, winning three.[7]

Hollywood rebooted dozens of comic book heroes during the twenty years after September 11, but it was Batman—not the plucky teenager Spider-Man, and not the alien deity Superman—who allowed superhero movies to take a more serious turn and become vehicles for the country's anxieties about war, surveillance, freedom, and dread. To see why this was possible for Batman and nobody else, it may suffice just to describe him and then see if that description reminds us of anything. Unlike other superheroes, Batman is an ordinary human man. He does not have any supernatural abilities. He can't fly or shoot lasers out of his eyes, and he wasn't subjected to any scientific experiments that made him unusually fast or strong. His superpower, if we can call it that, is money. Known to most people as Bruce Wayne, Batman is the scion of Gotham's wealthiest and most powerful family. The public views him as decadent, dissipated, and lazy, albeit handsome. He shows up late to five-star dinners with a supermodel on one arm and a prima ballerina on the other, and he is also the not-very-engaged owner of the family business, Wayne Enterprises, a globe-spanning conglomerate that invests heavily in technological research while outsourcing its manufacturing to Asia. It is Wayne's limitless wealth that allows him to build Batman's gadgets: the armored suit, the combat tools, the hip-holstered rappelling gear, the bombproof car, the motorcycle, the small airplane/hovercraft. The city police are suspicious of Batman's vigilantism. They're trying to keep order by using a traditional set of rules that everybody understands, and they're reluctant to accept the help of this anonymous man who delivers justice while refusing to answer to laws other than his own. They can never decide whether to put him in handcuffs or give him a medal. Eventually, though, they wise up: The threats are too great, and only Batman has the money and the military hardware required to deal with them.

Presenting himself to the public as a vapid playboy so as to avoid suspicion, Bruce Wayne is actually all that keeps Gotham from collapsing into chaos, violence, and tyranny. Without Batman's high-tech arsenal and bottomless reserves of self-sacrificing generosity, Gotham would be nothing more than a playground for gangsters and madmen. Maybe you see where I'm going with this? Batman appealed to Americans after September 11 because in Nolan's films, Gotham is the world, and Batman is the United States.

It was September 11 that really made the analogy work, because the other important thing about Batman is that his heroism is the product of boyhood trauma and victimization. Many of the war on terror Batman movies have reminded their viewers that "Master Bruce," as his English butler calls him, was once attacked by bats after tumbling down a well on the grounds of the family estate. He lay there cowering until his father, a doctor constantly imparting lessons about the importance of putting your wealth to good use by helping the poor—for the purposes of the analogy, think of this as "international aid"—climbed down into the well and brought his son back into the daylight. These lessons were cut short, however, when a mugger, an ungrateful member of the very class the Waynes had spent millions trying to aid, killed both of Bruce's parents right in front of him. The adult Bruce vowed to fight crime in Gotham because crime is what deprived him of parental love, and in becoming a fighter in his own right, he hopes to exorcise the shame he feels at not having been able to save his mom and dad. That was just the kind of hero America wanted to see as it grappled with its own failures to save the thousands who died in New York and Washington. Wayne is even more admirable in that he embraces his shame rather than running from it, taking on the bat identity because bats are what he fears most. And finally, so as not to visit his own formative trauma on any other innocent children, no matter how repulsive their criminal parents may be, Wayne decides that for all his weaponry and training, Batman will never kill anyone. Thus is limitless technological and financial power tempered by wise restraint.

For a country that had invaded Iraq despite the disapproval of most of the rest of the world, a figure like Batman was extraordinarily appealing. At the end of *The Dark Knight*, Batman agrees to let the people of Gotham think that he murdered their crusading district attorney in cold blood. He didn't, but he and the police commissioner both understand that the real story—the DA had a psychotic break and tried to kill a little boy in front of his parents—is too awful to ever be made public. As a wounded Batman flees the scene, knowing that all the cops in Gotham will soon be hunting for him, the little boy he saved asks why he is running: "He didn't do anything wrong." "Because he's the hero Gotham deserves," Commissioner Gordon says, "but not the one it needs right now." Sometimes, in other words, a hero needs to be unpopular, even despised, in order to save those who don't know enough to be grateful for his sacrifice and devotion. In 2008, that sentiment would have been comforting to citizens of a country that was bogged down in an unpopular war of its own making.

But Batman wasn't popular just because he came up with a flattering explanation for the unpopularity of America's foreign policy. Along with all of the other comic book heroes who crowded into cinemas like circus performers in a clown car during the war on terror, Batman helped to answer some of the war's most pressing questions: What kinds of fighters would America need to mobilize in order to win? What would the mythological frontier hunter need to do, and what equipment would he need to bring with him, in order to ensure that the terrorists never threatened the homeland again? What did the ideal American soldier look like in the twenty-first century, and how did he fight? Batman, Iron Man, and the rest of the gang at Marvel and DC Studios provided an entertaining and glamorous answer to those questions, but other answers could be found by switching on CNN and Fox News. While Batman patrolled Gotham in multiplexes across the country during the first decade of the war, America's Special Forces units—Navy SEALs, Army Rangers, Green Berets, and the like—fanned out across the globe. They carried with them not just technologically sophisticated arsenals of their own but the country's distilled fantasies of national superiority. The main thrust of these fantasies, which Batman and other superheroes embodied on the screen, was that the special ops soldier's synthesis of training, human ingenuity, and cutting-edge technology would make the United States all but invulnerable in the fight against terrorism. Whether this vision of invincibility could survive the realities of war depended largely on just how vulnerable America's soldiers turned out to be.

· · ·

In 2003, an academic journal published a study covering the early stages of America's war in Afghanistan. It was titled "A Different Kind of War?"[8] Seven years later, an Army research center published a report with the same title, except that the question mark had been removed: *A Different Kind of War.*[9] That was the earliest consensus to coalesce around the war on terror, that it would be unlike any prior conflict in the country's history. "This was not Desert Storm, in which victory could be proclaimed once Iraqi troops were driven from Kuwait," one journalist wrote under the headline "What Would 'Victory' Mean?" "This was not a struggle against a conventional guerrilla force, whose yearning for a national homeland or the satisfaction of some grievance could be satisfied or denied."[10] "This is different," Secretary of State Colin Powell said. "The enemy is in many places. The enemy is not looking to be found. The enemy is hidden. The enemy is, very often, right here within our own country. And so you have to design a campaign plan that goes after that kind of enemy."[11] Donald Rumsfeld cautioned that such a campaign would not be able to rely on the old strategy manuals, according to which one prevailed by attacking areas with the highest concentrations of enemy personnel or infrastructure. "The terrorists don't have targets of high value," he said. "They don't have armies and navies and air forces that one can go battle against. They don't have capital cities with high-value assets that they're reluctant to lose."[12] (If you squint hard enough, this could also read as a description of Vietnam, but Bush administration officials generally avoided raising the specter of that particular defeat.) "This will be a different kind of conflict against a different kind of enemy," President Bush said in a radio address, "a conflict without battlefields or beachheads."[13] Al-Qaeda, Vice President Cheney said, was not a conventional military force with conventional ranks of conscripts and recruits. It was more like "an Internet chat room," a place where people could "come and participate . . . for one reason or another," even though they sometimes had "different motives and ideologies."[14] Such an unfamiliar enemy would require an unprecedented response. "It's a new kind of war," Rumsfeld said. "It will be unconventional, what we do."[15]

Rumsfeld and other members of the Bush administration had already spent years preparing for new and unconventional conflicts, as well as a new role for the United States in world affairs. They hadn't needed to explain their thinking to the public at the time, nor did they envision that something as horrible as September 11 would set their plans in motion, but now they had everyone's attention, and they weren't going to let the opportunity go to waste. Their boss had campaigned for president as a foreign policy moderate. In debates with then–Vice President Al Gore, Bush disavowed what he called "nation building," praised the Clinton administration for not sending U.S. troops to intervene in the Rwandan genocide, and voiced concern over the U.S. military being overextended.[16] The United States had been the world's lone superpower for a decade, just long enough to get used to it, and its foreign policy grandees understood the country's role as privileged but essentially managerial. America would step in when this or that rogue state got too far out of line, as Saddam Hussein had in 1990, but its primary task was just to keep the wheels of the global free market turning, a job that could mostly be handled by the bureaucrats at the International Monetary Fund and World Bank.

Once in office, however, Bush staffed his White House with foreign policy advisers who had a more expansive vision. Absent September 11, these neoconservatives might well have spent the Bush years nibbling at the edges of the Washington consensus, pushing at small opportunities to advocate for a more interventionist stance, and otherwise grousing to one another behind the scenes about the stubbornness and mediocrity of Congress or the State Department. But because September 11 *did* happen, they were able to realize their vision on the largest possible scale, all at once.

Their foreign policy program was motivated by the same anxieties that September 11 had brought to bear on the country as a whole. In 2000, Robert Kagan, a former State Department official with the Reagan administration, and William Kristol, the editor of the conservative *Weekly Standard,* published a collection of essays titled *Present Dangers: Crisis and Opportunity in American Foreign and Defense Policy.* The volume included contributions from several thinkers who would eventually take positions under Bush, including Richard Perle (adviser to Donald Rumsfeld), Elliott Abrams (National Security Council), and Paul Wolfowitz (deputy secretary of defense). These men had spent their careers helping to steer the most powerful ship of state in world history, but in *Present Dangers* all they could see on the horizon were "growing threats to the American peace established at the end of the Cold War." Elliott Abrams, for instance, thought that America's pursuit of a peace settlement between Israel and the Palestinians under George H. W. Bush and Bill Clinton had been the product of "naive optimism." Rather than fooling themselves into believing that Palestinians were ready for democratic self-rule, he wrote, America's policymakers should decelerate their pursuit of a Palestinian state and focus instead on what really mattered: "[avoiding] the creation of another radical Arab state that would weaken Jordan and Israel and perhaps Egypt while it draws close to Syria, Iraq, Libya, or Iran." Democracy, human rights, and addressing the Palestinians' so-called legitimate grievances would have to take a backseat to bolstering Israel's defenses and making sure the Middle East's more troublesome rulers understood that America was not going to cede its position of regional preeminence to an alliance of fundamentalist governments without a fight.[17]

Kristol and Kagan wanted the country to adopt "a foreign policy of 'benevolent hegemony' as a way of securing that peace and advancing American interests and principles around the world."[18] By "benevolent," they meant that America's interests were the world's interests. "Americans should understand," they wrote, "that their support for American pre-eminence is as much a strike for international justice as any people is capable of making."[19] And by "hegemony," the authors meant that the United States should be so powerful that no other country would even *think* about challenging it, much less actually try. One contributor argued that the United States needed to maintain a "two-war standard," meaning a military sufficiently large to wage full-scale wars with two powerful opponents at the same time. "What good would an American [security] guarantee be," he wrote, "if our allies knew that once the U.S. military became embroiled in a crisis elsewhere, it would not be able to come to their defense should they face attack? Any strategy that seriously aimed at deterring both current and future challenges had to be based on at least a two-war capability."[20]

Present Dangers brooded over old humiliations, as well as potential humiliations to come. The United States had easily defeated Iraq in the first Gulf War, but it had "failed to see that mission through to its proper conclusion: the removal of Saddam from power in Baghdad."[21] It warned that Hussein was "on the verge of breaking free from the international constraints imposed upon him"[22] (a fanciful idea), and it fretted about "a disturbing principle in the post–Cold War world: that dictators can challenge the peace, slaughter innocents in their own or in neighboring states, threaten their neighbors with missile attacks—and still hang on to power. This constitutes a great failure in American foreign policy, one that will surely come back to haunt us."[23] And while the Indian war cries grew louder at the edge of the woods, the United States was mired in "passivity and drift,"[24] a complacent stupor: "The simple fact is that today's U.S. armed forces are smaller, less well prepared for combat, and operating older equipment than those of a decade ago."[25] The appropriate response to these dangers could no longer be the halfhearted attempts to patch up a crumbling international stability that had characterized prior years. "What is needed," the authors wrote, "is not better management of the status quo, but a fundamental change in the way our leaders and the public think about America's role in the world."[26] Kagan wrote that he hoped for "a broader and more forward-looking conception of the national interest."[27] His goals, if realized, would amount to a revolution in international affairs. When the United States sent its first Special Forces into Afghanistan in the middle of September 2001, weeks before the larger invasion began on October 7, the revolution was under way.

The neoconservative project was not without its own internal contradictions, however. These contradictions looked surmountable at the outset, but in the end they helped doom the United States to failure in Afghanistan and Iraq. First, while the Bush administration was proposing a massive expansion of the military's role around the world, it could not effect that expansion in the traditional way—adding hundreds of thousands of soldiers—without a draft. This was a nonstarter. The trauma of defeat in Vietnam had poisoned subsequent generations of Americans against compulsory military service, and politicians were also wary of the opportunities a draft provided for protest should the war not go as planned. Second, Americans were not going to accept the sort of war that resulted in high casualties or disrupted daily life in a sustained, material way. Indeed, the government had started promising just the opposite within days of September 11, with Bush urging Americans to see their summer vacations as expressions of patriotic defiance ("Get down to Disney World").[28] Bush was trying to rebuild the country's shattered faith in the safety of commercial air travel, but his remarks also harmonized with the more general sense that to change daily life in any real way would be to "let the terrorists win."

The third contradiction was the most consequential: Secretary of Defense Donald Rumsfeld had taken office promising to transform the military by making it *smaller* while still extending its reach. He adhered to a set of theories and reforms that went under the name revolution in military affairs, or RMA. Proponents of RMA believed that recent technological advances, especially those relating to information and communications, were transforming conflict. Because the U.S. military already enjoyed such an enormous technological advantage over any of its rivals, it followed that it should fully embrace these transformations. By leaning further into an area it could already count as a strength, the United States would extend the gap separating its armed forces from those of other countries and compound its advantages on the battlefield. Instead of columns of soldiers crashing into and steadily destroying each other, modern warfare would be characterized by speed, precision, and up-to-the-second situational awareness. The famous fog of war would be reduced to one of history's curios.[29] This kind of combat meant satellite communication, twenty-four-hour drone surveillance, light armored vehicles racing through the landscape in search of enemy combatants, massive air support called in on targets marked by lasers, and, crucially, fewer ground forces. The appeal of such theories to Rumsfeld and his Republican colleagues was obvious: Fewer ground troops would mean fewer casualties, every one of which constituted a small but real public relations disaster for an administration trying to sustain polling support for the war effort. Rumsfeld pushed his cheerleading for RMA reforms far past what his army's commanders were comfortable with, but he was in charge, so they would have to make do. In preparing to invade Iraq, General Tommy Franks requested a force of about half a million U.S. troops. Rumsfeld gave him 170,000.[30]

Technology was the linchpin of the whole program. Just as technology made it possible for Batman to take on the entirety of Gotham's criminal underworld by himself, it was technology that allowed the Bush administration to claim with a straight face that the United States could fight a war spanning the globe without conscripting a large number of its citizens into service. It was technology that made it possible for the United States to topple one of the world's most stable military dictatorships over the course of just a few weeks in the spring of 2003, and it was technology that let the country's civilians believe that their lives at home would not change at all while people around the world bore the brunt of America's fury and vengeance. The media emphasized the military's technological prowess at every opportunity. The Iraq War began on the evening of May 19, 2003, in the United States, with a televised countdown to invasion leading up to President Bush announcing a full-scale military assault. The United States then launched several cruise missiles from warships floating in the Persian Gulf, attempting a series of "decapitation strikes" that would take out Saddam Hussein, members of his inner circle, and important figures within the Iraqi military hierarchy. The strikes only managed to kill dozens of civilians[31]—as in the run-up to the war, Americans struggled to distinguish good intelligence from bad—but that wasn't known in real time, and on CNN the strikes looked like a prelude to the massive bombardment that was to follow, live and literally in prime time. When the full "shock and awe" campaign then failed to begin that evening, the network's anchors, audibly puzzled and disappointed, passed the time by describing the precision and sophistication of America's weapons. Digital images of planes and missiles appeared on the screen, accompanied by excessively detailed information on their technical capabilities. The Nighthawk stealth fighter, viewers learned, had a top speed of 650 miles per hour and a range of 690 miles, and it was equipped with "various laser-guided bombs and GBU-27 'Bunker Busters.'" The Tomahawk cruise missiles that had just been launched into Iraq used "terrain contour matching, digital scene matching, and GPS to reach targets." And the B-2 Spirit stealth bomber had a range of more than 7,000 miles to accompany its "$2.1 billion price tag." No planes had been used at all in the evening's attacks, and CNN didn't explain what "terrain contour matching" meant, but the point was to impress, not to inform. In the digital renderings, the planes and missiles were literally haloed in golden light.[32]

Digital and information technologies were developing at a rapid pace. The dot-com bubble was in the process of bursting on September 11, with the tech-heavy Nasdaq exchange falling by more than 75 percent between March 2000 and October 2002.[33] But the five years of euphoria that preceded the crash had injected wild amounts of capital into Silicon Valley, and both the military and the defense manufacturers who built the weapons were eager to adopt the tech companies' new toys as quickly as they could. Less than a month after the attacks, with the Pentagon preparing to receive billions of dollars' worth of emergency funding from Congress, the Defense Department's shopping lists were making the rounds. Bombs would be "smarter," surveillance systems "more sensitive," and communications networks "more sophisticated" than before. "Small groups of foot soldiers"—that is, Special Forces units—"sent into Afghanistan on commando missions" would strap themselves into "prototype soldier helmets" that featured "a built-in video camera, an infrared camera for night vision, a microphone for voice communications and a display unit linked to global positioning satellites to show the soldiers' location, that of fellow soldiers and of suspected enemy positions." As these beta testers for Google Maps closed in on the enemy, they would be armed with "modified M-4" rifles equipped with "lasers for calculating distance and a thermal imaging system for seeing a heat-producing target through smoke or foliage." And that's not to mention the many forward leaps in "covert communications systems" or "easily concealed sensors" that the military wasn't willing to discuss for fear of losing the element of surprise. "All I'd say is that there have been big improvements," one defense industry CEO said. "We're a lot more prepared than most people realize."[34] Even more tantalizing than the new military hardware the public could see was the hardware that beckoned just out of view. The country was excited to see this twenty-first-century military deployed against Afghanistan's "ancient traditions of guerrilla warfare."[35]

The new technologies also enabled fantasies of a more humane kind of war. In the new century, precision targeting would make civilian casualties, which the military had long since euphemized as "collateral damage," a thing of the past. Three months after the invasion of Afghanistan, *The New York Times* recounted a "pivotal moment in the siege of Kunduz." A commander with Afghanistan's opposition forces had "pleaded" that the United States launch air strikes against a mass of Taliban fighters who were assembling along a ridge outside the city.

He asked that the attack take place within twenty-four hours. The Americans needed less than twenty minutes:

> A Special Operations ground spotter immediately radioed an American command center in Saudi Arabia, which ordered a nearby B-52 to rain 16 cluster bombs on the enemy forces. Flying at 30,000 feet, the bomber never saw its prey. But the spotter used a laser pointer to guide the bombs, which carried new devices that kept them on course through buffeting winds, enabling them to spew antiarmor bomblets with deadly precision.

This was just one episode of many. America, the *Times* wrote, was conducting "a relentlessly accurate bombardment . . . day and night, under clear and cloudy skies alike." The effects on enemy morale were said to be devastating. Taliban and al-Qaeda prisoners had "confirmed that the precise bombing from planes they often could not see or hear broke the will of battle-hardened troops." At the same time, the campaign's uncanny accuracy was keeping civilian casualties to a minimum, helping the United States "maintain the support of friendly Islamic nations." "This is a new pattern of warfare," an Air Force historian explained. "There's not that image of uncaring, rampant destruction."[36]

Peering further into the future, cheerleaders for the technological revolution could envision a time when Americans themselves would suffer no casualties at all. As robots started to replace human workers in the manufacturing and services industries, it was thought that they could also relieve human bodies of war's many burdens. The machines were coming to the battlefield. P. W. Singer, the author of a 2009 book on new military technologies, quoted a *Times* article on the work performed by robots assisting with the rescue mission at Ground Zero. The headline read "Agile in a Crisis, Robots Show Their Mettle":

> These rescuers are unaffected by the carnage, dust and smoke that envelop the remains of the World Trade Center. They are

immune to the fatigue and heartbreak that hang in the air. They are, literally, robots: small, mobile machines that whir, blink and burrow alongside the emergency workers and rescue dogs, combing the debris.[37]

Looking at the explosive growth of the military and homeland security budgets since September 11, Singer thought it was only a matter of time before robots took up combat positions. He wrote about a four-legged robot that could "run a four-minute mile for five hours, while carrying 100 pounds," yet was "agile enough to fit through a doorway and go up stairs," speculating that its manufacturer "may well be on its way to becoming the Ford or GE of the twenty-first century."[38] Profiling a second company, which he found to be "even more revolutionary" than the first, Singer described a robot called SWORDS, "akin to a Transformers toy made just for soldiers." SWORDS was capable of carrying "pretty much any weapon that weighs under three hundred pounds, ranging from an M-16 rifle and .50-caliber machine gun to a 40mm grenade launcher or an antitank rocket launcher."[39] Soldiers of the future, "much like a football quarterback," would "call the 'play' for robots to carry out, but like the players on the field, the robots would have the autonomy to change what they do if the situation shifts."[40] All of this would keep American humans out of harm's way. "Our major role is to sanitize the battlefield," one airman told Singer, to "make sure our own guys aren't walking into danger."[41]

In the early 2000s, however, robot armies were just a twinkle in a defense executive's eye. For the time being, real soldiers would still have to put their bodies on the line. As the invasion of Afghanistan commenced and the pursuit of bin Laden pushed toward the Tora Bora cave complex in the White Mountains, the media increasingly turned its attention to one kind of soldier in particular. From the doughboys of World War I to the Top Gun fighter pilots of the 1980s, the American public had a long tradition of distilling the country's vast military apparatus down into representative individual types. In the war on terror, it was Special Forces—the Army Rangers, Marine Force RECON units, and Navy SEALs, among others—who came to stand for the military as a whole. The Special Forces represented everything Rumsfeld and his fellow RMA believers wanted the U.S. military to be. The machines might be taking on some of the war's grunt work, but there were certain crucial tasks that still required an incredibly skillful human touch. Trained to within an inch of their lives (deaths during training exercises are rather common), each Special Forces soldier represented an astonishing investment in a single unit of human capital. They worked in small groups of a dozen or so, and they moved quickly and in silence. They were the first units into Afghanistan, deployed in secret several weeks before the bombing campaign began, and when the Army withdrew its conventional troops in 2015, it was the Green Berets who stayed behind.[42] Journalists embedded with the chatty recruits of the Army's regular units could feel the quiet intensity of Special Forces soldiers emanating from the darkened corners of barracks and mess halls. Tucking into a dinner of macaroni and ground beef at the Army base outside Kandahar, one reporter was able to identify a table of operatives "by their dusty beards and deep suntans. Shunning press attention, those soldiers were back from extended operations in faraway villages, largely to gather intelligence."[43]

As to the details of what the Special Forces did once their helicopters took off and disappeared, who could say? Either the public found out after the mission was complete, as when SEAL Team Six raided bin Laden's compound and killed him in 2011, or it didn't find out at all. Journalists more accustomed to the government announcing the deployment of regular troops or reservists found themselves arriving in Kurdish-controlled Iraq or rural Afghanistan and learning that some platoon of Army Rangers had already been in country for weeks. Less than a month after the beginning of the Iraq War, there were nearly ten thousand Special Forces operating "in nearly every corner of the country and penetrating even the streets of Baghdad." With little to no access to these elite soldiers and their commanders, reporters were at the mercy of the military's public relations machine, but Special Forces so fascinated audiences back home that it wasn't hard for the Army to get its press releases published in major newspapers essentially unchanged.

A long article published in *The New York Times* in April 2003 under the headline "Covert Units Conduct a Campaign Invisible Except for the Results" must have pleased the top brass. It was still early days in Iraq, yet the Special Forces were well ahead of the curve, doing everything from "organizing Kurdish militia in rugged northern Iraq" to "scouting for suspected Scud missile launchers in the vacant west" (these were Boone-like figures from the outset, lone hunters confronting a hostile wilderness). Though their campaign was "largely invisible," it was "remarkable for its breadth and complexity." The RMA obsession with information and networks made its de rigueur appearance, with "information from the spies, analysts, surveillance planes and satellites of the intelligence agencies . . . linked more directly than ever before to commandos on the ground." Masters of their terrain, commandos had "conducted reconnaissance," "cleared mines," "carried out precise strikes in urban settings," and occasionally played their "huge trump card: American air power." They trained Kurdish forces in the north as well, using their "mortar specialists" to help the Peshmerga "tighten down their shot groups," in the words of one commander. In sum, according to one brigadier general, these units were "doing things that have never been done on such a large scale and have produced phenomenal results."

In a sense, they were better than robots. Special Forces combined the best of human courage, training, and adaptability with the sorts of advanced digital technology that wouldn't make it into civilians' consumer goods for years. That's why so few of them could accomplish so much. "We are able to use a fairly small force to leverage an incredible amount of technology," one military officer said, "to bring that technology to bear on the battlefield."[44] This is part of what made them unnerving. Even in street clothes, Special Forces soldiers intimidate. Unlike America's regular troops and reservists, many of whom flew off to combat out of shape and with no more than basic training,[45] Special Forces, to a man, were awesome physical specimens: tall, bearded, and heavily tattooed, with muscles like wrapped steel. At home, they were notorious for starting (and finishing) bar fights. Sheathe men like that in the most elegant and lethal technology there is, and you have a truly frightening spectacle, a band of Greek heroes moving through the night, bristling with deadly weapons and encased in flexible black armor, with night-vision goggles protruding out of their faces like alien eyestalks. The *Times* reporters picked up on the fear these soldiers inspired, although they didn't address it directly. They described the commandos working in "furtive teams," "creeping in larger numbers toward Baghdad," on a "hunt" for key members of Saddam's regime. The military itself called them "the black side" of its campaigns.[46] These were not people one would want to encounter in a bad mood back home, but that was part of the appeal. They wouldn't have been the warriors America needed unless they also exuded menace everywhere they went.

· · ·

Not content to rely on the goodwill of journalists to publicize the appeal of the twenty-first-century soldier, the military also put its considerable resources to work on getting the message out directly. Since 1980, "Be All You Can Be" had been the Army's primary recruiting slogan, a good choice for that decade's obsession with individual achievement. In 2001, however, that slogan was changed to better reflect the way that technology could now amplify a single recruit's powers beyond all previous reckoning. The first commercial produced to advertise this new version of America's military debuted during a broadcast of the network sitcom *Friends.* It opened on a lone soldier running across the desert. "Even though there are 1,045,690 soldiers just like me, I am my own force," the soldier said. "With technology, with training, with support, who I am has become better than who I was. . . . The might of the U.S. Army doesn't lie in numbers. It lies in me." The new tagline flashed on the screen at the end: "An Army of One."[47] At one point during the soldier's sprint across the Mojave, he ran past another group of recruits going in the opposite direction, like Batman tracking the Joker while the bumbling Gotham police scurry in the other direction in pursuit of some bogus lead. The Army would lean into the superhero associations as time passed, eventually producing an ad campaign in which different kinds of soldiers were reimagined as a camo-clad Avengers squad. A woman working on encryption appeared as "The Code Fighter," a communications specialist became "The Wavelength," and a chef, with a halo of knives rotating behind him and flying onions falling under his blade, became "The Replenisher."[48]

The stories that appeared on-screen in between the commercials also bore the military's direct influence, to the point that some of them functioned as advertisements in their own right. The Department of Defense consulted on Hollywood films and network TV productions during the war on terror, lending its equipment and expertise to producers in exchange for the ability to demand changes to the script if a given film didn't paint the military in a sufficiently rosy light. The scale of this involvement could be breathtaking; the Pentagon provided more than a billion dollars' worth of equipment, shooting locations, and uniformed extras for director Michael Bay to use in *Transformers,* an action blockbuster based on a line of children's toys from the 1980s.[49]

Among the military's most successful collaborations during this period was its work on *Iron Man,* the first installment in the Marvel Cinematic Universe, which is now the most profitable movie franchise in history. *Iron Man* is where the technologically enhanced Special Forces super-trooper took on his most hyperbolic form. Played by Robert Downey Jr. in three separate movies released between 2008 and 2013, Iron Man is Tony Stark, a billionaire genius playboy who runs an international technology conglomerate focusing on weapons and security. Stark first appears on the screen in Afghanistan, drinking whiskey in the back of a Humvee while rolling through Kunar province. He is celebrating the successful demonstration of his firm's new super-missile, the Jericho, so named because, like the Israelites in the book of Joshua, it can bring the walls of a great city crashing to the earth. Stark's audience of Army officers had been thoroughly impressed, especially when he sweetened the deal by promising to throw in a refrigerated bar cart with every purchase of $500 million or more.

In the Humvee, he is flirting with the female soldiers up front and fielding selfie requests when the convoy is ambushed by terrorists, who take Stark prisoner. Trapped in an underground cave complex, Stark escapes by building a prototype Iron Man suit out of the scrap metal he finds lying around, though not before discovering that his company's weapons have fallen into the terrorists' hands. The suit is heavy and cumbersome, but it is also powerful, immune to the terrorists' machine guns, armed with flamethrowers, and capable of flight. When he is safely returned to the States, the first thing Stark requests is "an American cheeseburger."[50]

Then he builds the real suit. Made out of gold and titanium and painted with red highlights, the suit can shoot lasers out of its hands and precision-guided missiles out of its shoulders. Its visor includes an augmented-reality display that keeps Stark informed on enemy positions, damage sustained, power levels, and biometrics. It moves at blinding speed and lends Stark superhuman strength. *Iron Man* includes a thin plot about the dangers of weapons proliferation, but the movie's focus, the reason people watch it, is Tony's relationship with the suit. Although it encases Stark entirely and clanks loudly against anything it touches, the suit does not weigh him down or restrict his movement in any way. It never gets hot inside, nor is there any risk that some malfunction could injure its human pilot. The operating fantasy here—and I mean "fantasy" in the crude sense, as in "something that doesn't exist in reality"—is one of a perfect, seamless integration of technology and flesh, of technology that only augments its user's human capabilities while eliminating his vulnerabilities. This is the RMA fantasy too, the idea that the right mix of equipment could remove danger, injury, weakness, and death from the American soldier's experience of war. The three *Iron Man* movies are fascinated by how easy it is for Stark to inhabit his invention. Each one pauses at some point to watch him put it on: Dexterous robot arms emerge out of the floor, or a walkway, or even just a briefcase, and build the suit around his outstretched limbs.[51] Armor plates lock into place, screws tighten, and Downey's expressive face disappears behind a stern mask with two glowing eyes and a horizontal slit for a mouth. Inside, Stark is both protected and deadly. As he will say later while testifying in front of a skeptical congressional panel, "The suit and I are one."[52]

• • •

Batman and Iron Man were perfect vehicles for America's militaristic fantasies because they weren't real people. But every time the media or government tried to imbue an actual soldier with those same fantasies, something went wrong.

In May 2002, Pat Tillman, a talented safety playing football for the Arizona Cardinals, declined a $3.6 million contract offer and enlisted to train as an Army Ranger. "My great-grandfather was at Pearl Harbor, and a lot of my family have . . . fought in wars," he said. "I haven't really done a damn thing as far as laying myself on the line like that."[53] He was a gift to the war effort, an ideal American who ticked every box. He was white, handsome, square-jawed, married to his teenage sweetheart, strong enough to deal out "bone-rattling hits" on the field of play, and smart enough to maintain a high grade point average in marketing at Arizona State University. "All the girls loved him," a classmate said of Tillman's high school days, "and all the guys wanted to be him." He had once been charged with felony assault as a teenager, but that could be excused on the grounds that he was "defending a friend," and he did not hesitate to take responsibility for his actions, pleading guilty and serving time on a "work farm" the summer before he started college.[54] Though Tillman refused interviews about his decision to enlist "for fear that [his] decision will be interpreted as a publicity stunt,"[55] friends said that September 11 had spurred him to action.[56] That he wanted to join an elite Special Forces unit only made it better. The media reported admiringly on the "nearly intolerable" training endured by aspiring Rangers "in conditions of swamps, jungles, mountains. . . . Rangers are sent to places where the danger is the worst."[57]

Tillman went to Iraq for the initial invasion less than a year after enlisting, and soon after that he was redeployed to Afghanistan. He was killed on April 22, 2004. The military said that while Tillman had been "patrolling one of the most dangerous areas of Afghanistan," a region near the border with Pakistan that "al-Qaeda and Taliban forces [were] known to infiltrate," his unit had been "ambushed by anti-coalition forces." The Rangers had been on "special alert" in the weeks leading up to the ambush, but the terrorists had found Tillman anyway, leaving his wife to mourn rather than celebrate their second wedding anniversary in a month's time.[58] Having now sacrificed his life on top of the comforts of his athletic career, Tillman became a national martyr, a secular saint. Here is the beginning of one obituary published shortly after his death:

> When nobody was around, Arizona State University football star Pat Tillman would climb the 10-story light tower at Sun Devil Stadium, certainly without permission, just to gaze at the buttes, the desert, the glow of Phoenix—and ponder the state of the world. A roughneck with a philosophical bent, Tillman never followed convention.[59]

One finds every element of the mythical frontier hero in that paragraph: the homegrown philosophizing, the communion with nature and the universe, the quiet individualism, and the refusal to ask for permission to do what needs doing. The obituary describes the American Southwest but just as easily summons up the image of Tillman surveilling the Khyber Pass from a mountain overlook, scanning a different landscape for signs of danger with his gun at the ready. His death sanctified the tale that journalists and his former employers at the National Football League started building around him the day he enlisted. No longer able to fight himself, Tillman was now an example to future soldiers who would retrace his path to the battlefield.

It wasn't until after the family held its nationally televised memorial service for Tillman that the Army admitted its story was false. Tillman's platoon had been patrolling along a canyon road when a Humvee broke down, forcing the unit to split into two groups. The first, which included Tillman, had made it down the canyon road "without incident," but the second group following behind encountered enemy fire. Tillman's group circled back and took up a position from which they could support their comrades as they attempted to get out of the ambush, but as the second group exited the canyon, it mistook Tillman's group for the enemy and opened fire. Tillman was killed by Americans, shot in the head three times from less than thirty feet away.[60] Making matters worse, the Army had known the real circumstances of Tillman's death almost from the very beginning but hid the truth from Tillman's family and the public. Tillman's fellow soldiers had burned his armor and uniform in an attempt to cover up what happened, and senior officers had recommended Tillman for a posthumous Purple Heart and Silver Star, as well as promotion to corporal. Officers even ordered the other members of Tillman's unit to lie to his family about what happened at the funeral.[61] What started as a propaganda coup for the government and the war effort turned into a shameful, drawn-out embarrassment for an Army that had killed one of its own and then lied about it for favorable press coverage.

This kind of thing happened several times as America's fantasies about its super-soldiers collided with reality. Journalists, Pentagon flacks, or politicians looking to keep pro-war sentiment at a rolling boil repeatedly latched on to some story of grace under fire or patriotic sacrifice—almost always involving one or another branch of the Special Forces—only to watch those stories crumble under the pressure of even mildly curious scrutiny. In the spring of 2003, the nineteen-year-old Army private Jessica Lynch was seriously injured in a car crash near Nasiriyah and then captured by Iraqi forces. A week later, the Pentagon announced that special ops teams had recovered Lynch in an operation the military described as a daring triumph, the first successful rescue of an American POW since World War II. At its press conference, the Pentagon screened a five-minute video of the rescue. Reporters saw the special operations team huddling over maps as they planned the operation and then loading up their trucks and rolling off into the desert. A night-vision camera then captured those same trucks pulling up at the hospital entrance and disgorging soldiers, who hurried inside as a man got on the radio to say, "This is impressive." The video then cut to inside the hospital, where soldiers crowded around the trembling Lynch's bed, gave her a flag to hug, and then whisked her back to safety.[62]

The Pentagon spokesman said that Lynch had been stabbed and shot in the attack, and that while captive she had been slapped and interrogated.[63] Eventually, speculation about the interrogations turned into a belief that Lynch had been tortured. "Those people—the Iraqi captors—were barbaric," an anonymous source told *People* magazine. "I have no doubt that with her injuries, and with what they had planned for her, she was going to die."[64] Tiny, blond, and white, Lynch looked like exactly the kind of American who might get tortured by savages, and the media emphasized her helplessness at every opportunity, glossing over the fact that she was a trained soldier as quickly as possible. As Susan Faludi wrote of the coverage, "She was said to be 'clutching a teddy bear.' She was said to favor applesauce and steamed carrots. She was said to be dreaming of washing her hair and styling it with the curling iron she 'calls her magic wand.' She was said to be 'asking for her mother.' "[65] Lynch's biographer went so far as to claim she had been anally raped, although the "records" he examined didn't specify whether the Iraqis had "assaulted her almost lifeless, broken body after she was lifted from the wreckage, or if they assaulted her and then broke her bones into splinters until she was almost dead."[66] Lynch had no memory of any such assaults, and she told her biographer that she "definitely did not want that in there."[67] He included the claim anyway, and he explained Lynch's inability to remember her sexual trauma by hypothesizing that her conscious mind, overwhelmed by the horror of the ordeal, had repressed it.[68]

The real story of Lynch's captivity was more mundane than her biographer's lurid fantasy of savagery and violated innocence. She was neither shot nor stabbed. The injuries Lynch sustained were consistent with exactly the kind of serious car wreck she had experienced. She was not mistreated but cared for. Her Iraqi doctors set her broken bones, used up some of the hospital's meager supplies of specialized equipment to treat her, and found her American-style food to eat when she didn't like the standard hospital fare. Lynch remembered one of her nurses, who sang to her, with special fondness. At one point, her doctors had even tried to physically return Lynch to the Army, loading her into an ambulance and driving over to a nearby U.S. military outpost. The soldiers there opened fire on the car as it approached, and the driver had to turn around.

While the revelation of the truth about Lynch's completely gratuitous "rescue" didn't provoke the same level of outrage as the Tillman cover-up, several other wrinkles that eventually came to light were controversial. Foremost among these was the fact that Lynch was one of *two* women soldiers who had been taken hostage that night. The second, Shoshana Johnson, was a single mother and the first Black woman to become an American POW. She, too, was returned safely home, but she received none of the media fanfare that attended Lynch's rescue. Also ignored was Lori Piestewa, a soldier who died fighting in the ambush that ended with Lynch's capture. She was the first Native American woman to die fighting for the United States in combat, as well as the first woman killed in the Iraq War. Lynch made a point of repeating that Piestewa was the real hero of the ambush, but that had little effect on a news media drawn to the story of an innocent white woman thrown into the lions' den. Ultimately, Lynch testified before Congress and roundly criticized the distortions to which her story had been subjected, and another effort to shoehorn the inglorious realities of war into a mythological template (helpless blond white woman saved by strong men) ended with a queasy, uncomfortable ambivalence.

As the Jessica Lynch and Pat Tillman stories filled newspaper columns across the country, another legend, more or less unknown outside the military, was constructing itself in Iraq. Chris Kyle was a sniper for the Navy SEALs. He served four tours of duty in the Iraq War, during which he racked up 160 "confirmed kills." In the words of his 2012 memoir, *American Sniper,* this made him "the most lethal sniper in U.S. military history." Kyle's memoir was one of several published by Navy SEALs and other former military officers around the same time, as a handful of veterans tried to kick-start their postwar lives with infusions of cash and fame. *American Sniper* spent the better part of a year on the *New York Times* bestseller list, and unlike Tillman or Lynch, Kyle was an enthusiastic participant in his own mythmaking. If Pat Tillman and Jessica Lynch found their respective analogues in Daniel Boone and the pious Mary Rowlandson, Chris Kyle was Davy Crockett, cheerfully meting out death across the wilderness. Crockett, one literary historian wrote, "was a hunter rather than a farmer, and the lust for killing was in his blood. With his pack of hounds he slaughtered with amazing efficiency. . . . His hundred and five bears in a single season, his six deer shot in one day while pursuing other game serve to explain why the rich hunting grounds of the Indians were swept so quickly bare of game by the white invaders."[69]

Kyle didn't become a legend because of his lethality as such. Any American who shoved bombs out of a plane during World War II or Vietnam likely had greater quantities of blood on his hands. But Air Force bombers are unskilled labor in comparison to snipers. Kyle appealed to the public because he was recognizably a hunter, and in Iraq he hunted Iraqis, or "savages," as he insisted on calling them. "Savage, despicable evil," he wrote. "There really was no other way to describe what we encountered there."[70] To much of the American right wing, he was the ideal soldier, a one-man army always ready to discuss the intricacies of his gear. "In 2004," he wrote, "I brought over a Springfield TRP Operator, which used a .45-caliber round. It had a 1911 body style, with custom grips and a rail system that let me add a light and laser combo. Black, it had a bull barrel and was an excellent gun."[71] A Christian with a crusader tattoo on his arm ("in red, for blood"), Kyle did not hesitate to describe the war in religious terms.[72] Though he had "never known that much about Islam" before the war, he "also knew that Christianity had evolved from the Middle Ages. We don't kill people because they're a different religion."[73] Where other soldiers might recite catechism about personal sacrifice and liberating the Middle East, Kyle's understanding of the job was simpler: "My country sent me out there so that bullshit wouldn't make its way back to our shores. I never once fought for the Iraqis. I could give a flying fuck about them."[74]

In Clint Eastwood's film about Kyle's life, the climactic battle scene ends with the hero calling home in tears. He misses his family, and he has finally had enough of war. "I'm ready to come home," he says.[75] This, however, appears to have been an invention on Eastwood's part, perhaps one designed to make Kyle more sympathetic. In the memoir, Kyle's battle hunger is never sated. "I loved what I did," he wrote. "I still do. If circumstances were different—if my family didn't need me—I'd be back in a heartbeat. I'm not lying or exaggerating to say it was fun."[76] He meant "fun" literally, in the manner of games. "We had so many targets," he wrote, "we started asking ourselves, what weapons have we *not* used to kill them? *No pistol kill yet? You have to get at least one.*"[77] The Iraq War killed roughly 250,000 civilians,[78] but Kyle insisted that he'd never killed someone who didn't have it coming. "Everyone I shot was evil," he wrote. "They all deserved to die."[79]

So long as he was on the battlefield—or at least within several hundred yards of it, peering down the sight of a long rifle—Kyle felt as though nothing could touch him. "I always seemed more vulnerable at home," he wrote. "After every deployment, something would happen to me, usually during training. I broke a toe, a finger, all sorts of little injuries. Overseas, on deployment, in the war, I seemed invincible."[80] This feeling turned out to be prescient. Kyle became vulnerable in several different ways once he returned to the States. Separated from the fellow soldiers who saw him as a warrior king—his nickname in Iraq was Legend—Kyle had to deal with journalists who started to point out that some of his stories were either highly unlikely or verifiably false. Kyle once claimed, for instance, that he and another man had driven down to New Orleans after Hurricane Katrina in 2005. They'd seen reports of looting on television, and they wanted to help keep the peace. Kyle said that while standing on top of the Superdome, the stadium where the NFL's New Orleans Saints play their home games, he and his companion set up their rifles and shot dozens of people who they thought were making trouble down on the ground. No reports of a sniper going on a killing spree at the Superdome ever emerged to corroborate this story.[81] If it is some consolation that a decorated Navy SEAL didn't actually murder victims of a natural disaster, that consolation is tempered by the question that naturally follows: What kind of decorated Navy SEAL thinks it would reflect well on him for people to think he did?

This kind of reputational vulnerability might be par for the course for someone publishing a bestselling memoir, but Kyle was also physically vulnerable in ways he failed to anticipate. After his final return home, he took to spending time with other veterans who were struggling with the adjustment to postwar life. In February 2013, one of these veterans shot and killed Kyle at a Texas gun range. He was hit from behind, and his gun was still holstered when he died. The funeral service was held nine days later at Cowboys Stadium in Arlington. People waved flags over the interstate as Kyle's body was taken to an Austin cemetery.

That Kyle was killed by a fellow veteran rather than an insurgent from Sadr City made his death disturbing rather than simply tragic. What are you supposed to think when the hero and his murderer are both products of the same institutions, the same training, the same system? Whatever the answer to that question was, it was *not* to seek revenge on the mentally ill veteran, because during the war on terror criticizing veterans has been more or less forbidden. This was a crucial part of America's post-9/11 militarism. If soldiers, particularly Special Forces soldiers, had been turned into symbols of the war effort as a whole, and if criticizing those soldiers was prohibited, then criticizing the war itself was prohibited as well. Politicians, shortsighted or stupid officers back in Washington, and the Army's indifference toward the welfare of its soldiers were all legitimate targets, but veterans themselves are the closest thing the country has to a sanctified class (as one slogan has it, "Love the warrior, hate the war").[82] In the early 2000s, critics of the wars in Afghanistan and Iraq could be disarmed by accusations that they did not "support the troops," and as of this writing in 2023 most commercial airlines still allow U.S. military personnel to board planes early, just after the disabled and parents with little kids but before everyone else. Too excessive to just be a simple expression of gratitude, the praise and thanks showered on veterans also helped to fend off the specter of Vietnam. Injured and mentally ill veterans of that war were often either left to rot in the fetid conditions of Walter Reed National Military Medical Center, or else abandoned to addiction and homelessness. The country felt ashamed of Vietnam—of both the war itself and how the country treated those who fought it. After September 11, Americans made an anxious and mostly tacit pledge that its soldiers would not be mistreated this time around. (When *The Washington Post* revealed in 2007 that veterans were *still* being neglected at Walter Reed, it prompted an outcry and congressional hearings.)[83]

Towns held parades when their soldiers returned. Politicians invoked their courage at the slightest opportunity, with the invocation becoming almost mandatory if they were giving a speech about foreign policy. Television networks interrupted the Super Bowl and other sporting events to show live video feeds of troops gathered around their own televisions, tuning in to the big game from overseas. The troops had not forgotten about life back home, and life back home was not going to forget about them. There was always a formulaic quality to these expressions of gratitude, an element of recitation or ritual. The most well-known formula, of course, was "Thank you for your service."

Curiously, one of these stock expressions used the vocabulary of finance. On Memorial Day in 2008, President Bush spoke at Arlington National Cemetery and invited the country to "pay tribute to all who have fallen—a tribute never equal to the debt they are owed."[84] On Veterans Day five years later, President Obama appeared at Arlington and affirmed that "we join as one people to honor a debt we can never fully repay."[85] This phrase is so common that it is easy not to think about it, but it takes only a brief pause to realize how strange it is: In the words of one ethnographer who interviewed soldiers on a military base, "to insist that we cannot repay a debt is, essentially, to default on it."[86] And as a second ethnographer pointed out (ethnographers spend a lot of time thinking about debt), what kind of debt are we talking about when the debtors are the only ones insisting it exists?[87] Over and over, the United States told war on terror veterans that it would never give them what they were owed, with the unsettling implication that it knew it would default on the debt when it took out the loan in the first place.

Veterans themselves were uncomfortable with this praise, and sometimes they tried to undermine it. Having to field constant expressions of gratitude from strangers while you're picking up groceries or sitting down at a restaurant is annoying. One soldier who was rehabilitating from his injuries at Walter Reed told a researcher about a conversation he'd had with a man his family was visiting. The soldier recalled, "I said to him, 'You're a carpenter, right? Well, imagine that you went out to a job and built some cabinets and all of a sudden on your way home, everyone was lining up and waving flags and saluting.'"[88] The same researcher also looked through a storage room holding gifts that grateful citizens had sent to Walter Reed for the soldiers. The gifts could be divided into two categories. First, there were daily essentials: diapers, toothpaste, socks, bottled water, Girl Scout cookies. These the soldiers were happy to have, and the closet's supplies often needed replenishing. "But the objects that most clearly exuded others' expressions of patriotic gratitude," the researcher wrote, "the painstakingly crafted red, white, and blue lap blankets and the saddle bags made of down-homey denim that could be Velcroed onto crutches, these things languished in their boxes and bins."[89]

One soldier, a veteran named Peter, took a more direct approach when a tour group walked up to him one day at Walter Reed. The VA man leading the group asked Peter if he would answer some questions. Peter agreed, but his answers were clipped and unfriendly, barely answers at all:

The man from the VA finally seemed to take the hint. He tried to close the awkward interaction, smiling politely and saying, "Well, you're fighting for our freedom, so thank you for your service." But before he could move on to Alec, Peter jumped in: "And your job." He said, "If we didn't get blown up, you wouldn't have a job." A nervous laughter rippled through the group of onlookers in the pause that followed. The man from the VA replied, "Well, yes, we prefer if you didn't get blown up."[90]

Peter wanted to make the group uncomfortable, and he did so by shining a spotlight on the thing they most wanted to ignore. He pointed to the fact that the tour group's gratitude and friendly curiosity and little presents, all of which did more to help them feel good about themselves than it did to help the patients at Walter Reed, depended on his being *vulnerable*—to injury and death, of course, but also to mental illness, drug addiction, and permanent physical disability. In just the first four years of the Iraq War, the military spent more than $23 million on prescription drugs for traumatic brain injury and post-traumatic stress disorder (PTSD), two of the most common diagnoses given to those who fought in Iraq and Afghanistan. It's now estimated that about a fifth of returning soldiers experience PTSD, and by 2010 suicide rates in the military had surpassed those in the rest of the United States.[91]

Superhero movies and splashy newspaper pieces about advances in military technology made it seem as though America's soldiers were invulnerable, and in a *relative* sense they basically were: From 2004 to 2009, more than twenty-seven Iraqis died for every American killed in the war.[92] But America did not fight the war on terror in a relative sense. Starting on September 12, 2001, it was fought overseas, thousands of miles away, which meant Americans could not look at the casket of a dead Marine, see the twenty-seven dead Iraqis in the background, and understand that the United States was getting the much better end of the exchange. All Americans could see when a soldier came off the flight home in a box was that an American was dead.

The body armor, reinforced Humvees, and other technological advances that were supposed to guarantee soldiers' safety at the war's outset actually made them *more* vulnerable in some ways. The armored vehicles sent to Iraq and Afghanistan in the early stages of those wars were good at protecting soldiers from small-arms fire coming from the street or a balcony, but their wide, flat undersides meant they absorbed the full force of any improvised explosive device (IED) that detonated underneath them, with devastating results for those inside. More soldiers survived these kinds of attacks than in prior wars, thanks to both improved body armor and advances in the logistics of military medical treatment. Medics could reach soldiers and begin treating their wounds more quickly than ever before, which saved many lives. The flip side of these improvements, however, was that soldiers became *more* likely to come home with awful and complicated injuries requiring months or even years of treatment and recovery that in many cases came with the risk of opiate addiction. In Vietnam or Desert Storm or even the Balkans, a significant percentage of these soldiers simply would have died. They came home from the war on terror, but their mangled bodies testified to what it was that war did to people.

Civilians consuming a steady diet of *Call of Duty: Modern Warfare* and action dramas about covert ops had a hard time reconciling this reality with myths about the invincibility of the country's armed forces. But soldiers themselves, who lived with their own vulnerability day to day, had a more practical understanding of what it meant. Don White, a Marine who served three tours in Afghanistan, was once asked whether he felt that his high-tech equipment really did keep him safe. He answered quickly, and his tone was matter-of-fact: "No." There was a pause, and then he burst out laughing:

So, to start, you get issued your protective gear, your personal protective gear. You get issued a whole gamut of that stuff. You get flame-retardant gloves, you get a flame-retardant uniform (depending on where you went). You get a flame-retardant face mask, you get a helmet that's designed to absorb impact if you bang your head against something. But the helmet that you wear is only rated to stop a 9-millimeter bullet. The Afghans are shooting at you with a 7.62 rifle bullet. It'll go right through that helmet. And then you're in this armored Humvee, so people would get the sense that, "Oh, these guys are in this Humvee with three-quarter-inch armor all around it, and it's invincible," when the reality is a five-gallon jug full of some HME [homemade explosives] would blow one of those things fifty feet up into the air and kill everybody inside of it. . . . You would get issued safety goggles; nobody wears safety goggles because it's one hundred and twenty degrees in Afghanistan.... You were given groin protecters, and no one ever wore that thing either, because it was made to stop shrapnel, but it was just this piece of Kevlar that hung down in front of your pelvis. And everybody knows that IEDs come from the ground up, so it literally does no good but cause chafing, so why would I wear it?

This perspective made White somewhat disdainful of the way civilians back home fetishized the technology that didn't really keep him safe overseas. He returned to the United States and saw that Toyota was selling a "desert tan" version of its Tacoma pickup truck, "the same color scheme that we used in Afghanistan and Iraq." He went to outdoor supply shops and saw hiking gear based on the same MOLLE system—for Modular Lightweight Load-Carrying Equipment—that troops used to customize how they carried their equipment on patrol. He saw men at shooting ranges with ludicrous accessories attached to their rifles. "They have things they don't even know what they're for," he said. He had a special contempt for civilians who put canted sights on their guns:

A canted sight goes on the side of your rifle at a forty-five-degree angle. The purpose of that is if you're using a scoped weapon, if that breaks, I have a secondary method to aim at my target. Or, if you have a multi-platform type of mission, like maybe you're going to be doing something kind of long-range, but then eventually you're going to need to clear a building, maybe you want a long-range sight and maybe you want a short-range sight. But the average person that says, "I have my AR-15 to protect my house," why do you have this gun decked out like you're gonna go kick down the door with Delta Force?

White understood that these accessories sold well because they were filling a psychological need. "There's tactical baby bags," he said,

"I guess for guys who are too insecure in their masculinity to carry a normal diaper bag? They need to look like they're going into a war zone."[93]

Soldiers like Don White understood that civilians had turned them into bit players in a larger fantasy about the country's invulnerability, and they resented it. The gifts and yellow ribbons and tributes at football games were always presented as simple acts of generosity, but the people making those gestures were taking at least as much as they gave. Civilians got the psychological reassurance they needed; so long as they could watch their countrymen storm through Baghdad on television and listen to people like Chris Kyle talk about how war made him feel invincible, they could get on a plane or go to the mall without having to worry about falling victim to al-Qaeda's next attack. But the soldiers got nothing comparable in return; boarding an airplane before everyone else in coach wasn't going to stop their nightmares or headaches, nor give them back their limbs. Back in 2003, when the prospect of a quick, clean victory in Iraq was still within the realm of plausibility, it might have been reasonable to hope that the war would end before the gap separating fantasy and reality became too obvious to ignore. But by the end of Bush's second term, the war on terror was going badly on all fronts, and the cognitive dissonance was getting hard to ignore. Bin Laden had disappeared into the mountains, and more than four thousand Americans were dead in Iraq. The vulnerabilities of the country's armed forces—and, by extension, of the country itself—were becoming more visible with each passing year. By the spring of 2008, more than 60 percent of Americans thought the invasion of Iraq had been a mistake.[94]

• • •

The final installments of the Batman and Iron Man trilogies were released in 2012 and 2013, respectively. Both movies saw their heroes struggling under the weight of their tasks. *The Dark Knight Rises* finds Bruce Wayne still spending his evenings patrolling Gotham in search of criminals. The job is taking a toll. His injuries are adding up, his family estate has burned to the ground, and his lifelong friend Rachel, with whom he was in love, has been killed. The city government continues to treat its savior with a mix of suspicion and small-minded ambivalence. "You're not living," his butler tells him. "You're just waiting, hoping for things to go bad again." He wants Master Bruce to leave Gotham, to give up Batman, to stop wasting his life defending a city that will never embrace him. But Bruce can't find a good reason to leave. "There's nothing out there for me," he says.

Meanwhile, Tony Stark is also feeling bad. A major battle in New York City has left him with PTSD. He has anxiety attacks and screams in his sleep. "Nothing's been the same since New York," he tells his girlfriend, Pepper. "I can't sleep. You go to bed, I come down here. I do what I know—I tinker. A threat is imminent, and I have to protect the one thing I can't live without. That's you." But it's precisely Tony's vigilance that is driving Pepper away, and she is fed up. If Tony is going to keep putting himself in danger, she's leaving. Soon after, Tony is attacked at home, without his Iron Man suit on. It is the first time in any of the Iron Man films that Stark appears to be genuinely, physically vulnerable, the first scene filmed so as to be frightening rather than exciting. Bruce and Tony have reached the limits of what technology can do to protect them. If they are ever going to have the normal lives and happy endings they deserve, they need to escape from their own alter egos.

Both films then arrive at the same ingenious solution. In *The Dark Knight Rises,* the faux-populist villain starts the countdown clock on a nuclear bomb hidden somewhere in Gotham. Batman locates the bomb in time but is unable to disarm it; one way or another, it is going to explode. Running out of time, Batman hitches the bomb to his Batplane, jumps in the cockpit, and flies out over the water, where the bomb detonates. Gotham is saved, but Batman is dead. A funeral is held on the Wayne family grounds, and the city, finally able to appreciate Batman now that he is gone, builds a statue to honor his sacrifice. Only at the very end is it revealed that Batman wasn't in the plane when the bomb exploded. He turned on the autopilot and bailed out in time, and now he travels Europe with his girlfriend, Catwoman, in contented anonymity. Gotham's final savior wasn't the Batman at all, but a small, unmanned aircraft.

Over in the world of *Iron Man 3*, Tony Stark makes some modifications to his suit while processing his trauma on a journey through rural America. Having reflected on his life, he then jumps back into the fray to save a dozen people who have been sucked out of a hijacked plane and are falling to their deaths. He gathers them up like ducklings and safely deposits them back on the ground. Then he gets distracted for a moment and gets smashed to bits by an 18-wheel truck. But Stark wasn't in the suit at all. It's a drone now, not an exoskeleton, and Stark is its pilot, perfectly safe in his remote command center. In the film's final battle, Stark summons the dozens of prototype suits he has built over the years, all remotely piloted by artificial intelligence, to fight for him. Like Bruce Wayne, he is able to put his fighting days behind him and enjoy his wealth and his woman in peace. If technology couldn't protect the good guys while their bodies were physically present on the battlefield, it could still do the next best thing: Keep them off the battlefield altogether.

Both of these films were released during Barack Obama's presidency. During his time in office, Obama steadily decreased the number of U.S. troops deployed around the world. Although he sent 70,000 additional troops to fight the Taliban in Afghanistan, all but 10,000 had returned home by the beginning of 2015, and even the initial increase was more than balanced out by the drawdown of America's military presence in Iraq. Troop levels there decreased from around 140,000 at the beginning of his first term to just 40,000 by the fall of 2011. As he pulled soldiers out of the line of fire, he replaced them with remotely piloted Predator drones, carrying out ten times as many drone attacks as his predecessor. Under the war on terror's second commander in chief, drones bombed Yemen, Pakistan, and Somalia more than five hundred times, with thousands of strikes in Afghanistan as well.

U.S. casualties dropped precipitously as a result of Obama's shift, falling from an average of nearly two thousand per year between 2004 and 2008, to about fifteen hundred between 2009 and 2012, to fewer than a thousand after 2013.[95] In some respects, this shift lessened the degree to which the Obama administration could make a patriotic spectacle out of America's militarism. While drones gave off the dark gleam of a techno-warfare future that had suddenly turned into a present-day reality, the original myths from which Americans derived their ideas about how the ideal soldier fought required that he be physically present on the battlefield, risking life and limb in theory even if his armor, weaponry, and air support made him all but invincible in practice. Drone pilots, by contrast, reminded people of nothing so much as gamers. But the shift had important benefits as well. Flag-draped coffins were the kind of thing that reliably made headlines, and in lowering the number of those boxes that newspaper editors could splash across their front pages each year, Obama made the war easier to ignore at home even as the fighting intensified in many parts of the world. That might have been cold comfort to those on the receiving end of a Predator drone's payload—it hardly made a difference to an Afghan farmer whether their son was killed by a missile or a Green Beret with an M4A1 rifle—but at home, drones helped to save the lives that actually mattered.

CHAPTER 3

I Think Security Is Very Tight, but I'm Still Concerned

Protect this house.
—slogan of athletic apparel company Under Armour,
introduced in 2003

I t was not enough for America to go abroad on a mission of revenge. The homeland, as people now called it for the first time in the country's history, had to prepare itself for war as well. Part of the humiliation of September 11 was the nagging feeling that the country should have seen it coming, that it should have done more ahead of time to prepare for the worst. How could the country's intelligence agencies have missed the signs of impending disaster? How could airport security have allowed the hijackers to carry knives and box cutters onto the planes? Why didn't the cockpits have reinforced doors, and why didn't New York have a plan to rescue people from the rooftops of its two tallest buildings? There were certainly real intelligence failures to criticize. To mention just one, in July 2001 an FBI agent working out of Phoenix had alerted the bureau's headquarters that an unusual number of possible al-Qaeda affiliates were attending commercial aviation schools in Arizona. No FBI managers saw the

memo until after September 11, and nobody acted on the agent's recommendations.[1] These failures should be kept in perspective, however: No terrorist had ever hijacked a commercial jet in order to crash
it into a building, and no skyscraper in human history had ever collapsed for any reason. But the *9/11 Commission Report*, the government's official account and analysis of the attacks, dissected America's
security failings in obsessive, self-flagellating detail. It noted every
failure of communication among the various air traffic control centers
that knew of the multiple hijackings.[2] It anatomized the FBI's and the
CIA's failures to share information on impending threats.[3] It quoted
memos that were ignored, suspects who slipped out of the government's view, and airport security screeners whose work was "marginal
at best."[4]

Congress declined to hold any government officials responsible
for these failures, but the *9/11 Commission Report* ended with a flurry
of recommendations for securing the country against the follow-up
attacks everyone was sure would be attempted in the future. These
recommendations included using biometric technology to screen
travelers trying to enter the country, making it harder to obtain birth
certificates and driver's licenses, instructing private-sector companies
to make substantial investments in securing their own facilities, and
mandating that airlines supply the government with the passenger information required to maintain national no-fly lists.[5] It was to be a
comprehensive effort to harden the country from the inside. At the
press conference introducing him as the first head of the brand-new
Homeland Security Office (which would eventually become a cabinet-
level department), the former Pennsylvania governor Tom Ridge said,
"We will find something for every American to do."[6]

Ridge was true to his word. Americans soon found themselves
learning how to navigate complicated security procedures in all kinds
of public spaces. The first really prominent exhibition for the country's new lockdown mindset took place in New Orleans, where Super
Bowl thirty-six was played on February 3, 2002. This was the first
post-9/11 Super Bowl, and inside the stadium, the NFL put on an exu-
berant celebration of America at war. The pregame festivities began

with Barry Manilow singing "Let Freedom Ring" from a stage at the fifty-yard line. As Patti LaBelle, Wynonna Judd, and James Ingram joined Manilow onstage, a pageant unfolded around them on the field. Police officers, firefighters, and members of the armed forces stood in a line holding dozens of American flags. A couple hundred women dressed in red, white, and blue Statue of Liberty costumes walked around on the Superdome's proprietary blend of artificial turf (officially named Mardi Grass) in tight formations. Teenagers in football pads wheeled an enormous replica of the Liberty Bell on to the field, with dozens of children dressed as soldiers, doctors, cheerleaders, and first responders trailing behind them. They were followed, in turn, by a gospel choir. At the song's climax, a little boy in head-to-toe camouflage hit the fake Liberty Bell with a mallet, turned to the camera, and waved.[7]

That was the first of *four* performances that preceded the game. Mary J. Blige and Marc Anthony sang "America the Beautiful." Paul McCartney performed an original number called "Freedom," which began with the words, "This is my right / A right given by God." He sang in front of a ninety-foot-tall mural by Keith Haring depicting the Statue of Liberty. "Anyone tries to take it away," he sang, "they'll have to answer." (One columnist was pleased to see that McCartney displayed "no hint of the naive peacenik of yore.")[8] Finally, Mariah Carey sang the national anthem to the accompaniment of the Boston Pops Orchestra. Three American flags made prominent appearances during her performance. One was presented by a color guard comprising a Marine, a Port Authority police officer, one representative each of the NYPD and FDNY, and a sailor assigned to the USS *Cole*, a destroyer that had been attacked by al-Qaeda in October 2000. The second was held by soldiers reenacting the famous photograph of Marines raising a flag over Iwo Jima during World War II. The third was the tattered flag that had survived the attack on Ground Zero.

There was more. Before kickoff, Fox aired a video package in which players from the two participating teams, the St. Louis Rams and the New England Patriots, read famous quotations by former presidents. Kurt Warner, the Rams' star quarterback, delivered one from John F. Kennedy: "A nation reveals itself not only by the men it produces but also by the men it honors, and the men it remembers." Troy Brown, a wide receiver for the Patriots, was assigned Teddy Roosevelt: "We admire the man who embodies victorious effort." These quotations were laid over video clips of Americana. A sepia-toned classroom of children reciting the Pledge of Allegiance gave way to a shot of a cheerful boy delivering the morning paper over a white picket fence. These scenes led into clips of soldiers, pilots, and lumberjacks, which alternated with images of Patriots and Rams finding glory on the field. As the play-by-play announcer Pat Summerall praised "the indelible spirit of Americans everywhere," the video ended with a shot of a soldier returning home and sweeping his daughter into his arms.

The network maintained this militaristic bombast and apple-pie sentimentality throughout the actual game. The broadcast's cutaway graphics and animations were studded with soldiers. Between plays during the game's opening drive, Fox put up partially computer-generated clips in which real members of the armed forces, identified by name and rank and looking dead serious, pushed buttons on futuristic displays to bring up each team's lineup. There was also the halftime show in which the Irish band U2 played through a few of its hits while the names of everyone killed on September 11 scrolled up a huge video board behind them, as though ascending to heaven. Even better, the on-field action lived up to the larger spectacle's nationalistic packaging. When the underdog New England Patriots, who were led by the clean-cut quarterback Tom Brady and had insisted on being introduced as a team rather than as individuals, upset the Rams, American sports had its first post-9/11 fairy-tale ending, something it had been pining for ever since the New York Yankees had been denied a World Series win by just a single game in November 2001.

But the only reason those inside the Superdome and the millions watching at home could spend the evening taking in this celebration of freedom was that the neighborhood surrounding the stadium had been turned into one of the least free areas in the United States. The year 2002 was by no means the first time that the Super Bowl had been turned into a militaristic spectacle. In 1991, just over a week into America's first Gulf War, tens of thousands of spectators had waved little flags and F-16s had flown over the stadium while Whitney Houston belted out a memorable rendition of the national anthem. But never before had the big game been protected by such an enormous, complex, and intrusive security apparatus. The 2002 Super Bowl was the first sporting event ever to be declared a National Special Security Event (NSSE) by the White House. This designation had previously been handed out to presidential inaugurations, national political conventions, general assemblies of the U.N., and, in 1999, the celebration of the fiftieth anniversary of NATO. NSSE status put the Secret Service in charge of the whole operation, which involved thousands of personnel from the Louisiana National Guard, the Louisiana State Police, and the New Orleans Police Department, among other agencies. The NFL consulted with the FBI, the Environmental Protection Agency, and the Centers for Disease Control and Prevention in the run-up to the game. The Federal Emergency Management Agency (FEMA), which became notorious a few years later for leaving thousands of New Orleanians stranded after Hurricane Katrina, oversaw the evacuation plan in case terrorists did manage to strike.[9] The mayor of New Orleans estimated that forty-eight different agencies were involved.[10]

If the inside of the Superdome was a football- and America-themed amusement park, the outside was fortified like a military base in enemy territory. The stadium was surrounded with concrete barriers and an eight-foot-tall fence, and National Guard soldiers carrying M-16 rifles patrolled the grounds along with bomb-sniffing dogs. Government agencies imposed a no-fly zone over the entire city, which meant there were no aerial shots of the stadium during the game—the skies were reserved for patrolling fighter jets.[11] The section of Interstate 10 that runs past the stadium was closed to trucks, and streets in the surrounding neighborhood were blocked off by Army vehicles. The teams' players, coaches, and staff were all subjected to metal detectors, pat downs, and identity checks. For the thousands of vendors, reporters, and other workers who make an event like the Super Bowl tick, the security gauntlet also included background checks beforehand and photo identification tags that had to be worn around the neck at all times.[12] Despite the NFL's assurances that spectators would enjoy a "seamless" game day experience,[13] the security process was expected to be so onerous that the stadium's gates were opened at 12:30, five hours before kickoff, and fans were encouraged to show up as close to 12:30 as they could.[14] (The expectation that tens of thousands of people would spend the afternoon trapped in the Superdome may explain why the NFL staged so many pregame musical performances; those fans had paid extravagant sums for their tickets, and they expected to be entertained the whole time.) Fans were also instructed to arrive with as few personal possessions as possible. Small cameras and binoculars were allowed, but the cases in which they might be carried were prohibited, as were any cameras with lenses measuring larger than six inches. Electronic devices were strongly discouraged, as inspecting them would take a while and slow down the line. Large bags, novelty footballs, foam "We're No. 1" hands, and banners and noisemakers of any kind were all confiscated at the gates.[15]

These highly visible security measures were impossible to miss. They were covered extensively by the press in the weeks leading up to the game, and they defined the experiences of those who attended the game in person. Yet government officials went to some lengths to suggest that there was a second network of *invisible* security measures in place as well. "There are some very interesting things being discussed," a spokesperson for the governor of Louisiana said two months before the game, "but I cannot get into specifics." The Secret Service echoed the sentiment. "Security at this Super Bowl will be like no other," a spokesperson said. "I cannot comment on any specifics, but most of the measures we deploy, fans will not see." Defense analysts working in the private sector helped reporters to fill in these tantalizing blanks. "It can be as simple as Army guys in ninja suits, lurking on tall buildings," one said. Others raised the possibility that the military would deploy a ring of portable anti-aircraft missile launchers on rooftops around the stadium. They warned, however, that while "such missiles could easily destroy smaller aircraft like a single-engine Cessna or a helicopter," they might be insufficient to take down "a wide-body commercial jet whose pilots were on a suicide mission." The problem with deploying larger arrays of more powerful weapons that *could* shoot down a passenger jet was that they would have to be stationed on city streets, where they would "stick out like a sore thumb."[16]

There was a prominent element of fantasy to the whole exercise. None of the articles outlining these security procedures suggested that the government's plans had been crafted in response to specific threats that actually existed. Instead, the Secret Service seemed to have made a list of every kind of attack that could occur and then deployed its personnel and technology with the intention of foiling every possible plot at once. The government "[had] not ruled out any possibility," according to the NFL's senior director of security. "We're looking in 360 degrees," one Secret Service chief said. "We're not protecting against a threat; we're protecting against all potential threats, whether it's Genghis Khan and his horde, Islamic terrorists, or Bill Jim Bob."[17] By game day, the government's list of potential threats apparently included attacks that could have been lifted from a James Bond movie. One Patriots fan said the men she was with had been made to change the time on their watch to prove that it wasn't a cleverly disguised bomb detonator. The only problem she had with this was that the same level of scrutiny had not been applied to women. "The women walked right in," she said. "So if there are women terrorists out there, we could walk right in." The same security that was supposed to make people feel safer about attending the game also emphasized all of the things that could go wrong. "I think security is very tight," another fan said, "but I'm still concerned."[18]

The woman's concerns about female suicide bombers highlighted an insoluble contradiction at the core of America's post-9/11 militarism: Every effort to make people feel safer by ramping up security also makes people more conscious of both real *and* imagined potential threats. Metal detectors, fenced-off city blocks, surveillance cameras mounted on lampposts, and camo-clad soldiers patrolling train stations with assault rifles all communicate a simple and unsettling message: Something bad might happen here. During the first decade of the war on terror, the United States built up internal fortifications the likes of which the country had never seen, including in many places where the realistic chances of a terrorist attack were essentially zero. These fortifications transformed many aspects of daily life, from commercial air travel and live entertainment to the experience of walking on a city street and the kinds of cars people bought. From a citizen's perspective, the results of this security buildup were wasteful in every sense. Not only did it fail to make people safer—it made them *feel* less safe as well. The result was a built environment in which Americans increasingly viewed the people around them as potential threats.

• • •

Given the ticket prices, most people were never going to experience Super Bowl security in person. But around 40 percent of Americans took at least one commercial flight each year, and for millions of white-collar workers, air travel was one of the basic parts of doing the job.[19] More than any other sector of the economy, September 11 had been a disaster for the airline industry. The attacks had begun the moment the terrorists set foot on the curb outside the departures area. Airline employees had checked the terrorists into their flights and handed over their boarding passes, and private contractors working for the airports had waved them through security. They had used airline property to kill nearly three thousand people and destroy one of the most densely populated neighborhoods in the country.

In the months after September 11, passengers and crews alike were terrified to fly. Flight demand dropped by around a third and didn't recover to pre-9/11 levels for two years, prompting a wave of bankruptcies, layoffs, and mergers that ultimately left around three-quarters of domestic flights in the hands of just four carriers.[20] One writer recalled taking his first post-9/11 flight into Reagan National Airport in Washington: "It was in the evening, already dark, and the grim voice of the pilot announced over the loudspeaker that no one was allowed to stand up or leave their seats for the last 30 minutes of the flight. Not even for the bathroom. No exception, he said repeatedly. . . . Looking out the window at the lights of the city at night felt like a transgression."[21] A flight attendant remembered that when she returned to work in late September, she and a colleague placed their own hands around their necks during takeoff, so that a hijacker sneaking up from behind wouldn't be able to slit their throats.[22] If air travel was ever going to recover—and by the time the federal government approved a $15 billion bailout for the industry less than two weeks after the attacks, there were plenty who thought it never would—the whole experience, all the way from check-in to security, takeoff, and landing, would have to be transformed. Airports became theaters in which the government staged performances demonstrating its new mindset. For passengers, arriving at the intended destination now depended on how well they could read their new lines and play their new parts.

The immediate effects of September 11 on the country's travel infrastructure were chaotic. Ticket prices plunged as airlines cut flights from their schedules and laid off workers.[23] Business associations canceled annual conventions because of the uncertainty surrounding whether attendees would be able to make it. Car rental companies were in disarray, their fleets scattered all over the country by travelers who drove home after the attacks stranded them at airports.[24] Security was managed by a scattershot network of private firms that varied from airport to airport, which meant there was no unified guidance to heed or standards to adopt as the industry tried to get back on its feet. Passengers found themselves at the mercy of screeners who didn't know what they were supposed to be doing now, only that it was not whatever they had been doing before. Often the screeners just telegraphed the newfound gravity of their jobs by spending a lot of time scrutinizing every object in everyone's bags. Half-baked suggestions came in from all directions. The secretary-general of Interpol wrote that airlines might need to consider "building a safe zone between the cockpit and the passengers," failing to understand that for a struggling industry that needed to squeeze ticket revenue out of every available square foot of cabin space, this was a total nonstarter.[25]

With wait times skyrocketing and public confidence in the industry at historic lows, Congress passed the Aviation and Transportation Security Act in November 2001. The bill ended the state of affairs whereby individual airports and airlines hired private security firms to handle passenger screening. Going forward, airport security would be federalized, with the newly created Transportation Security Administration (TSA) overseeing the whole process (as well as security procedures for trains and intercity bus travel). Airports would now be divided into "sterile" and "non-sterile" zones. Passage into the sterile zone would require a trip through metal detectors, inspection of carry-on items by TSA agents, and X-ray examinations of all checked bags. Ticket counter agents were also required to pose two questions to anyone who wanted to check a bag: (1) "Have any of the items you're traveling with been out of your immediate control since the time you packed them?" and (2) "Has anyone unknown to you asked you to carry an item on board the aircraft?" Standards for employment as a screener were minimal, requiring only that applicants speak English and "possess basic aptitudes and physical abilities," including the ability to perceive colors.[26]

Over the following years, the TSA built a large and complex security apparatus on top of this foundation. Protective measures were removed from the larger program only on rare occasions; the normal procedure was to keep layering new safeguards on top of the ones that were already in place. In December 2001, a man named Richard Reid tried and failed to detonate explosives packed into the shoes he'd worn on a flight from Paris to Miami. The TSA responded by asking passengers to send their shoes through the X-ray machines along with their carry-on bags. By April 2003, pilots who wanted to were allowed to carry handguns on their flights, the TSA had begun training crew members on how to use firearms mid-flight, and cockpit doors were reinforced. The government also deployed increased numbers of plainclothes air marshals who would sit on commercial flights with handguns concealed under their sport coats and watch for hijackers. In the summer of 2006, following the disruption of a plot to bomb North America–bound flights with liquid explosives concealed in brand-name plastic beverage containers, the TSA banned liquids, gels, and aerosols from carry-on luggage. When this new restriction prompted an outcry, the TSA modified its requirements, allowing non-solid hygiene products so long as they were held in containers of 3.4 ounces or less, and so long as those containers were held in a one-quart clear plastic bag with a zip top. The TSA added canine teams to its airport security program in 2008. In 2009, an al-Qaeda operative named Umar Farouk Abdulmutallab tried to bomb a Christmas Day flight to Detroit with explosives concealed in his underwear. From that point on, the TSA began subjecting passengers to full-body scans, which allowed them to perform a visual pat down on everyone looking to enter the gate area. Anyone unwilling to step inside the full-body scanner machines was allowed to request a physical pat down instead, but this did not always prevent tensions from boiling over. In 2010, a thirty-one-year-old libertarian blogger made the national news when he recorded himself telling a TSA agent, "If you touch my junk, I am going to have you arrested." The TSA agent paused for a few seconds to consider this. "Actually," he said, "we are going to have a supervisor here because of your statement."[27] (There were also any number of reports that women had been inappropriately touched by TSA agents in the security line, but it was the male blogger's story that got the most attention.)

The post-9/11 security program became so complex that some people worried about whether Americans had the brainpower to comply even if they wanted to. "The message is a pretty sophisticated one," the chairman of the Business Travel Coalition said, "and it's a lot for the average person who is traveling for the first time in months to remember."[28] The TSA made some attempts to simplify the process, mounting a public information campaign around its "3-1-1" policy to help travelers understand the rules (*three*-ounce bottles in *one* clear plastic bag, with *one* bag allowed per person). But the rules changed so frequently, and were enforced in such a scattershot way, that airports became very tense places.

The airports themselves, as physical structures, were somewhat to blame for this. Airports take a very long time to build. They require huge amounts of land, which can be hard to come by in a metropolitan area large enough to justify having an airport in the first place. Complicated negotiations among city governments, the airlines whose planes will use the airport, and the vendors that will fill the retail space can drag on for years, even decades. The result is that new airports are often out of date by the time they open. When the 700,000-pound Boeing 747 jet was introduced in 1969, people had only just come to grips with the needs of the earlier generation of jets that preceded it, and airports like Atlanta's found themselves having to expand the runways and parking aprons of their brand-new facilities in order to accommodate the behemoths.[29] Similarly, America's airports were not ready for post-9/11 security. In the fall of 2001, the newest airport in the country was Denver International, which opened in 1995. It was the country's first completely new large airport in more than two decades, and as of this writing it remains America's newest. With no space allocated for the crowds that built up as wait times increased, lines could stretch all the way back to the ticket counters. Body scanner machines took up so much more space than their metal-detector predecessors that some airports had to decrease the number of lines moving through the security area. Someone who had trouble taking off their shoes while standing could cause a bottleneck. All of this meant that passengers who were already more frightened of flying than they had been before September 11 were now also frustrated and angry when they got to the gate.

This was a problem for the TSA, because crowds of agitated passengers made the other elements of their security program more difficult to implement. The TSA wasn't satisfied with searching people's luggage, shoes, and toiletries. It also wanted to scrutinize passengers themselves—their body language, their gestures, the way they did or did not make eye contact when buying a ticket at the counter—in the hope of sussing out who might try to mount an attack even if they didn't have a box cutter in the side pocket of their roller bag. For years before September 11, Massachusetts State Police had used various behavior detection techniques to identify people who might be transporting drugs through Logan International Airport in Boston. So in

2002, the department hired Rafi Ron, who had run security at Ben Gurion International Airport in Tel Aviv, and Paul Ekman, a social scientist who claimed to have developed a list of facial cues that indicated someone was lying. The TSA liked the results of the trial run, and so in 2005 it expanded the program to twelve other airports. The program was called SPOT, for Screening Passengers by Observation Techniques. TSA agents selected for the program received four days of classroom instruction and three days of field training.[30]

The idea that criminals might reveal their intentions in advance of any wrongdoing began to take its place in pop culture with the 2002 film *Minority Report,* and by the end of the Bush administration it was inspiring TV shows. In the opening scene of *Lie to Me,* which premiered on Fox in 2009, Dr. Cal Lightman, an expert on body language and "microexpressions" who contracts out to various law enforcement agencies, interrogates a white supremacist and divines the location of a pipe bomb in less than two minutes, much to the chagrin of the skeptical FBI agents who watch the interview from behind a one-way mirror. "Emotion looks the same whether you're a suburban housewife or a suicide bomber," Lightman says. "The truth is written on all our faces."[31] That's almost exactly how the head of the TSA, Kip Hawley, justified the agency's use of behavioral detection: "It doesn't matter what race, ethnicity, age or whatever a person is. It's got to do with the human condition, that humans express certain emotions unknown to them that you can detect."[32]

But if everyone at the airport was stressed out, agitated, and angered by the difficulties of navigating the security line, then it wouldn't be possible for behavioral detection agents to spot the one passenger who is agitated because he's on a suicide mission. As Hawley described it, the SPOT program picked out suspicious passengers on a relative basis rather than an absolute one. "We know what normal is," he said. "We know what a hassled business traveler looks like. We know what somebody who's just had a fight with their girlfriend or boyfriend or whatever looks like. We know what the normal experience is. So you build on top of that." That meant the passenger who merited more focused scrutiny would not be the one whose behavior could be judged in a vacuum; it would be the one who behaved *differently* from everyone else, who demonstrated "deviations from baseline behavior," as the TSA put it.[33] In this sense, the TSA had decided that behavioral detection aimed at large crowds was analogous, more or less, to a lie detector test, in which the interview subject is asked to provide truthful answers to ordinary questions about their life and job in order to provide a baseline against which to judge the answers where the subject would be more likely to lie. This meant that airports needed to lower the emotional temperature of the airport as a whole. "We need to calm down the checkpoint," Hawley told a group of aviation reporters. "If we can calm down the process so the baseline data is lower, then it makes it easier for the other to pop out."[34] This need brought new changes to airport design. Terminals built a few years or more after September 11 allocated more space to the security area. Post-security retail stores went upscale, in an acknowledgment that shopping is a common way for Americans to relieve stress (if the shops could be seen from the security line itself, all the better—passengers might find it easier to remain calm if they could see the treat they would get once they made it through the line). The TSA installed blue lighting at a security checkpoint in Indianapolis International Airport, believing it would have a "calming effect."[35]

Combined with the technological security measures, the SPOT program meant that for passengers hoping to make it through the airport with a minimum of hassle, it was not enough to simply not be someone who intended to commit terrorism. One also had to look and sound and act like someone who did not intend to commit terrorism. Airports became stages. Passengers did their best to follow the government's script for how an innocent traveler behaved, and the TSA pounced on performances that weren't up to the correct standard. The TSA was explicit about this. "*You* already know you're not a threat," the narrator said in an instructional video shown near airport checkpoints during the 2007 holiday season. "*Show us* by packing smart." Packing "smart" meant folding the clothes in your suitcase and separating clothes and electronics into separate layers so that TSA agents could rifle through your things more quickly and efficiently. It also meant having your boarding pass and identification card already out and ready for inspection when you approached the checkpoint. The TSA video included a scene where an attractive white woman takes forever digging through her purse, annoying the agent at the kiosk as well as all of the delayed passengers stuck behind her in line.[36] Passengers were expected to make themselves easy to inspect, to be as transparent as possible, to help the government's agents find out who they were and where they were going and what they were carrying with them. It wasn't just that the TSA was going to invade your privacy—you were going to behave as though you liked it, too.

Passengers were also expected to take the process seriously. The slightest criticism of a TSA agent, the smallest hint of irritation at having to go through the body scanner rather than the metal detector, could be enough to have a supervisor called over to provide extra scrutiny. Jokes were totally out of the question, as a matter of official policy. In 2004, a young British woman joked to a TSA agent in Miami that she had "three bombs" in her luggage. When asked to repeat herself, she repeated the joke two more times, at which point she was arrested. "After what happened on 9/11, you cannot just come on flights and make these types of jokes," a Miami police detective said. "They will not be tolerated and we have to take enforcement action."[37] After another incident in which a French pilot joked about having explosives in his shoes, a TSA spokesperson emphasized to the media that "we have zero tolerance for these kinds of comments."[38] For passengers who missed that particular press conference, signs were posted at airports around the country. A placard at LAX read, "ATTENTION! Making any jokes or statements during the screening process may be grounds for both criminal and civil penalties. All such matters will be taken seriously. We thank you for your restraint in this matter."[39]

As you might expect, the NO JOKING signs and other security measures were terrific fodder for jokes. A theater group in Kansas City took to a popular outdoor shopping mall, posted signs reading NO JOKING ZONE on one side and THANK YOU FOR NOT LAUGHING on the other, silently stood guard, and watched people react. The *New Yorker* writer Calvin Trillin went on *The Daily Show* after the attempted shoe bombing and said, "There's one Arab terrorist with a sense of humor, and he said, 'I bet I can get them all to take their shoes off in airports.' If the next one is called, because of his M.O., 'the underwear bomber,' you'll know I'm on to something."[40] Three years later, when a real underwear bomber appeared in the form of Umar Farouk Abdulmutallab, Trillin wrote an article titled "Crystal Ball." "Nobody has mentioned that I predicted this turn of events," he wrote. "How many dead-on predictions does a person have to make to get a little credit around here?" The terrorists, he wrote, were "engaged in an elaborate scheme to embarrass us to death."[41]

For those who didn't stick to the script, however, the results could be quite serious. The British woman who joked about bombs in her luggage at the Miami airport was threatened with a fifteen-year prison sentence. A woman was charged with harassment after complaining about a lengthy interrogation at Honolulu International Airport,[42] a place where screeners referred to some of their co-workers as "Mexicutioners" because of their habit of flagging Hispanic passengers for questioning.[43] A mother trying to travel out of Reagan National Airport in Washington was detained and threatened with arrest after she spilled water from her son's sippy cup. Air marshals shot an unmedicated bipolar man at Miami International Airport. An "agitated" passenger in Vancouver was cuffed and tased multiple times, and he died lying on the terminal floor. A woman in Phoenix on her way to a rehab center was late for a connecting flight, became angry with the gate attendant, and was then arrested and put in a holding cell, where she died.[44]

A ruthless utilitarian might argue that these deaths were worth it given the hundreds or thousands of other deaths that were prevented by thwarting terrorism, but there is little to no evidence that *any* of the post-9/11 security measures made air travel safer. In a 2010 report by the U.S. Government Accountability Office, the TSA said it was "not known if the SPOT program has ever resulted in the arrest of anyone who is a terrorist, or who was planning to engage in terrorist-related activity."[45] Given the government's eagerness to publicize every instance in which a terrorist plot was stopped in its tracks, it is safe to infer from that statement that the SPOT program never caught anybody. A Department of Homeland Security project manager testified before Congress that he wasn't even sure that behavioral detection worked at all. "The research in this area is fairly immature," he said. "We're trying to establish whether there is something to detect."[46] Passenger and baggage screeners have a similarly thin record of success. In 2003, a college student named Nathaniel Heatwole decided he would try to help the TSA identify the weaknesses in its security program. He repeatedly bought plane tickets and then packed box cutters, knives, and liquid bleach in his luggage, which he successfully smuggled through the checkpoint on each occasion. When he emailed the TSA to let them know, he was fined $500 and put on probation.[47] Not wanting to rely entirely on the public to find out how ineffective their screeners were, the TSA established its own unit of undercover testing agents, which it called the Red Team. In operations carried out at LAX and O'Hare, the Red Team tried to smuggle fake bombs through security. Seventy-five percent of them made it through unnoticed in Los Angeles, and 60 percent slipped through in Chicago.[48] In 2015, the TSA did even worse: In sixty-seven out of seventy cases, Red Team agents were able to get weapons through the checkpoints, a failure rate of 96 percent. That same report also found that despite spending more than half a billion dollars in six years to buy the latest technology for screening checked luggage, the TSA had failed to make any improvements in that area, either.[49]

In this light, people's frustrations with airport security seemed more or less justified. If the TSA wasn't using its scanners and X-ray machines to actually find weapons, and if its behavior detection agents weren't spotting any terrorists—in short, if the government hadn't managed to stop a *single* terrorist plot at its airport security checkpoints—then what was the point? Why not just let passengers' relatives back into the gate area to greet or say goodbye to their loved ones? Why not let people keep their shoes on? Who cares if someone forgot and left a pair of scissors in their toiletry bag? After all, there was nothing to stop a terrorist from detonating a suicide vest while standing in the security line. Checkpoints were now the most crowded parts of the airport, and such an attack would cause almost as much terror as another midair hijacking.

Yet nothing like that had happened, which made one begin to suspect that the terrorist threat as a whole had been overhyped. People started to use the phrase "security theater" to describe the situation, the idea being that successfully staging the appearance of safety was a higher priority than actually making the airports secure. But this rationale doesn't hold up under scrutiny, either. While public opinion polling is an inexact science at best, the evidence suggests that the post-9/11 security program did not make a meaningful difference in how people perceive the safety of air travel, a fact that might be explained by noting that security and safety are not the same thing.[50] Safety is the feeling that you are not threatened. Security is the feeling that you *are* threatened but that you are protected from the threat. That makes security a double-edged sword; it emphasizes the dangers people face as much as the steps taken to protect against them. Safety means living in a place where you feel that you can leave your doors unlocked when you leave the house or go to sleep. Security means you shell out for the best locks money can buy and spend a lot of time peering at the street through your blinds.

• • •

Along with the halftime show and the game itself, there is a third crucial element to the Super Bowl's status as America's biggest media spectacle: the commercials. A thirty-second slot during the big game is the most valuable advertising real estate in the world. For large corporations like Anheuser-Busch, Coca-Cola, and the Ford Motor Company, there is no better opportunity to remind everyone in the country that you are still on top. Upstart firms, meanwhile, can blow a whole year's media budget on a single ad and go from total unknown to household name overnight. The Super Bowl of football is also the Super Bowl of American consumerism. In February 2002, thirty-second ad slots sold at an average price of $1.9 million.[51]

Advertisers found themselves in a complicated spot after September 11. On the day itself, the major news networks had all decided to forgo commercials entirely. Nobody wanted to hear about the stain-fighting power of Tide laundry detergent (or whatever) while they watched Manhattan burn. On the other hand, consumerism occupies an exalted place in American culture. No other country spends more on consumer goods, and nowhere else do people derive so much meaning from the things they buy. By the time news networks returned to regular commercial programming on September 15, 2001, it felt as if a welcome sense of normalcy was being reestablished. When the Super Bowl came around five months later, advertisers had their first big chance to grapple with how to sell things to people who were now at war.

The commercials that aired during Super Bowl thirty-six took a cautious approach, with only three directly addressing terrorism. The first saw New York City Mayor Rudy Giuliani thanking America for its support, after which the name of Monster.com, a job-seeking website, flashed briefly on the screen. The second, an ad for Budweiser beer, saw a group of beautiful horses pulling a wagon through the American landscape, traversing snow-covered fields and making their way through small towns before finally arriving in New York and respectfully bowing to the Statue of Liberty. The third was part of a government antidrug campaign and listed the amounts of money the September 11 hijackers spent on various parts of their plan: $3,000 for a fake ID, $2 for box cutters, $100 for phones, and so on. "Where do terrorists get their money?" the ad asked. "If you buy drugs, some of it might come from you." That commercial was laughed out of the room, and the campaign was short-lived. It is indicative of the expectations Americans have for each year's batch of ads that one national newspaper led its coverage of the commercials with a headline remarking on how few of them were explicitly pro-America: "Patriotism Barely Gets off the Bench."[52] But this was something of a misreading. Post-9/11 anxieties could be felt in several of the ads, even those that didn't wave a flag in your face and then slap a logo on it. The frontier myths that organized the country's understanding of what the attacks meant were all over three commercials for Cadillac's new lineup of cars and SUVs.

In one, a man driving a vintage Cadillac convertible sits in gridlocked city traffic. Steam billows out of manhole covers, office drones trudge by in identical trench coats and fedoras, and except for the lipstick-red body of his car, everything in sight is the same shade of dull gray-brown. He looks around, fed up with the monotony of the grind, and drives out of the city as Led Zeppelin fades in on the soundtrack. Suddenly he is in the American Southwest, speeding through a wild landscape of cacti, mesas, and dusty two-lane highways. In the place where America's pioneers found new lands in which to settle, abundant natural resources, and natives who could be dispossessed with a minimum of fuss, the driver finds brand-new Cadillacs. A blond woman speeds by him in a silver sedan, a guy at a roadside gas station fuels up his black SUV, and as he waits for a freight train to thunder past at a railroad crossing, a miraculous kind of transposition takes place, lifting him out of his old ride and into a 2003 convertible. By leaving the filthy, soul-destroying city behind and returning to the place where America forged its national identity, he is able to redeem his individuality, cast off the shackles of the past, and drive into the future behind the wheel of an XLR. The tagline at the end sat uneasily with the fact that every person in the commercial was white: "The legendary bloodline is about to boil."

Consumerism served two purposes after September 11, one of them general and the other more specific. In general, the Bush administration just wanted Americans to spend as much money as they could. The first dot-com crash had sent the country into a recession, and the attacks had thrown the stock market, along with America's travel and tourism industries, into chaos. The tech-heavy Nasdaq stock exchange didn't bottom out until late 2002, and one research institute estimated that the attacks cost the United States more than 650,000 jobs, with those losses concentrated in tourism, travel, and entertainment.[53] The government needed to stoke consumer demand by any means, and with the country experiencing its biggest surge of patriotic feeling since the first Gulf War, why not connect the two? The issue was so pressing that President Bush brought it up as soon as the evening of September 11, 2001, trying to reassure Americans that the country remained "open for business." Dick Cheney, in his inimitably unfeeling way, expressed the hope that Americans wouldn't let the attacks "in any way throw off their normal level of [economic] activity." Businesses themselves were also quick to yoke their efforts to the war everyone knew was coming. The Ad Council argued that patriotic consumption was well established in American history, reminding people that the council "was originally founded as the War Advertising Council during World War II in the aftermath of the bombings of Pearl Harbor."[54] The Federal Reserve dropped interest rates by more than a full percentage point by the end of the year in the hope of spurring investment and spending, and rates wouldn't return to their pre-9/11 levels until 2005. The Steve Madden shoe company started selling a line of sneakers called the Bravest. They were white trainers with a chunky sole and a rhinestone American flag on the side. They retailed for $49.95, and the company pledged to donate all proceeds to the families of dead firefighters.[55]

The results of these efforts were mixed. On the one hand, media commentators derided Bush and Cheney's pleas for Americans to fight terrorism by opening their wallets as insensitive and crass, a bit of moneygrubbing when what people needed were appeals to the country's loftiest democratic ideals. On the other hand, Bush and Cheney might have been more clear-eyed about what America stood for than the pundits. There could be no doubt, after all, that al-Qaeda hoped to strike at the America-led global economic order. Why else would they have attacked the two buildings that most symbolized the country's financial power? In that light, why not ask Americans to do their part by consuming a little more?

The various charity initiatives that businesses supposedly undertook to support victims and their families also sometimes fell apart under scrutiny. In February 2002, it came out that although Steve Madden had generated more than half a million dollars in profit from its star-spangled sneakers, none of that money had actually found its way to the families of any dead firefighters. When journalists called up the company to ask about where the money was going, Steve Madden pledged that 10 percent of those profits would go to the fire department. And when asked whether 10 percent wasn't a rather stingy amount, the company's CEO was defiant. "We have stockholders, so we walk the line between what is good for the stockholder and the company and doing these good deeds," he said. "The most patriotic thing we can do is make money."[56] Despite the Federal Reserve lowering interest rates, investment remained very sluggish for at least a year. By the end of 2002, the U.S. economy's growth rate was an anemic 1.7 percent, and it remained below 3 percent through 2003.[57]

On the other hand, there is some evidence that while corporations failed to keep up their end of the bargain after September 11, American consumers went above and beyond in opening their wallets, which might have cushioned the economy against some of the worst effects of the attacks. Consumer spending from October through December 2001 was up 6 percent over the same period a year earlier, a massive increase.[58] To hear retailers tell the story, this could be at least partially explained by the fact that Americans just found it comforting to shop. A Walmart manager spoke to the media and said that "the day of the attacks, we had many people who were alone come into the store because they wanted to be around other people and have someone to talk to."[59] And in addition to the camaraderie, there were deals. People jumped at the chance to finance new car purchases with no interest. General Motors made the first move, launching a patriotic advertising campaign offering 0 percent interest to "keep America rolling," the slogan echoing the famous "Let's roll" rallying cry that was thought to have launched the passengers' effort to fight the hijackers on Flight 93. Ford soon followed suit, promising to "do their part to keep America moving forward" by offering the same interest-free financing. Thirty-year mortgage rates also fell sharply, reaching an all-time low of 5.26 percent by the middle of 2003, helping to fuel a boom in new home purchases and construction (we'll discuss some of the consequences of this housing boom in a later chapter).[60] During World War II, Americans were asked to help the war effort by saving their money, restricting personal consumption, and forgoing certain luxuries they'd become accustomed to regularly buying. During the war on terror, they were asked to spend up to and then beyond their available means. In both cases, they answered the call.

Consumerism's second purpose in the post-9/11 period was to encourage Americans to open their wallets and buy things that made them feel more prepared to confront the dangerous, violent world in which they now lived. Gun sales increased, with the FBI announcing that background checks for gun purchases had increased by nearly half a million over the prior year. Alighting on the angle that was the most likely to frighten his readers, a *New York Times* columnist reported that even northeastern college feminists were scooping up firearms. "A generation ago, women here at Mount Holyoke College defied convention by burning bras and moving in with boyfriends," Nicholas Kristof wrote in March 2002. "These days, some women here are shocking the campus by embracing something even more dangerous than men—guns."[61] Gun manufacturers knew full well, however, that the majority of their clientele were not university radicals. Beretta advertised a new nine-millimeter pistol called United We Stand that included an attractive wooden finish on the grip and an American flag etched onto the side, and Tromix won some notoriety for itself by previewing a new .50-caliber rifle called the Turban Chaser (it's unclear whether the gun was ever actually sold).[62] The media reported on this increase with trepidation, claiming that the sales increase couldn't be explained away as the country's long-standing gun owners rounding out their arsenals with an AR-15. "This is different," one Los Angeles shooting range worker said. "The mindset of people has changed." Gun store owners around Southern California said that the majority of first-time permit seekers were women, and that these women were also buying up gas masks so as to protect their families from anthrax attacks.[63]

Changing mindsets among women were also thought to be a driving force behind the most dramatic shift in post-9/11 consumer habits. By 2003, for the first time, data indicated that women were the main decision makers behind more than half of all car purchases in the United States, and market research had demonstrated for years that for women the ability to sit high above the road was an important factor in deciding what to buy. Auto manufacturers began to cater more to women's preferences than they had in the past, with Jeep designing a new SUV specifically to keep women happy. "The real key for women was to sit high," a Jeep executive said. "The new Jeep Liberty feels like I'm driving around on stilts, and there's a very important marketing reason for that."[64]

The notion that women were gravitating toward SUVs because they made them feel safe dovetailed nicely with another figure who came to prominence in the run-up to the 2004 presidential election between George Bush and Senator John Kerry: the so-called security mom. Her vague outline first appeared as the United States invaded Iraq, with *The Washington Post, Washington Monthly, Philadelphia Inquirer, Time* magazine, and other publications all running articles claiming that women were more concerned than men about the possibility of future terrorist attacks.[65] And she officially stepped out in June 2003, when *Time* ran a cover story headlined "Goodbye, Soccer Mom. Hello, Security Mom":

> She used to say she would never allow a gun in her house, but now she feels better if her airline pilot has one. She wanted a nuclear freeze in the 1980s and was a deficit hawk in the 1990s, but she now believes the Pentagon should have whatever it wants. Her civil liberties seem less important than they used to, especially compared with keeping her children safe.

One of the security moms interviewed for the article had voted for Bill Clinton twice, prioritizing liberal policies on abortion and welfare spending in choosing her favored candidates. That was all over. "Since 9/11," she said, "all I want in a President is a person who is strong."[66] There's evidence that the security mom was more of a media invention than a real phenomenon, but she exerted a strong cultural influence during the Bush administration. Picture the security mom in your mind, and you are likely to see an affluent suburban woman. She is competent, trim, and well put together, and she is sitting behind the wheel of the biggest passenger vehicle you've ever seen. Between September 11 and the election of Donald Trump, SUVs and pickup trucks became the most popular cars in the country.

The shift from station wagons and minivans to the SUV as the car of choice for suburban families was already under way before September 11, but the war on terror accelerated that shift and made it stick. The SUV got its start in World War II, when the Army decided it wanted a small truck that could transport troops plus a heavy machine gun. The "jeep" (as soldiers eventually nicknamed the vehicle) fit their needs, and the Army ordered half a million of them. Attempts to market jeeps to civilians after the war ended were unsuccessful, but in the mid-1980s a group of researchers at Ford decided the time was right for a four-door SUV that would be marketed to families rather than tradesmen, people who could get by just fine with a minivan or station wagon but would be happier if their car didn't immediately identify them as suburban drones with yammering children hanging from their shirtsleeves. The first Explorer rolled off the factory line in 1990. Because these cars would be marketed primarily to people living in urban and suburban areas, most of the features that distinguished SUVs from minivans were totally unnecessary. As one marketing executive at Jeep said, "All of the SUV market was psychological, there was no actual customer need for four-wheel drive."[67] But that wasn't the point. By catering directly to the collective midlife crisis of the country's affluent boomer parents, the Ford Explorer launched a revolution in how Americans got themselves from place to place. The rest of the country's automakers spent the rest of the decade trying to catch up.

September 11 put the SUV into a new, even more profitable context. Its appeal no longer had to rely on perpetually unfulfilled fantasies of using your vacation days to tame the wilderness instead of visiting the in-laws. Now the world was a dangerous place where terrorists could strike without warning, and SUVs, because they were taller and heavier than anything else on the road, made people feel secure. The vehicles' military origins returned to the foreground— this was the car to drive when the homeland was a potential war zone. An arms race began, with SUVs and then pickup trucks growing in size, putting on weight, and sporting ever more intimidating and aggressive designs with each passing year. In 2001, a Ford Explorer weighed between thirty-eight hundred and forty-one hundred pounds, depending on which features were included. By 2010, the lightest Explorer available for purchase weighed almost forty-five hundred pounds, and by 2015 the heaviest came in at nearly forty-nine hundred. Meanwhile, the Ford F-150, the bestselling truck in the country, ballooned to around fifty-five hundred pounds by 2010. A glance at how the design of these vehicles changed over that period makes the appeal obvious: They look more like combat vehicles with each passing year. Their grilles got taller and more imposing, and what had been sinuous curves at the end of the 1990s hardened into sharp angles.

The advertising used to sell these behemoths only amplified the impression given by the vehicles themselves, which is that America's streets and parking lots were battlefields. In 2014, Ford described the body of its new F-150 model as "military grade" and guaranteed its "toughness" based on the "torture-testing" to which it had been subjected.[68] Market research repeatedly confirmed that people liked SUVs because they thought they needed protection from the outside world. "The world is becoming a harder and more violent place to live, so we wrap ourselves with the big vehicles," said one SUV owner in California. Another said, "It gives you a barrier, makes you feel less threatened."[69] Another study even found that drivers liked how high SUVs sat up off the ground because "it's easier to see if someone is hiding underneath or lurking behind it."[70] SUVs and pickups were not just family automobiles but urban assault vehicles, fortresses, survival tools. Their model names often recalled the glory days of the militarized frontier: Trailblazer, Defender, Pathfinder, Warrior, Cherokee, Navajo, Tahoe, Yukon, and so on. The vehicle that went the furthest in embracing the SUV's military styling was the Hummer H2, which weighed around sixty-five hundred pounds and used up a gallon of gas every twelve miles. With ads touting its "military-derived DNA," it became the bestselling large luxury SUV in the country.[71]

SUVs were controversial throughout their ascendancy, pitting those who found their appeal to be self-evident against those who thought they symbolized an unappealing and specifically American mix of arrogance, wastefulness, and insecurity. Perceptions of increased safety were central to SUVs' appeal as the category took off in the 1990s, but just as the purported benefits of tightened airport security tended to evaporate under scrutiny, it soon became clear that SUVs were significantly less safe than ordinary cars. The fact that they sat so high off the ground made it easy for drivers to see the roads around them, but it also gave the vehicles such high centers of gravity that they sometimes rolled over while making turns and killed their occupants. That problem was eventually addressed, but lower rollover rates did not solve the problem that while SUVs might have offered safety to their occupants, they were extremely dangerous to anyone who wasn't sitting inside them. Because women tend to drive smaller cars than men, they are now seriously injured in car wrecks at higher rates than the men piloting the equivalents of small tanks from their homes to the golf course.[72] The tall, squared-off grilles that have become de rigueur in SUV design also produce enormous blind spots directly in front. One local TV station conducted an investigation and discovered that the blind spot in front of a 2019 Cadillac Escalade was more than ten feet long. To translate that into the number of people who might be killed because of a design choice, the reporter was able to put twelve seated children in a line directly in front of the car before the driver was able to see the top of the thirteenth child's head.[73] SUVs also nudged the people sitting inside them toward more dangerous driving behavior. A 2017 study found that men and women were both more likely to not wear their seat belts, blow through red lights at intersections, and look at their phones while behind the wheel of an SUV than while driving a smaller car.[74] For some people, the only way to feel safe with so many of these monsters careening around the streets was to give in and buy a Suburban or F-150 of their own. One social worker from Maine told a reporter that while he'd prefer to drive a "compact car," he has post-traumatic stress disorder from a prior crash, so he drives a big truck, too. "Everyone else in my town does," he said, "and it's the only way I can get around without feeling like I'm gonna die."[75]

The most controversial thing about SUVs and pickups during the early years of the war on terror, however, was their fuel efficiency. Poor gas mileage has been a signature feature of SUVs since the 1970s, when their designation as light trucks instead of passenger vehicles allowed them to skirt congressional fuel efficiency standards. By the early twenty-first century, that regulatory regime had been significantly weakened, and SUVs and pickups could use up all the fuel they wanted. In 2005, a Ford Explorer got fifteen miles to the gallon, a Chevrolet Tahoe got sixteen, and the SUV/pickup hybrid version of the Cadillac Escalade managed just thirteen miles.[76]

As the United States launched an aggressive war in Iraq that many of its critics believed was motivated by the Bush administration's desire to secure American dominance of some of the Middle East's largest oil reserves, the country's growing embrace of SUVs came to look like the manifestation of some collective death wish. Everyone knew that America's dependence on foreign oil made it vulnerable to the political vicissitudes of the Middle East, and Al Gore's 2006 documentary film and book, both titled *An Inconvenient Truth,* had put the dangers of climate change in the national spotlight for the first time in years. Why, then, was America doubling down on its love affair with these extravagantly wasteful machines?

It didn't make sense, and protests broke out at various points, both online and on the streets. The Hummer was the favored target, giving rise to websites such as StopSUVs.org and FUH2.com. In August 2003, someone from the radical environmentalist group Earth Liberation Front went further, breaking into a Hummer dealership in the middle of the night and torching twenty new H2s, spray-painting "gross polluter" and "fat, lazy Americans" on many of the burned-out wrecks for good measure. That was a step too far for some of the more prominent critics of SUVs. "What these people are doing isn't activism—it is vandalism, and I strongly oppose it," said the media mogul Arianna Huffington, who was running for governor of California at the time. The dealership owner, a man named Ziad Alhassen, said he would not be deterred by the "terrorist acts." "They burn gas—so what?" Alhassen's lawyer added. "That's not the way to look at it. A lot of people buy these cars because they're safe. A lot of women buy them for that reason. They've got a patriotic feel to them, especially after 9/11."[77]

The key sentence there is "They burn gas—so what?" SUVs appealed to some consumers *because* they were wasteful, not in spite of it. Americans had made a collective promise that September 11 wouldn't be allowed to change their "way of life," and part of that way of life was uninhibited, unembarrassed consumption of material goods. SUVs were not just expensive and eye-catching toys guaranteed to turn heads as you drove down the street. They were consumers in their own right, chugging down gasoline in utter defiance of the geopolitical vulnerabilities. Anyone who had a problem with that could take it up with the U.S. military, whose own Hummers had taken up defensive positions around the oil fields of Iraq. SUV advertisers knew full well that excess was part of the appeal. "OK, it's massively over-engineered for the school run," one Jeep ad conceded. "And the problem with that is what, precisely?"[78] An ad for the H2 read, "Excessive. In a Rome at the height of its power sort of way." That text accompanied a close-up picture of the vehicle from directly in front of its left headlight, as though the cameraman had just managed to get the shot off before being run over.[79]

• • •

Super Bowl security wasn't content to remain inside and around the arena. According to the logic of the war on terror, victory required more than hunkering down and sealing the borders; the country also needed to project force out into the world. In a similar way, the security apparatus that protected the big game each year slowly expanded out beyond the turnstiles and parking lot and into the neighborhoods of the country's cities.

It started somewhat modestly. For Super Bowl thirty-six in New

Orleans, the government established an eight-mile no-fly zone over New Orleans, shut down a stretch of the interstate that ran by the stadium, and barricaded the streets in the surrounding neighborhoods. This was a major inconvenience to New Orleanians, albeit a temporary one; once the Patriots finished celebrating on Bourbon Street and flew back to Boston for their parade, the skies and the highways reopened. With each passing year, however, the security program expanded. By the beginning of the following season, local authorities in Baltimore were running evacuation and triage drills in case someone released chemical weapons into the air at the Ravens game. "We have never done anything on this scale before," a hospital spokesperson said. "After September 11 this has all taken on more of a sense of importance."[80] In 2005, Coast Guard ships patrolled the waters off Jacksonville, Florida, in preparation for Super Bowl thirty-nine. Jet Skis were banned from the St. Johns River, and divers inspected the undersides of five cruise ships docked at the city's port.[81] The year after that, authorities imposed a *thirty*-mile no-fly zone over Detroit, which stretched across the border into Canada, and brought in some ten thousand people to protect Ford Field. In 2010, thirty-three federal agencies were involved in security preparations for Super Bowl forty-four in Miami, which was "eight more than the previous Super Bowl."[82] In 2011, Indianapolis installed locking manhole covers throughout the city, at a cost of $2,000 each, in advance of Super Bowl forty-five.[83]

City governments compete to host the Super Bowl just as hard as NFL teams compete to play in it. It is an unjustified but persistent article of faith among municipal officials and "pro-growth" lobbyists that hosting a Super Bowl will generate jobs, bolster people's sense of civic pride, and make a city more attractive to tourists picking out their destination for the next year's holiday. The NFL has a notoriously long and detailed list of requirements for what cities must provide to the league in exchange for the privilege of hosting the year's biggest game. Some of these requirements are nothing more than demands for handouts. For Super Bowl fifty-two in 2018, for example, the NFL's list of demands included "the reservation of three (3) top quality 18-hole golf courses, at the same site or in close proximity to one another, for use by the NFL Foundation Golf Classic"; "the reservation of up to two (2) top quality bowling venues at no rental cost for use by NFL Foundation"; the reservation of "all convention centers, arenas, and concert sites in the Host Community with one thousand (1,000) or more seats"; and a commitment from the city's fire and building departments that any requests for help from the NFL would take "top priority."[84]

This orgy of taxpayer-funded party favors comes to an end once the game clock hits zero each year, but requirements pertaining to security can be longer lasting. The NFL now requires that new stadiums for NFL teams meet the league's requirements for hosting a Super Bowl at some point down the road, and the security measures demanded by the league are extensive. Cities must be able to establish and enforce "clean zones" around the stadium and other key downtown areas in which only officially licensed NFL merchandise will be sold. In Jacksonville, city officials hired private security firms to install "approximately 100 VPN encrypted video cameras throughout the city," a system "designed to 'expand,' 'stay for decades,' and 'go beyond the Super Bowl for other needs.'"[85] Facial-recognition cameras and surveillance programs that can track specific license plates as they move around a city have also been installed at the NFL's behest. In order to host the Super Bowl in 2018, Minneapolis had to confirm that its police department had the resources and equipment to establish a "hardened security perimeter," including concrete barriers, around the entirety of the stadium.[86] And by requiring cities to have all of this equipment ready and on hand for the Super Bowl, the NFL tacitly encourages the cities where its teams play to keep using it for years once the big game has pulled up stakes and left town. By militarizing the biggest game on its annual calendar, the NFL has helped to militarize public space around the country.

• • •

For a decade after September 11, no public space carried more symbolic weight than Ground Zero. After the Alfred P. Murrah Federal

Building in Oklahoma City was bombed by two white supremacists in 1995, the government demolished the building's remains and built a memorial in its place. What had been destroyed would be remembered but not rebuilt. That was never an option for New York. A sixteen-acre plot of land in one of the densest neighborhoods of the country's largest city could not just be left empty—the humiliation would be too great. The rebuilding effort turned the World Trade complex into the most publicized and most hotly debated construction project of the twenty-first century. People believed, in the words of one anthropologist who wrote a book about the process, "that whatever we decided to build here would reveal nothing less than what makes us American."[87]

There seemed to be no limit to the number of interest groups with strong views on what should be built and how. There was Larry Silverstein, the developer who had purchased the Twin Towers in July 2001 for $3.2 billion, which was then the largest real estate deal in the history of New York. He needed whatever replaced the towers to make him money. He agreed that a memorial should be part of the rebuilt site, but that wasn't his focus. Less than two weeks after the attacks, he gave a press conference at which he announced that the Twin Towers would be replaced by quadruplets: four towers, fifty stories each. Thus would all of the lost office space be replaced without creating attractive new targets for al-Qaeda to attack.[88] There were also the families of the firefighters and police officers who had died in the failed rescue attempts on September 11. The buildings collapsed with such force that many people's remains had never been recovered. In the eyes of some families, that meant the complex needed to be recognized as a grave site in perpetuity—they did not want the final resting place of their loved ones to be rebooted as a hotbed of commercial activity. City and state officials hoped to mediate these conflicts as quickly and efficiently as possible. The last thing they needed was for the rebuilding process to get swallowed up in bureaucratic labyrinths of red tape, zoning laws, and political bickering. And there was also everyone else in America. They'd been attacked by al-Qaeda as well, albeit not physically, and they wanted a say in how the country responded. When the

Lower Manhattan Development Corporation held an open competition for 9/11 memorial designs, it received more than five thousand entries, including submissions from forty-nine states and sixty-three nations.

New York's governor, George Pataki, eventually forged an uneasy truce among the project's various power brokers. David Childs, chairman of the architectural firm Skidmore, Owings & Merrill, would be in charge of designing the "Freedom Tower," a 1,776-foot-tall skyscraper that would replace the Twin Towers as the climax of lower Manhattan's skyline. Larry Silverstein would retain the rights to build several office towers on the site, but the Freedom Tower itself—which later took the official name One World Trade Center—would belong to the Port Authority of New York and New Jersey, which had a long-standing presence at the WTC complex. Daniel Libeskind, the architect who had won the competition to design the master plan for the sixteen-acre site, would "meaningfully collaborate" with Silverstein and Childs, and he would also continue to be one of the public faces of the project, the man who lent the whole endeavor the artistic credibility it needed to avoid being seen as totally dominated by commercial concerns.[89] The Israeli American architect Michael Arad would design the memorial, two enormous pools outlining the Twin Towers' vanished footprints, with water cascading down their vertical gray walls into an abyss. The first responders' families won a victory as well. Since their loved ones had run into the buildings while everyone else had tried to run out, they thought that firefighters, police officers, and medical personnel should receive special recognition. The media treated them with a mixture of sympathy and irritation; one day they were victims whom the city was duty-bound to support in perpetuity, the next people who stubbornly refused to let any other considerations intrude upon the wild intensity of their grieving. Arad's memorial design eventually wound up with all of the victims' names carved into the stone that surrounded the pools, but he agreed that first responders would be grouped and identified by their unit numbers.

This plan was vastly scaled down from Libeskind's original ambitions. In the design he'd submitted to the competition, the Freedom

Tower would be topped by an enormous, twisting spire that shot up out of the place where the building's west side joined the roof, a pointed symbolic echo of Lady Liberty holding her torch aloft out in New York Harbor. That design was scrapped due to the cost, and Childs's reworked tower was a glass-sheathed, corporate banality, un-remarkable in every way except for its size. But it was a plan that ev-erybody could live with, and it even made an attempt to solve some of the biggest problems of the original World Trade Center complex. While the Twin Towers now symbolize the greatest loss in New York's history, many architects hated them while they stood. The problem wasn't entirely with the towers themselves. They had been built around a vast marble plaza, which, though very impressive in photographs, was alienating in person. Loudspeakers pumped canned music over its expanse all day, and the winds that accelerated as they funneled between the towers were so bad that people sometimes had to use ropes just to walk across it. The new design restored the neighbor-hood's older street grid, which would hopefully steer people and life toward a part of lower Manhattan that many people worried would languish for decades under a cloud of grief and fear. Even One World Trade Center wasn't so bad if you squinted hard enough at the render-ings. No, it wasn't going to win any architectural awards, but it could have been worse, and at least it sent the clear message that New York still wanted to be home to the tallest buildings in the world.

But people couldn't shake the anxiety that as soon as the tower's final steel girder was hoisted into the air and welded into place, al-Qaeda would bring the whole thing down again. This fear had been expressed for years by pundits and city officials worrying that even if the city did build a monumental skyscraper to replace the Twin Tow-ers, they wouldn't be able to find anyone to fill the office space. The economy was anemic, firms had been relocating to midtown Manhat-tan, and were companies really going to ask their employees to go to work in what would surely be the most attractive target for terror at-tacks in the country? It took nearly ten years for the magazine pub-lisher Condé Nast to announce that it would be moving its operations from Times Square down to 1 WTC, a major coup for the project. With *Vogue*'s editor, Anna Wintour, stalking the halls and *The New Yorker*'s soft-spoken, elegant eccentrics tending to their drafts while gazing down on the Hudson River, the Port Authority could feel much better about the prospects of its investment paying off. The tower itself would be a focal point for the glamour of the city's media industry, and the larger complex would teem with workers and tourists.

In reality, though, this vision had died well before Condé Nast signed its lease. The earliest iterations of the Freedom Tower's design planned for a building that would meet the security standards for a federal courthouse. Shortly after Governor Pataki laid the tower's cornerstone at a press conference, however, the NYPD let it be known that federal courthouse standards weren't going to cut it. They thought the building was too close to West Street, a busy, six-lane thoroughfare that turned into the West Side Highway as it wound up Manhattan along the Hudson. Setting buildings closer to streets makes them more a part of the public life that surrounds them, and the Freedom Tower's original design also called for wide staircases to cascade down to street level from the entirety of the building's west side, which would have invited people in from the sidewalk. But police thought that the tower's proximity to the street, along with the gently sloping stairs, would make the building a more inviting target for car and truck bombs like the one terrorists had detonated in the parking garage under the Twin Towers in 1993. Childs and Libeskind had initially taken that worry into account by planning to reduce West Street from six lanes to four, with an express road tunneled underneath that would shuttle cargo trucks up to the West Side Highway. But the investment bank Goldman Sachs objected to that plan. It felt the tunnel entrance would cause traffic buildups in front of the new headquarters it was planning to build on the other side of West Street, and it threatened to pull out of lower Manhattan entirely if the tunnel wasn't killed. That wasn't acceptable. Goldman's presence was seen as essential to the economic revitalization of the area. So the Pataki administration killed the tunnel and provided Goldman Sachs with a fifth of the $8 billion in tax-free bonds that New York had received from Congress for rebuilding. West Street would keep all six of its lanes.[90]

That satisfied Goldman but worried the police. In addition to pushing the tower back from street life, the NYPD wanted some of the architectural features of the tower's base to be changed. The original plan was for the first twenty floors to be wrapped in prismatic glass, which would allow people to see into the building from the street, make parts of its steel structure visible, and cast attractive flecks of rainbow light into the lobby. The rest of the tower would then emerge gracefully out of a base of shimmering iridescence. The department's deputy commissioner for counterterrorism thought the glass had to go; in the event of an explosion, it would shatter into thousands of deadly shards, maiming and killing anyone unfortunate enough to be in the lobby or on the adjoining sidewalks when the bomb went off. If Silverstein, Childs, and Libeskind wanted their building to survive September 11 part two, then they would have to redesign the tower in accordance with different, stricter standards: those applied to American embassies overseas. In other words, the tower needed to be built to survive in a war zone.

From an architectural standpoint, the results were catastrophic. Instead of a light-filled base, the bottom twenty floors were wrapped in blast-resistant concrete, making the building look as though it were sitting on top of a granite pedestal. The architects tried to justify the redesign on artistic grounds by claiming modernist sculpture as a source of inspiration, but the architecture critic for *The New York Times* accurately dismissed that argument as sophistry: The redesigned tower looked like a bunker. "The darkness at ground zero just got a little darker," he wrote.

> Somber, oppressive and clumsily conceived, the project suggests a monument to a society that has turned its back on any notion of cultural openness. It is exactly the kind of nightmare that government officials repeatedly asserted would never happen here: an impregnable tower braced against the outside world.[91]

His judgment was harsh but correct. The diaphanous quality that was supposed to evoke the transparency of democratic pluralism was gone. The concrete base was intimidating, and even when the designers tried to improve things by covering it in glass panels that were louvered in the manner of window blinds, the panels still repelled more than they attracted, flashing aggressively in the sunlight without allowing anyone to see what was happening inside. Even at the two main entrances, one couldn't see what was going on in the lobby; tall partitions inside the doors blocked the view of anyone passing by. The steps that were supposed to welcome people in from the sidewalk running along West Street were also gone, replaced by an elevated plaza that could be accessed only by walking around to either end of the block. The tower stood away from and above the street, as though it were scared of the urban bustle it was supposed to anchor. Looking at it today, one wonders why it doesn't just move to a suburb, where it would at least be able to relax.

Things didn't get any better as you walked through the rest of the rebuilt complex, either. The streets that Libeskind's master plan had been so careful to restore so as to undo the mistake of the original Trade Center's windswept plaza were rebuilt, but not as actual streets that the public could use. They looked like streets, with asphalt surfaces and lane markings and traffic lights, but all of them were closed off to everyday traffic. Booths housing security guards were placed on their corners, with surveillance cameras mounted on poles nearby. The streets were also equipped with giant toothed barricades that emerged out of the concrete to block off access. In theory, those barricades can retract down into the ground. In practice, they are almost always up.

People who lived in the area were dismayed by these developments. Even before September 11, the Trade Center's vast plaza had made them feel cut off from the rest of lower Manhattan; stitching their neighborhood back into the larger fabric of the island was going to be crucial to any real community recovery. "We can examine innovative ways to manage streets and traffic downtown, reinforcing the feeling that this is one place," New York City's mayor, Michael

Bloomberg, had said in December 2002. "Getting around easily means community, and that's what we're trying to create." Now residents saw that expansive vision slipping away. The former vice president of the Lower Manhattan Development Corporation was particularly acerbic regarding the police department's plan, saying the security measures made "a complete mockery" of the work people had done over the preceding few years. The police themselves were quite touchy about these criticisms. Richard Daddario, the department's deputy commissioner for counterterrorism, told a *New York Times* journalist that "pedestrians and bicyclists will be able to enter the site and travel along its streets and sidewalks just as they can everywhere else in the city. Vehicles and tour buses having business at the site will have access after screening to guard against the threat of a car bomb."[92] These remarks were printed in full in the *Times* article, but a different deputy commissioner then felt moved to send a letter to the editor in which he repeated everything his colleague had said the first time around, nearly word for word. "Pedestrians and bicyclists will be able to enter the site and travel its streets and sidewalks as never before," he wrote. "Taxis, cars and tour buses having business at the site will have access after screening to guard against the threat of a vehicle bomb." He then chided the *Times* for making "only passing reference to the trade center's destruction on 9/11," as though the people who lived in the neighborhood (or anyone else, for that matter) might have somehow forgotten. He did not address the fact that his description of the situation, which he presented as a self-evident improvement on the previous state of affairs, was exactly what residents were angry about.[93]

Time demonstrated that the residents' concerns were not misplaced. As late as 2019, the Port Authority's official stance was that "the streets of the World Trade Center campus are all managed streets with controlled access. There is no intention to ever re-open the streets to public vehicle traffic."[94]

The Trade Center remains almost entirely vehicle-free today, and in a certain light that might appear to be a good thing. New York's streets have been choked by traffic for years, and with research showing that decreasing the number of cars improves quality of life for a city's residents, large municipalities are trying out various schemes to give their roads back to pedestrians and cyclists. But the new World Trade Center is not a pedestrian's paradise or exemplar of twenty-first-century urbanism. Mazes of police barricades that seem to shift around at random from day to day make it difficult to navigate, and in the middle of a city that otherwise continues to give cars free rein, the impression given by the complex is ominous, not welcoming. Surveillance cameras become visible everywhere as soon as you start to look for them, and the heavy police presence never seems to flag. It is a simulacrum of a public space rather than the real thing. The memorial and adjacent September 11 Museum are usually thronged with tourists, and white-collar workers disappear into One World Trade Center in their thousands each morning, but people who live in New York do not spend time there. As a public space, the rebuilt World Trade Center is a dead zone.

Or, to be more precise, it is a security zone. That is the term for an urban area in which governments have decided that security concerns take precedence over street-level commerce, cultural expression, eating lunch on the steps of a building, the right to free assembly, hanging out, and the hundreds of other uses to which city residents might want to put their public spaces. Security zones have proliferated throughout the United States in the years since September 11, and their existence constitutes a direct assault on the public's ability to encounter, understand, and express itself *as a public.* Just as airports are now environments in which your physical surroundings let you know that it's unsafe to act like anything other than the stereotypical business traveler, so are security zones places that tell their inhabitants that strange, odd, or flamboyant behavior will not be tolerated (if you are nonwhite and poor, it may be best to avoid these places entirely, no matter how you behave). They are characterized by the constant presence of law enforcement, intensive use of CCTV cameras and other surveillance technologies, and physical barriers that restrict when, where, and how people are allowed to move through and occupy public space.

In 2010, a pair of academics studied two prominent neighborhoods in New York City—the Financial District, home to the New York Stock Exchange, and Civic Center, where city hall and other government buildings are located—and quantified exactly how much of the available public space had been given over to security. Their findings were astonishing. In Civic Center, more than 20 percent of the district's available public space had been closed, and when the researchers included the areas in which access had been limited if not entirely closed off, the figure rose to more than a third. Even more surprising to the study's authors was the fact that more than 17 percent of the public space in the Financial District had been converted into security zones, even though there are few government buildings in the area. This led them to the insight that corporations and other private firms have been just as enthusiastic as governments about the post-9/11 security regime. While security zones popped up around all buildings that might be considered obvious targets of an attack, such as the Stock Exchange, they also appeared around "high-value private buildings" such as the headquarters of Goldman Sachs, built thanks to the State of New York's panicked largesse. "The diminution of the public realm was palpable in both neighborhoods," they wrote. "Few open public spaces remain for the hundreds of thousands of workers and residents who live in or near Civic Center and the Financial District." The authors argued that security zones were now so ubiquitous that they should be considered an entirely new category of land use.[95]

New York and Washington, the two cities attacked on September 11, have been among the most enthusiastic proponents of destroying public spaces by militarizing them. New York now has cameras that can read license plate numbers installed on all bridges and tunnels in and out of Manhattan, and navigating the fenced-off streets of D.C. on foot, especially in the vicinity of the National Mall, requires uncommon amounts of patience, agility, problem solving, and stamina. But the securitization of public space is a national phenomenon. After September 11, Chicago proposed a budget including $76 million in funds for terrorism prevention and security. Nationally, a majority of American cities with more than 100,000 residents—there are more than three hundred such cities—have tightened security for infrastructure, government buildings, airports, and schools.[96] Neighborhood Watch, a volunteer crime prevention program that has deputized suburbanites to be on the lookout for suspicious people and activity since 1972, has long been notorious for encouraging hostility toward people of color who wind up walking down a sidewalk in the "wrong" neighborhood. The program was partially rebranded as a terrorism prevention effort after September 11, and between 2002 and 2005 the number of local watch groups in the United States increased by 85 percent.[97]

In cities like San Francisco, the combination of security-minded local governance and rapidly expanding tech companies looking to cordon off more of the city for themselves brought the erosion of public space to crisis levels. In 2015, an activist group spent six months putting together a map of all the public spaces that had disappeared from San Francisco over the previous several years. Increased police presence at BART stations made them less safe for homeless people— who are also part of the public, as much as some people would like you to believe otherwise—looking for somewhere to spend the night. Large stretches of downtown San Francisco were closed each year so that tech companies could pitch huge tents for their conferences and fairs. A private developer used a city grant to install surveillance cameras along the historic Mission Miracle Mile. Recycling centers, an important source of income for the city's homeless population, were closed down to make way for private development, and public bus stops and parking spaces were commandeered by tech companies that wanted to transport affluent, city-based workers to their suburban office buildings.[98] The result was a city in which non-wealthy residents got squeezed on both sides. Spiking rents and real estate prices made homes more and more difficult to afford, while the securitization and privatization of public space also made it harder to gather outside the home. This is an environment in which the public can barely function at all.

The twenty-first century saw "new urbanism," with its goals of re-vitalized cities centered on mixed use, walking, and public transporta-tion, become a kind of gospel among urban planners and liberal politicians. But under the unlucky star of the terrorist threat, the re-sults have frequently reproduced the forms of new urbanism without any of their content, resulting in parks and plazas that gleam appeal-ingly from a distance but are unpleasant, difficult, or impossible for the public—which is to say, everyone, not just the white and/or affluent—to actually use. The armed guards and surveillance cameras that now ring so many of the country's public spaces let their inhabit-ants know that use of those spaces is a privilege, not a right, and that the privilege can and will be revoked at any moment. Government officials responsible for imposing these security measures have always justified them as necessary to protect the public, but the experience of the past twenty years suggests that they really do the opposite, that militarism and a robust public life are at odds with each other by defi-nition.

One of the paradoxes of post-9/11 security zones is that everyone secretly knows they don't work. The bollards, surveillance booths, and sally ports surrounding the new World Trade Center don't matter, be-cause anyone with explosives strapped to their body could still walk (or bicycle) down one of the brand-new, car-free streets, give a wave to some of the cops as they pass by, take up a position in a crowd of tourists by the memorial, and hit the detonator. This is true all over the country. The militarism that suffused public life in the United States after September 11 did nothing to make people safer, and it didn't make people *feel* safer, either. If anything, by emphasizing and reemphasizing the potential dangers of being out in public, it did the opposite. In 2006, a researcher writing for the *Journal of Homeland Security and Emergency Management* noticed that "many antiterror-ism measures may actually intensify and reinforce public perceptions of vulnerability and fear." He found that the more visible the security elements in a public area were, the worse his study participants felt about being there. The researcher seemed to be puzzled by these find-ings, speculating that "such responses may be caused by a comparative lack of understanding of the nature and predictability of terrorism."[99] But it's more likely that people understood the situation just fine. When the terrorist threat has been so wildly exaggerated, the only remaining explanation for the security zones is that their purpose is to monitor the public itself.

PART II

Islam Is Peace

CHAPTER 4

Keep Quiet and Stay in Your Home

It gives me a reason to hate them more.

—visitor at Ground Zero

I t wasn't just New York. Americans built September 11 memorials all over the country. Just southwest of the Pentagon in Washington, D.C., the architects Julie Beckman and Keith Kaseman designed a memorial comprising 184 benches, one for each person who died in the Pentagon and on American Airlines Flight 77. Each bench was engraved with one of the victims' names and poised above a small, rectangular pool of illuminated water. Naperville, Illinois, dedicated its 9/11 memorial in 2003. It included a steel beam from one of the Twin Towers, perched on top of a pentagon-shaped marble pedestal. Other beams acquired by a church in Albuquerque were blessed by a Roman Catholic bishop, and a church in Palos Hills, Illinois, installed a large piece of the Trade Center in its entryway. Green Bay, Wisconsin, erected two thirty-foot-tall stainless-steel towers next to the Fox River, replacing a statue of a Green Bay Packer catching a football while standing on top of a gigantic football. And a town in New Jersey built life-size statues of a fireman, police officer, emergency medical services worker, stockbroker, and rescue dog, all gathered together on a pedestal engraved with the words "Hope," "Bravery," and "Peace."[1]

For the most part, the organizers behind these memorials worked hard to avoid any suggestion of whatever it was people meant when they said the word "politics." In New York, suspicions that politics were infiltrating the rebuilding process at Ground Zero were constant stumbling blocks. Earlier plans for the rebuilt World Trade Center complex included not just the September 11 Museum but also a cultural and educational center where people could learn about how tolerance, diversity, and liberty had been achieved throughout hundreds of years of human history. It was the brainchild of Tom Bernstein, the president of a sports and entertainment complex on the west side of Manhattan as well as a personal friend of George W. Bush, and it was going to be called the International Freedom Center (IFC).[2] Spotlighting the highs as well as the lows of humanity's march toward liberty and justice, the center promised to be a knotty but ultimately inspiring counterpoint to the memories of loss and grief that would forever swirl around the larger site.

Almost as soon as the project was announced, however, family members of some of the first responders voiced outrage. In addition to covering great moments of human achievement and liberation, the proposed IFC would include exhibits on slavery, the Holocaust, and the Native American genocide. To Debra Burlingame, whose brother had been the pilot on American Airlines Flight 77, that was unacceptable. She was furious at the idea that Ground Zero would become "a playground for culture and art," and a separate group of 9/11 families voiced similar concerns in a petition sent to Governor Pataki. "We, the undersigned," they wrote, "believe that the World Trade Center Memorial should stand as a solemn remembrance of those who died on September 11th, 2001, and not as a journey of history's 'failures' or as a debate about domestic and foreign policy in the post-9/11 world. Political discussions have no place at the World Trade Center September 11th Memorial."[3] The proposal was scuttled, and the Freedom Center was never built.

Not everyone held the view that politics should be kept away from memorials. In Shanksville, Pennsylvania, the September 11 crash site that people were likeliest to forget, local residents constructed a temporary memorial in advance of the official commemoration of Flight 93. A large wooden cross was erected close to the crash site, and a nearby chain-link fence was hung with hundreds of flags, notes, teddy bears, and bumper stickers. The signs changed from week to week and month to month, but they voiced a much wider range of political sentiment than would have been acceptable to the top-down organizers of the memorials in New York and Washington. One researcher visited the site in 2005 and saw the following messages, among others: "America No. 1, Thank God," "It's Not Just a Flag, It's a Way of Life," "Red State Insurgency," "Guns Don't Kill People, Abortion Clinics Kill People," and "Back to the Bible or . . . Back to the Jungle!"[4]

You could find things like this in New York, too, if you knew where to look or just spent enough time hanging around. Back when Ground Zero was still a cleanup zone and then a construction site, it was surrounded by plywood walls to keep onlookers at bay. These walls quickly became repositories of sadness, consolation, and hope, but also anger. One message, written in large black letters, read, "Bomb Afghanistan." Another person wrote, "Our grief is not a call for war," to which yet another responded, "Fuck you, you left-wing coward piece of shit." One writer met an Israeli couple who had come to visit the site during the first winter after the attacks. She asked them why they had come, and one of them said it was "a reason to hate them more." When the writer asked, "Who?" the woman responded, "Arabs."[5]

In Shanksville, the publication of plans for the official memorial did not dispel the Islamophobic sentiments that were simmering away at the unofficial site. Instead, it intensified them. In September 2005, the Flight 93 Advisory Commission announced the winners of its design competition, which had attracted more than a thousand entries. Paul and Milena Murdoch would make their design, "Crescent of Embrace," a reality. With much more room to work with in rural Pennsylvania than officials had in lower Manhattan and Washington, the Murdochs presented a sprawling design that included a tower filled with wind chimes, a black slate wall to mark the place where Flight 93 crashed into the ground, and a crescent-shaped pathway lined with red maple trees, with forty additional groves of trees planted nearby. People liked the tower and the wall, but for one of the jurors, the crescent was a major issue. Tom Burnett Sr., whose son died in the crash, told his fellow jurors that the crescent "goes back centuries as an old-time Islamic symbol." He thought the shape would turn the memorial into a celebration of the religion that had killed his son and that the jury would "be a laughingstock" if the project were allowed to go forward.[6]

Burnett's objections were more or less dismissed at the outset, but then a conservative blogger took up the cause. Where Burnett had seen the crescent shape as an unintentional mistake on the architects' part, Alec Rawls, who maintained a site called Error Theory (and who was also the son of philosopher John Rawls), thought the Murdochs knew exactly what they were doing. He started up a new website, CrescentOfBetrayal.com, where he explained that the crescent shape of the maple-lined pathway was just the tip of the iceberg—the whole memorial was a coded celebration of Islamic extremism. His site alleged that the crescent was geographically oriented toward Mecca, the holy city that observant Muslims face during prayer. He thought the tower of wind chimes had drawn inspiration from "an Islamic sundial" and that the top of the tower resembled a minaret, "from which Muslims are called to prayer." He then employed numerology to allege that the site was honoring the plane's four hijackers along with the forty passengers and crew who were killed. Rawls and those who signed his petition demanded that the original design be investigated and that the jury choose a new design that was "not tainted with Islamic symbolism."[7]

President Bush had gone out of his way after September 11 to say that the war on terror was not a war on Muslims as such. America was going after a certain group of Muslims who espoused violent and extreme beliefs, but that was not the true face of the religion. "Islam," he said, "is peace." But people like Burnett and Rawls suspected that Bush was just being polite for the cameras. They thought it was perfectly obvious that Muslims were America's enemies everywhere in the world, including in America itself. Such views could not be voiced in the mainstream media or polite company, but they were shared by millions of Americans, some of whom worked for police departments, the military, and the Federal Bureau of Investigation. Muslims living in the United States have been targets ever since.

The war on terror gives the lie to or at least complicates the old expression about how wars "come home," the idea that the way a country practices military violence overseas will eventually show up in its policing, or how traumatized veterans will wreak havoc in their communities upon their return from foreign battlefields. Well before Barack Obama inaugurated his drone warfare campaign across the Middle East and the Horn of Africa, before the Bush administration started agitating for the invasion of Iraq, and even before the United States dropped a single bomb on Afghanistan, the government began rounding up Muslims inside its own borders, and vigilantes across the country sought out mosques to vandalize and people on the streets who appeared to be Muslim or Arab to harass and intimidate. On September 12, 2001, a mob of hundreds of angry white people marched on a mosque in Chicago. Some of them brought weapons, and others chanted "Kill the Arabs" as they walked. The crowd came back the following two nights as well, and more than a hundred police officers had to encircle the neighborhood to keep the mob away from residents. One of the marchers spoke to a reporter and said, "I'm proud to be an American and I hate Arabs and I always have."[8] Over the following two months, police officers and FBI agents arrested and detained at least twelve hundred and perhaps as many as five thousand Muslim, Arab, and South Asian men. Many of these detainees were not told why they had been arrested, nor were they allowed to communicate with attorneys.[9] All of this happened *before* U.S.-backed Northern Alliance forces drove the Taliban out of Kabul and took the Afghan capital on November 13. The war on terror never "came home." It started there.

Hate crimes spiked dramatically. On September 15, a Sikh American named Balbir Singh Sodhi was planting flowers outside the gas station he ran in Mesa, Arizona. In accordance with his faith, he wore a turban and a beard. Mistaking him for an Arab Muslim, forty-two-year-old Frank Silva Roque, who worked as a mechanic in a Boeing repair facility, drove his truck to Sodhi's gas station and shot him five times with a handgun, killing him. Earlier in the day, before the shooting, Roque had donated $75 to a Red Cross fund for the relief workers at Ground Zero.[10] Then he drove to a different gas station and shot at the Lebanese American cashier he found there, though he fortunately missed. Still not satisfied, he moved on to his former home, which a local Afghan family had bought, and shot at the outside of the house. He bragged about the killing afterward at a bar, reportedly saying, "They're investigating the murder of a turban-head down the street." When he was arrested the next day, he was still defiant. "I stand for America all the way!" he yelled. "I'm an American. Go ahead. Arrest me and let those terrorists run wild!"[11]

The day Frank Roque was arrested, a thirty-one-year-old white supremacist named Mark Stroman, a member of the Aryan Brotherhood of Texas, walked into a Dallas convenience store called Mom's Grocery and killed its forty-six-year-old owner, Waqar Hasan, who had emigrated from Pakistan and moved to the area earlier that year. Hasan was grilling hamburgers when he was killed. Five days later, Stroman shot a Bangladeshi immigrant, Rais Bhuiyan, at a gas station, and two weeks after that he killed an Indian immigrant named Vasudev Patel at a different gas station. After his arrest, he told police that his sister had died in the North Tower on September 11, though no evidence was ever found to support his claim. He said he had done no more than what every other American wanted to. He was convicted of murder and sentenced to death. Bhuiyan, the only one of his victims to survive, spent the rest of Stroman's life protesting his would-be-killer's death sentence, going so far as to sue in an attempt to stop the execution. When asked why he was trying to save Stroman's life, Bhuiyan said, "I was raised very well by my parents and teachers. They raised me with good morals and strong faith." He said that contemplating Stroman's impending execution made him "very emotional and very sad, and makes me want to do more."[12]

In 2003, a thirty-year-old New Yorker named Larme Price rampaged through Brooklyn and Queens over a period of seven weeks, shooting five men point-blank in the head, four of whom died. All of them were immigrants, though only one was from the Middle East. In California, someone tagged a mosque in Conejo Valley with the message "Jesus is the Lord and Allah is the Devil." A man drove his car through the front of an Islamic center in Cleveland, Ohio, and in Virginia bricks were thrown through the windows of an Islamic bookstore. In the six calendar years preceding September 11, the Federal Bureau of Investigation never recorded more than 32 anti-Muslim hate crimes in the United States in a given year. In 2001, that number rose to 481, and over the following seven years it never dropped below 100.[13] Muslim and Arab Americans faced a national, slow-moving pogrom after September 11, and in the years since they have never known anything like the relative peace they enjoyed during the twentieth century. The version of America that existed for those communities before September 11 is gone.

The vigilante violence and government roundups constituted a national tragedy for Muslim and Arab communities in the United States, but they also revealed the government's hysterical determination to *exaggerate* the scale of the terrorist threat rather than focusing on the threats that really existed. Again and again, immigrants who committed minor violations to remain in the country were treated as sleeper cells awaiting activation, and unremarkable criticisms of the country's foreign policy were interpreted as the beginning of a plot to bring down the government. And in many cases, the FBI and other law enforcement agencies made up terrorist plots out of whole cloth and then used paid undercover agents to persuade innocent Muslims to participate in them, carrying out a campaign of mass entrapment that continued for years.

For Muslims and Arabs themselves, one of the most devastating effects of these campaigns was that it became difficult and sometimes impossible to participate in civic life—to speak your mind freely in a student group, attend public discussions at a mosque, respond to a bigot on a Facebook thread about politics, or even argue with someone who was being a jerk in public. With respect to the agencies that carried out these campaigns, however, the most pressing question is, why bother? The government didn't need to invent terrorists living in upstate New York in order to justify its war; real terrorists had already destroyed lower Manhattan and attacked the Pentagon. The worst attack in the country's history hardly needed to be padded out with a handful of imaginary small-time plots to vandalize a synagogue or mail a pipe bomb to an Army base.

The first decade of the war on terror is filled with liberal commentators accusing the Bush administration of cynically exploiting the country's fears in order to drum up support for military action, but it seems just as likely, if not more so, that exaggerating the terrorist threat responded to a genuine *internal* need rather than a fictional external one. In the context of the country's longer history and mythology, Americans have good reason to be anxious about what non-whites might have planned for them. The United States was founded on the dispossession and genocide of Native Americans, and it was built on the backs of enslaved Africans who still function as the country's permanent underclass. America's whole mythology, from Mary Rowlandson down through the cowboys and the Texas Rangers, is an attempt to justify that dispossession and to manage the attendant guilt that is always trying to make its way to the surface. There is a grim relief, a perverse wish fulfillment, in convincing yourself that the punishment you've long dreaded has finally arrived.

After September 11, Muslim and Arab Americans paid the price for their country's uncontrollable anxieties. In order for Americans to feel that the war was justified, the enemy needed to be omnipresent, vicious, irrational, devoid of scruples, and capable of bringing down the country from the inside. When it turned out that actual Muslim and Arab Americans were not that kind of enemy, the government fantasized the enemy into being. The result was the steady exclusion of Muslims and Arabs from public life in the United States, a degradation of citizenship that would eventually be expanded to other populations as well.

• • •

On the "Hate Crimes Statistics" page of its official website, the FBI lists a number of ways in which its data sets might be useful to the wider public. Most of them are matter-of-fact—"supply the media with credible information," "help researchers in determining trends in hate crimes"—but one of them suggests that the bureau sympathizes with victims and wants to help end their persecution: "show hate crime victims that they are not alone."[14] This is ironic, because it would be hard to think of an institution that did more to isolate and persecute Muslim Americans during the war on terror than the FBI.

In late October 2001, Congress and President Bush passed and signed the USA PATRIOT Act, which is partially styled in all-capital letters because it is an impressively torturous acronym: the Uniting and Strengthening America by Providing Appropriate Tools Required to Intercept and Obstruct Terrorism Act. The bill granted law enforcement expansive new powers. It allowed government agents to make lists of organizations they suspected of supporting domestic terrorism, and to jail and deport anyone who materially supported those organizations, all on the basis of evidence that could be kept secret. It also allowed them to jail anyone who committed a crime that, in the government's view, was intended to "intimidate or coerce a civilian population" or "influence the policy of a government by intimidation." Citizens and noncitizens alike could be detained as enemy combatants, held without bail and without access to lawyers. These people could be tried before military tribunals as opposed to the normal criminal courts. And finally, the bill authorized the government to build detention camps, at which people could be held indefinitely.[15]

The immediate post-9/11 dragnet was swift and expansive, and must count as one of the most shameful episodes in the country's history. The more than twelve hundred detentions didn't result in a *single* terrorism conviction. What they did instead was rip hundreds of immigrants away from their families and lives on the basis of minor violations. The detainees' families often had no idea where their loved ones had been taken or why. Many of them didn't see their husbands, brothers, and fathers—almost all of those detained were men—for years. Some of them, in cases that ended in deportation, never saw them again (President Trump's policy of separating immigrant children from their parents at the southern border was by no means an innovation). And while the FBI never again matched the volume of detentions and deportations that it managed in the months after September 11, the practice continued for years, without the mass protest mobilization that greeted Trump's Islamophobic policies starting in 2017.

One of the people eventually caught up in the FBI's longer-term dragnet was a sixteen-year-old New Yorker named Adama Bah. She was a sophomore at Heritage High School in Manhattan. She'd been born in Koubia, a small town of just a couple thousand people in the West African country of Guinea. She came to the United States with her mother when she was a toddler, and eventually the rest of her family joined them. She had no memories of Guinea, and New York was her home. She lived with her parents; her brothers, Abdoul, Mohammed, and Saydu; and her sister, Mariama. In a documentary made about her case in 2011, two things are obvious: The family is very poor, and the siblings are very close. They joke and fight a lot. "The only thing Mohammed loves," Adama says, "is GameCube and Game Boy, and he loves Muslims." Of Mariama, all Abdoul has to say is, "She dance too much."[16]

Adama's father, also named Mohammed, wasn't all that religiously observant, but after she graduated from junior high, he sent her to an Islamic boarding school. It was too strict for her, and she missed her home, but she liked that she was able to learn about her religion. "They taught how a woman should act, how a man should act, everything. The hijab and the face veil was a choice for the girls." After returning to New York and public school, she wore a niqab for a few months, along with colored contacts for a bit of pizzazz. "If you can't see my face, look at my nice eyes!" she said. There were lots of jokes with her classmates about the mystery of what she looked like, which she remembers as good-natured and not hostile. Then she switched out the niqab for an abaya, and her high school friends said, "Oh, you're not ugly! You have nice teeth."[17] Adama remembers that on September 11 she was confused. "Who is this Osama bin Laden guy?"

she thought. "What is he up to? Why would he do this?" None of her friends knew who bin Laden was, either, but one of them made a joke that stuck with her. "Your name is very close to his name," they said. "Adama, Osama."[18]

One Thursday morning in March 2005, FBI agents, along with police and Department of Homeland Security officers, appeared at her family's apartment at dawn. They woke everybody up, herded the family into the living room, and searched the apartment. After a while, Adama's father entered the apartment in handcuffs; the police had arrested him at the mosque. He told his family that they were going to take him away. Adama saw the police take her mother, Aissatou, into the kitchen, and she heard them yell at her. Aissatou didn't speak much English, but Adama heard the agents yell, "We're going to deport you and your whole family!" Adama had suspected for a while that not everything was in order with her father's immigration papers, so his arrest wasn't a total shock, but then they told *her* to pick a pair of sneakers and put them on. "You're coming with us," they said. She didn't know where they were going, and neither did her parents.

They put Adama and her father in a car. Once they arrived at the jail, Adama was put in a cell by herself, though she could still see her father. Then she was interrogated. The agents had told her father that he needed to sign a form consenting to their interviewing Adama, who was underage. It didn't seem as though he had a choice in the matter, so he signed it. For her part, Adama didn't know she had the right to a lawyer or to remain silent, and the people interviewing her never mentioned it, so she tried to be as honest as possible. When asked how she felt about President Bush, she said, "I don't like him."[19]

It was at the jail that Adama learned for the first time that she wasn't a legal resident of the United States. "I didn't know I wasn't an American," she said, "until I was sixteen and in handcuffs."[20] It was at this point that her father, who had to his detriment been overly accommodating to the government agents so far, decided the stakes were too high not to resist. An interrogator handed them a document laying out the process for seeing a Guinean consular officer. Mohammed could read English, but he asked his daughter to pretend to be translating the document into Pular, their native language. Then he told her, "Whatever you do, do not say you can go back to your country. They will circumcise you there." Female genital mutilation was common in Guinea. Adama's mother had been subjected to it as a girl, and she and Mohammed feared it so much for their daughters that they never returned to Guinea, not even for a short visit.

As Adama was being fingerprinted, she saw a girl from her mosque. Tashnuba Hayder was also sixteen, and like Adama she'd been arrested by FBI and Homeland Security agents that morning. While they knew each other well enough to say "hello," they weren't friends. The sight of Tashnuba threw Adama into a panic. "What the hell is she doing here?" she thought. "Who am I gonna see next?" As Adama's interrogation proceeded, she began to figure out what was going on. The agents said that the founder of Tashnuba's religious group at the mosque was suspected of terrorist involvement. Adama wasn't a part of the religious group, but she knew about it, and that sounded crazy to her. "The study group . . . was all women," she said. "So it was women learning about religion, women's empowerment, why we cover, how we do the prayer, when to pray, things like that."[21] She said it was mostly a group for converts, people new to Islam who needed to be shown the ropes. It made no sense to her that anyone would try to recruit jihadis out of a group of people who barely knew which direction they were supposed to face while praying.

But the FBI agents said that Tashnuba had written down Adama's name on a list of potential suicide bombers. That was a shock to Adama. Why would someone she barely knew identify her as a terrorist recruit? She would later learn that the agents told Tashnuba the inverse, that Adama had written *her* name down on a list. The FBI and Homeland Security never produced any evidence that either girl had produced such a list,[22] and today it is still unclear why the two girls were detained in the first place. The agents did their best to intimidate Adama, telling her they'd go through her computer and find whatever it was she was hiding there. Adama knew there was nothing on her computer that was even remotely connected to terrorism, but the interrogations could make you feel crazy, as though maybe you really *were* dangerous and had tricked yourself along with everyone else. She kept having to remind herself, "Wait a minute, I'm not this person. What are they talking about?"[23] Then the interrogators harassed her about choosing to cover, just as her schoolmates had, though with more hostility.

When Adama emerged from the interrogation room, her father was gone. They told her he was going to see an immigration judge that day, but they wouldn't tell her anything beyond that. Then they put Adama and Tashnuba in a black Escalade—years later, Adama said she still found it traumatic to see black Escalades on the street—and drove off, first to another facility in Manhattan and then to a juvenile detention center in Pennsylvania. Upon arrival, a guard told the two girls that they would be strip-searched. When they protested, saying it was against their religion, the guard said, "It's either that or we hold you down." Tashnuba went first, and then it was Adama's turn. She recalls crying the whole time. "It must be against some law for you to do this to me," she said. "No, it's not," the guard replied. "You no longer have rights." When she was finished, she was given some new clothes to wear and was told she had five minutes to shower. "I knew I only had five minutes," she said, "but I just sat at the corner of the shower and held myself and cried."

> I was thinking, *I cannot believe what I just went through.* I was just crying and crying and crying. I don't know how long, but then I just told myself that I had to get up. I washed myself really quickly. I've never felt like I needed God more than I did on this day. So, I did ghusl, which is like a special shower for prayer. I prayed, "God, you've got to hear me for this one. I've never asked for anything that I desperately needed but this one."[24]

After she dressed, the guards took away her headscarf. She and Tashnuba stayed up late that night in their cell, getting to know each other and marveling at their predicament, laughing and then crying and then laughing again. It seemed like a cruel and elaborate prank.

The next day, Adama was told to salute the American flag and say the Pledge of Allegiance before breakfast. She refused. "I'm like, 'Fuck the American flag. I'm not saluting it.'" Soon after, *The New York Times* published an article recounting the girls' arrest, including the FBI's suspicions of terrorist involvement. The news got around to Adama's guards, who then increased the frequency of the strip searches to three times a day. This made Adama furious. She wanted to make herself repulsive so that the guards would leave her alone. Using the bathroom, she'd think, "I hope I stink this place up, I pray that my shit would make this place close down or something." She left toilet paper stuck to her ass as a nasty surprise for the guard to find when it was time for the next search. She even tried not wiping at all. She was trying to force the guards to share in her degradation.

Adama was held at the juvenile detention center for six weeks. For the first three, her family had no idea where she was. Once they located her, a lawyer was hired and sent to the detention center to work on her release. That took another three and a half weeks. Adama turned seventeen in prison. When the release was finally secured, the terms stipulated that she would have to wear an ankle bracelet twenty-four hours a day. The FBI and Homeland Security seemed to have forgotten all about their prior belief that Adama was an aspiring suicide bomber, but they still wanted to pursue a case against her for being in the country illegally. As she left the detention center on the day of her release, a guard called her a "fucking n***** terrorist."[25] She also said goodbye to Tashnuba, who, along with her mother, was also in the country illegally. Tashnuba and her mother were deported to Bangladesh immediately after her release, and Adama never saw her again.

Adama's classmates were delighted to see her return to school, but that reunion was short-lived. After sixteen months in prison, Mohammed Bah was deported to Guinea in 2006. Adama saw him only once before he left, in a brief, wrenching visit at the New Jersey facility where he was being held. He told her to take care of the family in his absence. "It's your job," he said, "you're the next person in line." Adama remembers her mother telling her, "It's all your fault, it's all your fault," and how upsetting that was to hear. But she tried to do what her father had asked of her. With her mother unable to work, Adama dropped out of school and took whatever babysitting and cleaning jobs she could find. She says that at certain points the family starved: "For days there would be no food in the house." A chance meeting with a social worker informed them that the family could apply for public assistance. That would have been good to know from the outset, but "nobody tells you about this stuff," Adama says. Not wanting her siblings to be deprived of the things she was being deprived of, Adama took sole responsibility for making money, working three, four, even five jobs over the course of a single day, and then racing home to make her 10:00 p.m. curfew. Miss it even once, she'd been warned, and you'll go back to jail. Adama and her friends drifted away from one another; they could no longer relate to her experiences, nor she to theirs. Her childhood was over.

She wore the ankle bracelet, which constantly made her heel hurt, for two and a half years. She and her mother attended immigration hearing after immigration hearing in the hope of Adama's being allowed to stay in the United States, but the decision kept getting postponed. In the meantime, someone at Child Protective Services caught wind of the Bah family's poverty and started an investigation, meaning that Adama's siblings now also had to worry about being sent into foster care. The hostility with which the family was treated by their adoptive country is breathtaking. For a time, Adama's younger brother was sent to live with an activist in Rockville, Maryland, so as to avoid foster care. He hated it. Suburban Maryland was boring, and he missed his siblings terribly. "I'd rather fight with Abdoul," he said.[26]

Adama finally got asylum in 2007, at her seventh and final hearing. An immigration judge agreed she would be at risk of mutilation were she to be sent back to Guinea, and she was granted an employment authorization card. Looking down and smiling after her ankle bracelet was removed, she said, "My feet look funny." She had decided to wear her headscarf to the hearing. This wasn't a foregone conclusion. She'd removed it before a previous hearing, hoping the judge would be more inclined to let her stay if she didn't look so Muslim. "But after I took it off, I was still treated like shit," she said. "So I went back, I wore my head scarf. This time I knew why and it was not coming off again. It's not me. I am a Muslim woman." She told the filmmaker who was documenting her experiences that while she'd previously been angry almost all of the time, she was now starting to accept that "God let it happen that way."

That may be, but it's hard to avoid feeling that Adama's anger is one of the reasons she survived her ordeal at all, and she kept it in reserve, ready for deployment, as the case continued to follow her over the next several years. In 2009, she tried to board a flight to Texas, where she and several friends were going to celebrate her asylum. When she arrived at the gate, an airline representative told her that she was on the federal government's no-fly list. She was put in handcuffs, taken to a back room, and held for thirteen hours. The next year, she tried to fly to Chicago with a family she was working for as a nanny. Worried about a repeat of the prior year's debacle, she had called her lawyer beforehand, and he had assured her there should be no problems. But the same thing happened again, and she lost out on the money she was going to make on the trip. "Something in me just triggered," she said. "I told myself, 'I'm done. I'm tired. I am not going to go through this again.' I told my lawyers, 'I want to sue these motherfuckers,' and so we filed a lawsuit against Attorney General Eric Holder, FBI Director Robert Mueller, and Director of the Terrorist Screening Center Timothy Healy."[27]

The lawsuit was filed by the American Civil Liberties Union, and Bah was one of thirteen Muslim plaintiffs, including four veterans, none of whom had ever been charged with any crime related to terrorism. In 2014, a federal judge ruled that the government's no-fly list was unconstitutional, ordering that procedures be implemented that would allow people to challenge their inclusion.[28] This was some measure of justice, but not the full one. No court could undo the deportation of her father. No judge could restore to Adama the days and nights she spent desperately trying to support her family instead of finishing her high school education and becoming an adult alongside her peers. No legislature could un-leak the government document that baselessly identified her as a potential suicide bomber. No jury could erase her memories of being shoved into a black Escalade and then subjected to strip searches. The time Adama spent under the watchful and punitive eye of the FBI and the federal judiciary destroyed her childhood, violated her human rights, and permanently altered the trajectory of her life, erasing pathways and opportunities that might otherwise have been available to her. And although the government's years of surveillance failed to identify any terrorist or uncover any plot, it does not follow that the FBI's efforts were wasted. The story's "happy ending" notwithstanding, the United States successfully delivered a message to Adama and people like her: You are not a full and equal member of our society. You are neither secure nor safe here. Whatever dreams and aspirations you might have cultivated as a child must now take a backseat to the smaller dream of staying out of trouble. The government delivered this message over and over and over after September 11, as though it wanted to make sure the lesson stuck.

• • •

What's most striking about the federal government's detention and surveillance of Muslim and Arab Americans in the period immediately following September 11 is how few terrorists they managed to catch. Hundreds and potentially thousands of people like Adama Bah were arrested on the flimsiest of pretexts, whether because they had made a donation to the wrong charity or because they were seen hanging out at the wrong bookstore and chatting with people there. In these early cases, however, the evidence connecting the government's suspects to terrorism either collapsed under the slightest scrutiny or just never appeared all. At this point, the government should have released the detainees, offered public apologies, and paid out civil damages. Instead, prosecutors and judges simply changed tack, pretending that terrorism had never been the primary concern and focusing instead on violations of immigration law to push for deportation. A program billed at the outset as a first line of defense against terrorists operating inside the United States turned out in practice to be little more than a new way for the government to persecute its immigrant population, particularly those immigrants who practiced Islam.

This kind of tool was genuinely useful to the government for a number of reasons that will be discussed at length later, but it still presented a problem. The premise of the war on terror was that Islamist extremists threatened Americans around the world *and at home.* So where, then, were the domestic terrorists? The war could be seen as legitimate only if the threat it claimed to combat was real. Law enforcement's early failures to secure a single terrorism conviction seemed like a bad omen, but as the war progressed toward the end of its first decade, the government's record on prosecuting domestic terrorism appeared to be improving. In 2010, the Department of Justice released a list of all the terrorism and terrorism-related convictions that had been obtained since September 11. The list included 403 entries. Suspects had been charged with crimes ranging from making false statements and passport fraud all the way up to conspiring to kill members of the U.S. military, and the government had obtained convictions across the country, in New York, Florida, Texas, Minnesota, Virginia, and elsewhere. Some defendants had been sentenced to nothing more than time already served, while others were put away for life.[29] Taken at face value, the list was an impressive document. To go by its calculations, the federal government was disrupting domestic terrorist plots at a rate of nearly four extremists every month.

In 2014, however, two civil rights lawyers analyzed all of the cases on the list and concluded that the government's successes in prosecuting domestic terrorism were almost entirely fictional. They found that federal law enforcement had decided to make up for a lack of real terror plots by essentially inventing them, sometimes out of whole cloth. In hundreds of cases, the FBI sent undercover informants into mosques, Islamic bookstores, and community centers to strike up conversations with potential targets. These targets were not people the government suspected of having already committed any crime, which meant the informants were tasked with proposing a fictional terror plot and then persuading them to participate, needling and cajoling their POIs, or "persons of interest," over weeks, months, and even years. POIs tended to fit a particular profile. People who had criticized U.S. foreign policy, whether online or in a mosque, were good targets. So was anyone who expressed even the slightest interest in jihad, or who conducted internet searches on weapons or combat training. Even in the absence of these specific activities, a relatively unattached, young Muslim man could make an excellent target, particularly if he needed money. By systematically combing through Muslim and Arab communities around the country, these informants carried out a campaign of mass entrapment. It was as though law enforcement, in the absence of real terrorist threats, needed to imagine them into being on the country's behalf.

The two lawyers, Stephen Downs and Kathy Manley, used the term "preemptive prosecution" to identify terror convictions that had been wholly or partially invented by law enforcement. They defined preemptive prosecution as follows:

Preemptive prosecution . . . is a law enforcement strategy, adopted after 9/11, to target and prosecute individuals or organizations whose beliefs, ideology, or religious affiliations raise security concerns for the government. The actual criminal charges are pretexts, manufactured by the government to incarcerate the targets for their beliefs. These pretexts include:

- Using material support for terrorism laws to criminalize activities that are not otherwise considered criminal, such as speech, association, charity, peace-making and social hospitality.
- Using conspiracy laws to treat friendships and organizations as criminal conspiracies, and their members as guilty by association, even when most members of the group have not been involved in criminal activity and may not even be aware of it.
- Using *agents provocateur* to actively entrap targets in criminal plots manufactured and controlled by the government.

- Using minor "technical" crimes, which otherwise would not have been prosecuted or even discovered, in order to incarcerate individuals for their ideology (for example, making a minor error on an immigration form, which is technically a crime; lying to government officials about minor matters; gun possession based on a prior felony many years earlier; minor tax and business finance matters).[30]

Using this definition as a starting point, Downs and Manley found that the DOJ's list of convictions was much less impressive than it seemed. They concluded that nearly three-quarters of the convictions were based on "suspicion of the defendant's perceived ideology and not his/her criminal activity," with another fifth involving the government inflating and manipulating instances of minor, non-terrorist criminal activity until they could win convictions on terrorism charges. That meant that just 5.8 percent of the cases on the list involved people who had embarked on terrorism-related crimes on their own and that the threat of domestic terrorism was largely a hysterical fiction.

Many of these convictions were obtained only because the government engaged in what is commonly understood as entrapment. The Department of Justice itself is very clear that entrapment is not a legitimate method of criminal investigation, stating on its website that "entrapment is a *complete* defense to a criminal charge" (emphasis added).[31] But federal prosecutors successfully carved out an exception for themselves in cases involving terrorism, arguing that defendants were ideologically "predisposed" to participate in terrorism even if they had nothing to do with formulating the plot and acquiring the materials necessary to put it into action. Unless a defendant had explicitly and affirmatively stated that they wanted nothing to do with the undercover informant's scheme, judges would not allow their attorneys to mount an entrapment defense. So long as the FBI's agents could keep stringing their targets along, it didn't matter how reluctant the suspect's participation was, it didn't matter how many times he tried to minimize his involvement, and it didn't even matter if he barely had a clue about what was going on: A conviction was all but certain.

Without this loophole, which rendered the entrapment defense functionally useless, prosecutors in many of these cases would have been laughed out of court. To give one example, in 2003, American soldiers in Iraq found the name, address, and phone number of an Albany imam, Yassin Aref, written on a piece of paper in a bombed-out encampment. Aref was a Kurdish refugee who had fled Iraq during Saddam Hussein's rule. Suspicious of Aref's ideology, the government carried out a sting operation, sending an informant into the mosque under the cover name "Malik." First, Malik persuaded a member of Aref's mosque, Mohammed Hossain, to accept a loan so that he could improve his rental properties, telling him that "the money for the loan came from the sale of a missile to a terrorist group."[32] Hossain told Malik that he had no interest in terrorism, but he needed the money, and he took the loan. Then Hossain asked Aref to witness the loan. This was Aref's only involvement with the whole scheme, and the government never produced evidence that Aref had any idea that the funds were derived from terrorism. The FBI even included a fake missile as part of the sting, which, as a weapon of mass destruction, would allow prosecutors to seek a harsher sentence. But the bureau never showed the missile to Aref, because they were pretty sure he would get scared and back out completely if they did. Neither of the two targets had any interest in supporting terrorism or killing Americans: One needed a loan for his work as a landlord, and the other wanted to do a favor for a congregant. Both were sentenced to fifteen years in prison.

In addition to preying on people's good intentions, the government could exploit their vulnerability. Shortly after September 11, the FBI sent an undercover informant named Mohamed Alanssi into Abdulrahman Farhane's House of Knowledge Islamic bookstore on Atlantic Avenue in Brooklyn. Farhane was the father of six children, and Alanssi had told the FBI that he held radical views on Islam. Alanssi struck up conversations with Farhane and told him that he was looking for a way to send money to Islamic fighters in Afghanistan and

Chechnya. Farhane told Alanssi that he would not personally be able to help, but he introduced him to a man named Tarik Shah. Shah, Farhane told Alanssi, could help get the money out of the country.

Tarik Shah was a jazz bassist and martial artist, and radical politics was part of his familial inheritance. His father was a lieutenant with Malcolm X, working out of the No. 7 Temple in Harlem, and as an adult Shah adopted the great man's religious commitment as well as the Black Panthers' belief in the importance of teaching Black people how to defend themselves in a racist society. His life in music wasn't any kind of spectacular success, but it was a real career. He toured Europe with the famous singer Betty Carter in the 1980s, and he also played with the pianist Ahmad Jamal, the singer Abbey Lincoln, and the towering saxophonist Pharoah Sanders. In 1993, as part of the Duke Ellington Orchestra, he played at Bill Clinton's inaugural ball. When he wasn't on tour and playing gigs, he taught martial arts at his Expansion of Knowledge Center in Harlem. Like much of the Black Panthers' work in the middle of the twentieth century, Shah's martial arts instruction was simultaneously a political project, a consciousness-raising exercise, and a community service. He taught everyone from children to police officers. He also sold homemade pies out of the back of his car.[33]

Alanssi spent *three years* trying to get Shah to do something illegal without any success, a protracted and consistent string of failures for which the FBI paid him about $100,000.[34] At that point, the bureau could have reasonably concluded that Shah simply wasn't interested in helping terrorists, but instead they sent in a second informant to work on him, a man named Saeed Torres, who went by the name Shariff. (For his part, Alanssi became so disillusioned and frustrated by his work with the FBI that in 2004 he stood outside the White House and set himself on fire.) Torres was a former Black Panther himself. In an interview, he recalled joining the party in the spring of 1967. "I was a little fly kid wearing fly clothes," he said. "I was interested in what they were saying: 'What the government can't supply we take upon ourselves to get to the people.'" He wasn't an informant then, because the Panthers, he said, killed informants. He became a

Muslim in the early 1970s, drawn to the same things that had appealed to Shah. "What drew me to Islam was more of that militant aspect," he said. "Not a jihadist but more of a stand up, take no bullshit." By the 1980s, the Panthers' revolutionary project was much diminished from its glory days, but Torres was still part of a neighborhood security council, walking the streets and driving off drug dealers during the height of the crack epidemic. "I was an asset to the community," he said. "I loved it. I loved it."

Then he did something stupid. He robbed a New York City subway booth. He says he committed the robbery not out of petty greed but because he was a "revolutionary activist," describing the places he targeted—post offices and banks were also on the list—as "institutions to be appropriated for our cause."[35] The money from the theft was given back to the community, but Torres got caught, and he was charged with grand larceny, impersonation of a New York City transit cop, and possession of a weapon. As he faced down a twenty-year sentence, the FBI approached him and said they could ensure his early release if he took a job as an informant. Torres took the deal, got out in 2000, and went to work. To keep his conscience clean, he told himself that he was helping to make amends for his prior mistakes by serving on the front lines of the war on terror.[36]

As "Shariff," Torres took a gradual approach in getting close to Shah. First he took bass lessons at his house, three times a week. Shariff never learned all that much about playing bass, but the two men struck up a rapport, and because Shah clearly loved to talk, Shariff could get by with little more than the monosyllabic responses that were required to keep Shah in the flow of his own speechifying. Shah bragged about his martial arts prowess, and he waxed eloquent on the West's persecution of Muslims, both around the world and at home. Shariff recorded all of it. Eventually, Shariff told Shah that he needed a place to stay, so Shah vouched for Shariff to his mother, who rented him a room in Shah's home. Eventually, Shariff learned that Shah had a major financial problem and no good way of solving it. Shah owed more than $70,000 in unpaid child support. He'd been making payments, but he couldn't keep up, and in 2000 the government had suspended his passport over the arrears. For a jazz musician who made his money touring, this was a disaster. The United States might have been the center of the jazz universe through the end of the 1960s, but as American audiences left jazz behind for other genres in the last decades of the twentieth century, the greater level of interest in jazz among European listeners, combined with the generous subsidies that European governments provided to the arts, meant that performing in Europe was just about the only way a non-superstar jazz musician could make a decent living. By revoking his passport because of his failure to make child support payments, the government all but ensured that Shah would never be able to make child support payments.

Shah dreamed of opening up his own martial arts training center, but he hadn't been able to find a suitable space, and even if he did find one, he didn't have the money to get it into shape. This gave Shariff the window he needed. He said that he had a space Shah could use, an empty warehouse building in Queens. He'd intended to use it for drumming and dancing lessons, but the dancers didn't like rehearsing on the warehouse's cold floors in their bare feet. Shah was welcome to it. He began to make plans. Wrestling mats could be brought in to deal with the concrete floors, and the warehouse was big enough to train people in all sorts of disciplines, from wrestling and jujitsu to sword fighting and archery.[37]

A short while later, Shariff came to Shah with another proposal. He said two friends—one from Saudi Arabia and one from Iran—were looking for a self-defense expert, and he asked Shah whether he'd be willing to meet one of them. Shah said he was. Shariff and Shah traveled to Plattsburgh, New York, to meet a man Shah thought was a terrorist recruiter (in reality, another undercover FBI agent). Shah listened to what the undercover agent had to say, bragged about his mastery of knife fighting, and ranted against the American police state. The meeting ended without any concrete plans being made.[38] The following month, agent and target traveled to Florida, to meet a doctor friend of Shah's. The FBI hoped to get him involved as well, but when Shariff and Shah arrived at Dr. Sabir's home, the physician was not there. Then a year went by, with Shah going about his daily life and doing nothing to advance the plot. Finally, in May 2005, Dr. Sabir flew to New York to visit Shah, and the two of them met with the "terrorist recruiter." He asked them to take an oath pledging allegiance to al-Qaeda, which they did. Shah and Sabir were arrested the following week.

Neither of the two men had actually provided any support or services to terrorists. Shah never taught a martial arts class to al-Qaeda recruits, and Dr. Sabir never treated any wounded Taliban fighters. As he sat in jail and considered the charge against him, however—a single count of conspiracy—Shah knew that his prospects for avoiding a guilty verdict were slim. He had spent a lot of time bragging during his conversations with Shariff, talking about moves that could cause someone to "drown in their own blood" and demonstrating how to use his upright bass as a weapon: "All I've got to do is, pop, flick it like, boom, move out the way," he said. "Flip, pop, pop, right in the middle of your head."[39] That kind of boasting can be heard every day in any martial arts studio in the country, but it wasn't going to sound good in the context of a terrorism trial, nor would the fact that he'd told Shariff that his life as a jazz musician would provide the "greatest cover" for his participation in the plot.[40]

The son of a Black Panther had been seduced by the fantasy of putting his fighting skills to use against the state that had persecuted his family and community for his entire life, and the FBI, discovering how easily Shah could be enchanted by his own visions of rebellion, had pounced. His vision might have been modest—America wasn't going to be brought to its knees just because some jihadists learned jujitsu in a Queens warehouse—but it was enough to bring criminal charges. For the government, Shah's Black nationalist politics provided all the "predisposition" they needed to send him to prison. Believing he would never receive a fair trial, Shah pleaded guilty. He was sentenced to fifteen years in prison. Dr. Sabir had more faith in the criminal justice system and decided to stand trial. He was found guilty and sentenced to twenty-five years.

• • •

If apolitical children like Adama Bah and radicals like Tarik Shah could be targeted by the post-9/11 crackdown on Muslim and Arab life in the United States, so could people whose professional and political activities were squarely within the mainstream. Until 2003, Rafil Dhafir's life looked like a textbook illustration of the American dream. Born in Iraq, Dhafir graduated from Baghdad University's College of Medicine in 1971 and immigrated to the United States the following year so that he could complete his medical studies. He was intellectually and professionally ambitious. He came to the United States because he'd been told it was "the best place in the world" to study medicine, and he chose to specialize in cancer research rather than cardiology because of how much work there was to be done in the field. "In those days there were no drugs available, nothing," he said.[41] He did a fellowship in oncology at the University of Michigan in Ann Arbor, and then he taught for a while at Texas Tech in Amarillo. Eventually, he wound up in Fayetteville, New York, just east of Syracuse. He opened a private practice in Rome, a forty-mile drive from his house, because the town had no oncology practice to speak of. He could have gone to work in Syracuse—it was closer and he would have made more money—but he wanted to provide help where help was needed. When his patients couldn't afford treatment, he treated them anyway and asked them to pay what they could. Dhafir also established himself at the center of Muslim life in Syracuse. He spent lots of time at the Islamic Society of Central New York, even becoming its spiritual leader for about seven years when the center was unable to find a full-time imam. His family, his work, and his religion were the three suns around which Dhafir's life orbited. Over the first thirty years of his time in the United States, he conformed to the immigrant ideal in every respect.

In the early 1990s, Dhafir's personal life collided with world events. After defeating but not deposing Saddam Hussein during the first Gulf War, the United States persuaded the United Nations Security Council to impose a harsh sanctions regime on Iraq. The sanctions banned almost all forms of trade with Iraq, and those categories of trade that weren't banned entirely, such as medicine and food, were strictly regulated. The precise extent of their impact has been hotly debated during the twenty-first century—one report said the sanctions killed more than half a million children, while other surveys arrived at a much lower figure—but there is no doubt that life under sanctions was devastating for Iraqis. Materials commonly used in the production of agricultural or medical equipment were kept out of the country because of the possibility that they would be used to make weapons. Restrictions on manufacturing equipment made it difficult or impossible for Iraqis to repair the damage caused by the war, meaning that bridges, roads, hospitals, schools, and water treatment facilities were left useless. Depleted uranium from bombs used during the war also worked its way into the food and water supplies, and within a couple years of the war's end, cancer rates in Iraq were going up at a horrible rate.

Having left Iraq in order to learn how to treat cancer, Dhafir felt he should do something to assist the people he'd left behind. He founded a charity called Help the Needy, and he began to raise money for food, clothing, and medical supplies to be sent to Iraq. The charity's aims were not political. Dhafir hated Saddam, but he did not want his charity work to bump up against the geopolitics of America's postwar blockade of Iraq. He just wanted to get aid to where it was needed. The charity was small and understaffed, with Dhafir and a few friends handling many different jobs themselves. A woman they hired as a tax preparer eventually refused to keep working with them because of how sloppy she found the charity's administrative practices, claiming that Help the Needy told donors their deductions would be tax-deductible before it had even applied for tax-exempt status.[42] This would eventually come to haunt Dhafir and his colleagues, but through the 1990s and the first couple years of the new century the work seemed to be going well. Help the Needy raised several million dollars and used an intermediary in Jordan to get the money to Iraq. They focused particularly on sending money around Ramadan and Eid so that people would have enough food to put on proper celebrations.[43] Despite the charity's disorganization, Help the Needy representatives did ask U.S. government officials at one point whether their humanitarian aid work was legal. They were told that it was.[44]

On February 26, 2003, Dhafir and several other men connected to Help the Needy were arrested. He was charged with violating U.S. sanctions laws and money laundering, and at the press conference announcing the arrests, U.S. Attorney Glenn Suddaby said that funds raised by Help the Needy had not actually been used for humanitarian aid. He would not say what evidence the government had to support that claim, but the charity's sloppy administrative practices made it easy for him to imply the worst. "You can move money through charitable means into Iraq if you do it in the right way," he said. "It kind of begs the question: You go through all this effort, why wouldn't you do it legally, if that truly was your intent?"[45] Other government officials were more explicit. On the day of the arrests, Attorney General John Ashcroft said the government had apprehended "funders of terrorism," and New York's governor, George Pataki, said the arrests proved the existence of "terrorists living here in New York among us . . . who are supporting and aiding and abetting those who would destroy our way of life and kill our friends and neighbors."[46]

The arrests landed in the wider community like a bomb. Dhafir's cancer patients were left scratching their heads at the locked doors of his medical practice, wondering how they were going to find a new doctor to pick up their treatment. Even if they could find one, they doubted he or she would have Dr. Dhafir's skill. "He was just an outstanding doctor," one patient said. "I had cancer and he cured it. . . . It was a 100 percent shock to me that something like this could happen."[47] And in addition to the arrest of Dhafir and his Help the Needy colleagues, nine government agencies, including the FBI and the Immigration and Naturalization Service, worked together to interrogate members of around 150 Muslim families in and around Syracuse. Some of those interviewed said government officials harassed and intimidated them, asking wide-ranging and invasive questions about their cultural and religious beliefs. They talked to reporters about their experiences, but anonymously; they worried that speaking out in public would get them deported or jeopardize their student visa status. An assistant U.S. attorney responded to questions about this harassment with the blithe assertion that "law enforcement is always sensitive to religious differences. I cannot imagine anyone in law enforcement would try to communicate with anyone who had difficulty understanding them."[48] And when members of the local Muslim community scraped together more than $1 million as a surety against the possibility of Dhafir's trying to flee the country, Dhafir was still denied bail four times.[49]

Indicted on charges of violating the International Emergency Economic Powers Act as well as twelve counts of money laundering, Dhafir faced a maximum sentence of 265 years in prison, but he refused to take a plea bargain. Whatever administrative errors Help the Needy had made were extremely common in the charity world, the kind of thing the government punished with small fines and other slaps on the wrist, not serious prison time. And as for the idea that Dhafir was a secret supporter of terrorism, that was outrageous, and the government had no evidence suggesting otherwise. Curiously, they hadn't tried very hard to find that evidence, either. Despite mounting a large and complex operation to interrogate what seemed like every Muslim in Syracuse, the prosecutor's office had not bothered to send anyone to Jordan or Iraq to track down where the funds it claimed were missing had actually gone. Dhafir was both furious and, as he describes it now, "stupid enough to believe in the American justice system."[50] He wanted his day in court.

When that day came, prosecutors had a surprise for Dhafir. Added to his indictment were twenty-five charges of Medicare fraud. The government claimed that although Dhafir had sometimes not personally been in the office when his patients received their chemotherapy and other treatments, the reimbursement forms submitted by his office all said he was present. That was all. There was no suggestion that any of Dhafir's patients had been improperly cared for, nor any evidence that Dhafir had benefited financially from the incorrect paperwork. The change in tactics made for a confusing trial. Cases like Dhafir's, in which some office administrator accidentally commits

Medicare "fraud" by filling out a form in the wrong way, usually resulted in little more than a reprimand, or maybe a fine if the mistakes
had been occurring for a long time or were particularly costly. But
here the government sought a conviction and prison time.

Dhafir's defense attorney wanted to tell the jury what was really
going on, that Dhafir had been arrested under suspicions of financing
international terrorism that the government quickly realized it had no
hope of substantiating. That would have made the prosecution look
bad from the start, and it would also have allowed the defense to further point out that the government's response to Dhafir's alleged violation of U.S. sanctions was also extreme. In recent years, an activist
group called Voices in the Wilderness had made headlines by *intentionally* violating sanctions laws, traveling to Iraq in person to deliver
food and medical supplies to Iraqis. Some of the group's leaders faced
steep fines, but none had been arrested, nor was the government trying to put any of them in jail. But the judge presiding over Dhafir's
trial ruled that the defense could not so much as mention the reason
why the FBI had investigated Dhafir to begin with. Nothing about terrorism, nothing about the government's failed efforts to track Help
the Needy's donations to extremists, and nothing about Ashcroft and
Pataki painting Dhafir as a key node in the global terrorism financing
network. Instead, the trial proceeded amid a cloud of unreality, as
prosecutors pretended to believe that a man whose administrative errors had neither enriched himself nor hurt his patients deserved to
spend several decades behind bars. As the trial dragged on, Dhafir
was kept in jail and classed as the highest level of "security risk," forbidden to attend Islamic classes and with strict limits on his outdoor
time. His refusal to undergo a strip search, which he said violated his
religious beliefs, also meant his jailers wouldn't allow him any physical contact with those who visited him. By the end of 2005, he hadn't
touched his wife in more than two years.[51]

Following Dhafir's conviction in 2005, the government suddenly
wanted to talk about terrorism again. In a sentencing memo submitted after the guilty verdict, the prosecution asked for a sentence of at
least twenty-four years and four months, citing Dhafir's links to ter-

rorism as a partial justification for the long prison term. "In the 1980s," prosecutors wrote, "Rafil Dhafir traveled repeatedly to Pakistan where he worked as a volunteer doctor in the mujihadin refugee camps on the border of Afghanistan."[52] The government did not mention that he was volunteering for Doctors Without Borders, though it did begrudgingly acknowledge in a footnote that the mujahideen were America's *allies* during the 1980s, when the United States was waging a proxy war to push the Soviet Union out of Afghanistan by funding the country's insurgents (to the tune of $630 million a year by 1987). The judge sentenced Dhafir to twenty-two years in prison, and the Department of Justice started including him on a list of successful terrorism prosecutions.[53] All of Dhafir's appeals failed in the following years, and he developed gout, high blood pressure, high cholesterol, and finally prostate cancer in prison.[54] He was released to home confinement in the spring of 2020 and fitted with an ankle bracelet so the government could track his movements. He will never practice medicine again.

• • •

The FBI never replicated the orgy of arrests and deportations that it carried out in the immediate wake of September 11, but government persecution of Muslims continued at a steady clip for years, keeping the government well supplied with scapegoats to hold up as examples of how much danger the country faced. As late as 2009, the FBI used an agent provocateur named Shahed Hussain to lure four ex-convicts, none of them more than marginally involved with Islam, into a plot to bomb two Bronx synagogues and shoot down military aircraft at an airport just west of Newburgh, New York. The four defendants participated only because the FBI's informant had posed as a wealthy Pakistani businessman, and they hoped to scam him out of his money. The FBI chose the targets, financed and planned the entire operation, and sought out the participants. Onta Williams, James Cromitie, David Williams, and Laguerre Payen did little more than occasionally ride around in a car the FBI owned. After their arrest, they spent four months in solitary confinement, twenty-three hours a day,[55] and New York's mayor, Michael Bloomberg, praised the FBI for its work. "The good news here," he said, "is that the NYPD and the FBI did exactly what they're trained to do and they have prevented what could be a terrible event in our city."[56] All four were convicted. At the sentencing hearing, the federal judge Colleen McMahon criticized the FBI. "The essence of what occurred here is that a government . . . created acts of terrorism out of [a defendant's] fantasies of bravado and bigotry, and then made those fantasies come true," she said. "The government did not have to infiltrate and foil some nefarious plot—there was no nefarious plot to foil." Hamstrung by the sentencing requirements of their conviction, however, and convinced that the defendants were virulent antisemites, Judge McMahon sentenced each of them to twenty-five years in prison. Their convictions were all upheld on appeal. (In 2023, it turned out that Judge McMahon was still upset about the FBI's behavior. She ordered the compassionate release of three of the Newburgh defendants, writing in her decision that "the real lead conspirator" in the case "was the United States.")[57]

The effects of cases like these stretched far beyond those who were personally caught up in them. By arresting, deporting, and incarcerating thousands of Muslims and Arabs who lived in the United States, the government drove millions more out of civic life. One could be Muslim or Arab in the United States, or one could fully exercise one's citizenship, but it became nearly impossible to do both.

This fact was driven home to people at the slightest excuse. In the summer of 2006, a man named Raed Jarrar, who had emigrated from Iraq and obtained a green card in the United States, tried to board a JetBlue flight from New York to the Bay Area. As he was eating breakfast in the terminal, a TSA agent approached him, asked for his information, and wrote it down. Then he told Jarrar that others in the airport were offended by his T-shirt. "I looked down at my T-shirt to see which one I was wearing," Jarrar said. "I'd just woken up that morning, put on a clean T-shirt and whatever, jeans, sneakers." The shirt said "We Will Not Be Silent" in English and Arabic. It asserted nothing beyond the idea that First Amendment rights applied to

Arabs along with everyone else, and now the TSA wanted Jarrar to take it off before he'd be allowed to board the plane. He refused, and the situation escalated. Hoping to calm things down, the JetBlue desk agent proposed what she called a "compromise." "We will buy you a T-shirt and put it on top of this one." "That's not a compromise," Jarrar replied. He needed to make his flight, so he agreed to put on the new shirt over his original one, but he told the officers that he would "pursue this case with a constitutional rights organization as soon as I arrive in California." The agents went over to a newsstand and debated which T-shirt to buy. "Should we buy him the I HEART NEW YORK T-shirt?" one said. "No," another replied, "we don't want to take him from one extreme to another." Jarrar later learned that the airline had seated a flight attendant behind him to watch his movements and take notes on the channels he watched. "I came to realize it was not an option for me to be just an American, even if I wanted to," Jarrar said. "The moment they put that T-shirt on me, that was the end of it, seriously. I came to understand my identity the hard way."[58]

It became much more difficult for Muslim Americans to associate in groups. Mosques, community groups, and Muslim Student Associations (MSAs) on college campuses either knew they were under surveillance or worried that they were, and it was hard for new members to overcome the reasonable suspicion that they were FBI informants. "When it came to the MSA and the activities we would do," a college student named Malaika said, "we tried to avoid all politics. We didn't know where that would lead and we wanted to keep it strictly educational."[59] Rather than participating in the political debates that would shape their lives, MSA members found themselves simply trying to explain, over and over, that they were just as American as everyone else. Anything more ambitious than a friendly, anodyne presentation explaining how Muslims celebrated different holidays could draw an immediate firestorm of media criticism. In 2013, the national activist group Students for Justice in Palestine (SJP) organized a group of students at Northeastern University to stage a walkout at an event where Israeli soldiers were speaking. In response to this ordinary act of political protest, the university condemned the students, forced them to produce a "civility statement," and put the campus SJP group on probation.[60] Three years before that, a twenty-year-old Egyptian American college student from Silicon Valley had taken his car in for an oil change and discovered a GPS tracker planted on the back. He took the device home and posted photos of it online. Two days later, FBI agents arrived, demanding that their equipment be returned. It became clear as he talked to them that the government had been monitoring his phone and email as well.[61]

Some Muslim and Arab Americans continued to protest, to criticize U.S. foreign policy in public, to organize actions opposed to the government's persecution of their communities. But as time passed, they became increasingly exceptional cases. For many, the safer, more reasonable response was to disappear from public life and retreat to the confines of the community or the home. "I also became more quiet," Talat Hamdani said. Her son, an EMT, had died on September 11 after rushing to the Twin Towers to help, after which the *New York Post* portrayed him as a terrorist who hadn't died but disappeared into the extremist underground. "I gave others a chance to talk as much as they could, to reveal themselves, what they're saying," she said. "Initially I was all mouth, I would talk and talk and talk. But after 9/11, going through that traumatic time, I don't trust anybody anymore. I just trust my sons. That's it."[62] Gurwinder Singh, a Sikh man who grew up in Queens, was eight years old on September 11. He was bullied relentlessly at school over the following months. "One time on the bus ride home, an African-American kid pulled my patka off my hair. I couldn't do anything; I was helpless." He withdrew as well. "Every time I got on the bus after that, I wondered, *Will it happen again?* Anytime I saw someone who might pick a fight, I got anxious. I wouldn't look at them at all. I just tried to disappear."[63] "I don't want to do anything even remotely questionable," said one Muslim participant in a sociologist's study. "If I'm about to get into an argument with someone about something stupid, like they sold me something defective, I'm thinking, 'Oh my God, if I start arguing with this guy, he's going to think that all Muslim people are argumentative.' . . . It's like you can't do anything wrong, because you're there for your whole community, and everyone's going to be branded in the mind of this person." The requirement wasn't just that people comport themselves with dignity and politeness for fear of reflecting badly on the wider community; Muslims and Arabs in post-9/11 America were expected to be submissive, silent, and self-effacing. "I have to be more careful in how I conduct myself," another study participant said.

> Like even something as simple as riding the subway. If somebody shoves you out of the way, you should be able to glare at that person. But since I feel like I have to represent all Muslims everywhere now, I feel like I have to smile at the person and say, "'Oh, I'm sorry, I must have been in your way.'"[64]

For others, even riding the subway or the bus became too much, no matter how hard they tried to blend into the scenery. Abdul, who lived in Colorado, stopped attending Friday prayers at the mosque. "What if somebody were to bomb this place if they're really angry? . . . It does scare me, and so I just wanted to stay home, just do my prayers at home rather than take the risk." Abdul was not the only one who made this calculation. As another Colorado Muslim said, "Everybody just basically locked themselves inside their homes."[65]

CHAPTER 5

I Do Break Regulations

So it was like we were crossing the line, but we should have crossed the line.

—Sergeant Javal Davis, guard at Abu Ghraib

We ought to be reasonable about this.

—Senator Chuck Schumer (D-New York)

Had George W. Bush decided to limit America's war to a campaign against al-Qaeda, it would have simplified things. To begin with, the enemy would have been easy to define. It was al-Qaeda that attacked the United States on September 11, and al-Qaeda was based in Afghanistan. Since Afghanistan, according to the Bush administration, was either unable or unwilling to root out bin Laden's organization, America would have to take care of the job on its own.

The ensuing twenty years revealed that invading Afghanistan and replacing its theocratic government with one amenable to liberal democracy was not as simple as all that, but at the time it made for a compelling and easy-to-digest argument: America was going after the people who had gone after America. Public support for the invasion was overwhelming. In a selection of thirty-one opinion polls conducted in the fall of 2001 on whether Americans approved of the war, *none* saw support for the invasion at less than 80 percent, and nine clocked support at 90 percent or higher. There were a handful of protests in American cities before the invasion, with around twenty thousand people marching in Washington, D.C., in late September 2001, as well as smaller actions in San Francisco, Los Angeles, and New York. But none of these protests disrupted much of anything other than car traffic, and they did not exert any material pressure on the country's politics.

But the Bush administration didn't stop with Afghanistan. It launched a global war instead. As an Israeli major general wrote in the spring of 2003, "The ultimate goal is the Middle East, the Arab world and the Muslim world. Iraq will be the first step in this direction; winning the war against terrorism means structurally changing the entire area."[1] Winning *that* kind of war required a definition of the enemy that included a lot of people who weren't members of al-Qaeda. Arriving at such a definition was tricky, though, because the project immediately ran up against the fundamental contradiction of the war on terror. On the one hand, President Bush said the country was fighting to liberate the peoples of the Middle East. In the televised address he delivered to announce the beginning of combat operations in Iraq, Bush said that "the hopes of an oppressed people" depended on the courage and honor of America's soldiers. Before the invasion, Vice President Cheney infamously said on *Meet the Press* that American forces in Iraq would be "greeted as liberators," and after the invasion Secretary of Defense Donald Rumsfeld changed the subject when asked by CNN's Wolf Blitzer about the fact that American troops had failed to locate any of the promised weapons of mass destruction (WMDs). "Anyone who goes into Iraq and sees those people who were liberated," he said, "and sees what a vicious dictatorship can do to people . . . it's so refreshing and wonderful to see their faces and what's happened, their circumstances so much improved."[2]

On the other hand, all nineteen of the September 11 hijackers were Muslim, and the government refused to discuss any nonreligious explanations for their motivations. Liberal or leftist commentators who offered political explanations for the attacks, whether by pointing to America's military bases in Saudi Arabia or to the country's long-standing support for Israel, were demonized as extremism's useful idi-ots, people so invested in their disagreements with how the United States carried out its foreign policy that they were unwilling to con-demn mass murder. Any attempt to *understand* why September 11 happened was immediately discounted as an attempt to *excuse* it. With politics and any other material grievances off the table, religion was the only explanation left.

When I describe these opposing views of the world's Muslims as the war's "fundamental contradiction," I don't just mean that they are incompatible with one another. I mean something a little more com-plicated and specific. A contradiction is an aspect of a historical pro-cess that both strengthens that process *and* undermines and destroys it. This can be a confusing idea in the abstract, but history is full of contradictions, and they become pretty easy to spot once you know how to recognize them. As one example, the invention of antibiotics in 1928 represented an important leap forward in the fight against disease, allowing doctors to easily treat a huge number of bacteria-caused illnesses that had previously killed many people. At the same time, the increased use of antibiotics over time has produced antibiotic-resistant bacteria, and antimicrobial-resistant infections are now associated with nearly fifty thousand deaths a year in the United States. We now live in a world in which antibiotics make it both easier *and* harder to treat bacterial infections, in which antibiot-ics may eventually become useless because of the overuse of antibiotics—that's a contradiction. Or you can take an example from economics. In our current economic system, job growth, lowered un-employment, and increased production of goods and services pro-duce a strong economy, in which most people have access to work and therefore the money to spend on goods and services, which keeps demand high and production humming along. At the same time, it is an article of faith among mainstream economists that as job growth and production accelerate, they eventually cause the economy to "overheat" and then fall into recession, which is when the economy contracts and unemployment increases. Strong economic growth is therefore the ultimate cause of weak economic growth, and unemployment that decreases too much is the cause of increased unemployment down the line. That phenomenon has been naturalized in our public discourse as the "business cycle," but it is a contradiction as well.

In the United States, the dual status of Muslims as both victims to be saved and barbarians to be eliminated made deciding when and how much to blame Islam itself for the extremist threat a delicate operation. Both views were necessary if the Bush administration wanted to fight the war on a *global* scale. If the United States were to acknowledge al-Qaeda as a group with political grievances and goals (no matter how abhorrent those goals might be to Americans), the United States would not have been able to justify expanding the war beyond Afghanistan. It would have been enough to deprive the group of its safe haven, bribe other governments into refusing to shelter its members going forward, and maybe entertain negotiations on reducing the country's military presence in Saudi Arabia. The United States might not even have been able to justify invading Afghanistan in the first place. (Remember that Bush turned down an offer from the Taliban to hand over bin Laden to a third country to stand trial.) But if al-Qaeda's political demands and religious beliefs were understood to be little more than a cover for its innate and irremediable barbarism, then terrorism had no rational explanations or causes whatsoever. Confronted with a threat like that—a group of people who were not only immune to reason but also believed that victory was to be found only in domination and destruction—the United States could claim that it had no choice but to pursue extremists to the ends of the earth, no matter the cost.

At the same time (and here's the contradiction), if the United

States wanted its allies to consent to a global war, and if the Bush administration wanted to cultivate popular support for a military project that was going to be much more complicated than a simple revenge mission, the world's Muslims had to be understood as innocent victims in need of saving, people who longed for liberation at the hands of America's armed forces. There is no more powerful current in U.S. political thought than the idea that America is *the* exceptional nation, that its system of government is perfect or at least on its way to becoming so, and that anyone in the world living under a different system would love to live in a U.S.-style democracy instead. Without the insistence that the people of Iraq and Afghanistan were helpless victims who longed for their countries to be remade in our image, Bush would not have been able to mobilize support for his goal of remaking the entire political structure of the Middle East.

Of course, both of these views are incorrect. The world's Muslims are not irrational savages, nor do they all yearn as a single people for the opportunity to live exactly as Americans do. And as we've learned over the past twenty years, the failure to establish stable democracies in Iraq and Afghanistan didn't pose an existential threat to America after all. We'll get to what the United States really wanted out of its global war in the book's third section, but for now it is important to look at how the United States tried to manage the difficulties of seeing Muslims as savages and innocents at the same time. Neither of the war's first two presidents managed to navigate those difficulties successfully, but the Bush administration did manage to buy itself some breathing room during the first years of the war. The mass arrests and deportation of Muslim Americans did little to foil plots or get would-be terrorists off the streets, but with much of Muslim America either intimidated into silence or reduced to politely soliciting the country's tolerance, pro-war government officials and journalists could expound upon the relationship between Islam and terrorism without having to worry about hearing too many objections from Muslims themselves.

Muslim or Arab writers who were critical of the Bush administration's preemptive warfare were largely shut out of national newspapers and magazines, while those who supported America's plan for remaking the Middle East—or, at a minimum, who were willing to denounce the backwardness and antidemocratic governments of Middle Eastern states—found themselves launched to prominence. Ayaan Hirsi Ali, a Somali-Dutch immigrant who sympathized with the Muslim Brotherhood in her youth, came to international attention in 2002 when she renounced religion and proclaimed herself an atheist. She moved to the United States in 2006 and took a position at the American Enterprise Institute, a conservative think tank. Television appearances and magazine and newspaper interviews filled up her professional calendar, and she used those opportunities to expound on the grave dangers that Muslim immigrants posed to the good-hearted but naively tolerant Western countries that hosted them. She once told *The New York Times* that if European countries failed to teach Muslims respect for the cultural heritage of the West, that heritage might soon vanish from the face of the earth. "The Netherlands is an art country," she said. "If the citizens of Amsterdam, 60 percent of whom will soon be of non-Western origin, are not made part of that, all of this will decay and be destroyed. When the municipality has to vote on whether funds go to preserve art or build a mosque, they may ask, 'Why should I pay for this stupid painting?' They may do a host of other things that are undemocratic, illiberal and unfriendly toward women and homosexuals and unbelievers."[3]

With the media framing sentiments like these as the correct view for Muslim and Arab Americans to have about the war, the Bush administration was able to pitch the occupation of Afghanistan, saber rattling aimed at Iran, and the invasion of Iraq as parts of a larger civilizational mission, in which the world's 1.5 billion Muslims were simultaneously enemies to be destroyed and victims in need of rescue, with America the only country strong enough and compassionate enough to do both. This message was produced not only for domestic consumption but also to persuade America's allies in Europe and the Middle East to contribute to the war effort or at least not object too strenuously. This precariously balanced narrative survived until the spring of 2004, when the world discovered what had been happening inside a prison about twenty miles west of Baghdad.

• • •

The revelations of torture and abuse at Abu Ghraib emerged in a twenty-first-century media environment in which images have a unique power to determine what becomes news and what passes without notice. It was in April 2004 that the CBS News show *60 Minutes II* turned Abu Ghraib into a metonym for the brutal excesses of American military power, but the story actually broke—or at least it tried to break—six months earlier. The main problem with the original version of the story was that it lacked photographs.

On November 1, 2003, the Associated Press published a report by Charles J. Hanley that detailed the abuse, torture, humiliation, and killing of detainees held in America's network of prisons and detention camps across Iraq. The article focused on three detention facilities, one of which was Abu Ghraib, and there were moments when it seemed a little squeamish about its own findings, twice insisting that however badly the Americans were treating their prisoners, things had been worse under Saddam. Nevertheless, the details provided by six former detainees were harrowing. Prisoners held in outdoor cages baked in 120-degree heat and were given only hot water to drink. At one camp, a thousand men were forced to share ten water taps, which made washing all but impossible. "They would come," one said, "and throw ice into the sand just to make us suffer psychologically." Punishment involved being made to lie facedown in the sand for hours, surrounded by razor wire in a small enclosure called the Gardens. Beatings were common. One prisoner was shot in the shoulder when he tried to help a woman who had been bound and left lying in the dust, and another saw the Americans kill a detainee who tried to approach a barrier. Prisoners fielded questions about the whereabouts of Saddam's relatives or the workings of the black market, and they waited in vain for their captors to explain why they were being held in the first place. "There's no law," Rahad Naif said. "It's up to them. It's arbitrary." One woman saw a squadron of American soldiers arrest all three of her sons in a single July night. They were freed in October and returned to their mother, but she struggled with her memories of what happened. "Death would be better than the Americans again," she said.[4]

The AP story was itself preceded by an Amnesty International report detailing abuses at America's prisons in Iraq, but neither effort won Abu Ghraib a place at the center of the so-called news cycle.[5] Major newspapers did not pick up Hanley's story—Hanley says the *Tulsa World* and *Akron Beacon Journal* were the largest publications to run it—and the Amnesty report was dismissed as so much hand-wringing from a group of peaceniks. Hanley couldn't even get the military to provide him with an official response to the allegations. Instead, he had to quote the brief denial a brigadier general had provided to an Arab television interviewer.[6] In January 2004, the military walked back its earlier protestations of innocence, with U.S. Central Command announcing in a press release that "an investigation has been initiated into reported incidents of detainee abuse at a Coalition Forces detention facility." No further details were provided, although several national newspapers finally took notice and published brief stories of their own about the investigation. Five days after the press release, a cable news network reported that the abuses had been photographed, and over the following two months *The Washington Post* noted that seventeen soldiers had been suspended, with six facing criminal charges.[7] But despite the existence of detailed allegations, confirmation from the military that an investigation was under way, and the meting out of suspensions and criminal charges, there was still no larger outcry.

That only changed when people saw the photographs. Some of them were made public for the first time on *60 Minutes II,* in a fifteen-minute broadcast that included nine images. In order, the photographs shown in the segment depicted the following scenes: a hooded man standing on a box, with wires trailing down from his outstretched hands; four naked men with black hoods over their heads, posed in front of a pale yellow wall; a pile of five naked men stacked on top of one another, photographed from behind; perhaps the same pile of men photographed from the opposite direction, with a guard visible in the background; two guards smiling and giving a thumbs-up gesture while standing over naked prisoners, one of whom has the word "RAPEIST" [*sic*] written on his right buttock; two prisoners being forced to simulate oral sex; a female guard pointing at a prisoner's genitals with one hand while giving the thumbs-up with the other; two guards sporting huge grins while standing behind the prisoner pile; and finally, the bruised corpse of an Iraqi man in a black bag, his body partially covered by plastic sheeting.[8]

Additional photos were released later that year, and dozens more became public in 2006. Some showed naked prisoners cowering in terror, their genitals tucked between their legs, as snarling, blurry guard dogs strained at their leashes. Another showed a naked prisoner from behind, standing with his arms outstretched in a crucifixion pose, his entire body smeared with what looked like shit or mud. There were pictures of prisoners chained to walkway railings and bunk beds, and one in which a detainee had been wrapped in a foam pad and then sandwiched between two military stretchers and left on the ground, his head the only visible part of his body. There was a small gallery of pictures of a prisoner who was naked except for the women's underwear that had been put over his head. There were photos of detainees doing push-ups under the supervision of a guard, photos of people chained together, and new angles of the naked human pyramid. In one photo, a guard with a mustache knelt beside a pile of prisoners, who were clothed, for once. His hands were sheathed in teal latex gloves, and one of his fists was cocked back as though readying for a punch. There were close-up photos of prisoners' injuries and photos of guards stitching up their captives' wounds. Some photos had no human subjects at all. One showed blood spattered on a detainee's robe that had been laid out on the floor. One showed a splash of blood on a wall, and another showed a large amount of blood that had been spilled on the floor.[9]

The guards who appeared in these pictures were all eventually convicted of crimes. The most notorious of the group were Specialist Charles Graner, Private First Class Lynndie England, and Specialist Sabrina Harman. The photos made all of them look like sadists, participants in a brutal fraternity hazing. Charles Graner, a former corrections officer in his mid-thirties, really does appear to have been as vicious as the photos made him out to be. He was the mustached guard with the thick glasses, the one rearing back to throw punches at the prisoners lying at his feet. The human pyramid had been his idea, and soldiers in his unit testified at Graner's trial that he had taken pleasure in beating inmates.[10] Another soldier, Specialist Joseph Darby, said that Graner liked to show off the photographs he took. He remembered one October morning when Graner approached him with a camera, saying, "Check this out, Darb." He showed Darby a photograph of "an inmate chained to his cell, naked, with a bag over his head," and what looked like water on the floor. Darby didn't see much wrong with it—chaining prisoners to their beds was common practice, and the inmate wasn't in a stress position—but Graner clarified things for him. "The Christian in me knows it's wrong," he said, "but the corrections officer in me can't help but love to make a grown man piss himself."[11] Graner showed photographs like this to his superiors as well, but none of them filed any kind of report or complaint about it.[12]

Lynndie England, the guard shown holding a naked detainee on a leash, attracted special attention once the photographs were released, probably because of her sex and tiny stature. She was from a small town in West Virginia, and she was celebrating her twenty-first birthday on the night that some of the most upsetting photographs were taken. She was Graner's girlfriend. The two had started a relationship on base back in the United States, and by the time she left Abu Ghraib, she was pregnant with his child. (The relationship didn't last; Graner eventually married another female guard from Abu Ghraib.) She was fourteen years Graner's junior, and in Iraq she mostly seems to have done whatever Graner told her to do. She said that from the beginning of their relationship Graner would photograph her while they had sex, after which he'd email the photos to friends or even, on one occasion, show them to England's parents.[13] That's not surprising, because many of the photographs Graner organized or took at Abu Ghraib remind a viewer of nothing so much as sadistic amateur pornography (and Graner did, at one point, force a nineteen-year-old female detainee to expose her breasts so that he could get a shot). The night England turned twenty-one, Graner told her that the tableau of masturbating detainees he'd assembled was a birthday present for her, and England also claimed that it was Graner who orchestrated the photograph with the leash.[14] "I'm just kind of holding the tie-down strap," she said. "You can see the slack in it. I know people said that I dragged him, but I never did."[15]

It does seem plausible that England would have been much less involved in the abuses without Graner's constant encouragement and goading, but she has also consistently rejected the idea that she has *any* reason to feel remorse about her time in Iraq. "Their lives are better," she said of the Iraqis. "They got the better end of the deal. They weren't innocent. They're trying to kill us, and you want me to apologize to them? It's like saying sorry to the enemy."[16] In 2009, a reporter with an English tabloid tracked down England in West Virginia as she signed copies of her authorized biography at a bookstore. Again, she didn't feel there was any need for contrition. "Sorry? For what I did? All I did was stand in the pictures," she said. England reserved most of her anger for Sergeant Joseph Darby, the soldier who had first handed the photos over to military investigators. "In war, you don't rat out your buddies," she said, adding that if she ever saw him again, she'd "beat the hell out of him."[17]

While Graner used photographs to express his sadism and England seemed to genuinely not believe that she had done anything wrong ("All I did was stand in the pictures"), Sabrina Harman's relationship to photography was a little more complicated. When the first rounds of Abu Ghraib photographs were made public, the image showing Harman giving a thumbs-up while leaning over the beaten corpse of an Iraqi seemed to be among the worst. It was certainly one of the strangest, because Harman's smile seemed to be so genuine and unclouded by malice. She had grown up in Northern Virginia, about twenty miles southwest of Washington, D.C. Her father was a homicide detective, and her mother was interested in forensics as an amateur. Crime scene photos often made their way back from work to the Harman residence, where the whole family would analyze them. Sabrina spent her entire childhood looking at photographs of dead people, and by the time she was in high school, she knew she wanted to be a police officer, which would allow her to become a forensic photographer. She joined the military to help pay for college, and her fellow soldiers all described her as someone who abhorred violence, despite her fascination with visual documentation of its aftermath. "Sabrina literally would not hurt a fly," one said. People thought she was too nice to make a good soldier.[18]

Harman wasn't interested in seeing combat in Iraq, but she was interested in seeing corpses, which she'd never done in person. "On June 23 I saw my first dead body," she wrote from Iraq during the summer of 2003. "I took pictures!"[19] She'd been in a town called al-Hillah, far from the front lines. She spent four months there, snapping photos the whole time. When Harman herself was photographed, she almost always flashed her toothy grin and a thumbs-up, no matter the situation. Her unit thought it would be sent home after four months, but instead it was relocated to Abu Ghraib, which received mortar fire almost every day. "I have a bad feeling about this place," she wrote to her wife. "I want to leave as soon as possible!"[20] Harman felt uncomfortable with the abuse almost from the moment it started ramping up, and she said so in her letters. But along with everyone else in her unit, it was her job to keep prisoners "stressed out" in between their sessions with the interrogators from military intelligence (MI), to make noise or march them around so that they didn't get too much (meaning enough) sleep.

Unwilling to blow the whistle on her buddies but just as unwilling to understand herself as one of the detainees' tormentors, she started bringing her camera to Tiers 1A and 1B, where the abuses took place. "The only reason I want to be there is to get the pictures and prove that the US is not what they think," she wrote. "But I don't know if I can take it mentally."[21] Still, whenever she appeared in the photos, she reflexively flashed that grin and put her thumb in the air. She didn't have any specific plan for publicizing what was going on, but the vague idea that she'd give the photographs to CNN at some point in the future, once she was out of the military, was enough to keep her from feeling too complicit. Through photography, Harman was trying to establish a morally and psychologically bearable relationship between herself and the things she was seeing, things so overwhelming that she once described them in the same terms bystanders used to talk about seeing the Twin Towers come down, terms that reflected the distant, dreamlike, and relentlessly media-filtered war as a whole: "It seemed like stuff that only happened on TV, not something you really thought was going on. It's just something that you watch and that is not real."[22] Wielding the camera allowed Harman to distance herself from the abuse; so long as she was observing and documenting it, she did not have to think of herself as participating in it. But if Harman had been determined to really distance herself from Abu Ghraib, she could have resigned from the military, sent the photographs to reporters, and blown the whistle. She didn't. Here, then, is yet another contradiction: Even as photography pushes the photographer away from the people and events that fill their lens, it also brings them closer. While others may pass through and participate without really paying attention to what's going on, the photographer scrutinizes, stares, considers, and changes position so as to get a better angle. Something about torture fascinated Harman, made her want to look closer, even at what she described in her letters home as a significant emotional cost ("I don't know if I can take it"). Keeping the camera in hand and making images of the horrors unfolding in front of her allowed Harman to rationalize her presence in the room where they were taking place. Once these images found their way back to the United States, Americans also became fascinated with looking at torture. And like Harman, they eventually used the images they consumed and produced to rationalize their own support or tolerance for abuse that would otherwise have been inexcusable.

• • •

The *60 Minutes II* segment on Abu Ghraib included an interview with General Mark Kimmitt, the deputy director of coalition operations in Iraq, who appeared on the broadcast to deliver the Army's official response. Asked about the photograph of the dead man packed in ice, the first thing Kimmitt said was, "It's reprehensible that anybody'd be taking a picture of that situation." Dan Rather pounced: "Reprehensible that anybody would *take a picture* of that situation? What about the situation itself?" Rather's response suggested he thought that Kimmitt was being evasive, or that he felt worse about documentation of the crimes than he did about the fact that crimes had occurred. To some extent, this was a fair suggestion; Kimmitt was playing the role of the public relations crisis manager, and he spent much of the segment trying to insulate the military from the blowback that was obviously coming, insisting repeatedly that the abuses did not reflect the Army's "values." But Kimmitt's reaction to the photographs shouldn't be understood only as a PR maneuver. The photographs were not just documents of a crime—the camera was one of the weapons with which the crime had been committed. Nothing communicated the viciousness and ghastly inventiveness of the American guards at Abu Ghraib more effectively than the fact that they wanted to photograph what they were doing. The content of the photographs showed the kinds of abuse that were meted out, but the existence of the photographs showed that at least some of the soldiers were proud of what they were doing and had fun while doing it. At the very least (in Harman's case), it showed that they were willing to stand by and not intervene. In that sense, the fact that someone had taken a picture of the dead man *was* the most reprehensible thing about the situation. It meant that beating a man to death wasn't enough. It meant the Americans wanted to commemorate their own brutality and bring digital trophies home from the war as well. They might as well have scalped him.

Back home, Americans became obsessed with looking at scenes of torture. Torture became more common in action films and TV shows, and the violence depicted therein also became more explicit, as though producers and directors were trying to figure out exactly how much their audiences were willing to take. Before September 11, prime-time television showed its viewers fewer than four scenes of torture each year, on average. After September 11, that number began to increase, and three years after Abu Ghraib there were more than a hundred torture scenes broadcast during prime time each year.[23] Understanding that viewers would identify with different characters at different moments—the hero, his woman, the villain, the captive—writers and directors considered torture from many different angles. What would it be like to torture someone? What would it be like to watch someone else torture someone? What if you loved the person being tortured? What if you hated them? What if it was yourself? Under what circumstances would it be justified?

The action drama *24* was at the heart of the country's fascination with torture, and its writers came up with many different circumstances under which torture was justified. Comparing its first season with the eight that followed is instructive, because the first season was written and filmed before September 11, and it takes place in a world where the threat of Islamist terrorism is a distant nonconcern. The villain, described at one point as "the key threat to the peace in Bosnia," a conflict about which most Americans knew very little, is motivated by personal animus rather than politics: The show's hero, the Counter Terrorist Unit (CTU) agent Jack Bauer, and the leading presidential candidate, David Palmer, were responsible for accidentally killing his wife and daughter years ago, and he wants revenge.[24] Bauer threatens to torture people at various points, but he never actually needs to go through with it. The threat is sufficient to persuade his captives to reveal their secrets. Bauer's daughter finds herself in perilous situations, and his wife develops amnesia and wanders around Los Angeles in a daze. Bauer tries to keep tabs on his loved ones while scrambling to prevent Palmer's assassination, and in the season finale he kills all of the bad guys in cold blood because he mistakenly believes they have killed his daughter. The operatic grief/vengeance climax caps off a paint-by-numbers action plot filled with internal enemies and explosive set pieces. If not for the clever conceit that the show happens in real time, with twenty-four hour-long episodes unspooling over the course of a single day, *24* might well have been just another action show in a network television schedule that was already full of them.

Things changed with the show's second season, which was written and filmed after September 11. Torture changed from an ancillary element of the show's violent atmosphere to the main focus, and as a result *24* became the most popular show on television. The second season begins with an absolutely gruesome scene. Set in South Korea, it depicts a man tied to an elaborate electrified rack. His feet have been placed in bags of yellow fluid. There are needles, wires, and buckets catching various kinds of bodily runoff, and his eyes are held open by metal devices, *Clockwork Orange*–style. The first spoken words are, "Talk and the pain will stop."

The torture works, and the South Korean jailer walks down a hallway to a room of American men. "When?" one of them asks, hoping for information on the timing of an impending attack. "Today," the torturer responds, and the American places a phone call to someone at the NSA.[25] Torture thus begins on *24* with the United States outsourcing the task to one of its allies, but Jack Bauer and company soon take matters into their own hands. In the following seasons, Bauer and his colleagues withhold medical treatment from a suspect (a radicalized white woman),[26] torture a female co-worker who has betrayed the Counter Terrorist Unit,[27] cut a terrorist with a knife until he passes out,[28] step on a computer programmer's bullet wound when he won't divulge information,[29] threaten to torture Jack's ex-girlfriend,[30] torture the adult son of the secretary of defense (with the secretary's approval),[31] torture a fellow CTU agent who they mistakenly think is a mole (they later apologize, and she goes back to work),[32] and torture the husband of Bauer's lover by electrocuting him.[33] At one point, Bauer temporarily resigns from the CTU so that when he illegally tortures someone, it won't officially be connected to the agency.[34] In the fourth season, they torture a child.[35] (Bauer himself also gets tortured from time to time, so as to keep one side from running up the score by too much.)

Hollywood movies embraced torture as well. In the fall of 2004, just a few months before the fourth season of *24* launched, a low-budget horror movie called *Saw* was released in theaters across the country. The debut feature by the writer-director team Leigh Whannell and James Wan cost just over $1 million to make. Its thin plot revolves around two men who wake up in a dank room with tiled walls and floors. Sickly fluorescent light flickers overhead, the tile is crumbling, and the toilet is filled with shit. One of the men is chained to a bathtub, and the other is chained up on the other side of the room. A dead body lies on the floor between them, an apparent suicide by gunshot. Neither man knows how he got there, but they soon deduce that they have been kidnapped by a serial killer known as Jigsaw, who subjects his victims to various "games"—all of them involving torture—as a way of punishing them for their sins and flaws. A woman who is addicted to heroin is forced to kill a man who has been knocked unconscious by an opiate overdose. "Most people are so ungrateful to be alive," Jigsaw tells her after she survives the ordeal. "But not you. Not anymore." One of the men in the bathroom is unable to find the key that unlocks his chains, so he has to cut off his own foot with a hacksaw to escape. He's a doctor, and he's been targeted due to his cold bedside manner as well as the affair he's having with one of his medical students.[36] With its cast of B-list actors, cheap sets, and gory stunts, *Saw* took in more than $100 million worldwide. With a return on investment of about 8,500 percent, it was one of the most profitable movies ever made.[37]

A new *Saw* film was released each year for the following six years. The franchise was extraordinarily influential, reviving what had been a marginal genre of extreme horror filmmaking. The 2005 film *Hostel* gave the *Saw* premise international scope, following a group of loud and naive American tourists whose backpacking jaunt through Europe sees them captured, tortured, and dismembered by a cabal of aristocratic European sadists.[38] *Hostel* turned itself into a franchise as well. In the second installment, one of the victims is eaten alive, and one of the heroines cuts off a man's penis and throws it into the open mouth of a snarling dog as she strides out of the room.[39] In the third, a psychotic surgeon uses a scalpel to remove a victim's face.[40] Torture made inroads with other genres as well. Mel Gibson's *Passion of the Christ*, released just two months before the publication of the Abu Ghraib photographs, focused overwhelmingly on the physical torture Jesus endured leading up to his crucifixion, and it became the highest-grossing Christian film of all time.[41] In 2006, one critic at *New York* magazine finally came up with a name for the category: "torture porn." "I'm baffled," the critic wrote, "by how far this new stuff goes—and by why America seems so nuts these days about torture."[42] But the only baffling thing about it was the critic's bafflement. By 2006, the country had spent nearly two years taking in as much torture as the studios could churn out, as though they were trying to build up a tolerance to the world in which they lived, a world where being a patriotic American now meant identifying with soldiers who beat people for fun and used markers to write slurs on their captives' bodies.

Saw, 24, and *The Passion of the Christ* came from two different media and three different genres, but each of them presented its audience with a world in which torture was effective, inevitable, and above all necessary. Bauer never wanted to torture anybody, but circumstances always found a way to force his hand. Halfway through the show's second season, Bauer captures a terrorist subject, ties him up, and shows him a live video feed on a TV. The terrorist's wife and children have been captured as well, and American agents are pointing guns at them. If the terrorist doesn't tell Bauer what he needs to know, the family will be killed. "I despise you for making me do this," Bauer says.[43] When the terrorist still refuses to reveal the location of the bomb, Bauer has one of his children shot. (The shooting turns out to have been staged, but neither the terrorist suspect nor the show's viewers know that at the time.) Bauer lives in a world where there is always a clock ticking down, a nuclear bomb waiting to go off, or an assassination plot waiting to unfold, and all the ticking time bombs turn the legal protections of due process into a civic luxury the country can no longer afford. Bauer is a hero because he's the only one strong enough to sacrifice his conscience on the altar of the greater good. "That's the problem with people like you," Bauer tells a colleague after shooting a suspect in cold blood. "You want results, but you never want to get your hands dirty."[44] Similarly, the people in the *Saw* movies didn't ask to be kidnapped by a psycho, and they certainly didn't ask to be locked inside a lethal escape room, but the will to survive justifies anything. This is even true in *The Passion of the Christ*. Jesus doesn't want to be tortured and killed. "Father," he prays, "if thou be willing, remove this cup from me." But God tells him that his ordeal, to which he must go willingly, will save the human race, make the forgiveness of sins possible, and usher believers into the kingdom of heaven. Gibson's film makes it clear that the torture, the ordeal, is what made Jesus's sacrifice so powerful. It wouldn't have been enough for a centurion to sneak up from behind and run him through with a sword. The torture sanctifies his death.

In 2007, Jane Mayer wrote a magazine profile of Joel Surnow, the executive producer of *24*. She spoke to Cyrus Nowrasteh, a hardline conservative screenwriter and one of Surnow's best friends. Nowrasteh told Mayer that he and Surnow thought of *24* as a post-9/11 fantasy, "a kind of wish fulfillment for America," in Mayer's words. "Every American wishes we had someone out there quietly taking care of business," Nowrasteh said. "It would be nice to have a secret government that can get the answers . . . even kill people."[45] Part of the wish being granted by *24* is the desire to see a good man sacrifice his own happiness to save the day (Bauer's love interests inevitably betray him, leave him, or die), but in the torture porn movies, evil frequently triumphs. The fantasy that unites *24, Saw,* and *The Passion of the Christ* isn't that the right side always wins; it is that heroes can do evil things without compromising their moral integrity, *so long as they are forced to do them.* That's how Americans rationalized what happened at Abu Ghraib and the CIA black sites. Even if the photos made it impossible to deny what U.S. soldiers had done, Americans could still cling to the belief that torture's victims bore the ultimate responsibility because of their inherent savagery. Yes, we tortured our prisoners, they said, but only because they made us.

• • •

In the realm of politics and journalism, there were two competing accounts of what made Abu Ghraib possible. The government's story was the first to get off the starting line. To hear General Kimmitt tell it on *60 Minutes II*, the guards at Abu Ghraib acted alone, with neither inspiration nor encouragement from their superiors. "Frankly, I think all of us are disappointed at the actions of the few," he said. When Dan Rather followed up by asking what he would say to the millions of Iraqis who were going to see the photographs, Kimmitt briefly went off message. "These are our fellow soldiers," he said. "These are the people we work with every day. They represent us." Then he seemed to realize his mistake and immediately said the opposite. "This is not representative of the 150,000 soldiers that are over here," he said. "Don't judge your Army based on the actions of a few." When asked at the end of the segment what he thought was the most important thing for Americans to know about Abu Ghraib, Kimmitt said, "Number one, this is a small minority of the military. And number two, they need to understand that is not the Army. The Army is a values-based organization. . . . These acts that you see in these pictures may reflect the actions of individuals, but by God it doesn't reflect my Army."

This became the official line. One couldn't escape the phrase "a few bad apples" for months on television or in newspapers. (This was ironic: The point of the folk saying is that a few bad apples spoil the whole barrel.) The press, however, soon arrived at a second, more expansive explanation for Abu Ghraib, tracing the story up through the chain of command. It became clear that even within the physical confines of the prison, Graner, England, Harman, and the other military police officers had been receiving guidance and encouragement from above. On the prison's military intelligence block, high-value prisoners were kept on Tier 1A, where they were regularly interrogated by

MI officers. These officers came and went as they pleased. They often arrived in civilian clothes with no name tags, which meant the Army MPs were unable to identify them later, and if asked which branch of the military or government they worked for, they'd provide only the mysterious designation "OGA," for Other Government Agencies. It was the MI officers who set the tone at Abu Ghraib, telling the guards to keep detainees awake, naked, stressed out, or some combination of the three in between interrogation sessions. "There were different regimes for different MI prisoners," an MP named Javal Davis said. "'Cell seven, no sleep.' Or, 'Wake up four o'clock, go to bed one o'clock, wake up three o'clock, go to bed five o'clock, wake up . . . '—like that, up and down, up and down." Along with the detailed schedule for interrupting the prisoners' sleep, the MI officers furnished the MPs with ideas for what to do in between periods of rest. "The Military Intelligence people would come up there and say, 'Hey, play music at this time, play it loud,'" Davis said. "If they fall asleep, throw water on them, wake them up. Slam the doors, run up and down with garbage cans, bang on them, make sure they stand up when you walk by, don't sit down, things like that."[46] While some MPs were happy to apply their own creativity to abusing the prisoners—Graner is alleged to have come up with "hell night," the practice of going hard at new prisoners during their first night in Abu Ghraib—Davis insisted that the MI officers provided most of the ideas. "I didn't invent any of these things," he said. "These were presented to us. I didn't jump out of bed in the morning saying, 'Hey, I want to go smack up a detainee,' or, 'Hey, I want to throw ice on people,' or, 'I want to play loud music.' Who would have thought of something like that?"[47]

It also seemed to the MPs that whatever happened to the prisoners in the interrogation rooms was a good bit worse than the abuse they were meting out in between rounds of questioning. "They put a sheet up over the door and for hours and hours and hours, all you would hear is screaming, banging, slamming, and just more screaming at the top of their lungs," Davis said. "When [the MI officers] were done eight, ten hours later, they'd bring the guy out, he'd be halfway coherent, or unconscious, you'd put him back in the cell and they'd say, 'OK, this guy gets no sleep. Throw some cold water on him. We'll be back for him tomorrow.' "[48] But the MI officers didn't wind up in the photos, and none of them ever faced any kind of prosecution.

The MI officers, in turn, had been enabled by prominent figures within the Bush administration and the CIA. In the months after September 11, Deputy Assistant Attorney General John Yoo, Assistant Attorney General for the Office of Legal Counsel Jay Bybee, and the White House lawyer David Addington, all committed members of the right-wing legal establishment, drafted and approved a series of memos that methodically removed nearly all of the protections that detainees would otherwise have enjoyed as either criminal defendants or prisoners of war. Yoo worked out of the Office of Legal Counsel, a department whose opinions are legally binding on the executive branch unless they are directly overruled by the attorney general. This meant that Yoo's fringe theories took on the force of law as quickly as he wrote them down, with neither congressional oversight nor judicial review stepping in to moderate his vision of what was permissible.

Criminal defendants are entitled to legal representation, to be told the charges they face, and to confront their accusers in open court. POWs are protected by the Geneva Conventions, which outline basic standards of care and prohibit such practices as torture, coercive interrogations, and hostage taking. But according to the Bush administration, war on terror detainees would be categorized as "illegal enemy combatants" instead. "The administration's lawyers created a third category," one international law expert said, "and cast them outside of the law."[49] Illegal enemy combatants could be detained in secret and held indefinitely without charges. Appeals could be made only to the president or secretary of defense, both of whom, as the journalist Jane Mayer wrote, "would simultaneously serve as the prosecuting authorities."[50] There would be no right to remain silent, defendants would not be entitled to see the evidence against them, and guilt did not need to be proved beyond a reasonable doubt. Legally, detainees became non-people. That meant the government could treat them however it liked.

Emboldened by its new legal powers, the Bush administration

ensured that detainees were subjected to the harshest possible questioning. The CIA expanded its use of "extraordinary rendition," a Clinton-era program under which suspected terrorists were flown to secret "black sites" in countries such as Egypt, Morocco, and Poland, places where CIA operatives could either torture detainees themselves, secure in the knowledge that the host country would turn a blind eye, or else delegate the task to the security and intelligence services of an allied authoritarian government. The U.S. detention camp in Guantánamo Bay became a favored destination for prisoners. Because the camp was located on a naval base in Cuba, the government was able to argue that people detained there could not be subject to U.S. law, and because it was located on an *American* naval base, they wouldn't be subject to Cuban law either. Detainees could be squeezed for whatever information they had at one of the black sites and then left to rot in Guantánamo's legal limbo.

At the same time, government lawyers were expanding the scope and violence of what American interrogators could do to their prisoners. In November 2001, the CIA's general counsel wrote an internal memo arguing that torture could be seen as "necessary to prevent imminent, significant, physical harm to persons, where there is no other available means to prevent the harm."[51] The government then secretly authorized a set of practices that it collected under the euphemistic umbrella term "enhanced interrogation techniques," including the use of painful stress positions, beatings, blasting loud music, sleep deprivation, waterboarding, sexual humiliation, slamming detainees into walls, subjecting them to extreme heat and cold, confining them to boxes the size of coffins, and withholding medical care. This was the playbook the MI officers drew from as they ordered the MPs at Abu Ghraib to keep the detainees awake, disoriented, and upset in between interrogations, and it was authorized at the government's highest levels.

The government and the press, then, advanced two competing and incompatible narratives about how Americans came to commit torture. In one, a group of low-ranking soldiers lost their heads in the desert heat and took out their frustrations on the nearest available targets, unprompted by their commanding officers and in contravention of everything the military had taught them to uphold. In the other, torture was a top-down phenomenon, a set of policies drawn up by paranoid officials far from the battlefield and then carried out by soldiers whose primary mistake was trusting that whatever command said was okay. The first explanation lets the government off the hook entirely, and the second paints the Bush administration as a malignant aberration that pushed its fear and anger down the chain of command until it found a way to express itself on the ground. In a sense, *both* stories blamed torture on "a few bad apples"—each just identified a different group of people as the apples.

Both stories had it wrong. The Torture Memos, the black sites, and the rendition program are settled matters of historical fact, but Americans began torturing detainees in Afghanistan and Iraq *before* John Yoo tried to make it legal, and the abuse was by no means confined to Abu Ghraib. Human rights organizations documented the first cases of U.S. troops abusing detainees within months of the American invasion of Afghanistan. In the spring of 2002, an Army interrogator named Chris Mackey (a pseudonym), who later wrote an unrepentant memoir about his time in Afghanistan, was transferred to work the jail at Bagram Airfield, about thirty miles north of Kabul. He was impressed by the Special Forces soldiers he met there, and by a military intelligence officer who liked to talk about how interrogation was a kind of science of human domination. The Special Forces guys wanted him to conduct tough interrogations that produced results quickly, and the MI officer encouraged him to use half-baked theories about body language to determine whether detainees were telling the truth. "There are certain hand gestures that are particularly suggestive of deception," Mackey wrote. "If a prisoner covers his mouth, or even lays a finger across his lips, it's often a sign that he is subconsciously trying to block what he is saying, perhaps trying to cover an untruth."[52] This is the stuff of network TV crime dramas such as *Lie to Me,* but it structured how Mackey went about deciding which prisoners would get off easy and which would be subjected to violence. Mackey and his unit eventually coined the term "monstering," which meant keeping prisoners in the interrogation booth for as long as it took, without interruptions, until either the prisoner or the interrogator "broke."[53]

Later that same year, Americans killed a twenty-two-year-old taxi driver being held at Bagram. Known only as Dilawar, he'd been driving through militia territory when he was stopped and then handed over to the Americans. He weighed just 122 pounds, and he died after being shackled to the top of his cell and repeatedly beaten for the better part of four days. He called out to God when the jailers beat him, and this seemed to amuse them. Other detainees recall the Americans making a game out of hitting him so that he'd cry out again.[54]

There was no single motivation for the abuse. Some soldiers in Iraq described abusing detainees out of frustration with how the war was going or to blow off steam. "I threw another human," one soldier said. "I picked [him] up and threw him. At that point [I] wasn't thinking about another human being—wasn't worried about how he thought, if he was embarrassed. I just picked him up and threw him in the back of the Humvee. At that point, I was thinking, 'That was fun—that was funny.'" Others tortured their prisoners because they resented having to guard them. "You have to watch these prisoners—they're the reason why you're in the damned country," one said. "They're the reason you're thirsty. They're the reason you're miserable. And here you have to babysit them."[55] Others tortured prisoners out of boredom. "Honestly, a lot of the things that were done to the detainees were . . . just someone's idea of a good time," an MP named Daniel Keller said. He recalled an officer telling him about an interrogation technique involving water that had been used to get information out of prisoners during Vietnam. "Then I went ahead and tried it," he said. "The difference was that I didn't want information. I just wanted to hurt [a prisoner]."[56] Part of what made the abuse acceptable at the time was its ubiquity. As Keller said, "It's not a few rogue people . . . there were a lot of us doing it."[57]

It is also worth considering the role that fantasy might have played

in pushing both ground-level soldiers and Bush administration officials to torture. Although torture is worse than useless as a way of
gathering intelligence—in 2007, the U.S. military went so far as to ask
the producers of *24* to stop depicting it as effective—the idea that bad
guys can be "made to talk" if subjected to sufficient levels of pain has
proved to have a tenacious staying power. And given the guilt that
America's intelligence services felt over having failed to prevent September 11, it is not hard to look at what happened at Abu Ghraib and
the CIA's black sites as an enactment of what intelligence officers felt
they *should* have done to suspected terrorists in the years leading up
to 2001. It doesn't work, of course. No matter how many times a detainee is beaten or humiliated or doused in freezing water, September 11 can't be undone. But the uselessness fuels the repetition: Unable
to get the satisfaction they need and exorcise their guilt, the torturers
are compelled to do it again and again.

The simplest explanation, though, is that men and women up and
down the chain of command, people who shared an understanding of
the wars in Afghanistan and Iraq as revenge missions, tortured their
detainees because they wanted to, out of sadism. In the immediate
wake of Abu Ghraib, Democrats and Republicans both needed to
avoid this conclusion, because they needed to portray torture as ancillary to the war. Whether torture was caused by a few maniacs working
at Abu Ghraib or ideologue lawyers working inside the Bush administration, it still needed to be seen as a deviation from the war's real
purpose as a global self-defense and liberation project. But this belief
could not survive a confrontation with the fact that soldiers had begun
to abuse and torture their captives spontaneously and voluntarily,
without the need for guidance from the top brass, from the war's earliest days. The actions of the earliest abusers suggested that sadism was
a part of the project from the very beginning, and in that light the
government's legalization of torture was not a deviation from the war's
purpose but an attempt to formalize an aspect of the war that had
been present at the outset. As this truth became harder to ignore, and
as the shock of the Abu Ghraib photographs began to wear off, some
officials across both parties, along with prominent figures from within

evangelical Christianity, began to shift their view on torture, moving first from condemnation to acceptance, and then from acceptance to endorsement.

• • •

Very few people tried to defend torture when the Abu Ghraib photographs first came to light. The images were too awful. The setting looked like a serial killer's lair, the dog piles of detainees looked like the damned in Hieronymus Bosch's depiction of hell, and the soldiers, squinting into the camera flash, posing like drunken coeds, and seemingly oblivious to the squalid horrors of their environment, reminded one of the photo galleries that students used to put up on Facebook the day after a fraternity rager. But that changed as time passed. Though Bush administration officials declared themselves disgusted by the idea that Americans might have tortured even a single detainee, they repeatedly blocked congressional efforts to investigate the abuse. In late 2004, Daniel Levin, who had taken up John Yoo's position at the Office of Legal Counsel, produced a new memo that was designed to replace Yoo's endorsement of torture. While the new memo denounced torture in strong terms—its first sentence read, "Torture is abhorrent both to American law and values and to international norms"—it also included a footnote that preemptively absolved the Bush administration of any wrongdoing.[58] "In the real world of interrogation policy," Yoo later wrote of this footnote, "nothing had changed."[59]

In June 2005, the Democratic senator Carl Levin delivered remarks on an FBI agent's email that had detailed U.S. torture techniques. If you didn't know the email was about an American facility, he said, "you would most certainly believe this must have been done by Nazis, Soviets in their gulags, or some mad regime—Pol Pot or others—that had no concern for human beings." He was pilloried for his comments, including by the Democratic mayor of Chicago. Little more than a week later, Levin appeared on the Senate floor to apologize for saying that torture was more befitting of Nazis than Americans. "I'm also sorry if anything I said in any way cast a negative light on our fine men and women in the military," he said.[60] In December of that year, the Republican senator John McCain added language to the Defense Department budget prohibiting military interrogators from using any techniques that weren't specifically approved in the U.S. Army Field Manual, even if ordered to do so by the president. McCain, who had been tortured himself as a POW during the Vietnam War, had more credibility on the issue than any other government figure, but Vice President Cheney still went to Capitol Hill to personally lobby against what became known as the Detainee Treatment Act. The act eventually passed, but Bush administration lawyers then issued further secret legal opinions undermining its provisions. And when the Supreme Court ruled in June 2006 that the Bush administration was in fact bound by the requirements of the Geneva Conventions, Cheney spearheaded the drafting and passage of the Military Commissions Act, which undid most of the consequences of the court's ruling. McCain had lost, and he voted for the bill.[61]

Emboldened by the administration's resistance to reform, some Republicans shifted their rhetoric away from minimizing the significance of torture at Abu Ghraib and toward what sounded much more like endorsing it. "If our guys want to poke somebody in the chest to get the name of a bomb maker so that they can save the lives of Americans, I'm for it," the Republican senator James Talent said. He accused critics of being "unduly sensitive to some of the interrogation techniques."[62] This rhetoric was always swathed in euphemism, but its import was clear. This shift—from downplaying the use of torture in the past to justifying its continued use in the future—was accomplished by describing terrorists as the kind of enemy that *needed* to be tortured in order to beat them. Politicians and commentators had always said the war on terror represented a new kind of military challenge. Terrorist groups were smaller, more flexible, more fluid, and more decentralized than conventional military forces, which meant one couldn't expect the United States to win with the kinds of large-scale confrontations that had worked in the past. But after Abu Ghraib, a different aspect of the war's novelty started to receive more attention.

This was a *religious* war, at least on one side, and the United States couldn't afford to assume that an army of zealots could be defeated in the same way as an army fighting under a national flag.

Torture focused and amplified the Islamophobia and racism of the war on terror. Soldiers used Islam to simultaneously explain and discredit the motivations of the enemy: The terrorists fought with so little regard for the rules of war because they were mindless fanatics, and because they were fanatics, the only useful response to their provocations was violence. "All of us were laboring under the belief that these individuals will chew hydraulic lines with their bare teeth if they had had the chance, to do anything possible to immolate themselves so they could kill Americans," one military lawyer recalled. He also remembered hearing at one point that "these are the kind of guys that, if they were in a prison infirmary, they could take a syringe and drive it into the eye of a nurse or corpsman—just out of sheer hatred of Americans."[63] "These were not nice people at all," an intelligence officer stationed at Bagram said. "They were very evil people who, you know, definitely had violent intentions."[64]

Notions of frontier justice and the necessity of moral flexibility when fighting a savage enemy in the wilderness blended with more specific stereotypes about the enemy's psychological vulnerabilities. Some of these stereotypes circulated through Washington and the military via *The Arab Mind,* a 1973 study of Arab psychology written by Raphael Patai, a Hungarian-born ethnographer and Orientalist who spent his adult life in Israel and the United States. According to Patai, Arab men were almost uniquely susceptible to sexual humiliation. A misogyny instilled in them from childhood, combined with the repressive strictures of family codes of honor, meant that Arabs would sooner spy on their closest friends than risk their loved ones seeing them sexually humiliated. Terrorists fantasized about being rewarded with virgins in paradise, in other words, because they basically *were* virgins, men so stunted in their sexual development and so terrified of women that an interrogator could save American lives just by forcing a detainee to masturbate in front of a female guard. And since Patai's book also emphasized that Arabs had an intense phobia of dogs, which they viewed as "unclean," why wouldn't interrogators use dogs to intimidate them?[65] Stationed far from home, charged with the care of people they feared and about whose culture they knew nothing, and guided in part by the musings of a racist academic, soldiers working in Iraqi and Afghan prisons slowly made out of suspected terrorists a new kind of Indian, a people born and raised so far from the heart of real civilization that violence and humiliation were the only languages they could be expected to understand.

Back in the United States, evangelicals led the way in using Islamophobia to justify Americans taking the gloves off as they launched their new war. Theirs were lonely voices at the beginning, but as Iraq devolved into insurgency, counterinsurgency, sectarian recrimination, and torture, they started to win people over. Evangelicals had some new advantages coming into the war. While they had influenced the highest levels of American government ever since Billy Graham's friendship with Richard Nixon, George W. Bush's ascent to the White House marked a new high point for the religious movement. Bush was an outspoken, born-again Christian (only the second to hold the presidency), and his faith moved to the center of his political identity the moment he said that his favorite philosopher was Jesus Christ at a debate during the Republican primary campaign in 2000. Other prominent members of his administration were evangelical as well, including Attorney General John Ashcroft.

With Bush in the White House, evangelicals like Pat Robertson, Franklin Graham (Billy's son), and Jerry Falwell had a president whose faith would win them droves of new listeners and viewers. They did not waste the opportunity. In 2001, Graham called Islam a "very wicked and evil religion," and Jerry Vines, the pastor at the First Baptist Church of Jacksonville, Florida, told attendees at the annual Southern Baptist Convention that violence and terrorism were *inherent* to Islam. "Allah is not Jehovah," he said. "Jehovah's not going to turn you into a terrorist that'll try to bomb people and take the lives of thousands and thousands of people."[66] He said Islam had been "founded by Muhammad, a demon-obsessed pedophile who had twelve wives, and his last one was a nine-year-old girl." Controversy followed Vines for months. He did not apologize. When asked on *60 Minutes* whether he thought Muhammad approved of terrorism, the televangelist and political activist Jerry Falwell said, "I do. I think Muhammed was a terrorist. I read enough of the history of his life, written by both Muslims and non-Muslims, that he was a violent man, a man of war."[67]

Evangelical accounts of Islam also framed the war on terror as a turning point in biblical history. In 2002, the televangelist Hal Lindsey published his book *The Everlasting Hatred,* which claimed the war was a harbinger of the Armageddon foretold in the book of Revelation.[68] Like all Christian Zionists, Lindsey believed that the founding of the state of Israel in 1948 was a fulfillment of biblical prophecy. He described a "blood feud" between Muslims and Jews that dated "back to the tents of Abraham," with the war on terror as the culmination of centuries of conflict that would finally settle the issue of who "owns Jerusalem" and usher in Christ's return.[69] America was "faltering" in its holy mission, he wrote, "because we have failed to understand Muslim beliefs and practices. We have set as our goal to turn these Islamic countries into democracies, even though a Western-style democracy is totally contrary to the kind of government taught in the Koran."[70] Islam had frozen Arab culture in the "seventh century . . . and raised it to the level of 'divine revelation' on how all people should live for all time," he wrote. "The modern concept of 'Jihad' primarily has to do with forcing this culture upon the whole world."[71] This tenacious antimodern religious imperialism could be fought only on its own premedieval terms. "We need to destroy their war making capability and leave," he wrote, and "warn them that we will destroy them if they are complicit in further terrorist attacks against us. This is the only language that Islamic fundamentalists understand."[72] He estimated that "at least" 10 percent, or 140 million, of the world's 1.4 billion Muslims were potential terrorists, which made Islam "the single greatest threat in the world to the survival of Western civilization."[73]

These were extreme ideas, and they were largely treated as such in public. The Bush administration found itself having to disavow prominent Christians who supported the invasion of Iraq as part of a larger civilizational conflict with the world's second-largest religion. But while the torture program was a disaster for America's relationships abroad, making it very difficult for the United States to maintain the moral high ground as it tried to advise other countries on the importance of human rights, it didn't do as much damage to the Bush administration at home, in part because the opposition expended little effort making an issue out of it. Senator John Kerry debated Bush three times during his doomed 2004 presidential campaign, but at no point in those debates did he say any of the following words: "torture," "Abu Ghraib," "detainee," "Bagram," or "waterboarding." These omissions are hard to understand. Bush had promoted the war as a moral crusade, and one could hardly think of a better opportunity to paint Bush as a hypocrite than the revelation that freedom's soldiers had instead taken photographs while forcing their captives to masturbate for laughs. Every time a Democrat spoke out too forcefully against torture, however, some conservative politician or commentator would accuse them of denigrating the country's troops as a whole, and before long the Democrat would either apologize, assuring voters that they had nothing but love and admiration for the troops, or else simply drop the issue. "It's no longer fashionable among those in the Democratic Party," one Republican political strategist said, "to engage in the bashing of American servicemen and women while they are in combat."[74]

Why should objecting to torture constitute an insult to everyone in the military? If the vast majority of soldiers abhorred torture, as commentators repeatedly reassured Americans during the early days of the Abu Ghraib scandal, wouldn't those soldiers want to see the torturers criticized and punished in the harshest possible terms? In 2019, the writer Elizabeth Schambelan published an essay on torture and the history of fraternity hazing that focused on the U.S. Military Academy at West Point, which trains the Army's officer class. In 1898, she wrote, a West Point plebe named Oscar Booz was beaten, tormented with hot wax, and forced to drink Tabasco sauce as part of the academy's hazing rituals. He died two years later, insisting that the Tabasco had brought on his tuberculosis, and the House of Representatives opened an investigation. It was the country's first university hazing scandal. At a hearing, one of the witnesses, Cadet Lewis Brown Jr., had what Schambelan calls "an unusually blunt exchange" with Congressman Walter I. Smith that made it clear why the United States would have so little success in eradicating hazing from its university campuses over the following century. Smith was asking about the practice of forcing plebes to engage in bare-knuckle boxing. The sport was illegal in every state, yet one West Point cadet acknowledged that it was common at the academy and that blood-soaked towels were usually sent over to the school laundry after a fight.

Rep. Smith: Where did you derive your right, sir, to override the rules and regulations made for the government of the Academy, except from your assumption?

Cadet Brown: I derive my right to do what hazing I do from custom.

Rep. Smith: From custom?

Cadet Brown: Yes, sir.

Rep. Smith: An unlawful and illegal custom forbidden by the rules of this Academy?

Cadet Brown: Yes, sir.

Rep. Smith: And you . . . do not think you are impudent, or arrogant, or conceited, or need anything to redress that trouble?

Cadet Brown: I don't wish to say anything about my own characteristics. . . . I do not think it is impudent or arrogant in a good many cases to break regulations.

Rep. Smith: You do not?

Cadet Brown: No, sir.

Rep. Smith: I presume, then, that if you should become an officer in the United States Army, that you would still deem it your privilege to override the laws of your country when you might think your wisdom greater than that of the law-making power?

Cadet Brown: I may have a great many different views then, and may be guided by those who have had more experience than I have.

Rep. Smith: But you decline to be guided by your superiors now in these matters . . . ?

Cadet Brown: If breaking regulations is declining to submit to the orders of my superiors, I would have to admit so, because I do break regulations.

Rep. Smith: And willfully break them?

Cadet Brown: Yes, sir.[75]

There's no hard evidence that soldiers took inspiration for specific torture techniques from the hazing they endured at school, but the rituals reinforced an attitude, a social order, that was derived from the history of American war making. As Richard Slotkin demonstrated in his trilogy of books on the frontier, the American military has fought unconventional wars—first against Native Americans, then in the Philippines, then in Vietnam—for a majority of its history. Texts such as Dennis Hart Mahan's *Elementary Treatise on Advanced-Guard, Out-Post, and Detachment Service of Troops,* in combination with a Swiss philosopher's early theorization of just war, *The Law of Nations,* were used to teach America's cadets that while native peoples and prisoners should be treated humanely if possible, it would also be necessary at times to engage in "the destruction of property and food supplies, the imposition of communal punishments, and the execution of particularly incorrigible individuals." Within this framework, rule breaking is inevitable and necessary. Orders handed down by a superior officer are to be obeyed, and the rules can't be discarded completely, but they have to be flexible in order for the military to fight in the manner it knows best, and commanding officers must be able to distinguish between insubordination and healthy expressions of creativity and initiative. Maintaining this balance requires everyone, officers and cadets alike, to know how to interpret things that don't actually get said. "When Brown said that 'custom' gave him the right to haze," Schambelan writes, "he was referring to everything that everyone at West Point understood, but that no one had ever written down—for instance, that when your superiors conspicuously fail to question the source of the blood that soaks the towels you've used in your illegal boxing matches, their silence itself is a message." Breaking rules in this way couldn't be taught in a classroom, because breaking rules was precisely about having the imagination to do things on your own, without being prompted by an instructor. "The very fact that hazing was prohibited," Schambelan writes, "was the core of its tacit pedagogy."

While few in the government wanted to formally endorse torture in the months after the scandal broke, neither Democrats nor Republicans wanted to go too far in actively prohibiting it, either, as though they understood that extralegal violence had a long-standing place in the country's military traditions. For Democrats trying to fend off accusations of being "soft" on terrorism as they tried to retake control of the federal government in 2004, that meant the smart political choice was to hedge whenever possible. The Democratic senator Chuck Schumer said in 2004 that the soldiers who abused detainees in the *specific case* of Abu Ghraib should be prosecuted, but he tried to preserve the more general principle that during times of war the rules would occasionally need to be broken. "I'd like to interject a note of balance here," he said at a hearing of the Senate Judiciary Committee:

> There are times when we all get in high dudgeon. We ought to be reasonable about this. I think there are very few people in this room or in America who would say that torture should never, ever be used, particularly if thousands of lives are at stake.

Take the hypothetical: If we knew that there was a nuclear bomb hidden in an American city and we believed that some kind of torture, fairly severe maybe, would give us a chance of finding that bomb before it went off, my guess is most Americans and most senators, maybe all, would say, "Do what you have to do."[76]

When the journalist Jane Mayer published her book on the Bush administration's torture program in 2008, its subtitle referred to a "war on American ideals." "As early as the Revolutionary War," Mayer wrote in the first chapter, "General George Washington vowed that, unlike the British, who tortured enemy captives, this new country in the New World would distinguish itself by its humanity." She claimed that this humanitarian impulse had remained at the center of U.S. policy making throughout the following two centuries, and that America's efforts to build a more humane world had been successful. "In fighting to liberate the world from Communism, Fascism, and Nazism," she wrote, "and working to ameliorate global ignorance and poverty, America had done more than any other nation on earth to abolish torture and other violations of human rights."[77]

In order to make this claim with a straight face, however, and in order to present the Bush administration as a radical break from the country's traditions, Mayer had to ignore large swaths of the country's history. During the Revolutionary period, patriots tortured loyalists in Boston, Connecticut, and Georgia, to name just a few instances, imprisoning them in pitch-black mines, forcing them to eat hog shit, and setting them on fire.[78] In the twentieth century, U.S. soldiers frequently tortured enemy captives in the Philippines, where America successfully put down an independence movement and installed a puppet government, and in Vietnam, where America failed to do the same.[79] And throughout the second half of the twentieth century, the United States either tolerated or secretly encouraged right-wing and military groups in Indonesia, Brazil, Chile, Guatemala, and elsewhere to torture and massacre communist civilians in their countries, a campaign of indiscriminate mass slaughter that resulted in at least a million deaths as well as some of America's most important Cold War victories.[80]

It is unlikely that Jane Mayer, one of the most decorated journalists of her generation, was unaware of these episodes when she wrote *The Dark Side*. A more probable explanation for the rose-tinted version of America's humanitarian record that appears in her book is that she wasn't primarily scandalized by torture as such, but by something else. "For the first time in its history," she wrote of the torture program, "the United States government sanctioned officials to physically and psychologically torment U.S.-held captives, making torture the official law of the land in all but name."[81] She didn't write that American soldiers had never previously engaged in torture, only that the government had never previously sanctioned the practice.

The history that Mayer decided to skip over makes it harder to characterize torture as a stark departure from America's values. Indeed, throughout their history, Americans have not only practiced and tolerated torture during periods of military conflict, they have also glorified a set of myth heroes whose genius partly derives from their willingness to break free from the strictures of law and civilized conduct when the threat is serious enough to require it—their willingness to, in Chuck Schumer's words, "do what you have to do." What happened at Abu Ghraib would have been an atrocity whether or not it ever became a matter of public record, but it only became a scandal because of the photographic evidence and the Bush administration's insistence on putting its endorsement of torture on the record. If Charles Graner and Sabrina Harman had left their digital cameras at home, and if the Bush administration had indicated the kinds of interrogations it desired via winks and nudges rather than official legal memoranda, it is likely that torture in Iraq would never have made the front page to begin with.

In the months leading up to the Abu Ghraib scandal, American society was just barely managing to balance the war's contradictory requirements of seeing Muslims as innocent victims while simultaneously seeing them as monsters. But the publication of the photos made that balance impossible to maintain any longer. No more could honest people pretend that the war was anything other than Islamophobic and racist at its foundation. This was obvious outside the United States, and particularly within the Middle East. Why should the world's Arabs and Muslims continue to tolerate American lectures on human rights when America's soldiers had so thoroughly documented their own barbarity? Why should anyone believe in America's vision for a democratic Iraq, when anyone who watched the news knew that what Americans really wanted was to humiliate Iraqis? Torture did enormous damage to America's global standing, making a mockery of U.S. pretensions to moral leadership, but the damage wasn't just a matter of image. In the following years, torture also served as a powerful recruiting tool for extremist groups, whose leaders now had images to back up their rhetoric about America's oppression of the Muslim world.

But despite the damage torture did to America's global standing, and despite the fact that it increased the popular appeal of the very groups America was trying to destroy, the United States could not discard or excise the war's Islamophobia and racism, because without them America couldn't fight the war at all. The belief that terrorists were irrational, savage fanatics gave the United States an excuse not to pursue diplomacy even when diplomacy was clearly the best path forward. It allowed the government to wage the war on a much wider scale than would have been palatable otherwise. And it allowed U.S. troops to target Muslim and Arab detainees with violence that would have immediately been seen as illegitimate were it ever applied to white Christians. Anti-Muslim bigotry had been baked into the war from the beginning, and it was Abu Ghraib that revealed the uselessness of trying to pretend otherwise.

Unfortunately for the United States, the man who succeeded George W. Bush was determined to pretend otherwise, and Barack Obama's party, country, and place in history would all pay the price for that determination in 2016, when voters picked someone to succeed him as president.

CHAPTER 6

Geronimo

I have seen Him in the watch-fires of a hundred circling camps;
They have builded him an altar in the evening dews and damps;
I can read His righteous sentence by the dim and flaring lamps.
His Day is marching on.

—Julia Ward Howe, "Battle Hymn of the Republic"

I n October 2008, the Republican senator John McCain held a town hall rally in Lakeville, Minnesota, a Minneapolis–St. Paul exurb. There was just a month to go before the electorate would choose between him and Democratic nominee Barack Obama, a charismatic senator from Illinois who had first come to prominence with a speech at his party's national convention in 2004. McCain's campaign was flailing. A quarter century older than his opponent, McCain spent the summer watching helplessly as Obama drew massive, ecstatic crowds everywhere he went. McCain was a decorated war hero, and he spent the early stages of the race hoping to paint Obama as insufficiently experienced to run the country's military. But during the summer, the financial crisis that had begun a year earlier with the collapse of America's housing market bubble finally came to a boil. In mid-

September, the financial services firm Lehman Brothers, which had invested heavily in risky mortgage debt, collapsed. Lehman's $600 billion bankruptcy filing was the largest in American history, and on the day it was announced, the Dow Jones Industrial Average suffered its largest single-session drop since the week after September 11. The war wasn't the country's primary focus anymore. With the economy not just in trouble but on the verge of breaking down entirely, McCain tried to get his hands on the reins of the situation by announcing on September 24 that he would suspend his campaign and return to Washington. He called on President Bush to convene a bipartisan "leadership meeting" to work out a congressional response. He asked Obama to suspend his campaign as well. He said that both candidates should attend the meeting and that any further debates between the two of them—including one scheduled for just two days later—should be postponed "until we have taken action." "Following September 11th," McCain concluded, "our national leaders came together at a time of crisis. We must show that kind of patriotism now."[1]

McCain's announcement backfired in almost every possible way. Insofar as McCain hoped to position himself as the only candidate with the leadership skills to pull the country through an economic disaster, the effect of his campaign suspension was something like the opposite. Obama said that his campaign would continue, and he insisted that the scheduled presidential debate go on as planned. "Part of the president's job," he said, just managing to conceal his glee at the meatball his opponent had lobbed over the plate, "is to deal with more than one thing at once."[2] To make matters worse, McCain had decided to stake the last days of his candidacy on an issue about which he knew very little and had displayed almost no interest over the course of his political career. He'd advocated for the standard low-regulation economic policies that the Republican Party favored throughout the late twentieth century, but he had little familiarity with the technical ins and outs of the liquidity crunch that was bringing the financial system to its knees. When the two candidates appeared at the Washington leadership meeting McCain had requested, Obama spoke fluently and knowledgeably about the tricky mechanics of the proposed bailout package, while McCain initially declined to say anything at all—"I'll wait my turn," he said. When Obama later insisted that McCain contribute, all the Republican senator could manage were a few generalities about the progress being made and the importance of reaching consensus. Secretary of the Treasury Hank Paulson Jr. later wrote that he could see Obama chuckling while McCain searched helplessly for something substantive to add.[3]

By the time McCain stepped onto the stage at the Lakeville auditorium a couple of weeks later, he was down by around seven percentage points in national polls, and the mood in the town hall was angry. McCain's attacks on Obama's character had increased since the debacle of his economic summit, with the campaign releasing an ad in early October focusing on Obama's alleged professional association with the "unrepentant terrorist" Bill Ayers, one of the founders of the Weather Underground. This kind of dog whistle was not hard to understand, aimed as it was at a Black man with a Kenyan father and the middle name Hussein, but McCain's supporters were not content with dog whistles. Following McCain's unsuccessful attempts to tamp down a number of audience outbursts, a woman took the microphone to say her piece. "I don't trust Obama," she said. She wore a red jacket and slightly wild hair, and as McCain listened to her, he looked every bit the politician who is sick of pretending to enjoy listening to randos on the campaign trail. "I have read about him," she said, her voice faltering momentarily, "and he's not, he's not—he's an Arab." "No, ma'am," McCain replied. "He's a decent family man, citizen, who I just happen to have disagreements with on fundamental issues, and that's what this campaign is all about." That line received a smattering of muted applause, but most of McCain's supporters didn't want respectful disagreements on fundamental issues. They wanted McCain to defend their way of life from terrorists, and in their eyes Obama was, at minimum, a terrorist sympathizer. McCain was booed so many times at the town hall that a campaign spokesman was reduced to telling reporters that it was actually a *good* thing for a candidate to get jeered by the people who were supposed to vote for him in a month. "He's never been afraid to get boos from his own audience," he said. "That's always been John McCain's thing."[4]

The media feted McCain extensively for his remarks and continued doing so for the remaining ten years of his life. The moment became a kind of lodestar for the importance of civility in politics, with McCain's refusal to stoop to the level of his basest supporters described as "harking back to a different moment in American politics, in which disagreements could be intense without becoming existential clashes in which the freedom of the country was at stake."[5] But the media might have oversold McCain's courage, because earlier that summer he'd selected Alaska's governor, Sarah Palin, to run as his vice president. A newcomer to national politics, Palin soon revealed herself to be astonishingly ignorant of almost every issue a president might be expected to address, but she made up for her lack of policy expertise with the powerful and vulgar charisma she brought to her stump speeches. She saw McCain's basest supporters as the base of their political success, and at rallies she created an atmosphere in which those on the right wing of the party felt very free to express themselves.

Soon after she joined the campaign, attendees at rallies could be heard responding to mentions of Obama's name by yelling "Traitor!" and "Hang him!" McCain could speak forcefully about the importance of respectful disagreement, but his choice of running mate all but guaranteed that the campaign's final months would be fueled, at least on one side, by a strong current of barely concealed racist vitriol. "This is not a man who sees America as you and I do—as the greatest force for good in the world," Palin said of Obama. "This is someone who sees America as imperfect enough to pal around with terrorists who targeted their own country."[6] McCain never said anything that incendiary on his own, but he wasn't above allowing his supporters to believe the worst of his opponent, so long as they didn't articulate those beliefs too crudely. Even at the famous Minnesota rally, McCain did not directly repudiate the bigotry at the core of his supporter's statement about Obama-as-Arab. He never disputed the idea that Arabs weren't to be trusted. All he said was that Obama *was not an Arab.*

If this aspect of McCain's performance received little attention, that may be due to the fact that more moderate or subtle expressions of Islamophobia had by 2008 been completely normalized, including at the highest levels of culture and scholarship. A number of intellectuals who spent the first decade of the twenty-first century denouncing the invasion of Iraq or the horrors of the Bush administration's torture program also spent those years producing work that affirmed one of the core premises of the war on terror: There was something rotten at the heart of the world's Muslim societies, and the only way to fix it was for the United States to send in the military.

Some of these intellectuals were even ahead of the curve, and they found their work launched to new prominence once September 11 made their racism politically useful. In 1993, the Harvard political scientist Samuel Huntington published an essay called "The Clash of Civilizations?"—soon expanded into a book—in the journal *Foreign Affairs.* Huntington's theory attracted much attention at the time of its publication, and interest surged again after September 11. The "clash of civilizations" theory was an attempt to map out the lineaments of the world order that was rapidly and chaotically constructing itself in the wake of the Soviet Union's collapse. The previous half century had been defined by a global conflict between two mutually incompatible political and economic systems, two visions for how the world's resources should be parceled out and how the world's governments should be structured. Now that conflict was over. The capitalists had won. Even China, the last remaining communist state of truly international heft and standing, was transitioning into something that more closely resembled state-managed capitalism. What would come next?

Huntington took as his premise a rough approximation of Francis Fukuyama's famous argument in *The End of History and the Last Man,* which was also first published in the early 1990s. With the Soviet Union and the global triumph of communism off the table for good, debates and conflicts about the best way to organize humanity's material wealth were over. The future would still involve squabbles and reforms, but it would be a capitalist future. Going forward, Huntington argued, major global conflicts would have their roots in cultural disputes, and they would take place between two or more of the world's culturally distinct "civilizations," of which there were nine (Western, Latin American, African, Buddhist, etc.). Huntington was particularly worried about conflict between a "universalist" West, of which he considered himself a partisan, and Islam.

Huntington thought the West needed to abandon its universalist aspirations in the interest of prudence, but he also thought the West needed to steel itself against Islam's mounting aggression. Even as the developed world's consumer goods and entertainments spread themselves across the globe, Islam's ideologues were plotting the downfall of Europe and the United States. "Somewhere in the Middle East," he wrote, "a half-dozen young men could well be dressed in jeans, drinking Coke, listening to rap, and, between their bows to Mecca, putting together a bomb to blow up an American airliner."[7] Thanks to their "extremely high rates of population growth," Muslims could be expected to account for "20 percent of the world's population about the turn of the century, surpassing the number of Christians some years later, and probably accounting for about 30 percent of the world's population by 2025."[8] "Some Westerners, including President Bill Clinton, have argued that the West does not have problems with Islam but only with violent Islamist extremists," Huntington wrote. "Fourteen hundred years of history demonstrate otherwise."[9] Wherever you looked around the world, "the relations between Muslims and peoples of other civilizations—Catholic, Protestant, Orthodox, Hindu, Chinese, Buddhist, Jewish—have been generally antagonistic. . . . Wherever one looks along the perimeter of Islam, Muslims have problems living peaceably with their neighbors."[10] If the West hoped to survive the twenty-first century, it would have to accept that its underlying problem was not Islamic fundamentalism but Islam itself, "a different civilization whose people are convinced of the superiority of their culture and are obsessed with the inferiority of their power."[11]

Shortly after September 11, another prominent academic, the Princeton Orientalist Bernard Lewis, published the book *What Went*

Wrong? Western Impact and Middle Eastern Response, which argued with Huntington's work in some places and elaborated on it in others. Lewis painted a picture of Islam in which a once great civilization, responsible for many of humanity's finest achievements in the fields of art, mathematics, and the natural sciences, slowly but steadily devolved into political stagnation, insularity, and violence. While he did not go so far as Huntington in portraying Islam as an existential threat to the West, Lewis agreed with Huntington that Islam was the sole author of its own difficulties. In an earlier essay, titled "The Roots of Muslim Rage," Lewis had written the following:

> There is something in the religious culture of Islam which inspired, in even the humblest peasant or peddler, a dignity and a courtesy toward others never exceeded and rarely equaled in other civilizations. And yet, in moments of upheaval and disruption, when the deeper passions are stirred, this dignity and courtesy toward others can give way to an explosive mixture of rage and hatred which impels even the government of an ancient and civilized country—even the spokesman of a great and ethical religion—to espouse kidnapping and assassination, and try to find, in the life of their Prophet, approval and indeed precedent for such actions.[12]

Like Huntington, Lewis rejected the idea that Muslim grievances had any real material or political justification. Instead, all of it was ascribed to something called "the religious culture of Islam," which had somehow maintained its basic essence even as the religion spread to almost every corner of the globe over the span of more than a thousand years. Lewis differed from Huntington, though, in his recognition that "fundamentalism is not the only Islamic tradition." The Wahhabists, ayatollahs, and suicide bombers might be capable of viewing the world only through the lens of violent struggle, but there were other strains within Islamic thought that, if they were to prevail, might allow the Muslim world to coexist more peacefully with the world's other civilizations. Crucially, though, Lewis specified in *What*

Went Wrong? that the West should not try to involve itself in what was essentially an internal struggle for Islam's future. The good Muslims (secular moderates) and the bad Muslims (radical fanatics) would have to square off on their own, and if the West knew what was good for it, every effort would be made to stay on the sidelines and hope for the best.

Lewis wrote *What Went Wrong?* before September 11—he said the book was already in page proofs on the fateful day—and afterward staying on the sidelines was out of the question. But the idea that there were "good" and "bad" Muslims, those who were able to resist the pull of the violent elements of Islam's timeless culture and those who weren't, persisted. It exerted a powerful influence in the fields of art and entertainment. American television networks and bookstores were filled with stories—many of them written by people who understood themselves to be well-meaning progressives, people who abhorred both explicit racism and the Bush administration's excesses—in which the narrative was driven entirely by the question of whether a Muslim character would turn out to be "good" or "bad." It often turned out at the end of an episode or season that the character in question was a good Muslim, a plot device intended to serve as a rebuke to Islamophobia and stereotyping, but the final plot twist could not always make up for the fact that the previous hour of television had been compelling only because viewers got to view a Muslim with suspicion. The list of shows that made use of this plot device is extensive, including, as the University of Michigan professor Evelyn Alsultany has documented, *Boston Public, The Education of Max Bickford, The Guardian, Law & Order, Law & Order: Special Victims Unit, NYPD Blue, The Practice, 7th Heaven,* and *The West Wing.*[13] On the 2005–6 Showtime drama *Sleeper Cell,* a Muslim FBI agent named Darwyn goes undercover to infiltrate an extremist group, assuring his colleagues that "these guys have nothing to do with my faith."[14]

Fiction writers made use of this tactic as well. The protagonist of Khaled Hosseini's blockbuster 2003 novel, *The Kite Runner,* is another good Muslim, an innocent boy who spends his adult life trying to atone for his failure to protect his best friend from the sexual predations of the Taliban. There's also Ahmad, the hero of John Updike's 2006 novel, *Terrorist,* a high schooler made vulnerable to the extremist teachings of an obscure New Jersey sheikh by his mother's failure to provide disciplinary structure, his school's failure to recognize his intelligence and steer him toward college, and a spiritually deadening American culture that privileges material wealth above everything else. He agrees to drive a truck bomb into the Lincoln Tunnel but abandons his plan at the last minute, returning instead to New Jersey with his newly acquired father figure, a Jewish guidance counselor. Stories like these gently pushed back against the idea that all Muslims were terrorists, but they accepted and strengthened one of the most corrosive premises of the war on terror, which is that there was something about Islam that merited a unique degree of suspicion. Updike ended *Terrorist* with Ahmad's complete exoneration: He gives up on extremism and will now have a go at muddling through a decent American life in the more conventional way. But the exoneration is preceded by three hundred pages in which the plot is driven entirely by the suspicion that a Muslim boy *is* going to be a terrorist. Even if some Muslims are innocent in these works, their writers legitimize reflexive suspicion, and that suspicion is the engine that drives everything along. Without it, there would be no story to tell.

Another popular strategy involved making the terrorist a white Muslim rather than an Arab, which allowed audiences to indulge in a kind of "non-racist" Islamophobia. In 2011, the cable network Showtime premiered a new espionage drama titled *Homeland,* starring Claire Danes as Carrie Mathison, a CIA operative with bipolar disorder, and Mandy Patinkin as Saul Berenson, the CIA's Middle East division chief and Carrie's professional mentor. *Homeland* was *24* for liberals (Obama called it his favorite show). The first season revolved around Nicholas Brody, a Marine sniper captured during the first days of the Iraq War and then held captive by an al-Qaeda commander named Abu Nazir for eight years. Brody is rescued and returned to the United States in the show's pilot, at which point Carrie becomes suspicious that he has been turned by the enemy and is now working as a terrorist secret agent. Carrie's co-workers initially dismiss her suspicions as paranoid, but there are troubling if inconclusive signs that something is wrong almost from the moment Brody returns to his home. The first time he has sex with his wife, he is sullen, withdrawn, and violent, and Carrie watches the whole thing thanks to the surveillance cameras she's had illegally installed in his home. Is he just overwhelmed by the experience and thinking about the years of marital intimacy that were stolen from him, or has he absorbed some of the misogyny that is supposed to define the extremist mindset? In the next episode, Brody wanders around alone in the woods, and then he strolls through a shopping mall with a blank look on his face. Is he reacclimating himself to normal life in America, or is he scouting a potential target? Early one morning, while his wife and children are still asleep, Brody sneaks out to the garage. It's the one place in his home that Carrie failed to bug, but *Homeland*'s viewers get to see what he's doing in there. He cracks the garage door, just enough for a beam of sunlight to get in, carefully washes his hands, and unrolls a mat on the floor. He begins to recite prayers in Arabic. Brody has converted to Islam in captivity, and nobody back home knows.[15]

In *Homeland*, Carrie's paranoia is the source of her professional genius, even as it always gets her into trouble. She watches Brody and his family on her video feed in the same way that actual people watched *Homeland*: late at night, slumped on a sofa, with Chinese takeout approaching room temperature on the coffee table and a glass of white wine in hand. The show intends its liberal viewers to experience some discomfort about Carrie's spying, but it also knows that guilt intensifies the pleasure in things that are bad for us. If *Homeland* were the anti-*24* that it claimed to be—the show's two producers both wrote for *24*—it would finally have to deny its viewers the pleasure of having their suspicions about a Muslim confirmed: Carrie would, in fact, be deranged and wrong. But all of Carrie's suspicions turn out to be justified. Brody was turned in captivity, and back in the United States he's planning an attack on the highest levels of government. As Carrie and Saul race around trying to prevent an attack, the show somewhat tediously depicts them rejecting the Bush era's brutality, thoughtlessness, and lack of cultural sensitivity. In the show's fifth episode, a CIA agent asks a Marine to assist in interrogating a terrorist operative. "One question," the Marine asks, hesitating. "Will he be tortured?" "We don't do that here," the CIA agent replies, and the Marine breathes a sigh of relief.[16] In the ninth episode, a character called Special Agent Hall arrives to help sort out the aftermath of a mosque shooting that leaves two innocent worshippers dead. Carrie and her colleagues discuss the delicate prospect of gathering information from the mosque's grieving community, but Hall, sounding like Donald Rumsfeld after three drinks, has simpler advice: "You people have rubber hoses, don't you?" When he walks into the mosque, Carrie looks down at his feet, looks up, and says, with indignation, "Would you mind taking your shoes off please?"[17] These rote avowals of religious tolerance allowed liberal viewers to just kick back and enjoy the war on terror for once, to immerse themselves in the paradoxically comforting atmosphere of paranoia and dread without having to worry about the war's less palatable aspects. In *Homeland*'s moral universe, strong opposition to torture provides cover for the very fears and myths that made torture possible. With the Bush administration's failures having discredited the neoconservative bombast that prevailed immediately after September 11, Hollywood came up with subtler ways of expressing the Islamophobia that was required to keep the war going.

In the later years of the Bush administration, a number of writers also discovered that one could launder Islamophobia by embedding it within what purported to be a larger critique of religion as such. In the three years after Abu Ghraib, four men separately published books criticizing religious belief and promoting atheism as the only path forward for the democratic West. The neuroscientist Sam Harris (*The End of Faith*, 2004), the evolutionary biologist Richard Dawkins (*The God Delusion*, 2006), the philosopher Daniel Dennett (*Breaking the Spell*, 2006), and the ex-socialist polemicist Christopher Hitchens (*God Is Not Great*, 2007) spent years promoting what became known as the New Atheism, traveling around the country, staging debates with religious writers, and telling anyone who would listen that religion was the source of many of the world's ills. It oppressed women, promoted hatred of homosexuals, countenanced political violence, exploited the poor, and repressed healthy adult sexuality while at the same time covering up the widespread sexual abuse of children. They became known, collectively, as the Four Horsemen.

None of these men were natural allies of the neoconservative or religious right. Hitchens was a former Trotskyist who thought the creation of the state of Israel had been a mistake. Dawkins identified himself as left-leaning and usually voted for Labour Party candidates in English elections. Harris was a registered Democrat who supported gay marriage and the legalization of drugs, and Daniel Dennett sought to avoid politics as much as possible.[18] They deplored the Bush administration's support of "faith-based" education, its free-market economic policy, and its reactionary views on sex. In one sense, the Bush presidency could even be seen as the prompt for the New Atheist project as a whole: Bush was perhaps the most overtly religious leader in American history, and his administration made no effort to hide the fact that it wanted religion to play a much larger material role in public life, the very thing the New Atheists opposed above all else.

On the issue of Islam, however, they often sounded like the evangelical leaders they most loved to denigrate. It wasn't giving Christianity short shrift in their critiques; even today, YouTube is filled with videos of Hitchens debating this or that Christian intellectual or theologian, armed always with his mellifluous fluency, seductive baritone, and instant recall of quotations and bons mots from literature and history. But Islam comes off worst of all in the New Atheists' books. If, in their view, religion distills and concentrates the world's most intractable problems, then it is Islam specifically that distills and concentrates the worst of religion. In *God Is Not Great,* Hitchens gave Christianity and Judaism the barest modicum of credit for undertaking reformations at different points in their history. The Catholic Church, he wrote, had (fortunately) "never recovered from its abandonment of the mystifying Latin ritual" at the Second Vatican Council in the early 1960s. The "Protestant mainstream . . . suffered hugely from rendering its own Bibles into more everyday speech." And despite the insistence of some "mystical Jewish sects" on speaking

Hebrew and playing "Kabbalistic word games" with the Torah, "the supposedly unchangeable rituals of antiquity" had been consigned to the annals of history, breaking the clergy's grip on believers' ability to understand faith for themselves. But not Islam. "Only in Islam," Hitchens wrote, "has there been no reformation."[19] Islam continued to insist on the exclusivity of its truth, the immutability of its laws, and the importance of spreading its faith around the world through violent conquest. " 'Reformation' has meant, for Jews and Christians, a minimal willingness to reconsider holy writ," Hitchens wrote. "But, at the very point when Islam ought to be joining its predecessors in subjecting itself to rereadings, there is a 'soft' consensus among almost all the religious that, because of the supposed duty of respect that we owe the faithful, this is the very time to allow Islam to assert its claims at their own face value."[20]

Even if Bush's evangelicalism provided the New Atheists with their initial spark, they only had September 11 to thank for their eventual success. Richard Dawkins's *God Delusion* begins with reference to a documentary series that aired on British television shortly before the book's publication. Dawkins, who presented the series, didn't care much for the title (*Root of All Evil?*), but he was very pleased with an ad that Channel 4 placed in the country's newspapers. "It was a picture of the Manhattan skyline with the caption 'Imagine a world without religion,' " he wrote. "What was the connection? The twin towers of the World Trade Center were conspicuously present."[21] Hitchens insisted that he'd been concerned about religion for years before the attacks, citing in particular the 1989 fatwa issued by Iran's Ayatollah Khomeini against the novelist Salman Rushdie. But he, too, described September 11 as "the critical day."[22] Sam Harris, similarly, wrote in his 2004 book, *The End of Faith*, that "Islam, more than any other religion human beings have devised, has all the makings of a thoroughgoing cult of death,"[23] and he wrote elsewhere that "while the other major world religions have been fertile sources of intolerance, it is clear that the doctrine of Islam poses unique problems for the emergence of a global civilization."[24]

Having framed their critique of Islam in these existential terms, the New Atheists went on to regurgitate many of the same stereotypes that American guards in Iraq had used to justify their abuse. Hitchens echoed one guard's conclusions about the sexual repression of Muslim men. He found it "revolting" that "the fanatics" could make it to adulthood "without ever having had a normal conversation, let alone a normal relationship, with a woman." "This," he wrote, "is disease by definition."[25] Harris trotted out the old saw about how nothing *but* religion could explain the existence of terrorism. "Anyone who imagines that terrestrial concerns account for terrorism by Muslims must explain why there are no Palestinian Christian suicide bombers," he wrote. "Islam contains specific doctrines about martyrdom and jihad that directly inspire Muslim terrorism."[26] Dawkins was more succinct, declaring that "Islam [is the] greatest force for evil today."[27] Given these views, it should not be surprising that the New Atheists swallowed their distaste for Bush's evangelicalism and made common cause with his administration. Christianity and Judaism might be mystifying and retrograde, but only Islam was a threat to the human race. Hitchens, in particular, saw the conflict in terms that he would probably be unhappy to hear described as eschatological. He felt "exhilaration" on September 11, he said, and envisioned "a war to the finish between everything I love and everything I hate."[28]

New Atheism was not intellectually rigorous. The books produced by the Four Horsemen between 2004 and 2007 are, on the whole, about as substantive as an undergraduate debate club, and they become similarly grating after a while. They assign great significance to cheap thought experiments, belabor at great length all of the most obvious paradoxes of religious belief—why yes, I *had* already considered that the Bible was not literally dictated to the prophets by God— and refuse to engage with any facts that complicate their belief that religion is the primary source of the world's ills. Toward the middle of *The God Delusion*, Dawkins announces that he's going to deal with the "calumny" that says that the men behind the two worst atrocities of the twentieth century, Adolf Hitler and Joseph Stalin, "were both avowed atheists,"[29] and Hitchens also devotes a passage to the era's great totalitarian rulers in the later pages of *God Is Not Great*. Unfortunately for them, the "calumny" is more or less correct. Stalin was an atheist in the absolute sense endorsed by Hitchens and the others, and while Hitler's case is more complicated, there is little doubt that the führer thought the most important truths were to be found not in a church but in the "natural science" of racial biology.

These weaknesses didn't matter to the books' millions of readers, however, because the New Atheists succeeded at doing something more important: They made life easier for people who supported the war on terror but cringed at having to associate themselves with the proud ignorance of the Bush administration. That gang of down-home Bible-thumpers might have chosen war through a combination of lying, hubris, and under-processed anger, but the New Atheists were men who'd clearly taken their educations seriously and who constantly peppered their antireligious broadsides with references to the glories of Western high culture (that Dawkins and Hitchens both oozed Oxbridge with every utterance cannot but have helped them with their American audiences). Theirs was an Islamophobia varnished with an appreciation for the arts, an avowed faith in the objectivity of science, and an insistence that their concerns lay with the defense of the historical legacy of the Enlightenment, rather than anything so petty as control of oil reserves or a narrowly defined national interest.

• • •

This was the atmosphere Obama confronted when he decided to run for president. More than five years after launching a series of wars that depended on racism to maintain popular support, the country found that it was losing those wars, and the possibility of defeat was only intensifying the racism. This racism was being expressed and amplified on every level of society, from conspiracy theorists with clumsily designed websites, popular entertainment, and law enforcement, all the way up to the highest echelons of academia and journalism. To run for office as a nonwhite candidate has been a dicey proposition in all periods of American history, but to run for the country's *highest* office amid a fundamentally racist war and a drastic increase in public expressions of bigotry is trickier still. If he wanted to win, Obama would have to appeal to an electorate that was reflexively suspicious of someone with his name and skin color. If he wanted to successfully govern, he would need to deal with a cultural climate that would keep hostility toward his administration at a fever pitch. Together, these two imperatives comprised the fundamental task of his political life.

So what was Obama's plan? In the first volume of his presidential memoir, *A Promised Land,* Obama recalls winning the South Carolina Democratic primary election in January 2008. The young Illinois senator had beaten Hillary Clinton in Iowa, lost to her in New Hampshire, and fought to an effective draw in Nevada, losing the popular vote but winning a majority of the state's Electoral College delegates. South Carolina was the first primary to be contested in the South, as well as the first in a Black-majority state, and pundits believed both factors would play to Clinton's strengths, given her husband's Arkansas roots and Black voters' long-standing loyalty to him. A debate between the two candidates a week before the election was acrimonious; Clinton accused Obama of failing to take responsibility for his votes in the Illinois legislature, and Obama called Clinton "a corporate lawyer sitting on the board of Wal-Mart." On election day, Obama won big-time, drawing twice as many votes as his rival, and the victory unlocked a string of major endorsements that confirmed the national viability of his campaign and eventually powered him to the White House. Speaking to supporters in a Columbia auditorium once the results came in, Obama "could feel the pulse of stomping feet and clapping hands." He squinted through the glare of the television lights and saw "college students mostly, white and Black in equal measure, some of them with their arms interlocked or draped over one another's shoulders, their faces beaming with joy and purpose." They were looking up at their candidate and repeating a chant that one could not possibly imagine coming out of the mouths of young progressives a decade later: "Race doesn't matter! Race doesn't matter! Race doesn't matter!"

Obama resisted the urge to correct his supporters, "to remind them that in the year 2008, with the Confederate flag and all it stood for still hanging in front of a state capitol just a few blocks away, race still mattered plenty, as much as they might want to believe otherwise."[30] But those college students had done nothing more than follow his lead. The Obama campaign was founded on a simple theory: If a half-Black, half-white Hawaiian, a man with a Kenyan father and an Arabic middle name, a man who'd spent some of his childhood years living in the most populous majority-Muslim country in the world, could become the president of the United States, it would prove that America wasn't fundamentally racist after all, that the country's history of genocide, enslavement, and Jim Crow hadn't sprung from some immutable part of the national identity. Obama articulated this theory again and again, starting with the most famous line from the 2004 Democratic National Convention address that first launched him to national prominence: "There is not a black America and white America and Latino America and Asian America—there's the United States of America."

The theory drew power from the fact that Obama was personally invested in proving it correct; it wasn't just something he liked to say to win votes. He wanted to discover and then cultivate "a politics that bridged America's racial, ethnic, and religious divides, as well as the many strands of my own life."[31] Obama understood himself to be "running against the implacable weight of the past; the inertia, fatalism, and fear it produced." That is a fancy way of saying that he was running against history itself. By embodying and manifesting the racial reconciliation for which his supporters longed, by challenging "America's reigning political assumptions about how divided we were," Obama thought he could establish a durable majority, "a new covenant between its citizens."[32]

The Obama campaign also organized itself around the counterintuitive belief that in order to found this new covenant, it was important to avoid addressing racism too explicitly. As a young community organizer in 1980s Chicago, Obama had watched Harold Washington, the city's first Black mayor, take a more confrontational approach, to which the white-dominated city council responded by blocking all of his proposed reforms. Washington spent the entirety of his first term trying to get a federal court to invalidate the city's racially gerrymandered political map, and though he finally succeeded and won reelection, he died of a heart attack seven months later. This taught Obama that "a political campaign based on racial redress, no matter how reasonable, generated fear and backlash and ultimately placed limits on progress."[33] As a brand-new senator in 2005, Obama went on television shortly after Hurricane Katrina made landfall in majority-Black New Orleans and insisted that racism had played no part in the Bush administration's incompetent response. "The incompetence was color-blind," he said.[34] When right-wing shock jocks such as Rush Limbaugh went on the air and called him "Osama Obama," he thought it better to shrug and "let them have their fun" rather than send even more media attention their way by responding.[35] He told voters that inner-city poverty was just as much a problem of indifferent parenting as it was of intentional government neglect, he sympathized with white people who thought affirmative action was unfair, and he was even willing to admit to racist views of his own. "If I'm honest with myself," he wrote in his campaign book *The Audacity of Hope*, "I must admit that I'm not entirely immune to . . . nativist sentiments. When I see Mexican flags waved at proimmigration demonstrations, I sometimes feel a flush of patriotic resentment. When I'm forced to use a translator to communicate with the guy fixing my car, I feel a certain frustration."[36] Obama's campaign advisers "made no apologies for de-emphasizing any topic that might be labeled a racial grievance, or split the electorate along racial lines," Obama wrote. "To them, the immediate formula for racial progress was simple—we needed to win."[37]

They did. In early 2009, as Obama took the oath of office while a crowd of nearly two million people stretched down the Washington Mall, his theory seemed pretty well vindicated. Eight years later, as Obama ceded the presidency to a man who'd first come to political prominence by promoting conspiracy theories about whether Obama was a natural-born citizen, it would lie in tatters. Obama was wrong about the centrality of racism to American political life. With respect to domestic policy, he was wrong in believing that Republicans would accept the legitimacy of his presidency or cooperate even a little with the implementation of his agenda (e.g., health-care and immigration reform) in exchange for policy concessions, no matter how generous. And with respect to foreign policy, he was wrong in thinking that his administration could continue to fight the war on terror without exacerbating the very racism that made implementing his domestic agenda so difficult. Obama's misreading of the situation on these two fronts, his belief that America's racism could be ignored or evaded rather than confronted, would turn out to be the central tragedy of his presidency. As a result of his misapprehension, almost all of the problems Obama vowed to ameliorate as president had only further intensified by the time he left office.

The first year of Obama's presidency was frantic. The inauguration had been a cathartic celebration of his triumphant campaign against the "implacable weight" of American history, but with millions out of work and the financial engine of the economy still making all kinds of ominous noises, there would be no time to bask in the afterglow. He signed a clutch of executive orders immediately after taking office, which he hoped would signal the shape of the broader policy reset his administration was preparing. He banned torture, announced that the detention center at Guantánamo Bay would be closed within a year, prohibited corporate lobbyists from taking jobs in the federal government, and established various White House offices, councils, and advisory boards dealing with urban affairs, women, and the economy. He nominated Sonia Sotomayor to serve as the first Hispanic woman on the Supreme Court, and he proposed a health-care reform law that would provide tens of millions of Americans with insurance. He also assembled an economic policy team that would spend months scrambling to prevent the global financial crisis from destroying the economy. The corporate bailouts his team designed were broadly unpopular, however, and combined with the administration's lack of meaningful assistance to the millions of Americans who lost their homes to foreclosure, they burned through a substantial amount of Obama's political capital. Two years later, the bailouts would give rise to the Occupy protest movement.

Of course, Obama had also run as an antiwar candidate, constantly bludgeoning Clinton and then McCain with their prior support for the invasion of Iraq (Obama had opposed it, and said so in a speech at a Chicago antiwar rally in 2002). Deciding exactly how to wind down the wars in Iraq and Afghanistan would take a while, with the Pentagon's planners needing months to puzzle out which troops could come home, and from where, and when, before any concrete de-escalation could take place. But there was an aspect of the war on which Obama felt he could act quickly. He'd been troubled by surveys indicating that a majority of the world's Muslims thought the United States was hostile to their religion "and that our Middle East policy was based not on an interest in improving people's lives but rather on maintaining oil supplies, killing terrorists, and protecting Israel." The administration decided that Obama would give a speech addressing the Muslim world at Cairo University in Egypt, and that its title would be "A New Beginning." As with his approach to domestic race relations during the campaign, Obama wanted to show the people of the Middle East that even as the United States waged two wars in Muslim-majority countries, Americans and Arab Muslims already shared significant common ground. "I told Ben," Obama wrote, referring to his speechwriter Ben Rhodes, "that the focus of our speech had to be less about outlining new policies and more geared toward helping the two sides understand each other." That meant praising the Muslim world's contributions to civilization in the fields of math, science, and art; acknowledging that the United States had coddled regional autocrats and helped to overthrow the Iranian prime minister Mohammad Mossadegh in 1953; and recognizing the burdens shouldered by Palestinians living under Israeli occupation. Obama believed that the Middle East's low expectations for American leadership would serve him well. "Hearing such basic history from the mouth of a U.S. president," he later wrote, "would catch many people off guard, I figured, and perhaps open their minds to other hard truths."[38] These truths included that terrorism was incompatible with modern progress, that Muslim leaders often fomented anti-American outrage so as to distract people from their

own failings, that Palestine would never liberate itself through violence, and that sexism was wrong. He delivered the address on June 4,
2009. It pointedly did not include the words "terror" or "terrorism."

In Europe and the United States, reactions were overwhelmingly
positive. The Republican House minority leader, John Boehner, said
that Obama should have gone easier on Israel and harder on Iran, but
he said that kind of thing all the time, and elsewhere in the American
press the speech was viewed as a bold diplomatic gambit that had the
potential to shift the region's politics. Sweden liked the speech so
much that it gave Obama the Nobel Peace Prize four months later.
Opinion in the Middle East, however, was more divided. Many commentators in the Arab press praised the speech and expressed the
hope that it would lead to concrete policy, and centrists in Israel and
Pakistan were pleased, but for officials who took a harder line, it left
much to be desired. Some of the region's problems, it seemed, would
require a more targeted approach than the new president's bromides
about finding common ground. For all Obama's rhetoric about the
importance of confronting "hard truths," he had skirted many of the
thorniest issues. In the section on democracy, Obama said he would
support all people who yearned for "the ability to speak your mind
and have a say in how you are governed; confidence in the rule of law
and the equal administration of justice; government that is transparent and doesn't steal from the people; the freedom to live as you
choose," and he also talked about "the struggle for women's equality"
throughout the world. But his speech had been preceded by friendly
visits with Saudi Arabia's King Abdullah and Egypt's president, Hosni
Mubarak, two of the world's most authoritarian heads of state. He
voiced support for a two-state solution to the Israel-Palestine conflict,
but he called on only one of those groups (the Palestinians) to "abandon violence." "Resistance through violence and killing is wrong and
it does not succeed. . . . For centuries, black people in America suffered the lash of the whip as slaves and the humiliation of segregation.
But it was not violence that won full and equal rights," he said. He insisted that America was at war with extremism, not Islam, and pointed
out that most of the victims of terrorist attacks were themselves Mus-

lim, but he did not grapple at all with the fact that the United States had killed many more Muslims over the prior eight years than the world's terrorist groups had.

As Obama rolled out his more concrete changes to how the war on terror would be fought under its second chief executive, it became clear that his war policy was based on a similar hypothesis as his candidacy. If America wasn't racist in some fundamental way, if racism only distracted people from the more urgent tasks of solving social problems, then what the country's domestic policy needed was a president who could serve as a living symbol of post-racial utopia and inspire people to set aside their prejudices and work for the greater good. And if racism was similarly ancillary to the war on terror, then what the world needed was an American head of state who could use military force to keep extremists in check without the abuses, renditions, and rhetorical excesses that stoked the fires of Islamophobia and racism in the affluent West. Obama thought of himself as someone who was good in a crisis, someone whose role in any delicate or tense political situation was almost always to lower the temperature in the room. In terms of war, lowering the temperature meant getting people to pay attention to something else. Where Bush's war speeches had called up images of cowboys meting out summary justice as they raced across the plains, Obama's war would be sedate and carefully managed. If things really went well, it might even be dull.

So: Torture was banned. Interrogations in real life would no longer resemble their violent, carnivalesque counterparts on prime-time television dramas. Instead, they would be unglamorous but effective exercises in patience, cunning, and ordinary human psychology. Guantánamo would be closed, and the people detained there would be released into anonymity, transferred to other countries far beyond the scope of America's daily consciousness, or tried in court like ordinary criminals. Most American soldiers would leave Iraq and return the country to its people, who would then be solely responsible for their own successes and struggles. Drones would replace troops wherever possible. Keeping American soldiers miles away from the battlefield would adjust the drumbeat of U.S. casualty reports to a distant, barely audible level. So determined was Obama to fix the war's image problem that he even gave it a new name. "War on terror" might sound like something out of *The Lord of the Rings,* but about two months after taking office, the Obama administration announced that the war would henceforth go under the dazzlingly boring title "Overseas Contingency Operations," which sounded like a phrase shipping companies might use in discussing potential solutions to supply chain issues. It did not catch on.

In many respects, these reforms carefully skirted issues that went more to the heart of the war's conduct. Although the administration withdrew all of John Yoo's legal memos regarding the interrogation of terrorist suspects and detainees, it left Yoo's memos regarding the broader use of military force against non-state actors, which provided the legally dubious but crucial justification for the war as a whole, in place. But the reforms had, at least for a while, their intended cooling effect on public discourse. Three days after his inauguration, *The Washington Post* published a dramatic headline: "Bush's 'War' on Terror Comes to a Sudden End." "With the stroke of a pen," the article said, "[President Barack Obama] effectively declared an end to the 'war on terror,' as President George W. Bush had defined it." In the very next paragraph, however, was this: "Obama says he has no plans to diminish counterterrorism operations abroad."[39]

Indeed, although he did carry out the promised troop drawdown in Iraq, Obama expanded those operations, occasionally on a breathtaking scale. With little to no official fanfare, drones, which under Bush had served to complement the military's troop deployments, became in many respects the country's primary instrument of war. Obama had been critical of the CIA's secrecy, brutality, and bad-faith legalese during the campaign, and among the first executive orders he signed were instructions to close all of the agency's overseas prisons and prohibitions against extraordinary rendition. But Obama simultaneously pushed for an aggressive expansion of the CIA drone program. Just three days after the inauguration, on January 23, 2009, a Predator drone launched a Hellfire missile at a compound in a remote area of Pakistan, killing nearly twenty people. The compound was thought to be inhabited by Taliban fighters, but the Obama administration didn't actually require the CIA to be sure. Obama's drone program leaned hard on a tactic known as the "signature strike," in which the CIA was authorized to fire at groups of suspected militants without having to make a positive identification.[40] Similarly, the administration decided that all "military-age males" killed by drones would be categorized as enemy combatants. That categorization could be changed if evidence emerged that a particular drone strike had killed civilians, but since many strikes took place in Taliban- or al-Qaeda-controlled areas near the mountainous Afghanistan-Pakistan border, such evidence was often impossible for journalists or human rights organizations to gather. By the end of Obama's first year in office, the CIA had carried out dozens of strikes in Pakistan alone, killing as many as 210 civilians in the process.[41]

Pakistan was a logical place for Obama to begin the expansion of his drone war. Many Taliban and al-Qaeda fighters had fled across the Afghan border into Pakistan's relatively ungoverned northwest region following the American invasion in 2001, and they had long since used the area's mountains and caves to regroup, train, and deploy fighters back to Afghanistan to rejoin the conflict. Declaring war on Pakistan was out of the question. The Pakistani government was officially an American ally in the war on terror, even though the ISI, the country's powerful intelligence agency, was known to be arming and providing sanctuary to extremist groups. But the administration's lawyers decided that drone strikes, which could be carried out in secret under the auspices of the CIA, didn't require a declaration of war, and Obama would not publicly acknowledge his own drone wars until after he won reelection in 2012. By then, drones had been deployed in many other countries, including Somalia, Yemen, and especially Afghanistan, which became the most droned place on earth during Obama's two terms.

Afghanistan became the center of Obama's longer-term military project. Like many of the voters who had elected him, Obama saw the global war he'd inherited as divided in two. First there was Iraq, the bad war. That war never should have happened at all, and Obama wanted to end it as quickly as his methodical, process-oriented management style would allow. Then there was Afghanistan, the good war, the one that correctly targeted the people who'd attacked the United States. President Bush had bungled his attempt to turn Afghanistan into a democratic state with his political clumsiness and inadequate troop deployments, but Obama believed that America's strategic goals were still salvageable, and so in 2009 he began to ramp up the troop levels. On the day of Obama's inauguration, the United States had fewer than 40,000 troops in the country. By 2011, that number had gone up to nearly 100,000, an increase paired with a command-level reshuffle that brought in Lieutenant General Stanley McChrystal, then the director of the Joint Chiefs, to replace General David McKiernan as the war's commanding officer.[42] The change was something of a gamble—no top general had been relieved from duty in the middle of a war for half a century—but the decision was well received by the media. McChrystal had assiduously cultivated a compelling warrior-monk persona, presenting himself as the kind of man who spent his predawn hours on strenuous runs and his evenings reading from his vast library of military theory and history. McChrystal was an advocate of a military doctrine called counterinsurgency, or COIN, which posited that when one conducted offensive operations in a failed state, it wasn't enough just to destroy the enemy. American troops would need to live among the Afghan people as well, potentially for a long time, and painstakingly build up the country's ability to govern itself. As one magazine profile of McChrystal put it, "The theory essentially rebrands the military, expanding its authority (and its funding) to encompass the diplomatic and political sides of warfare: Think the Green Berets as an armed Peace Corps."[43]

Though the raw numbers of the troop increase received lots of media attention, the shift in the Army's goals with respect to Afghanistan took place with almost as little fanfare as the expansion of the drone war. With almost no public discussion, Obama's new commanding officer had made the military project in Afghanistan almost as ambitious as the one Bush had disastrously undertaken in Iraq. This decision was a grave mistake. As the military historian Andrew

Bacevich notes in his book *America's War for the Greater Middle East,* the U.S. war in Afghanistan had already been lost by the time Obama took office. After toppling the Taliban government in Kabul, the Bush administration had decided to keep troop levels low in Afghanistan, averaging out to just eighteen thousand per year.[44] These skeleton crews were supposed to "chase down al-Qaeda remnants" and anyone else referring to themselves as "Taliban," while a horde of NGOs and "twenty-six U.N. agencies" established offices in Kabul and went about trying to build a new Afghan state. But despite some improvements that looked good on television, such as formal elections and a draft constitution, "substantive improvements lagged," and the only thing that really developed in Afghanistan through the end of 2008 was the country's opium sector, which came to account for 90 percent of global production. "The disparity between what the occupiers promised and what they delivered," Bacevich writes, "created an opening for the Taliban and al-Qaeda to make a comeback."[45]

The military brass wanted troop levels boosted in Afghanistan to counter a Taliban offensive they expected to come in the summer of 2009, and even with the extra troops many within the Pentagon believed that "the war could not be won militarily."[46] They knew full well that the war required a political solution, in the form of a state structure and ruling class that could both defend itself and win the allegiance of the Afghan people. Bringing that state into being wasn't the U.S. military's job, though; their task was just to hunker down, pick off insurgents, and wait for Afghanistan's saviors to materialize. The biggest problem with this remit was the last part. Who were the saviors going to be? Where would they come from? Nobody knew, nor did anyone have good reason to expect they would *ever* arrive. The likeliest outcome was always that the Taliban would bide their time and then seize power whenever the Americans decided they were tired of spending money and losing troops in a faraway country of low to moderate strategic importance, which is exactly what happened in 2021. Although Obama sold the Afghanistan surge with a much greater show of thoughtfulness and deliberation than Bush could muster before the invasion of Iraq, his plan was just as strategically incoherent as his predecessor's. The most prudent course would have been to accept defeat, withdraw all American troops, treat the reestablishment of the Taliban's seat of power in Kabul as largely irrelevant to America's interests, and focus exclusively on tracking down Osama bin Laden. Instead, Obama allowed the Afghanistan war to become the longest in American history.

Finally, Obama oversaw a secret government surveillance apparatus that reached deep into the private lives of Americans, targeting not just those suspected of terrorism but hundreds of millions of innocent civilians. Though not in office when these systems were built, he made a conscious choice to allow them to continue operations without any public scrutiny. It was not until almost five years into Obama's presidency that Edward Snowden, a former contractor for the National Security Agency, revealed that the NSA had constructed a bulk surveillance program that was monitoring the phone calls and emails of millions of Americans, not to mention those of millions more around the globe (the Snowden leaks would push German-American relations, for example, to their lowest point since before the Iraq War). The scale of the NSA's surveillance operation, code-named STELLAR-WIND, was incredible, in some respects too large for an individual to comprehend. No government in human history had ever gathered so much information about so many of its citizens.

Obama's reaction to the Snowden revelations deserves some discussion in its own right, as an example of how his confidence in his own procedural and managerial acumen could cloud his judgment. It was easily the biggest political scandal of Obama's presidency. On the campaign trail in 2008, Obama had promised that his would be the most transparent government in history. Now it seemed that his government had done something like the opposite, making the private lives of hundreds of millions of Americans transparent to the government instead. His initial responses to the publication of Snowden's leaked files were angry and paternalistic. Ever process oriented, he said that Snowden should have gone through the government's formal system for whistleblowers rather than taking his objections to

NSA policy to the press, neglecting the fact that had Snowden gone through the formal system, he would have been entrusting his revelations to an agency whose primary purpose was not to inform the public but to protect the secrecy of classified NSA data. He said the American people would have been better off had they never learned about the NSA's surveillance programs. He said that his administration had conducted a review of the government's intelligence practices "before Mr. Snowden made these leaks," though he provided no details on what the review had scrutinized, nor what its findings were, nor what changes were implemented as a result. He disputed Snowden's description of himself as a patriot. He defended the agency's bulk collection of telephone data, pointing out that the NSA did not actually record the calls. The surveillance, he said, only "provides a record of phone numbers and the times and lengths of calls," as though Americans should not worry themselves at all about the government knowing the time and date on which almost every phone call in the country had been made, as well as the number to which the call had been placed.[47] "My preference, and I think the American people's preference, would have been for a lawful, *orderly*, examination of these laws," he said at a press conference, the tone of his voice communicating the effort involved in not exploding too angrily at a group of people who just couldn't understand that he knew better than they did.[48] In a speech delivered seven months after Snowden's disclosures, he declined to address Snowden's allegations about military intelligence officers regularly circulating people's sex photos around the office, claiming instead that "the men and women of the intelligence community, including the NSA, consistently follow protocols designed to protect the privacy of ordinary people." He also resorted to what is perhaps his favorite rhetorical technique, claiming that despite a full year's worth of anger and controversy, Americans didn't actually disagree with the country's surveillance practices as much as they thought they did. "The basic values of most Americans when it comes to questions of surveillance and privacy," he said, "converge a lot more than the crude characterizations that have emerged over the last several months."[49] As with racism during the campaign, Obama hoped to resolve the debate around surveillance by convincing people that there wasn't much of a debate to have in the first place.

• • •

By institutionalizing and in some ways expanding the war he had promised to end while campaigning, Obama helped to fuel the racist anger of a right wing whose sole political aspiration during his presidency was to delegitimize him as a leader. The right understood better than Obama's Democratic Party the fundamental truths that wars are sustained by rage and that rage seeks an object. In the war on terror, that object was Muslims.

By trying to rebrand the war rather than taking the political risk of tearing it out by the roots, Obama provided those on the right with all the space and energy they needed to organize, spread, and amplify their ideas. Whenever Obama spoke about an attack perpetrated by "violent extremists," Republicans flocked to cable news to wonder why it was so hard for the president to call the enemy by its real name, "Islamic terrorism." When he decided that detainees could no longer be waterboarded, beaten, or threatened with electrical wires, when he said of such practices, "That's not who we are," conservatives accused him of failing to understand who the *enemy* was instead. If terrorists remained enough of a threat to justify carrying a global war into its second decade, as Obama clearly believed, why force your own soldiers into battle with one of their hands tied behind their backs? The terrorists certainly weren't going to consult the text of the Geneva Conventions before they decided what to do with any Americans they captured. And when Obama announced that Khalid Sheikh Mohammed and four others who planned September 11 would be transferred out of Guantánamo Bay and tried in a New York federal court, conservatives *and* moderates went ballistic. New York City officials, including Michael Bloomberg, objected on the grounds of disruption and security costs. "It would be great if the federal government could find a site that didn't cost a billion dollars," Bloomberg said. "It's going to cost an awful lot of money and disturb an awful lot of people."[50] For conservatives, the objection was more visceral: KSM was an enemy, not a criminal. The government had sent Special Forces soldiers and intelligence officers to capture him, not a squad car from the First Precinct. To try a monster like Mohammed in the same civilian court that meted out punishment to bankers who made a few million from insider trading was to misunderstand, once again, the nature of the threat. As Dick Cheney said in a CNN interview a few months after Obama's inauguration, "When you go back to the law enforcement mode, which I sense is what they're doing, closing Guantánamo and so forth . . . they are very much giving up that center of attention and focus that's required, that concept of military threat that is essential if you're going to successfully defend the nation against further attacks."[51] Obama's election threw the Republican Party into chaos in many respects; the radical Tea Party movement would spend years wreaking havoc on moderate Republican incumbents in primary campaigns. On the issue of terrorism and Obama's insufficient willingness to fight it, however, conservative messaging was impressively disciplined.

The right's biggest victory during Obama's first term also took place in lower Manhattan, though it had nothing to do with KSM. In December 2009, *The New York Times* broke the news that two Muslim men—one an imam, the other a real estate developer—were going to build a fifteen-story Islamic cultural center in the Financial District, two blocks north of the site of the World Trade Center. Located at 45-51 Park Place, the center would be called Cordoba House, and in addition to a prayer space that could fit more than a thousand worshippers, it would include a lavish array of other community amenities: theater, gym, child-care room, swimming pool, basketball court, art studio, food court, and bookstore, plus a September 11 memorial. The Burlington Coat Factory that stood on the site had been abandoned since September 11, and Muslims were already using the derelict building as a place of worship on Fridays. Imam Feisal Abdul Rauf envisioned a neighborhood and community revival. It would send "the opposite statement to what happened on 9/11," he said. "We want to push back against the extremists." (Feisal had previously assisted the FBI in its counterterrorism efforts.) Though the *Times* noted the possibility of a backlash thanks to the project's proximity to Ground Zero, success seemed to be possible and even likely. Imam Feisal had the support of the city government; a mayoral spokesperson said, "The building owners have a right to do what they want." Feisal's wife was on an advisory team for the National September 11 Memorial and Museum. A prominent Upper East Side rabbi supported the project, as did the mother of one of the men killed on Flight 93. She called it "a noble effort."[52]

Cordoba House never stood a chance. Within weeks, most Americans who knew about the project knew it by the name that had been foisted on it by a group of right-wing activists led by Pamela Geller. She'd worked in newspaper publishing and advertising during the 1980s and 1990s, but September 11 radicalized her, and in 2004 she started a blog called *Atlas Shrugs*. "There's no gray area with me," she once told a reporter from *NY Jewish Week* before storming out of the interview yelling, "Shame on you!"[53] Her post-9/11 career was dedicated to stopping what she called the "Islamic takeover" of America, and she had a knack for going viral on the pre-social-media internet. "Here I am in my chador, my burka," she said in one of her videos, wearing a bikini while bobbing around in the ocean. "There is a serious reality check desperately needed here in America and I'm here to give it to you." The blog won enough fans to make Geller a bête noire on the margins of the Bush-era conservative movement, but Obama's election and the Cordoba House announcement turned her into a national star. She founded another website, this one called "Stop Islamization of America," and became the country's leading voice against what she insisted on calling the "Ground Zero Mosque." She bought ads on the sides of New York City buses. They juxtaposed a picture of the September 11 attacks with a picture of a mosque, with the question "Why here?" between the two. When "Ground Zero Mosque" wasn't sufficient, she called it the "Ground Zero Mega Mosque." Her campaign won the full-throated support of Liz Cheney, daughter of the former vice president and future Wyoming congressional representative, as well as former Speaker of the House Newt Gingrich, who said that building Cordoba House in its planned location would be akin to putting Nazi signs outside the Holocaust Museum in Washington, D.C. (Geller, in search of a cynical metaphor to call her own, said it was like building a Ku Klux Klan shrine next to a Black church in Alabama.)[54] Obama spoke out in support of the project at an iftar dinner the White House hosted in August 2010. "This is America," he said, using his under-control-but-furious-father voice again. "Our commitment to religious freedom must be unshakable. . . . The writ of the founders must endure."[55] Substantive action did not follow from this portentous rhetoric, however. So, with about 70 percent of Americans opposed to the project, and with congressional Democrats, including some from New York, breaking party ranks to oppose it as well, Cordoba House was allowed to die. Imam Feisal was removed from the project, and his real estate developer partner built some luxury condominiums instead.

That the right wing was able to mobilize so *quickly*, and with such force, around its racist opposition to Cordoba House, and that such a huge majority of Americans agreed with them that the construction of a mosque and community center would in some way dishonor the memories of the victims of September 11, should have sent a clear and ominous signal to the Obama administration that its attempt to move past racism by ignoring it was failing. Sidestepping difficult issues and always seeking to "lower the temperature" may work well during election season, when voters are looking for a candidate onto whom they can project their rosiest fantasies about the country's character and potential. It works even better if your candidate is perhaps the greatest political orator of his generation. But it didn't work once Obama assumed office and began the work of governing, and based on the evidence of *A Promised Land*, Obama did not spend much time wrestling with the reasons why. He was well aware that the simple fact of "a Black man in the White House" had "spooked" "millions of Americans," and there wasn't much he could do about that.[56] But his memoir contains no reflections on how maintaining and even expanding a war powered by the country's long-standing fears of nonwhite barbarians threatening the homeland might have fueled the racism that became the organizing principle of political efforts to destroy his presidency. Obama spent less than a full page writing about Cordoba House, and the majority of his brief discussion of the episode is devoted to his arguing with Chief of Staff Rahm Emanuel about whether to speak out at the upcoming iftar dinner. Rahm tells the president to avoid the subject; if he says anything, it will just give conservatives even more ammunition to use during the upcoming midterm elections. "I'm sure you're right," Obama said, "but if we can't speak out on something this basic, then I don't know what the point is of us being here."[57] And that's where Obama the memoirist leaves things, with an image of Obama the president determined to give a principled speech even if it costs him politically. He doesn't tell his readers what he did to support Cordoba House after the speech—nothing—nor does he note that the project was never built. Instead, the next paragraph begins with Obama discussing how much he likes his family's vacations on Martha's Vineyard.

• • •

Obama would get a big win of his own the following spring, although the victory would turn out to be a Pyrrhic one. On the evening of May 1, 2011, news organizations suddenly reported that the president would soon be making a televised announcement. This was unusual. It was after 10:00 p.m., and White House staff would say nothing about the content of Obama's hastily arranged national address other than that it was a big deal and had to do with foreign policy. More than an hour passed in speculation. Some thought the announcement might have to do with Libya, against which Obama had launched air strikes nearly two months prior. But as reporters worked their contacts on Capitol Hill, it became clear that the announcement concerned something even more consequential.

At 11:35 p.m., Obama walked up to a lectern stationed in the East Room of the White House. "Good evening," he began. "Tonight, I can report to the American people and to the world that the United States has conducted an operation that killed Osama bin Laden, the leader of al-Qaeda, and a terrorist who's responsible for the murder of thousands of innocent men, women, and children." He went on to offer a brief and almost sunny history of the wars America had launched in response. "The American people," he said, "came together" on September 11. "On that day, no matter where we came from, what God we prayed to, or what race or ethnicity we were, we were united as one American family." This was dishonest, but what else was he going to say? "We went to war against al-Qaeda," Obama said, and "thanks to the tireless and heroic work of our military and counterterrorism professionals . . . we've disrupted terrorist attacks and strengthened our homeland defense. . . . Around the globe, we worked with our friends and allies to capture or kill scores of al-Qaeda terrorists." Earlier that day, Obama said, a "small team of Americans"—meaning a group of Navy SEALs—had "launched a targeted operation" against "a compound deep inside of Pakistan," in the suburbs of a city called Abbottabad. They'd breached the compound, killed bin Laden, and taken his body. "Let us think back to the sense of unity that prevailed on 9/11," he said, returning to his earlier theme. "I know that it has, at times, frayed. Yet today's achievement is a testament to the greatness of our country and the determination of the American people." The speech lasted for just under ten minutes.[58]

I watched this address on television from my apartment in Brooklyn, New York, along with Rachel, my good friend and roommate. I was twenty-four years old. Flipping over to the city's local news station after the speech, we learned that people were gathering at Ground Zero. "I kind of want to go," she said. For a few minutes, I kept scrolling around on my computer in silence, and then I realized I wanted to go as well. We found a taxi. As we rode over the Brooklyn Bridge and looked at the city, I received a text message from my mother: "Such thrilling news, but sobering, too, as counterattacks are anticipated. Hope you'll be extra vigilant and try to avoid iconic locations in NY during the next few days (e.g., Times Square, etc.)." I cannot remember whether I replied; I was pretty confident that the members of New York City's Islamist sleeper cells needed more than a day or two to organize a suicide attack. As our cab pulled up in the Financial District and let us out, the driver said, "There's supposed to be retaliation attacks." He'd apparently been following the same news coverage as my mother. A few blocks away, we found the crowd, milling around on a street adjacent to the Ground Zero construction site. We could see the unfinished Freedom Tower beginning to rise out of the ground. The cranes surrounding the tower were illuminated from below by klieg lights, and camera flashes sparkled all around us for the duration of our stay. Television reporters huddled in little groups to share intelligence on who might be worth talking to, then dispersed in search of their next interview. One of them, from CNN, stood a few feet to my right, a big camera on his shoulder, and complained to his co-worker, "I'm trying to get on Twitter, but it's hard because I'm holding this camera." Later, I heard him say, "Okay, I'm on." The crowd was young. They seemed uncertain as to what a crowd like this was supposed to do, which makes sense to me in retrospect; it was the first time in their lives that Americans had assembled to celebrate, rather than protest, a foreign policy development. They compensated for their inexperience by borrowing gestures and attitudes from the kind of crowd with which they were more familiar: fans at sporting events. I watched two men who probably weren't out of college shimmy up a telephone pole. Clutching the sign for Church Street with one hand each, they held up and waved an American flag between them, to cheering. Then they displayed a cardboard sign that read, OBAMA—1, OSAMA—0, to more cheering. Then, to loud, extended cheering, they popped open two bottles of champagne and sprayed the people below them.

Three young women down on street level were unhappy with the attention being paid to the street sign boys. "Why aren't we looking at the monument?" one of them said, referring to the Freedom Tower. "Why are we looking at two douchebags waving flags around? I just feel like it's not respectful." Every so often, someone struck up the national anthem, and people sang along. The second or third time through, Rachel said it would be great if people could sing "Battle Hymn of the Republic" instead, though of course nobody knows the words. I agreed. The melody *is* much more exciting, even if the lyrics do focus a bit too much on Jesus Christ and war. A little before 1:00 a.m., Rachel and I left, looking for someplace to have a beer. I noticed my footsteps falling in rhythm to the "Battle Hymn" playing inside my head—*mine eyes have seen the glory of the something dum-dee-dum.* By the time we got to the bar, I was in a bad mood.

Bin Laden's death should have ended the war on terror. Despite the Bush administration's megalomaniacal stupidity, and despite the willful moral blindness of Obama's drone campaign, ten years of bombing and special ops raids had, in fact, beaten the group that had carried out September 11. Al-Qaeda no longer posed a serious threat to large numbers of Americans, and the threat it still did pose was not remotely sufficient to justify dragging the war into its second decade. Even before Rachel and I hailed our taxi to Manhattan, however, I knew the war would not be ending, because Obama had said the following in his speech: "His death does not mark the end of our effort. There's no doubt that al-Qaeda will continue to pursue attacks against us. We must—and we will—remain vigilant at home and abroad." Having accomplished the war's only goal that was both concrete and achievable, Obama decided the country would continue to pour money and blood into a project whose only remaining function was to fuel bigotry and anger.

The next morning, I clicked over to the *New York Times* website and learned something. The military's code name for bin Laden during the operation had been Geronimo. When they killed him, what they'd radioed back to the White House Situation Room was, "Geronimo EKIA"—enemy killed in action. Just as they'd shaped the country's unconscious response to September 11, so were the country's Indian Wars hovering in the background at the moment of America's revenge, and so would they continue to serve as one of the unacknowledged legislators behind the decision to keep America's troops in the Middle East for at least another ten years. If their memory, along with all of its attendant historical traumas, still drove the country's government toward violence and failure even after bin Laden's death, it also made those failures easier to bear. SEAL Team Six had ventured into the wilderness and scalped the savage—one shouldn't underestimate the consolation provided by a moment of cathartic violence that rhymes so perfectly with your own history.

The real Geronimo was an Apache shaman and famous warrior. For more than thirty-five years in the nineteenth century, he led raids against colonizers in both the northern states of Mexico and the American territories of New Mexico and Arizona. The Apaches had been driven onto reservations after the Mexican-American War, and Geronimo would not stop trying to break out. White settlers called him "the worst Indian who ever lived." One girl his band captured on one of their raids was found hanging from a meat hook, which had been driven into the base of her skull. Geronimo surrendered in 1886 and became a permanent prisoner of war. He and other Apaches were shuttled first to Texas, then to Florida, then to Alabama, and finally to Fort Sill in Oklahoma, where, though not free to leave, they were allowed to build villages and farm the arid land. Geronimo's fame did not dissipate with his captivity, however, and he soon became a traveling, government-sponsored tourist attraction. He was brought to an international exhibition in Omaha, Nebraska, and he was also given a role in one of Pawnee Bill's traveling vaudeville entertainments, where he demonstrated how the Indian had been tamed.

In 1905, he and five chiefs were included in Teddy Roosevelt's inaugural parade, after which Geronimo asked Roosevelt to free the prisoners at Fort Sill and allow them to return to their homes in Arizona. Roosevelt refused. He said Geronimo and his people "were not good Indians." Geronimo spent five more years living at Fort Sill. One cold night, he was thrown from his horse while riding. Someone eventually found him and brought him back to Fort Sill, but the ordeal had taken its toll, and Geronimo contracted pneumonia. Lying on his deathbed, he asked to see his nephew, who later said that the great man's last words were, "I should never have surrendered. I should have fought until I was the last man alive."[59] After Geronimo passed away on February 17, 1909, the *Chicago Daily Tribune* ran an article about him. The headline read, "Geronimo Now a Good Indian."[60]

PART III

Growth, Stagnation, Surplus

CHAPTER 7

Our Little, Imaginary World

*They tell you it's the oil but I know it is not the oil, I just
can't figure out what the hell it is we are here for.*
— American soldier in Baghdad, August 2003[1]

The first leader of post-Saddam Iraq was a white American in khaki chinos, a navy-blue blazer, and combat boots. Paul Bremer—or "Ambassador L. Paul Bremer III," as his name appears on the cover of his memoir—grew up in Connecticut. His father was the president of Christian Dior Perfumes, and his mother taught art history at a university. His education was about as elite as it gets: elementary schooling at New Canaan Country School, which as of 2023 charged more than $45,000 in tuition for kindergarten;[2] high school at Phillips Academy Andover; and college at Yale University. After college, he studied business at Harvard and politics in Paris. He began his career in the Foreign Service in 1966, then moved over to the State Department. In 1989, he joined Henry Kissinger's consulting firm, advising multinational corporations on which countries were too unstable to invest in and which were just unstable enough. By

2003, Bremer had spent nearly four decades in diplomacy and international relations, and he still looked the part of an energetic Ivy Leaguer with a spot on the squash team and a can-do spirit. He had a boyish face, bright eyes, and hair like a Kennedy. He favored conservative tailoring and spoke with a reedy but confident voice. He was six feet four inches tall.

Bush appointed Bremer as presidential envoy to Iraq on May 6, 2003. He arrived in Baghdad six days later. It was the first time he had ever set foot in the country. "I did read as much Iraqi history as I could in the very brief time before I went, which was only a couple of weeks," he said years later. "Would it have mattered greatly if I had known more? Perhaps. . . . I have never seen a convincing argument that my lack of deep Iraqi experience actually made a difference."[3] By June, he was the head of the newly formed Coalition Provisional Authority (CPA), the country's chief executive. The provisional government was fully established by mid-July. In his memoir, Bremer wrote that he was "the only paramount authority figure—other than dictator Saddam Hussein—that most Iraqis had ever known." This claim suggests that his "lack of deep Iraqi experience" did matter after all, because there were in fact millions of living Iraqis (as in, everyone over the age of about thirty) whose memories would have stretched back to before Saddam's 1979 assumption of the presidency.[4] Bremer's mandate was to oversee both the reconstruction of a devastated country and the birth of a new democratic government. He held the job for fourteen months and basically answered to no one. He liked to wake up at 5:00 a.m. and go for a run through the gardens of Saddam's presidential palace,[5] and he accessorized his suits with a pair of Timberland boots his son had given to him on the eve of his departure, along with a note reading, "Go kick some butt, Dad."[6]

Bremer did not kick some butt. He spent a bit more than a year in Iraq, and when he left in June 2004, basic services were still unreliable, the temporary Iraqi Governing Council was a hornet's nest of competing agendas, and popular discontent was in the process of developing into civil war. It would take a further three years for the military to bring the violence under any semblance of control. Bush awarded Bremer the Presidential Medal of Freedom several months after his return, but even back then he was generally seen as a failure.

Today, a similar judgment is often made about the war on terror as a whole. Despite the political benefits of rallying Americans around the flag in fits of nationalist enthusiasm, both parties found the war to be an enormous headache. George W. Bush had to mount an expensive and elaborate propaganda campaign to convince voters that Iraq was worth invading, and even with all that time and effort, the public remained on his side for little more than two years. By July 2005, a majority of Americans recognized that Bush had misled them about Saddam's weapons of mass destruction,[7] and during the awful summer of 2008, Bush had the lowest approval ratings of any president since Harry Truman, with just 24 percent of Americans believing he'd done anything resembling a good job.[8] His successor's enthusiasm for the war is even harder to understand in terms of politics. Obama's decision to increase America's troop levels in Afghanistan alienated the base of his popular support and did nothing to appease his conservative antagonists. When he took office, just a quarter of Americans thought that invading Afghanistan had been a mistake. When he left, that figure was almost 50 percent.[9] The larger war continued to strain America's relationships with many of its most important allies, boosted Iran's influence in the region thanks to the Shia takeover of Iraqi politics, and seeded outbreaks of violence and social unrest across the Middle East. In 2008, a Nobel laureate in economics and a former CFO for the Department of Commerce calculated that the Iraq War alone had cost America more than $3 trillion, more than a fifth of the country's GDP for that year.[10] And in addition to the political and financial costs, a 2021 report found that roughly fifteen thousand American service members and private contractors lost their lives fighting the war, a figure that doesn't even begin to reflect the real human cost to the United States. Add in the veterans who came home permanently disabled, or who took their own lives following their deployments, and you get a number in the hundreds of thousands.[11] For most of its existence, the war on terror was unpopular at home and counterproductive abroad, diminishing rather than enhancing America's standing and influence around the world.

To be blunt about it, governments do not often spend trillions of dollars doing something that is both politically unpopular and seemingly harmful to their global interests. So what was the point? Why did the war on terror continue for so long?

Over the past twenty years, there have generally been two answers to that question. Those who supported the war saw the project as a kind of crusade, an effort to rid the world of evil, make the Middle East safe for political and economic liberalism, and cement the United States atop the world order for at least the rest of the twenty-first century. After that project failed, first in Iraq and then in Afghanistan, these supporters changed their account of the war's meaning without giving up their belief in its righteousness. Now they gilded the war with the nobility of a doomed quest. America's soldiers had not failed, they said—failure was impossible by definition. American troops were the greatest fighters in history, and if they had come home without completing their mission, the correct place to lay blame was at the feet of the officers, politicians, journalists, and protesters who lacked the fortitude required to see the task through. By this logic, the war persisted for so long because the men and women who fought it refused to give up even as the society they defended turned its back on them.

The best distillation of this worldview can be found in the 2013 film *Lone Survivor*. Mark Wahlberg, a man who once had to apologize for saying that September 11 would have gone down differently if *he* had been on one of the planes that day, took the lead role as the real-life Navy SEAL Marcus Luttrell.[12] In 2005, Luttrell led a small group of fellow SEALs on a disastrous mission in search of a small-time military leader named Ahmad Shah. Stumbling around in the mountainous landscapes of Afghanistan's Kunar province, Luttrell's team was quickly located by Afghan fighters, who pinned them down with gunfire and then relentlessly pursued them down the mountain. Luttrell's three fellow team members were all killed, as were ten SEALs who were shot down in a helicopter while trying to execute a rescue operation. Luttrell himself appeared in the movie as an extra, playing one of the SEALs who dies in the helicopter, and he also delivered the film's final lines in a voice-over monologue: "No matter how much it hurts, how dark it gets, or how far you fall, you are never out of the fight."[13] That's probably not the most accurate way to sum up a badly planned operation of negligible strategic importance that left everybody dead except for Mark Wahlberg, but the film's harrowing action scenes, appealing cast, and heart-swelling post-rock soundtrack made it a hit. *Lone Survivor* did so well on its opening weekend that one Texas movie theater canceled screenings of *Anchorman 2* and *The Wolf of Wall Street* in order to accommodate the extra demand.[14]

Those who opposed the war told a different story: America did it for oil. The slogan "No blood for oil" could be seen and heard everywhere at protest marches during late 2002 and early 2003. It sought an explanation for the war in the field of economics, envisioning the conflict as part of a zero-sum competition for access to industrial resources. At the time of the invasion, Iraq was believed to have at least the fifth-largest oil reserves of any country on the planet, and that was a conservative estimate. No one would really know what Iraq had until Western oil companies were allowed to fly in with their equipment and expertise and start looking around. In a report published two months after the invasion, a writer at the Brookings Institution noted that while the consensus put Iraq's known and commercially viable reserves at 112 billion barrels, other estimates by *The Petroleum Economist* magazine and the Federation of American Scientists had the number closer to 200 billion barrels, and another study had gone as high as 300 billion. If the high-end estimate was correct, then Iraq was home to a quarter of all the drillable oil on earth.[15]

Despite halfhearted demonstrations of indifference, Dick Cheney's office was not very successful in concealing its interest in these oil fields. Even before September 11, the vice president instructed the National Security Council to work with the Energy Task Force he had established shortly after taking office. As Jane Mayer wrote in *The New Yorker,* Cheney wanted the two groups to work on combining "two seemingly unrelated areas of policy: 'the review of operational policies towards rogue states,' such as Iraq, and 'actions regarding the capture of new and existing oil and gas fields.'"[16] This was before technological advances in horizontal well bores made hydraulic fracturing, better known today as fracking, profitable on a large scale. Fracking eventually turned the United States into one of the largest fossil fuel producers in the world, but the technology wasn't yet commercially viable in 2001, and pundits and think tank researchers often warned of an impending oil supply crunch and its attendant high prices (the U.S. government knows very well that its car-dependent citizenry will not tolerate expensive gasoline for any sustained period of time). As the antiwar collective Retort observed, one private intelligence firm wrote in a report that invading Iraq would constitute "a 'sublime' opportunity to 'scoop up cheap assets.'"[17] What you had in 2003, then, was (1) a country gripped by anxiety about oil shortages, which (2) invaded Iraq, a country home to (3) perhaps the largest unexplored and unexploited oil reserves in the world. It's not unreasonable to put those facts together and conclude that the explanation for the Iraq War is obvious.

And yet, as Retort wrote, "it is one thing for an explanation to be vivid, another for it to be crushingly obvious. We tire of detectives solving crimes the criminals have never bothered to conceal."[18] Though persuasive at first glance, the blood-for-oil thesis loses much of its explanatory power the closer one looks. The idea that the government worried only about the price of oil going too *high* forgets that the oil market includes sellers as well as buyers. Oil companies are constituents, too, and the more prevalent worry within the industry was that a supply glut would drive prices so low as to make their operations unprofitable. That's the whole purpose of the OPEC+ cartel: to allow industry players to regulate prices and keep profits stable by coordinating the opening and closing of their respective spigots, a mechanism used just as often to set a floor beneath which prices may not fall as to keep a lid on any spiraling price increase. Second, while the oil companies would have been pleased to learn that America's military had made enormous new reserves available for exploitation, it is not obvious that those same companies would weigh the benefits against the risks and come out in favor of invasion. Investment in oil production is very capital-intensive, and it requires years, even decades, to turn a profit. Risk is a normal part of doing business, but invading Iraq was not a normal risk. Designed as it was to remake the political order of the entire region, invading Iraq threatened to upend a fifth of global supply. It's hard to make confident investments in new wells or exploration when you don't know whether some armed group is going to storm the halls of government next month. Finally, the blood-for-oil thesis paid too much attention to Iraq and not enough to all the other countries the United States bombed, invaded, or surveilled as part of the war on terror, to say nothing about all the money America sent to its allies to fund counterterrorism training and operations. Whatever oil might be able to explain about the Iraq War in particular, it cannot do the same for a twenty-year occupation of Afghanistan, drones over Pakistan or Yemen, or a quiet but persistent campaign of special operations exercises and training across Somalia, Niger, and much of the Sahel.

This is not to deny that oil helped to shape America's cost-benefit analysis; as one of the most important commodities in the world, it could hardly do otherwise. But proponents of the blood-for-oil thesis erred in treating oil as the Bush administration's primary motivating force rather than as one part of a larger economic project. This chapter, along with the two that follow, is about that larger economic project.

In trying to look at the economic forces underlying the war from a sufficient altitude, one needs to remember the part of the war's official name that is often omitted in conversation (as well as books like this one): *global* war on terror. The United States didn't become the world's most powerful country solely on the strength of its national economy after World War II, even if that economic strength was staggering (in 1960, the United States accounted for 40 percent of the world's economic activity).[19] What made the United States so powerful was its ability to superintend the global economy as a whole, to shepherd twentieth-century capitalism through its decades-long conflict with the Soviet Union, write the rules of global trade and finance, and enforce those rules when some malcontent got out of line. This enforcement often took place at gunpoint, as in the cases of Korea, Vietnam, Chile, Argentina, or any number of other countries in which the United States decided that legitimate governments needed to be replaced with rulers who would more readily accommodate America's requirements and preferences. But the United States also won countries over to its side by spreading around the wealth generated by its manufacturing prowess, with the reconstruction of Europe under the Marshall Plan as the most famous example. It shared the wealth at home as well, to a certain extent, permitting the growth of the powerful industrial unions whose labor advocacy created the vaunted American middle class and turning Americans into the most voracious consumers in world history.

For twenty-five years after World War II, America's leadership of the world economy was a success, at least from the perspective of Americans and other inhabitants of the affluent north. Beginning in the 1970s, however, the world's economic engine began to sputter. Global growth slowed down, and the mutually beneficial ties of trade and exchange that held together the American-led world system started to fray. By the end of the twentieth century, these ties had frayed to such an extent that a number of structural adjustments had to be made in order to sustain the American project through the twenty-first. To begin seeing the contours of that project, it will be helpful to look at what Paul Bremer tried to do with Iraq after Saddam was gone.

• • •

During his time in Baghdad, Bremer lived in what came to be known as the Green Zone, a fortified, ten-square-kilometer compound nestled into a bend in the Tigris River. Completely surrounded by blast walls and barbed wire, the Green Zone was the safest place in the city, home to soldiers, private contractors and mercenaries, civilian administrators, translators, and other Iraqi support staff. Except for the al-Rashid Hotel and the Baghdad Convention Center, Iraqis not employed by the occupation were excluded from the Green Zone.[20] Its inhabitants were young and overwhelmingly male—one journalist estimated the ratio at ten to one, and also characterized the atmosphere there as verging on "rampant sexual harassment"—a group of inexperienced and ambitious twentysomethings looking to make a name for themselves in Iraq and kick-start Washington careers back in the States.[21]

Many of them never set foot outside the Green Zone while in Iraq. Why would they? Outside its walls, the streets were choked with traffic and debris, the brutal heat was inescapable, and the risk of being kidnapped or caught in some firefight was high. Inside, however, were all the amenities of home: air-conditioning, swimming pools, movie nights, laundry service, bars, a dance club, and boxes of sugary Froot Loops and Frosted Flakes at the breakfast table. The cafeteria, operated by Halliburton, was managed by a "rail-thin twenty-two-year-old" with pimples on his forehead.[22] In the middle of a Muslim-majority city in which almost nobody ever ate pork, the Green Zone cafeteria menu often featured bacon, sausage, and spare ribs. Bible study happened on Wednesdays at 7:00 p.m. The "Hash House Harriers" organized group runs around the compound.[23] On Freedom Radio, 107.7 FM, an Army DJ played classic rock from a playlist approved by military higher-ups (hip-hop and country were forbidden).[24] Women deployed to the Green Zone sometimes packed hot pants and heels for dancing at the al-Rashid on weekends.[25]

Hermetically sealed off from life in the city around them, Bremer and the young guns who worked for him found it easy to move fast and dream big. Bremer's first official act as head of the CPA, known as Order 1: De-Ba'athification of Iraqi Society, eliminated at the stroke of a pen what had been for decades the most important political entity in the country. All senior members of the former dictator's Ba'ath Party were "hereby removed from their positions and banned from future employment in the public sector." In addition, all senior-level managers holding positions in any government ministry, Iraqi corporation, university, or hospital would be questioned regarding "possible affiliation with the Ba'ath Party." If investigators found any such affiliations, those questioned would be fired as well.[26] Former party members would also be investigated and possibly prosecuted for past criminal activity. CPA Order 2, "Dissolution of Entities," disbanded the Iraqi Army along with all other regular military organizations.[27] As Thomas Ricks pointed out in his account of the occupation's first two years, *Fiasco*, Orders 1 and 2 "threw out of work more than half a million people and alienated many more dependent on those lost incomes. Just as important, in a country . . . possessing few unifying national institutions, Bremer had done away with two of the most important ones."[28] One in fifty Iraqis lost their jobs, which caused exactly the kind of anger you would expect if someone flew into America, outlawed both the Democratic and Republican Parties, and fired six and a half million of the country's most experienced officials. While there certainly were some Saddam loyalists within the Ba'ath Party ranks, a situation made ominous by the fact that the United States had no idea where the dictator was at the time, Bremer did not opt for a targeted approach. Instead, he carpet bombed Iraqi civil society, effectively destroying the foundation of the country's ability to govern and defend itself. This made America's already formidable task that much harder. Now the CPA would have to build new foundations from scratch.

• • •

As the insurgency gathered steam during the two years following Saddam's downfall, CPA staffers weren't the only ones spending most of their time inside the Green Zone bubble. Journalists were cooped up as well. Quick visits to restaurants or markets to do local color reporting and man-on-the-street interviews now required advance preparations, security details, and finding a car that was sufficiently run-down to not be a temptation to kidnappers. This left foreign reporters dependent on CPA press conferences and official statements, and it made it difficult for journalists to know what was really going on in the city they were covering. For readers, however, there were options other than the major papers and wire services. Independent blogging was exploding in popularity, and after the invasion a number of

English-speaking Iraqis began recounting their experiences of war and occupation on the internet. Their chatty public diaries provided a valuable counterpoint to the officialese that emanated out of the Green Zone, and a few Iraqi bloggers attracted a large base of American readers. Salam Abdulmunem, who wrote under the pseudonym Salam Pax, was a twenty-nine-year-old Iraqi architect who learned English in Vienna as a child. He named his blog *Where Is Raed?* after a friend who was studying for a master's in Jordan and often didn't respond to Salam's emails. There was also "Riverbend," an anonymous Iraqi woman in her mid-twenties who worked in computer science and began publishing *Baghdad Burning: Girl Blog from Iraq* shortly after the invasion. *A Family in Baghdad* was a group blog with contributions from Faiza Al-Araji and her three sons, Raed, Khalid, and Majid. The sons translated their mother's Arabic posts, and of the non-contributing father and husband, they said only that "Azzam is not interested." These writers used their websites to document what was happening to their city, track and comment on developments in the news, correspond with people around the world, and articulate their grief and anxiety. Sometimes they poked fun at their loved ones. "Where are you mam?" son Raed posted one day on *A Family in Baghdad*, teasing Faiza for failing to post. "Start blogging for god's sake."[29] Sometimes they posted holiday greetings. "It is going to be a great year, no question," Salam wrote as New Year's Eve approached. "Go get drunk and promise you will not watch the news for the next three days, it's all bad anyway. Peace, out!"[30] Sometimes they just wanted to let people know they were still alive. "I'm female, Iraqi, and 24," Riverbend wrote in August 2003. "I survived the war. That's all you need to know. It's all that matters these days anyway."[31]

They also kept a close eye on what Bremer was up to inside the Green Zone. The big guy's year abroad remains instructive today, and not only as a case study in how not to do a post-invasion reconstruction. Bremer was America's most powerful overseas official at the precise moment when the country's dreams for what the war could accomplish were at their most utopian and grandiose. Afghanistan was drawing up a new constitution in the spring of 2003, and in less than two years its people would hold their first direct presidential election. Yes, Osama bin Laden had slipped through the U.S. dragnet on the Af-Pak border, but he would be found one way or another, and in any case he would be running scared for however many days remained to him on earth. In Iraq, Saddam's forces had melted away in the face of the U.S. military with a speed that surpassed analysts' most optimistic projections. The invasion had ruffled some European feathers, but that sclerotic continent liked to whine about almost everything America did. They would come around—and quickly—once they saw what America was capable of now that the twentieth-century politics of caution, triangulation, and realism had been swept off the board. Iraq was a blank canvas on which Bremer would outline the contours of a second American century.

Bremer approached the Iraqis themselves with a proud father's alternating feelings of benevolence and frustration. His memoir suggests that he did not see them as fully adult. Saddam's regime had been violent and oppressive, but the Ba'ath Party's "command economy," to use Bremer's phrasing, had coddled Iraqis for decades, with state monopolies and price controls keeping the costs of fuel, heating, food, and medical care "artificially low."[32] This government-induced dependency made it hard for Iraqis to take the kind of grassroots political initiative that was crucial to the country's hopes for a democratic future. "Most Iraqis have had no experience with free thought," Bremer recalled telling President Bush. "They vaguely understand the concept of freedom, but still want us to tell them what to do."[33] Hoping to instruct the people, Bremer set up a kind of liberal democracy kindergarten in the middle of Baghdad. He flew in the president of Michigan State University and began holding Monday-night seminars on the basic principles of free-market economics, which became "quite popular among people from the ministries, Iraq's nascent 'private sector,' and younger potential political leaders." He used real-world examples to reinforce the classroom lessons. At one meeting, he asked the country's new oil minister, a Shell executive named Phil Carroll, about the long lines he was seeing at gas stations. Carroll explained that the artificially depressed price of oil was making it impossible for refineries to produce enough fuel to keep up with demand, which had been surging since the "Liberation," a word Bremer always capitalized in his writing. "Huge subsidies distort activity," Bremer replied for the benefit of his students. "Economics 101."[34]

This lesson was applied to people working in every sector of the Iraqi economy, though Bremer seems to have grappled only rarely with the implications of hiking the prices of a country's most important staples immediately after overthrowing the government and firing half a million civil servants. In late May 2003, Bremer jumped the price of grain to $105 per ton while executing the sale of that year's wheat and barley harvests to the United Nations. The change would provide for an immediate injection of $150 million into Iraq's economy, but in Bremer's view the longer-term effect of "beginning to move toward market prices" was just as important. Though he sometimes made concessions to a less hard-line version of economic policy—"cascading bad economic news" forced him to approve a $100 million, government-funded "public works program" in June 2003[35]—these were understood to be exceptional responses to exceptional circumstances. Once things calmed down in the near future, Iraq's economy would operate according to the tenets of free-market orthodoxy. You've got your freedom now, Bremer told Iraqis, but that means the end of the free ride. On his first day in the country, Bremer saw "looters roaming freely through the streets of Baghdad." He suggested they be shot.[36]

The most detailed description of Bremer's vision for the new Iraq—and, by extension, of America's vision for the war on terror as a whole—can be found in the 100 Orders. As we've already seen, Orders 1 and 2 eliminated the Ba'ath Party and disbanded the army. But that was just the beginning. Between Bremer's arrival in the country and June 28, 2004, ninety-eight additional orders were hashed out and put into effect without any formal input from the Iraqi people. They were designed to remain in place forever, with stipulations prohibiting any future Iraqi government from modifying or rescinding them. This should have been illegal, as lawyers working for the Coalition Provisional Authority noted at the time. In his wonderful book on the early

days of the occupation, *Imperial Life in the Emerald City,* the journalist Rajiv Chandrasekaran wrote, "Article 43 of the second section of
the Hague Convention of 1899—the first set of international treaties
that attempted to create laws of warfare—requires an occupying
power to respect all the laws of the occupied country except when it is
necessary to promote public order and safety."[37] But the CPA had a
work-around. While Bremer sprayed Orders across the country and
rushed around trying to get a handle on whatever new crisis had
erupted overnight, the CPA was also guiding the drafting of Iraq's new
constitution, the Transitional Administration Law (TAL). In its final
form, the TAL specified that the Orders would remain in effect even
after the Americans left and returned sovereignty to the Iraqis. Orders
could be overturned or rescinded, but doing so would require the
votes of the president, the two vice presidents, and a majority of the
government's ministers. These ministers were handpicked by the CPA
and endowed with five-year terms,[38] which meant that Iraqis wouldn't
have a meaningful say as to whether the orders should remain in force
until the end of the decade. By then it would be too late, in many
cases, to turn back. "You set up these things and they begin to develop
a certain life of momentum of their own," Bremer said, "and it's harder
to reverse course." A less abstract way of putting that would be to say
that if you sell a state-owned university to private buyers in 2003,
you're not going to be able to buy it back in 2009.[39]

The Orders generally fell into three categories. The first might be
called the Emergency Orders. These were laws designed to keep violence at acceptable levels while the CPA and the Army worked to
clean up the mess they'd caused by invading. Order 14, "Prohibited
Media Activity," prohibited news organizations from broadcasting or
publishing any material that advocated "alterations to Iraq's borders
by violent means" or that incited "violence against any individual or
group . . . civil disorder, rioting, or damage to property."[40] Order 3
spelled out who was allowed to have weapons ("Coalition forces,"
"Iraqi security forces," and those authorized by the CPA to have a
weapon) and who wasn't (everyone else). Bremer knew perfectly well
that Iraq didn't stand a chance if America couldn't tamp down on

chaos in the streets. The violence was so bad that in order to leave the Green Zone for a meeting or site visit, he had to ride in a convoy comprising "two armored Humvees, a lead armored Suburban with Blackwater 'shooters,' my armored car, another armored Suburban with more shooters, and two following Humvees."[41] He brought in Bernard Kerik, former commissioner of the New York Police Department, to help set up the Iraqi police force. "Training professional, well-equipped Iraqi police," Bremer wrote, had to be "our top priority."[42]

Riverbend thought that was a joke. Though Baghdad was full of unemployed, military-age men following the dissolution of the Iraqi Army, "men were reluctant to apply to the Iraqi police," she wrote, "because they weren't given weapons! The Iraqi police were expected to roam and guard the hellish cities without weapons . . . to stop looters, abductors, and murderers with the sheer force of an application to their warped sense of morality."[43] The CPA eventually did arm Baghdad's cops, but in Riverbend's estimation it didn't help things much. "We see Iraqi police every once in a while," she wrote, "but their numbers are ridiculous compared to the situation. They wear light blue shirts, dark pants, and these black arm bands with IP written on them and the flag. They get to carry around these little 7mm Berettas that look tiny in their hands."[44] With fundamentalist militias roaming the streets and gangs making a living off kidnapping people for ransom, it was no longer safe for women to commute to school or work. Riverbend spent a month trying to persuade a neighbor to allow her nineteen-year-old daughter to attend a pharmaceutical college. "Her mother was adamant," Riverbend wrote, "and demanded to know what she was supposed to do with her daughter's college degree if anything happened to her. 'Hang it on her tombstone with the consolation that my daughter died for a pharmaceutical degree??? She can sit this year out.'"[45] In a post on *A Family in Baghdad,* Khalid explained why he couldn't go to college anymore, either. "The hi-tech USA cant garantee that your college will not be bombed any moment..daah. now tell me..is there anyone out there who still doesnt wana be librated yet?"[46]

In February 2004, on the fourth day of Eid, Riverbend's family gathered for dinner at an uncle's house. At the end of the meal, her cousin's husband, A., stepped out for a moment to drop off his parents at their house, fifteen minutes away. When he hadn't returned an hour later, people started to worry. The next morning, the family learned that A. had been abducted and was being held for a $15,000 ransom. "We panicked," Riverbend wrote. "The whole house broke down. L. fell to the floor crying and shouting that they'll kill him—she just knew they'd kill him like they were killing others." They debated going to the police but decided against it. "In some areas," she wrote, "the police were actually working with abductors for a certain amount of money and there was nothing they were willing to do anyway." They paid the ransom on the third day after A.'s abduction. He didn't come home until the fifth day. "I won't describe the crying, screaming, shouting, jumping, hobbling (A. was limping) and general chaos that followed A.'s entrance," Riverbend wrote. Even with a gash on his head, bruises all over his body, and bloody feet, A. was able to crack jokes. "They actually only wanted $5,000," he told his family, "but I was outraged—told them I was worth AT LEAST $20,000."[47]

Iraqis who managed to avoid the gangs, fundamentalists, and kidnappers still had to worry about the occupying American army. "Our house was searched by Americans," Salam wrote in August 2003. "I wasn't home, but my mother called the next day a bit freaked out." Soldiers arrived around midnight, hoping to surprise the "criminal Ba'athi cell" that they apparently believed was in Salam's family home. At first they tried a quiet approach, but when the front gate rattled, Salam's brother went outside to see what was going on:

> When the silent entrance tactic failed they resorted to shouty entrance mode. So they shouted at him telling him that he should get down on his knees, which he did. He actually was trying to help them open the door, but whatever. Seconds later around 25 soldiers are in the house my brother, father and mother are outside sitting on the ground and in their asshole-ish ways refused to answer any questions about what was happening. My father was asking them what they were looking for

so that he can help but as usual since you are an Iraqi addressing an American is no use since he doesn't even acknowledge
you as a human being standing in front of him. . . . Anyway so
my brother and father start talking to the medic and he tells
them what this is about. They have been "informed" that there
are daily meetings the last five days, Sudanese people come
into our house at 9am and stay till 3pm, we are a probable
Ansar cell. My father is totally baffled, my brother gets it. These
are not Sudanese men they are from Basra the "informer" is
stupid enough to forget that there is a sizeable population in
Basra who are of African origin. And it is not meetings these 2
(yes only two) guys have here, they are carpenters and they
were repairing my mom's kitchen. Way. To. Go. You have great
informers.

To save face, the Americans then rifled through some papers, pretending to be interested in the fact that Salam's father had attended
professional conferences in the past. One of the soldiers emptied a
bottle of Johnnie Walker into his flask. The commanding officer then
allowed Salam's family back into their home and told them to verify
that nothing was missing. "I don't want any complaints filed later on,"
he said. "They came," Salam wrote, "freaked out my mother, pissed off
my father, found nothing and left."[48]

The second category of Bremer's edicts could be called the Bureaucratic Orders. These established ministries and departments in
areas of government neglected by Saddam, and they also brought
the shape of Iraq's new government more in line with that of its American protector. Order 7, on the penal code, suspended capital punishment and prohibited torture, both hallmarks of Saddam's grim rule.
Order 18 remade the Iraqi central bank in the image of the Federal
Reserve, allowing it to independently set interest rates and make other
decisions on monetary policy without needing the approval of the
country's politically appointed finance minister.[49] Order 44 established the Ministry of Environment and provided it with a mandate to
"address environmental concerns" in a number of areas. Amusingly,

the first area listed, before waste management, biodiversity, or even air and water pollution, was "radiation control." The dream of Saddam's elusive weapons of mass destruction would die hard among the Americans who spent their days in the Green Zone.

These orders weren't pernicious on their face, but to Baghdad's bloggers, the people selected to govern the country and run the ministries mattered just as much as the separation of powers or whether the central bank could be politically influenced. Riverbend was particularly caustic on the subject of the Governing Council, a collection of nine Iraqis selected by the CPA to rubber-stamp Bremer's edicts until the United States pulled out and Iraq ratified a new constitution. Bremer and the council were unable to settle on a single leader, so instead they settled on the most awkward solution available. "The funny thing is that the 9 get to govern Iraq alphabetically," Riverbend wrote.

> The only reason for this seems to be that Bremer found them all equally ingratiating, dishonest, and incompetent so he was hard-pressed to make a decision. The way it will work is that each one will have their chance at governing Iraq, and at the end of the nine-month period, Bremer will decide which one of them best represents American assets in the region and he will become "The Chosen One." . . . Insiders say that all 9 members of the council hate each other. The one thing they do agree on is that Bremer is God. His word is Scripture.

She called them "the Puppets."[50] Iraqis had very little confidence that the nine council members could advocate for anything other than their own sectarian interests, and their constant bickering made them incapable of acting on behalf of the country as a whole. "The various bodies that have been installed here don't seem to have much coordination between them," Salam wrote. "We all need to feel that big sure and confident strides forward are being taken; it is not like this at all."[51]

Finally, there were Bremer's Economic Orders. Most of the 100 Orders fell into this last category. In just over a year as Iraq's head of state, a time during which the most immediate problems facing the country had to do with violence and the provision of daily necessities like electricity, fuel, and water, Bremer expended most of his legislative firepower on transforming Iraq into an exemplar of free-market liberalism. In doing so, he tore out the material foundations of Iraqi society at the roots. The notorious Order 39, "Foreign Investment," clearly articulated the CPA's goal of facilitating Iraq's "transition from a non-transparent centrally planned economy to a market economy characterized by sustainable economic growth through the establishment of a dynamic private sector." The first clause of Section 3 left no room for doubt about the scope and ambition of Order 39: "This Order replaces all existing foreign investment law." Where Iraq's economy had previously been closed off to foreign capital, with heavy industry owned and controlled by the government, the country was now open for business, 24/7. "A foreign investor shall be entitled to make foreign investments in Iraq on terms no less favorable than those applicable to an Iraqi investor," the Order said. "The amount of foreign participation in newly formed or existing business entities shall not be limited." Foreign investment would be permitted in all sectors of the Iraqi economy and in all geographic areas, with just a few exceptions carved out in order to appease the natives (banking, insurance, and the earliest stages of the oil extraction process would remain under Iraqi control for the time being). Foreign businesses that deposited the tiny sum of $100,000 in an Iraqi bank could conduct retail sales in the country. If an investor decided it was time to pull out of the country without warning, for whatever reason, or if a company believed that its Western shareholders deserved a fat dividend payout that year, that was no problem. The Order authorized companies to "transfer abroad without delay all funds associated with its foreign investment." And while the Order was otherwise insistent that foreign and domestic capital compete with each other for investment opportunities on a level playing field, Bremer also sought to help foreigners preserve any advantages that were already baked into the rules and regulations of the global economic system. "Where an international agreement to which Iraq is a party provides for more

favorable terms with respect to foreign investors undertaking investment activities in Iraq," Section 143 read, "the more favorable terms
under the international agreement shall apply."[52]

If the new Iraq was going to do business with the rest of the world,
it would have to run its internal economic affairs more like the rest of
the world—that is, more like the United States—as well. Otherwise,
there wouldn't be any attractive investment opportunities for the foreign investors to invest in. Order 30 eliminated Saddam's system of
patronage via government employment and established a new regime
for public-sector workers, making it easier for government agencies to
fire people or withhold raises.[53] Order 29, recognizing that post-
invasion chaos had made it impossible for many Iraqis to pay their
rent, suspended all residential eviction proceedings against tenants
who fell behind on payments between April and December 2003.
Tenants who had failed to pay rent *before* the war could still be kicked
out, however, no matter their current economic circumstances, and
rent increases were allowed to resume on October 16, 2004, by which
point (as the Bush administration then believed) the United States
would have returned full sovereignty to Iraqis and left the country.
The order thus helped to preserve the value of landlords' real estate
investments while simultaneously postponing any unrest over evic-
tions until it would no longer be America's problem.[54] Order 37 lowered the corporate tax rate from 45 percent to 15 percent "for 2004
and subsequent years."[55] Iraq would be the ideal buyer's market. Businesses from anywhere on the planet could parachute in, make a bunch
of money, pay essentially nominal taxes, and then take their profits
wherever they wanted without having to worry about any legal or regulatory strictures that would bind their investments to the longer-
term fate of the country.

Finally, Bremer set about rooting through the storeroom in search
of enticing items to place in Iraq's shopwindows. Little more than a
month into his tenure, he started telling any journalist who would listen that he was going to sell off the dozens of state-owned companies
that formed the bedrock of Iraq's economy. Steel manufacturers and
food packaging businesses alike would be handed over to the private

market.[56] The Iraqi State Company for Water Transportation would lose its exclusive license to manage the country's ports, and would henceforth have "to provide maritime agency services in competition with other companies."[57] A monthly food allowance previously handed out to all Iraqis would be replaced with a $15 cash payment, and state subsidies to unprofitable companies would end. These changes would be painful in the short term, as the withdrawal of state funding would doom companies that couldn't compete on the open market. Bremer thought the pain was worth it.

Today, it is usually leftists who are stereotyped as believing that economics lies at the foundation of all meaningful political change, but in 2003 it was Bremer, a man who looked like what an AI image generator would produce if given the prompt "20th-century middle-aged Ivy League Republican," who thought that Iraq's transition to democracy depended entirely on the success of his economic reforms. "Getting inefficient state enterprises into private hands is essential for Iraq's recovery," he said.[58] "If we don't get their economy right, no matter how fancy our political transformation, it won't work."[59] Everyone remembered the collapse of the Soviet Union and the subsequent privatization of the dead republic's state-owned enterprises, which had constituted perhaps the biggest orgy of corruption and greed in living memory. But that, too, was an acceptable price to pay. In any case, the Bush administration made sure that if any "mistakes" were made, American companies would not be caught up in the blowback. Two months after the invasion, Bush secretly signed Executive Order 13303, granting U.S. persons and corporations working with either the Development Fund for Iraq or the country's oil industry immunity from civil or criminal charges that might arise as a result of their participation in Iraq's economic rebirth. When the anticipated chaos did occur, that was fine as well. Beginning in 2004, a scandal erupted when Congress realized that $8.8 billion worth of money had disappeared into Iraq's U.S.-controlled government ministries. When pressed on the missing funds by a congressional panel in 2007, Bremer's financial adviser didn't seem too exercised about it. "Yeah, I understand," he said. "I'm saying what difference does it make?"[60]

It made a difference to Iraq's bloggers. When they looked at Bremer's vision for their country's economy, they didn't see an economic miracle in the making—they saw a continuation of the looting that had plagued Baghdad in the days after Saddam's downfall. "For Sale," Riverbend wrote in September 2003:

> A fertile, wealthy country with a population of around 25 million . . . plus around 150,000 foreign troops, and a handful of puppets. Conditions of sale: should be either an American or British corporation (forget it if you're French) . . . preferably affiliated with Halliburton. Please contact one of the members of the Governing Council in Baghdad, Iraq for more information.[61]

It wasn't just the indignity of having your national wealth sold off to a bunch of foreign vultures. It was the surrealism of watching Bremer pretend that Iraq would be a globalized economic powerhouse within a year or two when the people of Baghdad couldn't count on the electricity to stay on for twenty-four consecutive hours. Eight months into Iraq's "reconstruction," *nothing* seemed to be getting better. "Visited the neighbours," Faiza wrote on *A Family in Baghdad.* "She said she wants to emigrate and sell her house. All of her children are outside (Iraq) and life here is difficult, with no hope of things improving in the near future. She's right! I wished that I think like her and then all of my psychological problems would end. But I am attached to this land."[62] The water system couldn't muster enough pressure for the pump at Riverbend's family home to fill the rooftop reservoir. Whenever the tank emptied, Riverbend and her brother would have to fill buckets from a trickling hose and then haul them up to the roof one by one. Blackouts were so persistent that if the electricity happened to come on in the middle of the night, everyone got out of bed to vacuum, do laundry, and check emails—who knew how long the next blackout would last? Filling up the car's gas tank took hours, whole afternoons. When gas stations ran out, people turned to the black market; the prices were outrageous, and you had to be wary of sellers who cut petrol with cheaper kerosene, but at least you could hold out until the gas station was open again. Those with enough money bought electrical generators and sold "subscriptions" to the other houses on their block, which helped people to deal with the unpredictable blackouts. Bremer then prohibited the purchase or sale of black-market gas. "The all-new Iraqi Police in their ham fisted ways have already managed to kill a guy selling gasoline," Salam wrote. "Idiots you are supposed to stop them selling gasoline not stop them breathing, they shot him dead, bang bang, just like that and all he did was sell gasoline on the side of the street."[63]

It was also obvious that whatever reconstruction was taking place wasn't benefiting Iraqis. In August 2003, Riverbend wrote about an episode from earlier in the year in which one of her cousins, an engineer, heard that the CPA was accepting bids to repair a bridge in southeast Baghdad:

> He got his team together, they went out and assessed the damage, decided it wasn't too extensive, but it would be costly. They did the necessary tests and analyses (mumblings about soil composition and water depth, expansion joints and girders) and came up with a number they tentatively put forward— $300,000. This included new plans and designs, raw materials (quite cheap in Iraq), labor, contractors, travel expenses, etc.
>
> Let's pretend my cousin is a dolt. Let's pretend he hasn't been working with bridges for over 17 years. Let's pretend he didn't work on replacing at least 20 of the 133 bridges damaged during the first Gulf War. Let's pretend he's wrong and the cost of rebuilding this bridge is four times the number they estimated—let's pretend it will actually cost $1,200,000. Let's just use our imagination.
>
> A week later, the New Diyala Bridge contract was given to an American company. This particular company estimated the cost of rebuilding the bridge would be around—brace yourselves—$50,000,000!![64]

The biggest irony here is that Bremer's fire sale of Iraq's state assets didn't even happen. It was not for lack of trying, but Bremer and his acolytes in the Green Zone slowly discovered that it is difficult to sell companies, factories, warehouses, shipping yards, and rail lines when all of those things are physically located in war zones.

The situation that confronted the United States during its first couple of years in Iraq was similar to that facing the European powers in the early stages of colonizing North America. By the middle of the fifteenth century, the Spanish, English, and French had laid claim *on paper* to almost the entirety of the North American continent, as will be familiar to American readers who remember the maps in high school history textbooks that illustrated the dividing up of what would later become the United States. But paper claims are not the same thing as territorial control, and in reality the colonists controlled almost nothing for a long time. "At midcentury," one historian wrote of the 1600s, "colonial settlements in North America consisted of some two dozen seaside towns and a handful of forts of little consequence on the coastal plains, secured only through massive loss of life."[65] America's claim to have "occupied" Iraq, with its usual connotations of administration and security, had a similarly hollow ring in 2003. The economic team responsible for orchestrating the sale of almost everything the state owned was tiny, whereas just one of the ministries they needed to work with employed 150,000 Iraqis. "Not only was the CPA's economic team too small," Chandrasekaran found, "it was hard to imagine any investor braving an eleven-hour drive from Jordan (Baghdad's airport was closed to commercial traffic) to see a factory that was not operating because it lacked electricity and employees." And when the CPA did have a sale they wanted to push through, they ran up against a bureaucracy whose workings they did not understand and whose employees thought they were hilarious. Chandrasekaran interviewed an Army reservist and former Wall Street banker named Glenn Corliss, whose job was to collaborate with the Ministry of Industry and Minerals. "The point of all of this is we could choose to privatize or not to privatize," he said. "It didn't matter."

We didn't have the power to privatize. We didn't have the power to do anything, 'cause we didn't have control of these assets. It's like one man walking into a country—a hugely militarized country—with a piece of paper and saying, "This piece of paper now says I run the country," and that country has twenty-four million people with weapons. They're just going to look at him and go, "Oh, why don't you sit down over there in the corner, crazy guy?" That's what the Iraqis were like to us. They were like, "What are you talking about? There's three of you. There's 150,000 of us. You haven't seen most of the factories. Why do you think that you're going to make any of the decisions?" So they just kept doing their thing, and we sort of played in our little, imaginary world over at the CPA.[66]

By the end of the year, the CPA admitted that its grand privatization scheme was on hold. It would not be able to move forward again, it acknowledged, until people stopped getting shot all the time.[67]

• • •

Even if the United States had been able to successfully privatize Iraq in 2003 and 2004, however, one still wouldn't be justified in characterizing the war as just an attempt to get Iraq's national resources and industrial assets into American hands. Oil, after all, was one of the only economic sectors that the CPA agreed to leave alone. That is not to say that the United States didn't hope to get its energy companies involved in Iraq's oil industry eventually, but it had the same hopes for non-American oil companies based in allied countries. Order 39 was quite clear on this larger principle: Iraq would be hospitable to foreign investment from everywhere, not just the United States. Why bother sending American soldiers into battle and putting their lives at risk if you're then going to share the spoils with the same Europeans who spent all of 2002 moaning about what a bad idea the war was?

America's nationalist economic self-interest was perhaps most visible in the area of military spending. Kellogg Brown and Root, DynCorp International, and Halliburton are just a few of the many American corporations that raked in huge piles of cash by providing food, transportation, housing, and other logistical services to the military in Iraq, often thanks to the extremely favorable terms stipulated in the no-bid contracts the government handed out like candy to its favored corporate partners. Criticism of these sweetheart deals usually included ominous references to President Eisenhower's 1961 farewell speech, which warned against the predations of what he famously called the "military-industrial complex." But without minimizing the scale of the profits defense contractors accumulated as a result of the invasion, and without excusing the corrupt manner in which those profits were achieved, one still finds it hard to make the case that the combined forces of oil lust and military-industrial rapaciousness can explain America's push toward Iraq. The invasion was a bonanza for defense companies, but Iraq was supposed to be a *brief* war. Bush declared that combat operations had ended less than two months after the bombs started falling, and Bremer made it clear upon his arrival that he thought America would be out of the country entirely within two years. A superpower like the United States does not take a geopolitical risk like toppling Saddam Hussein just so it can spoon-feed six months' worth of high profits to a handful of defense companies that make up less than 3 percent of the S&P 500's market capitalization.

But you can learn a lot from your own dreams even when they don't come true. Bremer did not successfully remake Iraq's economy during his year abroad, and by 2006 the United States had abandoned its utopian dreams for the country's economic future, focusing instead on managing violence and containing the regional fallout from America's occupation. But if we ignore the clumsiness with which Bremer pursued his goal and instead look closely at the goal itself, we can start to see what the global war on terror was for. The 100 Orders were not designed to turn Iraq into a source of profits for the United States; they were meant to turn Iraq into a source of profits for the whole developed world. By the twenty-first century, America's national self-interest was much more *internationalized* than the blood-for-oil partisans understood. Individual Orders regarding seemingly mundane issues such as central bank independence, requirements that company board members act in the company's best interest rather than their own, free repatriation of profits, the suspension of tariffs and duties on imports and exports, dispute resolution, and adjustments to copyright and trademark law take on a deeper resonance when considered alongside one another. America wanted to turn Iraq into a country that functioned just like all the other countries that counted themselves members of the modern global economy. It wanted to integrate Iraq into a system. America did not control what occurred within that system by fiat, but it exercised more influence over the rules that governed it than any other nation, and it was the only country with the military, political, *and* economic strength to superintend the system as a whole. Al-Qaeda understood this perfectly well, as illustrated by their choice of targets on September 11: the Capitol or White House (seats of political power), which Flight 93 failed to hit; the Pentagon (nerve center of military power); and the World Trade Center (global symbol of America's economic power). The invasion was an attempt to force Iraq to join the twenty-first-century capitalism club, to make it subject to the same incentives and rules and pressures that structured the economies of all the other countries that had accepted the fact of America's global leadership. It was never an attempt to bolster Iraq's national sovereignty. Iraq had already been sovereign under Saddam Hussein's autocratic (and, it should be said, secular) rule. In America's eyes, that was exactly the problem.

The larger question, then, is why the United States waited until the first decade of the twenty-first century to make the attempt. It's not as if there hadn't been good opportunities in the past. In August 1990, Saddam Hussein ordered Iraq's military forces to invade the tiny, oil-rich nation of Kuwait, launching what is known in the United States as the first Gulf War. After diplomatic negotiations in the fall and winter failed to persuade Saddam to pull out, America sent the Army in January 1991. Within weeks, the Iraqi Army had been forced out of Kuwait. There was nothing to stop the U.S. military from pursuing Saddam's forces across the desert to Baghdad and ending the dictator's twelve-year reign. Iraq was a pariah state. Its leadership had even launched missiles at Israel, hoping that an Israeli military response would pull the region's other Arab nations into the conflict on Saddam's side. When that gambit failed, everyone knew the game was up. Yet George W. Bush's father held back. Without going into the details of Bush the Elder's geopolitical calculations, it is enough to simply note that in 1991, America declined a golden opportunity to topple Iraq's government and help usher the country into the global community of modern capitalism.

A little more than a decade later, America felt differently: Saddam had to go, even in the face of much greater risks than what confronted the United States in 1991. Something about America's superpower status had changed by the beginning of the twenty-first century, something momentous enough that the United States took a chance on militarizing its relationship to much of the rest of the world. In order to see what that something was, the next chapter will take a brief trip back through five hundred years of economic history.

CHAPTER 8

The Sign of Autumn

The unraveling of the neoconservative Project for a New American Century has for all practical purposes resulted in the terminal crisis of US hegemony—that is, in its transformation into mere domination.
    —Giovanni Arrighi, *The Long Twentieth Century*[1]

I n the modern global economy, there is one statistic that stands above all others as a measure of how things are going. That statistic is GDP growth. GDP, which stands for gross domestic product, is extraordinarily complicated to calculate, whether for a single country, an economic region like North America or eastern Europe, or the world as a whole. What GDP purports to measure, however, is simple: It is the monetary value of everything produced and sold in a given territory in a given year, encompassing both goods (clothing, appliances, groceries, raw materials, televisions) and services (health care, legal work, performances of all kinds, restaurants, educational instruction, and nail salons). When the Ford Motor Company sells a $35,000 car in the United States, U.S. GDP goes up by $35,000. When a barber cuts someone's hair for $35, GDP increases by $35. And while the absolute level of GDP is important in its own right—in the United States, that level came in at $25.46 trillion in 2022—it is the change in GDP over time, or growth, that really matters. Growth is calculated by measuring total economic output at a given point and then comparing that figure with the level of output that existed a year earlier. When journalists and economic officials announce that growth currently stands at 2 percent, they mean that the total value of what an economy currently makes, buys, and sells is 2 percent greater than what that same economy made, bought, and sold a year earlier. When GDP growth is high enough, an economy is said to be in an expansion, which is generally what people want, so long as the expansion isn't accompanied by something like undesirably high inflation. If GDP growth is negative over two consecutive financial quarters—that is, the economy is shrinking rather than growing—you have a recession, which everyone is always trying to avoid. If GDP growth is positive but too low to make people happy, an economy is said to be stagnating. Stagnation is almost as bad as recession. In some cases, it's worse.

That growth should be *the* measure of an economy's success or failure is a relatively new idea. Today it is such an omnipresent object of concern and discussion that one might be forgiven for assuming that it has always been so, that ancient, feudal, and other premodern economies were also directing their economic efforts squarely at driving up the production and consumption numbers. That assumption would be wrong. Human economic output barely increased at all until a few hundred years ago. What growth increases societies did manage were so minor, and occurred over such a long period of time, that they were completely imperceptible to the people who lived through them. The vast majority of the people who have ever lived experienced their worlds and societies as more or less unchanging, with human technological progress too halting and uncertain to transform much of anything over the span of a single lifetime. There is not much reason to try to measure something if you're not aware it's happening to begin with, and so it makes sense that GDP wasn't even invented as an object of statistical interest until 1934, when the economist Simon

Kuznets presented Congress with the first-ever calculation of the national income between 1929 and 1932. Within a quarter century, GDP growth would reign over economic policy the way the transit of Venus reigns over our love lives in astrology, with the ideal or "correct" levels of inflation, unemployment, and other economic metrics all derived at least in part from the one big number. In 1962, Arthur Okun, an economist with President Kennedy's Council of Economic Advisers, decided that for every 2 percent increase in GDP, unemployment would drop by 1 percent. Economists were so confident by this time in the hard reality of GDP, and so certain in the predictive value of their models, that the idea quickly acquired the impressive name Okun's law.

Economic growth went officially unnoticed until the interwar period not because people had failed to pay attention over the previous millennia but because growth really had taken up an unprecedented role in how people made and consumed the things their societies needed to function. Unlike all prior economic systems, capitalism, which began to develop in the fifteenth century but only started to achieve its explosive potential with the Industrial Revolution, is wholly dependent on growth. Its unique innovation was to mandate that the profits secured by any process of economic production—whether the harvest of a successful crop, the construction and sale of new housing, or the invention of a groundbreaking medical treatment—be invested *back* into the production process, thus enabling that process to expand. The mandate wasn't formal. No laws stipulated that non-expanding business enterprises would be shut down. But by subjecting all economic production to the requirements of the market more thoroughly and rigorously than any prior economic system, capitalism ensured that if firms failed to grow, they would soon find themselves undercut by competitors and driven out of business. Growth is the *point* of capitalism. Like an engine in a car, it makes the economy go. It is a very powerful engine if conditions are right; capitalist economic growth transformed human existence more comprehensively and at greater speed than any other invention in history. But it comes with a downside as well. To complete the analogy, if the engine breaks down—that is, if growth slows too much—the car can't go anywhere.

This basic fact is a crucial bit of context for those who want to understand why the United States launched the war on terror. In the years following the invasion of Iraq, commentators offered a wide range of explanations for the Bush administration's decision. As we saw in the last chapter, some people said the invasion was a play for tighter control over the world's oil supply. Others found an explanation in the realm of Freudian psychology, arguing that Bush wanted to succeed where his father had failed and get rid of Saddam for good. Still others saw it as a kind of national foreign policy reflex. Writing for *The New York Times Magazine* in September 2003, the Canadian academic and liberal politician Michael Ignatieff wrote that Iraq needed to be placed "in the long history of America's overseas interventions." "From the very beginning," he wrote, "the American republic has never shrunk from foreign wars."[2] But this explanation rather begged the question. Explaining that America invaded a foreign country because it has always invaded foreign countries doesn't help anyone understand *why* America does that. There were also those who offered cynical, borderline-conspiracist, wag-the-dog-style explanations for the war, arguing that Bush was working Americans into a militarist frenzy so as to distract voters from his domestic policy failures. But none of these mainstream commentators ever noted the larger economic and geopolitical situation that framed the whole project: The war on terror was launched thirty years into an alarming and steady slowdown in global economic growth, and this slowdown threatened America's ability to remain the world's most powerful country.

For our purposes, the second thing to know about capitalism is that throughout its five-hundred-year history, there has always been one political entity that is more or less in charge of the whole system. I say "political entity" rather than "country" because the early history of capitalism predates the invention of the nation-state, particularly the nation-state in its modern form. Some 150 years before the 1648

Peace of Westphalia began to shape our ideas of statehood and sovereignty, a number of Italian city-states, including Venice and Genoa, began to use long-distance trade and high finance in such a way as to give birth for the first time to the recognizable features of a capitalist system. In his history of global capitalism, *The Long Twentieth Century,* Giovanni Arrighi explains that between 1450 and 1650, "the Italian city-states in general and Venice in particular" were able to seize "monopolistic control over a crucial link in the chain of commercial exchanges that connected Western Europe to India and China via the world of Islam."[3] As the Spanish Empire found itself embroiled in a series of escalating (and very expensive) religious wars in the Islamic world as well as intra-European military conflict back home, innovative Italian merchant-bankers, working hand in hand with the respective ruling families of their city-states, skillfully navigated one crisis after another. Their banks lent huge sums of money to the warring Iberians at the same time as their own armies and traders established control over the trade routes that were providing all of western Europe with its wool, silk, and other valuable commodities. With the Spanish dependent on the Genoese to fund their imperial wars, and with much of the rest of the Mediterranean world dependent on Italian trading networks for goods, money and trade both concentrated themselves in the city-states. As the cumulative profits from the twinned practices of banking and trade accumulated, they could be invested back into the further expansion of banking and trade. As a result, the city-states emerged as the first recognizably capitalist powers in history. This was a new model of state power, one that would eventually supplant (at least in part) an older one centered on the direct seizure and control of land, or territory. "Territorialist rulers tend to increase their power by expanding the size of their container," as Arrighi puts it. "Capitalist rulers, in contrast, tend to increase their power by piling up wealth within a small container and increase the size of the container only if it is justified by the requirements of the accumulation of capital."[4] This is obviously a generalization: Nations have continued to pursue the expansion of their physical territory through the present day, as Russia is currently attempting in Ukraine.

But it is a useful generalization because it centers our focus on what has become the primary driver of geopolitical power over the last few centuries. It is not the country with the largest landmass or the largest population that gets to sit on top of the pyramid; instead, it is the country that can both amass the most capital within its borders *and* effectively deploy that capital throughout the world economic system. Capital accumulation is the key.

One of Arrighi's key insights is that capital accumulation happens in cycles rather than in a straight line that slopes upward at a constant rate. The Italians were in charge of the first cycle, and we'll discuss the other three shortly. Arrighi also breaks down each cycle into two stages. First, there is the material expansion. That is when the leading power's accumulation produces gains in the real economy—that is, more goods, more trade, and more access to the things and services that people use in their daily lives. When the Italian trade networks resulted in the increased production and use of wool, that was part of the city-states' material expansion. Eventually, however, an expansion's material phase runs up against some hard limits. One of these limits is increased competition. After watching the Italians amass enormous commercial and political power via their trade routes, other groups established their own competing trade networks, or else they sent their ships along the routes the Italians had already established in order to siphon business away from the city-states. This competition makes it harder to be confident that you'll get the returns you want on the capital you invest. If your company invents a new product that people love, your initial profits are going to be high, because people are clamoring to get their hands on the thing that no one else makes, and you can basically charge whatever you want for it, within reason. But once there are ten other companies making their own versions of the same thing, profits go down as companies struggle for pricing or efficiency advantages around the margins. But capital can't just sit around in a Genoese savings account either, because then its returns drop even further, essentially to zero. *Something* has to be done with it, because capital has to keep moving to survive. Its movement, or circulation, is what makes it capital. When a venture fund invests $1 million in a start-up, it is deploying capital; when an eccentric great-aunt hides $1 million in $100 bills under her floorboards, it's just cash.

That's where the second stage of an expansion begins. Sitting on top of a big pile of money but facing a dearth of sufficiently profitable real-economy opportunities for investment, the city-states gradually abandoned the commerce that had made them into great powers in the first place and started using their capital to finance the real-economy projects of other people instead. Over the course of the fifteenth and sixteenth centuries, the Genoese "switched from commodities to banking" and eventually "withdrew from commerce."[5] Now their profits would come not from raw materials or other goods but from the interest they could charge on loans made to others (among other financial instruments). Arrighi calls this stage the "financial expansion," and in agreement with the French historian Fernand Braudel, he calls the switch from material to financial expansion a "sign of autumn," a clear signal that the city-states' power had matured, was now on the wane, and would eventually end.[6]

But just because the city-states went into decline didn't mean that capitalism was declining as well. Capitalism's longer-term expansion was just beginning. While the Italians spent the final years of their preeminence lapping up the profits to be had from high finance, other nations were making use of that money to establish the beginnings of capitalism's second cycle of material expansion. By the end of the sixteenth century, it was clear that the United Provinces, known today as the Netherlands, would be in charge of this second cycle. An eighty-year war for independence from the Spanish crown, which ended with the Peace of Westphalia, had sparked the Dutch ascent to the top. After Spain invaded the Provinces to enforce the collection of taxes, the Dutch rebelled and took to the water, using piracy and privateering—the latter term referring to state-sanctioned piracy—to drain money and resources from the Spanish and stock up the coffers back home. In addition, the Dutch were located in an ideal spot from which to control the trade routes that traversed the Baltic Sea, and these would become increasingly important to the European economy as a whole as the Mediterranean trade network managed by the Italians reached the point of exhaustion.[7] By the time the Dutch achieved full recognition as an independent state in the mid-seventeenth century, piracy had made them rich, the Baltic trade network had made them an indispensable center of European commerce, and nearly a century of maritime fighting had made them some of the most skilled sailors on earth at a time when the fortunes of both commerce and warfare were primarily determined on the seas. The Dutch were ready to take charge.

You don't become the new leader of world capitalism by doing the same things your predecessors did. In addition to their geographic luck, the pirated wealth that made them rich from the outset, and their naval prowess, the Dutch were successful because they innovated. They commissioned the jurist and philosopher Hugo Grotius to write the book *Mare liberum*, an important early document of international law, which argued that the seas were international territory and thus free to use by any nation that wished to engage in trade. The Dutch also synthesized commercial, financial, and political power in ways the city-states had not. Venice, as one example, had established commercial, political, and military self-sufficiency, but at the cost of limiting itself to regional (as opposed to continental or global) power. Genoa, as a second, had projected its commercial and financial power across Europe and out into the wider world, but it was dependent on the Spanish Empire for military and political influence. The Dutch, by contrast, were the first capitalist power to establish the self-sufficiency of a modern state *and* project influence across the globe. Ships in the employ of the two major Dutch trading enterprises, the Dutch East India Company and the Dutch West India Company, could be chaperoned wherever they went by the large and technologically sophisticated Dutch navy. That navy could also enforce the administration of the global network of colonies from which traders returned to market with their goods, a network that included large swaths of Southeast Asia, portions of India and South Africa, and a big chunk of the present-day American mid-Atlantic, including New York City, which the Dutch founded as New Amsterdam. Just as important, the Dutch ensured that the money and goods generated by their trading empire, however far-flung their origins might be, eventually circulated back through the Provinces. Amsterdam became not just the political but also the physical center of world commerce. Its famous warehouses could store enough grain to feed all of Holland for a decade without beginning to run out of room, and its stock market—the first in history to remain in permanent session—attracted what Arrighi calls "idle money and credit" from all over Europe.[8] Nowhere else could that money be put to good, profitable use so quickly. This degree of ease in buying and selling company stock was unprecedented, and investors enamored of Amsterdam's user-friendly financial system poured money into Dutch commerce, enabling even more expansion. As the author of *Robinson Crusoe* famously put it when not writing novels,

> The Dutch must be understood as they really are, the Middle Persons in Trade, the Factors and Brokers of Europe . . . they *buy* to *sell* again, *take* in to *send* out, and the greatest Part of their vast Commerce consists in being supply'd from All Parts of the World, that they may supply All the World again.[9]

The Dutch demonstrated to the other European powers the benefits of centralizing within a single political entity all the component parts of long-range commerce, including the financing of large corporate enterprises, the use of military force to protect commercial interests, and the purchase, transport, storage, and sale of goods. Having watched the Dutch successfully implement this centralization, however, other powers began to imitate it, at which point the material phase of the Dutch expansion, like its Italian predecessor, hit its limits. Just as the Italians had, the Dutch sought to overcome these limits by switching their focus from commercial trade to financing the commercial efforts of others. Expensive and escalating conflicts among the European powers, which culminated in a wave of revolutions that swept across the continent in the eighteenth century, meant that there was plenty of demand for all the money the Dutch had to lend out.

From the perspective of Dutch financiers, it was a time of exuberance, but there was ultimately no getting around the fact that autumn had arrived for history's second great capitalist power. Eventually drawn into Europe's intra-continental wars, the Dutch saw their navy destroyed, their commercial influence diluted by competition, and demand for their financing eroded.

It was the British who destroyed the Dutch navy in the Fourth Anglo-Dutch War of 1780–84, and it was the British who replaced the Dutch at the top of world capitalism through the end of the nineteenth century. Building on the innovations pioneered by the Italians and the Dutch—the synthesis of trade, profit seeking, and high finance in the first case, with the additional backing of domestic military strength in the second—the British exploited Dutch weakness to make London the new financial center and then revolutionized how the world produced and transported goods with its technical advances in heavy industry. The revolution started in the field of what are called capital goods—that is, the things people need to build in order to be able to make lots of other things. Railways are capital goods, as are machines that produce textiles and the iron that goes into a steam engine, and the British were at the vanguard of all three. Iron smelting came first, and although England soon had the capacity to produce more iron than could be profitably employed at home, this surplus capacity was a powerful spur to economic growth in two ways. First, iron producers went looking for new ways to use the materials they could now manufacture on a large scale, and they found what they were looking for in railways and steamships. Second, England's liberal trade policies helped the ironworks to expand beyond their domestic market and create demand for capital goods all over the world. Wherever British capital goods gained a foothold, other kinds of commerce could soon follow, from the export of British textiles *to* new markets to the import of raw materials and other commodities *from* those new markets. These transactions often took place at gunpoint, if not always literally. Like the Dutch, the British used their formidable navy to clear away obstacles to the spread of their economic empire, and in cases of particularly tenacious resistance, British administrators were installed to keep recalcitrant peoples in line. By the early twentieth century, the British Empire was the largest in world history, administering colonies and territories that accounted for about a quarter of the world's land surface.

By that point, however, autumn had arrived again, and in the usual manner. Beginning around 1870, the global expansion of trade and commerce that had been kicked off by Britain's colonialism and technical advancements in mechanization began to generate competition. "An increasing number of business enterprises from an increasing number of locations across the UK-centered world-economy," Arrighi writes, "were getting in one another's way in the procurement of inputs and in the disposal of outputs, thereby destroying one another's previous 'monopolies'—that is, their more or less exclusive control over particular market niches."[10] As competition drove down profitability, those who held the U.K.'s capital began to shift their focus away from the material expansion of the real economy and toward the allure of high finance, while in the meantime ongoing economic competition slowly but steadily escalated to the generalized conflict of the world wars. The U.K. would retain its position atop the financial world well into the twentieth century, but the material center of global capitalism was already shifting across the Atlantic Ocean. The American century was under way.

It was only when the United States took up its leadership position at the head of global capitalism that world GDP growth truly exploded. Although retroactively ascribing growth figures to economies that did not think in terms of growth is a somewhat dicey exercise, estimates combining data from the World Bank with research from the Organisation for Economic Co-operation and Development (OECD) can help to sketch a general picture. Over the entirety of the first millennium of the Common Era, world GDP barely increased by 15 percent, expanding from $182 billion in the year 1 (in 2011 dollars) to $210 billion in the year 1000, for an annual growth rate of just over one-hundredth of 1 percent (on a per capita basis, there was no growth at all, because population growth kept pace with the millennium's meager increases in economic output). Over the subsequent five hundred years, growth more than doubled to $430 billion, but annual growth of two-tenths of a percent would still have been more or less imperceptible over the course of a human life. The combined efforts of the Italians, Dutch, and British made it possible for growth to quadruple between 1500 and 1870, but it was only after 1870, with America's post–Civil War industrialization and arrival on the world stage as an economic force, that growth began to accelerate at the rates we've all become used to over the last century. By 2000, the level of total world GDP stood at more than $63 trillion, eighteen times its level when the twentieth century began.[11]

To live through the hundred years from 1870 to 1970 was to experience the fastest and most profound transformation of daily life in history. As Robert J. Gordon puts it in his book *The Rise and Fall of American Growth,*

> Manual outdoor jobs were replaced by work in air-conditioned environments, housework was increasingly performed by electric appliances, darkness was replaced by light, and isolation was replaced not just by travel, but also by color television images bringing the world into the living room. Most important, a newborn infant could expect to live not to age forty-five, but to age seventy-two. The economic revolution of 1870 to 1970 was unique in human history, unrepeatable because so many of its achievements could happen only once.[12]

That it was America that got to lead the world through this historically unrepeatable series of transformations cannot be chalked up to any kind of national genius, nor can we credit the Italians, Dutch, and British with "deserving" their periods at the top of the economic hierarchy more than their competitors. It would be more accurate to say that capitalism itself, an economic *system* that operates according to a number of internal and impersonal laws, went "looking" for a new leader as its old one failed, like a parasite—please excuse the word's pejorative connotations—that goes looking for a new host after the old one has outlived its usefulness. America was in the right place at the right time. Because it was connected to Europe by ties of ancestry, diplomacy, and trade, the United States was able to share in the fruits of Great Britain's technological advances without too much delay. And because it was separated from Europe by an ocean as well as the Monroe Doctrine of 1823, the United States was not subject to the same competitive pressures that constrained other nations that might otherwise have looked to supplant the British Empire. Much has been made of the fact that America didn't pursue a colonial empire in the manner of the European powers, but to really believe this requires a degree of historical amnesia. Americans spent centuries fighting to displace the hundreds of Native societies that were spread across the continent when the first colonists arrived. What distinguishes the United States from the European empires, then, isn't its supposed lack of interest in colonies but rather its unique willingness to follow the colonization process all the way to the end. This process of "internal" expansion also provided the United States with abundant and cheap land, which both made it possible for the country to accept huge numbers of immigrant workers and helped to serve as a release valve for social pressures and conflicts in the major urban-industrial centers. Combined with the government's relatively more isolationist policies until the Japanese bombing of Pearl Harbor, these advantages made it possible for American capitalism to grow and develop secure in the knowledge of its territorial inviolability while the rest of the capitalist world tore itself apart in military conflict.

These advantages had essentially fallen into America's lap, but America made good use of them. Britain's advances in mechanization had made the dream of mass production possible, but it was Americans who made the dream real. The railway and telegraph facilitated the transport and distribution of goods across an entire continent. Frederick Taylor and Henry Ford invented manufacturing systems that made mass production much more cost effective than operating on a smaller scale. And the advent of advertising agencies, chain stores, and nationally distributed mail order catalogs made it possible to sell goods directly to anyone in the country. Urban and rural Americans alike were being integrated into an economic project that was producing and distributing goods at the fastest pace in history. And the effects of this integration cannot be understood simply in terms of the numbers of shoes or cars or even complete, ready-to-assemble houses (yes, really) that were sold by the Sears, Roebuck catalog during the first half of the century; the American capitalist expansion fundamentally changed people's relationship to the economy. Many goods and services that had been either produced within the home for domestic use or else exchanged only among members of the same community were folded into the logic of mass production and profit seeking. Instead of sewing clothes at home, families began to purchase their outfits from companies that might be located thousands of miles away. Fireplaces and kerosene lamps, each of which had to be individually maintained and monitored, gave way to networked electricity grids woven through the infrastructure of entire cities. Local musicians lost work to professionals whose performances could now be recorded and heard anywhere in the world. In sum, a whole universe of household tasks that had previously required enormous expenditures of time and muscle power could now be completed using cars, boilers, washing machines, vacuum cleaners, and dozens of other appliances that are categorized today as "consumer durables," meaning relatively expensive consumer goods that are expected to last for years after purchase. The Italian, Dutch, and British expansions had all effected historic transformations in how commerce worked, how governments and economies interacted, and how the capital goods that made large-scale manufacturing possible were produced. But under none of those three empires did capitalism make itself felt in people's homes and daily lives the way it did under the Americans.

As the United States rode the consumer durables expansion up the ladder of world power during the first half of the twentieth century, patriotism itself became entwined with the economic miracle the country was in the process of engineering. It would not be completely unfair to describe the "American dream" as fundamentally a vision of life made comfortable by the availability and affordability of various consumer durables, particularly the car and the appliance-filled, owner-occupied, single-family dwelling. As this vision shored up national self-belief at home, it also advertised the American way of life to people around the world. Just because America would not be pursuing a formal empire in the British manner did not mean it would put any less effort into projecting influence abroad. If the American economy was going to grow at its full potential, it would have to integrate as much of the rest of the world as possible into its system of manufacture and trade.

By placing itself at the head of a global economic system rather than trying to function as a self-contained economic powerhouse, the United States would accomplish two things. First, being able to sell manufactured goods to the rest of the world protected the United States in the event that domestic demand alone couldn't soak up everything America's factories were turning out, shielding the United States from the kinds of rapid price fluctuations and profitability squeezes that can throw a more isolated economy into crisis. Second, the more America invested and sold internationally, the more it familiarized other countries with the standard of living it was achieving domestically, which in turn made it easier for the rest of the world to accept America's economic and political leadership. As Arrighi points out in *The Long Twentieth Century,* this is a crucial step for a capitalist power to take. All dominant powers use coercion and violence to get what they want, but they can't *only* use coercion or violence without triggering a general war that will see them supplanted at the top of the pyramid. They must also *credibly* claim to be acting on behalf of larger, more general interests, such as market liberalization or economic prosperity for all. This claim is "always more or less fraudulent," Arrighi writes—that is, the dominant power's self-interest will always come first—but if it is "at least partly true and adds something to the power of the dominant group," then a state can be said to have achieved hegemony, the biggest geopolitical prize there is.[13]

The United States achieved hegemony with the end of World War II. The old order had been consumed by fire, and America was the only industrial power in a position to put a new one in place. Europe and East Asia were substantially in ruins, and decolonization was swallowing up the remnants of the old empires. But America had sacrificed much less than the war's other combatants in terms of people and matériel, it had used the war as an opportunity to expand its manufacturing capacity, and the geographic protection afforded by two oceans had left its domestic infrastructure almost totally unscathed by combat. Even before the war's formal end, the United States set out to remake the shattered economies of Western Europe and East Asia in its own image. The Bretton Woods Conference in 1944 saw representatives from forty-four Allied nations agree to a new monetary regime under which countries would guarantee the stability of exchange rates between their own currencies and the U.S. dollar, which at a stroke turned the dollar into the currency that no one in the world could afford to do without. The United States spent billions of dollars on postwar reconstruction in Europe, guaranteeing demand for American materials and products for decades, and the outbreak of the Korean War gave the United States an excuse to invest heavily in Japan as well. (Within thirty years, Germany and Japan, America's primary antagonists during the war, would be two of the most dynamic economies in the world.) Finally, the enormous levels of military spending made possible by the beginning of the Cold War allowed the United States to pump even more money into the world economy.

The result of all of this was twenty-five years during which the world economy grew at the fastest rates ever recorded. The French, rounding the time frame up by five years, simply named the period *Les Trente Glorieuses.* In the 1950s, world real GDP—"real," as opposed to "nominal," being the version of GDP that accounts for the distorting effect of inflation on output figures—grew at an average annual rate of 4.5 percent. In the 1960s, that figure jumped to roughly 5.5 percent, which is astounding.[14] A car company that started the decade making some 100 cars a week and then grew at a rate of 5.5 percent each year would be making some 170 cars a week ten years later, a 70 percent increase. Apply that increase to the economic production of *everything in the world,* and it is not hard to understand why so many people felt themselves to be living in the midst of an economic miracle. Anxieties regarding the Soviet menace made the

United States willing to export capital investment as well as technical know-how to Germany and Japan, kicking off a global manufacturing boom that consistently routed healthy profits back to American firms.[15] And at home, the government took halting but ultimately effective steps to maintain social peace by routing enough of the windfall back to the workers who ultimately made it possible. Part of this was accomplished through the GI Bill, which funneled immediate financial benefits to war veterans and all but guaranteed broad access to education, employment, and homeownership. Another part saw the government cultivating stable relationships with the country's major labor unions, which in turn kept their rank and file in line and avoided the kinds of disruptive labor actions that had defined the period between the two world wars. A third part was accomplished by the civil rights movement, which was to a significant extent an effort to win for Black Americans an acceptable share of the postwar boom's benefits.[16]

This approach was so successful that it was easy to miss the source of its fragility, which was that the whole thing depended on growth continuing to increase at its spectacular pace. Beginning in the 1970s, however, the American expansion, just like the three major capitalist expansions that preceded it, hit its limits, and growth began to slow down. Manufacturing outside the United States had advanced to the point that international firms no longer served just to satisfy the excess demand for manufactured goods that American firms lacked the capacity to produce. Now those firms began to compete directly with American companies for market share, including in the previously impregnable American domestic market. As low-cost firms began to eat into the profits that American manufacturers were by this point accustomed to, Aaron Benanav writes, "rates of industrial output growth in the U.S. began to decline starting in the late 1960s."[17] This was the beginning of the deindustrialization process that came to dominate American political debate during election campaigns. The United States responded by taking the dollar off the gold standard and dismantling the Bretton Woods monetary system in 1971. The hope was that eliminating the dollar's gold peg and allowing its price to fall would make American-manufactured goods more competitive internationally (the more expensive your currency, the more expensive your exports will be to international buyers). That worked to an extent for a little while, but ultimately it generalized the problem rather than solving it. Competition for manufacturing market share increased around the world, and the resulting decline in profits discouraged new investment.

People didn't know it at the time, but the world had entered what is now a full half century of slowing global growth, and the trend shows no signs of reversing. Average annual GDP growth was just over 4 percent in the 1970s, a decline of nearly 1.5 percent from the prior decade. In the 1980s, it fell further, to around 3 percent. In the 1990s, it barely topped 2 percent.[18] The global economic pie has continued to grow since the 1970s, but at a slowing pace that is insufficient to keep the capitalists happy. Reluctant to invest in new business lines or expanded capacity that can't provide the required rates of return, business have instead routed growing shares of their capital into asset markets, whether through share buybacks, increased dividend payouts, or other financial instruments. These investments are certainly profitable, but the only thing they grow is paper wealth. Financialization does nothing to grow the part of the economy that actually makes things for people to use. The economic historian Robert Brenner sums it up well:

> The fundamental source of today's crisis is the steadily declining vitality of the advanced capitalist economies over three decades, business cycle by business cycle, right into the present. The long-term weakening of capital accumulation and of aggregate demand has been rooted in a profound system-wide decline and failure to recover the rate of return on capital, resulting largely—though not only—from a persistent tendency to over-capacity, i.e., oversupply, in global manufacturing industries.[19]

In short, the world has too many factories, not enough demand to buy all the things those factories are capable of producing, and declining growth as a result, which only compounds the problem. Individual companies and countries have still found success in this environment, but only at the expense of others; slow growth turns the global economy into a zero-sum game that produces at least one loser for every winner rather than growing the pie quickly enough for most people to do well. One of the terms economists use for this situation is "secular stagnation."*

The growth slowdown has caused all kinds of problems, some of which I'll discuss shortly. But the first problem to highlight is the threat that secular stagnation poses to America's position of global leadership. To be a little crude about it, America became the most powerful country in the world because it was the first country that figured out how to manufacture consumer durables like cars and washing machines on a large scale and how to do so at sufficiently low cost that many people could afford to buy them. Then it not only sold those goods to the rest of the world, but it also provided enough capital investment and technical expertise for other countries to learn how to make those goods themselves. Thus permitted to hitch their wagons to America's growth engine, countries in Western Europe and East Asia (today they're referred to as "developed nations") helped to support the United States as the lead player in global power politics.

But as growth slows and the benefits of *voluntary* subordination to American interests decline, that support becomes harder to ensure. The world basically has enough cars and washing machines—far too many cars, in fact—and America can't reignite global growth by pro-

---

* This phrase reveals a lot about the extent to which capitalists have naturalized an economic system that is, in reality, man-made. In finance-speak, "secular" means anything not pertaining to the business cycle, which is the term for the process by which capitalist economies grow, eventually overheat, suffer some kind of crisis, struggle through a recession, and then begin to grow again. One expects growth to fall in the latter stages of the business cycle, but if growth falls even once the effects of the business cycle have been accounted for, then you have a "secular" decline in growth. What's revealing about the term is what it doesn't say. If anything not related to the business cycle is "secular," then the business cycle itself is divine.

ducing more of them. The problem is that nobody seems to know what America should produce instead, what combination of goods and services and raw materials can not only satisfy some hitherto unnoticed global economic need but also help America maintain its competitive economic advantages. But just because an economic solution to the problem of secular stagnation hasn't presented itself doesn't mean it's not worth trying political or military solutions instead. At its foundation, that's what the war on terror is: a potential solution to the problem of slowing global growth and America's declining power.

• • •

The most important economic problem caused by slowing global growth is one that economic statistics don't do a very good job of capturing. One consequence of increased competition in manufacturing is that the amount of money firms spend on wages for human employees declines relative to the amount of money they spend on technological improvements to the production process. This is because spending x amount of money on upgrading the machines in your factory will produce a greater increase in output and productivity—the latter defined as output per worker—than spending that same amount on hiring more workers. Pursuing cost efficiency above all else in an effort to eke out a higher profit margin, companies can reduce the relative share of their spending that goes to labor costs in two ways. One is to focus on outsourcing and replace the workers you currently employ with workers elsewhere—say, in China—who will do the same job for less money. Another is to hire fewer workers than you used to. Since the 1970s, capitalists have done both. They've chased pools of inexpensive labor all over the globe, dividing up the production process into a bunch of little parts and then sending each individual part to wherever it can be completed on the cheap. And they have also shifted away, wherever possible, from employing people full time, relying instead on contract labor, piecework, interns, adjuncts, and so on. The result has been a stunning increase in the number of people globally who cannot survive on the amount of work that is available to them in the formal economy, and who must piece to-gether a constantly changing series of part-time and temporary jobs, none of which include benefits or robust worker protections, in order to get by.

It is this global collapse in stable, full-time employment that eco-nomic statistics have failed to capture. In his recent book, *Automation and the Future of Work,* Aaron Benanav notes that when growth first began to slow in the 1970s, unemployment rates went up in a number of wealthy countries, and "outside of the United States, they remained stubbornly high for decades."[20] This was a serious problem for gov-ernment unemployment insurance programs, which had all been de-signed to handle temporary unemployment increases resulting from the normal ups and downs of the business cycle rather than perma-nently elevated unemployment caused by the fact that the golden age of manufacturing was over. "To coax the unemployed back to work," Benanav writes, "governments began to reduce labor market protec-tions and scale back unemployment benefits" (President Clinton's "welfare reform" initiative is probably the most notorious example of this phenomenon in the United States). With the safety net disappear-ing, Benanav writes, "few workers remain unemployed for long. No matter how bad labor market conditions become, they still have to try to find work, since they need to earn an income in order to survive."[21] Shunted out of full-time or union jobs into at-will employment and part-time work, these workers find themselves caught in the teeth of a brutal shift in the labor market, but one that unemployment statistics do not reflect. That's because unemployment figures primarily count people who are both not currently working *at all* and actively in search of full-time work. If your work life consists entirely of driving a car for Uber a couple of hours each week, you don't count as unemployed, no matter how much trouble you're having paying the bills, and no mat-ter how desperately you're searching for a salaried job with benefits. And if you become so discouraged by the whole thing that you give up and drop out of the workforce entirely, you don't count as unem-ployed, either, even though "unemployed" is exactly what you are. The result is persistent *underemployment* rather than unemployment, a situation in which the economy's vanishing core of full-time jobs is replaced by gig work that may provide a means of temporary survival but cannot offer the kinds of security and stability around which it's possible to build a dignified life.

And that's in the *wealthy* countries. In middle- and low-income nations, the consequences of secular stagnation have been catastrophic. In his 2006 book *Planet of Slums,* the great historian and political writer Mike Davis pointed out that since the 1970s the world's poor countries have urbanized at a rate that puts Europe's experiences of nineteenth-century urbanization to shame.[22] But whereas those European experiences of urbanization were part of an industrial revolution that saw growth accelerate dramatically, the more recent urbanization of what used to be called the Third World has largely occurred in places where economic growth is either low, slowing down, or nonexistent. Megacities such as Lagos (home to 20.7 million people in 2002), Cairo (14.2 million), Manila (26.4 million), Mexico City (24.7 million), São Paulo (22.7 million), and Jakarta (28.6 million) have grown so much not because they are hotbeds of economic opportunity but because the best way for people to survive when they cannot find secure, salaried labor is for them to live around as many other people as possible. The growth of these sprawling urban agglomerations accounted for some two-thirds of the world's human population increase between 1950 and 2006, and the expectation is that after 2020 or so, population growth will happen entirely within cities until peaking at around 10 billion near the midpoint of the twenty-first century. These megacities are not monuments to the possibilities of human achievement, however. An urban archipelago centered on Lagos and running along the Gulf of Guinea from Benin to Accra, for example, now has a population comparable to that of the East Coast of the United States, with 60 million people living on a six-hundred-kilometer strip of land. Back in 2006, Davis predicted that by 2020 this supersize urban agglomeration would "probably" constitute "the biggest single footprint of urban poverty on earth."[23]

The term for the people who live in this global slum archipelago is "surplus population." That sounds offensive, but it is not meant in any kind of moral sense. They are surplus with respect to the economic system they inhabit, surplus in the sense that the economy has no need for their labor and is unable to grow at a rate that would provide them with formal employment. Of course, their labor remains necessary in a few respects. For one thing, mega-retailers such as Walmart, Amazon, and Alibaba often rely on byzantine networks of subcontracting and outsourcing to manufacture the cheap goods they sell to middle- and high-income consumers, and researchers have found on multiple occasions that these networks extend into slums and other places that members of the surplus population call home. For another, people still need to eat even if they cannot get hired. Those who are shut out of the formal economy will rely instead on informal work—domestic labor, scavenging, temporary construction work paid in cash, or small-scale buying and selling on the gray or black markets. Davis estimated that the global surplus population numbered around one billion in 2006.[24] He expected that number to grow quickly, and in 2018 the United Nations reported that two billion people—*more than 60 percent of the world's workers, and more than a quarter of the total human population*—earned their livelihoods primarily through informal work.

Because these people are not technically unemployed in the eyes of those who tabulate labor statistics, this surge in informal work is not reflected in standard forms of economic data. But it is the single most important economic phenomenon of the past several decades, and it defines the gap separating the world's rich countries from its poor ones. When you hear the terms "developed countries" and "developed markets," it is useful to understand them as meaning "places where people have comparatively more access to formal employment." "Emerging markets" are places where people have less access, or none. The UN found that in Africa, 86 percent of employment is informal. In Asia-Pacific, it's 68 percent, and in the Americas it's 40 percent, with the vast majority of informal work concentrated in countries other than the United States. In Arab states, 69 percent of workers are stuck in the informal economy.[25]

Perhaps you can see where I'm going with this. While terrorism has existed for centuries—with John Brown as America's first celebrity terrorist—many historians argue that the contemporary version first emerged in 1972, when members of the Palestinian group Black September invaded the Olympic Village at the Munich Summer Games, killed two Israeli athletes, and took nine others hostage. That was the first time a terrorist group could rely on a global mass media to publicize their attack to the whole world in real time. That attack inaugurated a new surge of terrorist activity around the world, one that has not yet abated today (though it might have peaked with al-Qaeda's attacks on the United States). The Munich attack took place just as the long global growth downturn was beginning, and it was a message from the future. Israel had occupied the Palestinian territories five years earlier at the conclusion of the Six-Day War, completely shutting out Palestinians from meaningful participation in the global or even regional economy. The occupation turned Palestinians into members of the global surplus population at a stroke.

It is exactly that kind of terrorism that America mobilized to fight beginning in the late summer of 2001. It is politically or religiously motivated violence. It alternately targets citizens of the developed world, symbols of the developed world's power, or domestic institutions or political officials who are seen as cooperating with the developed world's economic sacrifice of poor and middle-income countries. Even when its targets are incoherent or its stated rationale conspiratorial, it expresses a version of the emerging world's anger and hopelessness in the most brutal way available. Just because it is neither politically constructive nor morally justifiable does not render terrorism incomprehensible, as most American political figures have claimed over the prior two decades. It is a demand that all of this be made to stop, and the people making the demand are sometimes willing to die in order to express themselves.

Since 2001, anyone suggesting that contemporary terrorism has anything to do with economic exploitation or inequality has been met with reactions ranging from pointed criticism to howling condemnation. Many of these reactions have simply been attempts by the American right to score political points by denouncing people like Susan Sontag or the Reverend Jeremiah Wright, Barack Obama's former pastor in Chicago. I don't think these critics deserve much serious consideration, given the extent to which they rely on crude moral denunciation in making their points. (It's like arguing that man-made climate change plays a role in the increased severity of flooding and hearing, in reply, "You're saying the flood victims deserved it!")

There is a different criticism of the economic explanation for terrorism, however, that deserves more attention. Objecting to the idea that terrorism amounts to a cri de coeur emanating out of the ranks of the global poor, a number of scholars have correctly noted that most terrorist leaders do not actually come from the poorest segments of their societies. Instead, they tend to be middle class and even educated. Osama bin Laden, after all, was not just middle or even upper class but full-on 1 percent rich. The son of a billionaire construction magnate in Saudi Arabia, bin Laden studied at elite universities in the Middle East and the U.K. and eventually inherited between $25 and $30 million from his father. This is a truly exceptional level of wealth, and it is by no means representative of terrorists on average. Nevertheless, it is true that most members of extremist groups were not languishing in poverty when they decided to start learning about homemade explosives.

To describe extremists as middle-class and dismiss the economic issue entirely, however, is to miss the fact that there are major variations in wealth and social status *within* classes. In 2011, the political scientist Alexander Lee published a paper investigating whether "poverty and lack of education play a role in participation in political violence." While conceding that many studies had "concluded that these groups are composed of people who are wealthier and better educated than the average member of the societies from which they recruit," Lee argued that researchers had missed some pretty important trees for the forest. Rather than situating terrorists within the class structures of their societies as a whole, Lee considered where extremists fell economically within the smaller group of people who were active participants in politics. He chose this as a starting point for his research because "terrorists . . . are not drawn from a random sample of the population but, rather, from those who have acquired information about the political process, are connected to politicized social networks, and are able to devote time and energy to political involvement." Around the world, the poor are relatively less politicized than the wealthier members of society, whether because they don't have the time to participate or because they don't see what the point would be (wealth and income are the best predictors of whether a given American votes or not). Lee found that terrorists tended to come from the bottom rungs of the politicized group.[26] In general, extremists are people who have just enough money and education to understand how the political system works and how they might get involved, but not enough to meaningfully influence its direction or improve their own lives. They live in a world in which low growth and soaring economic inequality are sucking the vitality out of the global economy, and they live in countries in which there are few political freedoms.[27] They may be educated, and they may have more money than the national average, but an education that isn't followed by opportunities to use it isn't worth much, as the persistent exodus of highly skilled university graduates from middle- and low-income countries suggests. Terrorists are people who are stuck. What's worse, they know it.

One of the defining features of terrorism in its contemporary form is the exploitation of mass media to disseminate news of attacks around the world and amplify the extremists' messages. But mass media has likely fueled terrorism as well. The period that saw the failure of the postwar dream of universal high growth is also the period during which mass media became truly global, allowing the rich West to blanket the earth with images of its consumerism and success. That combination is a perfect recipe for resentment, which the writer Pankaj Mishra has described in his 2017 book, *Age of Anger,* as one of the defining sentiments of our age. Although resentment-fueled extremism has flourished all over the world in recent decades, the Middle East proved to be particularly susceptible to its lure, not because of any belief inherent to Islam, but because the geopolitical pressures on the region have been especially brutal for the people who live there. Studded with American military bases, menaced by a hostile Israel, predominantly ruled by authoritarians (some of them dynastic) who enjoy the backing of this or that rich Western government, and reliant on oil exports to a degree that stifles productive investment in other kinds of economic growth, many Middle Eastern societies have essentially been frozen in place, leaving their citizens with no way to share in the material prosperity and freedom of political action they see on their television and computer screens every day. In this light, religion doesn't so much provide the basic motivation for political violence as it constructs an edifice of meaning and redemption around social frustrations that already permeate daily life. The moment when people decide there is no hope for constructive change or progress in this world is also the moment when they will begin to listen to those who can promise to deliver those things in the next world. "Those who perceive themselves as left or pushed behind by a selfish conspiratorial minority," Mishra writes, "can be susceptible to political seducers from any point on the ideological spectrum."[28] In the case of al-Qaeda and similar groups, those seducers arrived brandishing a Koran.

Of course, violent fundamentalist groups aren't the only problem associated with stagnant global growth. Low growth also produces increased numbers of migrants, as people look to escape from their exploited homelands and make a new life in the rich countries that have benefited the most from our inequitable global economic arrangements. It produces political instability as well, because autocratic leaders who cannot offer their citizens jobs or prosperity even if they want to find themselves relying more and more on violence and repression to maintain the political order that keeps them in power. And it produces the slums that Mike Davis described so vividly—places in which housing is inadequate, basic utilities are unreliable, socioeconomic betterment is a pipe dream, and local governance is often managed by competing groups of violent gangs.

It is in the light of these wider problems of global governance that the economic rationale behind America's war on terror becomes even more compelling. To say it plainly: In the wake of September 11, the United States found itself at the head of a global economic order that had been founded on a growth surge that was slowly but surely running out of steam. To stand back and watch as China took the top spot for itself was unthinkable, nor was it an option to find a more equitable way to share control over the functioning of the world economy. For one thing, the benefits of being on top were just too great, allowing Americans to develop and sustain levels of consumption that far outstripped those of any other group of people in world history. For another, "sharing" isn't how capitalism works on the global scale. With those options off the table, the United States faced a whole series of problems stemming from the kinds of authoritarian political rule, endemic urban poverty, and social instability that plagued the countries where growth had failed most spectacularly. The government's military planners often refer to these countries as weak or failed states, and while the United States believed for some time that the problems facing these states could be kept more or less at arm's length, September 11 was thought to reveal that belief as illusory. Going forward, America would need to confront these problems more directly, with a decentralized, expansive, and flexible military effort that wouldn't be bound by any conventional definitions of victory or defeat. That's where the expanded war on terror came from. It might not be able to solve the problems facing a low-growth world, but it could at least tolerably insulate the United States from their effects. The war is a tool for managing the very surplus populations that the end of American-led economic prosperity helped to create, people whom the United States now finds itself unable and unwilling to help.

• • •

America's military planners didn't use the term "surplus populations" as they outlined how the country should respond to the rising instability of the late twentieth and early twenty-first centuries, nor did the Bush administration talk about slowing global growth as it made the case for the war on terror. Neither omission should be surprising. Strategists and soldiers aren't tasked with curing the maladies that afflict the parts of the world in which America has decided it has a vital economic or social interest. Their job is to use military force to get rid of the symptoms, whether those be food riots carried out by poor people or suicide attacks planned by religious young men who resent the fact that society failed to reward their efforts to get educated with a reliable income. And for George W. Bush and Barack Obama (or any president, for that matter), acknowledging that slowing global growth was a characteristic tendency of capitalism as an economic system was out of the question. That idiosyncratic problems might pop up over the course of capitalism's journey through history—whether recessions, waves of speculative frenzy, or market crashes—was fine. Those could be talked about and addressed. But to suggest that some of these problems might be inherent to the system itself, requiring not just targeted interventions or reforms but potentially replacement by a new system, was impossible.

Despite this code of silence around some of capitalism's more deeply rooted problems, however, Pentagon strategists were clear-eyed about the kind of world they confronted and open about their desire to manage the surplus populations whose numbers were increasing almost everywhere. Following the 1993 Mogadishu debacle, in which Somali forces shot down three Black Hawk helicopters and killed eighteen American soldiers, Army theoreticians and eggheads working for the RAND Corporation began to churn out all kinds of papers and memoranda on how the military might reorient itself toward prolonged, sporadic, low-intensity urban conflict. Three years after Mogadishu, the house journal of the Army War College, *Parameters,* published an article on the swiftly emerging era of urban conflict. Major Ralph Peters began with a flourish:

> The future of warfare lies in the streets, sewers, high-rise buildings, industrial parks, and the sprawl of houses, shacks, and shelters that form the broken cities of our world. We will fight elsewhere, but not so often, rarely as reluctantly, and never so

brutally. Our recent military history is punctuated with city names—Tuzla, Mogadishu, Los Angeles, Beirut, Panama City, Hue, Saigon, Santo Domingo—but these encounters have been but a prologue, with the real drama still to come.[29]

Peters called cities "the post-modern equivalent of jungles and mountains—citadels of the dispossessed and irreconcilable," and he wrote that "a military unprepared for urban operations across a broad spectrum is unprepared for tomorrow." One year later, a National Defense Panel review imagined what the world might look like in 2020 and then identified several areas of concern that the U.S. military would need to address if it wanted to be able to cope with this coming world. One was terrorism; "missile proliferation and a host of transnational dangers may play a more prominent role," the panel warned. Another was "the need to prepare ourselves to conduct operations in urban environments."[30] Without ever actually using the term, the panel highlighted the world's growing surplus populations as one of the key threats that would menace American supremacy through the first decades of the twenty-first century. The report cited "social and demographic trends that threaten to outstrip the ability of many countries to adapt," including "rapid population growth in regions ill-prepared to absorb it, refugee migration and immigration, chronic unemployment and underemployment, and intensified competition for resources, notably energy and water."[31]

The RAND Corporation warned about the "urbanization of insurgency,"[32] and a theoretical journal run by the U.S. Air Force described the difficulties involved with carrying out combat operations in slums, a kind of battlefield that is "decreasingly knowable because it is increasingly unplanned."[33] The Bush administration might have tried to convince Americans that the war on terror and especially the invasion of Iraq would go smoothly, conjuring visions in which grateful throngs of the world's oppressed peoples would toss flowers and garlands at America's soldiers before embarking on the construction of dynamic market economies. But the military theoreticians who tried to delineate the contours of the coming era were less optimistic, and they occasionally slipped into dystopian gloom. "Consider just a few of the potential trouble spots where US military intervention or assistance could prove necessary in the next century," Peters wrote.

> Mexico, Egypt, the sub-continent with an expansionist India, the Arabian Peninsula, Brazil, or the urbanizing Pacific Rim. Even though each of these states or regions contains tremendous rural, desert, or jungle expanses, the key to each is control of an archipelago of cities. The largest of these cities have populations in excess of 20 million today—more specific figures are generally unavailable as beleaguered governments lose control of their own backyards. Confronted with an armed and hostile population in such an environment, the US Army as presently structured would find it difficult to muster the dismount strength necessary to control a single center as simultaneously dense and sprawling as Mexico City.
>
> ... In fully urbanized terrain ... warfare becomes profoundly vertical, reaching up into towers of steel and cement, and downward into sewers, subway lines, road tunnels, communications tunnels, and the like. ... The broken spatial qualities of urban terrain fragments units and compartmentalizes encounters, engagements, and even battles. The leader's span of control can easily collapse, and it is very, very hard to gain and maintain an accurate picture of the multidimensional "battlefield."

Peters's litany of difficulties continued for an additional twenty-five hundred words, without any evident improvement in his mood. "Noncombatants, without the least hostile intent," he wrote, "can overwhelm the force." "Atrocity is close-up and commonplace." "Casualties can soar. ... [U]rban operations result in broken bones, concussions, [and] traumatic impact deaths." Soldiers with "untempered immune systems" would also confront "a broad range of septic threats" resulting from "the appalling sanitation in many urban environments." "Soldiers will die simply because they were looking the wrong way, and even disciplined and morally sound soldiers disinclined to rape can lose focus in the presence of female or other civilians." "Vertical fighting is utterly exhausting."[34]

What you have here is a detailed and more or less accurate description, before the fact, of the war on terror that the United States spent the first two decades of the twenty-first century fighting. Like the war itself, Peters's list of places where the United States might have to send its military spans every continent except for Antarctica, and each location is home to at least one of the mega-slums that we have identified as a signature product of stagnating growth within global capitalism. His description of urban conflict, with America's troops shooting their way through tower block stairwells and blind alleyways, reads like the script for a *Call of Duty: Modern Warfare* game. His emphasis on the dangers of concussions anticipates the rise of traumatic brain injury as the signature combat wound of the Iraq War. And his chilling warnings about the difficulties of distinguishing enemy combatants from civilians in urban combat environments—"atrocity is up-close and commonplace"—have been more than borne out by the results of the past twenty years.

There is one other curious aspect of Peters's essay that I would like to discuss. Throughout the paper, Peters emphasizes the importance of training to prepare the U.S. military for urban conflict. He captures perfectly the juncture at which the Army found itself immediately after September 11. "The modern and post-modern trend in Western militaries has been to increase the proportion of tasks executed by machines while reducing the number of soldiers in our establishments," he writes. "We seek to build machines that enable us to win while protecting or distancing the human operator from the effects of combat. At present, however, urban combat remains extremely manpower-intensive—and it is a casualty producer." Fully mechanized war might be feasible in the long term, but for now the front lines would remain the responsibility of real, human soldiers, and those soldiers would need a lot of new equipment to keep them safe.

Soldiers would need "new forms of armor," "eye protection . . . given the splintering effects of firefights in masonry and wood environments," and "protective headgear" that could guard against "accidental blows from falls or collapsing structures" just as well as they guarded against "enemy fire." Guns would have to be "compact and robust, with a high rate of fire and very lightweight ammunition." In addition, soldiers would need the capability for "thermal or post-thermal imaging" to help them see through walls and around corners, perhaps even equipment that could "differentiate between male and female body heat distributions and that will even be able to register hostility and intent from smells and sweat." This panoply of gadgets would have to be balanced, however, against the need to reduce the amount of weight each soldier carries "dramatically . . . since fighting in tall buildings requires agility that a soldier unbalanced by a heavy pack cannot attain." Still, the equipment would inevitably add up, meaning that "soldiers will need more upper body strength." Again, we see here an aspect of the war on terror fantasized into being in advance of its realization, as Peters conjures up the image of the Special Forces super-soldier that has become such an icon of twenty-first-century conflict.

In the paper's second-to-last paragraph, however, a different kind of fantasy, or perhaps nightmare, appears. Following a list of bureaucratic reforms that might help to facilitate the military's transition to twenty-first-century warfare, Peters returns to the issue of training: "None of the sample measures cited above is as important as revolutionizing training for urban combat." But *where* to train these soldiers? Current facilities, designed to teach recruits to fight in "villages or small towns," were clearly inadequate. Peters briefly raises the possibility of "building realistic 'cities' in which to train" but concludes that such an endeavor would be "prohibitively expensive." Then Peters has a better solution in mind. "Why build that which already exists?" He writes,

In many of our own blighted cities, massive housing projects have become uninhabitable and industrial plants unusable. Yet they would be nearly ideal for combat-in-cities training. While we could not engage in live-fire training (even if the locals do), we could experiment and train in virtually every other regard. Development costs would be a fraction of the price of building a "city" from scratch, and city and state governments would likely compete to gain a US Army (and Marine) presence, since it would bring money, jobs, and development—as well as a measure of social discipline.

At the very end of a paper otherwise focusing entirely on the difficulties facing American troops as they try to navigate the dangerous, seething cities of the rest of the world, we are suddenly presented with a shocking vision of the hopeless state of America's own cities. These are apparently places where "locals" engage in "live-fire training"— presumably in the course of carrying out their violent gang wars—and governments are so desperate for not only "money, jobs, and development" but also a modicum of "social discipline" that they would welcome and even "compete" to host an occupying force of U.S. military trainees.

How did things get so bad at home, anyway? That larger question is beyond Peters's remit, but his description still offers some clues as to what the answer might be. As one ideal training site, we have the "unusable" "industrial plants" that huddle ominously on the outskirts of America's urban landscapes. As another, we have "housing projects." These projects might once have symbolized the optimism of Lyndon Johnson's Great Society, a project undertaken when America's growth engine was roaring, but now they are "uninhabitable," although Peters must know that many people do, in fact, continue to inhabit them. The factories became unusable because growth slowed and the corporations that built them stopped investing in their operation, and the projects, which once housed a class of people referred to as the working poor, are now little more than decrepit containers in which to store people who are still impoverished but increasingly struggle to find any work at all.

This pessimistic vision may seem like a non sequitur, a somewhat paranoid conception of domestic social decay shoehorned into what is otherwise a coherent (if very contestable) account of what the United States will need to do to maintain its global dominance in the twenty-first century. It is not. Underneath the racism that animates the passage, Peters also gestures toward an awareness that global stagnation is producing deindustrialization, persistent underemployment, and growing surplus populations *inside* the United States as well. During the first decade of the war on terror, the kinds of training, tactics, and equipment Peters urged the military to develop would be tested and refined throughout Iraq, Afghanistan, Yemen, Pakistan, Somalia, and elsewhere. Following the global financial crisis, however, many Americans would come to realize that economic stagnation and precarity were coming for them as well. In turn, the government realized that this new kind of war fighting also had many useful domestic applications. If the military the United States had built and the tactics it had developed could be sent to foreign countries to manage surplus populations and their attendant problems—from political instability to guerrilla insurgencies to migration—then those same tactics could also be used to manage urban poverty, the discontent of the chronically underemployed, and unwanted migrants at home.

CHAPTER 9

Borders, Squares, Real Estate, Streets

I can't breathe.

—protester recovering from tear gas exposure in
Tahrir Square, Cairo, Egypt, 2011[1]

I can't breathe!

—protester arrested at Occupy Wall Street,
New York City, 2011[2]

I CAN'T BREATHE!

—chant heard at Black Lives Matter protests,
United States, 2014–20

Americans don't use the phrase "surplus population" when they talk about the un- and underemployed people who try to make their way to the United States each year. Instead, they talk about "illegal immigrants," and they talk about the country's southern border. In the early spring of 2005, hundreds of journalists, outfitted with their usual array of notepads, audio recorders, and video cameras, began to gather in Tombstone, Arizona. Situated about thirty miles from the Mexican border, Tombstone had been a boomtown for silver mining during the late nineteenth century, as well as the site of the legendary O.K. Corral gunfight in 1881. A ghost town for much of the twentieth century once the silver ran out, Tombstone's population barely surpassed a thousand in the twenty-first, a number the visiting journalists, American and international alike, might well have doubled all on their own. They had come to report on the national coming-out party of the Minuteman Project, a group established, in the words of one of its founders, to "launch a movement against illegal immigration" and "demand action from the federal government."[3] A six-month recruiting drive had summoned nearly a thousand volunteers to Tombstone (now the town's population had nearly tripled). They were there to carry out a monthlong "border watch" along a several-dozen-mile stretch of desert. They sat on lawn chairs in combat fatigues, peering into Mexico through binoculars and keeping their sidearms at the ready. They were there to hunt for migrants. With the Minuteman-to-journalist ratio sitting close to one to one, they had little trouble getting out their message.

The group was founded by two men. Chris Simcox was a former kindergarten and grade school teacher from Los Angeles. He had a failed marriage and a teenage son. Following September 11, his exwife filed for sole custody after Simcox began leaving angry voicemail messages on her phone, ranting about the impending nuclear destruction of Los Angeles and the necessity of teaching their son how to use firearms. "I will no longer trust anyone in this country," he said in one message. "My life has changed forever, and if you don't get that, you are brainwashed like everybody else."[4] He moved to Tombstone, turned the local newspaper, the *Tumbleweed,* into a forum for his anti-immigration views, and began running small border watch operations in 2002. He couldn't get himself into the national media, however, until he linked up with Jim Gilchrist a couple of years later. A Vietnam veteran and retired accountant, Gilchrist contacted Simcox after being impressed by one of his interviews and proposed the national border watch event.⁵ Their meeting catalyzed a plan for action that had been building inside Gilchrist for years. It was on September 11, he wrote, that "he realized that he was, in effect, an American without a country. . . . As the events of that day unfolded, they revealed that the murderers were Islamo-fascist terrorists who had overstayed their visas and were living in the United States illegally. If immigration laws had simply been enforced, the lives lost that day might have been spared."⁶

Drawing from various parts of American mythology, from the militia-driven rebelliousness of the Revolution to the flinty-eyed determination of the frontier days, the Minuteman Project made for compelling and effective political theater, which was good, because it wasn't terribly effective at anything else. The news media oohed and aahed over the handful of migrants the Minutemen spotted during their initial monthlong border watch, but false alarms and long, boring nights out in the desert chill would become much more common than genuine sightings, which occurred, on average, only once every fifty hours on patrol.⁷ Even when a patrol did find migrants, they couldn't pursue and apprehend them. That was the U.S. Border Patrol's job, and the Border Patrol wasn't about to tolerate a group of self-selected and untrained vigilantes stopping Mexicans at gunpoint or attempting to carry out citizens' arrests. As the Project's leaders knew, that was for the best, because the organization's volunteers were not exactly paragons of youth, health, or fitness. Veterans and law enforcement officers made up a large portion of the group's ranks, but not veterans of the war on terror, and not on-duty police officers who had taken time off in order to serve their country at the border. The veterans had served in Vietnam or even Korea—one Minuteman was eighty-three—and the police officers were retirees.⁸ They were people whose careers or marriages or military service had ended long ago, and they were hardly in any condition to chase down young migrants desperately fleeing Mexico in search of work. When they did see migrants moving through the landscape, the most they could do was phone it in to Border Patrol and, if they were close enough, shine flashlights at them. Their effect on the number of migrants who successfully crossed the border landed somewhere between "negligible" and "none."

That is not to say the patrols served no purpose at all. In addition to the many column inches and hours of television coverage the Minutemen won for their cause, the patrols allowed those who participated to feel as though they, too, were helping to fight America's war, even if military service or police employment were no longer available to them. The sociologist Harel Shapira, who spent time with the Minutemen both at their camp and on patrol and then wrote a very informative and entertaining book about the experience, found that even as they failed to catch migrants, they succeeded at creating a nostalgic fantasy world in which they could live dangerously and heroically. Men and women in the group were expected to fill their traditional gender roles, with men going out on patrol and women handling food preparation and camp administration, even though patrolling almost never involved anything more physically arduous than sitting in a lawn chair, bundling up against the nighttime cold, and holding a pair of binoculars up to one's face.[9] The volunteers' very presence at the camp also constituted an act of resistance against what they universally regarded as a disturbing deterioration of the national character. "Being a citizen does not mean sitting on the sofa with a can of beer and bag of potato chips while watching football," one said. "The sad thing is that for many Americans today that is what it has come to mean."[10] Volunteers wore military fatigues, amassed impressive caches of weapons, and adopted nicknames like the ones soldiers had in the army. ("Legolas" saw himself as a skilled tracker,[11] while "Blowfish," who had served in Vietnam as a Green Beret, commanded more respect and deference than anyone else.)[12] Any military-grade thermal scopes or night-vision goggles that made their way into the group's equipment stores became instant objects of fascination and desire.[13] Collectively, the high-tech gear, rugged desert setting, military argot, and largely imaginary sense of danger allowed the Minutemen to feel as though they were frontiersmen, Indian hunters, and soldiers in the new century's first great war. "I was ready to enlist," one said of the days following September 11. "I got this bum leg, but I would serve my country in a heartbeat."[14] And another: "I can't go and fight in Iraq, but I can come down here and make sure these borders are secure. . . . You better believe those terrorists are trying to come through over here."[15]

On the ground, all of this produced scenes like something out of a Coen brothers film. One volunteer mistook cows for migrants so many times that someone else put up a sign at camp: a picture of a cow below the words "To all people on the line: this is bovine in nature, and not to be confused with Illegal Aliens."[16] One day on patrol, a trio of Minutemen who had invited the sociologist to tag along became convinced that the firefight they'd long anticipated was finally popping off. I'll quote Shapira's account at length:

> I'm standing with Andrew. We're facing the empty stretch of desert that is Mexico. And suddenly a helicopter comes at us. It is coming from our left, to the west, over the top of a mountain. It shuttles toward us, straddling the barbed wire fence that separates one stretch of desert from another.
>
> . . . Mark rushes toward us. "Hey, did that helicopter have any writing on it?" There's desperation in his voice. Andrew says it did not, seemingly happy that his own observations have been confirmed. "Yeah, that's what I thought," Mark continues in haste. "It was fucking unmarked. It was a Mexican fucking military helicopter."
>
> Jack races to his truck. He takes out two pistols from inside, and with his back [against] the driver's side door he cocks them both. Mark makes a run to his own truck, pulls out his bulletproof vest, and proceeds to strap it on. Andrew hobbles in haste. He falls on the way. I help him up. He gives me an admiring glance. We make a run for Jack's truck, where Mark is now also hunkered down. The exhilaration is contagious. The fear, the excitement, is intense. Everyone has at least one gun in their hands. Jack yells out, "They're coming at us tonight, they're fucking coming at us." Mark puts a fresh clip into

his gun. "There's gonna be a god damn shoot-out tonight." All of us are crouching beside Jack's truck.

The helicopter disappeared, and the attack failed to materialize, but the trio were not dissuaded from their theory that it was undercover Mexican military. They hypothesized instead that the Mexicans had deployed aircraft to scout the Minutemen. "Maybe they also want to know where we are so they know where to bring the illegals so they can cross," Mark said.[17]

Part of what made the Minuteman Project volunteers so ludicrous, aside from the slapstick hijinks, is that none of them seemed to understand what the border really is. The United States no longer has a border that one can see on a map. What it has is a border system, a set of physical barriers, surveillance techniques, law enforcement agencies, and checkpoints that allow the country's security apparatus to scrutinize the public and intimate lives of impoverished migrants and business travelers alike, and whose agents are authorized to enforce the country's migration laws not just at the border but deep in the heartland and in foreign countries thousands of miles away. Two decades after September 11, thwarting terrorism remains the government's primary justification for this system, but its real function is to insulate the United States from the human consequences of the economic regime it manages. With growth slowing and no good solutions on offer, the global economy has in a sense decided that it simply has no use for as many as two billion of the earth's inhabitants. As the steward and prime beneficiary of that economic system, the United States has decided in turn that those two billion people and their attendant problems will need to be monitored, tracked, and kept out of the homeland whenever possible.

That immigration could have inspired the kind of mediagenic and carnivalesque political theater that unfolded near Tombstone would have seemed unlikely during the 2000 presidential campaign. The 1990s had seen a concerted government effort to harden border security in California and Texas. By the end of the decade, however, the issue had largely fallen out of the conversation, as indicated by the fact that immigration never came up even once during the three presidential debates between Bush and Gore.[18] Little seemed poised to change in that respect during the first eight months of the Bush administration. If anything, the pressures on the Republican Party had more to do with *easing* immigration restrictions and carving a path toward legal residency for the millions of undocumented migrants who lived and worked in the country. Bush had received just a third of the Hispanic vote in 2000, and conventional wisdom held that Democrats enjoyed a natural electoral advantage with Latinos that would only increase with time. If Bush wanted a chance at a second term, he would need to do something significant to attract Hispanic support. Accordingly, legislation that would legalize the presence of the country's undocumented migrants sat among his highest priorities heading into the second half of 2001, and supporters had reason to be optimistic about its passage. Major labor unions, Democrats, and self-identified "compassionate conservatives" might have disagreed on the details of the legislation, but all agreed that immigration reform was achievable in one form or another. "The entire political climate seems in hindsight almost unrecognizable," as Daniel Denvir writes in his book on American nativism. "States like Utah, North Carolina, and Tennessee were issuing driver's licenses to undocumented immigrants."[19]

This sense of openness and possibility surrounding immigration reform had vanished by the morning of September 12. Among the many painful bits of news to absorb over the following months were two reports that helped to revive immigration as a live issue on a national scale. First, while all nineteen of the September 11 hijackers had entered the country legally, variously bearing student, tourist, or business visas, the conservative journal *National Review* retrieved fifteen of those visa applications and found that none had been filled out properly, which should have resulted in their denial.[20] Second, the Immigration and Naturalization Service had approved student visas for two of the hijackers six months *after* they rather famously died while crashing planes into America's most important buildings.[21] Not only was immigration policy too welcoming, but the people in charge of implementing it were incompetent as well.

With the country's immigration laws and enforcement apparatus facing simultaneous crises of legitimacy, the federal government made a number of sweeping changes to both, and not the kinds Bush was talking about in the summer of 2001. On March 1, 2003, the U.S. Customs Service, the Immigration and Naturalization Service, and the entire U.S. Border Patrol were reorganized under the same new parent agency, the Department of Homeland Security. This all but guaranteed that the government's immigration officials and policy makers would now be much more focused on keeping immigrants out than on identifying the best ways to let them in. Visions of can-do strivers making their way to the United States in search of peace and prosperity were out. Now the rhetoric more closely mirrored that of people like Attorney General John Ashcroft, who said in 2002, "Our enemy's platoons infiltrate our borders, quietly blending in with visiting tourists, students, and workers."[22] In order to repel these platoons, the government increased the budget and swelled the ranks of the Border Patrol, which now lived under the parent agency Customs and Border Protection (CBP). In 2002, federal appropriations to the Border Patrol stood at $1.4 billion, already more than a fivefold increase from 1990. They would grow to $3 billion by 2010 and $3.8 billion by 2015.[23] The number of people working for the Border Patrol more than doubled over the same period.[24]

The Border Patrol became perhaps the most powerful and ubiquitous domestic law enforcement agency in the country. Part of this has to do with the extraordinary size of its jurisdiction. While you or I might think that a commonsense definition of America's border region goes something like, "the parts of the country that are within a few miles of Mexico or Canada," that is not how the government defines it. According to a regulatory measure instituted in 1953, the U.S. "border" comprises all inland territory within *one hundred* miles of the country's international borders and coastlines. It is a thick outline drawn around the continental United States and Alaska. Because of its small size, Hawaii is *entirely* borderland. Within this jurisdiction, which includes some two-thirds of America's roughly 330 million residents, the Fourth Amendment of the Constitution does not fully apply, because Customs and Border Protection officials are permitted to search anyone's belongings without needing to obtain a warrant.[25] The range of tasks performed by Border Patrol agents is expansive: They establish vehicle checkpoints throughout the Sunbelt, question passengers on Amtrak trains and Greyhound buses about their citizenship, and conduct training missions in more than one hundred foreign countries, including Iraq.[26] As for the 100 million Americans who don't live within the Border Patrol's jurisdiction, they still fall under the authority of Immigration and Customs Enforcement (ICE), whose tens of thousands of officers operate throughout the country's interior. Both organizations began to recruit heavily among veterans as soldiers started returning from Iraq and Afghanistan late in the first decade of the twenty-first century, and as the numbers of these Army grunts turned immigration cops increased, they brought with them the military tradition of coining derogatory nicknames for the enemy. In the 1960s and 1970s, North Vietnamese fighters had been referred to as "gooks." In Iraq and Afghanistan, they were "hajjis" and "ragheads." On the border, migrants were "tonks." "Tonk" is the sound a migrant's head makes when you hit it with a flashlight.[27]

In March 2005, President Bush gave a joint press conference with the Mexican president, Vicente Fox, as part of his doomed effort to pass immigration reform. Asked about the Minuteman Project, Bush said, "I'm against vigilantes in the United States of America. I'm for enforcing the law in a rational way." The Minutemen and their handful of Republican supporters in Congress reacted with outrage. The House member Tom Tancredo said that Bush should be made to write "I'm sorry for calling you vigilantes" on a chalkboard and then erase it with his tongue. In addition to alienating a wing of his party whose power would only grow in the coming years, Bush's remarks indicated either an unwillingness or an inability to understand that groups like the Minutemen were an entirely logical product of the immigration enforcement policies he had promoted ever since September 11. The Minutemen went to the border because they had been told again and again that terrorists were trying to get in. They had felt it necessary to form their own group in part because they were no longer young or healthy enough to join the actual Border Patrol, whose work they fervently admired and whose approval and validation they always anxiously courted. And while Bush was right to be concerned about what a group of untrained and heavily armed anti-immigration ideologues might get up to if left to their own devices in the desert, five thousand volunteer Minutemen could not have wreaked even a tenth of the havoc that the Border Patrol and ICE inflicted on immigrant communities during his presidency. Border Patrol recruitment drives in areas where much of the population had Mexican heritage forced young people to weigh the best chance at stable employment they were likely to see against the guilt involved with pursuing and locking up their own. The hardening of the borders in California and Texas did little to reduce the absolute numbers of migrants entering the United States each year, but by leaving the brutal Arizona desert as the only available route, it made the journey more dangerous. Paradoxically, making it more difficult to cross the border might have actually *increased* the country's undocumented population, because Mexicans who had previously come to the United States for seasonal work and then returned to Mexico when the harvest was done now had little choice but to sit tight and remain undetected until it was time to work again. Massive workplace raids decimated immigrant communities in the country's interior, and persistent harassment and intimidation by immigration officers ground some migrants' daily lives down to nothing. One undocumented woman who lived in a South Carolina trailer park became reluctant to leave for fear of being pulled over by the police officers who seemed to be stationed outside the entrance twenty-four hours a day. Her son told a journalist that he hadn't left the trailer park in a year.[28]

As is probably becoming clear, catching terrorists constituted an infinitesimally small part of what CBP and ICE did on a daily basis. An official CBP report acknowledged as much, noting that "encounters of watchlisted individuals at our borders are very uncommon."[29] Instead, the vast majority of Border Patrol time, money, and manpower was spent pursuing, apprehending, and deporting people who had crossed the border not to set off a pipe bomb but simply to find work. The agriculture jobs they sought were not glamorous, stable, or particularly safe, and they often paid wages so low that Americans themselves could not be induced to work for them. But low wages and exploitative conditions were preferable to the total dearth of gainful employment that prevailed in the migrants' countries of origin. These workers made up the surplus populations of Mexico and Central America. The purpose of the supercharged post-9/11 border control apparatus was to control, manage, and discourage them.

If Bush seemed ignorant of the fact that the vigilantes he criticized had been emboldened by his administration's own policies, then the country's political system as a whole seemed equally ignorant of the fact that the surplus populations the Border Patrol hunted were to a substantial degree an American creation as well. Since the 1990s, much of the unauthorized migration across the southern border has been a consequence of the North American Free Trade Agreement (NAFTA), negotiated among the United States, Canada, and Mexico and officially implemented under President Clinton in 1994. NAFTA eliminated almost all of the import tariffs that Mexico had long used to protect its domestic agricultural production from penetration by American agricultural goods, which were usually cheaper because they were produced on a much larger scale. The prices of many goods and staples dropped in Mexico as a result. This development is sometimes credited with aiding the growth of the Mexican middle class, who became able to afford goods that had previously been out of reach. But those benefits are only from the perspective of consumers, whereas the consequences for Mexican workers were disastrous. As A. Naomi Paik writes in her useful primer on twenty-first-century migration, "NAFTA led to the loss of 1.3 million jobs in Mexico's agricultural industry, which employs one fifth of the country's workforce." Manufacturing jobs increased as American firms outsourced production to the enormous maquiladoras, or duty- and tariff-free factories, that emerged in Mexican border towns, but those new jobs could not compensate for the agricultural shortfall, and they were low-paying and exploitative in their own right. In the previous chapter, I discussed how in an environment of slowing global growth, economic development turns into a zero-sum game. As capital circulates from place to place in search of the cheapest labor and lowest production costs, any benefits that accrue to one country almost necessitate losses in another. Under NAFTA, this meant that manufacturing gains in Mexico produced a further hollowing out of America's industrial workforce, while increased market share for America's agricultural behemoths devastated Mexican industries such as corn production. As Paik notes, this chain of consequences put downward pressure on wages in both countries while inflating corporate profits, which happens to be the precise formula for widening inequality. "The wealthiest 10 percent of Mexicans," she writes, "has increased its share of national earnings, leaving everyone else behind. A 2005 World Bank report showed that extreme rural poverty spiked from 35 percent in 1992–94 to 55 percent in 1996–98."[30]

NAFTA is a perfect example of how the developed world responded to slowing growth in the years following 1970. This response goes by a number of different names. One is "globalization," and another is "neoliberalism." Whichever term you use, the broad idea is the same. Since the cause of the growth slowdown was overcapacity in manufacturing and companies' consequent reluctance to invest in new production, governments in wealthy countries have worked to make capital investment as easy and frictionless as possible, in the hope of enticing firms to increase their capital outlays and get growth going again. Duties, tariffs, worker protections, community resistance, or anything else that makes it difficult for capital to do what it wants have been systematically removed. But while NAFTA and similar treaties have promoted the free movement of capital and goods across international borders, they have not accorded similar freedom to workers, who have remained at the mercy of their governments' restrictive immigration policies. The United States is by no means the only country that has promoted this state of affairs, but as the leader of the global economy it benefits the most, and no other country is more invested in perpetuating it.

America's hardened border is among the largest of its investments in keeping the economic system running even as it weakens. As of 2014, Border Patrol and ICE employees made up 80,000 of the 200,000 people working for the entire Department of Homeland Security, with some 650,000 local police officers also tasked to immigration enforcement.[31] To put that into context, there are only four militaries in the world with more people on active duty than the number of Americans working on border enforcement alone.[32] Similarly, "the $18 billion spent on border and immigration enforcement in 2012 outguns the budget of all other federal law enforcement bodies *combined*."[33] Since 2004, federal courts have filed more prosecutions for immigration violations than for any other crime. Over its entire history, the United States has deported roughly fifty million people. Forty-five million of those deportations, or 95 percent of the total, have taken place since the long economic downturn began in the early 1970s.[34]

The militarization of America's borders did not begin with the war on terror, but the war has both accelerated and expanded the process. If you think of "borders" as mechanisms of control as opposed to just lines, it is now paradoxically the case that America's actual borders extend far beyond the borders you can see on a map. In 2003, the members of the 9/11 Commission wrote in their final report that "9/11 has taught us that terrorism against American interests 'over there' should be regarded just as we regard terrorism against America 'over here.' In this same sense, the American homeland is the planet."[35] They meant it literally. Since September 11, there has been what one Border Patrol representative called an "exponential" increase in America's efforts to stop migrants from crossing international borders even when they were nowhere near the United States. In addition to sending CBP units to organize border patrol operations in Afghanistan and Iraq as part of the reconstruction processes there, the United States has trained border patrol and homeland security agents in Kenya, Tanzania, and Uganda, among other countries. At least sixty new border walls have also been built around the world since the collapse of the Soviet Union, two-thirds of which were constructed after September 11.[36] In Mexico, border police now act as adjuncts to the

American government in exchange for aid and training, apprehending, detaining, and deporting migrants from Honduras, Guatemala, and other Central American countries long before they get anywhere close to the United States. In 2015, for the first time, Mexico deported more Central Americans than the United States did.[37]

At every international airport that services flights to the United States, passengers must also contend with the American "border" even before they board a flight. As Todd Miller writes, America's "National Targeting Center was founded on September 11, 2001, according to former acting CBP commissioner Thomas Winkowski, when 'two people jumped in a booth or cubicle and began targeting.'"[38] It now employs hundreds of people who analyze the data of a quarter million inbound foreign passengers each day, with any discrepancies in their documents or outré political sentiments in their social media histories prompting more focused scrutiny. There are also now CBP "Preclearance" operations at fifteen international airports scattered across six countries, from the United Arab Emirates to Canada. These Preclearance stations require U.S.-bound passengers to submit their documents for inspection and be interviewed by a CBP agent before they actually make it to American soil. An official CBP video explaining the process suggests that the main function of Preclearance is to help passengers "relax," a point it makes three times, using that exact word, in the space of seventy seconds.[39] But in practice, Preclearance is often extremely invasive, with agents demanding the passwords to passengers' phones or asking Muslim passengers detailed questions about their religious beliefs (CBP is one of the only federal agencies that is exempted from laws prohibiting racial profiling). In late 2016, a thirty-year-old man from Canada attempted to fly from Vancouver to New Orleans to visit his boyfriend. CBP demanded that he unlock his phone and then interrogated him about the contents of his profile on a dating app for gay men, asking what it meant when he described himself as "looking for loads." The man was so embarrassed that he left the airport. When he attempted the trip again a month later, he had deleted all of the apps and emails and text messages on his phone, but CBP remembered who he was, and the blank phone only made them more suspicious. They accused him of being a sex worker and turned him away.[40] CBP wields expansive discretionary powers at these checkpoints. Even a valid and fully processed visa no longer guarantees entry into the country. All it allows, in the words of a CBP spokesperson, is for a "foreign national to come to a U.S. international airport and present themselves for inspection, where a CBP [agent] will determine the traveler's admissibility."[41] There are dozens of legal grounds for turning someone away, including their lack of health coverage, which would require the U.S. government to foot the bill for any medical emergencies. Those who do make it through Preclearance at Vancouver International, however, get to walk under a sign reading, WELCOME TO THE USA.[42]

The primary purpose of America's complex, labor-intensive, and costly border surveillance system isn't to deter terrorists; it is to shield and insulate Americans from the negative consequences of the economic system from which they benefit more than any other people on earth. Just as not hearing about the working conditions under which Apple's iPhones and Nike's sneakers are produced makes it easier for Americans to keep spending money on iPhones and Air Force 1s, not having to confront the human refuse of the global economic system makes it easier to continue supporting that system. The border system tries to keep out migrants whose poverty might complicate that support just as an individual's psychological defense mechanisms try to shield them from intrusive feelings of anxiety or guilt.

In late 2010, however, Mohamed Bouazizi, an impoverished twenty-six-year-old fruit vendor who lived in the Tunisian city of Sidi Bouzid, decided he couldn't stand any more police harassment and set himself on fire. The revolutions and civil wars that followed threw much of the Middle East into crisis, and for a brief time the plight of surplus populations in the Arab world, at least, would be impossible to ignore.

• • •

When the Bush administration voiced its hopes that toppling Saddam Hussein would inspire a wave of democratic reforms across the Middle East, it did not have something like the Arab Spring in mind. As Cheney, Wolfowitz, and the other neoconservative true believers peered into the future from the spring of 2003, they saw Iraq setting an example for the rest of the region that would inspire and terrify in equal measure. People like Ayatollah Khamenei in Iran would understand that their days of impunity and repression had come to an end, that refusal to participate in global politics and the world economy on America's preferred terms would have consequences much worse than economic sanctions. Chastened by Saddam's downfall and awed by America's rejuvenated global prestige, they would eject the hard-liners from government, make their economies more receptive to international capital, and bring their own political systems more in line with that of the world's unquestioned superpower.

What happened instead was that an explosive series of social and political revolutions toppled leaders across the region. Within a month of Mohamed Bouazizi's self-immolation, protests had spread from Tunisia to Yemen, Egypt, Oman, Jordan, Morocco, and Syria. The Tunisian government was overthrown on January 14, 2011, and President Zine El Abidine Ben Ali fled to Saudi Arabia with his wife and children. A week and a half later, thousands of protesters began to fill Tahrir Square in Cairo. In February, protests spread to Iraq, Bahrain, Libya, and Kuwait. The Algerian president agreed to lift a state of emergency that had been in effect for nineteen years, the sultan of Oman agreed to some economic reforms, the king of Jordan dismissed his prime minister along with the entire cabinet, and Hosni Mubarak resigned as president of Egypt, transferring his powers to the military. Through the end of the spring, Oman's elected legislature gained the power to make laws; the Yemeni president, Ali Abdullah Saleh, survived an assassination attempt; Jordan undertook a process of constitutional reform; and the protests in Syria turned into a violent uprising. Morocco held a constitutional referendum in July, and Libyan rebels captured Tripoli in August. By the end of the year, the prime minister of Kuwait had resigned, and the Libyan president Muammar Gaddafi was dead. The Syrian uprising was declared a civil war by the Red Cross in July 2012. It would soon become one of the bloodiest conflicts of the twenty-first century, and it is ongoing as of this writing.

The Arab Spring was one of those rare periods when it is possible to watch decades of history unfold in a matter of weeks. Many Americans watched it online with the same rapt attention people had given to their televisions on September 11. Events moved at such a blistering speed that managing things in any one of the affected countries would have been a tall order for President Obama and his State Department. But they all happened at the same time, meaning that in most instances there was little for the United States to do aside from observe, decide whether to offer or withhold statements of support for this or that political actor, and hope for the best. From the zero-sum perspective of American power calculations, what Obama got might not have been the worst possible outcome, but there wasn't much for him to smile about, either. The United States was not sorry to see Saleh and Gaddafi removed from power; the former had been a thorn in Saudi Arabia's side for years, and the latter was one of America's most outspoken enemies. But Tunisia, Jordan, Egypt, and Kuwait were all committed American allies. President Mubarak, in particular, had benefited more from American support and largesse than any other Arab leader aside from the Saudi monarchy, receiving more than $2 billion each year in military aid and equipment (as well as near silence regarding his government's political repression) in exchange for Egypt's not making noise about Israel and amplifying America's demonization of Iran.[43] For thirty years, the Mubarak alliance was one of the pillars of U.S. foreign policy in the Arab world, and it crumbled to nothing in less than three weeks. To make matters worse, a decade of U.S.-instigated war against extremism in the region had, if anything, put Islamist political parties in a much stronger position than they had occupied on the eve of 2003. When Egyptians revolted again in 2012, deposed the general who had replaced Mubarak seventeen months earlier, and successfully held a presidential election, they elected Mohamed Morsi, an Islamist with strong ties to the Muslim Brotherhood. America's diplomatic power in the Middle East seemed to be fading, and quickly.

Because this book is focused primarily on how the war on terror changed life in the United States, I won't be engaging in any detailed analysis of the Arab Spring's vast political consequences for the region. But there are a few aspects of what transpired in 2011 and after that had a significant impact back home, whether on the political dynamics of the federal government, young people's collective feelings about the country in which they were becoming adults, or individual experiences of daily life. I want to mention a few of them.

First, the Arab Spring made the weaknesses of Obama's foreign policy painfully visible. It exposed the vacuity of the hazy promises Obama made in his Cairo speech and revealed his administration's inability to foresee the obvious consequences of America's support for regional tyrants. And with Obama's sclerotic State Department unable to respond creatively to the upheaval, the United States then exacerbated a migration crisis that consumed the airwaves for months and made it all but impossible for Obama to advance the remaining components of his unfulfilled agenda.

These missteps also had devastating consequences for Libyans and Syrians in particular. In Libya, Obama seemed to sleepwalk into leading a military intervention of the exact kind that the wars in Afghanistan and Iraq had supposedly discredited. Although protests emerged in Libya at around the same time as elsewhere, and although their intensity also grew in line with how events unfolded in countries like Egypt, Gaddafi was determined to maintain his grip on power, meaning there could be no bloodless transition to a new government. Protest turned to more widespread unrest, which in turn turned into violent confrontation and civil war, and by the summer of 2011 the situation was extremely fluid. For a time, it seemed the Libyan rebels would successfully oust the dictator, but then Gaddafi's forces, who were always better armed, regrouped and retook a number of major cities. All the while, the rhetoric coming out of the ruling camp darkened and eventually turned eliminationist, with Gaddafi urging his supporters to fight rebels he described as "cockroaches" who were high on hallucinogenic drugs.[44] Gaddafi's son, for his part, assured the world that his father's government and military would fight "until the last bullet."[45]

In March 2011, the Libyan army began to close in on the city of Benghazi, a crucial rebel stronghold. The United States and its allies were almost certain that a massacre would take place if Gaddafi managed to retake the city, and so on March 19 the UN Security Council voted for military intervention, demanding a ceasefire, imposing a no-fly zone, and authorizing the use of force to protect civilians. As America's Tomahawk missiles began to fly, Obama and other members of his administration assured the media that regime change was not among their goals. "The task that I assigned our forces [is] to protect the Libyan people from immediate danger and to establish a no-fly zone," Obama said. "Broadening our military mission to include regime change would be a mistake." But the hypothetical "mistake" had already been made—it was, in fact, part of the plan. Almost from the beginning of the intervention, NATO forces conducted air strikes that could only be explained as personally targeting Gaddafi, including one that hit a presidential compound. When asked how journalists were supposed to square the idea that Gaddafi wasn't a target with the missiles landing less than fifty yards from the president's residence while the president was inside, the director of the Joint Staff would only say, "Yeah. But, no, we're not targeting his residence."

This was a pretense, and one that administration and military officials didn't seem too concerned with maintaining once rebel forces found Gaddafi, sodomized him with a bayonet, and shot him dead. Reflecting on the war after leaving his position as secretary of defense, Robert Gates said, "I don't think there was a day that passed that people didn't hope he would be in one of those command-and-control centers." And then, to dispel any lingering doubt about what the intervention's purpose had been, Secretary of State Hillary Clinton, upon learning of Gaddafi's death, said, "We came, we saw, he died!" Questioned about this remark years later at a hearing, Clinton said it was an "expression of relief that the military mission undertaken by NATO and our other partners had achieved its end."[46] As with his antiwar-ish stance during the 2008 campaign, Obama had failed to back up what Sarah Palin called his "hope-y change-y" rhetoric with a new set of principles for how the United States should interact with the rest of the world. Instead, the United States responded to the Arab Spring by playing the old hits: regime change in Libya and humanitarian intervention in Syria. The returns on those strategies had long since diminished to nothing, and in 2011 they produced only chaos and destruction.

Obama would later describe the intervention in Libya as his administration's worst mistake. While the United States and its partners were happy to bring NATO's overwhelming firepower to bear on the conflict, and while they were equally happy to let Egypt funnel advanced weapons and other military equipment to rebel groups in defiance of an embargo that had been in place for thirty years, Obama drew the line at permitting any American ground forces to enter Libya. The Security Council resolution prohibited any foreign occupation, and Obama still had a reputation to uphold as a commander in chief who wouldn't be as reckless with the lives of American soldiers as his predecessor had been.

But in trying to avoid launching the same kind of war as Bush, Obama made many of the same errors. If the war's purpose had actually been limited to the protection of civilians, the intervention might have worked. NATO air strikes repelled Gaddafi's army from Benghazi within days of commencing operations and devastated the military's logistical infrastructure, providing the rebels with the breathing room they needed to either fortify their positions, escape, or begin to explore options for a negotiated settlement. But since the United States was really pursuing regime change under the banner of its purely humanitarian rationale, it needed a plan for what might come next once the regime had in fact changed. There was no such plan.

In Iraq, President Bush's insufficient allocation of ground forces in the months after the invasion allowed an insurgency to organize itself and gather strength, meaning that by the time the United States realized its mistake and increased its troop levels, the country had already spiraled into civil war. In Libya, it was worse than that. The rebels there did not constitute any kind of unified opposition. The forces fighting Gaddafi comprised a variety of militias that disliked each other almost as much as they disliked the dictator, and they had no hope of peacefully forming a government once Gaddafi was gone. This was obvious to any competent observer, but as with Bush in Iraq, the Obama administration managed to fool itself into believing that a coherent political leadership would emerge out of the postrevolutionary chaos and quickly bring order to the country. Instead, Libya spiraled, with competing militias wreaking havoc for years afterward. The country became one of the most fertile hotbeds for extremist recruitment in the world, and a resurgent extremist group known as the Islamic State (or else as ISIS, ISIL, or Daesh) established operations there. In 2015, a British envoy to Libya said the country was on its way to becoming a "Somalia on the Mediterranean."[47]

In Syria, things got even worse, with governments on three different continents making self-interested, amoral decisions that produced one of the most horrifying catastrophes of the young century. The Syrian civil war should never have happened in the first place. Protests broke out in 2011, as they did throughout the region, but the protesters were not seeking the downfall of President Bashar al-Assad. The dissidents were reformists, not revolutionaries, and their demands were entirely reasonable, including the end of emergency law (justified by a permanent "state of war" with Israel), the release of political prisoners, the removal of a regional governor who allegedly allowed the torture of teenagers by police, and an end to the bribes and harassment and other daily humiliations of life under authoritarian rule.

It was Assad who made the first mistake, responding to these entirely peaceful demonstrations with beatings, water cannons, and live ammunition. His forces killed protesters, and then they killed mourners at the dead protesters' funerals. This was egregious, inflammatory, and barbaric, and although the pro-democracy protesters did not reach for their rifles en masse, they were gradually overtaken and displaced by more than three thousand different militias, defectors from the military who established the Free Syrian Army (FSA), and an al-Qaeda-affiliated group of Sunni fundamentalists who saw the escalating chaos as an opportunity to topple Assad's Alawite regime. This turned a reform project into a revolutionary one, but as in Libya the revolutionaries had no shared vision for what the new Syria would look like, and the visions they did have were incompatible with one another, ranging from secular democracy to a theocratic state under Sunni rule. Though one can hardly blame the anti-Assad forces for escalating the situation given Assad's violent response to the protests, their lack of any substantive political commonality made that escalation a mistake as well. One Syrian journalist who reported on the Battle of Aleppo said there was a moment in 2012 during which the Free Syrian Army, had it been able to muster a unified force of a few hundred, could have seized city hall and "proclaimed Aleppo a liberated city." It didn't.[48]

Other countries should have seen these fissures in the rebellion as a reason to stay away and allow the conflict to exhaust itself. Instead, they made the third mistake, viewing the rebellion's weaknesses as an opportunity to use it for their own varied ends. Saudi Arabia saw an opportunity to roll back the democratic tide in the Middle East and weaken Iran, its primary opponent and Assad's most important supporter in the region. Iran saw Assad's Syria as a key arm of its regional influence. The strategically insignificant but very wealthy country of Qatar bet on the rebels in hopes of winning increased influence after Assad's fall, pumping nearly $3 billion into the rebellion during the first two years of the war. Turkey, following its unenthusiastic and unsuccessful pursuit of EU membership, thought that helping the FSA to overthrow Assad would help it establish a diplomatic power center in the east instead. Russia lavished the Assad regime with military and economic aid, and its air strikes helped to turn the tide against the rebels in 2016. Britain and France thought toppling Assad would help to stymie Iran, and having apparently learned nothing from the misadventure in Libya, they provided rebels with arms and communications equipment, as well as carried out bombing raids of their own.

As for the United States, Obama seemingly *had* learned something from Libya, and he was extremely reluctant to involve America too deeply in another regional conflagration. But he couldn't quite let go of the idea of America as the world's chief of police, and in 2012 he told the White House press corps that any use of chemical or biological weapons by Assad would be a "red line for us." He used the "red line" phrase twice, the clear implication being that direct military intervention would follow. But one year later, when chemical weapons were launched at rebel-held positions in Ghouta, it turned out that Obama's calculus would stay the same, and the expected air strikes never came. This might have been a wise decision on its own, but it could not compensate for the recklessness of having made the "red line" remarks in the first place. Opposition forces had spent a year digging in and escalating the conflict in the expectation that the American cavalry would soon arrive, and its failure to do so left the FSA in the lurch. The Islamic State soon seized the initiative that the FSA could no longer hold. All the while, the United States continued to pursue regime change. Hillary Clinton undermined peace talks that didn't include Assad's removal as a condition in 2011, and the CIA assisted rebels with training, arms, ammunition, and supply routes along the Turkish border. The Islamic State, which by 2014 had replaced al-Qaeda as America's preeminent terrorist bogeyman, served as a useful excuse for America's clumsy meddling.

The result of all this venality and shortsightedness was the destruction of Syria as a functioning state and the murder of hundreds of thousands of its citizens. Much of Aleppo, one of the oldest continuously inhabited cities on earth and one of the region's architectural and cultural jewels, was reduced to rubble. A country with a strong national identity and a tradition of religious tolerance—including a dozen Christian denominations along with esoteric sects like the Druze—was transformed into a place of bitter sectarian violence. Life expectancy for Syrians dropped by more than twenty years, from roughly seventy-nine to fifty-six. Around half a million people died in Syria through the end of Obama's presidency, with another two million wounded, in a country whose prewar population amounted to just more than twenty million.

For those who survived, the only sensible option was to flee. This brings us to the Arab Spring's larger impact on U.S. politics. As a result of the war, more than half of Syria's population was forced to leave their homes, including some six million who were internally displaced and almost five million refugees. This was in addition to the million or so Libyans who fled, primarily to Tunisia but also across the Mediterranean to Europe. Between 2011 and 2016, successive waves of migration, along with the social crises they produced as migrants reached the shores of Europe, supercharged nativist political sentiment both on the Continent and in the United States, kicking off a process of right-wing anti-immigrant radicalization that would culminate in the "Muslim ban" Trump instituted upon his arrival in the Oval Office in 2017. In 2011, people fled Libya at a rate of a thousand every *hour,* and across the region some two million people fled their homes as a result of the Arab Spring through the winter of 2012. Egypt and Tunisia maintained open border policies during this period, accepting about half a million migrants as well as an additional half a million nationals who had decided to return home. When some forty-five thousand migrants arrived in Europe, however, they received a chillier reception. About twenty-five thousand Tunisian refugees made the journey to Lampedusa, Italy's southernmost port. As *The New York Times* reported, "Italy tried to get rid of them by issuing many of the Tunisians six-month temporary residency permits entitling them to travel to other European countries." Most of them went to France—Tunisia had been a French protectorate until 1956—but once they arrived, French officials refused to recognize their documents and turned them away.[49] The EU tightened its border security and even briefly considered suspending the treaty that guaranteed freedom of movement within the EU.[50]

This initial wave of Arab Spring migration was just a preview of what was to come once the Syrian civil war reached the full extent of its horrors, but it was enough to energize European nativists who had long viewed Muslim immigrants as harbingers of civilizational decline. In July 2011, a Norwegian man named Anders Breivik, who described himself as a Nazi and fascist, killed seventy-seven people in a single day, including sixty-nine people, most of them teenagers, on an island summer camp run by the Norwegian Labour Party. Shortly before the attack, he released a fifteen-hundred-page manifesto railing against "cultural Marxists" for allowing Muslims to infiltrate the

European homeland. Though Breivik had planned his attack for years before the Arab Spring, crediting his white nationalist political awakening to NATO's pushing the Serbs out of Kosovo in 1999, which he described as helping an "Islamic terror organization" to conquer the city, his manifesto echoed all of the fears that American activists and writers on the hard right had been voicing about the coming Islamic subjection of an innocent West.[51] To a large extent a collage of plagiarized passages and citations of other writers, the manifesto quoted a number of right-wing American bloggers who had come to prominence for their anti-Islamic writing after September 11. Among these were Pamela Geller, whose blog, *Atlas Shrugs,* attracted a wide readership thanks to its racist criticisms of the Cordoba House project in New York, and Robert Spencer, whose Jihad Watch website Breivik cited more than a hundred times. Spencer replied by denying that Breivik's massacre had "anything remotely to do with anything we have ever advocated," while Geller made the more creative choice to rebut allegations of Islamophobia with more Islamophobia. "If anyone incited him to violence, it was the Islamic supremacists," she wrote.[52]

The initial wave of refugee panic caused by the Arab Spring subsided somewhat in 2012 and 2013, when many Tunisians and Libyans returned to their respective countries. Anti-refugee sentiment didn't go away entirely, but one might say it remained at a simmer rather than boiling over. In 2015, however, violence escalated dramatically in Syria, and Syrians fled their homeland en masse. Around 1.3 million refugees sought asylum in Europe that year, the highest number since World War II. The stress these migrant inflows placed on the social service capacities of European countries (Germany, Bulgaria, France, and Italy in particular) breathed new life into the continent's nativist political parties, who painted the migrants' desperate search for safety as the beginnings of a civilizational conquest. Right-wing congressional representatives and pundits, in turn, pointed to Europe as an example of what might befall the United States so long as its feckless Democratic president refused to take drastic steps to secure America's own borders against the coming flood of extremists.

To be clear, Obama had not been any more lenient with respect to immigration than his Republican predecessor, and in some respects his policies had been harsher than those of Bush the Younger. Like Bush, Obama sought to pass wide-ranging immigration reform, and he hoped that by hardening enforcement, he could attract sufficient Republican support to move an immigration bill through Congress. An act signed into law by Bush in 2006 had required hundreds of miles of fencing to be installed along the southern border. That construction proceeded under Obama, and as he made his reform pitch in a 2011 speech in El Paso, Texas, he boasted that the fence was now "basically complete." The remark drew boos and a call to "tear it down!" from his audience, but Obama continued to enumerate all of the ways in which he had complied with Republicans' stated wishes and cracked down on immigration:

> We tripled the number of intelligence analysts working at the border. I've deployed unmanned aerial vehicles to patrol the skies from Texas to California. We have forged a partnership with Mexico to fight the transnational criminal organizations that have affected both of our countries. And for the first time—for the first time we're screening 100 percent of south-bound rail shipments to seize guns and money going south even as we go after drugs that are coming north.[53]

If anything, Obama was being modest. He did not tell his El Paso audience that he had tripled the budget for ICE, nor did he mention that he had expanded a program that helped ICE to locate and deport undocumented migrants being held in local jails and prisons across the country. Some of those deportees had been convicted of serious crimes, but others had done nothing worse than violate traffic laws, and nearly 70,000 of the 375,000 people deported under the program hadn't been charged with a criminal offense. By the end of his presidency, Obama had deported some three million people.[54]

Despite these efforts to court the opposition, Obama's immigration reform bill failed to pass. He gave Republicans almost all of the things they were willing to demand out loud, but Obama would not give them that which they desired most: He refused to demonize migrants. In his speeches touting reform, he invariably made the point that the vast majority of migrants were "just trying to earn a living and provide for their families." He did not think it was okay for them to break the rules and "cut in front of the line," but he encouraged Americans to sympathize with their plight, admire their determination, and share his concerns regarding undocumented migrants' vulnerability to "unscrupulous" business practices on the part of their employers.

That sympathy was too much for the right wing, many of whom, as adherents to the "birther" conspiracy theory that Obama was not really a natural-born citizen, believed the president was an illegal immigrant himself, as well as an illegitimate president. It did not matter to them that Obama's hard-line actions on immigration belied his empathetic rhetoric. During the first three quarters of 2015, as Europe absorbed staggering numbers of Syrians, Obama refused to increase America's Syrian refugee quota, which stood at the laughably low level of two thousand people for the entire year. When Obama announced in September 2015, following diplomatic pressure from European capitals and domestic immigration activists, that the United States would accept ten thousand Syrian refugees in 2016—still a drop in the bucket when compared with the scale of the problem—the right went ballistic. "Our enemy now is Islamic terrorism," said the Republican congressman Peter King, "and these people are coming from a country filled with Islamic terrorists."[55]

The anticipated refugee attacks never materialized in the United States, but two months after Obama's announcement, on November 13, Islamists killed 130 people and injured more than 400 more in a series of coordinated attacks around Paris, detonating three suicide bombs outside the Stade de France during a football match, firing guns at crowded cafés and restaurants, and massacring 90 concertgoers at the Bataclan theater. The Islamic State soon claimed credit for the attacks, and although most of the participating terrorists had been born and raised in Europe, a number of them, including the attack's leader, had spent time in Syria fighting for ISIS before slipping across Europe's borders into France.[56] While Obama's stump speeches to that point had been at least moderately successful in building public sympathy for unauthorized migrants, the Paris attacks cemented the idea, at least on the right, that any relaxation of America's border enforcement policies constituted an invitation for terrorists to wreak similar havoc on the country's urban centers.

Like all politicians trying to convince the public of a policy proposal's benefits, Obama laced his stump speeches with anecdotes about sympathetic individuals. But for those looking to understand how immigration, the war on terror, and the long economic slowdown intertwined during the first two decades of the twenty-first century, a broader view is more instructive. Just as the growth slowdown and its concomitant decline in formal employment opportunities played a role in pushing migrants from Central and South America toward the southern border of the United States, so did a lack of economic opportunity in Arab countries fuel much of the discontent that exploded into protest, revolution, and civil war in 2011. A senior expert with the UN's International Labour Organization pointed out that youth unemployment rates in the region averaged over 23 percent, adding that "for young women, the average unemployment rate of 31.5 percent is even worse." Further inflaming the situation was the fact that young Arabs who did manage to find work still faced "low wages, little social protection, lack of secure contracts and career prospects, and weak or lacking trade unions to give them a voice."[57]

Nor were these problems confined to the poor and uneducated segments of society. Young adults who had completed their university education, and even young adults with secondary professional degrees, routinely found upon graduation that all the work they and their parents had invested in their education was for nothing: There were no jobs for them to take, no government plans to create jobs, and no social service or welfare provisions to prevent them from sinking into destitution while they waited for a surge of economic growth they had no reason to believe would ever arrive. They came to understand that the governments and economic systems that ruled their lives viewed those lives as disposable surplus, and in 2011 many of them made the decision to raze those governments to the ground.

• • •

As every working journalist in America seemed to note in 2011, the Arab Spring marked the first time in history that protesters and revolutionaries across an entire region could use social media to organize, plan, make strategic and tactical decisions, and broadcast their experiences to the entire world in real time. This became particularly crucial in Egypt, a country where 60 percent of the population was under thirty years old in 2011. As these young people gathered in the hundreds of thousands in Cairo's Tahrir Square, they dominated online discussion, with Twitter alone seeing nearly a quarter of a million posts about Egypt during the week before Mubarak stepped down. Western journalists might have exaggerated the extent to which social media made the protests possible—they often ignored the years of political activity and organizing that preceded 2011—but the protesters themselves were happy to acknowledge that the internet was a useful tool. As one wrote, "We use Facebook to schedule the protests, Twitter to coordinate, and YouTube to tell the world."[58]

This is where the Arab Spring's third impact on life in the United States comes into play. In the United States, young Americans who had recently graduated into the worst economic conditions in more than eighty years watched young people thousands of miles away risk their lives in the hope of bringing about a future worth the name. As they scrolled along with the protests unfolding on their computer screens, many of them realized that they didn't just admire the courage and ingenuity of the Egyptian protesters—they identified with their grievances as well. Several months later, in September 2011, some of them began to gather in lower Manhattan. They said they were angry with the banks.

The standard explanation for the 2008 global financial crisis that eventually prompted the rise of Occupy Wall Street—the one offered by the 2011 findings of the federal government's Financial Crisis Inquiry Commission and in films such as *The Big Short,* for example—blames the disaster on avarice and failures of regulation. Beginning in the early years of the twenty-first century, this explanation goes, bankers at a number of financial institutions came up with the idea to sell mortgages to people who were never going to be able to pay them down, and government regulators fell asleep at the switch and failed to spot the disaster that was obviously coming. Both of these things are true, but they hardly constitute an explanation for *why* the housing boom and subsequent bust took place, because they ignore some more specific questions such as "Why *then*? And why *in the United States*?" Greed, for instance, is timeless. Bankers are always greedy. So why didn't they start selling subprime mortgages and raking in the cash back in the 1990s, or even the 1980s? Why did financial regulators choose 2002–3 as the time to start turning a blind eye to practices that threatened the very foundations of the system they were supposed to guard?

The real roots of the crisis go back to the late twentieth century, and as with the migration crises that have unfolded during the war on terror, the housing bubble needs to be understood in the context of the long slowdown in GDP growth. In the mid-1990s, following economic crises in Mexico and Japan that threatened the stability of the global economy, the Clinton administration decided that America's decades-long effort to fuel economic growth with high levels of government spending—that is, Keynesianism—had run its course. Going forward, the government would cut its spending, balance the federal budget, and, by fully embracing globalization and internationally integrated supply chains, unleash capital to seek profits on whichever continent they might be hiding. As part of this plan, the Federal Reserve, led by Chairman Alan Greenspan, decided that it would no longer steadily raise interest rates in the normal way over the course of an economic expansion. Instead of making it progressively more expensive to borrow money in an effort to prevent the economy from overheating, interest rates would be kept low so as to allow the expansion to build up momentum. While this package of reforms did nothing to solve the problem of global excess manufacturing capacity or zero-sum economic competition between countries, the persistence of low-cost borrowing, backed by a tacit guarantee from the Fed that interest rates would drop further at the slightest hint of market turbulence, sent the stock market on a historic tear. For corporations and wealthy households, this was a kind of paradise. As corporations watched their valuations rise, they could borrow even more cheap money to invest. And as rich households saw the numbers at the bottom of their portfolio statements increase, they could save less and spend more on consumption. In his brilliant and surprisingly fun essay "What Is Good for Goldman Sachs Is Good for America," Robert Brenner described the situation well: "Instead of supporting growth by increasing its own borrowing and deficit spending—as with traditional Keynesianism—the government would thus stimulate expansion by enabling corporations and rich households to increase *their* borrowing and deficit spending by making them wealthier (at least on paper) by encouraging speculation in equities." Brenner called this new economic strategy "asset price Keynesianism."[59]

The problem with asset-price Keynesianism is that it is very easy for equity markets to behave in ways that aren't justified by what's actually going on in the economy. Stock prices are essentially predictions about the future. Someone who buys shares of a company at $50 does so because they believe that the price will eventually be higher than $50, just as someone who sells shares at $50 believes the price will eventually fall below that level. This makes the stock market as a whole vulnerable to people and companies that can tell a convincing or appealing story about the future even when they lack the expertise, revenue, or profit margins to make that story come true. That's what a stock market bubble is: when too many people start believing in a story that isn't sufficiently grounded in economic reality. In the 1990s, the story that investors liked the most had to do with how internet technology was going to provide a new foundation for worldwide GDP growth and secure America's economic dominance well into the new millennium. The racks at airport newsstands were filled with magazines like *Wired,* their cover stories touting the arrival of an economic revolution, and it seemed that all one had to do in order to get listed on the Nasdaq-100 was start a business that seemed to be normal in every way except that it had the words "dot-com" at the end of the name.

The problem was that many of these companies were nowhere close to profitable, nor did their executives have workable plans for becoming profitable in the future. Their growth was based not on sustainable revenue streams (no one had figured out yet how to effectively monetize the internet) but on the seemingly limitless availability of cheap credit and stock market valuations that had fully detached themselves from the fundamentals of good business practice. So when problems appeared in other segments of the real economy, particularly a strengthening dollar that made American exports more expensive and therefore less competitive with the rest of the world, the foundations of the dot-com boom crumbled quickly. U.S. export growth collapsed from 13 percent in 1997 to just 0.6 percent in 1998, and corporate profits dropped. Greenspan and the Fed intervened twice to reassure the markets, prompting one last spectacular run for the bull market. As Brenner notes, "By the first quarter of 2000, the total value of the equities of US non-financial corporations . . . had reached $15.6 trillion, more than triple its level of $4.8 trillion in 1994." During that same six-year period, corporate profits had increased by just 41.2 percent, meaning that roughly 80 percent of the stock market climb was based on little more than blind faith in the dot-com revolution. Though the information technology sector accounted for just 8 percent of the national GDP, it "accounted for no less than *one-third* of the growth of GDP between 1995 and 2000." So when the bubble finally burst in 2000 following a number of disastrous corporate profit reports, the consequences were stunning. The S&P 500 fell by nearly half, and the tech-heavy Nasdaq fell by almost *80 percent*. The United States entered a brief recession, and the story about how digital technology could reverse the long growth slowdown was revealed, at least for a while, as the fantasy it had always been.

Fortunately, the U.S. economy soon had a new and even more appealing story to tell. Interest rates dropped dramatically following the dot-com crash, hitting just 1 percent by November 2003, a low that hadn't been seen since the 1950s. Since Silicon Valley was still strewn with the picked-over carcasses of all the firms that went bankrupt when the Nasdaq crashed, this decline in rates wasn't going to reignite a tech boom. But information technology isn't the only sector of the economy that is extremely sensitive to interest rates. With East Asian economies buying huge amounts of dollar-denominated assets in order to suppress their own exchange rates and stimulate U.S. demand for their cheap exports, long-term interest rates declined precipitously as well, and suddenly it became very easy to take out a mortgage on a new house.

The mechanics of the 2007–8 crisis, from the bailout of Bear Stearns to the collapse of Lehman Brothers to the liquidity freeze that paralyzed global markets, has been told many times, and I won't narrate that story again here. What hasn't received quite as much attention, however, is the novelty of the preceding boom, the scale of its economic impact *before* the crash, and its function in the wider context of a U.S. economy that was steadily losing its vitality and dynamism.

On the issue of its novelty, between the end of World War II and the late 1990s, housing prices had *never* experienced an increase that meaningfully outpaced inflation; the cost of housing went up at the same steady rate as the cost of groceries, cars, and everything else. Beginning in the late 1990s, that changed. An unprecedented flood of cheap credit, combined with the increased paper wealth of households that had invested in the stock market, sent housing to the moon, with the rate of home price growth increasing by nearly 100 percent between 1999 and 2007. With home prices increasing by as much as 10 percent a year during this period, people began to treat their homes, in Brenner's words, "like the proverbial ATM machine," taking out loans against their home equity so as to fund higher levels of personal consumption. Household debt doubled between 2000 and 2007, and the U.S. savings rate collapsed.

Because homeownership is so much more widely distributed than stock ownership, the benefits of the housing-driven expansion were shared much more broadly than those of the dot-com boom. Wealthy and middle-income families alike increased their personal consumption by record amounts during the early years of the century. In addition, the housing boom seemed to enjoy an advantage over its dot-com predecessor by virtue of the fact that all houses are *real*. Dot-com companies might have juiced their stock valuations by making promises they would never be able to keep, but strong demand for housing mobilizes many labor-intensive sectors of the economy, especially construction. This appeared to put the U.S. economy on more secure footing. By making homeownership available to as many Americans as possible, the government hoped to unleash consumer demand like never before, which would help grow the economy, which would spur further demand for housing, and so on. Here was the new story about how America would overcome stagnating growth, and during the early years of the war on terror it appeared to be working very, very well. Together, personal consumption and investment in housing accounted for *98 percent* of the increase in U.S. GDP between 2001 and 2006.

Nevertheless, the economy as a whole seemed to just tread water during the early years of the housing expansion. GDP growth averaged an anemic 1.6 percent between 2000 and 2003. Housing prices could rise only so much before people stopped being able to afford them, after all, and interest rates could go only so low before the Fed would lose its ability to help the economy recover from a recession. (When a downturn hits, central banks generally lower interest rates to help get the economy going again, but they can't do that if interest rates are already about as low as they can go.) But the housing boom was too important an opportunity to waste, and so the Fed, in Brenner's words, "adopted a conscious policy of lowering the standards for playing the game of mortgage borrowing . . . nurturing the newly emerging market in subprime and other kinds of nonconforming mortgages, which had been specifically designed to open up the housing market to as many buyers as possible who could not meet the prerequisites for a standard prime/conforming loan." Rather than caution lenders against handing out mortgages to people who could manifestly not afford them, Alan Greenspan encouraged the banks, asking them to provide lenders with "greater mortgage alternatives to the traditional fixed rate mortgage." The banks were only too happy to oblige, and with credit cheaper than it had been in decades, they also took it upon themselves to repackage those mortgages as securities and sell them back onto the market, a process that few knew about and even fewer understood. Without the expansion of subprime lending, the housing boom would have ended in 2004, a year in which the origination of normal mortgages dropped by 50 percent. Instead, subprime mortgages picked up the slack, rising to 20 percent of the total mortgage market by 2004. As subprime mortgages also made homeownership available to segments of the working-class population that had previously been excluded, they provided the wider economy with more than enough fuel to keep the good times rolling for another couple of years. In 2004, 42 percent of first-time buyers made no down payment at all on their homes.

When all of this came crashing down in 2007 and 2008, a few things became clear. First, not only had the United States failed to solve the problem of stagnating growth, but it had not even made a good-faith attempt to solve it. The government had based fifteen years of economic policy on the tacit premise that the kinds of capital-intensive manufacturing industries that produced real economic growth and stable jobs had left the United States behind for good. But rather than acknowledge and attempt to manage this situation, America had turned to asset-price inflation as a means of papering over the economy's fundamental weakness. The wealthy didn't mind this state of affairs. They were the ones who owned most of the country's financial assets, and they benefited the most from the government's obsessive focus on making sure the markets kept going up. A stock market crash might deal a significant blow to their net worth, but it wasn't going to threaten their ability to feed and house themselves, and as a rule they had sufficient financial reserves to get back in the game once market indexes started climbing again. But for middle-class investors who had put their retirement savings into dot-com stocks, or whose modest wealth was locked up in a home purchased with an adjustable-rate mortgage, the impact was much more severe. Nearly ten million people lost their homes to foreclosure between 2008 and 2014. Around nine million lost their jobs,[60] and the number of Americans living in poverty topped forty-five million for the first time, an increase of around fifteen million since the year 2000.[61] As low- and middle-income Americans struggled to navigate this wreckage, they also had to watch as the federal government spent hundreds of billions of dollars rescuing the very financial institutions whose malpractice had crashed the economy.

The global financial crisis made it clear to millions of people that all of the biggest economic success stories of the prior fifteen years had been a mirage. When you stripped out the housing bubble's two main contributions to the country's economic performance—housing itself and the consumption made possible by people taking equity out of their homes—the true picture of the American economy was dismal. Without the bubble, U.S. GDP growth between 2000 and 2005 stood at just 1.6 percent, easily the least dynamic business cycle since World War II. The bubble also accounted for half of all the jobs created during the same period, because corporate investment in sectors other than housing, as well as net exports, had failed to grow at all. In other words, the economy had become entirely reliant on a surge of economic growth that turned out to be fake. All the while, corporations had continued to pursue their campaign against worker power, laying off 20 percent of the country's manufacturing workforce between 2001 and 2007 and *cutting* total real compensation (the number of employees multiplied by the money spent paying them, adjusted for inflation) by an average annual rate of 1.9 percent. Many of these laid-off workers simply joined the ranks of the permanently unemployed. Between 2007 and 2015, the labor force participation rate dropped by a full four percentage points, meaning that about twelve million working-age Americans just stopped looking for full-time work.[62] Those who continued to seek employment often found that the only jobs on offer were insecure and low-paid gigs in the services sector, whereas the cost of essential services such as college education and medical care continued to skyrocket.

Occupy Wall Street took off, in part, because hundreds of thousands of Americans watched the Arab Spring protests and realized that from the perspective of the global economy, they felt disposable, too. The result was the largest protest movement since Vietnam, with marches and occupations taking place in more than six hundred cities around the country. In New York, the movement's epicenter, nearly 80 percent of the protesters had at least a bachelor's degree, and a substantial portion lived in households with an annual income greater than $100,000. These facts, however, cannot be used to discount the protesters as trust-fund kids who only took to the streets in search of a cheap thrill. For one thing, a third of the protesters had recently been laid off or lost a job, and a similar number had significant credit card or student loan debt.[63] This was a key line of continuity between New York and Cairo, for many of the young Egyptians who gathered in Tahrir Square in early 2011 were also well educated. The issue wasn't education itself but what the economy allowed or didn't allow people to do with the educations they had spent so much money to acquire. In both countries, the protesters were part of a group that commentators had begun to call the "precariat," people with university degrees who found themselves unable to find secure jobs amid the slowest economic recovery on record. They might not be part of the world's surplus populations yet, but they didn't have to look very far into the future to see a world in which they, too, might be completely at the mercy of the capricious flows of international capital. The financial crisis seemed to have accelerated that world's arrival. Feeling betrayed by the societies that raised them, and unwilling to submit quietly to lives of permanent instability, they took to the streets instead.

Occupy Wall Street marked the return of leftist mass politics in the United States after several years during which it could seem hard to tell whether large-scale protest had gone into temporary hibernation or disappeared for good. Following the spectacular failure of the Iraq War protests to influence the Bush administration's plans, the antiwar movement had disappeared from public consciousness. That is not to say that antiwar organizers gave up. Groups such as Code Pink could still attract a brief spell of media attention by interrupting government hearings with chants and signs. What they could not do, however, was attract large crowds, much less the enormous masses of people that had filled city streets around the world in late 2002 and early 2003. As early as March 2004, mainstream news outlets such as NBC began to publish articles with headlines like "What Happened to the Antiwar Movement?" And while the writer of that piece described an activist community that was still plugging away despite the decline of its visibility, the headline painted a less optimistic but more accurate picture of a movement that had lost its grip on the public.[64]

Occupy Wall Street, by contrast, left a more durable impression on political life in the United States. Anger over the country's shocking levels of wealth and income inequality, as well as the increasing difficulty of getting by for those excluded from the economy's upper echelons, dominated the 2012 presidential election, turned the social democrat Bernie Sanders into a viable national candidate in 2016 and beyond, and seeded the emergence of leftist groups such as the Democratic Socialists of America. In addition, Occupy provided an intense and lasting education in political action for a generation of young Americans who had come of age amid a devastating recession and shrinking prospects for economic stability, allowing other protest movements to flourish in its wake. The most influential of these successors has obviously been Black Lives Matter (BLM), an antiracist movement that first emerged in 2013 to protest the frequent killing of unarmed Black Americans by police officers. Like Occupy, Black Lives Matter proved to be much more durable than the antiwar protests of 2003, permanently altering how the American political system oriented itself around issues of racism and proving capable of reappearing with even greater force when police killings flared up again, as they did during the first year of the COVID-19 pandemic.

I will take a closer look at each of these movements in the book's final section, but for now it may suffice to propose an answer to just one question: Why did the antiwar movement find it so difficult to sustain its momentum, and what did Occupy and Black Lives Matter do differently? Part of the answer has to do with nostalgia. In the United States, the antiwar movement of 2002 and 2003 semi-consciously modeled itself on the Vietnam-era protests of the 1970s. Contemporary musicians released a number of singles and albums objecting to the invasion of Iraq—Green Day's concept album *American Idiot* was the most prominent—but the soundtrack to the marches themselves was decades old, with Vietnam-era stalwarts like John Lennon, Bob Dylan, and Bob Marley predominating.[65] And for all their size, the protests against the Iraq War were also orderly and non-disruptive, as though their organizers had been influenced more by the mythology of the Vietnam-era protests than by what actually transpired. Their routes approved days or weeks in advance, the Iraq protests assembled huge numbers of people to chant, sing, and walk down streets that had been cordoned off by police the night before, then disperse without disrupting in any real way the war machinery that was roaring to life in Washington. It was fitting, in an unsettling way: The war on terror had begun with an attack that the vast majority of Americans had experienced only as a series of images, and now those protesting the war appeared to believe that equally spectacular images of protest, emptied of their disruptive substance, would be enough to bring the whole thing to a halt.

Antiwar organizing did not stop entirely following the failure of the Iraq War protests to stop the invasion. In 2006, high school and college students around the country revived the famous 1960s group Students for a Democratic Society (SDS), and the new SDS spent the next several years organizing demonstrations, marches, and sit-ins against the war. While these marches attracted many fewer participants and much less media attention than their prewar predecessors, they provided a political home for young people who weren't willing to just give up and head back inside once the mega-marches of 2002 and early 2003 dispersed. They continued their political education, experimented with different tactics, and waited for a time when Americans would decide they were ready to hit the streets once again.

That time arrived with Occupy Wall Street and Black Lives Matter, both of which avoided the antiwar movement's earlier missteps. Occupy took physical space and held it, successfully making Zuccotti Park their home for nearly two months until the New York Police Department cleared the park in the middle of the night on November 15. Black Lives Matter protesters halted traffic on the Brooklyn Bridge, fought with police and the National Guard in Ferguson, Missouri, and flipped over cop cars in Rochester, New York.[66] Rather than gathering in one place, voicing their concerns, and assuming that the government would listen to them, Occupy and BLM protesters attempted to force their government leaders to behave differently. When they didn't, leftist political candidates challenged them in both local and federal elections, scoring a number of major victories, as when a twenty-eight-year-old Alexandria Ocasio-Cortez defeated Congressman and Democratic Caucus chair Joe Crowley in a New York primary. These movements have also struggled to ensure lasting reforms—wealth inequality continued to accelerate in the United States, and police killings have proceeded at a steady clip—but they have not vanished from public view. Even if they failed to achieve their immediate goals, they succeeded in permanently politicizing a large mass of people.[67]

Occupy and BLM might also have proved more durable than the 2003 antiwar movement because they saw more deeply into their shared historical moment. As we've seen, the antiwar movement organized itself around the slogan "No blood for oil," the idea that America had launched its new war primarily as a means of securing natural resources from the Middle East. That idea was wrong. Oil was and is one of the key nodes of the world economy, but the United States was not in danger of losing access to sufficient oil supplies in the early years of the twenty-first century, nor were oil companies clamoring in unison for the United States to completely upend the politics of the world's most important oil-producing region. By focusing so intently on oil, the antiwar movement missed the larger economic forces that were shaping people's lives in the early twenty-first century. Occupy Wall Street and Black Lives Matter did not make the same mistake. Occupy Wall Street was a movement against two of the primary symptoms of the growth slowdown that has afflicted the entire world since the 1970s: the increase in wealth inequality, on the one hand, and the steady disappearance of well-paid, stable employment, on the other. Four years later, Black Lives Matter emerged as a protest against a key component of America's response to the economic effects of that slowdown: the use of excessively well-funded and militarized police forces to manage and incarcerate those who had been abandoned by the economic system in which they live.

It is no coincidence that as police forces in the United States have come to resemble occupying armies, American soldiers abroad have increasingly been used for police functions, managing and containing scattered outbreaks of violence and instability rather than pursuing the capture of a given territory or some other, clearly delineated military goal. This, more than anything else, is why it is a mistake to think of the war on terror as something that happened overseas whose effects just happened to filter back into the homeland. Police violence against poor Black Americans at home, military violence against impoverished populations abroad, and the globally widening wealth inequality that is a necessary consequence of America's ongoing program of asset-price Keynesianism are *part of the same project*, the same larger effort to preserve American supremacy at the expense of the global poor even as America loses the economic capabilities that legitimized its global leadership in the first place. In that sense, Occupy Wall Street and Black Lives Matter were successful in large part because they were the first protest movements of the twenty-first century to identify and target the war on terror's true foundations.

PART IV

Impunity Culture

CHAPTER 10

The Iraq War Debate
Did Not Take Place

*What I'm saying is that to walk the road of peace, sometimes
we need to be ready to climb the mountain of conflict.*
    —Simon Foster, minister for international development,
        In the Loop (directed by Armando Iannucci)

A s he traveled around the United States for nine months in
1831, the twenty-five-year-old French aristocrat Alexis de
Tocqueville noticed that Americans loved to argue with one
another. "To set foot on American soil is to find oneself in tumultuous
surroundings," he wrote in his great two-volume travelogue, *Democracy in America*. "A confused clamor proceeds from every quarter. A
thousand voices assail the ear simultaneously, each giving expression
to some social need." The variety of social needs that people argued
about was endless. Whether to build a school, what to do with a criminal, how best to plan the route for a highway—it seemed that nothing
in life could not be made the topic of animated discussion at a town
meeting. "Citizens meet for the sole purpose of announcing that they
disapprove of the policies of the government," Tocqueville wrote,
"while others hail the men now in office as the fathers of the country."

He saw this fever pitch of civic engagement as a fundamental part of the new country's identity. "In the lives of Americans," he wrote, "to take an interest in and talk about the government of society is life's most important activity and, in a way, its only pleasure." He found this interest making itself known no matter the setting and no matter the situation. "Americans do not converse," he wrote; "they argue."

Tocqueville also found that this love of debate filtered up from streets and towns into the highest levels of government. "The great political fervor that keeps American legislatures in a state of constant agitation," he wrote, "is merely an episode in something much larger, and in a way an extension of it: something that begins in the lowest ranks of the populace and from there spreads through all classes of citizens one after another."[1] Civic engagement was infectious, in other words, and its means of contagion was the press. "The press is, par excellence, the democratic instrument of liberty," Tocqueville wrote.[2]

> It carries the currents of political life into every section of this vast country. Ever vigilant, it regularly lays bare the secret springs of politics and obliges public men to appear before the court of public opinion. It is the press that rallies interests around certain doctrines and formulates the creeds of the political parties. It is through the press that the parties speak to one another without meeting face-to-face and understand one another without direct contract.[3]

In Tocqueville's reading, the press had the power to shape public opinion, but it was also the institution that converted public opinion into a real political force. It was the press that allowed Americans' passion for debate to exercise influence, often decisively, over how they were governed. Journalists and pundits might use the press to broadcast their individual opinions, of course, but the primary importance of a free press to a democratic society was its function as a loudspeaker for the beliefs of the people.

That might have been an accurate description of how the press worked in the first half of the nineteenth century, and Tocqueville's qualified but admiring view of the United States remains an important element of the country's self-image. But his account of the relationship among Americans, the press, and the government does not apply to the United States in the years following September 11. While the American *people* had strong and varied opinions about the wisdom of invading Iraq—as evidenced by their turning out in the hundreds of thousands for antiwar marches in Washington, San Francisco, Seattle, and elsewhere—it was only the pro-war side of the population whose views got a fair hearing in the country's major newspapers and on the airwaves of the country's biggest news stations. During the first two weeks of February 2003, for example, little more than a month before the invasion began, 267 current or former government officials appeared as guests to discuss Iraq on ABC's *World News Tonight*, CBS's *Evening News*, NBC's *Nightly News*, and PBS's *NewsHour with Jim Lehrer*. Just *one* of those guests expressed skepticism about the invasion, and even that one guest, the Democratic senator Edward Kennedy, talked as though the war were a foregone conclusion.[4] As the Bush administration marched the country toward war, and as Congress did as little as it could to get in Bush's way, the news media, for the most part, marched alongside it in lockstep.

Over the following several years, of course, it became clear that invading Iraq had been a mistake. The military failed to locate any stockpiles of nuclear or biological or chemical weapons. The country devolved into civil war instead of rallying around secular democracy and economic liberalism. Saddam Hussein's ouster and subsequent execution did not inspire a wave of democratic reforms across the region. As the scale of America's failure in Iraq sank in, it provided Americans with the opportunity to indulge another of their favorite pastimes: blaming the media for things. Americans did not just believe that their political leaders had pushed the country into a foolish war; they believed the media helped with the pushing. The year in which the United States invaded, 2003, is the last year in which a majority of Americans told Gallup that they had a "great deal" or "fair amount" of trust and confidence in the mass media, and that trust has declined steadily ever since, from a pre-invasion high of about

55 percent to just 34 percent in 2022.[5] Two decades later, resentment of the media remains at a fever pitch across the political spectrum, with Donald Trump making attacks on "fake news" a staple of his rallies and speeches, and left-wing users of the social media platform formerly known as Twitter regularly castigating journalists who supported the invasion. Journalism's failure to cast more doubt on the wisdom of invading is our era's paradigmatic example of what happens when television networks and national newspapers get caught prioritizing the concerns of the people they cover above those of their audiences.

Journalists themselves got in on the criticism as well, with most major newspapers eventually running at least a few op-ed pieces detailing the media's failures. For individual pundits who got the war wrong, the "Iraq apology essay" became a professional rite of passage. In the spring of 2004, the editorial board of *The New York Times* went a few steps past that, undertaking a kind of internal struggle session and then publishing an anguished package enumerating its failures of editorial judgment and emphasis. After "reviewing hundreds of articles written during the prelude to war and into the early stages of the occupation," the *Times* found "a number of instances of coverage that was not as rigorous as it should have been." The editors regretted the paper's performance during the months leading up to the invasion. "In some cases," they wrote, "information that was controversial then, and seems questionable now, was insufficiently qualified or allowed to stand unchallenged." While the editors still believed the paper had produced "an enormous amount of journalism that we are proud of" during that period, they thought the *Times* should have squinted a bit harder at the government's prewar arguments: "Looking back, we wish we had been more aggressive in re-examining the claims as new evidence emerged—or failed to emerge."

While this lengthy recitation of the paper's mistakes gave the impression of an institution that was determined to hold itself accountable, the editorial board let themselves and their colleagues off the hook in a few important ways. To begin with, they did not specify *how* the *Times* would avoid making similar mistakes in the future: Their report included nothing about changing editorial procedures, punishing the reporters whose shoddy work pushed misinformation onto the paper's front page, firing the editors who failed to oversee the reporters, or instituting any new policies regarding anonymous sourcing. All the *Times* promised to do was "continue aggressive reporting aimed at setting the record straight." In addition, the paper made a point of emphasizing that its reporters and editors had not been alone in making such errors. For example, the *Times* said it had been misled by "a circle of Iraqi informants, defectors and exiles bent on 'regime change' in Iraq," people whose self-interest the paper had failed to account for when evaluating the veracity of their claims. To make matters worse, the "best American intelligence sources available at the time" also fed *Times* reporters information that turned out to be false (or at least unverified), particularly concerning Iraq's alleged possession of aluminum tubes that were to be used in the manufacture of enriched uranium. These missteps were unfortunate, but the editorial board implicitly painted them as understandable: "Administration officials" and "many" other "news organizations" had also been taken in by the exiles, and the *Times* certainly wasn't alone in publishing the bad American intelligence.[6]

To hear the *Times* tell it, the newspaper participated in an intense national debate and, despite its collective expertise and the best of intentions, arrived at the wrong conclusions. It pursued the truth in good faith and struggled to weigh good information against bad at a time when things were moving fast and much was uncertain. It made a series of honest mistakes along the way, but so did the rest of the news media, as well as the Bush administration itself. But that explanation is self-serving in the extreme. *The New York Times* and the rest of the national news media did not stage an honest debate and then come down on the wrong side. The media refused to stage a real debate at all. Its errors went far beyond giving too much credence to opportunistic defectors or making educated guesses that turned out to be incorrect. From the beginning, mainstream news organizations treated the invasion of Iraq as a foregone conclusion, going out of their way to avoid seriously considering any evidence or information that would have made the war look like a bad idea. Such evidence and information was not hard to find. As the hundreds of thousands who took to the street in protest saw clearly, the Bush administration's case for war was laughably weak, ridiculous on its face. The judgment that news organizations made was not that the evidence for invading outweighed the evidence against, but that the evidence against the war didn't need to be aired at all. In 2013, Thomas Ricks, who reported on the military for *The Washington Post* in 2002, recalled the bosses spiking his articles criticizing the planned invasion. "There was an attitude among editors," he said: "'Look, we're going to war, why do we even worry about all this contrary stuff?'"[7]

In the nineteenth-century America of Tocqueville's travels, the press forged a connection between the wider population and their representatives in government by transmitting opinion from the former to the latter. In the buildup to Iraq, the press severed that connection. In doing so, it earned the intensifying contempt of Americans for twenty years and counting. When today's press warns about the spread of "misinformation," as became fashionable during the election campaign that put Donald Trump in the White House, it is usually talking about foreign influence campaigns and other malign actors on social media. But when many Americans talk about the problem of "misinformation," they're talking about the press itself.

As we'll see, journalism's failures in 2002 and 2003 also made it easier for Congress to ignore the people it was representing as it considered whether to invade. The cumulative effect, both in the news media and in the halls of government, was a bit surreal. On the streets, in schools and workplaces, and in conversations with friends and family, one could hear and see the "confused clamor" of democratic contention everywhere. But in the news and on Capitol Hill, one saw instead a set of phrases and gestures that had the form and appearance of debate without any of the real content, a debate in the uncanny valley, a disjointed performance of deliberation in which the crucial decisions had already been made. What resulted was the most conformist cultural climate the United States had experienced since the 1950s, under an executive branch acting with a degree of impunity the country had not seen in decades.

• • •

The first type of conformity to be established after September 11 was emotional. On September 16, *The New Yorker* published a series of reflections on the attacks, including a short contribution by Susan Sontag:

> The disconnect between last Tuesday's monstrous dose of reality and the self-righteous drivel and outright deceptions being peddled by public figures and TV commentators is startling, depressing. The voices licensed to follow the event seem to have joined together in a campaign to infantilize the public. Where is the acknowledgment that this was not a "cowardly" attack on "civilization" or "liberty" or "humanity" or "the free world" but an attack on the world's self-proclaimed superpower, undertaken as a consequence of specific American alliances and actions? How many citizens are aware of the ongoing American bombing of Iraq? . . . A lot of thinking needs to be done, and perhaps is being done in Washington and elsewhere, about the ineptitude of American intelligence and counterintelligence, about options available to American foreign policy, particularly in the Middle East, and about what constitutes a smart program of military defense. . . . Those in public office have let us know that they consider their task to be a manipulative one: confidence-building and grief management. Politics, the politics of a democracy—which entails disagreement, which promotes candor—has been replaced by psychotherapy. Let's by all means grieve together. But let's not be stupid together.[8]

Sontag was one of the most prominent and well-established public intellectuals in the country, which meant that she could not be driven entirely out of public life for her impertinence and lack of sentiment. But that did not stop a number of people from trying, and Sontag briefly became the most hated writer in the country. Her piece prompted several memorable tantrums. The conservative blogger Andrew Sullivan called her a "pretentious buffoon" who had revealed herself as "contemptible."[9] In *Newsweek,* the commentator Jonathan Alter called it ironic that Sontag and other left-wing writers, "the same people always urging us to not blame the victim in rape cases[,] are now saying Uncle Sam wore a short skirt and asked for it," which is a pretty creepy way of characterizing a debate about foreign and military policy.[10] Not to be outdone, a *New York Post* columnist named Rod Dreher laid out a sadomasochistic fantasy in which he imagined personally humiliating Sontag in front of the heroes she had disparaged: "I wanted to walk barefoot on broken glass across the Brooklyn Bridge, up to that despicable woman's apartment, grab her by the neck, drag her down to ground zero and force her to say that to the firefighters."[11] This criticism continued for weeks. Sontag was called a "moral idiot" and a "traitor."[12] *The New Republic,* a magazine that had previously run her work, published an article with the opening line "What do Osama bin Laden, Saddam Hussein, and Susan Sontag have in common?"[13] When she appeared on *Nightline* to discuss the controversy, the other guest, a man from the conservative Heritage Foundation, said something to the effect that Sontag should no longer be "permitted" to speak in "honorable intellectual circles."[14]

What exactly were these people mad about? The substance of what Sontag wrote was neither inflammatory nor particularly controversial. That was the first thing that Sontag noticed, anyway. "I mean, I am aware of what a radical point of view is," she told an interviewer a month after her piece was published. "But I did not think for a moment my essay was radical or even particularly dissenting. It seemed very common sense."[15] She had not written that the people inside the Twin Towers and the Pentagon deserved to die. She had not praised the hijackers. She had not criticized a single government policy or official action. What she had done was complain about the tone struck by pundits and political leaders after the attacks, a tone of hazy sentimentality and consolation that seemed to leave no space for the kinds of hard thinking that a disaster like September 11 required. She had written the piece after binge-watching cable news for two days after the planes hit. "What I published in the *New Yorker* was written literally 48 hours after the Sept. 11 attacks," she said. "I was in Berlin at the time, and I was watching CNN for 48 hours straight. You might say that I had overdosed on CNN. And what I wrote was a howl of dismay at the nonsense that I was hearing."[16] With the whole Atlantic Ocean between herself and the city she called home, what Sontag wanted from CNN—and what she did not get—was debate: "a lot of thinking," "the politics of a democracy," "disagreement," and "candor," as she wrote in *The New Yorker*. To her critics, that desire in itself, totally separate from any judgments she might have made about the best course of action going forward, was unpatriotic at best and possibly treasonous at worst.

Many people contributed reflections on September 11 to the *New Yorker* issue in which Sontag's essay appeared. Adam Gopnik, for example, made the strange decision to compare the smell that pervaded lower Manhattan in the aftermath of the attacks to "smoked mozzarella," a scent he described as "not entirely horrible from a reasonable distance." That is at least as offensive as anything Sontag wrote, but readers could forgive his *haute bourgeois* aestheticization of September 11's brutal violence because the tone was right, his feelings appropriate. The article was pensive, mournful in a gentle way, totally apolitical. Gopnik lost himself in the library of his own mind, quoting Edgar Allan Poe, Auden, and E. B. White. He appreciated the birds in Central Park and noticed a now-ironically cheerful advertisement on the street for a "Wayne Thiebaud show at the Whitney." He walked down Seventh Avenue and felt "a surprising rush of devotion to the actual New York, Our Lady of the Subways, New York as it is."[17] His piece was a perfect example of "confidence-building and grief management," the very thing Sontag had criticized. A couple of writers made fun of him for the line about cheese, but on the whole, the media gave him a pass.

The imperative to focus on grief management extended into the "entertainment" sectors of the media as well. In March 2003, on the eve of invasion, the all-female country music trio the Dixie Chicks performed a concert in London. Public opinion in England, as in the rest of the world outside the United States, was overwhelmingly against the war. Before playing a song about an American soldier who dies in Vietnam, singer Natalie Maines talked to the audience. "Just so you know, we're on the good side with y'all," she said. "We do not want this war, this violence, and we're ashamed that the President of the United States is from Texas."[18] The crowd cheered and the concert continued, but when *The Guardian* reported on Maines's remarks, Americans went ballistic. People referred to the group as "Saddam's Angels" and "the Dixie Sluts." The band's song "Travelin' Soldier" dropped from the No. 1 position on the country music chart down to No. 63. Radio stations stopped playing the group's music and suspended DJs who didn't comply. They lost an endorsement deal with a tea company, and their bus driver quit in protest. Maines had to move from Austin to Los Angeles because of death threats, at least one of which the FBI decided was credible.[19]

Musicians didn't even have to say anything about the war to see their careers harmed. In the week following the attacks, program directors for the radio broadcasting conglomerate Clear Channel, which owned stations across the country, received a suggested list of more than 160 songs to *not* play. The origins of the list were unclear, and Clear Channel denied that it ever issued an outright ban on the songs that were included, but many DJs stopped playing them anyway. Whatever the truth of its origins, and whatever the level of enforcement, the list's message came across: It was no longer appropriate to give musical expression to certain ideas and feelings in public. *Every* song by the left-wing rock band Rage Against the Machine was included; there was no longer any room for criticism of America's politics. John Mellencamp's "Crumblin' Down," the Dave Matthews Band hit "Crash into Me," and Carole King's "I Feel the Earth Move" were all banned, presumably because their titles and lyrics might inadvertently cause listeners to dwell on the events of September 11. John Lennon's pacifist anthem "Imagine" was on the list, too: The only thing Americans were going to imagine for the time being was the satisfaction they would take in retribution. But emotional management didn't just mean discouraging people from thinking about negatives like death, destruction, and war. The list wanted to guard against people feeling too positively, too, and that meant that Louis Armstrong's "What a Wonderful World" and Sam Cooke's "Wonderful World" were out as well. The controversy surrounding the list was a silly episode and a public relations headache for Clear Channel, but it illustrated the extent to which media companies saw their audiences as people who couldn't be trusted to manage their feelings about September 11 on their own.[20]

Today, when many people get their news and entertainment primarily from individually curated social media feeds and streaming services rather than national newspapers and a monolithic complex of corporate television and radio networks, one runs the risk of underestimating the effect that episodes like the Sontag controversy and Clear Channel's do-not-play list had on the cultural climate. The internet is now so central to how information gets disseminated and discussed that it can be hard to remember just how embryonic the digital world was two decades ago. A critic for *The New York Times*, for example, recently wrote that "Sept. 11 was the first world event experienced communally online,"[21] but that's not even close to correct. It might have been for a tiny, dedicated cadre of early adopters, but television, not the internet, is where most people experienced September 11. None of today's major social media platforms existed on September 11 or even when the Iraq War began. In early 2003, 89 percent of Americans were still using television as their primary news source, as were 87 percent of America's internet users. The internet lagged behind not just television but print newspapers and radio as well.[22] This meant that when something published in the country's most prestigious magazine prompted comparisons between the writer and Osama bin Laden, people heard about it. And when the nation's largest radio conglomerate banned "Imagine," many people simply weren't going to be listening to "Imagine" for the foreseeable future.

The attempted cancellation of Susan Sontag served as a model for conservatives and center-left liberals who wanted to police any deviations, no matter how minor, from the scripted morality play of mourning, national innocence, and vengeance. The television host Bill Maher, for example, who was otherwise happy to join the New Atheists in singling out Islam for demonization, made the mistake of furrowing his brow at the reflexive description of the hijackers as "cowards." President Bush had used the term in the very first public sentence he uttered about the attacks—"Freedom itself was attacked this morning by a faceless coward"—and the rest of the media had quickly followed suit. Maher didn't get it. "*We* have been the cowards," he said on *Politically Incorrect* just under a week after the attacks. "Lobbing cruise missiles from two thousand miles away—*that's* cowardly. Staying in the airplane when it hits the building, say what you want about it, not cowardly." He apologized multiple times during the ensuing uproar, but his show was canceled within a year.

Local newspaper columnists in Texas and Oregon were fired for criticizing President Bush's peripatetic behavior on the day of the attacks. A New York performance of music by the loopy German composer Karlheinz Stockhausen—who once told a newspaper he was educated at the Sirius star system—was also canceled after he described the attack on the World Trade Center as "the greatest work of art imaginable for the whole cosmos." The reaction to all of these comments was excessive; a couple of grumpy newspaper columnists weren't going to prevent the invasion of Afghanistan from going forward, and the idea that a European composer of atonal art music could undermine feelings of national unity in a country as indifferent to high culture as the United States was laughable. But the firings and boycotts and cancellations enforced the kind of emotional conformity that now made up the texture of the country's public life, affirming that it was ridiculous to suggest that America's response to September 11 required debating anything at all. President Bush's press secretary, Ari Fleischer, spelled this out when he drew the following lesson from Bill Maher's comments at a White House press conference: "People have to watch what they say and watch what they do."[23]

By the spring of 2002, the shock of September 11 had slightly worn off and American soldiers had taken Kabul. The Bush administration now had the time to shift its focus from enforcing emotional conformity to cultivating the political conformity that would be required to realize its dream of war with Iraq. This effort required one of the most forceful propaganda campaigns in the country's history. Nationally, the debate revolved around three questions:

1. Did Saddam Hussein's government have any direct connections, or had it ever provided material assistance, to al-Qaeda or any other extremist group?
2. Did Iraq possess, or was it on the verge of possessing, weapons of mass destruction, whether chemical, biological, or nuclear?
3. Would overthrowing Hussein's government and attempting to replace it with liberal democracy serve America's strategic interests?

As the Bush administration made its case for war, it answered all three of these questions in the affirmative, but the second was the most important. If Saddam possessed WMDs and was hiding them from United Nations inspection teams, then he was an "imminent threat," and America would be justified in taking him out. As everyone knows now, and as many people understood at the time, Hussein didn't have anything that needed to be hidden from the U.N.—the case for war was built *entirely* on lies. But in addition to the stalwart support of Fox News and other conservative news organizations, the Bush administration got crucial assistance from *The New York Times,* which, despite its status as a favored punching bag of the right wing, might have done more to aid the push for invasion than any other newspaper in the country.

The *Times* was instrumental in legitimizing the false claim that

Iraq either possessed or was pursuing WMDs. Relying on the allegations of Iraqi defectors looking to advance their own political interests at Hussein's expense, the *Times* reporters Judith Miller and Michael Gordon wrote a notorious front-page story in September 2002 alleging that Iraq had purchased aluminum tubes specifically designed for use in uranium enrichment. Miller talked to White House officials she described as administration "hard-liners," writing that "the first sign of a 'smoking gun,' they argue, may be a mushroom cloud."[24] Vice President Dick Cheney cited the story on *Meet the Press,* and Secretary of Defense Donald Rumsfeld and National Security Adviser Condoleezza Rice did the same on other television programs. Miller also interviewed a defector who said he had "personally worked on renovations of secret facilities for biological, chemical, and nuclear weapons . . . as recently as a year ago."[25] In response to intelligence analysts who voiced doubts about the evidence for Hussein's pursuit of WMDs—doubts that weren't even mentioned until the story's ninth paragraph—Miller cited anonymous administration officials who "insisted" that "this was a minority view."[26]

Miller's father was a nightlife impresario who was famous for persuading Elvis to play hundreds of shows in Las Vegas starting in 1969,[27] and just like her dad, Miller built a career on her ability to book A-list talent—in her case, as sources. Like most reporters at major newspapers and networks, Miller needed to maintain access to powerful people in order to perform the basic functions of her job, which meant that criticizing those officials or casting doubt on their honesty in public always came with a high potential cost. Miller was an extremely well-sourced reporter, and unlike Elvis, the talent she booked preferred to keep their names off the marquee, allowing the *Times*'s reputation to lend their claims a credibility they would have lacked had readers known the identities of the people making them. Ahmed Chalabi, exiled leader of the dissident Iraqi National Congress, was a key source for Miller's reporting on Hussein's alleged weapons of mass destruction program, and Vice President Cheney's chief of staff, Scooter Libby, supplied her with the name of an undercover CIA agent, Valerie Plame, whose subsequent public outing became a prolonged scandal (it was widely believed at the time that someone associated with the Bush administration had leaked the agent's identity in retaliation for an op-ed written by her husband, who thought the evidence for Hussein's pursuit of WMDs was flimsy). The eventual controversy surrounding Miller's reporting put a stop to her professional ladder climbing, but she managed to make a home for herself as a commentator on Fox News. "My job isn't to assess the government's information and be an independent intelligence analyst myself," she later said. "My job is to tell readers of *The New York Times* what the government thought about Iraq's arsenal."[28] This was a very convenient bit of self-exonerating sophistry. By devoting just two paragraphs out of sixty-one in her first article on Hussein's nonexistent nuclear program to those who expressed doubts that Iraq was much of a threat, Miller made it perfectly obvious that she had "assessed" the government's claims to be credible. And by describing her work as something close to stenography, she revealed herself as a megaphone for the Bush administration rather than any kind of independent observer or analyst.

The news media was similarly lax in scrutinizing the case Secretary of State Colin Powell made for the invasion at the United Nations. The presentation that Secretary Powell gave on February 5, 2003, as well as the extent to which other Bush administration officials had to bully him into giving it, is now notorious, and I won't recount the details of that story in too much detail. Taking place just over a month before the invasion, Powell's speech was the administration's single most effective bit of salesmanship in its campaign for war. Powell was one of the most admired men in the country, a moderate Black conservative with a distinguished record of military service and a sober, statesman-like bearing. Commentators often wondered when he would mount a campaign for the presidency, an idea rendered even more appealing by Powell's obvious reluctance to pursue the office. His presence among the ideologues populating the rest of the Bush administration was reassuring to the press. "George W. Bush's intention to name Colin Powell as secretary of state . . . instantly enhances his coming administration," the *Times* editorial board wrote in December 2000.[29] That perception was the single best reason for Bush to send him to the U.N. "You've got high poll ratings," Powell later remembered Dick Cheney telling him before the speech. "You can afford to lose a few points."[30] As far as the media was concerned, the performance Powell delivered to the Security Council was in keeping with his stature. "Colin Powell convinced me," wrote the future Obama appointee Steven Rattner. The *Newsweek* columnist Jonathan Alter didn't buy Powell's arguments about the link between Iraq and al-Qaeda, but he found the secretary of state "persuasive on Iraq's efforts to obtain nuclear weapons."[31] The *Times* editorial board found in Powell everything that was lacking in Bush, describing the presentation as "powerful," "convincing," and "all the more convincing." It thought Bush's decision to send Powell to the U.N. was "wise."[32] The speech was a public relations coup. By the time journalists and other world leaders came around to the realization that almost all of it was based on false or at least faulty intelligence, Hussein was gone and it was too late.

What's most striking about the presentation today, though, is how *unconvincing* it is if you don't start from the assumption that the man delivering it deserves an enormous benefit of the doubt. Supplementing his speech with audio clips from intercepted phone calls as well as a forty-five-card slideshow, Powell put the translated text of allegedly suspicious Iraqi phone calls on a screen and then exaggerated the content of the translations while reading aloud, turning remarks that seemed innocuous or ambiguous on their face into damning evidence of malign schemes. One of the intercepted messages Powell read was translated as follows: "And we sent you a message to inspect the scrap areas and the abandoned areas." Then Powell put a more exciting gloss on the recording, restating it as "And we sent you a message yesterday to *clean out* all the areas, the scrap areas, the abandoned areas—*make sure there is nothing there*" (emphasis added). He also showed satellite surveillance photos documenting the fact that trucks and other kinds of equipment had been moved from place to place. Those photos were rendered suspicious by Powell's reference to an Iraqi defector who claimed the Hussein government had "mobile biological resource laboratories" that could be hidden in shipping containers and transported anywhere by truck. Of course, the satellites couldn't see inside the trucks or the shipping containers they towed, and Powell admitted that none had yet been found, but then *of course* they wouldn't have been found; because the labs were mobile, they would be easy to hide. "The mobile production facilities are very few, perhaps 18 trucks that we know of—there may be more—but perhaps 18 that we know of," he said. "Just imagine trying to find 18 trucks among the thousands and thousands of trucks that travel the roads of Iraq every single day."[33] Powell did not explore the possibility that people moving trucks and equipment around was a normal occurrence everywhere in the world.

Powell's presentation was built solely on speculation, an insistence on making the worst possible assumption about any piece of circumstantial evidence, and his stellar reputation among the press corps and diplomatic community. It included no direct evidence of a nuclear, chemical, or biological weapons program. It was very effective. Despite what should have been the obvious shortcomings of his presentation, Powell still managed to place the onus on Iraq's government to prove the negative proposition that it *wasn't* pursuing a weapons program (these were the exact terms in which the U.N. drafted its resolutions demanding Iraqi disarmament).[34] To read the positive reviews of Powell's performance in newspapers the next day, or to watch them delivered on television news that evening, was to feel that the entire debate had entered a zone of unreality.

• • •

Opinion writers could have helped to mitigate some of the damage being done by their reporter colleagues over at the news desk, but as journalists like Judith Miller decided to prioritize access and close relationships with their powerful government sources over documenting the truth, many liberal and centrist pundits seemed to decide that criticizing the Bush administration's war effort wasn't worth the professional risks. The editorial board of *The New York Times,* for example, is made up of about fifteen people, give or take a few. The names of the head and deputy editors of the editorial page are listed on the paper's masthead, but the names of the board's other members are harder to track down. They have two jobs. The first is to produce unsigned articles that express the newspaper's official, institutional opinion on the events of the day. The second is to commission and edit signed opinion pieces authored by guest contributors and columnists. They work in strict isolation. Members of the board are not allowed to discuss their work or views with colleagues in the newsroom, nor are they permitted to know what those colleagues will be reporting on over the coming days and weeks. The separation between news and opinion is supposed to be total, like church and state. During the first years of the twenty-first century, legacy publications were still enjoying the final years of their unquestioned dominance, and *The New York Times* was the most important and widely read newspaper in the country. That lofty status made the members of its editorial board something like the high priests of American public opinion. They were among the most influential semi-anonymous writers in the English-speaking world.

In 2002 and early 2003, the *Times* devoted many hundreds of column inches in its opinion pages to the question of whether the United States should or should not invade Iraq, depose Saddam Hussein, and install a democratic government in his place. It was odd, though: Very few of those column inches were actually devoted to evaluating the case for war on the merits. Hardly a week went by without the *Times* addressing Iraq in one way or another, but the board seemed to fixate in a rather manic way on President Bush's sales tactics while paying little attention to the thing that was up for sale. On July 25, 2002, one op-ed noted the likely costs associated with a full-scale invasion. "There is a case to be made that these costs are worth sustaining," the two guest contributors wrote. "But if so, we need Mr. Bush to make it. He has not yet done so."[35] The board would keep up this anxious drumbeat throughout the following seven months. August 3: "There may be a compelling case to be made for war with Iraq. The administration has not yet made it."[36] August 11: "It is not too late for Mr. Bush and the nation to consider basic questions about Iraq."[37] August 16: "Mr. Bush and his aides may yet be able to make a solid case for military action in one of the most volatile parts of the world."[38] August 24 saw a special guest appearance from Bill Keller, who would become the paper's executive editor in July 2003. "When the time comes, the president . . . needs to lay out his evidence," he wrote.[39] September 5: "Mr. Bush seems to realize that he has a lot of work to do if he hopes to present a more coherent policy."[40] September 20: "At this stage Congress and the American people deserve some time to ponder the matter."[41] October 3: "The debate should be a moment for the American public to take stock."[42] October 8: "Mr. Bush still has work to do if he hopes to persuade Americans of the need to use military force to disarm Iraq."[43] January 10, 2003: "There can be no wavering from the goal of disarming Iraq, but all chances of doing so peacefully should be explored before the world is asked to decide on war."[44] January 28: "The world must be reassured that every possibility of a peaceful solution has been fully explored."[45] February 2: "The administration owes the American people and the rest of the world a more careful and consistent approach."[46] March 7: "Diplomacy should be given a chance to rescue the Security Council from damaging paralysis, and to present Baghdad with one last opportunity to change course."[47] March 17: "This page remains persuaded of the vital need to disarm Iraq. But it is a process that should go through the United Nations."[48] The war began three days later.

It's not as if the *Times* didn't make up its mind about the war; by the spring of 2003, its editors clearly believed that Hussein was hiding a WMD program, and they thought that invading was worthwhile in the event that he refused to cooperate with United Nations inspectors. But the board never spelled out how it came to that belief. It didn't address the skeptics who thought the evidence for Iraq's WMDs was actually pretty thin, and it didn't reflect on the Bush administration's failure to substantiate Hussein's alleged links to al-Qaeda and what that failure said about the larger issue of the administration's credibility. Instead, the *Times* appeared to drift into a pro-war position, like an unmanned boat tugged down one river fork rather than another by an invisible current, even as the editors fetishized proceduralism and chided the president over his lack of enthusiasm for international consensus. The more it wrote about the invasion, the less interested it seemed in what that invasion would entail, or what its consequences might be. That's not the kind of writing one would like to expect from the opinion leaders of the English-speaking world.

The quality of argumentation was even worse at conservative outlets such as Fox News and *The Wall Street Journal.* Those organizations played their expected roles, praising Bush's every move, laying out the evils of the Hussein government in exhaustive and exhausting detail, and keeping a neurotically vigilant watch for anyone with a bad word to say about the proposed war. But even if individual writers at centrist and liberal publications didn't want to join in on the orgy of bloodthirsty jingoism that characterized conservative media, they still displayed a striking reluctance to oppose an administration that many of them had been happy to criticize for the first eight months of its existence. In places like *The New York Times* and *The New Yorker,* the Iraq debate was dominated by a group of ostentatiously reluctant hawks. When one surveys the editorials, symposia, panel discussions, and narrative journalism this group produced in 2002 and 2003, the consistency of tone is remarkable. Almost without exception (the exception is Christopher Hitchens), liberal support for the invasion was solemn, even melancholy, accented with flourishes of moral seriousness and high-minded anger directed toward the antiwar left. In March 2003, Hendrik Hertzberg published a comment in *The New Yorker.* Caught between two groups of loud partisans, each "equally convinced of their moral rectitude," Hertzberg counted himself among the "great many who hold their views in fear and trembling, haunted by the suspicion that the other side might be right after all."[49] The magazine's editor, David Remnick, was one of these many, and so was the writer Paul Berman, who was frustrated that Bush refused to describe the war as a defense of democratic civilization in general. "We're going into a very complex and long war disarmed," Berman told the *Times,* "in which our most important assets have been stripped away from us, which are our ideals and our ideas."[50] One month before the invasion, Thomas Friedman wrote, "I feel lately as if there are no adults in this room (except Tony Blair). . . . I side with those who believe we need to confront Saddam—but we have to do it right, with allies and staying power."[51] Leon Wieseltier broke with his fellow editors at *The New Republic,* the house organ of the Washington consensus, in displaying no eagerness for war, but he still thought there would need to be a war. "We will certainly win," he said, "but it is a war in which we are truly playing with fire."[52]

The liberal hawks were clearly at pains to distance themselves from the drum-beating patriots over at places like the *National Review.* In *The New Yorker,* Hertzberg disdainfully referred to "the sort of evangelical-Christian conservatives who contemplate Armageddon with something like rapture." But they were equally concerned that people not associate them with the antiwar left, or, as Hertzberg described them, "traditional pacifists and the sort of angry leftists for whom any exercise of American military power, because it is American, is wrong."[53] These were distinctions based on style, but when it came to substance—that is, the question of whether the United States should take out Saddam—there was little to separate the liberal hawks from the war's most enthusiastic proponents. They did not challenge the Bush administration's central contention that Saddam Hussein either already possessed or was actively working to acquire weapons of mass destruction. They did not point out the fantastical lunacy of the government's plan for shipping democracy to Iraq like so much flat-packed Ikea furniture. They failed to note that without a real, workable plan for rebuilding Iraq after Saddam's fall, the war was doomed to failure. They also refused to grapple with the Bush administration's obvious bad faith. It wasn't just that Bush, Cheney, Rumsfeld, and the rest were lying. It was how little they seemed to care that everyone could tell they were lying. For all the energy the Bush administration put into its propaganda effort, it hardly seemed concerned with whether the propaganda was any good. The Republicans believed they could get what they wanted without having to trouble themselves with a sophisticated strategy or a narrative that the average informed person would be likely to accept as accurate; they thought their goals were achievable through sheer shamelessness and force of will. In light of the liberal hawks' performance during 2002 and 2003, the Republicans were right.

There was one little corner of the media landscape where the public could find something like a real debate on the war. In the early years of the twenty-first century, a number of journalists and commentators—prominent, obscure, and upstart alike—began to publish their writing on independent blogs. For established journalists, blogging allowed them to communicate with readers more quickly and in a more colloquial tone than would have been allowed in the pages of a magazine or newspaper. For the up-and-comers, blogging allowed them to build up loyal audiences and get their byline into circulation by posting several times a day, commenting on events in real time, and lacing their posts with jokes, links to funny videos, wry expressions of disgust, and howls of outrage. Within the space of a few years, bloggers like Ezra Klein, Matthew Yglesias, Andrew Sullivan, and dozens of others built their own coherent world, one with its own rhythms, tics, preoccupations, and insider terms of art. A map of this world could be found in the blogrolls, the list of other sites that each blog would post on the side of the page to indicate whom they were in conversation with. Because many of them didn't do any original reporting of their own, the relationship between establishment publications and bloggers resembled that between sharks and the remoras that cling to them—without the mainstream media, the bloggers would not have had anything to comment on. But they were separate from it, too, like a group of quick-witted, intellectually unformed, and sometimes arrogant boys who sit in the back of the hall and keep up an insistent running commentary throughout the professor's lecture. For people who spent a lot of time reading these blogs during the Bush presidency, a roll call of their names is likely to inspire mixed feelings of nostalgia, amusement, and exhaustion: *Eschaton, Alicublog, Firedoglake, Instapundit, Allahpundit, Tapped, Pandagon, Little Green Footballs, Hullabaloo, Daily Kos.*

This medium for commentary was a recent development, very much in its infancy in 2002. Comments sections weren't introduced until 1998, and news organizations were slow to adopt them. Permalinks, which gave individual blog posts unique URLs that could be bookmarked and shared, were only invented in 2000.[54] The bloggers weren't exclusively focused on the war. They wrote about whatever was happening in the news that day, from international trade deals and minor congressional scandals to musings on the return of professional baseball to Washington, D.C. For the first several years of their existence, however, Iraq and the war on terror were the biggest stories in the world, so that's what they focused on. One could argue that Iraq was *the* event around which the internet learned to talk to itself, and audiences, for their part, found that the internet was very useful for keeping up with news on the war. Even if people weren't yet ready to give up their newspaper and cable subscriptions, more than three-quarters of Americans used the internet in some capacity to find or share information about the war, and their ranks grew as time passed. At the beginning of 2001, less than half of Americans used the internet at all. By 2007, when President Bush initiated the "surge" in response to America's failure to pacify Iraq following Saddam's ouster, 75 percent did.[55]

There was plenty of pro-war sentiment in Blogworld. Andrew Sullivan, for example, a gay British American conservative who idolized Margaret Thatcher and had edited *The New Republic* in the 1990s, was Susan Sontag's most dedicated critic. He started his blog, *The Daily Dish,* in 2000, and spent the next decade as one of the most influential commentators in the country. Though he turned against the war after the invasion, his defense of the Bush administration before the spring of 2003 was so strident as to merit the adjective "hysterical." He was quick to hand out his "Sontag Award" to any commentator who deviated from what he viewed as the only acceptable response to the attacks: unqualified sympathy for the Americans, unlimited hatred for the hijackers, and boundless love for America's ideals. When *The Guardian* published an opinion piece in which the writer Charlotte Raven described her ambivalent feelings toward the United States— "It is perfectly possible to condemn the terrorist action and dislike the US just as much as you did before the WTC went down"—Sullivan went into a rage.[56] "A new low in hatred for America," he wrote. "It is beneath response. But we might as well be aware of the enemy within the West itself—a paralyzing, pseudo-clever, morally nihilist fifth column that will surely ramp up its hatred in the days and months ahead."[57] The pro-war camp also included people like Matthew Yglesias (now a Twitter/X lightning rod as well as a star independent blogger), who started blogging as an undergraduate and swiftly climbed the ranks of the media power hierarchy. Yglesias spent a lot of his time writing irritatingly fine-grained disquisitions on arguments among pundits—"I'd meant to do a post a little while back about how I'd read a post from Oxblog's Afghan correspondent which answered about 75 percent of what had puzzled me about Peter Bergen's 'things are better than you think in Afghanistan' op-ed," is how he began one post in September 2004[58]—but occasionally he would drop the hair-splitting and just say what he thought. In January 2002, after President Bush characterized Iraq, Iran, and North Korea as making up an "axis of evil" in his State of the Union address, Yglesias wrote that "we should take them *all* out" (emphasis added).[59]

The difference between Blogworld and the traditional media, though, was that Blogworld had a place for antiwar voices, too, people whose contempt for the Bush administration was matched only by their loathing of the more established pundits who were falling over themselves to lend the neocons' geopolitical strategy a veneer of seriousness that it did not deserve. Duncan Black, who wrote under the pseudonym Atrios, used his talent for neologism to annoy his mainstream media superiors on his website, *Eschaton*. In 2006, Atrios coined the term "Friedman Unit," meaning six months, in reference to the *New York Times* columnist Thomas Friedman's funny habit of repeatedly claiming that "the next six months" would be crucial in determining the outcome of the Iraq War, which he'd done at least twelve times over the previous two and a half years.[60] "The dominant view among the crowd in Washington is that the next 6 months is a critical time in Iraq," Atrios wrote. "As it has always been. They're all Tom Friedman now."[61] David Rees produced a web comic titled *Get Your War On,* in which he attached profane speech bubbles to public domain clip art drawings of office workers talking to each other. A strip from October 2001 read as follows:

Man 1: If you could say one thing to God right now, what would it be?

Man 2: I think I would say, "Thank you, God, for your healing gift of religion." What about you?

Man 1: I'd say, "God, I regret to inform you that U.S. policy now dictates we bomb the fuck out of You up in Heaven."[62]

One of the most important nodes in Blogworld technically wasn't a blog at all. It was more like a collection of several dozen blogs, all housed together under the same name. The website *Slate* was founded in 1996 by Michael Kinsley, who had co-hosted the cable news talk show *Crossfire* in the early 1990s. *Slate* ran lengthy exchanges among its editors and contributors that covered much of the spectrum of opinion on Iraq. Liberal hawks gave voice to their ambivalence, the conservative columnist and former Reagan speechwriter Peggy Noonan qualified her support for invasion with the line "Ultimately it's all a big gut call," and the progressive historian and media critic Eric Alterman wrote that the war was "unnecessary and potentially ruinous."[63] David Plotz admitted that he supported the war in spite of finding arguments against it to be very compelling. "I haven't been able to explain to myself (much less anyone else) *why* I support it," he wrote.[64] Jonathan Alter said the United States should invade to preserve its credibility, and the pro-war journalist Jeffrey Goldberg telegraphed seriousness by breaking up his prose into as many clauses as possible and using a semicolon when a comma (or even no punctuation at all) would have worked just fine: "I will try, instead, to return to the essential issues: the moral challenge posed by the deeds of the Iraqi regime; and the particular dangers the regime poses to America and its allies. Everything else, to my mind, is commentary."[65] A few other writers said that the Bush administration's disdain for international law had cemented their opposition to the war. Midsize magazines such as *The New York Review of Books* also criticized the Bush administration's pro-war publicity campaign and detailed the recklessness and incoherence of the president's foreign policy, focusing in particular on his determination to undermine the same set of international rules that had benefited the United States more than any other country on earth over the previous half century.

Like traditional media, Blogworld was predominantly white and male, but its diversity of style and tone was crucial to its appeal, along with its speed and disregard for the conventions of legacy journalism. This disregard wasn't contrarianism for its own sake; traditional journalism really did seem ill-equipped to chronicle what was unfolding during President Bush's first term. In less than two years, Bush had lost the popular vote, been installed in the White House by the Supreme Court, and then been confronted with the worst disaster in the country's history. Given his lack of a popular mandate and the modesty of his campaign promises, one might have expected a president in Bush's position to respond to September 11 with caution. Instead, his administration revealed itself as the most radical in living memory, proposing to upend the country's foreign policy as well as the balance of power between the presidency and the other branches of the federal government. In light of the Bush administration's radicalism and the country's panicked mood, did it really make sense, as *The New York Times* maintained, to prohibit the inclusion of swear words in a news article? Blogs did a better job keeping up with the news as it unfolded, and their more rambunctious and emotional style was better suited to the disorienting and frightening times. The emotionally neutral stance on which newspapers prided themselves might have worked most of the time, but after September 11 that detachment sounded more like the dissociated monotone of someone who is unable to come to grips with events. The bloggers' emotionalism told readers that they, too, were struggling to make sense of it all.

For all their democratic, argumentative energy, however, the bloggers had a limited impact on the wider national debate. They simply didn't have the funds or the infrastructure to match the audience numbers of organizations like the *Times* and CNN. Their influence would grow as legacy publications began to imitate the independent blogs, whether by launching blogs of their own or hiring some of Blogworld's star performers to write under their mastheads. But the bloggers selected for promotion to the legacy media big time were not the firebrands, not the ones who had said from the beginning that invading Iraq was a mistake. They were people like Ezra Klein, the wunderkind who supported the invasion as a college student and then dutifully apologized for supporting it a decade later. "Ezra is an incredible operator," one editor said of him in 2013. "He is always looking upward at things. You only have to watch him work a party. He moves right to the most important people there."[66] Or consider Matthew Yglesias, who was glad to explain in 2021 that careerism fueled his undergraduate support of the war. "I was a senior in college when the war started, but I was an early adopting blogger," he said.

> I was looking to graduation, I was looking to my job, I was looking to my aspiration to become, you know, a Frank Foer kind of person. And I was aware that in sophisticated political commentary circles, these things that my friends around the dorm thought were considered incredibly naive and dumb ways of looking at it. I thought that I had developed this much more sophisticated view from reading all these wise professionals.[67]

While Blogworld's most valuable contributions in 2002 and 2003 came from people who were willing to say that the mainstream media had abdicated its role as social and political watchdog, the individual bloggers who enjoyed the most success within mainstream media later were those who knew from the beginning that in some cases, with respect to certain debates, the best course of action was to imitate and flatter one's professional superiors. This is one reason why, for all the promise of the bloggers' "disruptive" energy in the early years of the twenty-first century, the foreign policy views of traditional media have changed very little since 2003.

• • •

Let's pretend for a moment that journalists hadn't made any of the mistakes described above. Let's say conservative opinion writers had merely disagreed with their opponents rather than accusing them of treason and fantasizing about making them walk across broken glass. Let's say Judith Miller's editors had refused to publish her pieces because of her overreliance on Iraq's self-interested exiles as sources, or that they had told her to spend more time interviewing those who were skeptical of Iraq's alleged WMDs. Let's say *The New Yorker*'s reluctant hawks had suddenly realized their reluctance was well founded, and let's say the editorial board of the *Times* devoted more attention to the merits of the case for war as opposed to impotently complaining about the Bush administration's failure to make the case for war. Would it have made a difference? Would it have made people less willing to watch the war drag on for year after year if serious doubts about the need to wage it had been raised at the beginning? Would it have weakened the Bush administration enough to deny him a second term? Would it have stopped the war from happening at all?

One way to answer these questions, which isn't quite as cheap and dismissive as it seems, is to reject their premise and note that the imaginary alternative was just that—imaginary. Not only did the media go along with the Bush administration's war planning, but it has continued to support presidential militarism ever since. Despite the public self-flagellation over its errors in reporting on Iraq, for example, the *New York Times* editorial board responded to Obama's 2009 plan to increase troop numbers in Afghanistan with the same fussy proceduralism they directed at Bush in 2002 and 2003. Dismissing out of hand the idea that the United States should give up and withdraw entirely (which would have been the correct decision), the editors would insist only that "Mr. Obama needs to explain the stakes for this country, the extent of the military commitment, the likely cost in lives and treasure and his definition of success."[68] And when Obama made the more egregious mistake of taking military action in Libya, disguising as a simple effort to protect civilians a military action that was in reality always designed to end Muammar Gaddafi's rule, the editors praised the decision, writing that "the United Nations Security Council resolution [authorizing] member nations to take 'all necessary measures' to protect civilians . . . was perhaps the only hope of stopping him from slaughtering thousands more."[69] Other outlets failed to live up to their post-Iraq commitments to subject the military actions of future presidents to more rigorous scrutiny even when the president in question was Donald Trump. When Trump ordered the launch of several dozen Tomahawk missiles into Syria in April 2017, the U.S. military's first unilateral involvement in the Syrian civil war, the CNN host and *Washington Post* columnist Fareed Zakaria described it as the moment Trump really "became President of the United States," as though it were impossible to embody the full majesty of the office without killing people over something of negligible strategic importance.[70]

The very idea that the American news media, in its current form, can just decide to cultivate a consistently adversarial relationship with the government it covers is a fantasy. Objectivity and editorial independence are valuable ideals that news organizations could never afford to abandon, and many young journalists still dream of one day taking down a corrupt presidential administration in the manner of Woodward and Bernstein. But the economic and social realities of producing daily journalism on a national scale often militate against putting those ideals into practice. President Bush's approval ratings never dropped below 57 percent between September 11, 2001, and March 2003,[71] and a majority of Americans supported invading Iraq from June 2002 right until the invasion began.[72] Why exactly would one expect the country's journalists and editors to have been less susceptible than the general public to the country's mythology of redemptive violence after September 11? Why would one expect pundits to have radically different views on the uses of American military power than their countrymen? The whole point of the word "mainstream" in the phrase "mainstream media" is that the people who voice their opinions on those platforms mostly have the same opinions as everyone else. Exceptional journalists and publications exist, of course, but to expect journalists *as a group* to be more perceptive and more measured in their judgment than the average citizen doesn't make a lot of sense.

In addition, national news organizations are corporate entities with budgets in the hundreds of millions of dollars. The competitive pressures are intense, and this makes it costly to espouse unpopular views for any sustained period of time. Journalism in the United States is battered on all sides by public opinion it cannot afford to ignore for long, the need to get a story published before the competitors do, and the laws of profitability. Compared with an as yet unrealized ideal of journalistic foresight and editorial independence, the media failed spectacularly in the months preceding the invasion. But with respect to the news media infrastructure that actually exists in the United States, journalism functioned about as well as you would expect it to.

For another way of answering the what-if questions about the media and Iraq, consider the institution that, unlike the media, literally had the authority to prevent the country from going to war after September 11: Congress. Anyone claiming that a more adversarial media response to the Bush administration's pro-war propaganda campaign in 2002 would have ultimately made a difference also presupposes a Congress that is responsive to public opinion and ready to debate issues on their merits. Congressional representatives are the only people in the federal government who are elected by direct popular vote, which means that the House and Senate are the parts of the federal government that should, in theory, be most responsive to "the will of the people." If an adversarial news media had turned people against war in 2002, it would still have been up to Congress to make their constituents heard at the federal level. Fortunately, Congress had more than sufficient authority to prevent the Bush administration from sending the military into Iraq, because in 1973, in an effort to reset the federal government's balance of power following decades of presidents waging undeclared wars in Korea and Vietnam, Congress had passed the War Powers Resolution Act over Nixon's veto. Designed to prevent future presidents from sending troops into combat on their sole authority, the law states that any troop deployment by the president must be preceded by a congressional declaration of war, except in cases of a national emergency or some other formal "statutory authorization" on the part of the legislature.

Three days after September 11, however, Congress decided to voluntarily abdicate its authority when it took up a bill called the Authorization for Use of Military Force (AUMF). The text of the bill was brief. It began, "Whereas, on September 11, 2001, acts of treacherous violence were committed against the United States and its citizens," and it ended with an assurance that "nothing in this resolution supersedes any requirement of the War Powers Resolution." In spite of that assurance, the rest of the AUMF rendered the War Powers Resolution all but irrelevant to America's foreign and military policy for the next twenty years and counting. "The President," it declared,

> is authorized to use all necessary and appropriate force against those nations, organizations, or persons he determines planned, authorized, committed, or aided the terrorist attacks that occurred on September 11, 2001, or harbored such organizations or persons, in order to prevent any future acts of international terrorism against the United States by such nations, organizations or persons.[73]

The implications of passing the AUMF were staggering. At a stroke, the executive branch would acquire nearly absolute authority to decide when, where, and how the U.S. military would fight. The choice of targets would be left entirely to the president's discretion, so long as he could claim with a straight face (he didn't even have to prove it, just claim it) that a newly designated enemy had at least "aided" or "harbored" anyone who had anything to do with any organization involved in September 11. And so long as Congress periodically agreed to reauthorize the authorization they had already given—not a big lift, politically—the executive's new war-making authority would be bound by neither time nor space. The war on terror has sometimes been called "the forever war." It was the AUMF that made the "forever" part possible.

The California congresswoman Barbara Lee was the only member of the House *or* the Senate to vote against the AUMF. "I am convinced," she said in a September 14 speech on the House floor, "that military action will not prevent further acts of international terrorism against the United States." She sounded nervous as she spoke. Her voice shook, her shoulders rose and fell as she took deep breaths between sentences, and she repeatedly clasped and unclasped her hands. She concluded by quoting a member of the clergy who had spoken at a memorial service earlier that day: "As we act, let us not become the evil that we deplore." She knew the AUMF's passage was a foregone conclusion, which meant that her vote was an act of genuine political courage. Her reward for that courage was to become the most vilified politician in the country. She became the Susan Sontag of Capitol Hill, and for the same reason. "Let's step back for a moment," she said in her floor speech. "Let's just pause, just for a minute and think through the implications of our actions today, so that this does not spiral out of control." Instead of a rush to war, she wanted deliberation and debate, and in response her office was flooded with so many death threats that the Capitol Police appointed bodyguards to look after her for twenty-four hours a day. The press turned her into a symbol of the American left's feckless pacifism. "Who Is Barbara Lee?" asked the headline of a September 17 editorial in *The Wall Street Journal,* written by the conservative pundit John Fund. The answer, in short, was that Congresswoman Lee was "someone who always blames America first," a representative whose district was "perhaps the most radical in the country," and a longtime antiwar activist whose supposed pacificism was really just "a cloak for her belief that when it comes to the use of American power, her country can never do right." At best, Lee and her ilk were "hopeless dupes." At worst—and Fund seemed to believe the worst—they were up to "something more sinister."[74]

During the Bush and Obama administrations, the AUMF was invoked *thirty-seven times* to launch military operations overseas. These included combat action in Afghanistan (2001); opening the notorious detention center at Guantánamo, as well as foreign military training in the Philippines, Georgia, and Yemen (2002); deployment to Djibouti and "maritime interception operations on the high seas" (2003); military operations in Iraq (2004); deployment (it's not specified where) to enhance the counterterrorism capabilities of "friends and allies" (2006); strikes targeting Somalia from both the air and the sea (2007); "working with counterterrorism partners to disrupt and degrade al-Qaeda and affiliates" (2010); the detention of some one thousand "al-Qaeda, Taliban, and associated fighters," plus the implementation of a "clear-hold-build strategy" in Afghanistan (2011); "direct military action . . . against al-Qaeda in the Arabian Peninsula," including in Yemen (2012); the capture of a single member of al-Qaeda in Libya (2013); and a campaign of air strikes against the Islamic State in Iraq and Syria, the use of U.S. troops to support Iraqi security forces, a series of strikes against the Khorasan group of al-Qaeda in Syria, and one air strike in Somalia (2014). The year 2015 saw U.S. support for anti-al-Qaeda operations in Afghanistan, U.S. support of a Kurdish Peshmerga rescue operation in Iraq, the deployment of U.S. forces to northern Syria, and the deployment of combat aircraft and personnel to Turkey.[75] Without the AUMF, Congress would have been obligated to debate and vote on these operations, making decisions for which they would have to answer to their constituents every two years. But Congress didn't want to have those debates and cast those votes. Perhaps they remembered what happened to Barbara Lee.

The passage of the AUMF was one of the worst self-inflicted wounds in congressional history, and given the importance of the House of Representatives in particular to the democratic character of the country's government, it was also a blow to American democracy writ large. Even before September 11, Bush's presence in the White House constituted a democratic crisis, regardless of one's political orientation. Receiving half a million fewer votes than Al Gore in 2000, Bush was the first president in 112 years to win an election while losing the popular vote, and his victory was only assured when five unelected members of the Supreme Court stepped in to make sure that not all of the votes were counted. The decision was a political one, and nakedly so, with five conservative justices overruling a lower court and handing the presidency to the Republican candidate (subsequent analysis revealed that a full statewide recount would have swung the election to Gore). Given the manner in which Bush took office, one might have expected Congress to be particularly aggressive in terms of oversight, because it was the only branch of the federal government that could claim substantive democratic legitimacy at the time. Instead, Congress responded to September 11 by rushing to give up its authority over military policy, as though it were only too grateful not to be responsible for making the big decisions. The result was that a president whose administration stood on the shakiest democratic foundations in more than a century also became the most powerful chief executive in modern times.

As Bush sought to expand the war on terror to Iraq in 2002 and 2003, the empowered executive branch pressed its advantage, asking Congress to pass a second AUMF that would apply to Iraq. Again, Congress failed to push back, never seriously considering the alternative passage of a full declaration of war instead. A declaration of war would have made it clear that Congress—and by extension, citizens— still had the final word on when and where America's armies went to fight. It would also have classified Iraq's soldiers, as well as the extremists Bush believed to be allied with Saddam, as "enemy combatants" under international law, with all of the protections that designation entailed. In addition, all of Congress's prior declarations of war, the last of which had been issued after the Japanese attack on Pearl Harbor, had at least formally adhered to the principle of nonaggression, declaring not that the United States was about to start an offensive war but that, because of the actions of another party, a state of war already existed. The illegality of aggressive wars is one of the basic pillars of international law. All of the above considerations made a declaration of war unacceptable to the Bush administration. They could not argue with a straight face that Iraq had brought a state of war into being, and Bush was determined that America's enemies not be granted the full protection of the Geneva Conventions. A second AUMF constituted the limit of what the Bush administration was willing to tolerate in terms of congressional participation, and his officials made it clear that the request for a second AUMF was an indulgence that Congress did not really deserve. As far as those officials were concerned, the *first* AUMF had provided them with all the authorization they needed. The second AUMF was just to let Congress save a little face.

For all the media's errors, it was Congress that really failed to debate the invasion of Iraq. The negotiations that took place over the Iraq AUMF never touched on the central question of whether the United States would go to war. It was a foregone conclusion that the United States would go to war. Even before Congress brought the AUMF to the floor of either chamber, the Democratic senator Dianne Feinstein said it was obvious that Bush "has the votes" to approve the invasion.[76] The way she saw it, her job was not to try to stop the Bush administration from launching a war but to pad the AUMF with language that would make it less embarrassing for skeptical Democrats like herself to get on board. Doing so would help to limit the amount of time the Senate had to spend debating the war in front of C-SPAN's cameras. This was not a very ambitious goal for a legislature that refers to itself as "the greatest deliberative body in the world," but it made sense in light of the midterm elections that were approaching in less than two months. The Democratic Party's strategy seems to have been to hedge their opposition and ensure that if the war went well, they would share at least some of the credit with their Republican counterparts. "I'm one that has been very concerned about a preemptive unilateral attack," Feinstein said, "in terms of America's perceived 'imperialist' culture that this administration has developed." Once the AUMF had been modified to include a few anodyne caveats, she voted for the preemptive unilateral attack, as did nearly 40 percent of her Democratic colleagues in the House and a majority of Democrats in the Senate.

Even the compromise AUMF, however, came with so many executive branch strings attached that its final form could hardly be said to represent a real exercise of congressional deliberation and oversight. Although the alleged link between Hussein and al-Qaeda was by far the weakest component of the Bush administration's argument for war, it was not one the neocons were willing to abandon. Less than a week before Congress began voting on the Iraq AUMF, Secretary of Defense Rumsfeld told reporters that America's evidence of the links between Iraq and al-Qaeda was "bulletproof," though he refused to share any details.[77] Holding to the Iraq–al-Qaeda hypothesis allowed the administration to argue that invading Iraq required no additional legislative approval whatsoever. So long as the official rationale for invading retained the claim that Saddam had aided al-Qaeda in some way, or that he had attempted to, or even that someone in his government had been in contact with them and then failed to help the free world bring the terrorists to justice, Bush could argue that the first AUMF had already granted his administration the authority to send troops to Baghdad. Under Attorney General John Ashcroft, the Office of Legal Counsel published a memorandum opinion arguing that "to the extent that the President were to determine that military action against Iraq would protect our national interests, he could take such action based on his independent constitutional authority; no action by Congress would be necessary."[78] And as a former lawyer with the State Department recently pointed out in *Lawfare,* the thinly veiled threats to bypass Congress entirely and rely solely on the 2001 AUMF "provided leverage in negotiations, limiting the extent to which some in Congress felt they could push back on the White House's demands."[79] Skeptics in Congress did succeed in adding language to the authorization stipulating that President Bush could only order the use of military force against Iraq once all diplomatic efforts had been exhausted, but they rendered their own stipulation toothless by also granting Bush the sole authority to determine when diplomacy was no longer useful. The AUMF also required President Bush to check in with Congress and submit reports on how things were going every sixty days. Other than that, he could do as he liked.[80]

A legislature doesn't just represent the views of its constituents. It also models the kind of government under which its constituents live. In 2002 and 2003, Congress modeled a kind of governance more akin to sleepwalking than democracy, a dissociated going through the motions of debating an issue that everyone seemed to agree had been decided well in advance. The *Times*'s editorial board didn't seem to have a problem with this. On the day it published an op-ed asserting that "no further debate is needed to establish that Saddam Hussein is an evil dictator whose continued effort to build unconventional weapons in defiance of clear United Nations prohibitions threatens the Middle East and beyond," congressional debate on the AUMF had not even *begun*.[81] Convinced that their job security was more important than the lives of the Iraqis and Americans who were going to die once the bombs started falling, congressional Democrats consistently pulled their punches, refusing to attack President Bush's case for invasion at the point where it was most vulnerable—its falsehood. Senator Hillary Clinton, for example, was widely believed to be unwilling to voice her own doubts about invading Iraq because she wanted to preserve her viability as a presidential candidate in 2008, a reticence that Washington insiders regarded as "shrewd and pragmatic," in the words of the columnist Maureen Dowd.[82] One exception was Representative Jim McDermott of Washington, who said during a visit to Baghdad that he thought President Bush was willing to "mislead the American people." A newspaper columnist described McDermott's interview as "the most disgraceful performance abroad by an American official in my lifetime,"[83] and Andrew Sullivan wrote that McDermott was "perilously close to treason" in a post that also described the antiwar movement as "obscene."[84] It didn't take McDermott long to walk back the remark, which set yet another useful example.

Foreign policy is often the sphere of government action that is the least accessible to democratic input, but even by those standards, what happened between 2000 and 2003 was extreme. The Iraq War might have been launched with the official approval of Congress, the United Nations, and public opinion, but this approval was semantic rather than substantive. The war was planned by an administration that was installed in the White House rather than elected. It was rubber-stamped by a legislature whose first act after September 11 was to abdicate its responsibility to steer the country's military policy. And it was applauded by a citizenry whose approval had been elicited with lies and who were stuck relying on a news media that didn't really want to bother with what Thomas Ricks's editor called the "contrary stuff." Whatever President Trump did to harm democracy between 2016 and January 6, 2021, what the Bush administration and the rest of the federal government did to get the war on terror off the ground was worse.

CHAPTER 11

Mom, Can You Not Read over My Shoulder?

And today, I run across a post on your Facebook page that you didn't think I'd be able to see. So since you want to hide it from everyone, I'm gonna share it with everybody.
—Tommy Jordan, North Carolina parent, in a video addressed to his daughter

There is a weird skyscraper on the east side of Church Street between Thomas and Worth in the Tribeca neighborhood of lower Manhattan. Formerly known as the AT&T Long Lines Building, it now goes by the more prosaic name of its address: 33 Thomas Street. Clad entirely in red granite, it is 550 feet tall and has no windows aside from those on the front doors. As the eye ascends from street level along the tower's monumental pilasters, the only thing that interrupts the brutalist facade is a series of huge ventilation ducts, with one set on the tenth floor and the other on the twenty-ninth. Constructed between 1969 and 1974, it was designed by the architect John Carl Warnecke to serve as the world's largest processing hub for long-distance phone calls. As an architectural school, brutalism insisted that a building's form should reflect its function in a straightforward way, and on that criterion 33 Thomas might be considered a minor masterpiece, its alienating lack of windows a forthright acknowledgment of the fact that it was built to be inhabited by machines rather than people. Built while hundreds of thousands of American troops were fighting and dying in Vietnam, it was also outfitted with prison-level security and backup systems that had backup systems. Dedicated water, gas, and food supplies could sustain fifteen hundred people for two weeks, and the structure was designed to withstand a nuclear fallout.[1] AT&T moved some of its equipment out of the building following an embarrassing central switch malfunction in 1991, but after September 11 it relocated some of the offices that had been destroyed at the World Trade Center to 33 Thomas.

September 11 was just the beginning of AT&T's new lease on life at Long Lines. In 2016, two reporters working for *The Intercept* found among the documents leaked by the whistleblower and NSA contractor Edward Snowden more or less conclusive evidence that 33 Thomas Street was also a crucial hub for the National Security Agency's mass surveillance operation. The documents in question referred to a New York City surveillance site code-named TITANPOINTE, and they also informed NSA employees planning to travel to TITANPOINTE that their visit would be supervised by a "partner" with the code name LITHIUM, which was the NSA's code name for AT&T. Along with the phone company's machines, according to the documents, the building contained a secure room with government equipment linked to AT&T's routers, and it was also equipped to capture satellite communications. "That is a particularly striking detail," the *Intercept* reporters wrote, "because on the roof of 33 Thomas Street there are a number of satellite dishes. Federal Communications Commission records confirm that 33 Thomas Street is the only location in New York City where AT&T has an FCC license for satellite earth stations."[2] Subsequent investigative reports identified eight other buildings around the country in which telecommunications companies had allowed the NSA to set up shop, most of them in the heart of major downtown areas: 1122 Third Avenue in Seattle, just a block away from the central branch of the public library; 611 Folsom Street in San Francisco;

420 South Grand Avenue in Los Angeles, also a block away from the library; 10 South Canal Street, in the West Loop Gate neighborhood of Chicago; 4211 Bryan Street in Dallas; 30 E Street SW in Washington, D.C., between Interstate 695 and the Capitol; 51 Peachtree Center Avenue in Atlanta, just north of the Georgia State University campus; and 811 Tenth Avenue, also in New York City. The NSA praised AT&T for its "extreme willingness to help."[3]

An AT&T representative half denied *The Intercept*'s report on 33 Thomas Street but conspicuously avoided actually saying that the NSA wasn't doing work in the building. When I wrote the first draft of this chapter in February 2023, one could find the "Titanpointe" label hovering above the address by zooming in far enough on Google Maps. By the time I revised the chapter in November 2023, the label had disappeared. I don't know who removed it, nor do I know whether the label was originally added by Google engineers, random users of Google Maps, or an unhappy NSA contractor, but it was a great source of amusement for the dozens of internet jokers who rated the facility on Google Reviews: "10/10 would be spied on again" (that review had also disappeared by November 2023). Government officials have had a harder time seeing the humor. On the day *The Intercept* published its investigation, someone—their name redacted in the government records—emailed the text of the article to James Clapper, who was then the director of national intelligence. They wrote, "And just why does America 'need to know' this???"[4]

Inside the Long Lines Building, one could find in miniature the structure of a great national surveillance network that spanned both the public and private spheres in monitoring almost every aspect of how people used technology to communicate with one another. The machines and nodes and secret information-sharing agreements that governed what happened in there were the products of a shared desire on the part of the federal government's intelligence apparatus and Silicon Valley technology firms to gather as much information as they could, about as many people as they could, as quickly as possible. Their goals were different—the government wanted to prevent further terrorist attacks, while the tech companies simply wanted to make money—but they could be achieved by the same means. Many Americans had begun to suspect that something like this kind of network was being constructed very soon after September 11, and their suspicions were confirmed a little more than a decade later when Edward Snowden leaked information about the government's domestic spying operation. Despite more than two decades during which to think about the implications of this operation, however, trying to understand the effects of surveillance on people's daily lives is a bit like staring at the blank walls of the Long Lines Building and wondering uselessly about what exactly goes on in there. The absence of windows makes it impossible to see inside, and all that comes out of the building are clouds of steam that swiftly dissolve into the Manhattan air. For all the information we now have on the technical and bureaucratic mechanics of mass surveillance, many of its social consequences remain hidden away in a black box.

There is a useful intellectual trick, however, that can help provide a foothold for thinking about the meaning of mass surveillance. If something persistently gets in the way of your efforts to understand something—in this case, the obstacle is the granite walls of the Long Lines Building—stop trying to think around or through the walls and start thinking about the walls themselves instead. Rather than focusing on what those walls are preventing you from seeing, focus on what they are showing and telling you. The windowless facade of 33 Thomas Street doesn't only prevent passersby from seeing what is going on inside. It also sends a message, which is that ordinary people *can't be trusted* to know what is going on inside. A windowless building produces feelings of either dread (as in the case of a mausoleum) or suspicion, and the suspicion derives from the building's evident hostility to those looking at it from the outside. For all of the difficulties entailed over the past twenty years in understanding exactly how NSA surveillance works and what the government does with the information it collects, that lack of trust has come through loud and clear. The consequences of America's lack of trust in its own citizens will continue to unfold for many years to come.

• • •

The government didn't start out quite so eager to hide its war on terror surveillance measures from the public. Even as the attacks were under way on September 11, television news commentators were discussing the need to roll back certain civil liberties that Americans took for granted, and for a few weeks afterward Congress was warmed by a remarkable spirit of bipartisan unity. Everyone agreed on the big things: The attacks marked a great turning point in world history, the United States would spare no expense in hunting down and killing those responsible, and security would have to be the government's top priority going forward.

In the first week of October, however, that unanimity hit a snag. Congress had been debating the package of antiterrorism legislation that would eventually be signed into law as the PATRIOT Act, and the Democratic senator Pat Leahy, chairman of the Judiciary Committee, was slowing things down. The bill was set to kick off the biggest expansion of law enforcement detention and surveillance powers in history, and Leahy was on board with most of it. He was on board with detaining immigrants who were suspected of but had not been charged with terrorism, and he was okay with new government powers to eavesdrop on communications carried out by computer. But he had a problem with a provision that would allow law enforcement agencies almost total leeway to share the results of their surveillance with American intelligence agencies, and he kept summoning Republicans to meetings to try to hash out a compromise. To Attorney General John Ashcroft, who was pushing the legislation on behalf of the Bush administration, this was not just frustrating; it was irresponsible. Everyone had agreed until then that poor information sharing between law enforcement and intelligence had gifted the terrorists valuable time in which to plan and execute the attack. Failing to open up the lines of communication between America's crime fighters and its spies would only make it easier for terrorists to carry out further attacks in the future, and as Jake Tapper recounted in an article published by

Salon, Ashcroft was keen to emphasize that the threats were numerous. "We think that there is a very serious threat of additional problems now," he said on *Face the Nation.* "The threat of more violence still exists," he said on *Late Edition.* "Individuals—not only those involved in the hijackings, but related individuals—making inquiries about crop dusting, and being observant of literature on how to disperse things in an aerosol way." He mentioned "threats of explosives," and then he started to list other specific threats before contenting himself with a summation: "There are all kinds of threats." Following a closed-door meeting with Republican senators, Ashcroft held a press conference alongside ranking Republican members of the Judiciary Committee and said America didn't have time for Leahy's hand-wringing. "I'm deeply concerned about the rather slow pace at which we seem to be making this come true for America," he said. "Talk won't prevent terrorism; tools can help prevent terrorism."[5]

When Ashcroft referred to "tools," he meant the kinds of things that tech entrepreneurs were building out in California's Silicon Valley. Within weeks of the attacks, Oracle's CEO, Larry Ellison, one of the world's richest men, made his way to Washington to offer his company's assistance in establishing a national system of identification cards. Oracle was a database company. It made software that allowed its customers to store, sort, and analyze huge amounts of information, and it maintained data storage facilities that clients could pay to use rather than having to shell out for hardware of their own. With the help of Oracle's software and technical expertise, Ellison proposed, the United States could build out a system in which each identification card could be matched to its holder's thumbprint and iris scan. The system would be optional for citizens, though adoption rates would increase as people realized how much easier the cards made it to get through airport security, for example. For noncitizen residents, and for any foreign nationals who wanted to enter the United States, the cards would be mandatory. Ellison met with Vice President Dick Cheney to discuss the proposal, and he won the support of both John Ashcroft and the Democratic senator Dianne Feinstein, who counted Larry Ellison as one of her constituents.[6]

The public was not very receptive to Ellison's proposal. A central database containing a scan of every American's eyeballs sounded a bit too much like something out of Orwell to be palatable. But the government's ultimate rejection of the database might have had more to do with the timing and the messenger than with the proposal itself. Culturally, Ellison was a direct ancestor of Elon Musk, an unpleasant playboy-nerd with a genius for self-promotion and creepy, eugenics-adjacent hobbies. (Musk has repeatedly cited his concerns about "population collapse" to justify his decision to father eight children, while Ellison invested millions into efforts to halt or reverse the process of human aging.) Like Musk, Ellison had a legion of fans who viewed him as a prophet of the digital utopia to come, but there is (fortunately) also a chunk of the population that is just always going to be turned off when a rich guy goes to a reporter and volunteers that he wants to live forever.[7] Ellison proposed the database so quickly that one couldn't help but assume that the ambition predated September 11, and it seemed hard to believe that he would not personally profit from the plan if it ever became a reality. While polling indicated reasonable levels of support for *some* kind of national identification system, that enthusiasm melted away in the face of a concrete plan. "A national ID card is one of those third-rail issues of national politics," one researcher explained at the time. "It tends to die pretty quick."[8]

In most other respects, however, the plan was just what the government wanted to hear. Its rollout became a cautionary tale in terms of public relations, but in terms of policy it was more like a beta test—something to build on rather than abandon. To begin with, Ellison's plan was based on the premise that the problem of post-9/11 security could be addressed with a technological fix. That was a relief. Addressing the *political* aspects of international extremism would have involved considering the shortcomings of America's foreign policy, its management of the global economy, and its alliances with authoritarians in the Middle East. All of that was off the table. The people who could provide technical solutions to America's surveillance needs, however, had spent the previous decade getting very good at making big promises that couldn't be fulfilled yet but would surely be possible in the future, and proposals like Ellison's poured into Washington. As the sociologist David Lyon outlined in his book *Surveillance After September 11,* they fell into four main categories:

- biometrics, the use of data extracted from the body, such as an iris scan, digital image, or fingerprint;
- identification (ID) cards with embedded programmable chips ("smart cards");
- Closed Circuit Television (CCTV), or video surveillance, often enhanced by facial recognition software;
- communicational measures, such as wiretaps and other message interception methods including Web-based surveillance.[9]

Washington's preference for technological as opposed to political measures is palpable in the "recommendations" section of the *9/11 Commission Report.* Reflecting on America's unpopularity in much of the Middle East, the *Report*'s authors resorted to vague hand-waving: "the U.S. government must define what the message is, what it stands for"; it should promote a "vision of the future" stressing "life over death";[10] it should "openly" confront "the problems in the U.S.-Saudi relationship"[11]—that kind of thing. The technological recommendations had much more to do with nuts and bolts, e.g., "the Department of Homeland Security . . . should complete, as quickly as possible, a biometric entry-exit screening system, including a single system for speeding qualified travelers."[12]

In addition, the kinds of surveillance the government wanted to implement dovetailed nicely with how Silicon Valley wanted to make money. The tech industry was near the bottom of a historic crash in the early years of the twenty-first century. After a decade of hype about how dot-com firms were going to revolutionize everything and reignite the engine of American growth, the markets had finally run out of patience waiting for those firms to start turning a profit. Yes, the internet made it easier to shop for certain kinds of goods, plus you could talk to people from all over the world at a moment's notice—but how were you supposed to *make money* there? Once a few big names declared bankruptcy, investors got skittish and became less willing to keep pumping money into the ecosystem as a whole, and despite a few substantial bear market rallies, the final magnitude of the crash was impressive.

Silicon Valley wasn't ready to give up on itself, though, nor was the government ready to abandon its dream of tech-driven growth and prosperity in the twenty-first century. For tech entrepreneurs, there was simply still too much money sloshing around Northern California. Many firms had been wiped out by the crash, but those that survived now had fewer competitors to worry about, and they wanted to get back to telling the old story about exponential growth and double-digit returns on investment. Washington was rooting for them, because where else was the growth going to come from? Corrosion proceeded apace in the Rust Belt, China was on its way to becoming the world leader in manufacturing, and it was impossible to wring the required productivity gains out of the domestic services sector, particularly with low-wage economies like India beginning to flex their muscle. The California nerds had hit a rough patch, but they were young, nimble, and unnervingly optimistic. Once they got back on their feet, the government would be there to help. And despite Silicon Valley's reputation as a hotbed of incorrigible social liberalism, born-again George W. Bush had mounted a significant outreach effort to the tech industry during the 2000 campaign. The historian Malcolm Harris describes the Bush campaign's divide-and-conquer tactics as follows:

> The team split its appeals by generation. For those under forty, there was Gregory Slayton, an energetic, wild-eyed evangelical Christian with a circle beard and a baseball cap who made millions selling a company to Silicon Graphics and was then CEO of an email marketing company called ClickAction that, naturally, contracted with GOP campaigns. Tim Draper, third in the Silicon Valley Draper [venture capital] line and grandson of Herbert Hoover associate General William Draper, took the

fortysomethings. The Netscape CEO Jim Barksdale took the next decade. Heading the whole operation and covering the old guys was E. Floyd Kvamme, an early Apple executive and Kleiner Perkins director.[13]

In order to launch a second phase of tech industry expansion, it wouldn't be enough just to use the internet to sell things to people. That was just retail business minus the costs of a brick-and-mortar storefront, not something that could produce growth in the necessary magnitude or at the required speed. What you needed was a way to monetize and commodify the increasing amounts of time and attention that people were spending on the internet, whether they were buying anything or not. The company that solved the puzzle was Google. The founders, Larry Page and Sergey Brin, derived their competitive advantage from the fact that Google's eponymous search engine allowed it to learn more things about more people than anyone else. The search engine itself surpassed competitors like Yahoo and Ask Jeeves because it was built around crawlers and scrapers, computer programs that trawled as much of the internet as possible and mapped out which sites were linking to which other sites, all in dizzying detail. These maps allowed Google to produce ranked lists of the websites that would probably be most useful to someone interested in a particular topic. If someone googled "New York Times," they would probably want to be shown the website that lots of other websites linked to when they talked about *The New York Times*: www.nytimes .com. And because Google also tracked what people clicked on when they used the search engine, its growing user base made the search engine better: If everyone searching for "Oscar nominations" kept clicking on the site that appeared fourth on the page, that site would eventually get bumped up to the top spot. Google began to place ads on the same page as its search results, because its scrapers could also figure out what people who searched for certain things were likely to buy. Then they launched an email client as well, Gmail, set their scrapers to work on the contents of people's emails, and started placing ads above the inbox that were tailored to what individual users were communicating about. Advertising with this degree of specificity was unprecedented, and Google's revenues soared (even today, ads bring in more than 80 percent of its money).[14]

This advertising model has been copied, tweaked, and retrofitted for different industries by any number of tech companies, and in every case the key is knowing as much as possible about your users: their name, age, sex, gender, race, ethnicity, income, zip code—the list of things it would be useful and profitable for Silicon Valley to know about you theoretically never ends. As it happened, the U.S. government was also interested in knowing as much as possible about as many people as possible following September 11. This was a happy coincidence. Washington and Silicon Valley were pleased to find that their respective projects required the same raw input materials.

I've already discussed the kinds of targeted surveillance and human intelligence operations that were carried out against American Muslim communities during the war on terror, but that was never going to be enough. The shock and surprise of September 11 had been just as humiliating and traumatizing as the property destruction and the casualties, and success going forward didn't look like "not many" successful major terrorist attacks. It meant *zero* successful major terrorist attacks, ever again. Given how few al-Qaeda operatives were involved in the operation and how simple their tools were (knives, box cutters, a few months of flight school), you weren't going to be able to prevent future attacks just by keeping track of who was shopping for the components of a dirty bomb. To really do the job right, you would have to surveil almost everyone to some extent; at a bare minimum, you needed to have the ability to surveil anyone at a moment's notice. It was nearly an article of faith among the national security establishment that September 11 would have been prevented if only they had been able to "connect the dots," as though everyone in Washington had simultaneously forgotten the truth behind the old saying about how hindsight is twenty-twenty, which is that the future is inherently unknowable. "The key to fighting terrorism is information," a high-level Defense Department official wrote. "Elements of the solution include gathering a much broader array of data than we do currently, discovering information from elements of the data, creating models of hypotheses, and analyzing these models in a collaborative environment to determine the most probable current or future scenario."[15] If I had put the second sentence of that quotation in the mouth of a start-up founder, no one reading this book would have noticed. Tech firms were beginning to make serious money by collecting billions and billions of those dots. That's where the state and Silicon Valley found their national security interests and corporate interests aligning. As Harris puts it, "The advertising technology (ad tech) industry and the NSA were looking for the same thing: information—specifically, all of it."[16]

Over the following years, the government and Silicon Valley built a vast electronic surveillance machine, one that took the form of a lucrative public-private partnership. As the military overseas leaned heavily on private contractors to build and staff bases, cook food, clean facilities, sort mail, and even shoot the guns, the Defense Department relied on tech giants to supply it with mountains of information on what Americans were up to. Silicon Valley couldn't offer up its services quickly enough. Oracle established a new division focusing on security and disaster recovery.[17] One of Oracle's partners, a direct-mail and telemarketing company called Acxiom, used its connections with former president Bill Clinton to get work supplying consumer data to a government project called Total Information Awareness (TIA).[18] Peter Thiel, the right-wing venture capitalist and co-founder of PayPal, started a data analytics company called Palantir, the name taken from the crystal balls in *The Lord of the Rings* that wizards used to see events on the other side of the world. He quickly won an injection of capital investment from In-Q-Tel, the CIA's venture capital outfit. Thiel also won the support of John Poindexter, a Defense Department official best known for lying to Congress about his role in the Iran-Contra affair in the 1980s. Poindexter was in charge of a new outfit called the Information Awareness Office (IAO), which housed the Total Information Awareness project. The IAO provided research funding to more than two dozen companies in its first year alone and also mounted an effort to compare airline passenger

ticket records against mountains of consumer data to look for suspicious patterns.[19] It would have been illegal for the government to collect all of this data itself, but Attorney General Ashcroft worked out a
loophole under which surveillance operations could make use of
whatever data they liked so long as they paid to purchase that data
from the private sector.[20]

None of this was public information at the time. As he had with
respect to torture, the Office of Legal Counsel appointee John Yoo advised the Bush administration that since the country was already at
war, Bush didn't need court approval to collect intelligence it judged
would be useful in fighting the war. "The Fourth Amendment declares
that 'the right of people to be secure in their persons, houses, papers,
and effects, against *unreasonable* searches and seizures, shall not be
violated,'" Yoo wrote, implying with his italics that everything the
Bush administration wanted to do was reasonable.[21] When the details
of Poindexter's work on TIA finally did become public toward the end
of 2002, the columnist William Safire described it as "the supersnoop's
dream," and public outrage scuttled the project (it didn't help that the
IAO's logo featured the Eye of Providence—the eye floating on top of
a pyramid that appears on the back of American cash—casting its
omniscient gaze across the globe).[22] Similar outrage greeted the Bush
administration's establishment of Operation TIPS, the acronym standing for "Terrorism Information and Prevention System." The idea was
that workers who had regular access to the private homes of civilians
or critical business or transport systems—postal workers, cable TV
installers, plumbers, telephone repair workers, train conductors, and
truck drivers—would be deputized to report to the government if
they saw or heard anything suspicious while doing their jobs. The
government hoped to eventually deputize at least 4 percent of Americans, which, as one investigative journalist noticed, would give the
United States a higher percentage of citizen spies than East Germany
under the Stasi.[23] Some Americans began to work as volunteer informants even before the government launched its Operation TIPS website (www.citizencorps.gov). A FedEx driver who worked in Brooklyn's
Bay Ridge neighborhood told a reporter that he made sure to place a

call whenever he found an apartment in which there were too many Arabs. "Whenever I would go to a place where there was a lot of them, I would tell the landlord, hey, you got nine people living up there or whatever, and they would call the F.B.I. and get them checked out." The reporter worried about the government deputizing workers who are "typically unarmed"—what happens if a repairman comes across a terrorist's "homemade rocket-launcher"?—but Congress worried more about the Bush administration promoting an official civic culture of spying and informing, and the program was killed.[24]

The Bush administration learned from these early mistakes, but the lesson it learned wasn't that it should scale back its plans. Instead, it learned that it would have an easier time implementing those plans if it just stopped publicizing them. After Congress withdrew funding for TIA, Poindexter and his colleagues secretly moved the project over to the National Security Agency. It was an inspired decision. When most people thought about American intelligence agencies, they thought about the CIA and the FBI, which sent agents into the field on missions, hired undercover operatives, and gathered a significant portion of the intelligence they generated in person. The NSA, on the other hand, focused solely on signals intelligence, or SIGINT, the monitoring, collection, and analysis of intelligence gathered electronically, whether via wiretap, satellite imagery, or digital surveillance. This was where the real action was now, because SIGINT was the only way to amass the quantities of data the government wanted. The NSA's low profile meant that Poindexter's programs could be continued and expanded without attracting undue notice. NSA head Michael Hayden was a technophile like Poindexter, and both shared the Bush administration's view that the United States was now in a permanent state of emergency. The NSA's technical infrastructure meant that it had the ability to surveil a substantial portion of the world's electronic communications in bulk, but its activities were restricted by law to foreign surveillance—spying on people inside the United States had always been legally out of the question.

That changed quickly as the NSA began to assume its post-9/11 shape. Bush told Hayden that going forward the NSA would have the authorization to spy on people inside the United States, including citizens, so long as the other person they communicated with was located elsewhere.[25] This authorization came straight from the executive branch. Congress, which would only have slowed down the process with its oversight concerns, was largely excluded from the process. Even more radically, the Bush administration asserted that the NSA didn't need to obtain a warrant from the federal court that dealt with foreign surveillance in order to set up a wiretap on someone, which meant the Justice Department was cut out as well. Flooding Washington with secret legal memos from John Yoo and future attorney general Alberto Gonzales, the Bush administration made quick work of the oversight mechanisms that had been put in place to restrain executive power following America's defeat in Vietnam. While certain aspects of the NSA's STELLARWIND program bubbled into view and provoked controversy over the coming years, its full extent remained hidden for nearly a decade.

With its new mandate in place, the NSA needed to expand, and at a quicker pace than what government agencies were accustomed to. At the end of the twentieth century, the agency was outdated, listless, and losing employees to Silicon Valley. The disappearance of the Soviet Union from the scene had deprived the NSA of its main reason for existing, it was too behind technologically even to store—much less analyze—the huge amounts of data that now hummed around the world on fiber-optic cables, and its public reputation among young people was overdetermined by the movie *Enemy of the State*, in which the agency tries to ruin Will Smith's life.[26]

But with Hayden in the director's chair, the NSA stopped moaning about California's tech companies and started imitating and working with them instead. Like other agencies within Washington's defense and security complex, it went on a hiring spree, pensioning off older public-sector analysts who were uncomfortable working with cutting-edge technology and replacing them with fresh-faced computer science graduates from the private sector. This contract-driven growth "made the area around Washington DC one of the only places where someone can show up with a new BA in communications or international relations, get hired at a full-time entry-level job, and sign the lease on a $2,000-a-month loft apartment the next day," as one analysis put it. "Between 2000 and 2010, as federal spending on contracts almost tripled, the area's population increased by three-quarters of a million people, most of them under 35."[27] The NSA also hired Silicon Valley and defense firms to set up and maintain the data storage facilities that would enable it to collect information at the required scale. At every step of the way, mass surveillance was a public-private collaboration in which the government purchased the tech industry's services while also adopting its core habits and traits, including speed, a growth-at-all-costs mentality, and a willingness to implement new and untested technologies first and ask questions about how well they worked later.

For tech firms emerging from the wreckage of the dot-com crash, the fat contracts amounted to a very welcome government stimulus package. In exchange for its largesse, the government wanted more than the private sector's workers and equipment; it wanted the data as well. Telecommunications firms had long handed over information on specific customers' activity on a case-by-case basis in response to government requests or warrants, but the NSA now believed that America didn't have the time to do things on a case-by-case basis. It wanted the country's largest tech and telecommunications firms to hand over their customer information in bulk, whether by sending it to the NSA themselves or (even better) by allowing the NSA to attach its own secret pipelines to company servers that would extract the information as it came in. Between 2007 and 2012, Microsoft, Yahoo, Google, Facebook, YouTube, and Apple all agreed to participate to some extent.[28] In 2011 alone, a group of phone companies that included Verizon, AT&T, Sprint, T-Mobile, MetroPCS, Cricket, and U.S. Cellular received at least 1.3 million government requests for customer data.[29] With these companies on board, the NSA had access to almost the entire telephone, email, and internet search history of the United States.

Here are some numbers to help flesh out what is meant by the term "mass surveillance." As of 2013, the NSA was collecting metadata—meaning the numbers on either end of a phone call, along with their location and the call's duration—on nearly five billion phone calls per day. Its databases also tracked the locations of "at least hundreds of millions of devices" in a sustained way, allowing the NSA to map the movement patterns and daily habits of all the people attached to those devices. The location data was thought by privacy advocates to be particularly sensitive because "the laws of physics don't let you keep it private. . . . The only way to hide your location is to disconnect from our modern communication system and live in a cave." When asked how many Americans, as opposed to how many devices, were having their locations tracked, an NSA official said, "It's awkward for us to try to provide any specific numbers," which is easy to believe.[30]

In addition, the NSA captured an unknown number of emails, Facebook posts, and instant messages, which it handed over to federal and local law enforcement agencies upon receipt of a court order. To give some sense of the size of this component of the surveillance operation, the NSA requested the private data of between eighteen and nineteen thousand Facebook users over the last six months of 2012 alone, according to Facebook's general counsel.[31] Further collection of raw internet traffic allowed the NSA to track who visited which websites and when.[32] The NSA was able to capture this data in real time, monitoring users from moment to moment as they clicked on links, chatted with friends, masturbated to porn, plugged in directions on Google Maps, filed their taxes, Facebook stalked a frenemy, and shopped for shoes or electronics or home goods or car parts. The NSA by no means tracked *everyone* in real time, but insofar as people lived their lives online, the NSA had the capability to reconstruct almost anyone's day-to-day digital existence should it decide they merited attention. As Silicon Valley claimed an ever-widening sphere of human experience as its domain—from commerce and communication to romance and play—the reconstructions at the NSA's fingertips grew in richness and detail.

• • •

Like the invasion of Iraq and the detention of "enemy combatants" at Guantánamo, mass surveillance was first implemented on a nakedly illegal emergency basis by the ideologues who staffed the Bush administration. Then it was allowed to continue after Barack Obama helped to varnish it with a gloss of constitutional legitimacy that did nothing to alter the project's core activities. In 2008, Congress passed and Senator Barack Obama voted for a series of amendments to the Foreign Intelligence Surveillance Act (FISA), a 1978 statute that originally imposed substantive restrictions on the intelligence services' ability to conduct wiretaps and other forms of electronic surveillance on foreign and domestic targets. The FISA amendments gutted these restrictions while pretending merely to update them. They permitted the attorney general and the director of national intelligence to authorize, without congressional approval, the targeting of non-U.S. persons who intelligence agencies "reasonably believed" to be located outside the United States (the NSA said it interpreted "reasonable belief" to mean that 51 percent confidence in a target's foreignness was sufficient). Targeting U.S. citizens was not permitted, but the amendments contained an enormous loophole: so long as the intelligence services' *intent* was to collect information on a foreign target, any "incidental" collection of information on Americans that might occur in the course of pursuing the foreign target was allowed. The amendments' other oversight provisions were similarly flimsy. The federal court tasked with approving government requests for surveillance was reduced to approving only the procedures the government planned to use in carrying out its surveillance, as opposed to the targets themselves, meaning that the FISA court was simply rubber-stamping the surveillance of targets whose identity, nationality, and location were unknown to it. In 2012, the government submitted 212 requests to conduct surveillance to the FISA court, and the court approved every one of them.[33] The court had no authority to track government compliance with its orders once a given operation was approved, and because its proceedings were entirely classified, individuals targeted by the government had no judicial recourse. The amendments, which Obama reauthorized twice as president, turned mass domestic surveillance into an established fact of American life, one that Americans had no direct way to legally challenge.

What did Americans think about this new facet of their lives? How did they feel knowing that their phone calls and text chats and shopping habits and love affairs and mundane frustrations were likely being stored away on a server farm and indexed so that some government contractor could comb through it all? Public opinion on mass surveillance was divided, although not in the strong way that people talk about when they use the word "polarization," which suggests an issue on which the public is split into two deeply held and mutually irreconcilable sets of belief. A better word for how people felt about mass surveillance is "ambivalent." On the specific issue of Snowden's whistleblowing, Americans were evenly divided, with 44 percent believing Snowden had done the right thing in taking his concerns to the press and 42 percent believing he had not. Views on Snowden's actions were split somewhat along party lines; with Obama in power at the time, Democrats were the only group that disapproved of the leaks, whereas a plurality of Republicans and independents approved of them. Given that one might reasonably expect conservatives to be more enthusiastic about expansive state police powers for the purpose of fighting terrorism, those numbers suggest that people's views on Snowden had more to do with their established political allegiances than any principled stance on the issue. Polls that asked broader questions about mass surveillance reinforce this impression. In 2006, with Bush in office, Republicans approved of the federal government obtaining phone records "in order to create a database of billions of telephone numbers dialed by Americans" by a margin of 72 percent to 22 percent, while Democrats disapproved by a margin of 76 percent to 20 percent.[34] By 2013, those numbers had flipped: Republicans now disapproved, 63 percent to 32 percent, and Democrats approved, 49 percent to 40 percent.[35] Even as partisan views shifted over this period, the overall national picture of public opinion on surveillance remained the same, with roughly equal numbers of people for and against it. The twenty-first-century polarization of America is usually said to indicate an era during which things are more political than usual, but here polarization seems to indicate something more like a frustrated antipolitics: Unable to take a view on the issue on its own terms, people shrugged their shoulders and threw in their lot with whatever political label happened to be close at hand.

In a certain light, this ambivalence regarding mass surveillance isn't so difficult to understand. It is hard to know what to think about an issue when it is impossible to know what kind of effect it might have on your life. For the first twelve years of the war, Americans hovered in a state of uncertainty. Given the Bush administration's aggressive rhetoric, it seemed like a safe bet that some kind of broad domestic surveillance was under way, but the details remained hazy, and the sheer scale of the program remained hidden. The government wasn't setting up any kind of hotline you could call to ask who was looking at your emails, and Congress was more focused on how the war was going overseas than the status of privacy rights back home. For most Americans, surveillance was not an immediate, pressing concern. Migrants, Muslim and Arab Americans, and antiwar activists understood the material consequences of surveillance very well; they were the ones experiencing early-morning raids, detention, deportation, and the persistent worry that the FBI's agents provocateurs were secretly undermining their communities from the inside. But with migrants excluded from any larger sphere of civic belonging, Muslim Americans constituting a tiny minority of the population (less than 1 percent), and activists carrying out a strategic retreat during the politically quietist interregnum between the invasion of Iraq and the beginning of Occupy Wall Street, most Americans had little trouble convincing themselves that surveillance didn't really have anything to do with them even if it did sound creepy. Government agents weren't coming to their homes and confiscating their hard drives. People weren't hearing clicking sounds in the background when they talked on their phones. Their emails didn't arrive with disclaimers attached reading, "For your protection, this communication has been reviewed by the National Security Agency." Surveillance was unobtrusive, discreet, largely invisible, and seamlessly integrated into people's normal routines.

At the same time, there *were* signs, hints, and both physical and digital traces of the country's expanding surveillance apparatus. Someone trying to navigate the clover-leaf intersection of the Baltimore-Washington Parkway and the Patuxent Freeway in Fort Meade, Maryland, might find their GPS suddenly on the glitch, trapping them in a frustrating tangle of U-turns and missed exits. That's because NSA headquarters sits just southeast of the interchange, and the signals it emits to confound hackers and spies didn't distinguish between personal navigation devices and the enemy's surveillance tech.[36] Two years before the Snowden leaks, the *Washington Post* journalists Dana Priest and William M. Arkin published a remarkable investigation into the country's post-9/11 surveillance programs. Titled *Top Secret America: The Rise of the New American Security State,* the book was in part an effort to catalog these physical traces, to find out just how close someone without a top secret clearance could get to the research facilities and office buildings where people spent their working days spying on their countrymen. Hollywood likes to depict America's spies and covert operators as working entirely outside the awareness of regular people, but most classified programs basically operate like normal white-collar jobs. The people who run them work in office buildings that have to be staffed and maintained by receptionists, security guards, repairmen, and janitors. They hire people by posting job listings online. They have conventions and other junkets where people spend their days networking in a windowless hall and their nights getting drunk with one another. And as with workers in any industry, they congregate in particular cities and neighborhoods, send their children to similar schools, and maintain their own rules of etiquette (for instance, not asking for too much detail about work when meeting people at a barbecue or a kid's birthday party). If America were being surveilled by just eight guys, or even eighty, it might be possible for them to set up shop in some rural warehouse and effectively disappear from public view. But when the Defense Department delivered its list of classified "special access programs"

(SAPs) to congressional leadership each year—a list containing *only* the programs' names—it was reliably three hundred pages long, and it doesn't even include "two other categories of deep secrets: 'waived SAPs' and 'unacknowledged SAPs,' neither of which the full committees have to be briefed on."[37] That's too many workers, office parks, and LinkedIn profiles for anyone to hide, no matter what level of classification is slapped on top (the levels, in ascending order of secrecy, are confidential, secret, and top secret).

So Priest and Arkin went and found some of them. Arkin spent several years combing through online job listings for positions that required a top secret clearance, with "top secret" legally defined as "information, the unauthorized disclosure of which reasonably could be expected to cause exceptionally grave damage to the national security."[38] A given search might reveal up to 15,000 such listings, and between 2006 and 2010 Arkin tallied up 182,000 of them. Looking through reams of government documents—"budgets, contracts, military directives, program descriptions, hearing transcripts," etc.—he began to encounter phrases that he realized were code words. Then he realized to his delight that the code words often appeared in the job listings, such as one from the intelligence consulting firm Windermere Group that sought applicants to work on "at least two of the following: ANCHORY, OCTAVE, SKYWRITER, SEMESTER, JAGUAR, ARCVIEW, e-WorkSpace, PINWALE, or HOMEBASE."[39] These programs were proliferating like crazy after September 11, but Priest and Arkin realized that the congressional oversight apparatus tasked with supervising the country's spy activities was not even beginning to keep up. At the House and Senate Permanent Select Committees on Intelligence and the House and Senate Appropriations Subcommittees on Defense, "the number of staffers [had] not grown much at all in the decade since the 9/11 attacks," and the number of staffers who were well informed on the NSA in particular had actually declined to just four. Similarly, Priest and Arkin found at the National Archives that the staff size of the agency in charge of ensuring proper classification practices had barely grown during the first decade of the twenty-first century, whereas the number of newly classified documents had "tripled to over 23 million."[40] At the heart of America's spy machine was the equivalent of an understaffed and overwhelmed office mail room.

Arkin's documents offered up addresses as well. While hunting for information on the Defense Policy Analysis Office (DPAO), a sub-operation of the Defense Logistics Agency, whose mission description he found to be suspiciously bland, Arkin came across a request for the installation of an encrypted line connecting the Pentagon, an office on the fifteenth floor of a building in the Crystal City neighborhood of Arlington, Virginia, and an Air Force organization in Rosslyn called XOIWS. Priest made the drive to Crystal City to see what she could find. The address housed a basement-level shopping mall with a food court, as well as dry cleaners and shoe-repair businesses that existed to serve the people who worked in the government-leased offices above them. Once your eyes adjusted to the fluorescent lighting and stopped being so distracted by all the signs, however, one also began to notice the people with identification lanyards draped over their business casual, the corridors that led to doors that could be opened only with a magnetic key card, the surveillance cameras tucked away in dim corners. Priest found a directory screen in the street-level lobby that listed a number of private companies known to do contracting work with the Defense Department, but the directory stopped at the fourteenth floor. When she stepped into the elevator, however, it turned out there was a fifteenth floor, and she pushed the button. She found a cardboard sign identifying the DPAO as the occupant of suite 1501, a door held shut by an electromagnetic lock, and another sign warning that "anyone without the proper clearance should leave." Then Priest located the not-very-well-hidden offices of XOIWS, their entrance identical to that of the DPAO in Crystal City except for a sign reading, FORCE PROTECTION CONDITION BRAVO. "This was Defense Department dialect for 'an increased or more predictable threat of terrorist threat,'" Priest wrote. "In reality, since the initial frenzy of September 11 had died out, the threat level had remained at bravo, much like Homeland Security's permanent shade of yellow." Following these discoveries, "secret doors seemed to be everywhere," Priest wrote. She returned to Crystal City with "new eyes," noticing all kinds of things she'd missed the first time around: armed guards, more corridors that required a badge for entry, more office directories with missing floors. "Some of the directories for twenty-story buildings," she wrote, "were completely blank except for the name of one convenience store in the lobby."[41]

• • •

Priest and Arkin's investigative work can help us begin to understand more about how post-9/11 surveillance degraded the country's public spaces. I've already spent some time in this book talking about certain kinds of physical public space, including airports, parks, and government buildings and plazas. These are places where fencing, bollards, security cameras, and police officers made public spaces unwelcoming. The documents Arkin scoured for addresses and acronyms were largely public, but it is hard to imagine that any meaningful segment of the public would ever come into contact with them. Even for a trained reporter like Arkin, someone who knew both how to use the Freedom of Information Act (FOIA) and how to decipher the hundreds of obscure acronyms that fill government reports, finding what he was looking for required years of training and work. Maybe a more accurate term for the kinds of documents he was working with is "semipublic," a word that also describes the buildings Priest visited. She didn't need any special clearance to wander around the basement-level shopping mall or stroll into the lobby, nor did she need a magnetic key card to take the elevator up to the office of the DPAO on the fifteenth floor. Those spaces, like Arkin's documents, were technically public. Unlike normal public places, however, the offices where different aspects of mass surveillance actually happened had no signs on the front doors and no entries in the lobby directories, nor could one type their names into Google Maps for directions. Truly public spaces are *legible*. Signs, labels, directories, and architectural styles help people to understand what goes on there, whether it is shopping for food, receiving an education, drinking, getting a haircut, borrowing a book, or anything else. But the unmarked buildings Priest visited create a dead zone in public life, taking up space without making any effort to let people know what goes on inside.

What mass surveillance did to a small set of public spaces in the Crystal City neighborhood of Arlington, it did on a much larger scale to a different kind of public space. Digital evangelists have long enjoyed describing the internet as a "digital town square," a place where people can encounter strangers they would never meet in their private lives and where platforms are equally available to anyone with the desire to speak. Like the agora in ancient Athens, the internet would be a place where people could gather whenever they wanted and freely discuss whatever concerned them. In reality, of course, the internet has never been public in the full sense: In the United States, streets, libraries, schools, and public parks actually belong to citizens and the government that represents them, whereas the internet has always been in private hands. The chaotic landscape of the internet's early days, however, allowed the dream of an online agora to flourish. Silicon Valley needed years to figure out how to monetize the time people spent online, and during that period people found that it really was pretty easy to build various kinds of communities, from message boards and forums that revolved around single topics such as music, video games, or parenting to group blogs, chat rooms, and online diaries. These communities worked best when their membership numbers were sufficiently low, and the amount of content they produced was sufficiently reasonable, that a regular but not obsessive user could keep up with the main personalities and primary threads of discussion without having to sacrifice too much of the time they spent offline. And because it was rare for a Google username or some other centralized identifier to follow you from site to site, people were able to explore a series of contained, independent spaces in which they could freely exercise different elements of their personalities and interests, as well as different ways of engaging with others, without the fear of seeming duplicitous. It's not hard to understand why so many thought the internet would be a boon to public life.

As time passed, however, Silicon Valley solved the puzzle of how to monetize attention for the purposes of selling ad space, and tech firms began working to channel the more freewheeling behavior of the early internet into the kinds of compulsive scrolling and posting that made real money. This transition—from bloggers' enormous grab bag of individually run websites to the infinite, ad-soaked, single-column scroll of Twitter (now called X) and Instagram—unfolded over several years, but it is now replicated in miniature every time Silicon Valley and its counterparts outside the United States launch a new social media platform. Facebook, Twitter, Instagram, Snapchat, and TikTok all followed the same playbook. Step one was to offer people a free-to-use platform that could be accessed with little more than a working email address. Step two was to allow early users to play around, learn the platform's strengths and weaknesses, and discover useful tools the company's developers hadn't even considered, as when a Twitter user began encouraging his friends who were also on the platform to start using hashtags to help organize conversations and make them searchable in 2007. Once the user base reached a critical mass, step three was to use their personal data to sell targeted ads. Step four was to discourage scrolling in chronological order, which made it easy for users to tell when they had run out of new posts to view, and to encourage the use of feeds sorted by proprietary algorithms, which allowed tech companies to better steer users toward the kinds of posts that generated the most engagement and maximized the time and attention people devoted to their platforms.

Americans who were teenagers on September 11 lived through this digital transition as they entered adulthood, while those who were young children or not yet born have known only a fully monetized social media landscape. The younger cohort in particular, and their relationship to social media, have been objects of intense interest for an army of commentators, sociologists, technologists, and childhood development experts looking to understand the consequences that social media could have for civil society over the next several decades. As the objects of larger anxieties about our new digital world, these teenagers have been described as everything from avatars of a more networked, informed, and curious future to a seething mass of narcissistic attention addicts. So long as teen internet use is considered in isolation, divorced from the historical moment in which it developed—a practice common to both the proponents and the critics of social media's effects on young people—there is no way to resolve the conflict between these polarized views. Either you like the way that digital natives seem to be turning out, or you don't. In the context of the war on terror, however, young people's willingness to carry out much of their social lives online looks more like a logical response to social conditions and less like a self-defeating, collective abandonment of real-world relationships. And because twenty-first-century tech companies are financially dependent on the same kinds of mass digital surveillance that drive NSA programs like STELLAR-WIND, this context also helps to shed light on the war's consequences for the practice of citizenship at all ages.

The war's erosion of public space in the United States hit young people the hardest. Even under the best of circumstances, teens start out at a disadvantage in terms of relative access to public space: They aren't allowed to spend time in bars or clubs, they can't drive before the age of sixteen and may not have access to a car afterward, and the adult world reflexively views them with suspicion if they assemble in large groups. After September 11, these difficulties were compounded by a host of new restrictions. Cities and towns cordoned off public parks and municipal plazas with fencing and upped the day-to-day police presence, which made them less appealing to young people— why bother escaping from parental surveillance at home just to swap it out for being watched by a cop who stares in your direction whenever somebody laughs too loud? Benches designed to be uncomfortable and impossible to lie down on, a measure increasingly adopted so as to exclude the bottom rung of America's surplus population (unhoused people) from public space, also decreased parks' appeal. Private owners of malls, movie theaters, and corporate plazas found it easier to impose regulations prohibiting teens from gathering in large groups than they had previously, because few were willing to challenge someone who cited "security" as the justification for a change in policy.

Safety was also the justification parents reached for when explaining why they afforded their own children so much less freedom than they had enjoyed as teenagers. For her book *It's Complicated: The Social Lives of Networked Teens,* the social media and technology scholar danah boyd (who styles her name without capital letters) interviewed teenagers from all over the country between 2005 and 2012, and parents provided her with endless variations on the theme of the dangers their children faced in public. "Bottom line is that we live in a society of fear; it is unfortunate but true," one Texas parent told boyd in an email. "As a parent I will admit that I protect my daughter immensely, and I don't let my daughter go out to areas I can't see her."[42] Another parent refused to allow his teenage daughter to attend sleepovers at friends' houses. He worried that other fathers and brothers would get drunk and try to sexually assault her.[43] "Even in urban environments," boyd writes, "where public transportation presumably affords more freedom, teens talked about how their parents often forbade them from riding subways and buses out of fear."[44] At the same time, studies consistently show that the dangers facing teenagers in public spaces have *dropped* dramatically over the past several decades, whether you measure in terms of violence, drug use, drinking, or almost anything else. Twenty-first-century teenagers are probably the safest and most well-behaved generation of young people in American history. That so many of their parents insisted that the opposite was true tells you something important about the cultural climate in which they were made to grow up.

Some parents felt bad about the restrictions they imposed on their kids, and tried to compensate by packing their schedules with after-school clubs, music lessons, sports, and other kinds of supervised, "constructive" activity. But the problem with trying to keep an eye on your kids all day and schedule out their lives in half-hour increments is that teenagers hate it, and with good reason. Spending unsupervised time in public with your peers is how you learn to be a member of the public and navigate the world in which you live. Schools, homes, and other youth spaces run by adults are places where the rules governing how people interact with one another are imposed from above, by the adults. In public with your friends and peers, however, learning the rules is a process of negotiation and improvisation. You watch the people around you, pick up cues from the built environment, and test out the limits of etiquette in encounters with friends and strangers. All teenagers know that their incomplete understanding of how to navigate different public environments—when to speak, when to listen, what to wear, how to move, how to acquire status, when to feel nervous, and when to feel safe—is one of the main things that separates them from adults, and they want very badly to catch up, to know how to read the hundreds of little social cues that present themselves to you every time you go for a walk or eat in a restaurant. It is "through engagement with publics," boyd writes, that "people develop a sense of others that ideally manifests as tolerance and respect."[45] There is a reason that the Athenian agora has for centuries figured so prominently in the work of philosophers and theorists writing about democracy: The public has to be able to encounter itself in order to forge the bonds of trust on which any functioning democracy depends. Without those encounters, and without that trust, there is little to check the spread of mutual fear and suspicion.

Locked up at home by their agoraphobic parents and overburdened with homework, chores, extracurricular activities, and after-school jobs, teens turned to the internet as a public space of last resort. The teenagers who talked to boyd were explicit on this point. "Teens told me time and again that they would far rather meet up in person," boyd writes, "but the hectic and heavily scheduled nature of their day-to-day lives, their lack of physical mobility, and the fears of their parents have made such face-to-face interactions increasingly impossible."[46] One sixteen-year-old named Amy told boyd that the only reason her mother had allowed her to be interviewed was that she "saw it as equivalent to a job because [boyd] was offering money for teens' time." Amy spent a lot of time on Myspace, and when boyd asked what she would rather spend her time doing, Amy said, "Just go anywhere. I don't care where, just not home. . . . I sit on MySpace and talk to people and text and talk on the phone, 'cause my mom's always got some crazy reason to keep me in the house."[47]

Part of the reason adults resent the time that teens spend online is that they can tell it is an attempt to get out from under their authority. In 2012, fifteen-year-old Hannah Jordan decided she was fed up and made a post on her Facebook wall. "To my parents," she wrote,

> I'm not your damn slave. . . . If you want coffee, get off your ass and get it yourself. If you want a garden, shovel the fertilizer yourself, don't sit back on your ass and watch me do it. . . . I'm tired of picking up after you. . . . Every day when I get home from school, I have to do dishes, clean the counter tops, all the floors, make all the beds, do the laundry and get the trash. I'm not even going to mention all the work I do around your clinic. . . . I go to sleep at 10 o'clock every night because I am too tired to stay up any longer and do anything else. I have to get up at five in the morning, to get ready for school. . . . Next time I have to pour a cup of coffee, I'm going to flip shit. I have no idea how I have a life.

Hannah's father, Tommy Jordan, found the post. His response was to film himself reading it aloud in the middle of a field. Wearing a salt-and-pepper goatee, jeans, and a wide-brimmed hat, he rebutted her points one by one—what did she have to complain about, when *he* had gone to high school and college at the same time while simultaneously working as a volunteer firefighter?—and he said that if Hannah thought she had it hard now, she was about to have it a lot harder. He got out of his Adirondack chair, pointed the camera at Hannah's laptop, which was lying on the ground, and then shot it seven times with a .45-caliber pistol. He said that if she wanted a new laptop, she could get a job and buy it herself, but only after she paid him back for the bullets.[48] Then he posted his video to Hannah's Facebook wall, where he hoped it would serve as an example to her friends of what happens when you act out.

Hannah never meant for her parents to see the post. Before writing it, she had blocked them on Facebook, but her dad worked in IT, and he was able to get around whatever restrictions Hannah had activated in her settings. Though the letter was addressed to her parents, that was just a rhetorical device; all Hannah wanted was for her friends to know that she was pissed off. She ran into a classic problem facing teens who have tried to find public space to inhabit online, which is that it is always difficult and often impossible to control whom you are speaking to. Facebook allowed users all kinds of ways to adjust the visibility of their posts, but its byzantine privacy settings menu changed all the time, and the site made little effort to educate users on its intricacies, because the site's preference was that everything be visible to as many people as possible. What Hannah tried and failed to do when she wrote her open letter was something called context switching, a universal social practice in which people behave and speak in certain ways with some groups and other ways with other groups. As one fifteen-year-old named Summer explained to danah boyd, context switching is easier in physical public spaces like parks, because in parks "you can see when there's people around you and stuff like that. So you can like quickly change the subject."[49] But Hannah had no way of knowing that her father was creeping up behind her and listening in, and her laptop paid the price.

Silicon Valley has not been sympathetic to people who would like online context switching to be a little easier. "Having two identities for yourself is an example of a lack of integrity," Facebook's co-founder Mark Zuckerberg said in 2010. "The days of you having a different image for your work friends or co-workers and for the other people you know are probably coming to an end pretty quickly."[50] As an ethics of collective social life, this idea is idiotic: Nobody actually believes that people should behave in exactly the same way at school, at home, in bed, at work, in the stands of a basketball game, at a bar, or at a funeral. But for an industry dependent on tracking and selling information about its users, the policy makes perfect business sense.

Teenagers flocked to social media because they were desperate for access to any kind of unsupervised public life, but once they arrived, they found that social media is subject to the same dynamics of surveillance and suspicion that had been eroding real-world public life to begin with. Complicated privacy settings make it hard to know who is listening to you, and fake accounts make it hard to know whose words you are reading. The increasing sophistication of targeted digital advertising further amplifies the feeling that someone you don't know is listening in; the internet is full of anecdotes where people describe mentioning some product out loud while in the same room as their phones and then seeing ads for the same product the next time they scroll through Instagram, even though they have never typed its name into any search engine. Adults aren't the only ones who worry about privacy on the internet. "We don't tell everybody every single thing about our lives," a seventeen-year-old called Waffles told boyd. "Every teenager wants privacy."[51]

But while adults have been more concerned with government and corporate surveillance online, teenagers tend to worry more about their online activity being surveilled by people with more immediate kinds of power over them: parents, teachers, college admissions officers, and peers. When danah boyd asked teenagers in 2012 why they preferred platforms such as Twitter, Tumblr, and Instagram to Facebook, she heard "a near-uniform response: 'Because my parents don't know about it.'"[52] These concerns become particularly acute when teens want to work out certain aspects of their identity—for example, their sexuality or gender—that they don't trust their parents or larger peer group at school to accept. Not sharing these struggles with anyone at all can be torture, but posting or texting or chatting about it always carries the risk of wider exposure. Teens attempting to avoid the adult world's suspicious gaze has been a major theme of popular culture going back at least half a century, but this isn't a same-as-it-ever-was situation. Having adopted the NSA's post-9/11 mindset as their own—*I will know where you are and what you're doing at every moment, for your own protection*—adults began to scrutinize children's social lives with an intensity they never came close to experiencing when they were children themselves. And with 40 percent of college admissions officers admitting that they reviewed applicants' social media profiles as of 2015, the stakes of this scrutiny can be very high.[53]

Further compounding the difficulties facing teenagers who sought both public life and a modicum of privacy online was the fact that the internet keeps a permanent record of everything you say. A stray remark made to a friend as you walk down the street may be forgotten by both parties by the next morning, but the same remark posted to Twitter lives on Twitter's servers forever, and if someone else screenshots the tweet, deleting it won't help. danah boyd calls this "persistence: the durability of online expressions and content," and she notes that a main consequence of this persistence is that "those using social media are often 'on the record' to an unprecedented degree."[54] In general, when a politician or celebrity speaks to a reporter on the record, they have to be very careful to say exactly the right thing, or at least they do if they know what's good for them. That means making their point as concisely as possible, avoiding speculation about subjects in which they lack expertise, and saying nothing that might make them look confused, uninformed, or weird. It is a strange and difficult way to communicate—so difficult, in fact, that there is an entire media coaching industry devoted to helping people do it well. It works for journalism, congressional committees, and courtrooms, but it doesn't really work anywhere else. If a member of a friend group gets criticized for always sounding as if he is "on the record," what his friends mean is that he sounds fake, that he isn't open to the normal exchanges of vulnerability or uncertainty that characterize meaningful friendship, that he doesn't trust the people with whom he is supposed to be close. Force young people out of real-world public life and into a digital town square that requires them to be on the record all the time, and what you get is a lot of young people with high levels of anxiety about saying the wrong thing.

It may sound like I'm about to start talking about cancel culture. I'm not. For one thing, the idea that cancel culture represents an existential threat to U.S. freedom of speech is fundamentally a product of right-wing grievance politics, promoted by conservatives who became upset during the politically acrimonious Trump administration that they could no longer say things like "Black people are less intelligent than white people" without having to fear professional or social consequences. For another, the cancel culture framework mostly revolves around and is fueled by professional political commentators, politicians, and celebrities, adults with professional standing to defend and prestige to preserve. I've been primarily interested in young people here, and not because the young are more politically or intellectually virtuous than the generations that preceded them. My focus on millennials and zoomers is due to the fact that those are the only generations of Americans who had to *become* citizens while the war on terror was under way, and my concern with the effects of surveillance on their ability to speak freely has more to do with how people figure out what their political views are than with how they express views about which they are already certain.

Allowing young people to explore, revise, and experiment with their views on how the world works is an indispensable prerequisite for a functioning public sphere. "Allowing" might be the wrong word to use, because teenagers are going to figure out what they think about the world whether or not they get permission. But post-9/11 surveillance, with its synthesis of widespread social anxiety and paranoia, aggressive government intelligence gathering, and Silicon Valley's money-driven hunger for personal information, has shaped the spaces teenagers inhabit in ways that make political self-determination much more difficult. Even as crime, substance abuse, and sexual assault rates extended declines that had begun in the last decades of the twentieth century, overblown fears of terrorist attacks allowed parents to feel justified in cutting off their children from public life. At the same time, the government worked with Silicon Valley to develop tools to keep a close watch over the daily lives of most Americans, with teenagers receiving special attention due to their supposed susceptibility to radicalization. The government used these tools for law enforcement, while tech firms used them to make money, but the effects were similar. They produced a social world founded on suspicion, one in which it is safer to be alone than to be with others, easier to go along than to object, and simpler to be quiet than to ask a question in good faith that might nevertheless attract the wrong kind of attention, whether from cops, peers, parents, or strangers.

Even in 2015, before the Trump presidency and before the media began fixating on cancel culture—before the term "cancel culture" had been invented, in fact—surveys were indicating that roughly half of college students felt unable to freely voice their opinions and beliefs in campus debates. Today's cancel culture watchdogs in the Republican Party and the right-wing media would have you believe that this is entirely a phenomenon of conservative students being bullied into silence by the intolerant left-wing ideology that dominates colleges and universities. But barely more than a third of the students surveyed by the polling company McLaughlin & Associates said their schools were more tolerant of liberal than conservative beliefs, and Republicans were only slightly more likely than Democrats to report feeling intimidated in the classroom.[55] That's not to say that campus debates are balanced perfectly in the center of the ideological spectrum, but the survey broadly paints a picture of a higher education environment in which anxiety about political self-expression had become *generalized*. That doesn't sound like a strategic campaign of political intimidation carried out on behalf of one political party. That sounds like a more pervasive social climate in which telling people what you really think carries heavier costs than it did before. It sounds like a society that views the truly free development of political ideas—that is, ideas not sanctioned in advance by one of the two ruling parties—as a threat rather than a source of strength and renewal.

Intelligence officials and the Washington political class have always insisted that the only intended purpose of mass surveillance was to catch terrorists, as though any other potential effects, like the collection of non-suspect Americans' personal data, were "incidental." One may take them at their word while still finding it curious that Washington has refused to abandon large-scale, tech-driven surveillance despite the growing pile of evidence that it doesn't catch terrorists after all. In 2020, seven years after the Snowden leaks, the Ninth Circuit Court of Appeals ruled that the NSA's warrantless collection of Americans' phone records was illegal. What's more, the opinion found that NSA surveillance had contributed nothing of significance to the government's successful prosecution of four Somali migrants who had been charged with fundraising for terrorism, a case the government had often cited as an example of the program's importance to national security. Reviews conducted over the prior fifteen years confirmed this finding: In more than two hundred cases where the government had successfully charged extremists with an act of terrorism since 9/11, the NSA's bulk surveillance program had contributed next to nothing of use, and "traditional investigative methods, such as the use of informants, tips from local communities, and targeted intelligence operations" had been much more important. In some instances, the program was *worse* than useless. FBI field offices were inundated with tips about "suspicious" phone numbers and email addresses, and agents became so frustrated with the amount of time they were wasting running those tips to ground that they told the NSA, "You're sending us garbage."[56] The NSA was in possession of the most sophisticated data sorting technology in the world, but the technology's promises have far exceeded what a CEO might call its deliverables. The network analysis tools used by the NSA as part of STELLARWIND, for example, were supposed to sift through phone and email records to find the nodes around which other suspicious characters revolved. But whenever the NSA identified such a node and looked more closely, it tended to find a pizza place rather than a radical mosque or an arms dealer.[57] Information is not the same thing as knowledge, and the idea that the two are equivalent is a lie that benefits no one who isn't working for Silicon Valley or the government's intelligence agencies.

The motivations behind Silicon Valley's pursuit of mass surveillance and bulk data collection don't need investigating: They did it for the money. So long as the venture capital funding continues to flow and the customers don't get too uncomfortable about handing over their personal information, the tech industry's collection of personal data will continue.

The dynamics underlying the government's surveillance program in spite of its uselessness, however, might be illuminated by Kat, a Massachusetts fifteen-year-old who spoke with danah boyd. "When I'm talking to somebody online, I don't like when [my parents] stand over my shoulder," Kat said. "I'll be like, 'Mom, can you not read over my shoulder?' Not that I'm saying something bad. It just feels weird. I don't like it." Kat didn't resent her mother's surveillance because she felt that any of her online activity needed concealing. She resented it because it communicated her mother's lack of trust in her judgment. In a relationship of equals, which is what democracy is supposed to be, trust has to go both ways. Instead, mass surveillance has primarily communicated the government's lack of trust in Americans. In the fall of 2001, 60 percent of Americans said they trusted the government to do the right thing most or all of the time, the highest figure recorded since 1969. The government did not reciprocate that trust over the following eight years, and Americans adjusted their views of the government accordingly. By 2008, just 17 percent of Americans said they trusted the government, and the average survey result hasn't topped 25 percent since then.[58] Commentators have worried over both the causes of this decline under Bush and its failure to reverse under Obama for years now, but the simplest way to account for it may just be to say that when it comes to mistrust and suspicion, it was the government that started it. In a 2022 polemic, the scholar Jonathan Crary wrote of "an array of platforms and applications [that] not only enable but reward sociopathic behavior," noting further that "at its most basic, the 'sociopathic' denotes what is *anti-social* or injurious to the existence of society."[59] He was talking about the internet as a whole, but it serves just as well as a description of STELLARWIND, the NSA, and the larger government impulse after September 11 to recast citizens as people who no longer deserved the freedom to encounter one another on their own terms.

CHAPTER 12

They Do This All the Time

I don't believe that anybody is above the law. On the other hand, I also have a belief that we need to look forward.

—Barack Obama

At the beginning of October 2016, with just over a month to go before the presidential election, the Republican nominee, Donald Trump, was trailing Hillary Clinton by three percentage points in the polls. He had managed to trim down his opponent's lead in the middle of September, after Clinton said that one could reasonably describe "half" of Trump's supporters as "a basket of deplorables" and also was caught concealing that she had been diagnosed with pneumonia. Her performance in the first general election debate on September 26, however, helped to reestablish the polling advantage she held throughout the entirety of the campaign. Still, a 3 percent lead was hardly comfortable, and not just because of the margin of error. Though Americans generally didn't have a favorable view of Trump, they didn't like Clinton, either, and the prospect of voters heading to the polls thinking of Clinton as the least bad option didn't inspire overwhelming confidence. If Clinton and her supporters were going to get any real sleep before Election Day, they needed something to break in their favor.

They got it. On October 7, *The Washington Post* published a video from 2005 that showed Trump in conversation with the *Access Hollywood* host Billy Bush. The two men were on a bus driving slowly through a parking lot, and although the camera was outside the bus, its audio feed was plugged into the microphones that Trump and Bush were wearing, and it captured everything they said. For thirty seconds or so, Trump recounted trying to sleep with a married woman who rebuffed his advances and then got breast implants. "She's totally changed her look!" he said. Then someone on the bus noticed the woman waiting for them in the parking lot and changed the subject, saying, "Sheesh, your girl's hot as shit!" General exclamations of agreement followed. While the other passengers disembarked, Trump and Bush stayed behind so that they could exit on their own and get the shot they wanted. Trump said he should eat some breath mints "just in case I start kissing her," and then he expanded on his tactics for sleeping with women:

> You know, I'm automatically attracted to beautiful—I just start kissing them. It's like a magnet. Just kiss, I don't even wait. And when you're a star they let you do it. You can do anything. Grab 'em by the pussy. You can do anything.

Bush, cackling along, said, "Yeah, look at those legs, all I can see is the legs." A few seconds later, the pair stepped onto the pavement, met the woman they had been ogling, and walked into the studio, where Bush asked her which of the two she'd take on a date if she had to choose.

The Republican nominee for the presidency had been caught on tape bragging about committing sexual assault. He was already trailing in the polls, he would have to face Clinton in a second debate later that weekend, and there was just a month left in which to undo the damage. Trump released a video apologizing that evening, but his tone made it clear the apology was strictly pro forma, and he also accused Bill Clinton of actually abusing women (as opposed to just talking about it) and Hillary of attacking her husband's victims. Nothing like it had ever happened during a presidential campaign before. Conservative commentators feared, and liberal commentators hoped, that what came to be known as the *Access Hollywood* tape would be the final "nail in the coffin" of Trump's political aspirations. As we all know, it wasn't. Another of Trump's remarks from earlier in 2016 turned out to be more prescient: "I could stand in the middle of Fifth Avenue and shoot somebody, and I wouldn't lose any voters, okay? It's, like, incredible!"

Trump was an unprecedented candidate in a number of ways, but to many commentators the real novelty of his campaign came down to his shamelessness, the eagerness with which he would admit serious and even criminal wrongdoing as though it were something to be proud of, his absolute indifference to being caught in a lie, his willingness to state the ugly parts of his appeal plainly rather than alluding to them, and his diamond-hard confidence that he would get away with and even be rewarded for his worst behavior. While much of Trump's self-regard is unjustified, that confidence was well founded. As the past fifteen years of American history had made clear, powerful people really could get away with almost anything.

• • •

In February 2006, Vice President Dick Cheney went on a hunting trip at Armstrong Ranch, a fifty-thousand-acre property to the southwest of Corpus Christi, Texas. He was accompanied by Pam Willeford, a longtime friend of the Bush family and then ambassador to Switzerland, and Harry Whittington, a lawyer and Texas politico who had worked for George W. Bush's father as far back as 1964. The trio were hunting for quail. It was late on a Saturday. The "hearty ranch breakfast," lunch "under a huge oak tree," and siesta that structured each day's fun had all come and gone. Cheney was waiting for the quail to flush from a covey when a single bird took off to his right. Willeford was to Cheney's left, and Cheney didn't know where Whittington was.

He turned toward the bird to fire his 28-gauge shotgun, and by the time he realized Whittington was standing there, it was too late. Cheney shot his friend in the face.[1] When Whittington was released from the hospital six days later, he spoke to the press wearing a navy suit and a tie the same color as the bruises that covered the right side of his head. Then Whittington apologized *to Cheney.* "My family and I are deeply sorry for all that Vice President Cheney and his family have had to go through this past week."[2] In his memoirs, Cheney wrote that he "appreciated the grace with which he handled the situation. He was a true gentleman."[3]

Just three months prior, a group of Marines had been on patrol in Haditha, a city in Iraq's Al Anbar province, when an IED exploded near their convoy, killing one soldier and wounding two others. In response, the Marines killed twenty-four unarmed civilians. They raided homes in a nearby village and killed everyone they found inside, including women, elderly people, and four children under the age of six.[4] At some point, the Marines also noticed a taxi approaching. The driver was bringing four students from the technical institute in Saqlawiyah to stay with one of their families for the weekend. When the driver threw the car into reverse and tried to retrace his route, the Marines opened fire and killed all of the passengers. The Marines initially lied to an Iraqi doctor about how the civilians had died, claiming that shrapnel from the IED was to blame, and then they lied to military investigators, saying that the IED explosion had been followed by a firefight with "insurgents."[5] Eight members of the squad were charged in connection with the massacre, but charges against six of the killers were eventually dropped, and a seventh was found not guilty. In 2012, the eighth, Staff Sergeant Frank Wuterich, was convicted of just one count of negligent dereliction of duty. His rank and pay were reduced, but he was not discharged from the military. He served no jail time.

In the summer of 2005, Hurricane Katrina hit the low-lying city of New Orleans, breaching its network of poorly maintained levees and putting 80 percent of the city under as much as fifteen feet of water. The Federal Emergency Management Agency was slow to send help, leaving people stranded in their homes and in a football stadium that became more squalid and chaotic with each passing day. When FEMA did finally send help, it was the wrong kind—the agency had spent the past several years preparing to respond to a terrorist attack, and authorities in Baton Rouge who had prepared a field hospital for victims were surprised to receive supplies for responding to a chemical attack, including the drug Cipro, which is used to treat victims of anthrax. Officials called in the Louisiana National Guard, but three thousand of its eleven thousand members, along with most of its heavy equipment, had been shipped over to Iraq.[6] Two days after the storm, a FEMA official emailed the agency director, Michael Brown, from the Superdome and said that people were likely to die within hours if help didn't arrive immediately. Brown's press secretary replied that the director wasn't available at the moment, writing, "It is very important that time is allowed for Mr. Brown to eat dinner."[7] On September 2, as New Orleanians remained trapped in their houses and the Superdome, Bush told Brown that he was doing "a heck of a job."[8] Brown resigned a week and a half later, transitioning into several years of work in disaster response for the private sector, plus a job as a talk-radio host.

In 1998, 120 countries voted to establish the International Criminal Court (ICC), a judicial body intended to serve as a venue for prosecuting people accused of war crimes. Though President Clinton refused to send the treaty to the Senate for ratification, citing America's "fundamental concerns" about the ICC, he was willing to sign the Rome Statute, a hopeful sign for the court's future. The Bush administration "unsigned" the statute in May 2002, and then Congress passed a law prohibiting the U.S. government from cooperating with the ICC in any way and authorizing the president to use "all means necessary," including military force, to free any American or allied person detained by the ICC. The bill was colloquially known as the Hague Invasion Act. The Bush administration then began signing Bilateral Immunity Agreements (BIAs) with allied countries, ensuring that "current or former government officials, military personnel, [and] citizens of the other party" could not be extradited to the ICC.

The United States had signed more than a hundred of these BIAs by 2018.[9]

The same year Congress signed the Hague Invasion Act, President Bush issued the notorious presidential memorandum denying al-Qaeda and Taliban POWs the protections required by the Geneva Conventions.[10] This was the crucial step in establishing the Bush administration's legalization of torture. Four years later, Congress passed the Military Commissions Act of 2006 to establish a replacement for the Combatant Status Review Tribunals that had been declared unconstitutional by the Supreme Court. The act prohibited both enemy combatants and detainees (that is, prisoners whose status had not yet been determined) from using habeas corpus to challenge their detention as unlawful. It applied going forward as well as retroactively—all pending habeas corpus cases in the federal judiciary were put on hold. Subsidiary provisions of the law allowed the government to present evidence in court that had been obtained through torture or other abuses, and it largely granted immunity to U.S. officials who had signed off on torture in the past.[11] John Yoo, the author of the February 7 memo, is now a law professor at the University of California, Berkeley, and those who had more hands-on involvement in torture also avoided punishment. Though the torture program spanned several continents, and though there has been no shortage of testimony from victims able to describe their experiences and the people who abused them in voluminous detail, John Kiriakou is the only CIA employee to serve prison time in connection with the agency's black sites program. He went to prison not for torturing anyone but for alerting journalists to the fact that torture was occurring in 2007. Before he went to the press, he went to his superior officers. "Look," he said, "I have a moral problem with this. I think there's a slippery slope, I think somebody is going to get killed. There's going to be an investigation. And a bunch of people are going to go to prison, and I don't want any part of it." He was wrong about a bunch of people going to prison, and he remains aghast that many of his co-workers are still walking free. Of Gul Rahman, the Afghan detainee who died after being stripped naked and chained to the wall of a thirty-six-degree brick factory the

CIA called the Salt Pit, Kiriakou says, "The man was murdered in cold blood, so where's the prosecution? You come home, you murder somebody in cold blood, you get a promotion and a $2,500 bonus."[12]

Many legal scholars, international observers, and human rights activists viewed the Military Commissions Act as an attempt to provide amnesty to Bush administration officials who were involved with the torture program. Between 2005 and the end of Bush's presidency, Human Rights Watch, the head prosecutor for the ICC, and the United Nations' special rapporteur on torture had all argued that prominent members of the Bush administration, including Bush himself, should be investigated and prosecuted for war crimes. As if torture and unlawful detention in the Middle East and Guantánamo weren't bad enough, the invasion of Iraq constituted a war crime in its own right, because wars of aggression are illegal under international law. The legal scholar and UN rapporteur on torture Manfred Nowak told German television in 2009 that Bush no longer enjoyed head of state immunity, meaning that President Obama was obligated to initiate legal proceedings against both the former president and his secretary of defense, Donald Rumsfeld. "The evidence is sitting on the table," he said. "There is no avoiding the fact that this was torture."[13] When the ABC News reporter George Stephanopoulos asked President Obama whether he would appoint a special prosecutor to investigate the Bush administration's potential war crimes, Obama began by saying, "I don't believe that anybody is above the law," but his very next sentence began with the words "On the other hand." He said, "I also have a belief that we need to look forward as opposed to looking backward." No federal legal agency ever opened investigations into Bush or any member of his inner circle during Obama's two terms. Obama also declined to push for the prosecution of any of the high-level financial executives whose reckless repackaging of junk mortgages into attractive and allegedly safe securities sparked the global financial crisis and put one out of every fifty-four American homes into foreclosure in 2008 alone.

Perhaps Obama hoped to set an example that his successor might be willing to follow as well, because Obama, not Bush, was responsible for the war's single most brazen assertion of executive authority. Anwar al-Awlaki was a Muslim American imam and U.S. citizen who led mosques in San Diego and Northern Virginia in the 1990s and early 2000s. Originally viewed by the government as exactly the kind of Muslim moderate the country needed, Awlaki fell under government suspicion shortly after September 11 when the FBI discovered that two of the hijackers had attended his sermons. He left the United States in 2002, first for the U.K., and then for Yemen, where he also had citizenship. His views became increasingly hard-line. He praised successful attacks against the United States and described America as the enemy of Islam around the world. Broadcasting his sermons over the internet, Awlaki cultivated a growing militant following. Though it never presented any evidence that Awlaki actually helped to organize any attack, the government became concerned that he was serving as a recruiter for al-Qaeda, and it began looking for a way to kill him.

Between January and April 2010, Obama and his lawyers decided that assassinating Awlaki was legal. The National Security Council signed off on the decision, and Awlaki was placed on Obama's notorious "kill list." He was killed in Yemen via drone strike on September 30, 2011, executed by a country that had never charged him with any crime, while living in a country with which the United States was not at war. Two weeks later, another drone strike killed Awlaki's sixteen-year-old son, Abdulrahman. The Obama administration said he was not the intended target, that he had simply been in the wrong place at the wrong time, but the former White House press secretary Robert Gibbs put the blame for Abdulrahman's death on his dead dad: "I would suggest that you should have a far more responsible father if they are truly concerned about the well-being of their children." Six years later, Donald Trump authorized a raid on a Yemeni village in which special operations forces killed between ten and thirty civilians. One of them was Nawar al-Awlaki, Anwar's eight-year-old daughter. Murdering one guy because he won't stop talking shit about you is one thing, but when the murderer then spends the next six years taking out two of the guy's kids as well, it starts to sound like something out of a mafia movie.

Evidence of war crimes continued to pile up throughout Obama's presidency. Amnesty International, Human Rights Watch, and *two* United Nations special rapporteurs all criticized the lack of transparency around Obama's drone warfare campaign in Pakistan and Yemen. This lack of transparency made it impossible for Yemenis and Pakistanis to seek justice for the wrongful deaths of their loved ones, and because Yemen and Pakistan were not "defined conflict zones" under international law, civilian deaths caused by drone strikes likely constituted extrajudicial executions. On top of that, Obama's drone fleet often carried out both "signature strikes" and what came to be referred to as "double taps." The former involved bombings that targeted people whose identities were unknown but whose behaviors were thought to indicate that they were insurgents. One of the most notorious signature strikes involved drone operators who obliterated a convoy of families in Afghanistan after they stopped to pray on the roadside, killing twenty-three people in the process. The latter were bombings that occurred in two stages. First, drones would target a building believed to contain Taliban or al-Qaeda fighters. Then they'd wait a little bit for rescuers to arrive and kill them as well.[14] Obama's drone strikes killed at least 324 civilians, and potentially more than 800.[15] No American has ever been charged or prosecuted in connection with these deaths.

Journalists and human rights advocates found the secrecy around Obama's drone program to be particularly galling. A minute after his 2009 swearing in, the White House website pledged that his administration would be "the most open and transparent in history." Then Obama spent the next eight years doing something like the opposite. His White House stalled on making improvements to operations at the federal government's Freedom of Information Act office and forcefully opposed FOIA requests at every turn. "Of the six [administrations I've worked with]," one Washington lawyer said, "this administration is the worst on FOIA issues. The worst. There's just no question about it." Egregiously high document retrieval and reproduction fees and confusing guidelines at agencies around Washington, especially the CIA and Department of Homeland Security, made it more difficult for the public to access government records. When whistleblowers took transparency into their own hands in order to publicize war crimes and illegal government surveillance, the Obama administration pursued them with a frightening intensity.[16] Edward Snowden, a Russian citizen as of 2022, can never return to the United States without risking life in prison. Julian Assange, the founder of the whistleblowing organization WikiLeaks, spent seven years living in Ecuador's London embassy, never setting foot outside, in order to avoid extradition to the United States. After Ecuador withdrew his asylum in 2019, the British government approved Assange's extradition, which he is appealing as of this writing. Chelsea Manning, who provided hundreds of thousands of government documents to WikiLeaks in 2010, was charged with aiding the enemy, a crime that carried a potential death sentence, and spent seven years in prison. None of the people who committed the crimes documented in the files released by these whistleblowers faced a similar degree of government antagonism.

In 2014, four former Blackwater contractors were convicted of first-degree murder and manslaughter for killing fourteen unarmed Iraqi civilians in 2007. In December 2020, President Trump pardoned all four of them. Trump also pardoned First Lieutenant Clint Lorance (convicted of murdering two Afghan civilians) and Major Mathew Golsteyn (charged with the 2010 murder of an Afghan civilian) in 2019, saying at the time that the pardons would provide America's troops with the "confidence to fight."[17] Other beneficiaries of Trump's forgiving spirit included Rod Blagojevich, the former governor of Illinois, who had been convicted of bribery, extortion, and wire fraud (among other charges) in connection with his efforts to sell a seat in the Senate; Bernard Kerik, former commissioner of the New York Police Department, who had committed tax fraud and made false statements in an attempt to conceal his involvement with a mobbed-up contractor; Scooter Libby, who committed perjury and obstruction of justice during his involvement with the Plame affair; Joe Arpaio, former sheriff of Maricopa County, Arizona, whose time in office had been dedicated to a vicious and racist campaign of harassing, humiliating, and "rounding up" immigrants; and Michael Behenna, a former Army first lieutenant convicted of murdering an Iraqi prisoner his superiors had ordered him to release.

The war on terror has involved criminal activity at every level, from its conception and legal justification in the White House all the way down to the actions of individual soldiers on the battlefield. The invasion of Iraq was an illegal war of aggression. John Yoo's memos justifying indefinite detention and torture violated both the Constitution and various treaties to which the United States is a signatory, particularly the 1948 Universal Declaration of Human Rights. American soldiers' treatment of detainees and civilians has in many instances involved assault and murder.

Yet despite the mountains of evidence and the clarity of the applicable laws, the architects and executors of the war on terror don't seem too weighed down by their misdeeds. George W. Bush remains a welcome guest at almost any ceremony, conference, panel discussion, or talk show he wishes to grace with his presence. His media image is that of an affable grandfather with an adorable hobby (painting), and former First Lady Michelle Obama considers him a "beautiful, funny, kind, sweet man."[18] Democrats miss Barack Obama so much that his wife is regularly urged to run for the presidency herself, the only way left to get Barack back in the White House in an official capacity. And Republicans have not just excused but embraced the brutality of the country's most bloodthirsty Special Forces operators. Chief Petty Officer Eddie Gallagher was accused by two fellow Navy SEALs of murdering an injured, seventeen-year-old Islamic State fighter with the last name Abdullah during the 2017 battle for Mosul. According to the SEALs, Gallagher said, "He's mine," over a radio, walked up to the boy and the medic treating him, and stabbed him with a hunting knife, after which he posed for photos with the body. Other soldiers testified that he killed at least two other Iraqis—the first an old man in a robe, the second a young girl—while working as a sniper and that he threatened to kill SEALs who were considering reporting his actions. Gallagher was acquitted of murdering Abdullah thanks to another SEAL who, after receiving immunity from the government, testified that he'd killed Abdullah himself, a story uncorroborated by any other testimony or physical evidence. After his acquittal, President Trump ordered the Navy to reverse Gallagher's demotion and called him "one of the ultimate fighters" at a campaign rally. Trump considered making him a speaker at the 2020 Republican National Convention.[19]

This is something larger than a collection of shoddy prosecutions, botched investigations, or powerful individuals tending to their self-interest. President Obama was not looking after a partisan ally when he declined to ask his Justice Department to investigate Bush, Cheney, Yoo, and Rumsfeld. This is a systematic refusal by the U.S. political system as a whole to pursue any measure of accountability for the crimes committed during a war that most people agree was detrimental to the country's international reputation and its capacity for global leadership. Accountability would have been very much in the larger national interest. Consistent prosecution of American soldiers who murdered Afghan and Iraqi civilians might have helped to uproot the hyper-macho culture of arrogance and unrepentant violence that many reporters agree now pervades the Special Forces. Jail time or, at a minimum, professional death for the legal architects of torture and mass surveillance could have allowed Obama to fully turn the page on the Bush administration's global messiah complex as opposed to spending most of his two terms finding new ways to rationalize and institutionalize it. And aggressive investigations of either Bush or Obama—which would have been fully justified by the principle of command responsibility in international law—could have diluted the corrosive concentrations of power amassed by the executive branch during the war's first decade.

Instead, most politicians with aspirations to national office over the past decade have made a series of promises to "change the system" while leaving it under the control of the exact same groups of people. That such accountability was not seriously pursued tells you something about the political system's lack of confidence in its own ability to adapt; a government that feels it cannot afford to hold serious malefactors responsible for their actions is a brittle government, one that understands itself as fragile despite the persistence of its outward trappings of strength and power. Insofar as the government's unwillingness to hold war criminals accountable manifested itself in other areas as well (as with the country's financial institutions after the financial crisis), one might say it became a part of the country's larger political culture. Call it impunity culture.

• • •

One might object that impunity culture isn't unique to the war on terror. Haven't governments attempted to evade responsibility for their wrongdoing throughout history? Don't many governments cover up crimes? Didn't the United States bomb Cambodia in secrecy, and didn't that campaign's architect, Henry Kissinger (RIP), still find himself invited to state dinners and lauded as a foreign policy wise man by bigwigs like Hillary Clinton? Maybe so, but impunity culture flourished during the war on terror because the war itself was impunity culture on a global scale, waged with no regard for international law, little regard for the civilian casualties the United States inflicted on other countries, and contempt for the idea that any other people or government might have legitimate grievances about the whole project. It represented a turn away from the Cold War era, a period during which American policy makers knew that military violence *on its own* would not be enough to defeat the Soviet Union. If communism's ambitions were to be checked, America would also have to demonstrate to other countries that capitalism's ultimate victory would benefit them as well, and not just the United States. After the fall of the U.S.S.R. and then especially after September 11, that kind of thinking disappeared from American strategic thinking. "Every nation, in every region, now has a decision to make," President Bush said on September 20, 2001. "Either you are with us, or you are with the terrorists." That's not diplomatic outreach or a sales pitch. It is a threat. America demanded allegiance from the rest of the world and offered nothing in return in 2001, because America no longer felt it owed the rest of the world anything—not democracy, not economic growth, and certainly not accountability when its drones blew up some farmers driving down the road or obliterated a wedding party. One of the war's fundamental goals was to confirm the hypothesis that in the twenty-first century the rest of the world would automatically defer to America, simply by virtue of America's overwhelming military strength.

As for Americans themselves, they certainly thought that impunity during the war on terror was something that needed addressing in its own right. *All* of the major protest movements that emerged following the invasion of Iraq have been focused squarely and specifically on impunity as such. Occupy Wall Street didn't set up camp in Zuccotti Park because banks crashed the financial system and threw the economy into a recession. The magnitude of the crash was clear by the end of 2008, and Occupy didn't start until the fall of 2011. What changed over those two and a half years was that it became clear that the Obama administration wasn't going to go after any of the bankers who caused the crash. There was more than adequate precedent for him to do so. After the savings and loan crisis of the 1980s, which contributed to a recession in the early 1990s but didn't cause anywhere near the damage wrought by the global financial crisis, more than *nine hundred* people went to jail. Only one executive saw prison time in the United States as a result of the financial crisis, and his trial didn't even take place until 2013.[20] In the early stages of the Obama presidency, many people believed that impunity culture was confined to the Bush administration rather than pervading the political system as a whole. When Obama's failure to punish the banks dashed those hopes, people's anger exploded.

Similarly, Black Lives Matter didn't take to the streets after George Zimmerman gunned down Trayvon Martin on the streets of a Florida suburb in February 2012. There were petitions and tweets and several protests, but nothing that coalesced into a movement. Black Lives Matter only got its name and turned into a national project after a jury acquitted Zimmerman of both second-degree murder and manslaughter. Several years later, impunity culture sparked a series of feminist protests as well. The Women's March was organized after the country put Donald Trump in the White House despite his being caught on tape bragging about committing sexual assault. #MeToo took off when it was revealed that Harvey Weinstein's methodical abuse of women hoping to work in his movies, abuse that was among the worst-kept secrets in the industry, hadn't done anything to harm his position as one of Hollywood's most powerful producers. These movements were all separate and distinct from one another in important ways, but it is not unreasonable to also think of them as a single, broad-based fight against impunity culture and its consequences.

One of the virtues of Occupy Wall Street was that it served equally well as a disruptive protest movement and as a self-renewing pedagogical project. It was confident and tentative at the same time, and both aspects of its personality increased its appeal. It was confident in the way it seized space without asking—and privately owned space at that. Zuccotti Park belonged to the commercial real estate firm Brookfield Properties, so in occupying it, the protesters realized on a small scale one of the movement's larger aspirations, which was to return the country's public and civic life to the actual public. The occupiers also didn't hesitate to make demands they knew were perfectly reasonable even if the political system was likely to reject them out of hand: a reversal of the Supreme Court's decision in *Citizens United v. FEC*, which had diluted citizens' free speech rights by extending them to corporations; forgiveness of student loan debt; increased taxation to narrow the country's surging wealth and income gaps; and relief for those whose homes were under foreclosure. (Many in the news media didn't even bother rejecting these demands. Instead, they just pretended to believe or else deluded themselves into thinking that Occupy didn't have any concrete proposals.) The movement was tentative insofar as many of the people who spent time in the park and participated in its general assemblies had no prior experience of a protest movement whose demands and actions hadn't been planned and scripted in advance. The leaderlessness of protest movements around the globe since the Arab Spring in 2011 has often been described as a mere aftereffect of the "revolution" that social media and the internet are supposed to have enacted on how people communicate with one another—why bother taking orders from some organizer when everyone can just decide that the march starts at 2:00 p.m. on Facebook? But for a generation of young people who grew up in the end-of-history 1990s or the fearful and politically repressive 2000s, that leaderlessness had a more substantial political valence. Leaderlessness forced protesters to take responsibility for the movements in which they took part, from small decisions concerning what the signs should say all the way up to larger questions about what the movement's goals were. It allowed protesters to experiment with flexing civic muscles that had atrophied over the prior two decades. One can't obey a leader's instructions and retain a feeling of self-respect unless one already has a sense of individual and collective civic selfhood. To constitute a public and make democracy happen in real time was a novelty, not the kind of thing one knows how to navigate in advance. The absence of charismatic authority figures meant the protesters had no choice but to educate themselves and one another.

The incremental learning process that unfolded between September 17 (when the park was occupied) and November 15, 2011 (when police cleared the park in a midnight raid), was sensitively documented in *Occupy! An OWS-Inspired Gazette,* a short-lived newspaper that published news reports, first-person accounts, polemics, cartoons, interviews, and historical essays from Zuccotti Park and other occupations around the country. The wonder and uncertainty of political discovery pervade the *Gazette's* articles. There was initial skepticism upon arrival. "The first day I arrived and, surveying the scene, was totally dispirited," one contributor wrote. "Same old same old, and not very substantial." September 17: "As 7 p.m. approached, my friends and I left thinking the cops would clear everyone out in no time." But as the occupation proved to have more staying power than originally assumed, optimism grew. September 25: "Nine days is nothing to sneeze at. I know people keep complaining that the occupiers don't have a platform, but any real deliberative convention takes time, and these folks were strangers nine days ago."[21] There were feelings of pleasure and exhilaration as the occupation maintained its organization and got more ambitious: "Maybe only someone as ignorant of strategy—of history—as I am would be impressed by this. But people—the ones who figured out how to do these things, the ones doing them now—are impressive!"[22] There were text message exchanges between friends trying to figure out where the next march was going, whether one could get arrested without getting fired for missing work the next day, how to find one another in the crowd. There were gripes about people who came to the park for entertainment rather than politics, such as the drummer who played for half an hour beyond the agreed-upon two-hour limit because "2 hours was not enough for my soul,"[23] or the woman who became the only protester the press had any interest in once she started walking around topless.[24] There were rumors, reports on other actions inspired by Occupy, op-eds analyzing key episodes from economic history or arguing against the folly of trying to dismantle the Federal Reserve. After ten years during which the government had gone out of its way to discourage any form of political expression more subversive than informing police officers about unattended luggage in a train station, the movement's slogan, "We are the 99 percent," was as much aspirational as it was declarative. If an atomized public wanted to reclaim its place at the center of political life, it would first have to learn how to recognize itself as a public. For just under two months, Zuccotti Park, along with dozens of other parks and plazas across the country, from Philadelphia to Oakland, was simultaneously a public square, a stage, and a school.

While the occupiers' confidence in their abilities to sustain a community, analyze the world around them, and describe what a better world might look like steadily increased, they had a harder time figuring out how to feel about the police. Why did the NYPD need to send so many officers to watch over entirely peaceful demonstrations? If Occupy was a movement of the 99 percent against Wall Street plutocrats, then weren't the cops potential allies? It's not as if cops had tens of millions of dollars stashed away in offshore accounts or drove Escalades to the station each morning. And if both the protesters and the cops understood their jobs as defending Americans' constitutional rights, what was to stop them from being on the same side? "Dear Police," one contributor wrote, addressing the NYPD directly, "You keep inserting yourself and distracting OWS. Could you please stay home? The conflict is between American citizens and concentrations of wealth."[25] Another writer advised occupiers to avoid confronting the police too directly, because doing so would likely provoke the cops to start assaulting and arresting people, which would in turn make it hard for Occupy to attract new participants and realize its goal of truly representing the 99 percent.[26] Others believed, in the words of a cardboard sign taped to Occupy's free library, that "mass arrests prove our power."[27] When confrontations did arrive, protesters also had to figure out how best to conduct themselves. Occupy was for many people their first experience of intentionally not doing something a cop told you to do. "Who do you protect? Who do you serve?" they shouted at the cops, their questions suggesting they thought that some officers might go home that evening, reflect on the day, and decide the protesters were right after all. One woman was arrested while trying to delay the opening bell of the New York Stock Exchange on November 17. "I was approached [by a cop] and asked if I wanted to comply," she wrote. "'We can do this the easy way,' the cop promised. I didn't answer and kept my head down. 'Okay,' he said and pulled my arm. I was flipped onto my stomach and zip-cuffed. I didn't know how to struggle or put up a fight beyond that initial resistance. Where should my arms flail?"[28] On October 1, hundreds of people decided they would march across the Brooklyn Bridge, both as a demonstration of their organizational power and to send the message that the crisis extended to all of the city's five boroughs, not just Occupy's home base in the Financial District. Police allowed them onto the bridge but then prevented them from completing the crossing and blocked the way from behind as well, making it impossible to retreat. Then they cuffed everybody. More than seven hundred people were arrested, making it one of the largest mass arrests of peaceful demonstrators in the country's history.[29]

Some segments of the federal law enforcement apparatus viewed Occupy as a terrorist event in the making. As demonstrations and encampments popped up in cities across the country, local law enforcement agencies deluged the Department of Homeland Security with requests for guidance on how to respond. While the DHS's Office for Civil Rights and Civil Liberties cautioned that "to a large degree, these protests are no different from any other protests/events from civil liberties, civil rights and privacy perspectives," it allowed that "persons demonstrating illegal or suspicious behavior and attempting to use the protests to obscure their activity could be reported."[30] Aside from the guy at DHS whose whole job was to worry about civil rights, however, the rest of the Department of Homeland Security, along with the FBI, had little problem with treating the Occupy movement like a violent threat from the beginning. As revealed in a report by the Partnership for Civil Justice Fund, the "DHS 'Threat Management Division' directed Regional Intelligence Analysts to provide a 'Daily Intelligence Briefing' that included reports on 'Peaceful Activist Demonstrations' along with 'Domestic Terrorist Activity.'" Regional "fusion centers" were tasked with collecting intelligence on the protests. In October 2011, the FBI's Jacksonville, Florida, office produced a domestic terrorism briefing on the "spread of the Occupy Wall Street Movement" (focusing on municipalities in which unemployment remained particularly high), while the Domestic Security Alliance Council, which facilitated cooperation among the FBI, the DHS, and the private sector, advised major financial institutions and other corporations on how to prepare for anticipated civil unrest.[31] The government even circulated a report by the International Council of Shopping Centers, a retail trade association, warning about the potential threat that Occupy Black Friday protests posed to retail sales (the "Specific Known Threats" identified in the report included "credit card cut ups" and "free non-commercial street parties").[32] If drawing an equivalence between protests for economic justice and September 11 seems tendentious, it was not a view that was confined to law enforcement. One maudlin opinion columnist felt that the protesters' very presence in lower Manhattan demeaned the memory of those who died on September 11. "The fact that Zuccotti Park had been covered knee-deep in ash and debris went unremarked," he wrote. "It was only a place to be occupied."[33]

It didn't take long for the NYPD to clarify which side it was on.

Shortly after 11:30 p.m. on November 14, Roots drummer Quest-love tweeted from a car traveling through lower Manhattan. "Omg, drivin down south st near #ows," he wrote. "Somethin bout to go down yo, swear I counted 1000 riot gear cops bout to pull sneak attack #carefulyall." The tweet was picked up by one of Occupy's main Twitter accounts, and a brief online discussion ensued. Some people thought it was just the usual midnight shift change. One person thought the riot gear cops were just movie extras, because the third installment in Christopher Nolan's Batman trilogy was being filmed in New York at the time. But Questlove was right. The bullhorns went off at around one in the morning, and hundreds of cops moved in. Officers told the occupiers that they had to "temporarily" leave the park so that all of the tents, chairs, tables, and other belongings could be cleared.[34] The protesters could return in the morning, but they wouldn't get their stuff back and couldn't bring any new stuff with them, which meant it would be impossible for Occupy to continue occupying. The NYPD did not want the public to see the raid. Barricades kept the public, as well as reporters, several blocks away. The airspace above lower Manhattan was shut down so that news helicopters could not get a shot. Those who had responded to Occupy's text alert about the raid and rushed to lower Manhattan were kept away by cops and told that there was nothing to see. When the protesters responded that clearly there was, some of them got maced. Gatherings and marches persisted for several weeks and months afterward, but the raid marked the beginning of the end of Occupy as a disruptive movement. The writer Astra Taylor was one of the people straining to see past the barricades that night:

> While we paced the street, seething and sorrowful, tents were trampled, people's possessions piled up, and occupiers arrested. Later I would come across a camper I had met earlier in the day sobbing on the sidewalk. A few blocks west, maybe thirty minutes after I arrived, the police line broke so two huge dump trucks could pass through. So that was it: We, and everything we had made and were trying to make, were trash.[35]

At a press conference the next day, New York City's mayor, Michael Bloomberg, justified the raid by claiming that the *protesters* had been infringing on the First Amendment rights of their fellow New Yorkers. "New York City is the city where you can come and express yourself," he said. "What was happening in Zuccotti Park was not that." He said Occupy had made the park "unavailable to anyone else."[36] It was an incredible piece of circular reasoning that did nothing to conceal, and which probably wasn't even intended to conceal, the purely repressive logic of the raid: The public, by spending time in a public space and welcoming anyone who wanted to join, had deprived the public of access to public space.

Black Lives Matter needed much less time to figure out its stance on the police: The police were the enemy. George Zimmerman, the man who shot Trayvon Martin in 2012, was not a cop—he worked in insurance—but he seemed to think of himself as one. He was the neighborhood watch coordinator for the Retreat at Twin Lakes, the gated community where he lived in Sanford, Florida. Obsessed with stamping out any signs of disorder in his neighborhood, he had a close relationship and obviously identified with the local police department, which he frequently called to report loud parties, potholes, trash on the street, and people whose presence in the neighborhood he viewed as suspicious. Having lost his home and his job while being tried for murder, Zimmerman might have been expected to reconsider this overidentification following the shooting and the acquittal. Instead, he doubled down. In 2016, he tried to auction off the gun he used to kill Martin, which he described as "a piece of American history," and he said the proceeds would be used to fight "violence against law enforcement officers."[37]

Two years after Martin's death, in July 2014, the forty-three-year-old Staten Island resident Eric Garner was killed by the NYPD officer Daniel Pantaleo, who was trying to arrest him for selling cigarettes on the street (a grand jury refused to indict Pantaleo, and it took the NYPD five *years* to take away his badge). Less than a month later, Ferguson police officer Darren Wilson shot and killed Michael Brown, an unarmed eighteen-year-old, for stealing a box of cigars from a convenience store. By the end of 2014, police had also killed Ezell Ford (twenty-five years old, Los Angeles), Laquan McDonald (seventeen years old, Chicago), Akai Gurley (twenty-eight years old, Brooklyn), and Tamir Rice (twelve years old, Cleveland), among others. No Black Lives Matter protester would ever claim, as some Occupy participants did, that they didn't have a fight with the police. The police were at the root of the whole problem. Eric Garner had been hassled by cops for much of his adult life, arrested some thirty times for selling loosies, driving without a license, and possession of marijuana, but he was the opposite of a detriment to his community. His neighborhood loved him. He was generous, kind, and calm; people called him Big E. On the day the police killed him, he had broken up a fight on the sidewalk. Asthma, heart disease, sleep apnea, and obesity made it difficult for him to get around, and they also made it hard for him to hold down a job. He'd worked for the city parks department off and on in the years leading up to his death, but he still had a wife and six kids to support even when he was out of work.[38] With Mayor Bloomberg's cigarette taxes driving prices through the roof, selling untaxed smokes on the street was a decent way to pull together some cash. He was proud of his life and family, proud to be Black. "He had me watching *Do the Right Thing* and *Malcolm X*," his daughter recalled of her childhood. After being subjected to a cavity search in broad daylight in 2007, he filed a complaint in federal court, and he told his lawyers at Legal Aid that he wouldn't accept any plea deals in the outstanding cases against him.[39] He was, to put it bluntly, part of America's surplus population. The formal economy had no use for him, he could not afford the medical care he needed, and the state wasn't going to step in to keep him on his feet. He cobbled together money and maintained his self-respect anyway, and that was his undoing. When the police approached him on July 17, he was fed up. "I'm minding my business, officer," he said. "I'm minding my business! Please just leave me alone." Less than fifteen minutes later, he was dead on the ground.

His dying words, "I can't breathe"—he repeated the phrase eleven times—became Black Lives Matter's first major rallying cry. The second came out of what happened in Ferguson, Missouri, the following month. Although the exact circumstances surrounding Michael Brown's death remain unclear today, everyone agrees that he was unarmed when Darren Wilson shot him, and in the immediate aftermath of the shooting some witnesses reported that Brown had his hands up when the bullets left Wilson's gun. Hence the second chant: "Hands up, don't shoot!" The protests that followed Eric Garner's death were almost entirely peaceful. The protests that swept through Ferguson after Michael Brown's were not.

If Eric Garner's death illustrated America's treatment of its surplus populations on an individual scale, Ferguson illustrated the same phenomenon on the scale of a whole municipality. In 2014, Ferguson was a city of some twenty-one thousand people, situated toward the north end of the St. Louis metropolitan area. Its population was nearly 70 percent Black, and its poverty rate hovered around 25 percent. As the Justice Department documented in an incendiary 2015 report, Ferguson city officials had systematized the exploitation of their most vulnerable residents, with the police department tasked not with maintaining public safety but with implementing what amounted to a municipal extortion racket. "City officials," the report said, "have consistently set maximizing revenue as the priority for Ferguson's law enforcement activity."[40] The city fined residents $102 for parking violations, whereas fines elsewhere in the St. Louis area were as low as $5. Citations for "weeds/tall grass" ranged from $77 to $102. City officials carefully tracked how much revenue law enforcement brought in, and treated any dips in income as potential municipal crises in the making. "Unless ticket writing ramps up significantly before the end of the year, it will be hard to significantly raise collections next year," the city's finance director wrote in a 2010 email. "Given that we are looking at a substantial sales tax shortfall, it's not an insignificant issue." The chief of police responded that he was in the process of hiring more police officers as well as tweaking shift schedules to keep as many cops on the street as possible, "which in turn will increase traffic enforcement per shift."[41] The police department made it clear to officers that they wouldn't be picky about *how* these fines and citations were imposed—the important thing was to keep the numbers up.

The result was a city in which residents effectively no longer had First or Fourth Amendment rights. Officers stopped people "without reasonable suspicion" and arrested them "without probable cause." If someone objected to being detained on the street for no reason, they would be charged with "failure to comply." In October 2012, Ferguson police pulled over a man and ticketed him for a broken brake light. The man knew this was nonsense, as he had replaced the brake light recently. The cops refused to let him out of his car so that he could demonstrate that the light worked. Detentions like these were fishing trips. Once they detained somebody, Ferguson police could run their name through the system for unpaid fines or outstanding warrants. One man was sitting at a bus stop when a police car pulled up:

Lieutenant: Get over here.

Bus Patron: Me?

Lieutenant: Get the fuck over here. Yeah, you.

Bus Patron: Why? What did I do?

Lieutenant: Give me your ID.

Bus Patron: Why?

Lieutenant: Stop being a smart ass and give me your ID.

When the officer failed to find any outstanding warrants for the man after running his name through the police database, he returned the ID and said, "Get the hell out of my face."[42] Another man was cooling off in his car after playing basketball at a public court one day in the summer of 2012 when a police officer approached. He "accused the man of being a pedophile . . . and ordered the man out of the car for a pat-down, although the officer had no reason to believe he was armed. The officer also asked to search the man's car. The man objected, citing his constitutional rights. In response, the officer arrested the man, reportedly at gunpoint." Among other things, the officer charged the man with making a false declaration because he'd said his name was "Mike" when it was really "Michael." The man lost his job as a result of the charges.[43] Another man was pulled out of his apartment by Ferguson police in August 2014. "You don't have a reason to lock me up," he said. The officer responded, "N*****, I can find something to lock you up on."[44] Ferguson was a place where police threats like these were also statements of fact.

Ferguson residents had learned to tolerate a lot, even if they'd never accepted police persecution as just or fair. But Michael Brown's death crossed a line. It wasn't just that Darren Wilson killed him. Police allowed Brown's body to lie on the pavement for four hours in the summer heat. When they finally did take him away, they left his blood on the street, in callous disregard of both Brown's family and the wider community.[45] Several months later, someone destroyed a memorial the community had built for Michael Brown, running it over with a car in the middle of the night. When a reporter called the Ferguson Police Department to ask whether there would be an investigation, a public relations officer said, "A pile of trash in the middle of the street? *The Washington Post* is making a call over this?"[46]

Ferguson residents knew exactly what their lives were worth to the people who ruled over them, and they responded accordingly. "It's a bunch of bullshit," one young woman told a reporter following the announcement that Officer Wilson would not be indicted for Brown's murder. "There's a lot that's going to go on to retaliate to this injustice. It's unreal. That's all it is. . . . They do this *all the time.* We have blacks getting pulled over *so much.*" The reporter asked if she lived in Ferguson. She said she used to. "*You don't want to be a part of a fucking community like this. This is a bunch of bullshit.*" Her eyes began to well with tears. The reporter asked how you move on from something like this. "You don't move on from something like this! With the Trayvon Martin case they moved on from 'something like this' and they let something else like this happen!" By this point her voice was breaking as well. "You're not supposed to move on from this. You're supposed to stand up for your rights."[47]

The city was consumed by protests well into 2015. Some of the protests were violent, though in a limited way. Protesters threw batteries, bricks, and rocks at police, and they also destroyed property, smashing the windows of several cop cars, looting a handful of businesses, and torching the gas station whose employees they falsely believed had called 911 to report Michael Brown on the day he died. This kind of property destruction is par for the course in countries with stronger contemporary traditions of worker protest, such as France. But American political officials responded as though the government's very survival hung in the balance, and for the first time, the arsenal the United States had amassed to fight the war on terror was deployed to its full extent on America's streets. Ferguson police patrolled Florissant Road in Humvees and BearCat armored tactical vehicles. The city imposed a curfew, making it illegal for anyone to be on the streets after midnight, and the airspace over the city was closed, keeping news helicopters away. The governor of Missouri twice called in the National Guard—the first time during the days following Brown's death, and the second in anticipation of the grand jury's decision not to indict Officer Wilson. Documents produced in the planning of the National Guard's operation referred to protesters as "adversaries" and "enemy forces." They urged the guard to use its intelligence capabilities to "deny adversaries the ability to identify Missouri national guard vulnerabilities," and they warned that the protesters had formidable intelligence-gathering capabilities of their own: "Adversaries are most likely to possess human intelligence (HUMINT), open source intelligence (OSINT), signals intelligence (SIGINT), technical intelligence (TECHINT), and counterintelligence capabilities," a fancy way of saying that protesters had the ability to read social media, access public documents, and listen to conversations being carried out on the street. Protesters and reporters were attacked with tear gas, beaten with clubs, and shot with rubber bullets. Hundreds were arrested. When asked about the guard's inflammatory rhetoric, a spokesperson said it was just the military's standard, boilerplate language, but Ferguson protesters had little difficulty figuring out what the troops thought of them. "*Y'all* learn how to be peaceful!" one protester yelled at police during the one-year anniversary vigil for Brown. "Don't keep telling us about being peaceful; *you* be peaceful. . . . We want the world to know that y'all are treating us like ISIS, and you wanna put a mic in front of my mouth and ask us how we feel? How the hell you think we feel?!"[48]

. . .

"The latest images of unrest in Ferguson, Missouri, evoke scenes from a battlefield," ABC News wrote: "heavily-armed officers in camouflage, carrying rifles in armored vehicles, firing at civilians."[49] "Ferguson police have deployed stun grenades, rubber bullets and what appear to be 40mm wooden baton rounds to quell the protests," *The Guardian* added. "The police response to a series of protests over [Brown's] death has been something more akin to the deployment of an army in a miniature warzone."[50] Police officers in camo gear pointed M-16s at protesters, and images of the two armored vehicles police brought to the protests each night proved to be particularly fascinating.

Across the country, police forces were outfitting themselves in gear that had originally been used by Marines patrolling in Mosul or Special Forces teams carrying out nighttime raids in rural Afghanistan. Beginning in 1997, the federal government had authorized a Defense Department initiative called the 1033 Program. Intended to provide Defense with a means of off-loading surplus equipment so as to lower inventory costs, it required branches of the military to make various kinds of gear available to local law enforcement agencies. Much of this gear was the sort of thing you would find at a hardware store or outdoor supply shop (flashlights, electrical wire, cold-weather clothing, sleeping bags), but much of it wasn't. The single most popular item requested by police agencies was a magazine cartridge, and Mine-Resistant Ambush Protected armored vehicles, or MRAPs, also proved a hit.[51] Originally intended to help police ramp up the war on drugs, the program was supercharged by America's shift to full-on war footing after September 11. A political mandate to retool policing toward combating "terror," along with the profligate distribution of federal grants to local law enforcement, meant that the federal government was giving police departments both the permission to outfit their officers like Navy SEALs and the money they needed to afford the makeover.

Local officials couldn't sign up quickly enough. In December 2011, the mayor of Keene, New Hampshire (a small city of around twenty-three thousand people), leaned toward one of his colleagues at a city council meeting and whispered in his ear, "We're going to have our own tank."[52] Keene, New Hampshire, didn't need a tank—the town had experienced only two murders since 1999—but terror hysteria meant that no expense was too great for law enforcement. "I don't think there's any place in the country where you can say, 'That isn't a likely terrorist target,'" a spokesperson for an armored vehicle company said. "How would you know? We don't know what the terrorists are thinking." Then, previewing the self-pitying logic that "Blue Lives Matter" conservatives would adopt toward the end of the Obama administration, he said, "I can't help but think that the people who are trying to stop this just don't think police officers' lives are worth saving."[53] Billions of dollars' worth of equipment have since been handed over to America's cops.[54]

Six years after Eric Garner's death, American law enforcement put on an even bigger spectacle while putting down a new wave of antiracist protests. The rallies, marches, and riots that followed the police murder of George Floyd in Minneapolis represent the peak of twenty-first-century American protest so far. Protests took place in all fifty states, with as many as twenty-six *million* people participating. Once again, people's disbelief at the impunity of America's police both amplified and focused anger at their treatment of African Americans. To watch George Floyd repeat Eric Garner's dying words as his life ended under the knee of the Minneapolis police officer Derek Chauvin—"I can't breathe"—was to understand that American law enforcement *still* regarded the scope of its punitive authority as unlimited. The repetition, in the words of the writer Tobi Haslett, "lent the instant rage and hurt a humiliated futility." This time, however, millions of Americans decided that it was the cops' turn to experience a little humiliation. Though still officially a "leaderless" movement, it is probably more accurate to say that Black Lives Matter in 2020 had more leaders than anyone could count—the protests demonstrated a flexibility of tactics and a level of institutional organization that hadn't been seen since Vietnam. In Minneapolis and Portland, protesters occupied downtown areas, barricaded them off, and announced that police were forbidden in the newly founded "autonomous zones," which they proceeded to successfully defend for weeks. On the West Coast, the International Longshore and Warehouse Union shut down ports for a day. In Minneapolis, protesters burned down the police station where Floyd's murderer worked, though it later became clear that the fire had been incited at least in part by members of a far-right white-supremacist group looking to kick off America's second civil war. In midtown Manhattan, where the streets had already been emptied out by COVID-19 lockdowns, things got even more surreal as blocks of glittering luxury storefronts were covered up by plywood in anticipation of looting. The word "protests" doesn't really capture what happened that summer. "Rebellion" and "uprising" hit closer to the mark. "The whole country seemed to tilt," Haslett wrote:

> Sacked shopping malls in Los Angeles and pillaged luxury outlets in Atlanta, a siege on New York's SoHo and flaming vehicles from coast to coast. Pictures of Philadelphia and Washington DC showed whole neighborhoods bristling with insurgency, crowds smashed the lordly windows in Chicago's Loop, and rioters set fire to the Market House, where slaves were bought and sold, in Fayetteville, North Carolina, the town where Floyd was born.

In just a few months, he continued, the rebellion spread to "one thousand seven hundred US towns and cities—the number was absurd," a number to make one laugh with elation, fear, or both.[55] For the first time in a young generation's living memory, ordinary people—poor people, especially—seemed to be the ones pushing history forward, and no one could say with any certainty where history would end up. The standard line that peaceful protest was the only kind

Americans would ever endorse also looked absurd in the summer of 2020: In a national poll asking Americans for their opinions on the destruction of the police station in Minneapolis's Third Precinct, 54 percent of respondents said the burning was justified.[56]

The government fought back with almost everything it had. While America's mayors and congressional representatives scrambled to assemble a package of reforms that would mollify the insurgents now making an open play for citizen control of the country's streets, the police and the military did their best to scare people back into quarantine. On June 1, several military helicopters hovered low over different crowds of protesters in Washington, D.C. The maneuver was ordered by President Trump and went under the official designation "Operation Themis," the name of one of the titans from Greek mythology. The ostensible purpose of hovering low was to use the powerful downdraft from the helicopter's rotors to disperse the protesters, blowing them away like so many leaves, but the maneuver was also simply a show of force. It was a way to make the protesters aware that they were vulnerable, that the full might of the world's most powerful military was close by and ready to strike. It was a death threat. A Predator drone circled over Minneapolis, and armored vehicles rolled through the streets of Salt Lake City. In one widely circulated video from Minneapolis, a woman filmed a Humvee rolling down her residential street, followed by a crowd of police officers in riot gear. In the video, she is standing on a porch with several other people. A sprinkler attached to a hose sits on the lawn. The strip of grass between the sidewalk and the street is overgrown, and the evening light is soft. "Look at this," she says, "they just keep coming." She says this in the same tone of voice one might use to point out a line of ducklings wandering down the block. She doesn't yet understand that the soldiers and cops and trucks are there *for her.* Then the police spot them and begin screaming at them to "get inside." When they hesitate, an officer says, "Light 'em up," and shots go off. The woman and her companions hurry indoors. One of them has been hit, by either a rubber bullet or a beanbag round. When the woman turns the camera back to the glass-paned door, a bright light is visible, shining up from the street. The police are waiting to see whether the "threat" will reemerge.[57]

In early June 2020, the Arkansas senator Tom Cotton published an op-ed in *The New York Times*. "The rioting has nothing to do with George Floyd," he wrote. "On the contrary, nihilist criminals are simply out for loot and the thrill of destruction." He called on the Trump administration and the rest of the federal government to "employ the military" to mount "an overwhelming show of force."[58] Perhaps he had not noticed that a majority of the country's governors were doing just that. More than thirty states mobilized some thirty-two thousand National Guard reservists to join the police in attempting to suppress the protests.[59] Short of using live ammunition, which would have escalated the situation past the point where it could still be contained, these soldiers and police officers made use of every means at their disposal. In Philadelphia, cops drove protesters off a highway running through Center City and then blasted them with tear gas and pepper spray while they were trapped against an embankment. In Iowa City, they threw flash-bang grenades at people who were kneeling on the street. In Indiana, they shot a reporter in the face with a tear gas grenade, causing him to lose an eye. In Salt Lake City, they pinned a homeless man to the ground and shot him in the back with an "impact projectile." They drove police SUVs into crowds in Brooklyn, and they surrounded protesters in the Bronx and then beat them with batons.[60] In Washington, law enforcement violently cleared protesters from Lafayette Square, after which President Trump walked through the area and posed in front of an Episcopal church while holding a Bible. Police partially blinded eight people across the country *in a single day*, and twelve over the course of that week.[61] In the four weeks from May 27 to June 22 alone, police arrested more than fourteen thousand people, with some outlets reporting arrest numbers as high as seventeen thousand. Less than 4 percent of that year's protests involved even property damage or vandalism, much less violence.[62] The arrests were more like roundups. More than seventy people who participated in the demonstrations were later convicted of federal crimes, receiving prison sentences that averaged just over two years.[63]

Protest activity decreased as the weather cooled, government officials promised reforms, and the second wave of the COVID-19 pandemic began to rip through a country that still lacked a working
vaccine. Police succeeded in pushing protesters whom President
Trump described as "domestic terrorists" out of their autonomous
zone in downtown Seattle; and they also succeeded in preventing new
autonomous zones from being established in Oregon, North Carolina,
and Tennessee.[64] As with Occupy Wall Street, the protests had been
too widespread and too consequential for politicians to dismiss them
wholesale after the fact, as much as many Republicans would have
liked to do just that. Local, state, and federal officials promised all
kinds of reform packages, including the establishment of citizen review boards that would have some kind of disciplinary authority in
cases of police abuse; the implementation of national policing standards; the end of qualified immunity, under which police officers cannot be held personally liable for violating the rights of citizens;
restrictions on the use of "no knock" warrants; and a mandate that all
federal police officers wear body cameras while on duty. At the federal
level, none of these reforms became law, because Senate Republicans
were able to block their passage. States and municipalities had slightly
more success, though mostly in the area of more rigorous training. In
response to Black Lives Matter's central 2020 demand, however—that
police departments throughout the country be substantially de-
funded, so as to decrease the influence police have over the daily lives
of the working poor—government at all levels delivered a clear, re-
sounding "no." Defunding the police was rejected by every major
presidential candidate during the 2020 campaign, including the democratic socialist Bernie Sanders. And while the country's fifty largest
cities reduced their police budgets by around 5 percent in 2021, that
was almost entirely due to wider post-pandemic cuts to municipal
budgets. As a share of total government spending, police funding increased.[65] By the end of 2022, police funding was increasing again in
absolute terms as well, a development championed by the Democratic
president, Joe Biden. "The answer is not to defund the police," he said
at his 2022 State of the Union. "It's to fund the police. Fund them!"[66]

This is not to say that police reform or even abolition is dead as a political project. But over the past decade, the government's response to two of the largest protest movements in the country's history has been telling. The central demand of Occupy Wall Street was an end to the wealth and income inequality that has turned daily life into a constant, low-grade anxiety attack for millions of people. That didn't happen. Wealth inequality has persisted and even worsened: From 2007 to 2019, household wealth decreased for all but the richest 20 percent of Americans, and the wealthiest 10 percent of households now own nearly 70 percent of the country's wealth.[67] Similarly, the central demand of Black Lives Matter was that police stop killing so many Americans. That didn't happen, either: The number of Americans killed by police increased *every* year between 2016 and 2022.[68] These two movements against impunity culture have had enormous and tangible effects on the country's political discourse, its citizens' understanding of the forces that shape their daily lives, and the views of millions of people. The government's specific remit, however, is policy, laws, and outcomes. On those counts, the government has made it clear that it is not willing to negotiate with its citizens at all.

• • •

I have tried in this book to use the war on terror to bring several distinct but related crises into focus, and to describe how those crises have shaped what it felt like to be an American during the early years of the twenty-first century. From drone campaigns over Pakistan to armored police vehicles idling outside government buildings, the war's militarism fueled a social climate of overriding anxiety and dread, and it made a mockery of the idea that democratic governments use military violence only as a means of last resort. The war's racism shored up and strengthened one of the ugly cornerstones of what one still must call (for lack of a better term) the national psychology. Forged in the crucible of a centuries-long race war that pitted white settlers driven by visions of unlimited wealth and freedom against dark natives who supposedly disdained the very idea of civilizational progress, America lurched into the new millennium hunting new groups of savages across unfamiliar landscapes abroad and obsessively scrutinizing and policing nonwhites at home for any signs of political dissent. The war exposed the country's inability to cope with slowing global growth and the end of America's unquestioned economic supremacy in a constructive way. Capitalists gobbled up a larger share of the national wealth even as they lost the ability to help it grow, and economic upstarts abroad were increasingly threatened with air strikes and occupation rather than wooed with financial incentives and treaties. The war was neither the sole cause nor the sole effect of any of these crises, but it has decisively molded all of them.

Historic militarism, resurgent racism, and levels of economic inequality that have no precedent in living memory have all made life worse for most people *and* made it harder for the political system to function. Despite the political destabilization wrought by these crises, however, the American system of government views their continuation as essential to its survival. With the United States unable to muster the economic strength to maintain even semi-consensual hegemony around the world, militarism is the next best option for managing discontents abroad and at home. If some growing portion of the globe's working-age population has to be excluded from formal employment due to slowing growth, racism provides the most efficient sorting mechanism for determining who is to be left out in the cold. Increased income and wealth inequality is a necessary consequence of the end of the twentieth-century economic expansion that launched the United States to superpower status, just as it was during the Gilded Age that signaled the approaching collapse of the world economic system centered on the U.K. and Europe.

Managing those contradictions is the purpose of impunity culture. A democratic government that was truly accountable to its citizens would never have suggested invading Iraq in the first place. It would not have discarded the whole edifice of human rights law in order to justify torture and the indefinite detention of thousands of people who were never charged with a crime. Its surveillance machine would have gone unbuilt, and its soldiers would have left Afghanistan at least a decade earlier than they actually did. Some portion of the obscene river of money that irrigates the Pentagon each year would have been diverted toward repairing the country's disintegrating social safety net and providing for the general welfare of its citizens with a national health-care program. Every single element of the alterative national history I've outlined in this book has enjoyed clear majority support from America's citizens, but impunity culture means that the government doesn't have to take its citizens' desires into consideration. By enabling and supercharging this impunity culture, the war on terror has degraded citizenship itself.

For all Americans, but perhaps especially for those Americans who came of age during the war, the rise of this impunity culture has been a dislocating and alienating experience. It has made voting in elections, the foundational act of democratic self-rule, seem hollow. It has made society something to be endured rather than shaped by the people who live in it, and it has made protest feel useless even as the reasons for protesting multiply. In 2014, two political scientists published a paper titled "Testing Theories of American Politics: Elites, Interest Groups, and Average Citizens." "Who governs?" they wrote. "Who really rules? To what extent is the broad body of U.S. citizens sovereign, semi-sovereign, or largely powerless?" The authors wanted to find out who actually influenced government policy in the United States. Measuring "key variables" for nearly eighteen hundred different policy issues, they found that wealthy people and business-based interest groups had "substantial independent impacts on U.S. government policy." They also found that "average citizens and mass-based interest groups"—the latter including protesters—"have little or no independent influence."[69] In other words, public opinion didn't change anything about how the government acted, nor did protest, nor did voting. What mattered, they found, were the desires of wealthy people and the businesses they owned.

The paper was an instant sensation, with news outlets from the political left, right, and center all reporting its findings with some variation of the headline "U.S. No Longer an Actual Democracy."[70] Some scholars criticized the study's methods,[71] and the pundit Matthew Yglesias wrote, with blithe self-assuredness, that it didn't matter: "Pining for a world in which policy outputs precisely reflect the views of the public is neither here nor there in terms of obtaining a better political system."[72] Nevertheless, the paper struck a nerve. People read about it, learned of its conclusion that American citizens exercised no material control over the national life, reflected on their own recent experiences of citizenship, and thought to themselves, "Yeah, that sounds about right." Whatever the paper's methodological weaknesses, that response is meaningful.

Prolonged exposure to impunity culture and the political paralysis it engendered was not sustainable. It was depressing and enraging for people to live in a place where they had little to no effective control over what happened to their lives, and when their lives also seemed to get harder with each passing year, the experience could be deranging. The past two decades have been characterized by the intensifying feeling that something has gone wrong with life in the United States. The last time 70 percent of Americans described themselves as "satisfied" with how things were going in their country was December 2001, immediately following the invasion of Afghanistan. The last time national satisfaction topped 50 percent was December 2003, the month America captured Saddam Hussein.[73] Except for these evanescent moments of militaristic exuberance, national satisfaction has trended down, averaging around 25 percent over the past fifteen years. The feeling wasn't so much that anything in particular had gone wrong as that *everything* had gone wrong, all at once, and it registered everywhere, from the surging popularity of dystopian television shows and novels to economists tracking the huge increase in "deaths of despair" since 2000, meaning all early deaths caused by suicide, drug and alcohol poisoning, and alcoholic liver disease and cirrhosis. In the early 2000s, music critics borrowed an idea from the French philosopher Jacques Derrida and began to identify aspects of something called "hauntology" in new popular music, referring to art haunted both by the irretrievable past and, more important, by the better future whose arrival now seemed to have been indefinitely postponed. One more optimistic Harvard psychologist felt compelled to rebut this feeling by writing an eight-hundred-page book arguing that things were actually better than they had ever been. That is not the kind of book one feels the need to write if things are actually going well.

During this period, a small group of isolated and predominantly young men decided they were going to lash out. Of the 148 mass shootings that have occurred in the United States since 1982, 115 of them, and 41 of the top 50 in terms of the death toll, took place during the war on terror. The first was in July 2003, when an assembly-line worker for the aerospace and defense giant Lockheed Martin shot fourteen and killed six of his co-workers with a shotgun at a plant in Meridian, Mississippi. The most recent, as of this writing, occurred in December 2023, when a sixty-seven-year-old academic named Anthony Polito shot and killed three faculty members at the University of Nevada–Las Vegas. The last year in which the country experienced only one mass shooting was 2003; in 2018, there were twelve. Mass shooters have targeted schools, workplaces, military bases, movie theaters, city streets, and music festivals. They have killed children as young as six at Sandy Hook Elementary School in Newtown, Connecticut; Black elders at Bible study at the Emanuel African Methodist Episcopal Church in Charleston, South Carolina; country music fans at the Route 91 Harvest music festival on the Las Vegas Strip; college students outside a sorority house in Isla Vista, California; and soldiers near the Fort Hood military base near Killeen, Texas. They have used handguns, revolvers, rifles, assault weapons, and cars. Some committed suicide after their murders, some were tried and put to death, and others are spending the rest of their lives in prison. Some wrote long manifestos or made disturbing remarks to family and friends before their attacks. Some singled out particular racial groups, some targeted women, and others killed indiscriminately. The motives of some mass shooters remain completely unknown.[74]

The causes of America's mass shooting epidemic have been hotly debated, with people broadly taking sides in line with their political allegiances. Democrats largely blame the country's gun laws, which made it easy for people to get their hands on assault weapons without so much as a background check. Republicans blame mental illness instead, arguing that the best America can do in response is to increase the number of metal detectors, police officers, and panic rooms inside the country's schools. Both explanations are weak. While Americans own more guns per capita than people in any other country, rates of gun ownership have actually declined over the past fifty years. In the late 1970s, roughly 48 percent of American households owned at least one gun. By 2014, that figure was down to 31 percent.[75] The 2004 expiration of the federal ban on private ownership of assault weapons, which gave Americans access to much deadlier firearms than had previously been available, is a very likely contributing factor, but a majority of the mass shootings committed since September 11 did not involve any kind of assault rifle, with handguns the weapon of choice instead.[76] As for mental illness, just 5 percent of the country's mass shootings were committed by someone who had ever been diagnosed with severe mental illness, a number that increased only to 25 percent even when researchers included nonpsychotic mental illnesses such as depression, diagnoses that in almost all cases were found to have been incidental to the killer's actions.[77] If mass shooters did have anything in common (other than their gender), it was their having experienced some kind of a life crisis shortly before their attack, whether the loss of a job, the end of a romantic relationship, or the death of a loved one.[78] Most of them did not decide to kill as many people as they could in a public place because they were psychotic or experiencing delusions or because they believed God had told them it was the right thing to do. They were largely in full possession of their mental faculties, and they killed people because they wanted to.

Why did they want to? People have always lost jobs and girlfriends and loved ones, and some people, overwhelmed by those crises, have always sought ways to lash out in public, to advertise their pain and anger, to make their problems everybody else's problems for once. The question isn't why people feel the need to lash out but why the mass shooting has become the preferred means of expression over the past quarter century. Different kinds of public crimes become attractive at different historical moments. During the Great Depression in the 1930s, Americans robbed banks, turning themselves into outlaw folk heroes by taking revenge on the institutions that had ruined the country's economy. Beginning in the late 1960s, they hijacked airplanes and demanded money or safe passage to Cuba or Rome or somewhere else in exchange for the passengers' safe return to earth. The promises of the revolutionary 1960s and the civil rights movement were curdling into cynicism, political violence, and economic malaise, and commercial air travel was still viewed as glamorous even as it was just becoming affordable for a plurality of Americans. To successfully hijack an airplane, therefore, promised both financial gain and escape from a country that seemed to be eating itself alive.[79] More than 130 commercial flights were hijacked between 1968 and 1972. Bank robbers and skyjackers gave voice to their anger by committing crimes they knew would resonate with millions of people. They did it for the money, but they also did it to be remembered, to create a spectacle. They understood themselves as performers and their countrymen as a captive audience.

Mass shooters operate at a higher pitch of desperation than bank robbers and hijackers—they generally don't expect to get away with their crimes—but in other respects they follow in their predecessors' footsteps. Their crimes are engineered for maximum media coverage and spectacular resonance, and as the bank robbers of the 1930s tailored their performances to audiences struggling through the Great Depression, twenty-first-century mass shooters perform spectacular suicide missions for a country that is drowning in endless war. Perhaps "resonance" is the wrong word. Resonance is the sound of a plucked guitar string gradually oscillating into silence. The kind of resonance mass shooters are after is the sound of that guitar plugged into an amplifier and gorging on its own feedback, rising in pitch, intensity, and distortion until it culminates in an unbearable shriek. The first shooter to make twenty-first-century America resonate in that way was probably James Holmes, who killed twelve people and injured seventy more at an Aurora, Colorado, movie theater on July 20, 2012. Holmes grew up in California, and unlike most mass shooters he had a long and well-documented history of both mental illness and unsuccessful attempts to treat it. Awkward and socially isolated since adolescence, he attempted suicide at just eleven years old, according to one of his defense attorneys.[80] He struggled with intrusive thoughts, both homicidal and suicidal, for years. He sought help from therapists, and he also tried to help himself. He graduated from the University of California, Riverside, and enrolled in the neuroscience PhD program at the University of Colorado, hoping he could learn how to repair what he described in a notebook as his "broken mind."[81] "I made it my sole conviction," he wrote, "but using something that's broken to fix itself proved insurmountable. Neuroscience seemed like the way to go but it didn't pan out."[82] Even as he acquired a fearsome arsenal of weapons—all purchased legally—in the months leading up to the attack, he continued to seek therapy and filled his private notebook with attempts at self-diagnosis, hoping that one of them would reveal a path to a normal life: "dysphoric mania," "generalized anxiety disorder/social anxiety disorder/OCD/PTSD (chronic)," "asperger syndrome/autism," "ADHD," "schizophrenia," "chronic insomnia," "psychosis," etc.[83] On page eighteen of the notebook, the journaling stopped. Over the following eight pages, Holmes just wrote the word "Why?" over and over, 249 times, the words increasing in size with each page. From then on, the notebook is dedicated to planning the attack: sketched maps of potential targets, lists of weapons with notes on their utility, different ways to kill a lot of people. On the third-to-last page, above a series of doodles and diagrams, he wrote, "embraced the hatred, a dark knight rises."[84]

In the late evening of July 19, Holmes bought a ticket for a midnight screening of *The Dark Knight Rises,* the third installment of Christopher Nolan's allegorical Batman trilogy about terrorism and the extralegal violence that is required to stop it. He sat in the front row, his bright orange hair rhyming with the terrorist Joker's green hair in *The Dark Knight.* About twenty minutes after the lights went down, he pretended to take a phone call and slipped out an exit door, propping it open behind him. He went to his car and put on tactical gear, some of which he had purchased on eBay: gas mask, vest, combat helmet, bullet-resistant leggings and throat guard, groin protector, and gloves.[85] He also gathered his weaponry, which included smoke canisters, a shotgun, a semiautomatic rifle, and a .40-caliber Glock. He returned to the theater, set off one of his smoke canisters, and started shooting. Some audience members initially assumed it was a prank, or maybe a publicity stunt organized by the movie studio for the midnight premiere. When he was done, he left the theater again and stood next to his car. He did not resist when the police arrested him. Soon after, police discovered that Holmes had also booby-trapped his apartment with explosives before leaving. After disarming the explosives with a robot and entering, they found dozens of home-made grenades, as well as a Batman mask.[86]

When Holmes stepped back into the movie theater that night after suiting up at his car, he simultaneously embodied both sides of the war on terror. First, he was a terrorist, someone who could suddenly transform a fun night out for hundreds of people into a waking national nightmare just by pulling a trigger a few dozen times. Whether or not it was a conscious part of his planning, Holmes understood that no other action would be capable of frightening so many people in so little time. The country's obsessive fixation on anticipating, imagining, and preventing future attacks had lent Holmes's plan an evil sheen, and he did not miss his chance to transform himself into an embodiment of everyone's worst fears. At the same time, Holmes stepped into the theater armed and armored like a member of the U.S. Special Forces, the most admired group of men in the country. He dropped the role as soon as the killing was over, making no attempt to escape, but for the few minutes he spent looking out from inside his gas mask, it would have been possible for him to feel that he was all-powerful, taking revenge on a world that had inexplicably forced him to feel the way he felt and be the way he was. The costume was nearly perfect; when police entered the theater after responding to a 911 call, they almost mistook him for a member of the SWAT team. "There was one particular piece of equipment that he had on him that was out of place," the Aurora police chief, Dan Oates, said, referring to his "non-regulation" gas mask. "I am so proud of my officers that they spotted that." Perhaps it was this aspect of his performance, the way Holmes swaddled himself in all the technology and accoutrements of militarized masculine power, that had the victims' families so concerned about his crime serving as an inspiration to others in the future. The parents of one of the victims in Aurora, a twenty-four-year-old man who died while shielding his girlfriend from the bullets, launched a campaign called No Notoriety, demanding that the media minimize the extent to which they published shooters' names or pictures of their faces. That didn't come until later, though, and in the meantime it wasn't just loners on 4chan who found that there were aspects of what Holmes did that they could identify with. A local gun rights activist said he thought civilian access to high-powered weapons made the United States "a stronger country," and he objected to proposed legislation that would limit the number of bullets someone could purchase at one time. "If I only had 6,000 rounds for my AR-15s, I'd literally feel naked," he said. "Two handguns, a shotgun, and a rifle," he continued, tallying up Holmes's arsenal. "That's the average male in Colorado."[87]

The first year in which the United States experienced seven mass shootings was 2012. Aurora was number four. The seventh took place in December, when Adam Lanza killed twenty-six people, including twenty children, at Sandy Hook Elementary School. Every year since, except for our locked-down 2020, there have been at least four mass shootings in the United States, and whether or not the perpetrators wear tactical gear and wield assault weapons, each one has restaged the war's two central traumas: the trauma of sudden and devastating victimization, on the one hand, and the trauma of committing mass violence, on the other. Like the war itself, mass shootings are now a normal part of the news cycle, something one expects to hear about from time to time, something one can almost forget about in between the rhythmic irruptions of a few days' headlines. After a 2018 shooting at Marjory Stoneman Douglas High School in Parkland, Florida, a sixteen-year-old student who went to Tallahassee to lobby for gun reform told a *New York Times* reporter that this time would be different. "Sandy Hook, they were elementary school kids who couldn't stand up for themselves. Virginia Tech was 2007, a different time," he said. "But this one, I just have a gut feeling—something is going to change."[88] It felt awful to read those words and judge the young speaker naive.

Cynicism is dangerous because, like all defense mechanisms, it is useful. It is a way of avoiding the pain of being surprised when something bad happens again. In the middle years of the war on terror, when President Obama was ramping up troop numbers in Afghanistan while trying to keep the conflict out of the headlines as much as possible, small but determined antiwar activist groups regularly warned Americans against becoming "numb" to the violence the U.S. military was continuing to deal out overseas. More recently, a new wave of mass shootings has given rise to the notion that Americans are now similarly "numb" to gun violence. But Americans are not numb—they are trapped. For more than twenty years, millions of them have appealed to their government to reduce the amount of violence it commits abroad and tolerates at home, and for more than twenty years those appeals have been ignored. That Americans have continued to make their appeals could easily be praised as persistence, but this persistence can also be unsettling. In 1914, Freud wrote an essay in which he outlined a psychological phenomenon he named "repetition compulsion," which refers to the way that people will unconsciously reenact traumas from earlier in life without realizing what they are doing. Someone who grew up feeling uncared for by an emotionally distant father may find themselves repeatedly dating emotionally distant men. A humiliating experience at school may later become the subject of recurring dreams or the basis of a sexual fetish. A child subjected to violence may hit their own children decades later. Someone under the sway of a repetition compulsion has not given up on the possibility of change—in fact just the opposite. In forcing themselves to relive or reenact a moment of fear or helplessness, they ultimately hope to master it, to produce a different result and triumph over a situation that previously wounded them. But this hope usually goes unfulfilled. The compulsion becomes self-sustaining, and visions of change and renewal are slowly replaced by anxious resignation: This is just what life is like.

One might think of the war on terror as a repetition compulsion carried out on a national scale. Those who launched and supported the war have carried out a series of failed attempts to exorcise the country's founding trauma of victimization by setting out into the wilderness in search of savages to dominate. Those who opposed the war have found themselves petitioning a government that has long made obvious its contempt for their desires. And those who mostly tried to take the Bush and Obama administrations' advice and live as though the war weren't happening in the first place have nevertheless found their lives gradually falling in time with its rhythms. For each of those groups, living through the war has felt like a single wish, a single desire, a single drive, pounding like a hammer that never stops. "Thus war effaces all conceptions of purpose or goal, including even its own 'war aims,'" Simone Weil wrote in her great essay on the *Iliad*. "It effaces the very notion of war's being brought to an end. To be outside a situation so violent as this is to find it inconceivable; to be inside it is to be unable to conceive its end."

Reality Principle

We can no longer afford to take that which was good in the
past and simply call it our heritage, to discard the bad and
simply think of it as a dead load which by itself time will
bury in oblivion. The subterranean stream of Western
history has finally come to the surface and usurped the
dignity of our tradition. This is the reality in which we live.
  —Hannah Arendt, *The Origins of Totalitarianism*[1]

Just before 3:30 p.m. on August 31, 2021, President Joe Biden stepped into the White House State Dining Room to deliver a speech. Over the prior two and a half weeks, the United States and its allies had staged a massive airlift, moving more than 120,000 people out of Afghanistan, including soldiers, contractors, diplomats, aid workers, other civilians, and thousands of Afghans whose safety in their home country could no longer be ensured. It had been almost exactly twenty years since George W. Bush promised to wipe the Taliban off the face of the earth, but in February 2020, Donald Trump negotiated a peace deal with the group, promising the withdrawal of American troops within fourteen months in exchange for the Taliban's commitment to preventing Afghanistan from becoming a staging ground for terrorist attacks. In the spring of 2021, with America appearing to be dragging its feet vis-à-vis withdrawal, the Taliban launched a stunning military offensive, overrunning the country on the way to Kabul, where they quickly deposed a government that had been lavished with U.S. aid and support for years. By mid-August, Kabul Airport was the only way out of the country. The other border crossings were all under Taliban control. As enormous C-130 and C-17 military planes took off with hundreds of people in their cargo holds and returned to take on hundreds more, twenty-four hours a day, U.S. embassy workers rushed to destroy the classified documents they could not take with them, and tens of thousands of Afghans scrambled to secure places on the departing aircraft for their friends, their relatives, and themselves.

President Biden characterized the airlift as a triumph. "More than 120,000 people evacuated to safety—that number is more than double what most experts thought was possible," he said. "No nation has ever done anything like it in all of history. Only the United States had the capacity and the will and the ability to do it, and we did it today." Several days earlier, 13 American military personnel, along with at least 170 others, had died when a suicide bomber attacked Kabul Airport, and once again a president reminded Americans that they were going to default on the blood debt they had been continually refinancing for nearly two decades: "We owe them and their families a debt of gratitude we can never repay." He said that no one could have expected the U.S.-backed government to fall so quickly in the face of a Taliban assault, much less that the country's president, Ashraf Ghani, would fill his pockets with cash and then flee the country in a helicopter.[2] But it was part of the American genius to be prepared for the unexpected, and Biden did his best to spin the hasty and chaotic retreat as a win for the U.S. military's logistical acumen. He wasn't so brazen as to literally claim that America had won the war, but that was the gist of the message. "Remember why we went to Afghanistan in the first place?" he asked. "Because we were attacked by Osama bin Laden and al-Qaeda on September 11th, 2001, and they were based in Afghanistan. We delivered justice to bin Laden on May 2nd, 2011—over a decade ago. . . . Then we stayed for another decade. It was time to end this war." He didn't spend any time dwelling on what America had been up to during the ten years that followed bin Laden's death—what would the point have been? The important thing was that the longest military conflict in American history was coming to an end. "I was not going to extend this forever war," Biden said.[3]

That last part wasn't just spin. In some ways, the war on terror really did come to a close under President Biden. One could even argue that it had ended sometime during the Trump administration, although not in terms of America's global military posture, which remained expansive. What changed under Trump was the war's centrality to the country's political life. Even as Trump polished up his image as commander in chief by overseeing campaigns against ISIS in Syria and Iraq, and even though one of his first major acts as president was to ban immigration from seven Muslim-majority countries, the war on terror steadily faded even further into the background under his administration. The new center of political life was Trump himself—his tweets, his lies, his grotesque and ever-changing cast of staffers and cabinet officials—and beginning in 2020 it was the COVID-19 pandemic, Black Lives Matter, and Trump's efforts to remain in the White House despite losing his reelection bid that dominated Washington politics. The media didn't bother to pay much attention to America's withdrawal from Afghanistan until things began to go wrong, and even then many commentators saw the chaos at Kabul Airport as an acceptable price to pay for the end of a war that had outlived its usefulness by at least a decade. Most major outlets published at least a few editorials arguing that failure in Afghanistan had long been inevitable, and that withdrawing was the only reasonable course of action.

That didn't mean everybody was happy with the withdrawal. Some politicians and commentators delivered righteous condemnations of the airlift. They said that by leaving, the United States had betrayed the people of Afghanistan, especially the thousands of Afghans who worked for American soldiers, corporate contractors, NGOs, and journalists. They said Biden had made it more likely that extremist groups would proliferate and one day regain the strength to mount an attack inside the United States. They said the United States had made it harder for allies to trust that America would honor its military commitments. They tended not to say what Biden should have done instead, and nobody expended much effort arguing that Biden should have ripped up Trump's negotiated settlement with the Taliban and maintained America's troop presence indefinitely. But they made it clear that Biden should have done *something* differently, anything that would have prevented the protracted national humiliation that was now broadcasting on television screens around the world. In the days after the withdrawal began, the evacuation's failures were emphasized to the point of fetishization. When reports circulated that a number of dogs owned by U.S. military contractors had been left behind in Kabul, the *New York Post* portrayed it as a stain on America's honor, with the president of a humane society describing herself as "devastated" that the Army could have abandoned "brave U.S. military contract working dogs to be tortured"—tortured!—"and killed at the hands of our enemies."[4] The chief foreign correspondent for MSNBC, who once wrote in his memoir about reporting on the Iraq War that "Iraq was a land where careers were going to be made," went on television to call the withdrawal "the worst capitulation of Western values in our lifetimes."[5]

It wasn't difficult to trace this note of hysteria back to its roots: The end of the occupation of Afghanistan reminded people of Vietnam, which stood alongside September 11 as postwar America's great humiliation. Once again, the United States had failed to replace a hostile government with one more amenable to its interests, even after more than a decade of trying. Once again, the foreign politicians it had ushered into the halls of power had proved to be unpopular and corrupt, turning tail at the first sign of physical danger. And once again, America's soldiers had been defeated by an army they massively outnumbered and outgunned. The wars had even ended in the same way, with airlifts undertaken in desperate haste as the two countries' respective capital cities fell to enemy forces. Many Americans could still remember the news footage of a single helicopter perched on top of an apartment building in the heart of what would soon be renamed Ho Chi Minh City, with a line of dozens of people stretching down a stairwell in the hope of securing a place on board. "It was swarms of helicopters," one American pilot said. "That's the only way you could describe it." Deck space became so limited on the two aircraft carriers from which these helicopters were dispatched that some of the choppers were simply pushed overboard, millions of dollars of the most sophisticated military hardware in the world dumped into the South China Sea.[6] Now people had to watch the same thing happen in Kabul, with the main difference being that fixed-wing aircraft had replaced the helicopters.

The similarities between Vietnam and the war on terror should not be overstated, though. Vietnam discredited overt American militarism for fifteen years. Street protests against both the draft and America's involvement in the conflict roiled the country's politics, from the 1967 March on the Pentagon through the 1968 Democratic National Convention riots, the 1969 Moratorium to End the War in Vietnam, and the 1970 killing of four student protesters at Kent State University. Congress also put constant pressure on the executive branch beginning in the late 1960s (the Watergate hearings were driven in part by congressional anger over Nixon's constant maneuverings to exclude the legislature from foreign policy decision making). In 1971, the Cooper-Church Amendment cut off all funding for American ground forces in Cambodia, and in the summer of 1973 Congress voted to stop funding any U.S. military involvement in Indochina.[7] The year 1973 also saw the passage of the War Powers Resolution over Nixon's veto. The law stipulated that a president could send American troops into action only when Congress made a declaration of war, except in cases of "a national emergency created by attack upon the United States." In addition, Congress successfully pressured President Ford into issuing a ban on government assassinations, and the 1978 Foreign Intelligence Surveillance Act mandated that all federal government domestic surveillance operations be supervised by the courts. As we've seen, all of these reforms were either dismantled or circumvented by the executive branch in the early twenty-first century, but at the time they constituted the most significant rebalancing of government powers in several decades.

By comparison, congressional opposition to the war on terror has been toothless, and no similar rebalancing of government forces seems likely in the near future. In his speech, Biden singled out Afghanistan as a theater in which military conflict had outlived its usefulness while continuing to endorse the larger premises of the war on terror. "The threat from terrorism continues in its pernicious and evil nature," he said. "It's changed, expanded to other countries. . . . We will maintain the fight against terrorism in Afghanistan and other countries. We just don't need to fight a ground war to do it."[8] Biden also indicated that even if the war on terror was ending in some larger sense—and he did refer to "ending an era"—the new goal was to repurpose American militarism rather than dismantle any aspect of it. "We have to shore up America's competitiveness to meet these new challenges in the competition for the 21st century," he said—"take on new threats that are here now and will continue to be here in the future." In case people didn't know off the top of their heads what these "new threats" were, Biden spelled them out: "There's nothing China or Russia would rather have, would want more in this competition, than the United States to be bogged down another decade in Afghanistan."

The war on terror may be winding down, but its legacy flourishes in America's refusal to see the world as something other than a battlefield. Vladimir Putin's decision to invade Ukraine in early 2022, for example, is already a humanitarian catastrophe, and it is unlikely to produce major strategic gains for Russia. Though Russia's annexation of some part of Ukraine through an eventual negotiated settlement would seem to be the likeliest outcome as of December 2023, it is not clear that the benefits of this territorial expansion will outweigh the costs of ruined relations with Europe and the United States. The invasion is also undoubtedly a criminal war of aggression. At the same time, it is worth noting that during the first two years of the war, America's response has been to escalate the conflict at every opportunity. Diplomacy has been used almost exclusively to expand the ranks of those countries fueling the war with money and weapons, and the Biden administration and Congress have lavished Ukraine with military aid while simultaneously looking to expand NATO's membership, a provocative decision given that anticipated NATO expansion contributed to Putin's original decision to invade. Meanwhile, commentators such as Anne Applebaum, Jeffrey Goldberg, and Timothy Snyder have decided to emulate Andrew Sullivan after September 11, describing America's support for Ukraine as a transhistorical defense of "civilization" and insisting that Vladimir Putin, like Osama bin Laden, is motivated solely by a hatred of freedom. The current situation is one that demands restraint, serious diplomatic engagement, and caution, especially given Putin's recent decision to revoke Russia's ratification of the global ban on nuclear weapons tests. That decision looks insane at first blush, but it is not without a logic. While the United States signed on to the treaty in 1996, Congress never ratified it, an outrageous blunder that has now made it possible for Putin to claim that Russia's withdrawal from the treaty is just an attempt to restore strategic parity with the United States.

But instead of calls to the negotiating table, America's response to the war is being shaped by Republicans, on the one hand, who would be happy to see Russia's Trump-friendly imperial autocrat humiliate western Europe's complacent parliamentarians, and Democrats, on the other, for whom the preferred outcome appears to be the collapse of the Russian state. More constructive requests to combine assisting Ukraine in its self-defense with diplomacy have been treated as so much Nazi appeasement. In October 2022, thirty progressive members of Congress sent a letter to President Biden. After praising Biden's support for "Ukraine's legitimate struggle against Russia's war of aggression," affirming their own continued commitment to "various appropriations of military, economic and humanitarian aid," and recognizing the "courageous fighting and heroic sacrifices" of the Ukrainian people, the authors urged Biden to undertake a "proactive diplomatic push" as well, so as to avoid prolonging the war any further. "If there is a way to end the war while preserving a free and independent Ukraine," they wrote, "it is America's responsibility to pursue every diplomatic avenue to support such a solution that is acceptable to the people of Ukraine." The response was furious, with the founder of a progressive news site accusing the representatives of "making common cause with Lauren Boebert, Marjorie Taylor Green [*sic*], JD Vance, and the rest of the MAGA crowd."[9] The letter's signatories published a retraction within twenty-four hours. The result of this militarized intransigence may well be several years of grinding, useless, stalemated conflict that fails to improve Ukraine's position when it inevitably negotiates a ceasefire.

The United States is also methodically escalating what could be an even more serious conflict with China, whose stunning economic ascent over the past several decades has reanimated the specter of great-power competition and increased the likelihood that the twenty-first century, just like much of the twentieth, will be dominated by a lengthy cold war. Similar to the war on terror, China is yet another example of domestic policy consensus across party lines in the United States even in the broader context of intensifying political polarization. Donald Trump has made criticism of China a staple of his political career since his first presidential campaign in 2016, and the Biden administration's National Security Strategy, published in October 2022, identifies China as America's "only competitor with both the intent to reshape the international order and, increasingly, the economic, diplomatic, military, and technological power to do it."[10] For at least the next ten years, the U.S. foreign policy establishment's highest priority will be to prevent China from replacing the United States as the world's primary superpower.

During this century's first decade, that replacement seemed to be inevitable. No country was better positioned than China to take advantage of the dramatic liberalization of global trade in the late twentieth century. As companies from wealthy nations sought to capitalize on liberalized trade rules by outsourcing production to places with cheaper labor than what was on offer in the affluent north, they found that China had a labor pool that was not just enormous but relatively high-skilled as well. Chinese manufacturing exploded, and the proceeds from the huge volumes of cheap exports that China sold to the

United States and other countries allowed the Chinese government to rapidly invest in the country's infrastructure. Between 1990 and 2020, Chinese per capita GDP growth, which had previously increased by less than $230 *total* over thirty years, jumped by an average $336 *per year,* rising from $318 to $10,409.[11] And between 2000 and 2011, total annual GDP growth never came in below 8 percent.[12] The projected date on which China's economy would officially become larger than America's seemed to get pushed up with each passing year.

The picture got more complicated after the global financial crisis. The resulting depression put a serious dent in Chinese export growth, the source of its enormous financial reserves and the foundation of its manufacturing expansion. As a result, China's central bank began to run up debt in order to keep infrastructure investment from drying up, and the government had to tighten its capital controls in order to keep private investors from sending their money abroad in search of higher returns. Over the past several years, this debt increase has caused a number of problems for the Chinese economy, not least in its overinflated real estate sector, and the country's economic growth, though still higher than the rest of the developed world on average, has been steadily slowing since 2008.[13] In 2007, China looked like a country preparing itself to take the reins of the global economy from the United States, perhaps as early as 2030. Now it looks more like any other country struggling to muddle through the persistent problems of overcapacity in manufacturing, high debt burdens, and slowing growth.

Nevertheless, the economic momentum of the "Chinese miracle" has not fully dissipated, and China retains several forward-looking advantages over the United States, including its still-inexpensive (though less so than before) and highly skilled workforce, its capacity for the rapid construction of infrastructure, and its deepening trade relations with countries across the global south. But at the moment it looks as though China's ascent was spurred by a happy historical coincidence—its possession of an enormous and inexpensive labor force—rather than any ability to lay the foundations for a new, qualitatively different wave of global expansion. This means that China and the United States will have to fight it out on the same playing field, navigating similar sets of economic difficulties while competing for slivers of relative advantage in a number of areas.

The first and most important of these areas, tech, is the one sector of the economy that policy makers around the world still believe could provide a solution to slowing growth, even though it has failed to do so thus far. When I say "tech" in this instance, I'm not referring to cryptocurrencies, the metaverse, or any of the other venture-capital-funded products for which "overpromise and underdeliver" seems to constitute the underlying business model. Instead, I'm referring to semiconductors, the tiny microchips that power everything from iPhones and the visual displays in automobiles to weapons systems and "smart" refrigerators. Semiconductors are now so vital to many of the world's goods and manufacturing processes that some commentators have started describing them as the "oil" of the twenty-first century, an analogy that doesn't work in all respects but still efficiently conveys their perceived importance to the modern economy. The United States is leaning hard on confrontation in the competition for semiconductor dominance, both to preserve the advantages it currently holds and to establish new ones in the future, and its attacks on China's economy have sharpened in recent years. As president, Donald Trump imposed hefty tariffs on Chinese exports in an effort to lessen America's trade deficit. The gesture was too scattershot to be effective, but it communicated a U.S. hostility to China's economic success that is now shared across party lines. Since taking office, Biden has ratcheted up the pressure even further, and his tactics are much less haphazard. The Biden administration has placed export restrictions on advanced semiconductors and other technologies in an attempt to slow the development of China's technology industry, a policy one analyst at the Center for Strategic and International Studies described as "strangling with an intent to kill."[14]

Tensions have also sharpened over the island of Taiwan, which China has sought to reabsorb ever since the Communist Party's 1949 victory over Chiang Kai-shek and his defeated Kuomintang party ended the Chinese Civil War. Taiwan is home to the most advanced semiconductor manufacturing plants in the world, and both China and the United States hope to secure control over that manufacturing capacity for decades to come. To that end, the United States agreed, in forming its new AUKUS partnership with the U.K. and Australia in 2021, to share nuclear submarine propulsion technology with the Australians, whom the United States hopes will serve as a check on China's ambitions to control regional shipping routes. Donald Trump also revived the Quad, a diplomatic project among the United States, Australia, Japan, and India, to counter Chinese influence in the Indo-Pacific, and Biden organized the first meeting of all four countries' leaders in 2021. Although the Biden administration has made some progress in improving relations with China following President Trump's untrammeled belligerence, the United States is unmistakably preparing itself for war. In early 2023, *The New York Times* published a guest op-ed by an analyst claiming that war between the United States and China is now more likely than at any time since World War II,[15] and a four-star general with the Air Force predicted that war would begin in 2025.[16]

Such a war would not only be devastating in terms of the immediate human and social costs. Another area in which China and the United States now find themselves at odds is the green transition, the complex of raw materials, manufactured goods, and energy distribution systems that will be required to move the world economy away from fossil fuels. The world is already well behind the reductions in carbon emissions that would be required to keep global warming at or below 1.5 degrees Celsius. To retain even the slightest hope of meeting that target, drastic action and close cooperation among all of the world's industrial powers are required, starting *immediately*. Together, China and the United States account for more than 40 percent of global carbon emissions, and China controls a high percentage of the raw materials required for the manufacture of crucial green-transition technologies, such as lithium-ion batteries. Should China retaliate against Biden's semiconductor export controls by imposing restrictions of its own on materials such as lithium, nickel sulfate, synthetic graphite, cobalt, and manganese—and as of November 2023 the Chinese government has announced policies to reduce exports of graphite—it will further slow a transition that is already hopelessly behind schedule.

Unlike terrorism or immigration, climate change really is an existential threat to everyone, and it is a problem that cannot be addressed at all without international cooperation. Instead, the United States and China are moving steadily toward a military confrontation that would make any meaningful cooperation impossible for years and possibly decades. Such a failure would all but guarantee that some of the worst effects of climate change will be realized in our lifetimes. By prioritizing its own continued economic supremacy over a just transition away from fossil fuels for everyone, the United States is pushing the planet toward a series of climate disasters that could render large swaths of the earth uninhabitable and destroy the lives of billions of people.

Finally, Israel's 2023 war on Palestine has revealed the extent to which America's relationship to the Middle East remains a dangerously militarized one. On October 7, Hamas and other Palestinian armed groups fired several thousand rockets and successfully breached the barrier separating Israel and Gaza, killing around 1,200 Israelis (including at least 845 civilians) and taking some 250 hostages. In response, Israel launched what is already one of the deadliest bombing campaigns in history, obliterating much of Gaza's northern half over six weeks, agreeing to a brief ceasefire that allowed for a prisoner exchange, and then starting work on destroying Gaza's southern half at the beginning of December. Israel has carried out a ground invasion of Gaza as well. More than 15,000 Palestinians have been killed as of early December 2023, with another 40,000 wounded. The dead include 250 health workers, more than 60 journalists and media workers, and at least 6,600 children.[17] With much of Gaza reduced to rubble, rescuers relying on little more than their bare hands to dig in search of casualties, and Israel making no genuine effort to avoid killing civilians, the real death toll is undoubtedly higher. Those who survive (for now) face a lack of clean water, insufficient food, a health-care system that has been largely destroyed, and no way out of the war zone.

Though the stated goal of Israel's war is to destroy Hamas and oversee the installation of a new political authority in Gaza, Israel's leaders are well aware that eliminating Hamas through military force is an impossibility. Hamas is fully embedded within the civilian population, its elaborate network of tunnels has at least some capacity to shield its fighters from the bombing, and Palestinians view the plausible replacements (such as the West Bank's governing Palestinian Authority) with disdain. Israel's actions since October 7 leave no doubt that its real goal falls somewhere between ethnic cleansing and genocide. This is not speculation. In mid-November, the finance minister for the Israeli prime minister Benjamin Netanyahu's far-right government explicitly called for ethnic cleansing, urging Palestinians to leave Gaza for other countries. "The State of Israel will no longer be able to accept the existence of an independent entity in Gaza."[18] And in early December, an Israeli newspaper reported that Netanyahu had asked one of his aides to "explore ways to 'thin out' Gaza's population."[19] This "thinning out" might be accomplished by driving Palestinians across the border with Egypt, but bombs can get the job done as well. Either way, Israel's campaign constitutes exactly the kind of war crime that international courts were established in order to prosecute. A professor of Holocaust and genocide studies has called Israel's campaign "a textbook case of genocide, unfolding in front of our eyes."[20]

The American government's support for Israel's campaign has been explicit and enthusiastic. The White House national security spokesperson John Kirby has affirmed on multiple occasions that the United States is "not drawing red lines" when it comes to Israel, and the United States also rejected a nonbinding resolution calling for a ceasefire at the United Nations. In addition to this rhetorical and diplomatic support, the United States has provided Israel with staggering amounts of military aid, totaling some $158 billion worth of equipment since the country's founding in 1948. Biden also promised that additional aid would be sent to Netanyahu's government after October 7. Without the weapons and diplomatic cover that Israel receives from its patron, it would never be able to maintain such a belligerent stance toward the Palestinians whose lives it controls, nor toward its neighbor countries in the region. "We need three things from the US," Netanyahu recently told a group of officials: "munitions, munitions, munitions."[21] So far, that is what Netanyahu is getting.

Within the United States, this support has provoked furious protests and increased the likelihood that Donald Trump will regain the White House in 2024. (Though Muslims and Arabs constitute just 1 percent of the country's population, they proved crucial to Biden's winning coalition in 2020, particularly in the Midwest. Support for Biden has plummeted among those groups since October 7.) It has also prompted concerns from anonymous officials within the Biden administration that Israel could ignite a broader and even deadlier conflagration across the region. Yemen's revolutionary Houthi group has begun launching drone and missile strikes at U.S. warships and commercial vessels, U.S. forces have been targeted by rockets in Syria and Iraq, and Israel's defense minister has suggested expanding the conflict to fight the Iran-backed group Hezbollah in Lebanon. "We should feel angry about how Netanyahu has literally put our reputation on fire to advance his personal political agenda," one State Department official said. "The collateral effects to American security are extremely consequential." Another official criticized news articles that tried to portray the United States as urging caution and restraint on the Israelis, saying, "It just feels like patting ourselves on the back while it increasingly seems like the IDF [Israel Defense Forces] are waging a campaign of ethnic cleansing."[22]

The campaign has also revealed the ease with which some of the social and political dynamics that characterized the peak years of the war on terror can come rushing back to the surface. In the years after September 11, for example, FBI informants and paranoid university administrators made it all but impossible for Muslim student associations to participate in political debate. In November 2023, Columbia University suspended Students for Justice in Palestine and Jewish Voice for Peace, student groups that had protested Israel's war without ever engaging in violence. After September 11, critics of the Bush administration were accused of supporting terrorism and actively undermining America. After October 7, commentators, politicians, and news organizations have routinely portrayed pro-Palestinian protests as antisemitic, falsely portraying antiwar activists as bigoted thugs roaming America's cities in search of Jews to harass and intimidate. After September 11, attempts to discuss the political roots of the attacks (for example, by Susan Sontag) were demonized as unthinking and reflexive anti-Americanism. After October 7, the House of Representatives overwhelmingly passed a resolution declaring that anti-Zionism—a political stance opposed to the legitimacy of a colonial state founded on one religious group's interpretation of its own scriptures—is the same thing as antisemitism. After September 11, officials and pundits exaggerated the scale of the domestic terrorist threat so as to maintain support for government surveillance of Muslim Americans, NSA bulk surveillance, and a psychotically aggressive foreign policy. And since October 7, the Israeli government has repeatedly disseminated false information about atrocities committed by Hamas, circulating stories about beheaded infants, fetuses ripped from their mothers' wombs, a systematic program of sexual violence, and the mass burning of children that it has consistently failed to substantiate with evidence. One might have thought that hundreds of murdered civilians would be outrageous enough on its own. Apparently not.

The analogy has limits, of course. The current climate of fear in the United States is still less intense than what prevailed in the fall of 2001; airports, for example, have not further tightened their security procedures because of Hamas. With that said, today's social and political climate is different only in degree, not in kind. In both cases, the people cheering on the slaughter drape their bloodlust in a hysterical rhetoric of civilizational defense against a horde of savages. In both cases, those who object to the killing are accused of being apologists for rape, murder, and torture. In both cases, the gap between public opinion and the government's rhetoric and actions is vast (as of early December, more than three-quarters of self-identified Democrats, and more than 60 percent of all voters, support a permanent cease-fire). Then and now, the goal would seem to be to recast a complex political question—in the current case, how to build peace between a nation of settler colonists and the people whose land they have occupied for decades—as a dark fairy tale, a morality play in which the only path to "peace" is the total displacement or annihilation of an ancient enemy.

Why would Biden be willing to risk the end of his presidency and the return of President Donald Trump to support a war that is so unpopular among his own supporters? One answer might be found in accepting as authentic Biden's self-presentation as someone who puts the national interest ahead of his personal success or party politics. As an ally, Israel can often seem to be more trouble than it's worth, but in the eyes of America's foreign policy establishment, it is indispensable. As Biden said in 1986 and repeated after October 7, "Were there not an Israel, the United States of America would have to invent an Israel." To be more specific, a *belligerent* Israel is a crucial component of America's strategy for the Middle East. It is an effective guarantor of American control in the region precisely because of its aggression. Its nuclear arsenal (one of the worst-kept secrets in the world) and potential willingness to use it constitute America's plan B should the United States fail to prevent Iran from acquiring nuclear weapons. Its intelligence agencies regularly assassinate members of Hezbollah, Palestinian Islamic Jihad, the Islamic Revolutionary Guard Corps in Iran, Hamas, and other groups that the United States is unable to engage directly. It is a snarling dog whose chain America threatens to loosen whenever some regional actor seems at risk of opposing the United States too strenuously. America has other regional allies, of course, including the autocratic governments of Egypt and Saudi Arabia. But it can never have full confidence in Egyptian or Saudi Arabian support, not least because of the popular discontent that the rulers of those countries must always be careful to suppress (most of the September 11 hijackers were Saudi Arabian, after all). Only with Israel, a fellow settler colony and a nation utterly dependent on American largesse, can the United States be sure it has an ally that will be there in good times and bad. It is the contemporary world's paradigmatic example of a client state.

Officially, the United States is also very concerned about the plight of the Palestinians, who for their part might be considered the contemporary world's paradigmatic example of a surplus population. Palestinians in Gaza and the West Bank are among the most surveilled, policed, imprisoned, exploited, and brutalized people on earth, subjected both to an Israeli occupation that is almost universally recognized as illegal (except by Israel and the United States) and, in the West Bank, to the predations of settlers who are always looking for an opportunity to encroach on Palestinian land, destroy the olive trees on which many Palestinians rely to make a living, and take possession of Palestinian homes. For decades, the United States has said it supports a two-state solution, meaning the formation of a Palestinian state along the borders that existed immediately preceding Israel's victory in the Six-Day War of 1967. Biden has reiterated his support for a two-state solution since October 7, and while there is no reason to doubt the personal sincerity of that support, U.S. rhetoric on the subject has long rung hollow in the ears of Palestinians and the rest of the Middle East. Israel has never negotiated in good faith to work toward an independent Palestinian state, and the United States has never pushed Israel to do so. The concrete proposals that have previously received American backing have all fallen well short of what Palestinians might reasonably consider justice, whether through an unfair division of land, the failure to affirm the right of Palestinian exiles to return to their homes, or an unwillingness on the part of Israel to grant Palestinians full sovereignty and self-governance.

American government concern for the Palestinians has had a similarly hollow ring to it since October 7. Following several weeks of unrestrained carnage, some government officials began to change their tune on whether there is a limit on Israel's right to "self-defense," persuaded by some combination of political protest in the United States, expressions of disgust from other world leaders (particularly in the global south), and the cumulative effects of spending day after day looking at images of death and destruction. Though continuing to resist calls for a ceasefire, Biden said on November 1 that he thought there should be a "pause" in the fighting so as to allow some amount of humanitarian aid to reach those trapped inside Gaza. Several weeks after that, following the humanitarian pause and subsequent resumption of hostilities, Vice President Kamala Harris visited the Middle East and announced that "under no circumstances" would the United States permit Israel to carry out the forced relocation of Palestinians from Gaza and the West Bank. Secretary of State Antony Blinken also said that Israel must have a "clear plan in place that puts a premium on protecting civilians." This rhetoric, however, has not been backed up with actions such as putting conditions on the military aid the United States provides to Israel.

As for Biden's insistence that "we need to renew our resolve to pursue this two-state solution," there are good reasons not to be optimistic, even beyond America's record of bias and insincerity in attempting to guide prior rounds of negotiations. Israel has a long history of establishing "facts on the ground" even when it knows the United States might not approve of its actions—a good pre–October 7 example is its relentless expansion of settlements in the West Bank—and then waiting patiently for the United States to decide that it can live with those facts after all. How much can a weeklong humanitarian pause matter if those who receive the aid are then immediately subjected to new rounds of bombing? What is the point of demanding that Israel have a "plan in place" for "protecting civilians" when any honest observer can see that Israel's plan is to subject the Palestinians to collective punishment? What good is insisting that the forced relocation of Palestinians will not be permitted when it is already clear that thousands of Palestinians will choose to flee rather than attempt to survive in a place that has been reduced to rubble and ash? Until the United States either threatens Israel with material consequences (such as the end of free weapons and other equipment) or attempts to extract real concessions from the Israeli government (such as the removal of its violent and fanatical settlers from the West Bank), all such rhetoric should be viewed as attempts to save face, not as constructive political engagement.

Indeed, until October 7, Biden's official plan for Palestine was to ignore it. This is yet another line of continuity between Trump and his successor. In 2020, the Trump administration finalized the Abraham Accords, an agreement under which Bahrain and the United Arab

Emirates agreed to formally recognize and establish diplomatic relations with Israel (in exchange for increased arms sales from the United States). Biden tried to build on this achievement upon taking office, tending to America's relationships with the Abraham signatories and attempting to persuade Saudi Arabia to recognize Israel as well. The hope was that by establishing productive diplomatic and trade relations among Israel and the more reactionary Arab states, the United States would be able to supervise the region from afar rather than directly. As one commentator explained, "Biden began to make good on the 'drawdown' promised by his predecessor—executing the pullout from Afghanistan while reducing troops and military assets in Iraq, Kuwait, Jordan and Saudi Arabia."[23]

The success of this plan depended, however, on the world's willingness to forget about Palestine as the United States, Israel, and its new allies enjoyed the fruits of their relationship. Rockets might still occasionally find their way from Gaza into Israel, and IDF soldiers might still "clash" with Palestinians along the border fence, but Palestinians would eventually submit to permanent occupation, and the Israelis would manage their wards judiciously, inflicting punishment when necessary but avoiding anything that might cause an international political crisis. That is the situation that Hamas exploded with its October 7 attack. And although one shouldn't underestimate America's ability to persuade the rest of the world to start looking the other way again, at the moment it would seem that there is no going back. Arab populations in the Middle East and Southeast Asia, along with South American countries such as Brazil, have reacted to the war with outrage and disgust. Bahrain, Jordan, Turkey, South Africa, Colombia, Chile, and other countries have either recalled their ambassadors to Israel or cut off diplomatic relations entirely. A significant and potentially irreparable rift has opened up between the mainstream of the Democratic Party and its left wing, and Israel itself will find it difficult or impossible to establish working relationships with its neighbors going forward. All of this has occurred because Palestinians refused to be abandoned to the occupation while the rest of the region pretended not to notice them and prepared to receive the next shipment of American military hardware. If things really are different going forward, if the fractures opened up by this war force the United States to put real pressure on Israel, for once—if and only if the ultimate result of this conflict is a just settlement for the Palestinians, then October 7 and all the carnage that followed might not have been for nothing.

In the meantime, however, Palestine, China, and Russia all indicate that the slow breakdown of the America-led world order is continuing. This is not to suggest that the United States will be out of the international power politics game in twenty-five, fifty, or even a hundred years. Nobody should blithely assume that Putin will succeed in restoring the Russian Empire to its former glory, nor that China will ever become the world's predominant superpower, nor that Palestine will have a nation to call its own by 2050. But the events unfolding in any one of these three parts of the world would be ominous for America's global standing on their own. All together, they make it hard to avoid the conclusion that America's grip on international affairs is loosening for good, that its ability to function effectively *as an empire* might have degenerated beyond repair. In order to retain their power over other countries, empires need to maintain their legitimacy. And in order to maintain their legitimacy, they need to be able to persuade the people who inhabit colonies and client states that the benefits of imperial exploitation and control outweigh the costs, even if those costs are high. Who could now call that an accurate description of America's relationship with the Middle East? To be sure, the benefits of empire remain obvious to Israel's colonists and the basket of autocrats who head up Saudi Arabia, Egypt, Bahrain, and other authoritarian states. But for the quarter of Egyptians who live in poverty, the migrant workers who keep Saudi Arabia's economy going, and the millions of Palestinians who live under Israeli rule, the United States today can be viewed as little more than a guarantor of their continued misery. The American empire may persist for many years to come, but its imperial legitimacy is quickly passing into the void of history. Even the dollar, one of the U.S. empire's most important instruments of power, isn't the behemoth it used to be. Brazilian president Luiz Inácio Lula da Silva recently called on the world's developing countries to conduct their trade in their own currencies instead, a shift that would meaningfully diminish America's power to impose its will via economic sanctions. "Who was it that decided that the dollar was the currency after the disappearance of the gold standard?" he asked in a speech at the New Development Bank in Shanghai.[24] Ending the dollar's reserve currency status is not a realistic proposition in the short term, but it is not something a politician like Lula could have dreamed of suggesting twenty years ago.

An important caveat: Just as a nation state's ascent from aspiring geopolitical heavyweight to imperial hegemon never unfolds along a smooth and always upward-sloping path, one should not expect a declining hegemon to gently slip back into the middle strata of world power politics at a regular, even rate. There are inevitably ups and downs along the way, moments when an ascending state will appear to have lost the plot and missed its chance at great power status, and moments when a declining power will have appeared to put the ship back on course. These "moments" can last for many years. The last time the global economic order broke down and reconstituted itself around a new leading power, it took three decades for World War II to complete the work that began with World War I, and the premonitions and consequences of that revolution in global affairs unfolded for decades on either side of that thirty-year period. With the United States posting strong GDP growth figures in 2021 and avoiding a recession entirely in 2023 despite the challenges posed by high inflation, it can be tempting to believe that the COVID-19 crisis inadvertently helped America to crack the code of twenty-first-century economic success: revitalized industrial policy focused on tech and renewable energy, tight labor markets, and monetary policy that keeps a firm hand on the reins of an economic expansion without panicking and driving interest rates high enough to stop that expansion in its tracks.

That conclusion, however, would be premature, because the central issues that have driven America's economic decline since the 1970s remain unresolved. Manufacturing overcapacity around the world is already causing difficulties for the green transition, with China's mammoth investments into electric vehicle production threatening to lower profitability for other manufacturers and discourage investment. The United States economy also remains dangerously reliant on asset price inflation, with home prices and rents increasing dramatically since the bottom of the 2020 downturn and the stock market overly reliant on a tiny handful of tech industry giants. In addition, the American empire cannot succeed on the back of domestic economic success alone. As superintendent of a global capitalist economy, the United States needs to fuel global economic activity, but the very policies that have strengthened the American economy over the past few years have only exacerbated the zero-sum dynamics of slowing global growth. Efforts to "decouple" America's economy from Chinese manufacturing have been a drag on China, the world's fastest-growing economy over the past twenty years, and the federal government's subsidies for green manufacturing at home have made green investment in Europe comparatively less attractive, with ominous implications for Europe's growth potential going forward. In short, even if some combination of green industrial policy, a slightly higher baseline level of inflation, and hard-nosed economic diplomacy makes it possible for the United States to maintain or even enlarge its own slice of the global economic pie, it will do nothing to change the fact that for the rest of the world, the pie is either shrinking or not growing fast enough. That leaves the United States where it was back in the early 2000s, increasingly relying on the military to manage crises and prop up autocrats around the world.

For the first time in a generation, the United States is looking around and finding itself part of a multipolar world, one that will be impossible to navigate without a concerted emphasis on mutually beneficial diplomacy. But the United States is not putting an emphasis on diplomacy, on discovering constructive ways to adapt to the coming end of its hegemony. Instead, it is rushing into a new cold war without the key economic advantage that secured its victory in the last one: its ability to fuel and coordinate global economic growth. Rather than exploring the productive roles it might play in this multipolar world order, America is doubling down on war on terror belligerence. For fifteen years, the war on terror defined the terms in which American politicians allowed themselves to think. Their apparent inability to start thinking in different terms now that the war has ended bodes poorly for the rest of the twenty-first century.

• • •

In epilogues to books like this one, authors are sometimes expected to propose a few reforms, to offer their readers hope that the problems they have just wrestled with for several hundred pages could be addressed with a few well-targeted laws and changes to the country's system of governance. In a book on America's declining life expectancy, a writer might advocate for the implementation of government-funded health care. In a book on gun violence, they might call for a ban on assault weapons and the imposition of universal background checks. A book on economic inequality would highlight increased union membership and higher income, wealth, and estate taxes as part of a potential solution. Since this is a book about the war on terror, the obvious way for me to meet this expectation would be to demand that Congress revoke its Authorization for Use of Military Force, stringently apply the provisions of the War Powers Act to the executive branch, shut down the intelligence community's mass surveillance operation, hold trials for anyone who participated in torture or extrajudicial assassination, ban the sale of military equipment to domestic law enforcement agencies, pay reparations to the immigrant families who were targeted by the FBI, and reduce the military's federal budget by at least 50 percent. If I also wanted to include a few more unlikely proposals in order to expand people's conception of what is possible, I might suggest that a Department of Peace be made a cabinet-level office within the executive branch. I would point out that some Americans have been advocating for such a department since 1793, when Benjamin Rush, who signed the Declaration of Independence, made the proposal in an almanac. In doing so, I would demonstrate that the solutions to America's problems can already be found in a neglected corner of American history, and that with a little publicity and organizational effort, those solutions might help to put the country back on the just and prosperous course its founders envisioned nearly 250 years ago.

I would be thrilled to see any and all of the above come to pass. Unfortunately, I don't believe that policy wish lists are adequate to the historical moment in which we're all currently living, and I don't think the answers to America's problems lie in America's past. In order to publish such a wish list, you have to believe that the government is capable, or could be capable in the future, of actually enacting the necessary reforms. I don't. Washington is a place where progressive reform is difficult even under the best of circumstances, and we have not been living under the best of circumstances in the twenty-first century so far. The Senate, which grants each state equal representation no matter the size of their respective populations, puts a heavy finger on the Republican side of the scale, giving the half a million conservative residents of Wyoming the same legislative clout as twenty million New Yorkers. Mitch McConnell, Senate leader of the Republican Party since 2007, has used his time in office to pack the federal courts with conservative justices, building a sturdy judicial firewall against any reforms that might happen to find their way through the legislature. Gerrymandering at the state level tips the scales even further toward reaction. And with power so concentrated in the executive branch, particularly power over foreign policy and military decision making, citizens have little to no say on issues such as where America's troops will go next. When people took to the streets and demanded reforms starting in 2015, conservatives took one of the words the protesters used to define their aspirations—"woke," meaning the awareness that systemic social injustices need to be addressed— and turned it into a slur. One prominent Republican governor with aspirations to national office has said he would like to turn his state into a place "where 'woke' goes to die."

The Republican Party is by no means some kind of unstoppable juggernaut. It has struggled with internal divisions since the failure of the Iraq War and the election of Barack Obama. The policy positions it most relies on to mobilize its base in primary elections, particularly the criminalization of abortion, are deeply unpopular among the wider public. Its last two presidents both took office after losing the national popular vote. Committed to a policy platform that cannot hope to win at the ballot box, the GOP now more or less consciously understands itself as a minoritarian political movement, one that must devote itself to restricting access to the vote and sowing doubt about the legitimacy of the electoral process whenever that process doesn't produce the desired result. Its standard-bearer is well past retirement age and facing multiple criminal indictments, and the pool of talent that might replace him is extremely shallow. The party is vulnerable, and those vulnerabilities are only going to increase over the coming years.

In terms of the war on terror, however, none of the above matters all that much, because the militarization of America's relationship to the rest of the world is one of the only remaining policy areas on which both major parties largely agree. (Republicans are now tired of funding Ukraine's self-defense and would be more or less content to see Russia come out of the war with some extra territory, but that position is not the product of any principled antimilitarism, as evidenced by some prominent Republicans' belief that the United States should combat drug smuggling by bombing or even invading Mexico.) The war on terror can help us to see the limitations of analyzing American politics in terms of "polarization." The most important political story of the past two decades isn't the intensifying conflict between Republicans and Democrats. It is the story of an empire, a world-spanning political and economic system, that clawed its way to the top of the global power hierarchy and is now determined to imprison and kill as many people as it needs to in order to stay there. If that sounds like hyperbole to you, take it up with the Afghans, Iraqis, Yemenis, Pakistanis, Somalis, Palestinians, Muslim and Arab Americans, and activists who have found themselves in the crosshairs of the war on terror over the past twenty years. During that time, both parties managed at some point to win control of the White House along with both chambers of Congress, but there have been no major reversals of America's ongoing militarization of the world. In the eyes of the government as a whole, there is no other choice. It is wedded to an economic system that is increasingly unable to provide most people with a stable material life, but it governs a population that demands unlimited and uninterrupted access to inexpensive consumer goods. It is America's privileged position at the head of that economic system that makes that access possible. As the global economy slows down and swells the ranks of the world's surplus population—and despite recent flashy growth figures in the United States, global growth continues to weaken—the United States has sent in troops and launched drones to manage them while drawing on its own racist mythologies in order to justify their deaths. When Americans have protested against the worsening conditions they see wherever they turn, the government has used militarized police forces to terrorize and beat them into submission. And as capital continues to spew carbon into the atmosphere and degrade the planet's habitability, the United States, as capital's chief political representative, will send its armies, cops, and surveillance technologies after the millions of refugees who are soon likely to find themselves wandering the earth in search of dry land. This response to climate migration is already a conscious part of the government's future plans: The Pentagon and the White House have been discussing climate change as a "national security threat" for more than fifteen years.[25]

It is an unpleasant fact of politics that the good intentions of individuals are decisively constrained by the systems in which they work. The American imperial system, which structures, guides, and restricts the lives of countless people abroad as well as its own citizens, is not interested in reforming itself. Indeed, its continued survival depends on its not reforming itself. Most people do not want to live in a militarized, surveillance-intensive world that has been rendered uninhabitable so that profit margins can be sustained at acceptable levels, but the American system that organizes the world is not primarily concerned with what most people want. Like all political-economic systems, and like all empires, it will come to an end eventually, but there is no way of knowing when, or how, or what exactly the decisive spark will be. What can be said of our moment is that we are living in a period of deep and widespread crisis, a situation the Italian thinker Antonio Gramsci defined as one in which "the old is dying and the new cannot be born." That is a tough spot to inhabit. In the short to medium term, the likeliest outcome for the United States and for much of the rest of the world is that things are going to get significantly worse—politically, economically, socially, and ecologically—before they begin to get better. Even if carbon emissions were to permanently drop to zero today, temperatures would continue to increase for some time, sea levels would keep rising for centuries, and it could well take a thousand years or more for temperatures to return to their preindustrial levels. That reality raises what I think is a sobering but unavoidable question for our shared historical moment: How should a person think and live in a world that offers hope, but potentially not for you?

• • •

One way to begin answering that question is to remember another phrase Gramsci liked: "pessimism of the intellect, optimism of the will." In other words, do not trick yourself into seeing things as better than they are, but behave and act as though justice were within reach. Over the past decade, activists have been our exemplary practitioners of optimism of the will. I've already talked in this book about the Arab Spring, Occupy Wall Street, and Black Lives Matter, but there is also a fourth protest movement that emerged during the Obama years, one I've not yet mentioned, which may prove to have a deep historical resonance. In December 2014, a Texas oil company called Energy Transfer Partners filed a federal application to build a twelve-hundred-mile pipeline. The proposed Dakota Access Pipeline would carry oil down from North Dakota to Illinois. Along the way, it would cross underneath Lake Oahe, which served as the primary source of drinking water for the Cheyenne River and Standing Rock Sioux nations. Indigenous leaders also objected on the grounds that the pipeline's construction would likely destroy several sacred burial sites. When those objections fell on deaf ears, a coalition of Standing Rock and other indigenous communities established a camp to block the pipeline's construction. As the Kul Wicasa scholar Nick Estes wrote in his book on the protests, it was the first time in more than a century that "all seven nations of Dakota-, Nakota-, and Lakota-speaking peoples" had gathered in one place to work toward one goal. And when North Dakota's governor, Jack Dalrymple, declared a state of emergency in August 2016 to defeat the protests and ensure the pipeline's completion, the camp began to attract supporters, indigenous and otherwise, from around the country and the world. "At its peak," Estes writes, "the camp was North Dakota's tenth-largest city. Its population surpassed 10,000 people, possibly reaching as many as 15,000."[26] The protesters called themselves "water protectors."

The Dakota Access protests took inspiration from Occupy, BLM, and the Arab Spring in focusing on occupying physical space for as long as possible (they held out for about eleven months). The war on terror had destroyed many of the country's public spaces and made it difficult for people to gather in the ones that remained, and protesters responded by conjuring new public spaces into being, places where people could speak, learn, care and be cared for, and collectively work toward discovering better ways to live. The people who lived at Oceti Sakowin fed thousands every day, handed out clothing, prayed together, provided medical treatment to the injured, trained new arrivals in protest tactics, and even established a school for children. The protest also drew a bright line connecting the concerns of local communities to the larger fate of the biosphere. The Dakota Access Pipeline specifically threatened the water on which the Sioux nations depended, but *all* fossil fuel pipelines are threats to the future habitability of the planet, no matter what part of the land they traverse. The Dakota Access protesters took that threat seriously. In doing so, they put up the stiffest resistance yet seen to the further expansion of the U.S. fossil fuel industry, and they also modeled the kind of society that might exist in a world no longer determined to burn itself to ash.

The government's response to Standing Rock was overwhelming. The last time the State of North Dakota had mobilized so many law enforcement and military personnel, it was to massacre nearly three hundred Lakota at Wounded Knee in 1890. Law enforcement from seventy-six separate jurisdictions traveled to Standing Rock, along with members of the National Guard and private contractors working for TigerSwan, a firm that got its start assisting U.S. military personnel in Iraq. Kitted out with surplus military equipment provided by the Defense Department's 1033 Program, the cops menaced protesters with assault weapons and MRAP vehicles. Using rubber bullets and beanbag rounds, they injured some two hundred protesters, and many had to be treated for hypothermia after being doused in pepper-spray-laced water in freezing temperatures. When law enforcement finally cleared the encampment in February 2017, they had arrested 832 people, and a few were sentenced to years in prison.[27]

More recently, in 2021, a group of activists inspired by Standing Rock's example began protesting the construction of a $90 million police training facility in the Atlanta forest. Calling themselves "forest defenders" and marching under the banner "Stop Cop City," these protesters tried to expand on the work done at Standing Rock by linking the fight against climate change to the struggle against America's militarized police forces. As Standing Rock pointed out that the threats from climate change scale all the way up from the local to the planetary, Atlanta's forest defenders have understood that a successful struggle to preserve the earth will have to run through the police powers the state mobilizes to protect fossil fuel extraction. Earlier in this book, I talked about Major Ralph Peters, who concluded in his 1996 article on the coming era of urban combat that "building realistic 'cities' in which to train would be prohibitively expensive." That conclusion turned out to be premature. The plans for Cop City, which is officially named the Atlanta Public Safety Training Center, include not just classrooms and a shooting range but also a whole model city, where police trainees will be taught how to suppress the kinds of urban protest movements that have exploded all over the country in the past decade. The forest defenders saw this clearly, too, and mobilized to shut down the project before it had a chance to get off the ground. This time the police response was even more extreme. The police arrested dozens of protesters in late 2022 and early 2023, and the State of Georgia eventually charged forty-two of them with "domestic terrorism," a crime that carries a thirty-five-year prison sentence. In January 2023, they also shot and killed the twenty-six-year-old activist Manuel "Tortuguita" Terán. The police claimed that Terán fired first. When Terán's autopsy report was finally made public three months after his death, it revealed that the police shot him fifty-seven times. A special prosecutor with the Georgia Bureau of Investigation supported the officers' version of events in an October 2023 report, but the state has refused to release the evidence on which the report's conclusions are based, a decision described by one civil rights attorney as "unique and chilling."[28] It was the first time in modern American history that police had killed an environmental activist.[29] It will not be the last. As people mobilize in the coming years to prevent climate change from forcing hundreds of millions into permanent homelessness, law enforcement in the United States and around the world will be waiting, armed with the training, heavy weaponry, and free rein to inflict violence that the war on terror provided to them.

What made the Standing Rock protest different from its immediate predecessors was the way it thought about sovereignty. Occupy Wall Street and (to a certain extent) the first iteration of Black Lives Matter articulated most of their demands as appeals for help from the U.S. government. Occupy asked the government to raise taxes on the wealthy, reverse the Supreme Court's decision in *Citizens United v. FEC,* and get big money out of the political process. Black Lives Matter asked federal, state, and municipal governments to ban abusive practices such as stop and frisk, require police officers to wear body cameras, and in some cases pull police officers off the streets entirely. Black Lives Matter included more radical actions as well, but both movements fundamentally believed that their goals could not be achieved unless the U.S. government was willing to cooperate. Standing Rock framed the situation in a different way. It is one thing to ask the government you recognize as legitimate to refrain from building any more oil pipelines. It is another to assert that the government never had the right to build any pipelines because it stole the land from your ancestors. In his book on the protests, Nick Estes quoted something his grandfather wrote in a history of the Kul Wicasa: "My people were civilized before the white man came and we will be civilized and be here after the white man goes away, poisoned by his misuse of the land and eaten up by his own greed."[30] Standing Rock didn't just dispute the wisdom of building a pipeline; it disputed the United States' claim to the land itself. It disputed the assumption on which the whole U.S. project rests, which is that the North American continent exists for the economic benefit of European settlers who built themselves a country out of the dispossession of the land's original inhabitants. "How can settler society, which possesses no fundamental ethical relationship to the land or its original people, imagine a future premised on justice?" Estes wrote. "Whatever the answer may be, Indigenous peoples must lead the way." At Standing Rock, they led by example, strengthening and publicizing a way of life that sees the water on which their community depends as a living part of that community rather than a resource to be exploited. "If the water, a relative, is not protected," Estes wrote, "then the river is not free, and neither are its people."[31] In the final chapter of his book, Estes posed a question. "Indigenous resistance is not a one-time event," he wrote. "It continually asks: What proliferates in the absence of empire?"[32]

I'm not claiming here that Standing Rock is a literal, practical model for how people will put their societies and ecosystems back on a sustainable path. The National Guard and various law enforcement agencies were able to bring the occupation to an end once they put their minds to it, and they are more than prepared to do it again if other occupations emerge. There is no one model for change, no single example for everyone to imitate, no skeleton key that will unlock a better future. Intellectually, however, to see and hear Standing Rock's vision not just articulated but realized, however briefly, opened up spaces for thought that hadn't previously been available, and it was personally clarifying to me as I struggled to understand the war I have lived through for a majority of my time on earth.

My public school civics education was basically founded on two premises. The first, as I've already discussed, was that history had ended: Humans had tried many different kinds of government over several thousand years, and U.S.-style capitalism and liberal democracy had turned out to be the best. Whatever happened going forward, it wasn't going to involve the kinds of revolutions and upheavals that characterized the past. The second premise was that the United States was something more than a country. Yes, it had a certain structure of government and a particular set of economic arrangements, but it also embodied an ethics, a belief in universal equality, a vision of human freedom—everything evoked by the famous seventeenth-century sermon about "a city upon a hill" and the moving opening words of the Declaration of Independence. September 11 disabused me of the first premise, but the second proved to be more tenacious. It's not that I believed the whole story about America's shining moral example. I knew about slavery and racism, segregation and sexism, My Lai and nuclear weapons, Japanese internment camps and the federal government's homophobic response to AIDS. But I had been taught to understand these things as mistakes, deviations from what the country actually stood for. In the early years of the war on terror— that is, during my adolescence—this was a common way for liberals and progressives, among whom I counted myself, to understand what was going on. When the investigative reporter Jane Mayer published her book on the Bush administration's torture program, its subtitle called the war on terror a "war on American ideals." That book came out in 2008, several months before Barack Obama won the presidency. At the time, I shared all of the assumptions embedded in that subtitle.

After the Democrats took control of both Congress and the White House in 2008, however, those assumptions made understanding the war more difficult. If torture violated America's commitment to universal human dignity, why wasn't Obama's Justice Department prosecuting anyone who had built the torture program? If the Iraq War violated principles of national sovereignty, why didn't Obama withdraw America's troops? If surveillance violated constitutional protections against unreasonable searches, why did the Obama administration facilitate an expansion of government surveillance? By 2012, I was so upset with Obama's expansion and institutionalization of the war that I couldn't bring myself to vote for his reelection. I was driving through Texas on Election Day, traveling from Los Angeles to Miami to conduct research for another book. I spent the day in a foul mood, listening to news on the radio as I worked my way east on Interstate 10 from El Paso to Austin. That night I stayed with a high school friend and accompanied him and a few other people to a bar to watch the results come in on CNN. I didn't tell any of them about not voting. I knew it was a useless gesture, and I also knew it didn't really matter, so why was it making me feel so bad? I didn't know why I had done it, and I didn't know what else I could have done instead.

The conclusion that I now believe I was avoiding back in 2012 is that it drastically oversimplifies things to say that the war on terror betrayed America's values. In many respects, it embodied them. Part of the reality that needs to be faced going forward is that notions of American ideals will not be sufficient to guide us through the rest of the century. As Richard Slotkin wrote, it is "through myths [that] the psychology and world view of our cultural ancestors are transmitted to modern descendants," myths that allow people to understand the values and ideals of the country in which they live.[33] Even a cursory look at the figures and characters who inhabit American mythology reveals a darker set of ideals than universal liberation and individual dignity. The "pioneers" who set out west in their covered wagons embodied ideals of unlimited economic expansion, internal imperialism that turned external once it gathered sufficient strength, and an economy so dynamic as to render the old constraints of time and space all but irrelevant. In James Fenimore Cooper's Hawkeye, we find a hero so proficient, skilled, and self-sustaining—whether hunting, tracking, or surviving off the land—that he has no real need of community. And in the cowboys, roughriders, and Indian fighters of the American West, we find a people for whom violence is not just a duty but a pleasure, a means of spiritual renewal, a bloody wellspring of national genius. At the end of his first book on American mythology, Slotkin stepped back and surveyed America's myth figures as a group. From a distance, he wrote, they "have an air of simplicity and purity that makes them seem finely heroic expressions of an admirable quality of the human spirit."

> But their apparent independence of time and consequence is an illusion; a closely woven chain of time and consequence binds their world to ours. Set the statuesque figures and their piled trophies in motion through space and time, and a more familiar landscape emerges—the whale, buffalo, and bear hunted to the verge of extinction for pleasure in killing and "scalped" for fame and the profit in hides by men like Buffalo Bill; the buffalo meat left to rot, till acres of prairie were covered with heaps of whitening bones, and the bones then ground for fertilizer; the Indian debased, impoverished, and killed in return for his gifts; the land and its people, its "dark" people especially, economically exploited and wasted; the warfare between man and nature, between race and race, exalted as a kind of heroic ideal; the piles of wrecked and rusted cars, heaped like Tartar pyramids of death-cracked, weather-browned, rain-rotted skulls, to signify our passage through the land.[34]

This is a horrifying description of what America "stands for," one that I imagine most Americans would rather reject or ignore. And yet reading it helps to make sense of the war on terror, and without denying the consolations of looking away and plugging one's ears, they cannot compete with the consolation of being able to see the world as it is. In the figure of Buffalo Bill, killing indiscriminately for pleasure and fame, one sees a reflection of the Navy SEAL Chris Kyle, the sniper who insisted that every single one of the dozens of Iraqis he personally killed deserved to die by his hand. In the exaltation of race war as "a kind of heroic ideal," one can hear Christopher Hitchens and the satisfaction he took in the prospect of "a war to the finish between everything I love and everything I hate." And the blasted landscape that concludes Slotkin's vision, scattered with mechanical wreckage and buffalo skulls, recalls news footage of Baghdad, Fallujah, Kabul, Mogadishu, and all of the other cities that have been visited by America's armies over the past twenty years. Keeping these images in mind as authentic representations of America's values also helps to clarify why it is that those Americans who excused or endorsed the worst abuses of the war on terror also have the easiest time understanding themselves as patriots. Why is it that people who supported the invasion of Iraq are also the most eager to embrace the flag? Why is it that those who endorsed or excused indefinite detention, extraordinary rendition, and torture also chant "U-S-A" the loudest? Why is it that the people who are quickest to identify themselves as pro-America are also more likely to think that Islam is incompatible with being American? For much of the war, I was told again and again that those people were simply deluded about what patriotism is and what American ideals are. The likelier explanation is that those people weren't deluded at all.

There are two issues at work here. One is nationalism, people's emotional and intellectual identification with their own country and its interests, especially to the exclusion or detriment of people living in other countries. The second is imperialism, which is how nationalism tricks itself into believing that its own interests are those of the whole world. Nationalism has had different associations, valences, and politics over time, but in the twenty-first century, and particularly in the imperial United States, it is an impediment to solving the global problems that confront us. There is no version of American nationalism that can help to solve the climate crisis (the quintessentially global issue), and there is no version of empire that can help us lessen America's military footprint around the world or do justice to the millions of climate refugees who will leave their homes in search of safety over the coming decades. The problem is not only that America's national and imperial interests are served by drone campaigns, special ops raids, and economic policies that exploit those living outside America's borders. It is that nationalism makes it harder to see that politicians' insistence on dividing the problems they confront into matters of foreign policy and domestic policy is based on a false separation.

As the United States moves further into the twenty-first century, Americans are going to make the painful discovery, again and again, that the problems they face at home and the problems they confront abroad are actually parts of the same problem.

In that light, the recent protests against Israel's war on Gaza have been remarkable. For more than a decade, America's major protest movements (and its most prominent progressive politicians) have been laser focused on the domestic, from Occupy Wall Street's obsession with *Citizens United,* to Bernie Sanders's "millionaires and billionaires," to the refusal by Black Lives Matter to notice that policing at home and U.S. militarism abroad are components of the same project. These blind spots were understandable in groups of activists trying to teach themselves how to protest almost from scratch, but they had to be overcome: Activists living in a country that is also an empire cannot afford the luxury of only trying to influence what happens inside their own borders, nor can they afford to think only in terms of what America's actions mean for Americans. With the protests against Israel, twenty-first-century American activists have become internationalist for the first time. While support for Israel and its war on Gaza is undoubtedly in America's strategic national interest, these protesters have decided that their own interests lie elsewhere, that they do not identify with their country's imperial ambitions, that their lives and those of the Palestinians are tied together, and that the barbarism in Gaza is an extension of the brutal treatment of surplus populations that harms their own communities (consider the chant "NYPD, KKK, IDF you're all the same").

The acuity of their insight may be measured by the viciousness with which much of the American government and many of the country's key institutions have responded. Prominent CEOs have vowed that their companies will not hire people who criticize Israel. Student activist groups have been banned from campuses, their members falsely accused of antisemitism, and the media seems to have accepted the lie that protesting on behalf of besieged Palestinians amounts to calling for the extermination of the world's Jews. In late November 2023, a white man approached three college students of Palestinian descent on the street in Vermont, two of whom were wearing keffi-yehs, and shot them. Meanwhile, university presidents testify before Congress and fall over themselves in agreeing that the alleged anti-semitism of student protesters is the real problem menacing student life. The same groups that have spent recent years cynically ringing the alarm about the death of free speech in the United States now ad-vocate for repression in defense of impunity for America's most val-ued client state.

It is by no means a certainty, but there is a real chance that by the time this book is published, Israel will have completed its ethnic cleansing of Gaza and the West Bank. It is almost a certainty that we will blow past the 1.5-degree threshold for warding off the worst con-sequences of our industrial recklessness. In my lifetime, we are likely to see small island nations and great coastal cities vanish beneath the waves, their inhabitants searching frantically for refuge. No one who has been paying attention can be surprised if the next fifty years bring intensifying conflicts between autocrats and insurgents, eruptions of violence as people fight for drinkable water, and a global right wing that continues to gather strength as it fortifies the border walls. For all their ingenuity, commitment, and courage, today's activists may see their goals thwarted, find that the moment of opportunity never ar-rives, that the political space they need in order to build something new simply refuses to open. But even if all that comes to pass, it will not diminish the importance of the work being done in our own time. Every thought, argument, protest, and occupation lays another stone in the foundation on which others will eventually stand. Each social movement that fails to achieve its goals in the near term still emerges with experience and knowledge that could not have been gained in any other way. Each frustrated effort to seek justice communicates something indispensable to the people who make the next effort. And the writing of history is not only an attempt to make the past intelli-gible to the present; it is an effort to turn the present into something the future can use. One day, the political space people need is going to open. By keeping that day in mind, and in working now to assist those who will seize the opportunities it presents, we can entertain the hope that our descendants will look back on us with something other than anger and shame.

There are many millions of people living in the United States who don't want to make war on Arabs, Muslims, or China to preserve America's economic privileges. They don't want to see protesters and refugees beaten, demonized, jailed, and killed. They don't want fossil fuels to lay waste to what remains of our biosphere, and they don't want the world's working poor to be sacrificed on the altar of unending American supremacy. In the decades to come, some of those people are going to find ways of changing and living in society that don't require a militarized world of SWAT teams, armored police vehicles, fortified borders, surveillance, night raids, secret prisons, and bombs, if only because they have no other choice. Today, it is impossible to say exactly what those solutions will look like, but we do know that they will not be imperial, for empire today can function only as a means of exploiting one half of the world for the benefit of the other. We also know (whether we want to or not) that with each passing year, each new border fence, each surveillance database, each drone strike, and each Special Forces raid, it becomes less likely that our descendants will use the word "American" to describe the solutions they eventually find.

ACKNOWLEDGMENTS

I would like to thank some of the people who have helped me to learn, think, and write about the war on terror over the past decade.

Thank you to everyone (and I do mean everyone) at *n+1*, my intellectual home. I'm grateful for the care and insight you have put into soliciting, editing, criticizing, and publishing my work. In particular, I want to thank the three people who have edited most of my writing on the war. The first is Keith Gessen, who told me, in response to my first piece on the subject, "You're a terrific writer, and you've pulled this off, but I don't approve." You were right, and I'm sorry. The second is Nikil Saval, who made sure I actually knew what I was talking about before abandoning me for politics and the glamour of Harrisburg, Pennsylvania. The third is Mark Krotov, who keeps giving me reasons to come back and write the next article. Writing is lonely—the three of you have made it less so.

Thanks also to those who assisted with the research for this book, including Lois Beckett, Andrew Cockburn, Rory Fanning, Thomas Gokey, Steve Graham, Sarah Harwell, Katherine Hughes, Lisa Ling, Kathy Manley, Tyler Maxin, Edward Menkin, Peter Romaniuk, Lyle Jeremy Rubin, and David Felix Sutcliffe.

Many people read drafts of the proposal and manuscript, entertained my questions and speculations, or even invited me to discuss aspects of the war in public. Their questions and suggested improvements were invaluable. Thank you to Atossa Araxia Abrahamian, Tim Barker, Lisa Borst, Matthew Shen Goodman, Elizabeth Gumport, Malcolm Harris, Tobi Haslett, Laura Kolbe, Simone Liu, Andrew Martin, Rachel Ossip, Sarah Resnick, and Stephen Squibb.

Thank you to my editor, Kevin Doughten, and my agent, Jim Rutman, for your support, wisdom, patience, and insight. I'm grateful for your belief in my writing and your determination to make it better.

Thank you to everyone else at Crown who shepherded the book through the publication process: Dustin Amick, Gillian Blake, Julie Cepler, David Drake, Mason Eng, Liana Faughnan, Deborah Foley, Anna Kochman, Andrea Lau, Amy Li, Carol McKenna, Dan Novack, Annsley Rosner, Stacey Stein, Ingrid Sterner, Christine Tanigawa, and Eldes Tran.

Thank you to Sally Snodgrass, my grandmother, who passed away in 2022. You taught me that the best way to take pleasure in life is to be curious about the world, the people around you, and yourself. That lesson is why I became a writer, and I miss you terribly.

Finally, thank you to Kelley Deane McKinney. It was true in 2015, and it's true now: You have all my love, for as long as you want it.

NOTES

Introduction: For the Beauty of the Earth

1. George W. Bush, Proclamation, "Declaration of National Emergency by Reason of Certain Terrorist Attacks, 2001, Proclamation 7463 of September 14, 2001," *Federal Register* 66, no. 181 (Sept. 14, 2001): 48199, www.govinfo.gov/content/pkg/FR-2001-09-18/pdf/01-23358.pdf.

2. "Military Decorations and Awards Review Results," U.S. Department of Defense, accessed Feb. 18, 2022, upload.wikimedia.org/wikipedia/commons/3/31/Military_Decorations_and_Awards_Review_Results_%28January_2016%29.pdf.

3. Authorization for Use of Military Force, Pub. L. No. 107-40, 115 Stat. 224 (2001).

4. Mark Landler, "20 Years On, the War on Terror Grinds Along, with No End in Sight," *New York Times,* Sept. 10, 2021, www.nytimes.com/2021/09/10/world/europe/war-on-terror-bush-biden-qaeda.html.

5. "Most Wanted Terrorist Dead: Bin Laden Killed in 'Targeted Operation,'" FBI News, May 2, 2011, www.fbi.gov/news/stories/bin-laden-killed.

6. Neta C. Crawford and Catherine Lutz, "Human Cost of Post-9/11 Wars: Direct War Deaths in Major War Zones," 20 Years of War: A Costs of War Research Series, Sept. 1, 2021, watson.brown.edu/costsofwar/files/cow/imce/papers/2021/Costs%20of%20War_Direct%20War%20Deaths_9.1.21.pdf.

7. "'Islam Is Peace' Says President: Remarks by the President at Islamic Center of Washington, D.C.," White House press release, Sept. 17, 2001, georgewbush-whitehouse.archives.gov/news/releases/2001/09/20010917-11.html.

8. Linda J. Bilmes, "Where Did the $5Tn Spent on Afghanistan and Iraq Go? Here's Where," *Guardian,* Sept. 11, 2021, www.theguardian.com/commentisfree/2021/sep/11/us-afghanistan-iraq-defense-spending.

9. Elisabeth Bumiller, "U.S. Lifts Photo Ban on Military Coffins," *New York Times,* Dec. 7, 2009, www.nytimes.com/2009/02/27/world/americas/27iht-photos.1.20479953.html.

10. Heidi Peltier, "The Growth of the 'Camo Economy' and the Commercialization of the Post-9/11 Wars," 20 Years of War, June 30, 2020, watson.brown.edu/costsofwar/files/cow/imce/papers/2020/Peltier%202020%20-%20Growth%20of%20Camo%20Economy%20-%20June%2030%202020%20-%20FINAL.pdf.

11. Alex Horton and Aaron Gregg, "Use of Military Contractors Shrouds True Costs of War. Washington Wants It That Way, Study Says," *Washington Post,* June 30, 2020, www.washingtonpost.com/national-security/2020/06/30/military-contractor-study.

12. Jessica Purkiss and Jack Serle, "Obama's Covert Drone War in Numbers: Ten Times More Strikes Than Bush," Bureau of Investigative Journalism, Jan. 17, 2017, www.thebureauinvestigates.com/stories/2017-01-17/obamas-covert-drone-war-in-numbers-ten-times-more-strikes-than-bush.

13. Donald Trump (@realDonaldTrump), Twitter, Oct. 9, 2019, 7:36 a.m., twitter.com/realDonaldTrump/status/1181896127471333381.

14. "Excerpts from Bush Speech on Travel," *New York Times,* Sept. 28, 2001, www.nytimes.com/2001/09/28/us/a-nation-challenged-excerpts-from-bush-speech-on-travel.html.

15. "The President's News Conference with President François Hollande of France," transcript, Nov. 24, 2015, www.govinfo.gov/content/pkg/DCPD-201500839/html/DCPD-201500839.htm.

16. Charles Krauthammer, "The Greater the Evil, the More It Disarms," *Time,* Sept. 24, 2001, content.time.com/time/subscriber/article/0,33009,1000889,00.html.

17. John Lanchester, *How to Speak Money: What the Money People Say—and What It Really Means* (New York: W. W. Norton, 2014), xiv.

18. Jonathan Nitzan and Shimshon Bichler, *The Global Political Economy of Israel* (London: Pluto Press, 2002), 2.

19. "Satisfaction with the United States," Gallup News, accessed March 7, 2022, news.gallup.com/poll/1669/general-mood-country.aspx.

20. R. J. Reinhart, "Terrorism Fears Drive More in U.S. to Avoid Crowds," Gallup News, June 20, 2017, news.gallup.com/poll/212654/terrorism-fears-drive-avoid-crowds.aspx.

21. Joel Rose and Liz Baker, "6 in 10 Americans Say U.S. Democracy Is in Crisis as the 'Big Lie' Takes Root," NPR, Jan. 3, 2022, www.npr.org/2022/01/03/1069764164/american-democracy-poll-jan-6.

22. Richard Falk, "Resisting the Global Domination Project," interview, *Frontline,* April 25, 2003, frontline.thehindu.com/cover-story/article30216662.ece.

23. David Johnston and Charlie Savage, "Obama Reluctant to Look into Bush Programs," *New York Times,* Jan. 11, 2009, www.nytimes.com/2009/01/12/us/politics/12inquire.html.

24. Mike Davis, "Thanatos Triumphant," *New Left Review,* March 7, 2022, newleftreview.org/sidecar/posts/thanatos-triumphant.

Chapter 1: No Time Zones

1. Garrett M. Graff, *The Only Plane in the Sky: An Oral History of 9/11* (New York: Avid Reader Press, 2019), 247.

2. Unless specified otherwise, all quotations from network and cable television news on September 11 can be found in "September 11 Television Archive,"

Internet Archive, accessed Sept. 12, 2023, archive.org/details/sept_11_tv
_archive. Jennings quotation from "ABC, Sept. 11, 2001 8:20 pm–9:01 pm,"
September 11 Television Archive, Internet Archive, archive.org/details/
abc200109112020-2101.

3. David Friend, *Watching the World Change: The Stories Behind the Images of 9/11*
(New York: Farrar, Straus and Giroux, 2006), 32.

4. Don DeLillo, *Underworld* (New York: Scribner, 1997), 94.

5. Brian Stelter, "How NBC's 'Today' Invented Morning TV," CNN, Jan. 14, 2017,
money.cnn.com/2016/01/14/media/today-show-creation-nbc/index.html.

6. Friend, *Watching the World Change*, 34.

7. "ABC, Sept. 11, 2001, 9:12 am–9:54 am," September 11 Television Archive,
Internet Archive, archive.org/details/abc200109110912-0954.

8. "ABC, Sept. 11, 2001, 9:54 am–10:36 am," September 11 Television Archive,
Internet Archive, archive.org/details/abc200109110954-1036.

9. Susan Faludi, *The Terror Dream* (New York: Metropolitan Books, 2007), 208.

10. Ibid., 213.

11. Richard Slotkin, *Regeneration Through Violence: The Mythology of the American
Frontier, 1600–1860* (Norman: University of Oklahoma Press, 1973), 78.

12. Ibid., 3.

13. Ibid., 95.

14. Ibid., 96.

15. Faludi, *Terror Dream*, 214.

16. Mary Rowlandson, *The Sovereignty and Goodness of God*, in *Plymouth Colony:
Narratives of English Settlement and Native Resistance from the* Mayflower *to
King Philip's War*, ed. Lisa Brooks and Kelly Wisecup (New York: Library of
America, 2022), 940.

17. Ibid., 942.

18. Ibid., 946.

19. Ibid., 976.

20. Ibid., 954.

21. Ibid., 982.

22. "ABC, Sept. 11, 2001, 10:36 am–11:18 am," September 11 Television Archive,
Internet Archive, archive.org/details/abc200109111036-1118.

23. "ABC, Sept. 11, 2001, 1:23 pm–2:04 pm," September 11 Television Archive,
Internet Archive, archive.org/details/abc200109111323-1404.

24. "ABC, Sept. 11, 2001, 12:41 pm–1:23 pm," September 11 Television Archive,
Internet Archive, archive.org/details/abc200109111241-1323.

25. Kevin Flynn, "60 Firefighters Who Died on Sept. 11 Were Off Duty," *New York
Times*, Jan. 27, 2002, www.nytimes.com/2002/01/27/nyregion/60-firefighters
-who-died-on-sept-11-were-off-duty.html.

26. "Common Valor," *Wall Street Journal*, Sept. 14, 2001, www.wsj.com/articles/
SB1000432905762754757.

27. William Langewiesche, *American Ground: Unbuilding the World Trade Center*
(New York: North Point Press, 2002), 160–61.

28. David Carr, "Rebutting a Claim of Tarnished Valor; Research Challenges
Account of 9/11 Looting by Firefighters," *New York Times*, March 23, 2003,
www.nytimes.com/2003/03/23/nyregion/rebutting-claim-tarnished-valor
-research-challenges-account-9-11-looting.html.

29. Faludi, *Terror Dream,* 66.
30. *9/11,* directed by James Hanlon, Jules Naudet, and Gédéon Naudet (Paramount, 2002).
31. Faludi, *Terror Dream,* 66.
32. Ibid., 67.
33. Deputy Commissioner Thomas Fitzpatrick, World Trade Center Task Force interview transcript, Oct. 1, 2001, 13–14.
34. EMT Faisel Abed, World Trade Center Task Force interview transcript, Oct. 12, 2001, 4.
35. EMT Jody Bell, World Trade Center Task Force interview transcript, Dec. 15, 2001, 12.
36. Firefighter Tiernach Cassidy, World Trade Center Task Force interview transcript, Dec. 30, 2001, 3.
37. EMT Mala Harrilal, World Trade Center Task Force interview transcript, Nov. 2, 2001, 3.
38. Interview with Bobby Senn, "A Heroic Death," *National Geographic,* Sept. 6, 2012, www.youtube.com/watch?v=fNyR2s2MKYc&t=1s.
39. Abed, World Trade Center Task Force interview, 9.
40. "FDNY Firefighter Bobby Senn: 'The Dead Guy That God Sent Home,'" *Easy Reader,* Sept. 9, 2021, easyreadernews.com/fdny-firefighter-bobby-senn-the-dead-guy-that-god-sent-home.
41. Captain Paul Conlon, World Trade Center Task Force interview transcript, Jan. 26, 2002, 8.
42. Langewiesche, *American Ground,* 135.
43. Ibid., 131.
44. Paramedic Manuel Delgado, World Trade Center Task Force interview transcript, Oct. 2, 2001, 22.
45. Abed, World Trade Center Task Force interview, 10.
46. *9/11,* directed by Hanlon, Naudet, and Naudet.
47. Bell, World Trade Center Task force interview transcript, 19–20.
48. "ABC Sept. 11, 2001, 11:59 am–12:41 pm," September 11 Television Archive, Internet Archive, archive.org/details/abc200109111159-1241.
49. Ibid.
50. "ABC Sept. 11, 2001, 12:41 pm–1:23 pm," September 11 Television Archive, Internet Archive, archive.org/details/abc200109111241-1323.
51. "ABC Sept. 11, 2001, 3:28 pm–4:09 pm," September 11 Television Archive, Internet Archive, archive.org/details/abc200109111528-1609.
52. Graff, *Only Plane in the Sky,* 81.
53. Richard Slotkin, *The Fatal Environment: The Myth of the Frontier in the Age of Industrialization, 1800–1890* (Norman: University of Oklahoma Press, 1985), 55.
54. Ibid., 60.
55. Timothy Flint, *Biographical Memoir of Daniel Boone, the First Settler of Kentucky, Interspersed with Incidents in the Early Annals of the Country* (New Haven, Conn.: College & University Press, 1967).
56. Slotkin, *Regeneration Through Violence,* 441.
57. James Fenimore Cooper, *Leatherstocking Tales,* vols. 1–2 (New York: Library of America, 1985).

58. Slotkin, *Regeneration Through Violence,* 300.

59. Umberto Eco, "Casablanca, or, the Cliches Are Having a Ball," in *Signs of Life in the U.S.A.: Readings on Popular Culture for Writers,* ed. Sonia Maasik and Jack Solomon (Boston: Bedford Books, 1994), 260–64.

60. "ABC Sept. 11, 2001, 6:14 pm–6:56 pm," September 11 Television Archive, Internet Archive, archive.org/details/abc200109111814-1856.

61. "ABC Sept. 11, 2001, 5:33 pm–6:14 pm," September 11 Television Archive, Internet Archive, archive.org/details/abc200109111733-1814.

62. "ABC Sept. 11, 2001, 6:14 pm–6:56 pm," September 11 Television Archive, Internet Archive, archive.org/details/abc200109111814-1856.

63. "CNN 9-11-2001 News Coverage 6:00 PM–7:00 PM," 911NewsCoverage, YouTube, www.youtube.com/watch?v=avLV11EvrPc.

64. Faludi, *Terror Dream,* 5.

65. Virginia Heffernan, "The Way We Live Now: 10-14-01: Aftermath; Getting Serious," *New York Times Magazine,* Oct. 14, 2001, quoted in Faludi, *Terror Dream,* 117.

66. Ginia Bellafante, "Being Single in New York Is a Little Lonelier Now," *New York Times,* Sept. 30, 2001, quoted in Faludi, *Terror Dream,* 119.

67. Phil McCombs, "Comeback of the Alpha Male," *Washington Post,* March 16, 2003, quoted in Faludi, *Terror Dream,* 9.

68. Danielle Braff, "The Great Pandemic Wedding Boom," *New York Times,* Feb. 6, 2021, www.nytimes.com/2021/02/06/style/the-great-pandemic-wedding-boom .html.

69. "Bush Rejects Taliban Offer to Hand bin Laden Over," *Guardian,* Oct. 14, 2001, www.theguardian.com/world/2001/oct/14/afghanistan.terrorism5.

70. "ABC Sept. 11, 2001, 6:14 pm–6:56 pm," September 11 Television Archive, Internet Archive, archive.org/details/abc200109111814-1856.

71. "ABC Sept. 11, 2001, 6:56 pm–7:38 pm," September 11 Television Archive, Internet Archive, archive.org/details/abc200109111856-1938.

72. "ABC Sept. 11, 2001, 8:20 pm–9:01 pm," September 11 Television Archive, Internet Archive, archive.org/details/abc200109112020-2101.

Chapter 2: Iron Men

1. "ABC Sept. 11, 2001, 6:56 pm–7:38 pm," September 11 Television Archive, Internet Archive, archive.org/details/abc200109111856-1938.

2. *Batman Begins,* directed by Christopher Nolan (Warner Bros. Pictures, 2005).

3. *The Dark Knight,* directed by Christopher Nolan (Warner Bros. Pictures, 2008).

4. *The Dark Knight Rises,* directed by Christopher Nolan (Warner Bros. Pictures, 2012).

5. *The Dark Knight,* advertisement, Movieposters.com, accessed April 2, 2021, www.movieposters.com/products/dark-knight-mpw-93991.

6. "Christopher Nolan: 'Dark Knight Rises' Isn't Political," *Rolling Stone,* July 20, 2012, www.rollingstone.com/tv-movies/tv-movie-news/christopher-nolan -dark-knight-rises-isnt-political-245401.

7. Box Office History for Batman Movies. The Numbers, accessed April 2, 2021, www.the-numbers.com/movies/franchise/Batman#tab=summary.

8. Colin McInnes, "A Different Kind of War? September 11 and the United States' Afghan War," *Review of International Studies* 29, no. 2 (April 2003): 165–84.

9. Donald P. Wright, *A Different Kind of War: The United States Army in Operation ENDURING FREEDOM (OEF) October 2001–September 2005* (Fort Leavenworth, Kans.: Combat Studies Institute Press, 2010), history.army.mil/html/bookshelves/resmat/gwot/DifferentKindofWar.pdf.

10. Serge Schmemann, "What Would 'Victory' Mean?," *New York Times,* Sept. 16, 2001, www.nytimes.com/2001/09/16/weekinreview/war-zone-what-would-victory-mean.html.

11. Todd Purdum, "Leaders Face Challenges Far Different from Those of Last Conflict," *New York Times,* Sept. 15, 2001, www.nytimes.com/2001/09/15/us/after-attacks-strategy-leaders-face-challenges-far-different-those-last-conflict.html.

12. Michael R. Gordon, "A New War and Its Scale," *New York Times,* Sept. 17, 2001, www.nytimes.com/2001/09/17/world/after-the-attacks-the-strategy-a-new-war-and-its-scale.html.

13. "Radio Address of the President to the Nation," Office of the Press Secretary, Sept. 15, 2001, georgewbush-whitehouse.archives.gov/news/releases/2001/09/20010915.html.

14. "The Vice President Appears on Meet the Press with Tim Russert," George W. Bush White House Archives, Sept. 16, 2001, georgewbush-whitehouse.archives.gov/vicepresident/news-speeches/speeches/vp20010916.html.

15. Todd S. Purdum, "Bush Warns of a Wrathful, Shadowy, and Inventive War," *New York Times,* Sept. 17, 2001, www.nytimes.com/2001/09/17/us/after-attacks-white-house-bush-warns-wrathful-shadowy-inventive-war.html.

16. "The 2000 Campaign; 2nd Presidential Debate Between Gov. Bush and Vice President Gore," *New York Times,* Oct. 12, 2000, www.nytimes.com/2000/10/12/us/2000-campaign-2nd-presidential-debate-between-gov-bush-vice-president-gore.html.

17. Elliott Abrams, "Israel and the 'Peace Process,'" in Robert Kagan and William Kristol, eds., *Present Dangers: Crisis and Opportunity in American Foreign and Defense Policy* (San Francisco: Encounter Books, 2000), 222, 234.

18. Kagan and Kristol, "Preface," in *Present Dangers,* vii.

19. Ibid., 24.

20. Frederick W. Kagan, "The Decline of America's Armed Forces," in Kagan and Kristol, *Present Dangers,* 245.

21. Kagan and Kristol, *Present Dangers,* 6.

22. Ibid., vii.

23. Ibid., 7.

24. Richard N. Perle, "Iraq: Saddam Unbound," in Kagan and Kristol, *Present Dangers,* 101.

25. Kagan, "Decline of America's Armed Forces," 241.

26. Kagan and Kristol, "Introduction: National Interest and Global Responsibility," in *Present Dangers,* 9.

27. Ibid., 14.

28. Kyle Smith, "Triumph of the Normal," *New York Post,* Sept. 11, 2011, nypost.com/2011/09/11/triumph-of-the-normal.

29. Andrew Bacevich, *America's War for the Greater Middle East: A Military History* (New York: Random House, 2016), 178–79.

30. Ibid., 248.

31. "Off Target: The Conduct of the War and Civilian Casualties in Iraq," Human Rights Watch, Dec. 11, 2003, www.hrw.org/report/2003/12/11/target/conduct -war-and-civilian-casualties-iraq.

32. "CNN Live Coverage—Start of Iraq War (7:00 p.m. E.T.–12:00 a.m. E.T.)," YouTube, Jan. 4, 2020, web.archive.org/web/20220507185855/www.youtube .com/watch?v=R3KNpswZyPc.

33. Tara Clarke, "The Dot-Com Crash of 2000–2002," Money Morning, June 12, 2015, accessed April 14, 2022, moneymorning.com/2015/06/12/the-dot-com -crash-of-2000-2002.

34. Barnaby J. Feder, "New Military Systems May Be Tested in Field in 'War Against Terrorism,'" *New York Times*, Oct. 1, 2001, www.nytimes.com/2001/10/01/ business/nation-challenged-weapons-new-military-systems-may-be-tested -field-war-against.html.

35. Joseph Fitchett, "U.S. Charts a High-Tech Strategy for Afghan War," *New York Times*, Oct. 3, 2001, www.nytimes.com/2001/10/03/news/us-charts-a-hightech -strategy-for-afghan-war.html.

36. Eric Schmitt and James Dao, "Use of Pinpoint Air Power Comes of Age in New War," *New York Times*, Dec. 24, 2001, www.nytimes.com/2001/12/24/world/ nation-challenged-air-campaign-use-pinpoint-air-power-comes-age-new-war .html.

37. Jennifer 8. Lee, "Agile in a Crisis, Robots Show Their Mettle," *New York Times*, Sept. 27, 2001, www.nytimes.com/2001/09/27/technology/agile-in-a-crisis -robots-show-their-mettle.html.

38. P. W. Singer, *Wired for War: The Robotics Revolution and Conflict in the 21st Century* (New York: Penguin Press, 2009), 24–25.

39. Ibid., 29–30.

40. Ibid., 133.

41. Ibid., 34.

42. Abigail Gage and Shawna Sinnott, "Closing the Chapter: Ending Afghanistan for US Army Special Forces," podcast, Modern War Institute at West Point, July 16, 2021, mwi.usma.edu/closing-the-chapter-ending-afghanistan-for-us -army-special-forces.

43. James Brooke, "Glimpse of Readiness to Fight Iraq at U.S. Copter Base in Afghanistan," *New York Times*, Sept. 10, 2002, www.nytimes.com/2002/09/10/ world/threats-responses-desert-warriors-glimpse-readiness-fight-iraq-us -copter-base.html.

44. Thom Shanker and Eric Schmitt, "Covert Units Conduct a Campaign Invisible Except for the Results," *New York Times*, April 6, 2003, www.nytimes.com/2003/ 04/06/world/nation-war-special-operations-covert-units-conduct-campaign -invisible-except-for.html.

45. Matt Kennard, *Irregular Army: How the US Military Recruited Neo-Nazis, Gang Members, and Criminals to Fight the War on Terror* (London: Verso, 2006), 127–32.

46. Shanker and Schmitt, "Covert Units Conduct a Campaign Invisible Except for the Results."

47. James Dao, "Ads Now Seek Recruits for 'An Army of One,'" *New York Times*, Jan. 10, 2001, www.nytimes.com/2001/01/10/us/ads-now-seek-recruits-for-an -army-of-one.html.

48. "What's Your Warrior | WHO WILL BUILD TOMORROW? | GO ARMY," advertisement, YouTube, Dec. 17, 2020, web.archive.org/web/20210520180252/ https://www.youtube.com/watch?app=desktop&v=7fiManEc2Tk.

49. Matthew Alford and Tom Secker, *National Security Cinema: The Shocking New Evidence of Government Control in Hollywood* (U.K.: Drum Roll Books, 2017), 5.

50. *Iron Man,* directed by Jon Favreau (Marvel Studios, 2008).

51. Ibid.; *Iron Man 2,* directed by Jon Favreau (Marvel Studios, 2010); *Iron Man 3,* directed by Shane Black (Marvel Studios, 2013).

52. *Iron Man 2.*

53. Andrew Murr, "A Heroic Life," *Newsweek,* May 2, 2004, www.newsweek.com/ heroic-life-128209.

54. Ibid.

55. Mike Freeman, "Tillman Leaves N.F.L. to Join Army," *New York Times,* June 1, 2002, www.nytimes.com/2002/06/01/sports/plus-pro-football-tillman-leaves -nfl-to-join-army.html.

56. Bill Pennington, "Former N.F.L. Player Killed in Afghanistan," *New York Times,* April 23, 2004, www.nytimes.com/2004/04/23/sports/former-nfl-player-killed -in-afghanistan.html.

57. Murr, "Heroic Life."

58. Pennington, "Former N.F.L. Player Killed in Afghanistan."

59. Murr, "Heroic Life."

60. Inspector General U.S. Department of Defense, *Review of Matters Related to the Death of Corporal Patrick Tillman, U.S. Army,* March 26, 2007, 4–5.

61. Sarah Seltzer, "Inside Pat Tillman's Life, and the Bush Administration's Cover-Up of His Death," *AlterNet,* Sept. 17, 2009, www.alternet.org/2009/09/ inside_pat_tillmans_life_and_the_bush_administrations_cover-up_of_his _death.

62. "Jessica Lynch Rescue Army Video," YouTube, June 25, 2010, www.youtube .com/watch?v=hYtmUx4nHco.

63. John Kampfner, "The Truth About Jessica," *Guardian,* May 15, 2003, www .theguardian.com/world/2003/may/15/iraq.usa2.

64. Stephen M. Silverman, "Jessica Lynch Story to Air as NBC Movie," *People,* April 11, 2003, web.archive.org/web/20210307004954/people.com/celebrity/ jessica-lynch-story-to-air-as-nbc-movie.

65. Faludi, *Terror Dream,* 185.

66. Rick Bragg, *I Am a Soldier, Too: The Jessica Lynch Story* (New York: Knopf, 2003), 96.

67. Faludi, *Terror Dream,* 191.

68. Bragg, *I Am a Soldier, Too,* 98–99.

69. Slotkin, *Regeneration Through Violence,* 555.

70. Chris Kyle, *American Sniper: The Autobiography of the Most Lethal Sniper in U.S. Military History* (New York: HarperCollins, 2012), 4.

71. Ibid., 144.

72. Ibid., 250.

73. Ibid., 98.

74. Ibid., 221.

75. *American Sniper,* directed by Clint Eastwood (Village Roadshow Pictures, 2014).

76. Kyle, *American Sniper,* 7.

77. Ibid., 272.

78. Philip Bump, "15 Years After the Iraq War Began, the Death Toll Is Still Murky," *Washington Post,* March 20, 2018, www.washingtonpost.com/news/politics/wp/2018/03/20/15-years-after-it-began-the-death-toll-from-the-iraq-war-is-still-murky.

79. Kyle, *American Sniper,* 430.

80. Ibid., 109.

81. Nicholas Schmidle, "In the Crosshairs," *New Yorker,* May 27, 2013, www.newyorker.com/magazine/2013/06/03/in-the-crosshairs.

82. Zoë Wool, *After War: The Weight of Life at Walter Reed* (Durham, N.C.: Duke University Press, 2015), 88.

83. Dana Priest and Anne Hull, "Soldiers Face Neglect, Frustration at Army's Top Medical Facility," *Washington Post,* Feb. 18, 2007, www.washingtonpost.com/archive/politics/2007/02/18/soldiers-face-neglect-frustration-at-armys-top-medical-facility/c0c4b3e4-fb22-4df6-9ac9-c602d41c5bda.

84. "President Bush Attends Arlington National Cemetery Memorial Day Commemoration," Office of the Press Secretary, May 26, 2008, georgewbush-whitehouse.archives.gov/news/releases/2008/05/20080526.html.

85. Chris Castel, "President Obama to Veterans: We Honor a Debt We Can Never Repay," *Oklahoman,* Nov. 11, 2013, www.oklahoman.com/article/3903578/president-obama-to-veterans-we-honor-a-debt-we-can-never-repay.

86. Kenneth T. MacLeish, *Making War at Fort Hood: Life and Uncertainty in a Military Community* (Princeton, N.J.: Princeton University Press, 2013), 221.

87. Wool, *After War,* 112.

88. Ibid., 108.

89. Ibid., 114.

90. Ibid., 112.

91. Ibid., 19.

92. David Leigh, "Iraq War Logs Reveal 15,000 Previously Unlisted Civilian Deaths," *Guardian,* Oct. 22, 2010, www.theguardian.com/world/2010/oct/22/true-civilian-body-count-iraq.

93. Don White, interview with the author, April 12, 2021.

94. Iraq (in Depth: Topics A to Z), Gallup, news.gallup.com/poll/1633/iraq.aspx.

95. "U.S. Active Duty Military Deaths by Year and Manner, 1980–2022 (as of August 2023)," Defense Casualty Analysis System, Defense Manpower Data Center, Aug. 2023, dcas.dmdc.osd.mil/dcas/app/summaryData/deaths/byYearManner.

Chapter 3: I Think Security Is Very Tight, but I'm Still Concerned

1. *9/11 Commission Report: Final Report of the National Commission on Terrorist Attacks upon the United States* (New York: Barnes & Noble, 2004), 272.

2. Ibid., 16.

3. Ibid., 267.

4. Ibid., 3.

5. Ibid., 383–98.

6. "Gov. Ridge Sworn-In to Lead Homeland Security," Office of the Press Secretary, White House, President George W. Bush, Oct. 8, 2001, georgewbush -whitehouse.archives.gov/news/releases/2001/10/20011008-3.html.

7. "Barry Manilow, Patti Labell [*sic*], Wynona [*sic*], James Ingram, Super Bowl," Música De archive, YouTube, May 20, 2020, www.youtube.com/watch?v=9_k -ahyKF8A.

8. John Hood, "Patriot Games," *Carolina Journal,* Feb. 2, 2002, www .carolinajournal.com/opinion/patriot-games.

9. Fred Mitchell, "Safe Spot? At Your Secret Service," *Chicago Tribune,* Feb. 4, 2002, www.chicagotribune.com/news/ct-xpm-2002-02-04-0202040144-story .html.

10. "Big Easy Gets Tough Security for Super Bowl," CNN.com, Feb. 2, 2002, www .cnn.com/2002/US/02/02/sb.superbowl.security/index.html.

11. Kimberly S. Schimmel, "'Violence-Complacent' to 'Terrorist-Ready': Post-9/11 Framing of the US Super Bowl," *Urban Studies* 48, no. 15 (Nov. 2011): 3281.

12. Mitchell, "Safe Spot?"

13. Mike Freeman, "The Super Bowl: Security, and Event, Will Be Extraordinary," *New York Times,* Dec. 1, 2001, www.nytimes.com/2001/12/01/sports/a-nation -challenged-the-super-bowl-security-and-event-will-be-extraordinary.html.

14. Mitchell, "Safe Spot?"

15. Brian Schmitz, "Security Keeps Game Safe, Sound," *Orlando Sentinel,* Feb. 4, 2002, www.orlandosentinel.com/news/os-xpm-2002-02-04-0202040230-story .html.

16. Freeman, "Super Bowl: Security, and Event, Will Be Extraordinary."

17. Schmitz, "Security Keeps Game Safe, Sound."

18. Mitchell, "Safe Spot?"

19. Lydia Saad, "U.S. Air Travel Remains Down as Employed Adults Fly Less," Gallup, Jan. 6, 2022, news.gallup.com/poll/388484/air-travel-remains-down -employed-adults-fly-less.aspx.

20. Leslie Josephs, "How the Sept. 11 Terrorist Attacks Forever Changed Air Travel," CNBC, Sept. 11, 2021, www.cnbc.com/2021/09/11/how-9/11-forever -changed-air-travel.html.

21. Peter Kujawinski, "Air Travel After 9/11: Just Get Through It," *New York Times,* Sept. 11, 2021, www.nytimes.com/2021/09/09/travel/airline-travel -september-11.html.

22. Josephs, "How the Sept. 11 Terrorist Attacks Forever Changed Air Travel."

23. Laurence Zuckerman and Laura M. Holson, "A Spartan New Set of Standards for Airlines and Most Passengers," *New York Times,* Sept. 18, 2001, www .nytimes.com/2001/09/18/business/nation-challenged-airlines-spartan-new -set-standards-for-airlines-most.html.

24. Joe Sharkey, "Tighter Airport Security Will Slow Business Fliers," *New York Times,* Sept. 13, 2001, www.nytimes.com/2001/09/13/us/after-attacks-travelers -tighter-airport-security-will-slow-business-fliers.html.

25. Ronald K. Noble, "Invest in Global Policing," *New York Times,* Sept. 15, 2001, www.nytimes.com/2001/09/15/opinion/invest-in-global-policing.html.

26. Aviation and Transportation Security Act of 2001, Pub. L. No. 107-71, 115 Stat. 597 (2001).

27. "CNN: John Tyner to TSA Security 'Don't "Touch My Junk,"'" CNN, Nov. 17, 2010, YouTube, www.youtube.com/watch?v=Laxmx4cE3aE.

28. Rachel Hall, *The Transparent Traveler: The Performance and Culture of Airport Security* (Durham, N.C.: Duke University Press, 2015), 117.

29. Alistair Gordon, *Naked Airport: A Cultural History of the World's Most Revolutionary Structure* (Chicago: University of Chicago Press, 2008), 218–19.

30. Hall, *Transparent Traveler,* 131–32.

31. Pilot, *Lie to Me,* YouTube, www.youtube.com/watch?v=bWyhsqh_e9s.

32. Joe Sharkey, "Giving Human Intuition a Place in Airport Security," *New York Times,* Aug. 21, 2007, www.nytimes.com/2007/08/21/business/21road .html.

33. Hall, *Transparent Traveler,* 140–41.

34. Ibid., 142.

35. Ibid.

36. Ibid., 112–14.

37. "Briton Jailed in US After Joking About Bombs," *Scotsman,* Jan. 21, 2004, www.scotsman.com/news/uk-news/briton-jailed-us-after-joking-about-bombs -2454136.

38. Hall, *Transparent Traveler,* 203.

39. Ibid., 171.

40. "Calvin Trillin Predicts Underwear Bomber Three Years Before," ryangawker, YouTube, Jan. 8, 2010, www.youtube.com/watch?v=WRco_Uh1rxc.

41. Calvin Trillin, "Crystal Ball," *New Yorker,* Jan. 10, 2010, www.newyorker.com/ magazine/2010/01/18/crystal-ball.

42. Gordon, *Naked Airport,* 262.

43. Hall, *Transparent Traveler,* 137.

44. Gordon, *Naked Airport,* 262.

45. "Aviation Security: Efforts to Validate TSA's Passenger Screening Behavior Detection Program Underway, but Opportunities Exist to Strengthen Validation and Address Operational Challenges," U.S. Government Accountability Office, GAO-10-763, May 20, 2010, www.gao.gov/assets/ a304517.html.

46. Hall, *Transparent Traveler,* 137.

47. Lisa Parks, "Points of Departure: The Culture of US Airport Screening," *Journal of Visual Culture* 6, no. 2 (2007): 189.

48. Bart Elias, "Airport Passenger Screening: Background and Issues for Congress," Congressional Research Service, April 23, 2009, 9, sgp.fas.org/crs/homesec/ R40543.pdf.

49. Justin Fishel et al., "Undercover DHS Tests Find Security Failures at US Airports," ABC News, June 1, 2015, abcnews.go.com/US/exclusive-undercover -dhs-tests-find-widespread-security-failures/story?id=31434881.

50. Gallya Lahav, "Mobility and Border Security: The U.S. Aviation System, the State, and the Rise of Public-Private Partnerships," in *Politics at the Airport,* ed. Mark B. Salter (Minneapolis: University of Minnesota Press, 2008), 96.

51. Greg Johnson, "Patriotism Barely Gets off the Bench," *Los Angeles Times,* Feb. 4, 2002, www.latimes.com/archives/la-xpm-2002-feb-04-fi-super4-story.html.

52. Ibid.

53. Sam Zuckerman, "Consumer Spending Kept Economy Going," *San Francisco*

Chronicle, Sept. 8, 2002, www.sfgate.com/business/article/9-11-01-Impact-on
-Business-American-consumers-2773356.php.

54. David L. Altheide, "Consuming Terrorism," *Symbolic Interaction* 27, no. 3
(Summer 2004): 298.

55. Marita Sturken, *Tourists of History: Memory, Kitsch, and Consumerism from
Oklahoma City to Ground Zero* (Durham, N.C.: Duke University Press,
2007), 66.

56. Ibid.

57. "GDP Growth (Annual %)—United States," World Bank, World Bank national
accounts data, and OECD National Accounts data files, accessed June 15, 2022,
data.worldbank.org/indicator/NY.GDP.MKTP.KD.ZG?locations=US.

58. Zuckerman, "Consumer Spending Kept Economy Going."

59. Sturken, *Tourists of History*, 57.

60. 30-Year Fixed Rate Mortgage Average in the United States, FRED Economic
Data, St. Louis Fed, accessed Sept. 19, 2023, fred.stlouisfed.org/series/
MORTGAGE30US.

61. Nicholas D. Kristof, "Chicks with Guns," *New York Times*, March 8, 2002, www
.nytimes.com/2002/03/08/opinion/chicks-with-guns.html.

62. Altheide, "Consuming Terrorism," 298–99.

63. Tina Dirmann and Timothy Hughes, "More Residents Taking Up Arms," *Los
Angeles Times*, Oct. 14, 2001, www.latimes.com/archives/la-xpm-2001-oct-14
-me-57133-story.html.

64. Keith Bradsher, *High and Mighty: The Dangerous Rise of the SUV* (New York:
Public Affairs, 2002), 105.

65. Faludi, *Terror Dream*, 156–57.

66. Karen Tumulty and Viveca Novak, "Goodbye, Soccer Mom. Hello, Security
Mom," *Time*, May 25, 2003, content.time.com/time/magazine/article/0,9171
,454487,00.html.

67. Bradsher, *High and Mighty*, 20.

68. "Ford Uses High-Strength Steel Plus High-Strength, Aluminum Alloys on
Toughest F-150 Ever," Ford Media Center, Jan. 13, 2014, media.ford.com/
content/fordmedia/fna/us/en/news/2014/01/13/ford-uses-high-strength-steel
-plus-high-strength--aluminum-alloy.html.

69. David Campbell, "The Biopolitics of Security: Oil, Empire, and the Sports
Utility Vehicle," *American Quarterly* 57, no. 3 (Sept. 2005): 958.

70. Ibid., 959.

71. Ibid.

72. Matthew L. Brumbelow and Jessica S. Jermakian, "Injury Risks and
Crashworthiness Benefits for Females and Males: Which Differences Are
Physiological?," *Traffic Injury Prevention*, Insurance Institute for Highway
Safety, Dec. 2021, www.iihs.org/topics/bibliography/ref/2219.

73. Andrew J. Hawkins, "Driving the 2021 Cadillac Escalade Was One of the Most
Stressful Experiences of My Life," The Verge, Oct. 19, 2020, www.theverge
.com/2020/10/19/21522959/cadillac-escalade-2021-first-drive-safety-oversized.

74. Peter Wallner, Anna Wanka, and Hans-Peter Hutter, "SUV Driving
'Masculinizes' Risk Behavior in Females: A Public Health Challenge," *Wiener
Klinische Wochenschrift* 129, no. 17 (2017): 625–29.

75. Angie Schmitt, "What Happened to Pickup Trucks?," *Bloomberg,* March 11, 2021, www.bloomberg.com/news/articles/2021-03-11/the-dangerous-rise-of -the-supersized-pickup-truck.

76. "Fuel Economy of 2005 Sport Utility Vehicle," U.S. Department of Energy, Office of Energy Efficiency and Renewable Energy, U.S. Environmental Protection Agency, www.fueleconomy.gov/feg/byclass/Sport_Utility _Vehicle2005.shtml.

77. Nick Madigan, "Cries of Activism and Terrorism in S.U.V. Torching," *New York Times,* Aug. 31, 2003, www.nytimes.com/2003/08/31/us/cries-of-activism-and -terrorism-in-suv-torching.html.

78. Campbell, "Politics of Security," 960.

79. Sturken, *Tourists of History,* 88.

80. Jon Morgan, "Drills Set for Today Simulate Attacks; Ravens Stadium to Be Part of Exercises to Prepare for Possible Terrorist Strike," *Sun,* July 13, 2002.

81. Ron Word, "Agencies Secure Jacksonville for Super Bowl XXXIX," *Ledger,* Jan. 24, 2005.

82. Schimmel, "'Violence-Complacent' to 'Terrorist-Ready,'" 3283.

83. Bill McCleery, "IPL: City Will Be Safe for the Super Bowl," *Indianapolis Star,* Nov. 22, 2011.

84. "Super Bowl LII Host City Bid Specifications and Requirements," National Football League, Nov. 2013, www.documentcloud.org/documents/1184220 -20140605190910.htm.

85. Schimmel, "'Violence-Complacent' to 'Terrorist-Ready,'" 3284.

86. "Super Bowl LII Host City Bid Specifications and Requirements," 29–30.

87. Elizabeth Greenspan, *Battle for Ground Zero: Inside the Political Struggle to Rebuild the World Trade Center* (New York: Palgrave Macmillan, 2013), xii.

88. Ibid., 20.

89. Ibid., 97.

90. Ibid., 101–2.

91. Nicolai Ouroussoff, "A Tower of Impregnability, the Sort Politicians Love," *New York Times,* June 30, 2005, www.nytimes.com/2005/06/30/nyregion/an -appraisal-a-tower-of-impregnability-the-sort-politicians-love.html.

92. David W. Dunlap, "With Security, Trade Center Faces New Isolation," *New York Times,* May 17, 2013, archive.nytimes.com/cityroom.blogs.nytimes.com/2013/ 05/16/world-trade-center-may-be-isolated-again-this-time-by-security -measures.

93. Paul J. Browne, "Security at the Trade Center, as the Police Dept. Sees It," *New York Times,* May 21, 2013, www.nytimes.com/2013/05/21/opinion/security-at -the-trade-center-as-the-police-dept-sees-it.html.

94. "Nosy Neighbor: Will the World Trade Center Streets Ever Reopen to Cars?," *Tribeca Citizen,* Jan. 17, 2019, tribecacitizen.com/2019/01/17/nosy-neighbor -will-the-world-trade-center-streets-ever-reopen-to-cars.

95. Jeremy Németh and Justin Hollander, "Security Zones and New York City's Shrinking Public Space," *International Journal of Urban and Regional Research* 34, no. 1 (March 2010): 20–34.

96. Gerda Wekerle and Paul Jackson, "Urbanizing the Security Agenda," *City* 9, no. 1 (April 2005): 41.

97. Ibid., 43.

98. Anti-eviction Mapping Project, "San Francisco for Sale," accessed June 22, 2022, www.antievictionmappingproject.net/publicspace.html.

99. Kevin R. Grosskopf, "Evaluating the Societal Response to Antiterrorism Measures," *Journal of Homeland Security and Emergency Management* 3, no. 2 (2006).

Chapter 4: Keep Quiet and Stay in Your Home

1. Erika Doss, *Memorial Mania: Public Feeling in America* (Chicago: University of Chicago Press, 2010), 160–64.

2. Greenspan, *Battle for Ground Zero,* 131–33.

3. Doss, *Memorial Mania,* 171.

4. Ibid., 153–54.

5. Greenspan, *Battle for Ground Zero,* 12.

6. Paula Reed Ward, "Designer of Flight 93 Memorial Receptive to Changes," *Pittsburgh Post-Gazette,* Sept. 16, 2005, web.archive.org/web/20221014054300/ https://old.post-gazette.com/pg/05259/572574.stm.

7. Alec Rawls, "Flight 93 Memorial Design Petition," Crescent of Betrayal, www .crescentofbetrayal.com/Flt%2093%20PETITION%20(Bill)%20both%20sides %20030508%20PDF.pdf.

8. Lori Peek, *Behind the Backlash: Muslim Americans After 9/11* (Philadelphia: Temple University Press, 2011), 29.

9. Tram Nguyen, *We Are All Suspects Now: Untold Stories from Immigrant Communities After 9/11* (Boston: Beacon Press, 2005), xvii.

10. Tanya Kaur Bindra, "Communities of Colour Remain Under Attack," *Al Jazeera,* Aug. 7, 2012, www.aljazeera.com/opinions/2012/8/7/communities-of-colour -remain-under-attack.

11. Peek, *Behind the Backlash,* 28.

12. Timothy Williams, "The Hated and the Hater, Both Touched by Crime," *New York Times,* July 18, 2011, www.nytimes.com/2011/07/19/us/19questions.html.

13. Peek, *Behind the Backlash,* 29–30.

14. "Hate Crime Statistics," Uniform Crime Reporting (UCR) Program, Federal Bureau of Investigation, www.fbi.gov/services/cjis/ucr/hate-crime, accessed Sept. 20, 2023.

15. U.S. Congress, House, *Uniting and Strengthening America by Providing Appropriate Tools Required to Intercept and Obstruct Terrorism (USA PATRIOT ACT) Act of 2001,* HR 3162, 107th Cong., 1st Sess., introduced in House Oct. 23, 2001, www.govinfo.gov/content/pkg/PLAW-107publ56/html/PLAW -107publ56.htm.

16. *ADAMA,* directed by David Felix Sutcliffe, 2011, vimeo.com/47204289.

17. Alia Malek, ed., *Patriot Acts: Narratives of Post-9/11 Injustice* (San Francisco: McSweeney's and Voice of Witness, 2011), 28–29.

18. Ibid., 27.

19. Ibid., 34.

20. Ibid., 25.

21. Ibid., 33.

22. Liz Brody, "This Woman Is Accused of Being a Terrorist—Her Story Is Beyond Important Right Now," *Glamour,* Sept. 27, 2017, www.glamour.com/story/ adama-bah-accused-of-being-a-terrorist.

23. Malek, *Patriot Acts,* 34.
24. Ibid., 38.
25. Ibid., 41.
26. *ADAMA,* directed by Sutcliffe.
27. Malek, *Patriot Acts,* 45.
28. Gail Sullivan, "Why the No-Fly List Was Declared Unconstitutional," *Washington Post,* June 25, 2014, www.washingtonpost.com/news/morning-mix/wp/2014/06/25/judge-rules-no-fly-list-unconstitutional.
29. "National Security Division Statistics on Unsealed International Terrorism and Terrorism-Related Convictions 9/11/01–3/18/10," U.S. Department of Justice, irp.fas.org/agency/doj/doj032610-stats.pdf.
30. Stephen Downs and Kathy Manley, "Inventing Terrorists: The Lawfare of Preemptive Prosecution," study by Project SALAM and National Coalition to Protect Civil Freedoms, May 2014, 3–4.
31. "645. Entrapment—Elements," Criminal Resource Manual, U.S. Department of Justice Archives, www.justice.gov/archives/jm/criminal-resource-manual-645 -entrapment-elements.
32. Downs and Manley, "Inventing Terrorists," B-5.
33. Mark Santora and Andrea Elliott, "A Seemingly Ordinary Friendship Held a Conspiracy, Authorities Say," *New York Times,* May 31, 2005, www.nytimes .com/2005/05/31/nyregion/a-seemingly-ordinary-friendship-hid-a-conspiracy -authorities-say.html.
34. Downs and Manley, "Inventing Terrorists," B-38.
35. *(T)error,* directed by Lyric R. Cabral and David Felix Sutcliffe (Film Collaborative, 2015).
36. Mattathias Schwartz, "The Informant and the Filmmakers," *New York Times,* Feb. 19, 2016, www.nytimes.com/2016/02/21/magazine/the-informant-and-the -filmmakers.html.
37. Alan Feuer, "Tapes Capture Bold Claims of Bronx Man in Terror Plot," *New York Times,* May 8, 2007, www.nytimes.com/2007/05/08/nyregion/08terror.html.
38. Ibid.
39. Ibid.
40. Alan Feuer, "Martial Arts Expert Pleads Guilty in Terror Case," *New York Times,* April 4, 2007, www.nytimes.com/2007/04/04/nyregion/04cnd-shah.html.
41. Rafil Dhafir and Osameh Alwahaidy, interview by author, July 22, 2021.
42. Mike McAndrew, "Dhafir Trial Hears Tax Preparer," *Post-Standard,* Dec. 2, 2004, B-3.
43. Maher Zagha, sworn statement, Aug. 24, 2005.
44. John Pilger, "The Political Trial of a Caring Man and the End of Justice in America," CounterCurrents.org, Nov. 11, 2012, www.countercurrents.org/pilger11112.htm.
45. John O'Brien, "U.S. Says CNY Charity Broke Iraq Sanctions," *Post-Standard,* Feb. 27, 2003, A-1.
46. Pilger, "Political Trial of a Caring Man and the End of Justice in America."
47. Glenn Coin, "Patients Unsure Where to Go for Care," *Post-Standard,* Feb. 28, 2003, A-8.
48. Renée K. Gadoua, "Up to 150 Questioned; Doctor Is Denied Bail—Muslims Afraid to Speak Out Publicly," *Post-Standard,* March 1, 2003, A-1, A-4.

49. Magda Bayoumi, "About Dr. Dhafir," *Syracuse Peace Newsletter,* Syracuse Peace Council, Sept. 2005, www.dhafirtrial.net/about-this-site/about-dr-dhafir.

50. Rafil Dhafir and Osameh Alwahaidy, interview by author, July 22, 2021.

51. Renée K. Gadoua, "Dhafir Claims Religious Persecution," *Post-Dispatch,* Nov. 14, 2005, A-10.

52. Sentencing Memorandum of the United States, Criminal Action No. 03-CR-64 (NAM), 3.

53. Karen Hughes, "Anatomy of a 'Terrorism' Prosecution: Dr. Rafil Dhafir and the Help the Needy Muslim Charity Case," *Truthout,* Jan. 31, 2012, truthout.org/ articles/anatomy-of-a-terrorism-prosecution-dr-rafil-dhafir-and-the-help-the -needy-muslim-charity-case.

54. Rafil Dhafir and Osameh Alwahaidy, interview by author, July 22, 2021.

55. Downs and Manley, "Inventing Terrorists," B-31.

56. Graham Rayman, "Were the Newburgh Four Really Out to Blow Up Synagogues? A Defendant Finally Speaks Out," *Village Voice,* March 2, 2011, www.villagevoice.com/2011/03/02/were-the-newburgh-4-really-out-to-blow -up-synagogues-a-defendant-finally-speaks-out.

57. Jesse McKinley, "Judge Orders Release of Three of 'Newburgh Four,' Criticizing FBI," *New York Times,* July 27, 2023, www.nytimes.com/2023/07/27/nyregion/ newburgh-four-terrorism-fbi.html.

58. Malek, *Patriot Acts,* 311–15.

59. Sunaina Marr Maira, *The 9/11 Generation: Youth, Rights, and Solidarity in the War on Terror* (New York: New York University Press, 2016), 66.

60. Ibid., 158.

61. Ibid., 208.

62. Malek, *Patriot Acts,* 66.

63. Ibid., 99.

64. Peek, *Behind the Backlash,* 156.

65. Ibid., 115.

Chapter 5: I Do Break Regulations

1. Ya'akov Amidror, quoted in Anatol Levin, "A Trap of Their Own Making," *London Review of Books,* May 8, 2003, www.lrb.co.uk/the-paper/v25/n09/anatol -lieven/a-trap-of-their-own-making.

2. "Interview with Donald Rumsfeld; Lugar, Dodd Talk About Post-war Iraq; Kissinger, Cohen Discuss Middle East Road Map," transcript, *Late Edition with Wolf Blitzer,* CNN, May 4, 2003, www.cnn.com/TRANSCRIPTS/0305/04/le.00 .html.

3. Christopher Caldwell, "Daughter of the Enlightenment," *New York Times,* April 3, 2005, www.nytimes.com/2005/04/03/magazine/daughter-of-the -enlightenment.html.

4. Charles J. Hanley, "Former Iraqi Detainees Tell of Riots, Punishment in the Sun, Good Americans and Pitiless Ones," Associated Press, Nov. 1, 2003, web .archive.org/web/20140222024344/http://legacy.utsandiego.com/news/world/ iraq/20031101-0936-iraq-thecamps.html.

5. "Iraq: Continuing Failure to Uphold Human Rights," Amnesty International, Index Number MDE 14/159/2003, July 22, 2003, www.amnesty.org/en/ documents/mde14/159/2003/en.

6. Greg Mitchell, "Four Years Later: Why Did It Take So Long for the Press to Break Abu Ghraib Story?," *Editor & Publisher,* May 8, 2008, web.archive.org/web/20140221090737/http://www.editorandpublisher.com/Article/Four-Years-Later-Why-Did-It-Take-So-Long-for-the-Press-to-Break-Abu-Ghraib-Story-.

7. Michael Gelter, "The Images Are Getting Darker," *Washington Post,* May 9, 2004, www.washingtonpost.com/archive/opinions/2004/05/09/the-images-are-getting-darker/815a7763-e385-4b46-a069-a53b8804d9ff.

8. "Abuse of Iraqi POWs by GIs Probed," *60 Minutes II,* CBS News, April 27, 2004, www.youtube.com/watch?v=onPH6Xkq2zQ.

9. Joan Walsh, "The Abu Ghraib Files," *Salon,* March 16, 2006, web.archive.org/web/20080306020142/http://www.salon.com/news/abu_ghraib/2006/03/14/introduction.

10. Richard A. Serrano, "Guard Enjoyed Beating Iraqis, Three Testify," *Los Angeles Times,* Jan. 11, 2005, www.latimes.com/archives/la-xpm-2005-jan-11-na-graner11-story.html.

11. Philip Gourevitch and Errol Morris, *Standard Operating Procedure* (New York: Penguin Press, 2008), 127.

12. Ibid., 128.

13. Tara McKelvey, "Lynndie England in Love," *American Prospect,* July 23, 2007, prospect.org/article/lynndie-england-love.

14. Gail Gibson, "Guards Say Abu Ghraib Abuses Went Beyond Photos," *Baltimore Sun,* Jan. 11, 2005, www.baltimoresun.com/news/bal-te.graner11jan11-story.html.

15. Gourevitch and Morris, *Standard Operating Procedure,* 137.

16. Adam Clark Estes, "Eight Years After Abu Ghraib, Lynndie England's Not Doing So Well," *Atlantic,* March 19, 2012, www.theatlantic.com/national/archive/2012/03/eight-years-after-abu-ghraib-lynndie-englands-not-doing-so-well/330398.

17. David Jones, "Why the Hell Should I Feel Sorry, Says Girl Soldier Who Abused Iraqi Prisoners at Abu Ghraib Prison," *Daily Mail,* June 13, 2009, www.dailymail.co.uk/news/article-1192701/Why-hell-I-feel-sorry-says-girl-soldier-abused-Iraqi-prisoners-Abu-Ghraib-prison.html.

18. Gourevitch and Morris, *Standard Operating Procedure,* 72–73.

19. Ibid., 74.

20. Ibid., 71.

21. Ibid., 111.

22. Ibid., 113–14.

23. Jane Mayer, "Whatever It Takes," *New Yorker,* Feb. 11, 2007, www.newyorker.com/magazine/2007/02/19/whatever-it-takes.

24. *24,* season 1, "Day 1: 7:00 p.m.–8:00 p.m.," directed by Stephen Hopkins, Fox, aired April 6, 2002.

25. *24,* season 2, "Day 2: 8:00 a.m.–9:00 a.m.," directed by Jon Cassar, Fox, aired Oct. 29, 2002.

26. *24,* season 2, "Day 2: 9:00 p.m.–10:00 p.m.," directed by Jon Cassar, Fox, aired Feb. 25, 2003.

27. *24,* season 3, "Day 3: 2:00 a.m.–3:00 a.m.," directed by Bryan Spicer, Fox, aired Feb. 17, 2004.

28. *24,* season 3, "Day 3: 3:00 a.m.–4:00 a.m.," directed by Kevin Hooks, Fox, aired Feb. 24, 2004.

29. *24,* season 5, "Day 5: 1:00 p.m.–2:00 p.m.," directed by Brad Turner, Fox, aired Feb. 6, 2006.

30. *24,* season 5, "Day 5: 9:00 p.m.–10:00 p.m.," directed by Jon Cassar, Fox, aired March 27, 2006.

31. *24,* season 4, "Day 4: 9:00 a.m.–10:00 a.m.," directed by Brad Turner, Fox, aired Jan. 10, 2005.

32. *24,* season 4, "Day 4: 4:00 p.m.–5:00 p.m.," directed by Brad Turner, Fox, aired Feb. 21, 2005.

33. *24,* season 4, "Day 4: 5:00 p.m.–6:00 p.m.," directed by Jon Cassar, Fox, aired Feb. 28, 2005.

34. *24,* season 4, "Day 4: 12:00 a.m.–1:00 a.m.," directed by Jon Cassar, Fox, aired April 18, 2005.

35. *24,* season 4, "Day 4: 9:00 p.m.–10:00 p.m.," directed by Bryan Spicer, Fox, aired March 28, 2005.

36. *Saw,* directed by James Wan (Lionsgate Films, 2004).

37. *Saw,* Box Office Mojo, accessed Aug. 1, 2022, www.boxofficemojo.com/release/rl2289010177.

38. *Hostel,* directed by Eli Roth (Lionsgate Films, 2005).

39. *Hostel: Part II,* directed by Eli Roth (Lionsgate Films, 2007).

40. *Hostel: Part III,* directed by Eli Roth (Lionsgate Films, 2011).

41. *The Passion of the Christ,* directed by Mel Gibson (Icon Productions, 2004).

42. David Edelstein, "Now Playing at Your Local Multiplex: Torture Porn," *New York,* Jan. 26, 2006, nymag.com/movies/features/15622.

43. *24,* season 2, "Day 2: 7:00 p.m.–8:00 p.m.," directed by Frederick King Keller, Fox, aired Feb. 11, 2003.

44. *24,* season 2, "Day 2: 8:00 a.m.–9:00 a.m.," directed by Jon Cassar, Fox, aired Oct. 29, 2002.

45. Mayer, "Whatever It Takes."

46. Gourevitch and Morris, *Standard Operating Procedure,* 93.

47. Ibid., 102.

48. Ibid., 99.

49. Jane Mayer, *The Dark Side: The Inside Story of How the War on Terror Turned into a War on American Ideals* (New York: Doubleday, 2008), 52.

50. Ibid., 87.

51. Yonah Jeremy Bob, "US Senate Report: CIA Used Israeli Courts as Precedent to Justify Torture," *Jerusalem Post,* Dec. 10, 2014, www.jpost.com/Israel-News/US-Senate-Report-CIA-used-Israeli-courts-as-precedent-to-justify-torture-384237.

52. Chris Mackey and Greg Miller, *The Interrogators: Inside the Secret War Against Al Qaeda* (New York: Little, Brown, 2004), 109.

53. Ibid., 289.

54. Joshua E. S. Phillips, *None of Us Were Like This Before: American Soldiers and Torture* (New York: Verso, 2010), 30.

55. Ibid., 63.

56. Ibid., 64.

57. Ibid., 67.

58. Daniel Levin, "Definition of Torture Under 18 U.S.C. §§ 2340–2340A," U.S. Department of Justice, Dec. 30, 2004, www.justice.gov/sites/default/files/olc/opinions/2004/12/31/op-olc-v028-p0297_0.pdf.

59. John Yoo, *War by Other Means: An Insider's Account of the War on Terror* (New York: Atlantic Monthly Press, 2006), 183.

60. Cynthia H. Cho, "'Torture' Fracas Draws Apology," *Los Angeles Times,* June 22, 2005, www.latimes.com/archives/la-xpm-2005-jun-22-na-durbin22-story .html.

61. Mayer, *Dark Side,* 324.

62. Alfred W. McCoy, *A Question of Torture: CIA Interrogation, from the Cold War to the War on Terror* (New York: Metropolitan Books/Henry Holt, 2006), 167.

63. Phillips, *None of Us Were Like This Before,* 74–75.

64. *Taxi to the Dark Side,* directed by Alex Gibney (THINKFilm, 2007).

65. Brian Whitaker, "'Its Best Use Is as a Doorstop,'" *Guardian,* May 24, 2004, www.theguardian.com/world/2004/may/24/worlddispatch.usa.

66. Richard Cimino, "'No God in Common': American Evangelical Discourse on Islam After 9/11," *Review of Religious Research* 47, no. 2 (2005): 162–74.

67. Mary Jayne McKay, "Zion's Christian Soldiers: Conservative Christian Says Founder of Islam Set a Bad Example," *60 Minutes,* CBS News, June 8, 2003, web.archive.org/web/20090210195101/http://www.cbsnews.com/stories/2002/ 10/03/60minutes/main524268.shtml.

68. Hal Lindsey, *The Everlasting Hatred: The Roots of Jihad* (Washington, D.C.: WND Books, 2011).

69. Ibid., 210, 70.

70. Ibid., 9.

71. Ibid., 124–25.

72. Ibid., 10.

73. Ibid., 6, 13.

74. Tom Curry, "Why Torture Issue Hasn't Had Political Traction," NBC News, Feb. 15, 2005, www.nbcnews.com/id/wbna6970081.

75. Elizabeth Schambelan, "Special Journey to Our Bottom Line," *n+1,* no. 34 (Spring 2019), www.nplusonemag.com/issue-34/essays/special-journey-to-our -bottom-line.

76. Eric Zimmerman, "Schumer on Torture 2004: 'Do What You Have to Do,'" *Hill,* May 14, 2009, thehill.com/blogs/blog-briefing-room/news/lawmaker-news/ 31978-schumer-on-torture-2004-do-what-you-have-to-do.

77. Mayer, *Dark Side,* 8–9.

78. George F. Will, "America's Shockingly Violent Birth," *Washington Post,* June 30, 2017, www.washingtonpost.com/opinions/americas-shockingly-violent-birth/ 2017/06/30/46a378fe-5cea-11e7-9fc6-c7ef4bc58d13_story.html.

79. William d'Ambrusco, *American Torture from the Philippines to Iraq: A Recurring Nightmare* (New York: Oxford University Press, 2021).

80. Vincent Bevins, *The Jakarta Method: Washington's Anticommunist Crusade and the Mass Murder Program That Shaped Our World* (New York: PublicAffairs, 2020).

81. Mayer, *Dark Side,* 7–8.

Chapter 6: Geronimo

1. "McCain Suspends Campaign to Focus on Economic Crisis," TPM TV, Sept. 24, 2008, YouTube, www.youtube.com/watch?v=aDWSFKnBIHg.

2. Elisabeth Bumiller and Michael Cooper, "Obama Rebuffs McCain on Debate

Delay," *New York Times,* Sept. 24, 2008, www.nytimes.com/2008/09/25/us/politics/25mccain.html.

3. Henry M. Paulson Jr., "When Mr. McCain Came to Washington," *Wall Street Journal,* Feb. 6, 2010, www.wsj.com/articles/SB10001424052748704022804575041280125257648.

4. Jonathan Martin and Amie Parnes, "McCain: Obama Not an Arab, Crowd Boos," *Politico,* Oct. 10, 2008, www.politico.com/story/2008/10/mccain-obama-not-an-arab-crowd-boos-014479.

5. Matt Bai, "A Turning Point in the Discourse, but in Which Direction?," *New York Times,* Jan. 8, 2011, www.nytimes.com/2011/01/09/us/politics/09bai.html.

6. Ben Smith, "McCain Camp: Obama Is 'Radical,' Pals Around with Terrorists," *Politico,* Oct. 4, 2008, www.politico.com/blogs/ben-smith/2008/10/mccain-camp-obama-is-radical-pals-around-with-terrorists-012797.

7. Samuel Huntington, *The Clash of Civilizations and the Remaking of the World Order* (London: Free Press, 2002), 58.

8. Ibid., 66.

9. Ibid., 209.

10. Ibid., 256.

11. Ibid., 217.

12. Bernard Lewis, "The Roots of Muslim Rage," *Atlantic Monthly,* Sept. 1990, www.theatlantic.com/magazine/archive/1990/09/the-roots-of-muslim-rage/304643.

13. Evelyn Alsultany, *Arabs and Muslims in the Media: Race and Representation After 9/11* (New York: New York University Press, 2012), 3.

14. *Sleeper Cell,* season 1, "Al-Fatiha," directed by Clark Johnson, Showtime, aired Dec. 4, 2005.

15. *Homeland,* season 1, "Grace," directed by Michael Cuesta, Showtime, aired Oct. 9, 2011.

16. *Homeland,* season 1, "Blind Spot," directed by Clark Johnson, Showtime, aired Oct. 30, 2011.

17. *Homeland,* season 1, "Crossfire," directed by Jeffrey Nachmanoff, Showtime, aired Nov. 27, 2011.

18. Carole Cadwalladr, "Daniel Dennett: 'I Begrudge Every Hour I Have to Spend Worrying About Politics,'" *Guardian,* Feb. 12, 2017, www.theguardian.com/science/2017/feb/12/daniel-dennett-politics-bacteria-bach-back-dawkins-trump-interview.

19. Christopher Hitchens, *God Is Not Great: How Religion Poisons Everything* (New York: Twelve, 2007), 125.

20. Ibid., 136–37.

21. Richard Dawkins, *The God Delusion* (New York: Mariner Books, 2008), 23.

22. Hitchens, *God Is Not Great,* 28.

23. Sam Harris, *The End of Faith: Religion, Terror, and the Future of Reason* (New York: W. W. Norton, 2004), 123.

24. Sam Harris, "Bombing Our Illusions," *Huffington Post,* Oct. 10, 2005, www.huffpost.com/entry/bombing-our-illusions_b_8615.

25. Hitchens, *God Is Not Great,* 55.

26. Sam Harris, "Mired in a Religious War," *Washington Times,* Dec. 1, 2004, www.washingtontimes.com/news/2004/dec/1/20041201-090801-2582r.

27. Richard Dawkins (@RichardDawkins), Twitter, March 1, 2013, 1:01 a.m., twitter.com/RichardDawkins/status/307369895031603200.

28. Ian Parker, "He Knew He Was Right," *New Yorker,* Oct. 8, 2006, www .newyorker.com/magazine/2006/10/16/he-knew-he-was-right-2.

29. Dawkins, *God Delusion,* 182.

30. Barack Obama, *A Promised Land* (New York: Crown, 2020), 127–28.

31. Ibid., 41.

32. Ibid., 127, 41.

33. Ibid., 17.

34. Barack Obama, *The Audacity of Hope: Thoughts on Reclaiming the American Dream* (New York: Broadway Paperbacks, 2006), 229.

35. Ibid., 122.

36. Ibid., 266.

37. Obama, *Promised Land,* 116.

38. Ibid., 358.

39. Dana Priest, "Bush's 'War' on Terror Comes to a Sudden End," *Washington Post,* Jan. 23, 2009, www.washingtonpost.com/wp-dyn/content/article/2009/01/22/AR2009012203929.html.

40. Greg Miller, "How Drones Became Obama's Deadly Weapon in a High-Altitude, Perpetual War," *Washington Post,* June 3, 2016, www.washingtonpost .com/graphics/national/obama-legacy/drone-program-strikes.html.

41. "Pakistan: Reported US Strikes 2009," Bureau of Investigative Journalism, web.archive.org/web/20200226232608/https://www.thebureauinvestigates.com/drone-war/data/obama-2009-pakistan-strikes.

42. "Afghanistan War: Trump's Allies and Troop Numbers," BBC News, Aug. 22, 2017, www.bbc.com/news/world-41014263.

43. Michael Hastings, "The Runaway General," *Rolling Stone,* June 22, 2010, www .rollingstone.com/politics/politics-news/the-runaway-general-the-profile-that -brought-down-mcchrystal-192609.

44. Bacevich, *America's War for the Greater Middle East,* 297.

45. Ibid., 298.

46. Ibid., 300.

47. "Obama's Speech on NSA Phone Surveillance," transcript, *New York Times,* Jan. 17, 2014, www.nytimes.com/2014/01/18/us/politics/obamas-speech-on -nsa-phone-surveillance.html.

48. "Obama: Snowden Was No Patriot," CNN, Aug. 9, 2013, YouTube, www .youtube.com/watch?v=wS9TXJqxkSQ.

49. "Obama's Speech on NSA Phone Surveillance."

50. Al Baker, "Bloomberg Wants Terror Trial Moved," *City Room* (blog), *New York Times,* Jan. 27, 2010, archive.nytimes.com/cityroom.blogs.nytimes.com/2010/01/27/a-growing-cry-to-move-a-terror-trial.

51. Katie Rooney, "Cheney's Opening Salvo," *Time,* April 28, 2009, content.time.com/time/specials/packages/article/0,28804,1889908_1893754_1893874,00.html.

52. Ralph Blumenthal and Sharaf Mowjood, "Muslim Prayers and Renewal near Ground Zero," *New York Times,* Dec. 8, 2009, www.nytimes.com/2009/12/09/nyregion/09mosque.html.

53. Doug Chandler, "The Passions (and Perils) of Pamela Geller," *NY Jewish Week,*

Sept. 1, 2010, www.jta.org/2010/09/01/ny/the-passions-and-perils-of-pamela
-geller.

54. Chris McGreal, "The US Blogger on a Mission to Halt 'Islamic Takeover,'"
Guardian, Aug. 20, 2010, www.theguardian.com/world/2010/aug/20/rightwing
-blogs-islam-america.

55. "Obama Backs Mosque near Ground Zero," Associated Press, Aug. 13, 2010,
YouTube, www.youtube.com/watch?v=EZOIBEEvbO0.

56. Obama, *Promised Land,* 672.

57. Ibid., 588.

58. Macon Phillips, "Osama Bin Laden Dead," transcript, White House, President
Barack Obama, May 2, 2011, obamawhitehouse.archives.gov/blog/2011/05/02/
osama-bin-laden-dead.

59. "We Shall Remain," *American Experience,* PBS, May 11, 2009, www.pbs.org/
wgbh/americanexperience/films/weshallremain.

60. Gilbert King, "Geronimo's Appeal to Theodore Roosevelt," *Smithsonian
Magazine,* Nov. 9, 2012, www.smithsonianmag.com/history/geronimos-appeal
-to-theodore-roosevelt-117859516.

Chapter 7: Our Little, Imaginary World

1. Salam Pax, "Tuesday, August 05, 2003," *Where Is Raed?,* Aug. 5, 2003,
dear_raed.blogspot.com/2003/08/i-know-what-we-have-done-is-right-and
.html.

2. "Affording Country School," New Canaan Country School, accessed Aug. 22,
2023, www.countryschool.net/admission/affording-country-school.

3. "L. Paul Bremer III Oral History," transcript, Miller Center, University of
Virginia, Aug. 28–29, 2012, millercenter.org/the-presidency/presidential-oral
-histories/l-paul-bremer-iii-oral-history.

4. L. Paul Bremer III, *My Year in Iraq: The Struggle to Build a Future of Hope,* with
Malcolm McConnell (New York: Simon & Schuster, 2006), 4.

5. Patrick E. Tyler, "Overseer Adjusts Strategy as Turmoil Grows in Iraq," *New
York Times,* July 13, 2003, www.nytimes.com/2003/07/13/world/after-the-war
-the-overseer-overseer-adjusts-strategy-as-turmoil-grows-in-iraq.html.

6. Bremer, *My Year in Iraq,* 21.

7. Iraq (in Depth: Topics A-Z), Gallup, "Do you think the Bush administration
deliberately misled the American public about whether Iraq has weapons of
mass destruction, or not?," news.gallup.com/poll/1633/iraq.aspx.

8. "Bush and Public Opinion: Reviewing the Bush Years and the Public's Final
Verdict," Pew Research Center for the People and the Press, Dec. 18, 2008,
www.pewresearch.org/politics/2008/12/18/bush-and-public-opinion.

9. Megan Brenan, "Americans Split on Whether Afghanistan War Was a Mistake,"
Gallup News, July 26, 2021, news.gallup.com/poll/352793/americans-split
-whether-afghanistan-war-mistake.aspx.

10. Joseph E. Stiglitz and Linda J. Bilmes, *The Three Trillion Dollar War: The True
Cost of the Iraq Conflict* (New York: W. W. Norton, 2008).

11. "Human Cost of Post-9/11 Wars: Direct War Deaths in Major War Zones," *Costs
of War,* Watson Institute for International & Public Affairs, Brown University,
watson.brown.edu/costsofwar/figures/2021/WarDeathToll.

12. Mark Memmott, "Mark Wahlberg: With Me Aboard, 9/11 Hijackers Would

Have Been Stopped," *The Two-Way,* NPR, Jan. 18, 2012, www.npr.org/sections/thetwo-way/2012/01/18/145404733/mark-wahlberg-with-me-aboard-9-11-hijackers-would-have-been-stopped.

13. *Lone Survivor,* directed by Peter Berg (Universal Pictures, 2013).

14. Erik Hayden, " 'Lone Survivor': Texas Theater Cancels Other Film Screenings due to Demand," *Hollywood Reporter,* Jan. 12, 2014, www.hollywoodreporter.com/news/general-news/lone-survivor-texas-theater-cancels-670140.

15. Gal Luft, "How Much Oil Does Iraq Have?," Brookings, May 12, 2003, www.brookings.edu/research/how-much-oil-does-iraq-have.

16. Jane Mayer, "Contract Sport," *New Yorker,* Feb. 8, 2004, www.newyorker.com/magazine/2004/02/16/contract-sport.

17. Retort (Iain Boal et al.), *Afflicted Powers: Capital and Spectacle in a New Age of War,* new ed. (London: Verso, 2006), 47.

18. Ibid., 10.

19. Mike Patton, "U.S. Role in Global Economy Declines Nearly 50%," *Forbes,* Feb. 29, 2016, www.forbes.com/sites/mikepatton/2016/02/29/u-s-role-in-global-economy-declines-nearly-50/?sh=7078db4d5e9e.

20. George Packer, *The Assassins' Gate: America in Iraq* (New York: Farrar, Straus and Giroux, 2005), 158.

21. "Interview: Rajiv Chandrasekaran," *Frontline,* PBS, Oct. 17, 2006, www.pbs.org/wgbh/pages/frontline/yeariniraq/interviews/rajiv.html.

22. Rajiv Chandrasekaran, *Imperial Life in the Emerald City: Inside Iraq's Green Zone* (New York: Alfred A. Knopf, 2006), 11.

23. Ibid., 10.

24. "Iraq War Remembered: Good Morning Baghdad," Channel 4 News, July 7, 2016, www.youtube.com/watch?v=jfK7QJdl0oA.

25. "Interview: Rajiv Chandrasekaran," *Frontline.*

26. "Coalition Provisional Authority Order Number 1—De-Ba'athification of Iraqi Society," Coalition Provisional Authority, May 16, 2003, web.archive.org/web/20040621014307/http://www.iraqcoalition.org/regulations/20030516_CPAORD_1_De-Ba_athification_of_Iraqi_Society_.pdf.

27. "Coalition Provisional Authority Order Number 2—Dissolution of Entities," Coalition Provisional Authority, May 23, 2003, nsarchive2.gwu.edu/NSAEBB/NSAEBB418/docs/9b%20-%20Coalition%20Provisional%20Authority%20Order%20No%202%20-%208-23-03.pdf.

28. Thomas E. Ricks, *Fiasco: The American Military Adventure in Iraq, 2003 to 2005* (New York: Penguin, 2006), 163.

29. Raed, "Wednesday, December 17, 2003–4:16 pm," *A Family in Baghdad,* Dec. 17, 2003, afamilyinbaghdad.blogspot.com/2003/12/where-are-you-mam-start-bloging-for.html.

30. Salam Pax, "Tuesday, December 30, 2003–2:01 am," *Where Is Raed?,* Dec. 30, 2003, dear_raed.blogspot.com/2003/12/it-is-going-to-be-great-year-no.html.

31. Riverbend, *Baghdad Burning: Girl Blog from Iraq* (New York: Feminist Press at the City University of New York, 2005), 5.

32. Bremer, *My Year in Iraq,* 28.

33. Ibid., 71.

34. Ibid., 63–65.

35. Ibid., 68.

36. Ibid., 128.
37. Chandrasekaran, *Imperial Life in the Emerald City*, 117.
38. Antonia Juhasz, "The Handover That Wasn't," *AlterNet*, July 20, 2004, web.archive.org/web/20100323171357/http://www.alternet.org/story/19293.
39. Rajiv Chandrasekaran and Walter Pincus, "U.S. Edicts Curb Power of Iraq's Leadership," *Washington Post*, June 27, 2004, www.washingtonpost.com/archive/politics/2004/06/27/us-edicts-curb-power-of-iraqs-leadership/20f3a3f5-efc6-4374-a4bb-975c0a4d6a53.
40. "Coalition Provisional Authority Order Number 14—Prohibited Media Activity," Coalition Provisional Authority, June 15, 2003, govinfo.library.unt.edu/cpa-iraq/regulations/20030610_CPAORD_14_Prohibited_Media_Activity.pdf.
41. Bremer, *My Year in Iraq*, 148.
42. Ibid., 128.
43. Riverbend, *Baghdad Burning*, 22.
44. Ibid., 62.
45. Ibid., 68.
46. Khalid, "Monday, December 22, 2003–10:03 am," *A Family in Baghdad*, Dec. 22, 2003, afamilyinbaghdad.blogspot.com/2003/12/so.html.
47. Riverbend, *Baghdad Burning*, 201–6.
48. Salam Pax, "Friday, August 29, 2003–12:43 am," *Where Is Raed?*, Aug. 29, 2003, dear_raed.blogspot.com/2003/08/our-house-was-searched-by-americans.html.
49. "Coalition Provisional Authority Order Number 18—Measures to Ensure the Independence of the Central Bank of Iraq," Coalition Provisional Authority, July 18, 2003, govinfo.library.unt.edu/cpa-iraq/regulations/20030707_CPAORD_18_Independence_of_the_Central_Bank_of_Iraq.pdf.
50. Riverbend, *Baghdad Burning*, 7, 26.
51. Salam Pax, "Friday, May 09, 2003–11:47 am," *Where Is Raed?*, May 9, 2003, dear_raed.blogspot.com/2003/05/5-us-dollars-for-single-hour-of.html.
52. "Coalition Provisional Authority Order Number 39—Foreign Investment," Coalition Provisional Authority, Sept. 19, 2003, govinfo.library.unt.edu/cpa-iraq/regulations/20031220_CPAORD_39_Foreign_Investment_.pdf.
53. "Coalition Provisional Authority Order Number 30—Reform of Salaries and Employment Conditions of State Employees," Coalition Provisional Authority, Sept. 8, 2003, govinfo.library.unt.edu/cpa-iraq/regulations/20030908_CPAORD_30_Reform_of_Salaries_and_Employment_Conditions_of_State_Employees_with_Annex_A.pdf.
54. "Coalition Provisional Authority Order Number 29—Amendment to Law of Estate Lease," Coalition Provisional Authority, Sept. 7, 2003, govinfo.library.unt.edu/cpa-iraq/regulations/20030907_CPAORD_29_Amendment_to_Law_of_Estate_Lease.pdf.
55. "Coalition Provisional Authority Order Number 37—Tax Strategy for 2003," Coalition Provisional Authority, Sept. 19, 2003, govinfo.library.unt.edu/cpa-iraq/regulations/20030919_CPAORD_37_Tax_Strategy_for_2003.pdf.
56. Edmund L. Andrews, "Overseer in Iraq Vows to Sell Off Government-Owned Companies," *New York Times*, June 23, 2003, www.nytimes.com/2003/06/23/world/after-war-economy-overseer-iraq-vows-sell-off-government-owned-companies.html.
57. "Coalition Provisional Authority Order Number 51—Suspension of Exclusive

Agency Status of Iraqi State Company for Water Transportation," Coalition Provisional Authority, Jan. 14, 2004, govinfo.library.unt.edu/cpa-iraq/regulations/20040114_CPAORD_51_Water_Transportation_.pdf.

58. Naomi Klein, *The Shock Doctrine: The Rise of Disaster Capitalism* (New York: Metropolitan Books, 2007), 345.
59. Chandrasekaran, *Imperial Life in the Emerald City*, 62.
60. Klein, *Shock Doctrine*, 345.
61. Riverbend, *Baghdad Burning*, 76.
62. Faiza al-Araji, "Tuesday, January 06, 2004–7:28 pm," *A Family in Baghdad*, Jan. 6, 2004, afamilyinbaghdad.blogspot.com/2004/01/friday-26122004-visited-neighbours.html.
63. Salam Pax, "Tuesday, December 23, 2003–12:53 pm," *Where Is Raed?*, Dec. 23, 2003, dear_raed.blogspot.com/2003/12/as-mr.html.
64. Riverbend, *Baghdad Burning*, 35.
65. Pekka Hämäläinen, *Indigenous Continent: The Epic Contest for North America* (New York: Liveright, 2022), 88.
66. Chandrasekaran, *Imperial Life in the Emerald City*, 119.
67. Rajiv Chandrasekaran, "Attacks Force Retreat from Wide-Ranging Plans for Iraq," *Washington Post*, Dec. 28, 2003, www.washingtonpost.com/archive/politics/2003/12/28/attacks-force-retreat-from-wide-ranging-plans-for-iraq/ee72c7cf-955a-4f5d-98f8-4e78dea11cb8.

Chapter 8: The Sign of Autumn

1. Giovanni Arrighi, *The Long Twentieth Century: Money, Power, and the Origins of Our Times* (New York: Verso, 1994), 379.
2. Michael Ignatieff, "Why Are We in Iraq? (And Liberia? And Afghanistan?)," *New York Times Magazine*, Sept. 7, 2003, www.nytimes.com/2003/09/07/magazine/why-are-we-in-iraq-and-liberia-and-afghanistan.html.
3. Arrighi, *Long Twentieth Century*, 41.
4. Ibid., 34.
5. Ibid., 5–6.
6. Ibid., 6.
7. Ibid., 134–37.
8. Ibid., 142.
9. Quoted in ibid., 140.
10. Arrighi, *Long Twentieth Century*, 168.
11. "World GDP over the Last Two Millennia," chart, Our World in Data, ourworldindata.org/grapher/world-gdp-over-the-last-two-millennia; and Angus Maddison, "The World Economy: A Millennial Perspective," Development Centre Studies, OECD, 2001, theunbrokenwindow.com/Development/MADDISON%20The%20World%20Economy--A%20Millennial.pdf.
12. Robert J. Gordon, *The Rise and Fall of American Growth: The U.S. Standard of Living Since the Civil War* (Princeton, N.J.: Princeton University Press, 2016), 1.
13. Arrighi, *Long Twentieth Century*, 30.
14. Robert Brenner, "What Is Good for Goldman Sachs Is Good for America: The Origins of the Current Crisis," Verso Blog, Nov. 13, 2018, originally published April 18, 2009, www.versobooks.com/blogs/4122-what-is-good-for-goldman-sachs-is-good-for-america-the-origins-of-the-current-crisis.

15. Aaron Benanav, *Automation and the Future of Work* (London: Verso, 2020), 24.

16. See Mike Davis, *Prisoners of the American Dream: Politics and Economy in the History of the U.S. Working Class* (1986; London: Verso, 2018).

17. Benanav, *Automation and the Future of Work,* 25.

18. Brenner, "What Is Good for Goldman Sachs Is Good for America."

19. Ibid.

20. Benanav, *Automation and the Future of Work,* 46–47.

21. Ibid., 47.

22. Mike Davis, *Planet of Slums* (2006; London: Verso, 2017), 2.

23. Ibid., 6.

24. Ibid., 178.

25. International Labour Office, United Nations, *Women and Men in the Informal Economy: A Statistical Picture,* 3rd ed. (Geneva: ILO, 2018), www.ilo.org/wcmsp5/groups/public/---dgreports/---dcomm/documents/publication/wcms_626831.pdf.

26. Alexander Lee, "Who Becomes a Terrorist? Poverty, Education, and the Origins of Political Violence," *World Politics* 63, no. 2 (April 2011): 203–45.

27. Alan B. Krueger, *What Makes a Terrorist: Economics and the Roots of Terrorism* (Princeton, N.J.: Princeton University Press, 2007), 79.

28. Pankaj Mishra, *Age of Anger: A History of the Present* (New York: Farrar, Straus and Giroux, 2017), 112.

29. Ralph Peters, "Our Soldiers, Their Cities," *Parameters* (Spring 1996): 43–50, cited in Davis, *Planet of Slums,* 203.

30. "Transforming Defense: National Security in the 21st Century," Synopsis, U.S. Army AMEDD Center and School, Fort Sam Houston, Tex., Dec. 1997, 11.

31. "Transforming Defense: National Security in the 21st Century," Report of the National Defense Panel, Chairman Philip A. Odeen, Dec. 1997, 6.

32. Jennifer Morrison Taw and Bruce Hoffman, "The Urbanization of Insurgency: The Potential Challenge to U.S. Army Operations," *Small Wars and Insurgencies* 6, no. 1 (1995): 68–87.

33. Troy Thomas, "Slumlords: Aerospace Power in Urban Fights," *Aerospace Power Journal* (Spring 2002): 1–15, cited in Davis, *Planet of Slums,* 204.

34. Peters, "Our Soldiers, Their Cities."

Chapter 9: Borders, Squares, Real Estate, Streets

1. Joshua Hersh, "Egypt: American Tear Gas, Policy Loom over Tahrir Square," *HuffPost,* Nov. 23, 2011, www.huffpost.com/entry/egypt-tahrir-square-tear-gas_n_1110292.

2. Joe Coscarelli, " 'Occupy Wall Street' Protesters Claim Excessive NYPD Force in Latest Arrests," *New York,* Sept. 20, 2011, nymag.com/intelligencer/2011/09/occupy_wall_street_protestors.html.

3. Jim Gilchrist and Jerome R. Corsi, *Minutemen: The Battle to Secure America's Borders* (Los Angeles: World Ahead Publishing, 2006), 6.

4. Susy Buchanan and David Holthouse, "Minuteman Civil Defense Corps Leader Chris Simcox Has Troubled Past," *Intelligence Report,* Jan. 31, 2006, www.splcenter.org/fighting-hate/intelligence-report/2006/minuteman-civil-defense-corps-leader-chris-simcox-has-troubled-past.

5. Gilchrist and Corsi, *Minutemen,* 5.

6. Ibid., 3.

7. Harel Shapira, *Waiting for José: The Minutemen's Pursuit of America* (Princeton, N.J.: Princeton University Press, 2013), 21.

8. Ibid., 19.

9. Ibid., 58–59.

10. Ibid., 19.

11. Ibid., 113.

12. Ibid., 6.

13. Ibid., 55.

14. Ibid., 109.

15. Ibid., 2.

16. Ibid., 62.

17. Ibid., 109–11.

18. Daniel Denvir, *All-American Nativism: How the Bipartisan War on Immigrants Explains Politics as We Know It* (London: Verso, 2020), 107.

19. Ibid., 110.

20. "State Dept. Lapses Aided 9/11 Hijackers," ABC News, Oct. 23, 2002, abcnews .go.com/WNT/story?id=130051&page=1.

21. Mark Potter and Rich Phillips, "Six Months After Sept. 11, Hijackers' Visa Approval Letters Received," CNN, March 13, 2002, web.archive.org/web/ 20220217055955/https://www.cnn.com/2002/US/03/12/inv.flight.school.visas.

22. "Attorney General Prepared Remarks on the National Security Entry-Exit Registration System," Department of Justice, June 6, 2002, www.justice.gov/ archive/ag/speeches/2002/060502agpreparedremarks.htm.

23. Denvir, *All-American Nativism,* 111.

24. Border Patrol Agent Nationwide Staffing by Fiscal Year (1992–2018), U.S. Border Patrol, www.cbp.gov/sites/default/files/assets/documents/2019-Mar/ Staffing%20FY1992-FY2018.pdf.

25. A. Naomi Paik, *Bans, Walls, Raids, Sanctuary: Understanding U.S. Immigration for the Twenty-First Century* (Berkeley: University of California Press, 2020), 69–70.

26. Todd Miller, *Border Patrol Nation: Dispatches from the Front Lines of Homeland Security* (San Francisco: City Lights Books, 2014), 22–23, 30.

27. Ibid., 107.

28. Ibid., 261.

29. Ronn Blitzer, "Border Patrol Caught 10 Terror Suspects at Border in July, New Data Shows," Fox News, Aug. 16, 2022, www.foxnews.com/politics/border -patrol-caught-ten-terror-suspects-border-july-new-data-shows.

30. Paik, *Bans, Walls, Raids, Sanctuary,* 11–12.

31. Miller, *Border Patrol Nation,* 17–18.

32. "Largest Armies in the World Ranked by Active Military Personnel in 2022," chart, Statista, www.statista.com/statistics/264443/the-worlds-largest-armies -based-on-active-force-level.

33. Miller, *Border Patrol Nation,* 26–27.

34. Paik, *Bans, Walls, Raids, Sanctuary,* 93, 76.

35. *9/11 Commission Report,* 362.

36. Todd Miller, *Empire of Borders: The Expansion of the U.S. Border Around the World* (New York: Verso, 2019), 32, 33.

37. Ibid., 177.

38. Ibid., 140.

39. "The Preclearance Experience," video, U.S. Customs and Border Protection, www.cbp.gov/travel/preclearance.

40. Miller, *Empire of Borders,* 132–33.

41. Ibid., 154–55.

42. Ibid., 132.

43. Justin Elliott, "How Did the U.S. Get in Bed with Mubarak?," *Salon,* Jan. 29, 2011, www.salon.com/2011/01/29/egypt_america_alliance.

44. Edmund Blair, "Up Close, but Not Very Personal, with Col. Gaddafi," Reuters, Feb. 25, 2011, www.reuters.com/article/idINIndia-55161720110225.

45. "Gaddafi's Son in Civil War Warning," *Al Jazeera,* Feb. 21, 2011, www.aljazeera .com/news/2011/2/21/gaddafis-son-in-civil-war-warning.

46. Micah Zenko, "The Big Lie About the Libyan War," *Foreign Policy,* March 22, 2016, foreignpolicy.com/2016/03/22/libya-and-the-myth-of-humanitarian -intervention.

47. Ian Black, "UK Envoy: If Libya Fails It Could Be Somalia on the Mediterranean," *Guardian,* Feb. 16, 2015, www.theguardian.com/world/on-the-middle-east/ 2015/feb/16/uk-envoy-if-libya-fails-it-could-be-somalia-on-the-mediterranean.

48. Charles Glass, *Syria Burning: A Short History of a Catastrophe* (New York: Verso, 2016), 121.

49. William Wheeler and Ayman Oghanna, "After Liberation, Nowhere to Run," *New York Times,* Oct. 29, 2011, www.nytimes.com/2011/10/30/opinion/sunday/ libyas-forgotten-refugees.html.

50. Khalid Koser, "Migration, Displacement, and the Arab Spring: Lessons to Learn," Brookings Institution, March 22, 2012, www.brookings.edu/opinions/ migration-displacement-and-the-arab-spring-lessons-to-learn.

51. Andrew Berwick (pseud.), *2083: A European Declaration of Independence* (self-published), 774.

52. Scott Shane, "Killings in Norway Spotlight Anti-Muslim Thought in U.S.," *New York Times,* July 24, 2011, www.nytimes.com/2011/07/25/us/25debate.html.

53. "Remarks by the President on Comprehensive Immigration Reform in El Paso, Texas," White House, Office of the Press Secretary, May 10, 2011, obamawhitehouse.archives.gov/the-press-office/2011/05/10/remarks-president -comprehensive-immigration-reform-el-paso-texas.

54. Paik, *Bans, Walls, Raids, Sanctuary,* 95–98.

55. Gardiner Harris, David E. Sanger, and David M. Herszenhorn, "Obama Increases Number of Syrian Refugees for U.S. Resettlement to 10,000," *New York Times,* Sept. 10, 2015, www.nytimes.com/2015/09/11/world/middleeast/ obama-directs-administration-to-accept-10000-syrian-refugees.html.

56. Jon Henley, Ian Traynor, and Warren Murray, "Paris Attacks: EU in Emergency Talks on Border Crackdown," *Guardian,* Nov. 20, 2015, www.theguardian .com/world/2015/nov/20/paris-attacks-france-launches-un-push-for-unified -declaration-of-war-on-isis.

57. "Youth Unemployment in the Arab World Is a Major Cause for Rebellion," International Labour Organization, United Nations, April 5, 2011, www.ilo

.org/global/about-the-ilo/newsroom/features/WCMS_154078/lang--en/index
.htm%3E.

58. Maeve Shearlaw, "Egypt Five Years On: Was It Ever a 'Social Media
Revolution'?," *Guardian,* Jan. 25, 2016, www.theguardian.com/world/2016/
jan/25/egypt-5-years-on-was-it-ever-a-social-media-revolution.

59. Brenner, "What Is Good for Goldman Sachs Is Good for America."

60. Colleen Shalby, "The Financial Crisis Hit 10 Years Ago. For Some, It Feels Like
Yesterday," *Los Angeles Times,* Sept. 15, 2018, www.latimes.com/business/la-fi
-financial-crisis-experiences-20180915-htmlstory.html.

61. "Figure 8. Number in Poverty and Poverty Rate: 1959 to 2020," U.S. Census
Bureau, Jan. 2022, www.census.gov/newsroom/stories/poverty-awareness
-month.html.

62. Civilian Labor Force Participation Rate, chart, U.S. Bureau of Labor Statistics,
Dec. 2, 2022, www.bls.gov/charts/employment-situation/civilian-labor-force
-participation-rate.htm.

63. Colin Moynihan, "In 'Occupy,' Well-Educated Professionals Far Outnumbered
Jobless, Study Finds," *City Room* (blog), *New York Times,* Jan. 28, 2013, archive
.nytimes.com/cityroom.blogs.nytimes.com/2013/01/28/in-occupy-well
-educated-professionals-far-outnumbered-jobless-study-finds.

64. Petra Cahill, "What Happened to the Antiwar Movement?," NBC News,
March 19, 2004, www.nbcnews.com/id/wbna4546739.

65. Sean Bell, "Everyone Lost: Protest Art and the Iraq War," *PopMatters,* March 7,
2013, www.popmatters.com/168763-everyone-lost-protest-art-and-the-iraq
-war-2495775122.html.

66. "Widespread Looting Preceded by Cars Set on Fire, Tear Gas Deployed at Violent
Rally in Rochester," *RochesterFirst,* May 30, 2020, www.rochesterfirst.com/news/
local-news/underway-black-lives-matter-rally-in-downtown-rochester.

67. Mapping Police Violence, mappingpoliceviolence.org.

Chapter 10: The Iraq War Debate Did Not Take Place

1. Alexis de Tocqueville, *Democracy in America,* trans. Arthur Goldhammer (New
York: Library of America, 2004), 278–79.

2. Ibid., 825.

3. Ibid., 212.

4. "In Iraq Crisis, Networks Are Megaphones for Official Views," Fairness and
Accuracy in Reporting, March 18, 2003, fair.org/take-action/action-alerts/in
-iraq-crisis-networks-are-megaphones-for-official-views.

5. "Americans' Trust in Media Remains Near Record Low," Gallup News, Oct. 18,
2022, news.gallup.com/poll/403166/americans-trust-media-remains-near
-record-low.aspx.

6. "The Times and Iraq," *New York Times,* May 26, 2004, www.nytimes.com/2004/
05/26/world/from-the-editors-the-times-and-iraq.html.

7. Howard Kurtz, "Media's Failure on Iraq Still Stings," CNN, March 11, 2013,
www.cnn.com/2013/03/11/opinion/kurtz-iraq-media-failure/index.html.

8. Susan Sontag, "Tuesday, and After," *New Yorker,* Sept. 24, 2001, www.newyorker
.com/magazine/2001/09/24/tuesday-and-after-talk-of-the-town.

9. Andrew Sullivan, "September 18, 2001," *The Dish,* Sept. 18, 2001, dish
.andrewsullivan.com/2001/09/17/september-18-2001.

10. Jonathan Alter, "Blame America at Your Peril," *Newsweek,* Oct. 15, 2001, 41.

11. Rod Dreher, "Painful to Live in Stricken N.Y.," *New York Post,* Sept. 20, 2001, nypost.com/2001/09/20/painful-to-live-in-stricken-n-y.

12. David Talbot, "The 'Traitor' Fires Back," *Salon,* Oct. 16, 2001, www.salon.com/2001/10/16/susans.

13. Lawrence F. Kaplan, "No Choice," *New Republic,* Oct. 1, 2001, newrepublic.com/article/64059/no-choice.

14. Talbot, " 'Traitor' Fires Back."

15. Ibid.

16. Ibid.

17. Adam Gopnik, "The City and the Pillars," *New Yorker,* Sept. 17, 2001, www.newyorker.com/magazine/new-york-journal/the-city-and-the-pillars.

18. " 'Shut Up and Sing': Dixie Chicks' Big Grammy Win Caps Comeback from Backlash over Anti-war Stance," *Democracy Now,* transcript, Feb. 15, 2007, web.archive.org/web/20071114015029/http://www.democracynow.org/article.pl?sid=07%2F02%2F15%2F1528222.

19. Jon Pareles, "The Dixie Chicks: America Catches Up with Them," *New York Times,* May 21, 2006, www.nytimes.com/2006/05/21/arts/music/21pare.html.

20. Allison Stewart, "The Fallout over Clear Channel's (Possibly Apocryphal) Do-Not-Play List Lasted Well Past 9/11," *Washington Post,* Oct. 8, 2021, www.washingtonpost.com/entertainment/music/clear-channel-911-list/2021/10/07/2dd3dee2-17d8-11ec-b976-f4a43b740aeb_story.html.

21. Dwight Garner and Jennifer Szalai, "Dread, War, and Ambivalence: Literature Since the Towers Fell," *New York Times,* Sept. 3, 2021, www.nytimes.com/2021/09/03/books/911-anniversary-fiction-literature.html.

22. Susannah Fox and Deborah Fallows, "The Internet and the Iraq War," Pew Research Center, April 1, 2003, www.pewresearch.org/internet/2003/04/01/the-internet-and-the-iraq-war.

23. Bill Carter and Felicity Barringer, "In Patriotic Time, Dissent Is Muted," *New York Times,* Sept. 28, 2001, www.nytimes.com/2001/09/28/us/a-nation-challenged-speech-and-expression-in-patriotic-time-dissent-is-muted.html.

24. Michael R. Gordon and Judith Miller, "U.S. Says Hussein Intensifies Quest for A-Bomb Parts," *New York Times,* Sept. 8, 2002, www.nytimes.com/2002/09/08/world/threats-responses-iraqis-us-says-hussein-intensifies-quest-for-bomb-parts.html.

25. Judith Miller, "Iraqi Tells of Renovations at Sites for Chemical and Nuclear Arms," *New York Times,* Dec. 20, 2001, www.nytimes.com/2001/12/20/world/nation-challenged-secret-sites-iraqi-tells-renovations-sites-for-chemical.html.

26. Judith Miller and Michael R. Gordon, "White House Lists Iraq Steps to Build Banned Weapons," *New York Times,* Sept. 13, 2002, www.nytimes.com/2002/09/13/world/threats-responses-baghdad-s-arsenal-white-house-lists-iraq-steps-build-banned.html.

27. "Booking Agent Who Brought Elvis Back to Las Vegas Dies," *Las Vegas Sun,* Dec. 12, 2002, lasvegassun.com/news/2002/dec/12/booking-agent-who-brought-elvis-back-to-las-vegas-.

28. Michael Massing, "Now They Tell Us," *New York Review of Books,* Feb. 26, 2004, www.nybooks.com/articles/2004/02/26/now-they-tell-us.

29. "The Bush Foreign Policy Team," *New York Times,* Dec. 16, 2000, www.nytimes .com/2000/12/16/opinion/the-bush-foreign-policy-team.html.

30. Michael Lewis, "Reluctant Warrior," *New York Times,* Nov. 26, 2006, www .nytimes.com/2006/11/26/books/review/Lewis.t.html.

31. Steven Rattner, "Roll Call," *Slate,* Feb. 19, 2003.

32. "The Case Against Iraq," *New York Times,* Feb. 6, 2003, www.nytimes.com/2003/ 02/06/opinion/the-case-against-iraq.html.

33. "U.S. Secretary of State Colin Powell Addresses the U.N. Security Council," transcript, White House, President George W. Bush, Feb. 5, 2003, georgewbush -whitehouse.archives.gov/news/releases/2003/02/20030205-1.html.

34. Resolution 1441 (2002), United Nations Security Council, Nov. 8, 2002, www .un.org/depts/unmovic/documents/1441.pdf.

35. Michael E. O'Hanlon and Philip H. Gordon, "Is Fighting Iraq Worth the Risks?," *New York Times,* July 25, 2002, www.nytimes.com/2002/07/25/opinion/ is-fighting-iraq-worth-the-risks.html.

36. "A Time for Candor in Iraq," *New York Times,* Aug. 3, 2002, www.nytimes.com/ 2002/08/03/opinion/a-time-for-candor-on-iraq.html.

37. "Steps Before War," *New York Times,* Aug. 11, 2002, www.nytimes.com/2002/08/ 11/opinion/steps-before-war.html.

38. "Warning Shots on Iraq," *New York Times,* Aug. 16, 2002, www.nytimes.com/ 2002/08/16/opinion/warning-shots-on-iraq.html.

39. Bill Keller, "The Loyal Opposition," *New York Times,* Aug. 24, 2002, www .nytimes.com/2002/08/24/opinion/the-loyal-opposition.html.

40. "Countdown to a Collision," *New York Times,* Sept. 5, 2002, www.nytimes.com/ 2002/09/05/opinion/countdown-to-a-collision.html.

41. "The Politics of War," *New York Times,* Sept. 20, 2002, www.nytimes.com/2002/ 09/20/opinion/the-politics-of-war.html.

42. "A Time for Debate and Reflection," *New York Times,* Oct. 3, 2002, www .nytimes.com/2002/10/03/opinion/a-time-for-debate-and-reflection.html.

43. "A Nation Wary of War," *New York Times,* Oct. 8, 2002, www.nytimes.com/ 2002/10/08/opinion/a-nation-wary-of-war.html.

44. "The Iraq Dossier," *New York Times,* Jan. 10, 2003, www.nytimes.com/2003/ 01/10/opinion/the-iraq-dossier.html.

45. "The Iraq Report," *New York Times,* Jan. 28, 2003, www.nytimes.com/2003/ 01/28/opinion/the-iraq-report.html.

46. "An Improvised March to War," *New York Times,* Feb. 2, 2003, www.nytimes .com/2003/02/02/opinion/an-improvised-march-to-war.html.

47. "The President Looks Toward War," *New York Times,* March 7, 2003, www .nytimes.com/2003/03/07/opinion/the-president-looks-toward-war.html.

48. "President Bush Prepares for War," *New York Times,* March 17, 2003, www .nytimes.com/2003/03/17/opinion/president-bush-prepares-for-war.html.

49. Hendrik Hertzberg, "Attack Anxiety," *New Yorker,* March 9, 2003, www .newyorker.com/magazine/2003/03/17/attack-anxiety.

50. George Packer, "The Liberal Quandary over Iraq," *New York Times Magazine,* Dec. 8, 2002, www.nytimes.com/2002/12/08/magazine/the-liberal-quandary -over-iraq.html.

51. Thomas L. Friedman, "Tell the Truth," *New York Times,* Feb. 19, 2003, www .nytimes.com/2003/02/19/opinion/tell-the-truth.html.

52. Packer, "Liberal Quandary over Iraq."

53. Hertzberg, "Attack Anxiety."

54. Michael Erard, "No Comments," *New York Times*, Sept. 20, 2023, www.nytimes
    .com/2013/09/22/magazine/no-comments.html.

55. "Percentage of Population Using the Internet in the United States from 2000 to
    2022," Statista Research Department, July 7, 2022, www.statista.com/statistics/
    209117/us-internet-penetration.

56. Charlotte Raven, "A Bully with a Bloody Nose Is Still a Bully," *Guardian*,
    Sept. 18, 2001, www.theguardian.com/world/2001/sep/18/september11
    .comment.

57. Andrew Sullivan, "Appeasement Watch," *The Dish*, Sept. 18, 2001, dish
    .andrewsullivan.com/2001/09/18/appeasement-watch-2.

58. Matthew Yglesias, "Afghan Optimism," *Matthew Yglesias: A Reality-Based
    Weblog*, Sept. 30, 2004, yglesias.typepad.com/matthew/2004/09/afghan
    _optimism.html.

59. Matthew Yglesias, "Hyper-hawkish TNR Editorial," *Matthew Yglesias*, Jan. 31,
    2002, web.archive.org/web/20201115173556/http://yglesias.blogspot.com/2002
    _01_27_archive.html#9239310.

60. "Tom Friedman's Flexible Deadlines," *FAIR*, July 1, 2006, fair.org/extra/tom
    -friedman8217s-flexible-deadlines.

61. Atrios, "The Six Monthers," *Eschaton*, May 21, 2006, www.eschatonblog.com/
    2006/05/six-monthers_21.html.

62. "Get Your War On 1–#8," *Get Your War On*, Oct. 9, 2001, www.mnftiu.cc/
    category/gywo/war1.

63. "Roll Call: Who's for War, Who's Against It, and Why," *Slate*, Feb. 19, 2003, slate
    .com/news-and-politics/2003/02/who-s-for-war-who-s-against-it-and-why
    .html.

64. David Plotz, "Make War, Help the Bourgeois," *Slate*, Oct. 3, 2002, slate.com/
    news-and-politics/2002/10/make-war-help-the-bourgeois.html.

65. Jeffrey Goldberg, "Aflatoxin," *Slate*, Oct. 3, 2002, slate.com/news-and-politics/
    2002/10/aflatoxin.html.

66. Julia Ioffe, "Ezra Klein: The Wise Boy," *New Republic*, Feb. 12, 2013,
    newrepublic.com/article/112366/ezra-klein-profile-wonkblogs-wise-boy
    -cannot-be-stopped.

67. "Fighting Words," *Slow Burn: The Road to the Iraq War*, podcast transcript,
    May 12, 2021, slate.com/transcripts/RHl5NGkrdkJoZS9pUzB6anBZQVRiekhIc
    XBhQ2xxT0NTSG1FRWZLd3dEdz0=.

68. "Mr. Obama's Task," *New York Times*, Nov. 18, 2009, www.nytimes.com/2009/
    11/19/opinion/19thu1.html.

69. "At War in Libya," *New York Times*, March 21, 2011, www.nytimes.com/2011/
    03/22/opinion/22tue1.html.

70. Mark Hensch, "CNN Host: 'Donald Trump Became President' Last Night," *Hill*,
    April 7, 2017, thehill.com/homenews/administration/327779-cnn-host-donald
    -trump-became-president-last-night.

71. Frank Newport, "Seventy-Two Percent of Americans Support War Against
    Iraq," Gallup News, March 24, 2003, news.gallup.com/poll/8038/seventytwo
    -percent-americans-support-war-against-iraq.aspx.

72. Jeffrey M. Jones, "Public Support for Iraq Invasion Inches Upward," Gallup

News, March 17, 2003, news.gallup.com/poll/7990/public-support-iraq
-invasion-inches-upward.aspx.

73. Joint Resolution to Authorize the Use of United States Armed Forces Against
Those Responsible for the Recent Attacks Launched Against the United States,
Public Law 107-40, 115 Stat. 224 (2001).

74. John Fund, "Who Is Barbara Lee?," *Wall Street Journal,* Sept. 17, 2001, www.wsj
.com/articles/SB122418640015141825.

75. Matthew Weed, "Presidential References to the 2001 Authorization for Use
of Military Force in Publicly Available Executive Actions and Reports to
Congress," Congressional Research Service, Feb. 16, 2018, sgp.fas.org/crs/
natsec/pres-aumf.pdf.

76. David Firestone, "Democrats Seek Compromise with White House on Iraq,"
New York Times, Oct. 1, 2002, www.nytimes.com/2002/10/01/us/threats
-responses-politics-democrats-seek-compromise-with-white-house-iraq.html.

77. Eric Schmitt, "Rumsfeld Says U.S. Has 'Bulletproof' Evidence of Iraq's Links
to Al-Qaeda," *New York Times,* Sept. 28, 2002, www.nytimes.com/2002/09/28/
world/threats-responses-intelligence-rumsfeld-says-us-has-bulletproof
-evidence-iraq-s.html.

78. "Authority of the President Under Domestic and International Law to Use
Military Force Against Iraq," *Opinions of the Office of Legal Counsel in Volume
26,* Office of Legal Counsel, U.S. Justice Department, Oct. 23, 2002, 152, www
.justice.gov/sites/default/files/olc/opinions/2002/10/31/op-olc-v026-p0143_0
.pdf.

79. Scott R. Anderson, "How the 2002 Iraq AUMF Got to Be So Dangerous, Part 1:
History and Practice," *Lawfare,* Lawfare Institute, Nov. 15, 2022, www
.lawfareblog.com/how-2002-iraq-aumf-got-be-so-dangerous-part-1-history
-and-practice.

80. Authorization for Use of Military Force Against Iraq Resolution of 2002, Public
Law No. 107-243, 116 Stat. 1498 (2002), www.congress.gov/bill/107th-congress/
house-joint-resolution/114/text.

81. "A Time for Debate and Reflection," *New York Times,* Oct. 3, 2002, www
.nytimes.com/2002/10/03/opinion/a-time-for-debate-and-reflection.html.

82. Maureen Dowd, "Can Hillary Upgrade?," *New York Times,* Oct. 2, 2002, www
.nytimes.com/2002/10/02/opinion/can-hillary-upgrade.html.

83. Chris Sullentrop, "The Anti-war Democrats," *Slate,* Oct. 2, 2002, slate.com/
news-and-politics/2002/10/the-anti-war-democrats.html.

84. Andrew Sullivan, "Whose Side Are They On?," *The Dish,* Sept. 30, 2002, dish
.andrewsullivan.com/2002/09/30/whose-side-are-they-on.

Chapter 11: Mom, Can You Not Read over My Shoulder?

1. "AT&T Long Lines Building," NYC Urbanism, www.nycurbanism.com/
brutalnyc/att-long-lines-building.

2. Ryan Gallagher and Henrik Moltke, "TITANPOINTE: The NSA's Spy Hub in
New York, Hidden in Plain Sight," *Intercept,* Nov. 16, 2016, theintercept.com/
2016/11/16/the-nsas-spy-hub-in-new-york-hidden-in-plain-sight.

3. Ryan Gallagher and Henrik Moltke, "The Wiretap Rooms: The NSA's Hidden
Spy Hubs in Eight U.S. Cities," *Intercept,* June 25, 2018, theintercept.com/2018/
06/25/att-internet-nsa-spy-hubs.

4. E-mail from [redacted] to James R. Clapper, Office of the Director of National Intelligence, FOIA Case # DF-2017-00119, Nov. 16, 2016, www.dni.gov/files/documents/FOIA/DF-2017-00119-TITANPOINTE.pdf.

5. Jake Tapper, "Squabbling Returns," *Salon*, Oct. 3, 2001, www.salon.com/2001/10/03/ashcroft_13.

6. Malcolm Harris, *Palo Alto: A History of California, Capitalism, and the World* (New York: Little, Brown, 2023), 505.

7. Jamie Doward, "Can Larry Go On Forever?," *Guardian*, June 24, 2001, www.theguardian.com/business/2001/jun/24/news.theobserver.

8. Joseph Menn, "National ID Card System Failing to Attract Supporters," *Los Angeles Times*, Oct. 24, 2001, www.latimes.com/archives/la-xpm-2001-oct-24-mn-60963-story.html.

9. David Lyon, *Surveillance After September 11* (Cambridge, U.K.: Polity, 2003), 68.

10. *9/11 Commission Report*, 376.

11. Ibid., 374.

12. Ibid., 389.

13. Malcolm Harris, *Palo Alto*, 503.

14. Ibid., 514.

15. Shane Harris, *The Watchers: The Rise of America's Surveillance State* (New York: Penguin Press, 2010), 178.

16. Malcolm Harris, *Palo Alto*, 519.

17. Ibid., 505.

18. Ibid., 517–18.

19. Shane Harris, *Watchers*, 197.

20. Malcolm Harris, *Palo Alto*, 518.

21. Shane Harris, *Watchers*, 167–68.

22. William Safire, "You Are a Suspect," *New York Times*, Nov. 14, 2002, www.nytimes.com/2002/11/14/opinion/you-are-a-suspect.html.

23. Ritt Goldstein, "US Planning to Recruit One in 24 Americans as Citizen Spies," *Sydney Morning Herald*, July 15, 2002, www.smh.com.au/world/us-planning-to-recruit-one-in-24-americans-as-citizen-spies-20020715-gdfgbq.html.

24. Andy Newman, "Citizen Snoops Wanted (Call Toll-Free)," *New York Times*, July 21, 2002, www.nytimes.com/2002/07/21/weekinreview/ideas-trends-look-out-citizen-snoops-wanted-call-toll-free.html.

25. Shane Harris, *Watchers*, 170.

26. "Only Collect," *n+1*, no. 18 (Winter 2014), www.nplusonemag.com/issue-18/the-intellectual-situation/nsa.

27. Ibid.

28. Malcolm Harris, *Palo Alto*, 581–82.

29. Andy Greenberg, "Here's How Often AT&T, Sprint, and Verizon Each Hand Over Users' Data to the Government," *Forbes*, July 9, 2012, www.forbes.com/sites/andygreenberg/2012/07/09/by-the-numbers-heres-how-often-att-sprint-and-verizon-hand-over-users-data-to-the-government/?sh=6b1328de5bb1.

30. Barton Gellman and Ashkan Soltani, "NSA Tracking Cellphone Locations Worldwide, Snowden Documents Show," *Washington Post*, Dec. 4, 2013, www.washingtonpost.com/world/national-security/nsa-tracking-cellphone-locations-worldwide-snowden-documents-show/2013/12/04/5492873a-5cf2-11e3-bc56-c6ca94801fac_story.html.

31. Ted Ullyot, "Facebook Releases Data, Including All National Security Requests," Facebook Newsroom, June 14, 2013, web.archive.org/web/20130804020113/ http://newsroom.fb.com/News/636/Facebook-Releases-Data-Including-All -National-Security-Requests.

32. Glenn Greenwald, "XKeyscore: NSA Tool Collects 'Nearly Everything a User Does on the Internet,'" *Guardian*, July 31, 2013, www.theguardian.com/world/ 2013/jul/31/nsa-top-secret-program-online-data.

33. "Are They Allowed to Do That? A Breakdown of Selected Government Surveillance Programs," Brennan Center for Justice, New York University School of Law, July 15, 2013, www.brennancenter.org/our-work/research -reports/are-they-allowed-do-breakdown-selected-government-surveillance -programs.

34. Jeffrey M. Jones, "More Americans Disapprove Than Approve of Government Collecting Phone Records," Gallup News, May 15, 2006, news.gallup.com/ poll/22789/more-americans-disapprove-than-approve-government-collecting -phone-records.aspx.

35. Frank Newport, "Americans Disapprove of Government Surveillance Programs," Gallup News, June 12, 2013, news.gallup.com/poll/163043/ americans-disapprove-government-surveillance-programs.aspx.

36. Dana Priest and William M. Arkin, *Top Secret America: The Rise of the New American Security State* (New York: Little, Brown, 2011), 73.

37. Ibid., 25–26.

38. "Executive Order 12356—National Security Information," Office of the Federal Register (OFR), National Archives, April 12, 1982, www.archives.gov/federal -register/codification/executive-order/12356.html.

39. Priest and Arkin, *Top Secret America*, 7–9.

40. Ibid., 22–24.

41. Ibid., 59–62.

42. danah boyd, *It's Complicated: The Social Lives of Networked Teens* (New Haven, Conn.: Yale University Press, 2014), 88–89.

43. Ibid., 97.

44. Ibid., 90.

45. Ibid., 201.

46. Ibid., 21–22.

47. Ibid., 90–91.

48. "Facebook Parenting: For the Troubled Teen," Tommy Jordan, Feb. 8, 2012, YouTube, www.youtube.com/watch?v=kl1ujzRidmU.

49. boyd, *It's Complicated*, 33.

50. Michael Zimmer, "Facebook's Zuckerberg: 'Having Two Identities for Yourself Is an Example of a Lack of Integrity,'" michaelzimmer.org, May 14, 2010, michaelzimmer.org/2010/05/14/facebooks-zuckerberg-having-two-identities -for-yourself-is-an-example-of-a-lack-of-integrity.

51. boyd, *It's Complicated*, 55.

52. Ibid., 59.

53. Alyson Klein, "Yes, College Admissions Officers Do Look at Applicants' Social Media, Survey Finds," *Education Week*, Jan. 13, 2020, www.edweek.org/ leadership/yes-college-admissions-officers-do-look-at-applicants-social-media -survey-finds/2020/01.

54. boyd, *It's Complicated,* 11.

55. McLaughlin & Associates, "The William F. Buckley Jr. Program at Yale: Almost Half (49%) of U.S. College Students 'Intimidated' by Professors When Sharing Differing Beliefs: Survey," press release, Oct. 26, 2015, mclaughlinonline.com/2015/10/26/the-william-f-buckley-jr-program-at-yale-almost-half-49-of-u-s-college-students-intimidated-by-professors-when-sharing-differing-beliefs-survey.

56. Lauren Kirchner, "What's the Evidence Mass Surveillance Works? Not Much," ProPublica, Nov. 18, 2015, www.propublica.org/article/whats-the-evidence-mass-surveillance-works-not-much.

57. "Only Collect."

58. Public Trust in Government: 1958–2022, Pew Research Center, June 6, 2022, www.pewresearch.org/politics/2022/06/06/public-trust-in-government-1958-2022.

59. Jonathan Crary, *Scorched Earth: Beyond the Digital Age to a Post-Capitalist World* (London: Verso, 2022), 25.

Chapter 12: They Do This All the Time

1. Dick Cheney, *In My Time: A Personal and Political Memoir,* with Liz Cheney (New York: Threshold Editions, 2011), 249–51.

2. "WHITTINGTON/CHENEY," CNN, July 21, 2016, YouTube, www.youtube.com/watch?v=wcFZgWqaMfM.

3. Cheney, *In My Time,* 251.

4. "Victims of Haditha Massacre," United for Peace & Justice, accessed March 7, 2022, web.archive.org/web/20071120021340/http://www.unitedforpeace.org/article.php?id=3283.

5. Ellen Knickmeyer, "In Haditha, Memories of a Massacre," *Washington Post,* May 27, 2006, www.washingtonpost.com/archive/politics/2006/05/27/in-haditha-memories-of-a-massacre-span-classbankheadiraqi-townspeople-describe-slaying-of-24-civilians-by-marines-in-nov-19-incidentspan/2c18d37f-071a-46e1-a0c2-30bbbcb0ba5f.

6. Julian Borger and Duncan Campbell, "Why Did Help Take So Long to Arrive?," *Guardian,* Sept. 3, 2005, www.theguardian.com/world/2005/sep/03/hurricanekatrina.usa1.

7. Jarvis DeBerry, "Almost 10 Years After Katrina, Michael Brown's Still Out to Lunch," *Times-Picayune,* June 1, 2015, www.nola.com/opinions/almost-10-years-after-katrina-michael-browns-still-out-to-lunch-jarvis-deberry/article_d50e5d7e-8ff8-5996-9aaa-74aa9f393e46.html.

8. "Katrina 10 Years Later: 'Brownie, You're Doing a Heck of a Job,'" C-SPAN, Aug. 18, 2015, www.c-span.org/video/?c4548480/katrina-10-years-later-brownie-heck-job.

9. Helen Clapp and Kathryn Sikkink, "From 'Invade the Hague' to 'Support the ICC': America's Shifting Stance on the International Criminal Court," Harvard University, Kathryn Sikkink personal website, April 27, 2022, scholar.harvard.edu/ksikkink/blog/%E2%80%9Cinvade-hague%E2%80%9D-%E2%80%9Csupport-icc%E2%80%9D-america%E2%80%99s-shifting-stance-international-criminal-court.

10. "Humane Treatment of al-Qaeda and Taliban Detainees," memorandum, White

House, Feb. 7, 2002, www.aclu.org/legal-document/presidential-memo-feb-7 -2002-humane-treatment-al-qaeda-and-taliban-detainees.

11. Military Commissions Act of 2006, Public Law 109-366, 120 Stat. 2600 (2006), www.congress.gov/bill/109th-congress/senate-bill/3930.

12. Andrew Jerell Jones, "Prison Dispatches from the War on Terror: Ex–CIA Officer John Kiriakou Speaks," *Intercept,* Jan. 19, 2015, theintercept.com/2015/ 01/19/cia-agent-jailed-john-kiriakous-long-road-era-torture.

13. Scott Horton, "U.N. Rapporteur: Initiate Criminal Proceedings Against Bush and Rumsfeld Now," *Harper's Magazine,* Jan. 21, 2009, harpers.org/2009/01/un -rapporteur-initiate-criminal-proceedings-against-bush-and-rumsfeld-now.

14. Jeffrey Bachman, "The Obama Administration May Be Guilty of War Crimes," *Guardian,* Nov. 5, 2013, www.theguardian.com/commentisfree/2013/nov/05/ obama-administration-drone-strikes-war-crimes.

15. Micah Zenko, "Obama's Final Drone Strike Data," Politics, Power, and Preventive Action, Center for Preventive Action, Council on Foreign Relations, Jan. 20, 2017, www.cfr.org/blog/obamas-final-drone-strike-data.

16. Josh Gerstein, "Obama's Muddy Transparency Record," *Politico,* March 5, 2012, www.politico.com/story/2012/03/obamas-transparency-stumbles-073606.

17. Karen DeYoung, "Trump Pardons Blackwater Contractors Convicted in Deaths of 14 Iraqi Civilians," *Washington Post,* Dec. 22, 2020, www.washingtonpost .com/national-security/trump-pardon-blackwater-contractors-iraq/2020/12/ 22/603da1f4-44b8-11eb-a277-49a6d1f9dff1_story.html.

18. Ashley Hoffman, "Michelle Obama on Her Bond with 'Beautiful, Funny, Kind, Sweet Man' George W. Bush," *Time,* Nov. 14, 2018, time.com/5454153/michelle -obama-on-george-w-bush.

19. Dave Phillips, "From the Brig to Mar-a-Lago, Former Navy SEAL Capitalizes on Newfound Fame," *New York Times,* Dec. 31, 2019, www.nytimes.com/2019/12/ 31/us/navy-seals-edward-gallagher-trump.html.

20. Matt Taibbi, "Turns Out That Trillion-Dollar Bailout Was, in Fact, Real," *Rolling Stone,* March 18, 2019, www.rollingstone.com/politics/politics-features/2008 -financial-bailout-809731.

21. Astra Taylor and Mark Greif, "Scenes from an Occupation," *Occupy! An OWS-Inspired Gazette,* Oct. 21, 2011, 2, www.nplusonemag.com/dl/occupy/Occupy -Gazette-1.pdf.

22. Elizabeth Gumport, "Back at Zuccotti Park," *Occupy! An OWS-Inspired Gazette,* Oct. 21, 2011, 8, www.nplusonemag.com/dl/occupy/Occupy-Gazette-1.pdf.

23. Astra Taylor, "Diary," *Occupy! An OWS-Inspired Gazette,* Oct. 21, 2011, 15, www.nplusonemag.com/dl/occupy/Occupy-Gazette-1.pdf.

24. Taylor and Greif, "Scenes from an Occupation," 2.

25. Mark Greif, "Open Letter," *Occupy! An OWS-Inspired Gazette,* no. 3, 2, www .nplusonemag.com/dl/occupy/Occupy-Gazette-3.pdf.

26. Jeremy Kessler, "The Police and the 99 Percent," *Occupy! An OWS-Inspired Gazette,* Oct. 21, 2011, 25, www.nplusonemag.com/dl/occupy/Occupy -Gazette-1.pdf.

27. Chloe Rossetti, photograph, *Occupy! An OWS-Inspired Gazette,* no. 3, 3, www .nplusonemag.com/dl/occupy/Occupy-Gazette-3.pdf.

28. Kathleen Ross, "Arrested," *Occupy! An OWS-Inspired Gazette,* no. 3, 3, www .nplusonemag.com/dl/occupy/Occupy-Gazette-3.pdf.

29. Matt Wells, "Occupy Wall Street—the Story of the Brooklyn Bridge 'Trap,'" *Guardian,* Oct. 3, 2011, www.theguardian.com/world/blog/2011/oct/03/occupy -wall-street-brooklyn-bridge-arrests.

30. "FW: Guidance Requested: Occupy Wall Street," email, in Occupy Wall Street Release 1—Homeland Security, Department of Homeland Security, Oct. 17, 2011, 6, www.dhs.gov/sites/default/files/publications/occupy-wall-street -redacted-1.pdf.

31. "The Crackdown on the Occupy Movement," Partnership for Civil Justice Fund, Aug. 31, 2015, www.justiceonline.org/ows-foia.

32. "Fusion Centers Approached 2011 Black Friday Consumer Boycott Like a Terrorist Threat," Partnership for Civil Justice Fund, June 1, 2014, www .justiceonline.org/fusion_centers_approached.

33. John Avlon, "How Occupy Wall Street Flashed New York Back to 9/11," *Daily Beast,* Dec. 30, 2011, www.thedailybeast.com/how-occupy-wall-street-flashed -new-york-back-to-911.

34. Jennifer Preston, "Surprise Eviction at Zuccotti Park? One Twitter-Friendly Celebrity Saw It Coming," *New York Times,* Nov. 15, 2011, archive.nytimes.com/ mediadecoder.blogs.nytimes.com/2011/11/15/surprise-eviction-at-zuccotti -park-one-twitter-friendly-celebrity-saw-it-coming.

35. Astra Taylor, "The Eviction," *Occupy! An OWS-Inspired Gazette,* no. 3, 2, www .nplusonemag.com/dl/occupy/Occupy-Gazette-3.pdf.

36. James Barron and Colin Moynihan, "City Reopens Park After Protesters Are Evicted," *New York Times,* Nov. 15, 2011, www.nytimes.com/2011/11/16/ nyregion/police-begin-clearing-zuccotti-park-of-protesters.html.

37. Brendan O'Brien and Colleen Jenkins, "Zimmerman Offers Gun Used to Kill Martin on New Auction Site: Report," Reuters, May 12, 2016, www.reuters.com/ article/us-usa-guns-zimmerman-idUKKCN0Y318Z.

38. Joseph Goldstein and Nate Schweber, "Man's Death After Chokehold Raises Old Issue for the Police," *New York Times,* July 18, 2014, www.nytimes.com/2014/07/ 19/nyregion/staten-island-man-dies-after-he-is-put-in-chokehold-during-arrest .html?_r=0.

39. "Profile: Eric Garner," BBC News, Dec. 5, 2014, www.bbc.com/news/world-us -canada-30350648.

40. "Investigation of the Ferguson Police Department," U.S. Department of Justice, Civil Rights Division, March 4, 2015, 9.

41. Ibid., 10.

42. Ibid., 17–18.

43. Ibid., 18–19.

44. Ibid., 73.

45. Andrea S. Boyles, *You Can't Stop the Revolution: Community Disorder and Social Ties in Post-Ferguson America* (Berkeley: University of California Press, 2019), 8.

46. Jose A. DelReal, "Michael Brown Memorial Destroyed Overnight," *Washington Post,* Dec. 26, 2015, www.washingtonpost.com/news/post-nation/wp/2014/12/ 26/auto-draft.

47. "A City Reacts: State of Emergency—Ferguson, Missouri (Dispatch 10)," VICE News, Nov. 27, 2014, YouTube, www.youtube.com/watch?v=TZxEyoplYbI.

48. Boyles, *You Can't Stop the Revolution,* 59.

49. Colleen Curry and Luis Martinez, "Ferguson Police's Show of Force Highlights Militarization of America's Cops," ABC News, Aug. 14, 2014, abcnews.go.com/US/ferguson-police-small-army-thousands-police-departments/story?id=24977299.

50. Jon Swaine and Amanda Holpuch, "Ferguson Police: A Stark Illustration of Newly Militarized US Law Enforcement," *Guardian,* Aug. 14, 2014, www.theguardian.com/world/2014/aug/14/ferguson-police-military-restraints-violence-weaponry-missouri.

51. Lindsey Cook, "Most Popular Items in the Defense Department's 1033 Program," *U.S. News,* Aug. 21, 2014, www.usnews.com/news/blogs/data-mine/2014/08/21/most-popular-items-in-the-defense-departments-1033-program.

52. Radley Balko, *Rise of the Warrior Cop: The Militarization of America's Police Forces* (New York: PublicAffairs, 2014), 253.

53. Ibid., 255.

54. Michael Shenk, "How Police Became Paramilitaries," *New York Review of Books,* June 3, 2020, www.nybooks.com/daily/2020/06/03/how-police-became-paramilitaries.

55. Tobi Haslett, "Magic Actions," *n+1,* no. 40 (Summer 2021), www.nplusonemag.com/issue-40/politics/magic-actions-2.

56. Matthew Impelli, "54 Percent of Americans Think Burning Down Minneapolis Police Precinct Was Justified After George Floyd's Death," *Newsweek,* June 3, 2020, www.newsweek.com/54-americans-think-burning-down-minneapolis-police-precinct-was-justified-after-george-floyds-1508452.

57. Tanya Kerssen (@tkerssen), Twitter, May 30, 2020, 10:37 p.m., twitter.com/tkerssen/status/1266921821653385225.

58. Tom Cotton, "Tom Cotton: Send in the Troops," *New York Times,* June 3, 2020, www.nytimes.com/2020/06/03/opinion/tom-cotton-protests-military.html.

59. Candice Norwood, "'Optics Matter': National Guard Deployments amid Unrest Have a Long and Controversial History," *PBS NewsHour,* June 9, 2020, www.pbs.org/newshour/politics/optics-matter-national-guard-deployments-amid-unrest-have-a-long-and-controversial-history.

60. "Black Lives Matter Protests," Amnesty International, June 23, 2020, www.amnesty.org/en/latest/news/2020/06/usa-unlawful-use-of-force-by-police-at-black-lives-matter-protests.

61. Meg Kelly, Joyce Sohyun Lee, and Jon Swaine, "Partially Blinded by Police," *Washington Post,* July 14, 2020, www.washingtonpost.com/investigations/2020/07/14/george-floyd-protests-police-blinding.

62. Valerie Pavilonis, "Fact Check: Thousands of Black Lives Matter Protesters Were Arrested in 2020," *USA Today,* Feb. 22, 2022, www.usatoday.com/story/news/factcheck/2022/02/22/fact-check-thousands-black-lives-matter-protesters-arrested-2020/6816074001.

63. Alanna Durkin Richer, Michael Kunzelman, and Jacques Billeaud, "Records Rebut Claims of Unequal Treatment of Jan. 6 Rioters," Associated Press, Aug. 30, 2021, apnews.com/article/records-rebut-claims-jan-6-rioters-55adf4d46aff57b91af2fdd3345dace8.

64. Tim Elfrink, Marisa Iati, and Derek Hawkins, "Seattle Mayor Blasts Trump's

Threat to 'Take Back' the City After Protesters Set Up 'Autonomous Zone,'"
Washington Post, June 11, 2020, www.washingtonpost.com/nation/2020/06/11/
trump-seattle-autonomous-zone-inslee.

65. Fola Akinnibi, Sarah Holder, and Christopher Cannon, "Cities Say They Want
     to Defund the Police. Their Budgets Say Otherwise," *Bloomberg,* Jan. 12, 2021,
     www.bloomberg.com/graphics/2021-city-budget-police-funding.

66. Grace Manthey, Frank Esposito, and Amanda Hernandez, "Despite 'Defunding'
     Claims, Police Funding Has Increased in Many US Cities," ABC News, Oct. 16,
     2022, abcnews.go.com/US/defunding-claims-police-funding-increased-us
     -cities/story?id=91511971.

67. Shehryar Nabi, "Charts That Explain Wealth Inequality in the United States,"
     Aspen Institute, Oct. 19, 2022, www.aspeninstitute.org/blog-posts/charts-that
     -explain-wealth-inequality-in-the-united-states.

68. "Policing in America," police shootings database, *Washington Post,* accessed
     March 14, 2022, www.washingtonpost.com/police-america.

69. Martin Gilens and Benjamin I. Page, "Testing Theories of American Politics:
     Elites, Interest Groups, and Average Citizens," *Perspectives on Politics,* Vol. 12,
     Issue 3, Sept. 2014, 564–81.

70. Brendan James, "Princeton Study: U.S. No Longer an Actual Democracy,"
     Talking Points Memo, April 18, 2014, talkingpointsmemo.com/livewire/
     princeton-experts-say-us-no-longer-democracy.

71. Dylan Matthews, "Remember That Study Saying America Is an Oligarchy?
     3 Rebuttals Say It's Wrong," *Vox,* May 9, 2016, www.vox.com/2016/5/9/
     11502464/gilens-page-oligarchy-study.

72. Matthew Yglesias, "Holding Politicians Accountable," *Boston Review,* July 2,
     2012, www.bostonreview.net/forum_response/holding-politicians-accountable
     -matthew-yglesias.

73. "Satisfaction with the United States," Gallup, news.gallup.com/poll/1669/
     general-mood-country.aspx.

74. Mark Follman, Gavin Aronsen, and Deanna Pan, "US Mass Shootings, 1982–
     2003: Data from Mother Jones' Investigation," *Mother Jones,* accessed Oct. 27,
     2023, www.motherjones.com/politics/2012/12/mass-shootings-mother-jones
     -full-data.

75. Tom W. Smith and Jaesok Son, "Trends in Gun Ownership in the United States,
     1972–2014," General Social Survey Final Report, National Opinion Research
     Center, 2014, www.norc.org/PDFs/GSS%20Reports/GSS_Trends%20in%20
     Gun%20Ownership_US_1972-2014.pdf.

76. Follman, Aronsen, and Pan, "US Mass Shootings, 1982–2023."

77. Ragy Girgis, "Is There a Link Between Mental Health and Mass Shootings?,"
     Columbia University Department of Psychiatry, July 6, 2022, www
     .columbiapsychiatry.org/news/mass-shootings-and-mental-illness.

78. Shaila Dawan, "What Are the Real Warning Signs of a Mass Shooting?," *New
     York Times,* Aug. 22, 2022, www.nytimes.com/2022/08/22/us/mass-shootings
     -mental-illness.html.

79. Brendan I. Koerner, *The Skies Belong to Us: Love and Terror in the Golden Age of
     Hijacking* (New York: Crown, 2013).

80. "The Latest: Courthouse Empties After Day 1 of Holmes Trial," Associated

Press, April 27, 2015, web.archive.org/web/20150428121706/http://bigstory
.ap.org/article/460d1a4541634e538a6161b857d2799b/latest-theater-shooters
-parents-arrive-courthouse.

81. "James Holmes' Notebook, Annotated by Dr. Jeffrey Lieberman," document, Marshall Project, June 2, 2015, 9, www.themarshallproject.org/documents/ 2091448-james-holmes-notebook-annotated-by-dr-jeffrey.

82. Ibid., 14.

83. Ibid., 9.

84. Ibid., 32.

85. "James Holmes Built Up Aurora Arsenal of Bullets, Ballistic Gear Through Unregulated Online Market," CBS News, Sept. 19, 2012, www.cbsnews.com/ news/james-holmes-built-up-aurora-arsenal-of-bullets-ballistic-gear-through -unregulated-online-market.

86. Noah Rayman, "Cops Found Batman Mask in Colorado Movie Theater Shooter's Apartment," *Time,* Oct. 24, 2013, nation.time.com/2013/10/24/cops -found-batman-mask-in-colorado-movie-theater-shooters-apartment.

87. "James Holmes Built Up Aurora Arsenal of Bullets, Ballistic Gear Through Unregulated Online Market."

88. Julie Turkewitz and Vivian Lee, "With Grief and Hope, Florida Students Take Gun Control Fight on the Road," *New York Times,* Feb. 20, 2018, www.nytimes .com/2018/02/20/us/parkland-students-shooting-florida.html.

Epilogue: Reality Principle

1. Hannah Arendt, *The Origins of Totalitarianism* (San Diego: Harcourt Brace, 1985), ix.

2. Eleanor Watson, "Ex–Afghan President Likely Did Not Flee Afghanistan with Millions, Report Finds," CBS News, June 6, 2022, www.cbsnews.com/news/ ashraf-ghani-likely-did-not-flee-afghanistan-with-millions-inspector-general -report.

3. Remarks by President Biden on the End of the War in Afghanistan, transcript, White House, Aug. 31, 2021, www.whitehouse.gov/briefing-room/speeches -remarks/2021/08/31/remarks-by-president-biden-on-the-end-of-the-war-in -afghanistan.

4. Yaron Steinbuch, "American Humane Group Says US Left Military Dogs Behind in Afghanistan," *New York Post,* Aug. 31, 2021, nypost.com/2021/08/31/ american-humane-society-say-us-left-military-dogs-behind-in-afghanistan.

5. Joseph A. Wulfsohn, "NBC's Richard Engel: History May Judge Biden's Withdrawal from Kabul as Dark Period for the US," Fox News, Aug. 30, 2021, www.foxnews.com/media/nbc-richard-engel-biden-afghan-withdrawal-worst -capitulation-of-western-values.

6. "The Fall of Saigon: 40 Years Later," CNN, April 29, 2015, www.youtube.com/ watch?v=vHLKFSWzImk.

7. Gabriel Kolko, *Anatomy of a War: Vietnam, the United States, and the Modern Historical Experience* (New York: New Press, 1994), 472.

8. Remarks by President Biden on the End of the War in Afghanistan, White House, Aug. 31, 2021.

9. Ryan Grim, "House Progressives Float Diplomatic Path Toward Ending

War in Ukraine, Get Annihilated, Quickly 'Clarify,'" *Intercept,* Oct. 25, 2022, theintercept.com/2022/10/25/house-progressives-letter-russia-ukraine -diplomacy.

10. President Joseph R. Biden, "National Security Strategy," Oct. 2022, 23, www .whitehouse.gov/wp-content/uploads/2022/10/Biden-Harris-Administrations -National-Security-Strategy-10.2022.pdf.

11. "GDP Per Capita (Current US$)—China," World Bank, accessed Dec. 5, 2023, data.worldbank.org/indicator/NY.GDP.PCAP.CD?locations=CN.

12. "GDP Growth (Annual %)—China," World Bank, accessed Dec. 5, 2023, data .worldbank.org/indicator/NY.GDP.MKTP.KD.ZG?locations=CN.

13. Victor Shih, "China's Credit Conundrum, Interview by Robert Brenner," *New Left Review,* no. 115 (Jan.–Feb. 2019): 59–74.

14. Gregory C. Allen, "Choking off China's Access to the Future of AI," Center for Strategic & International Studies, Oct. 11, 2022, www.csis.org/analysis/choking -chinas-access-future-ai.

15. Ross Babbage, "A War with China Would Be Unlike Anything Americans Faced Before," *New York Times,* Feb. 27, 2023, www.nytimes.com/2023/02/27/opinion/ a-war-with-china-would-reach-deep-into-american-society.html.

16. Charlie Campbell, "U.S. General's Prediction of War with China 'in 2025' Risks Turning Worst Fears into Reality," *Time,* Jan. 31, 2023, time.com/6251419/us -china-general-war-2025.

17. Ali Sawafta, "More Than 15,900 Palestinians Killed in Gaza Since Oct. 7—Palestinian Health Minister," Reuters, Dec. 5, 2023, www.reuters.com/ world/middle-east/more-than-15900-palestinians-killed-gaza-since-oct-7 -palestinian-health-minister-2023-12-05.

18. "Israeli Minister Calls for Voluntary Emigration of Gazans," Reuters, Nov. 14, 2023, www.reuters.com/world/middle-east/israeli-minister-calls-voluntary -emigration-gazans-2023-11-14.

19. "Netanyahu Wants to 'Thin Out' Gaza by Pushing Population into the Sea: Report," *Middle East Eye,* Dec. 2, 2023, www.middleeasteye.net/live-blog/live -blog-update/netanyahu-wants-thin-out-gazas-population-pushing-them-sea -report.

20. Raz Segal, "A Textbook Case of Genocide," *Jewish Currents,* Oct. 13, 2023, jewishcurrents.org/a-textbook-case-of-genocide.

21. John Paul Rathbone, "Military Briefing: The Israeli Bombs Raining on Gaza," *Financial Times,* Dec. 6, 2023, www.ft.com/content/7b407c2e-8149-4d83-be01 -72dcae8aee7b.

22. Akbar Shahid Ahmed, "U.S. Officials Privately Raise Fears of Israel-Gaza Conflict Sparking a Broader War," *HuffPost,* Dec. 7, 2023, www.huffpost.com/ entry/israel-gaza-war-lebanon-iran-us-yemen_n_65724dd5e4b001ec86a76c9a ?gae.

23. Oliver Eagleton, "Imperial Designs," *New Left Review,* Nov. 3, 2023, newleftreview.org/sidecar/posts/imperial-designs.

24. Joe Leahy and Hudson Lockett, "Brazil's Lula Calls for End to Dollar Trade Dominance," *Financial Times,* April 13, 2023, www.ft.com/content/669260a5 -82a5-4e7a-9bbf-4f41c54a6143.

25. Steve Holland, "Obama Says Climate Change a Matter of National Security,"

Reuters, Dec. 9, 2008, www.reuters.com/article/us-usa-obama-gore/obama
-says-climate-change-a-matter-of-national-security-idUSTRE4B86R920081210.

26. Nick Estes, *Our History Is the Future: Standing Rock Versus the Dakota Access Pipeline, and the Long Tradition of Indigenous Resistance* (New York: Verso, 2019), 2–3.

27. Ibid., 54–55, 64–65.

28. Timothy Pratt, "Georgia Refuses to Release Evidence from Police Shooting of Cop City Activist," *Guardian*, Oct. 16, 2023, www.theguardian.com/us-news/2023/oct/16/georgia-cop-city-police-shooting-evidence-manuel-paez-teran.

29. Timothy Pratt, "'Cop City' Activist's Official Autopsy Reveals More Than 50 Bullet Wounds," *Guardian*, April 20, 2023, www.theguardian.com/us-news/2023/apr/20/manuel-paez-teran-autopsy-cop-city.

30. Estes, *Our History Is the Future*, 13.

31. Ibid., 256.

32. Ibid., 248.

33. Slotkin, *Regeneration Through Violence*, 3.

34. Ibid., 565.

INDEX

ABC, xi–xii, 444
  Good Morning America, 4–8
  Nightline, 350
  World News Tonight, 345
Abdulmunem, Salam, 247, 252–53, 259
Abdulmutallab, Umar Farouk, 89, 94
Abrams, Elliott, 49
Abu Ghraib, 166–73, 180–81, 185–86, 191, 196–97
  rationalization of, 178–79, 182–83, 194–95, 211
Access Hollywood, 419–20
accountability, xxviii–xxix, 426, 428–30, 451, 484
Addington, David, 181
advertising, 59–60, 96–100, 390–92, 406, 412
Afghanistan, 34–36, 129, 223–24, 247, 463–64
Afghanistan war, 38–39, 47, 155, 161, 243, 374–75
  criticism of, 69, 239
  drone strikes in, 221
  invasion of, 56, 129, 160, 163, 165, 453
  U.S. troops in, 57, 222–24, 239, 370
  U.S. withdrawal from, 462–65
airports, xxvi, 51, 69, 79–80, 86–96, 313–14
Alanssi, Mohamed, 145–46
Alhassen, Ziad, 107

Ali, Ayaan Hirsi, 165
al-Qaeda, xx, 42, 48, 160–61, 163, 378
  in Afghanistan, 55, 223
  in Pakistan, 221
  and September 11, 8, 20, 38–39, 263, 463
  and Syria, 320
Alsultany, Evelyn, 205
Alter, Jonathan, 350, 358, 367
Alterman, Eric, 367
Amnesty International, 167, 426
anti-immigration, 301–3, 309, 323–24
antisemitism, 476, 498
Apaches, 234
Arab Spring, xxvi, 315–24, 327–28, 336, 432. *See also individual countries*
Arad, Michael, 111
Arafat, Yasser, 24
Araji, Faiza Al-, 247, 251, 258
Aref, Yassin, 145
Arizona, 39, 129–30, 301–5, 309
Arkin, William M., 401–4
Arrighi, Giovanni, 269–71, 273, 275, 279
Ashcroft, John, 152, 189, 307, 378, 385–86, 393
Assad, Bashar al-, 320–22
Assange, Julian, 427
Associated Press, 7, 166–67
AT&T, 381–84, 396
Atlanta, Georgia, 90, 383, 446, 490–91

Atlas Shrugs (Geller), 228, 324
Aviation and Transportation Security
    Act, 88
Awlaki, Anwar al-, 425

Bacevich, Andrew, 222–23
Baghdad Burning: Girl Blog from Iraq
    (Riverbend), 247
Bah, Adama, 134–41, 150
banks
    bailouts of (2008), 200, 216, 332, 335
    robberies of, 147, 455–56
    and subprime mortgages, 333–34
    See also Occupy Wall Street
Batman, 42–47, 52, 59, 62, 75–77, 437, 457
Beckman, Julie, 125
Ben Ali, Zine El Abidine, 315
Benanav, Aaron, 281, 285
Berman, Paul, 362
Bernstein, Tom, 126
Bible, 15, 40, 209, 211–12, 448
Biden, Joe, 17, 449, 467–69, 471–72, 475,
    477–80
    and Afghanistan withdrawal, xxii,
    462–65
bin Laden, Osama, xx, 10, 35–40, 160, 289,
    463–64
    death of, 230–33
    pursuit of, 56–57, 75, 163, 224, 248
Black, Duncan, 366
Black Lives Matter (BLM), 337–40, 431,
    438–39, 445–48, 497
    demands of, 449, 491
    in Ferguson, Missouri, 339, 438–444
Blackwater, 251, 427
Blinken, Antony, 479
Blitzer, Wolf, 161
blogging, 246–47, 251–54, 258, 364–69,
    406
Bloomberg, Michael, 115–16, 155, 226–27,
    438
Boone, Daniel, 28–31, 37, 67
border security, 18, 301–14, 325, 327
Boston, Massachusetts, 15, 40, 81, 90, 108
Bouazizi, Mohamed, 315
boyd, danah, 408–9, 411–13, 416–17
Braudel, Fernand, 271
Breivik, Anders, 323–24
Bremer, Paul, 237–39, 244–51, 253–60,
    262

Brenner, Robert, 282, 330–34
Bretton Woods Conference, 280–81
Britain, 274–78, 321, 472
Brown, Lewis, Jr., 192–94
Brown, Michael (FEMA), 422
Brown, Michael (Ferguson shooting), 438,
    440, 442–44
Buffalo Bill, 495
Bumppo, Natty, 29–30
Burnett, Tom, Sr., 128
Bush, Billy, 419
Bush, George H. W., xxi, 49, 264
Bush, George W., 48–49, 51, 128, 257, 366,
    368
    accountability of, 424, 429, 431
    and Afghan war, 222, 462
    approval ratings of, 239, 371
    and consumerism, 98–99
    and evangelicals, 189
    and Hurricane Katrina, 422
    and immigration reform, 308–10,
    325
    and Iraq War, xxi, 53, 129, 262, 268,
    377–79
    media image of, 428
    and Paul Bremer, 238–39, 248
    propaganda campaign of, 163–66, 239,
    355–56, 363
    on September 11, 2001, xxii–xxiii, 17,
    25–26, 33–35, 39, 40–42
    and surveillance programs, 393–95,
    400
    and torture program, 191, 195–97,
    423–24
    and 2000 election, xxiii–xxiv, 306,
    375–76, 389–90
    and veterans, 70
    and war on terror, xx, 48, 160–61

Cadillac, 97–98, 105–6
California, 18, 40, 131, 425, 464
    border patrol, 205, 309, 325
    Los Angeles, 161, 383
    San Francisco, 119, 161, 382
    See also Silicon Valley
Call of Duty: Modern Warfare, 73,
    296
Cambodia, 430, 466
Canada, 18–19, 310, 313
cancel culture, 354, 413–15

capital accumulation, 270–71, 282
capitalism, 202–3, 243, 263, 430, 493
   history of, 267–69, 271–81, 283
   in low-growth world, 292–93, 296,
    299
captivity narratives, 13–16, 27–28, 31
Casablanca, 32–33
CBS, 8, 166
   Evening News, 345
   Face the Nation, 386
   60 Minutes, 166–67, 173, 179, 190
Chalabi, Ahmed, 356
Chandrasekaran, Rajiv, 250, 260–61
Chauvin, Derek, 445
Cheney, Dick, 48, 99, 227, 356, 386,
   420–21
   and Iraq invasion, 161, 241–42, 315
Chicago, Illinois, 18, 118, 129, 214–15, 383
Childs, David, 111–14
China, 202, 284, 292, 467–73, 481, 483
   manufacturing in, 389
Christianity, 186, 189–90, 209–11, 322,
   363, 389
CIA, xxi, 80, 181, 221–21
   black sites, 178, 182–83, 185, 423
Citizens United v. FEC, 432, 491, 497
Clapper, James, 383
Clear Channel, 352–53
climate change, 106, 472–73, 487–88, 490,
   496, 498
Clinton, Bill, 48–49, 102, 182, 203, 213,
   420
   economic policies of, 310, 329–30
   and surveillance, 392
   and welfare reform, 285
Clinton, Hillary, 213, 217, 318, 322, 379,
   430
   and 2016 elections, 418–20
CNN, 47, 53, 351, 369
   Crossfire, 367
   Late Edition, 386
Coalition Provisional Authority (CPA),
   238, 245–51, 254–56, 259–61
Cold War, 49–50, 196, 280–81, 430
colonial America, 11–16, 27–31, 195, 260,
   277
colonization, 260, 269, 272–75, 277
Colorado, 456–59
Columbia University, 475
comic books, 44–47

communism, 195, 202, 430
Condé Nast, 112
conformity culture, 349, 354—55
consumerism, 96–101, 107, 244,
   290
consumption, 292, 330, 332–33, 335
Cooper, James Fenimore, 29, 494
Cordoba House, 227–30, 324
Corliss, Glenn, 260–61
Cotton, Tom, 448
COVID-19, 337, 446, 449, 464, 482
cowboys, 11, 28, 132
Crary, Jonathan, 417
Crockett, Davy, 31, 37, 67

Daddario, Richard, 116
Dahler, Don, 6–7, 9
Dakota Access Pipeline, 488–89
Dalrymple, Jack, 489
Davis, Mike, xxix–xxx, 286–87, 291
Dawkins, Richard, 208–12
DeLillo, Don, 3
Democratic Party, 191, 194, 214, 466, 480,
   486
Dennett, Daniel, 208–9
Denvir, Daniel, 306
deportations, 133–34, 138, 141–42, 155,
   164, 312–13
detentions, 181, 183–84, 191, 385, 451
   at Abu Ghraib, 166–73, 178–83, 185–86,
    191
   PATRIOT Act, 133–34, 141, 155, 164
Dhafir, Rafil, 150–55
displacement, 28, 277, 320, 322, 477
dispossession, 28, 30, 98, 132, 294,
   492
Dixie Chicks, 352
dollar, U.S., 280–81, 481–82
dot-com bubble (2000), 53, 98, 330–33
Downs, Stephen, 142–44
Dreher, Rod, 350
drone strikes, 77–78, 129, 219–21, 243,
   426, 486
Dutch empire, 271–74, 276, 278
DynCorp International, 262

Eagleburger, Lawrence, 35
economy, world, xxvii, 275–81, 389, 451
   slowing growth of, 282–84, 292–93, 299,
    311–12, 487

Egypt, 40, 49, 217, 477, 481
  and Arab Spring, 315–16, 319, 323, 328,
    336
  Cairo, 286
Eisenhower, Dwight, 262
Ellison, Larry, 386–88
employment, 284–88, 340, 451
enemy combatants, 191, 221, 296, 376
Enemy of the State, 395
England, Lynndie, 169–70
Eschaton, 364, 366
Estes, Nick, 489, 492
Europe, 218, 283, 326–27, 451, 467–68,
    483
  reconstruction, 244, 280
  and refugee crisis, xxvi, 323–24, 326
evangelicals, 189–90
extraordinary rendition, 182–83, 220
extremism, xx, 142, 162, 290–91, 387
  war against, 218–19, 316

Facebook, 328, 396–97, 410–12, 433
Fahrenheit 9/11, 25
Faludi, Susan, 11–13, 21, 36, 65
Falwell, Jerry, 189–90
Family in Baghdad, A (Araji), 247, 251,
    258
FBI, xx, 131, 133–56, 158, 228, 484
  and Anwar al-Awlaki, 425
  and Occupy Wall Street, 436
  and September 11, 79–80
Federal Emergency Management Agency
    (FEMA), 83, 421–22
Feinstein, Dianne, 377, 386
Filson, John, 29, 31
financial crisis, global (2007–8), xxvi,
    198–99, 299, 328, 336, 470
  prosecutions of, 424, 431
Florida, 17–18, 25–26, 39, 108
Floyd, George, 445–46, 448
Ford, Ezell, 439
Ford Motor Company, 56, 96, 100, 103–4,
    106, 265
Foreign Intelligence Surveillance Act
    (FISA), 398, 466
Fox News, 47, 355, 357, 362
France, 321, 323–24, 326–27
Franks, Tommy, 52
Freedom of Information Act (FOIA),
    426–27

Freedom Tower, 111–16, 323
Freud, Sigmund, 268, 460
Friedman, Thomas, 362–63, 366
Fukuyama, Francis, 202
Fund, John, 374

Gaddafi, Muammar, 315–20, 371
Garner, Eric, 438–40, 445
Geller, Pamela, 228–29, 324
gender, 37, 101–3, 208–9, 218, 303, 327
Geneva Conventions, 181, 187, 226, 376,
    423
genocide, 126, 474–75, 498
Germany, 224, 280–81, 288, 324
Geronimo, 233–34
Giuliani, Rudy, 20, 97
Goldberg, Jeffrey, 367
Goldman Sachs, 113–14, 118, 330
gold standard, 281, 482
Google, 54, 390–91, 396
Gopnik, Adam, 351–52
Gordon, Michael, 356
Gordon, Robert J., 276
Gore, Al, 48, 106, 306, 375–76
Graham, Billy, 189
Graner, Charles, 169–70, 196
Green Day, 338
Greenspan, Alan, 329, 331, 334
green transition, 472–73, 483
Ground Zero, 20, 23, 43, 55, 81, 127
  redevelopment of, 109–13, 126, 227–29,
    232
Guantánamo Bay, 182, 216, 219, 226,
    374
Gulf War, first, 50, 83, 98, 150, 269, 263–64
guns, 88, 101, 454–55, 459
Gurley, Akai, 439

Hague Invasion Act, 422–23
Halliburton, 245, 258, 262
Hamas, 473–74, 476–77, 480
Hanley, Charles, J., 166–67
Harman, Sabrina, 169–72, 196
Harris, Malcolm, 389–90, 392
Harris, Sam, 208–11
Haslett, Tobi, 445–46
Hastert, Dennis, 40
Hatch, Orrin, 35–36
hate crimes, 129–31, 133
Hawley, Kip, 91–92

Hayden, Michael, 394–95
Hayder, Tashnuba, 136–38
Healy, Timothy, 140
Heatwole, Nathaniel, 95
Heffernan, Virginia, 37
hegemony, 49–50, 279, 451, 482–83
heroism, 19–20, 28–29, 31–32, 36,
    44—47, 63
Hertzberg, Hendrik, 362–63
Hezbollah, 475, 477
Hitchens, Christopher, 208–12, 362, 495
Holder, Eric, 37–39, 140
Hollywood, 12, 31, 60–61, 176–78, 401,
    432
  heroes, 29, 43–44, 46
  and Islamophobia, 207–8
  and September 11, 21–22, 27, 33
Holmes, James, 456–59
Homeland, 206–8
Hosseini, Khaled, 205
Hostel, 176–77
housing market bubble, 100, 198–200, 329,
    332–35
Human Rights Watch, 424, 426
Humvee, 72–73, 251, 443, 447
Huntington, Samuel, 202–4
Hurricane Katrina, 68, 83, 215, 421–22
Hussein, Saddam, 48, 50, 53, 263–64, 345,
    363
  and al-Qaeda, 355, 358, 361, 377–78
  capture of, 262, 453
  regime of, 238, 244–46, 248, 253, 263

Ignatieff, Michael, 268
immigration, xxvi, 300–12, 326, 464
imperialism, 190, 260, 269, 272–75, 377,
    494
  American, 277–80, 481–83, 486–87, 496
impunity culture, xxix–xxx, 349, 430–32,
    451–53, 498
Indian Wars, 12–13, 28, 31, 233
indigenous people, 11–15, 27–31, 126,
    132, 193, 277
  and pipeline project, 488–89
inequality, wealth, xxvi, 288–91, 311, 451
  and Occupy Wall Street, 337, 339–40,
    432, 434–35, 450
Instagram, 406, 412
International Criminal Court (ICC),
    422–24

Iran, 49, 165, 217–18, 239, 315, 477
Iraq, 150–52, 154, 250, 253–54, 263–64,
    315
  Baghdad, 248–49
  Coalition Provisional Authority (CPA),
    238, 245–51, 254–56, 259–61
  economic reforms in, 248–49, 255–63
  Green Zone, 244–47, 251, 254
  oil industry in, 241–43, 257, 261
  reconstruction of, 259, 262–63, 312
Iraq War, 53, 58, 69, 161–62, 239, 246
  and Authorization for Use of Military
    Force (AUMF), 375–78
  cover-ups in, 63–66
  debate over, 345–70, 362–67, 372–80
  failure in, 75, 345
  and oil, xxvii, 241–43, 268
  protests against, 241, 336, 338–39, 345,
    431
  U.S. troop levels in, 77, 319
  veterans of, 72, 239
Iron Man, 46, 60–62, 75–77
Islam, 147, 218, 226, 269, 291, 496
  and peace, xx, 128
  and terrorism, 162–64, 174, 190
  and violence, 128, 188–89, 203–6, 211
Islamic State, 320, 322, 326–27, 375
Islamophobia, 127–41, 188–90, 197,
    205–12, 219, 324
Israel, 91, 162, 190, 217–18
  conflict with Palestine, 49, 288, 473–81
  and protests, 157, 476, 497–98
Italy, 269–72, 276, 278, 323–24

Jeep, 102–3, 107
Jennings, Peter, 3, 8–10, 17–19, 24–26, 34,
    40–41
Johnson, Shoshana, 66
Jordan, 49, 315–16
journalism, 17, 20, 328, 344, 368, 371–72
  and Abu Ghraib, 166–67, 173, 179, 196
  failures of, 346, 348, 358–63
  and Iraq War coverage, 57, 246, 345–50,
    357–64, 368, 371–72

Kagan, Robert, 49–51
Kaseman, Keith, 125
Keller, Bill, 361
Keller, Daniel, 184
Kellogg Brown and Root, 262

Kennedy, John F., 4, 82, 267
Kerry, John, 102, 191
Keynesianism, 30, 329, 340
Kimmitt, Mark, 173, 179
Kinsley, Michael, 367
Kiriakou, John, 423–24
Kissinger, Henry, 237, 430
Klein, Ezra, 364, 369
Kristof, Nicholas, 101
Kristol, William, 49–50
Kuznets, Simon, 266–67
Kyle, Chris, 66–69, 75, 495

Lanchester, John, xxvii
Langewiesche, William, 20
Lanza, Adam, 459
Last of the Mohicans, The, 29–30
Lee, Alexander, 289–90
Lee, Barbara, 374–75
Levin, Carl, 34, 186–87
Levin, Daniel, 186
Lewis, Bernard, 203–5
Libeskind, Daniel, 111–15
Libya, 49, 315–19, 320, 323–24, 375
Lie to Me, 91
Lindsey, Hal, 190
Lone Survivor, 31, 240–41
Luttrell, Marcus, 240–41
Lynch, Jessica, 64–67
Lyon, David, 388

Mahan, Dennis Hart, 193
Maher, Bill, 354–55
Manley, Kathy, 143–44
Manning, Chelsea, 427
manufacturing, 277–78, 281–85, 389,
    469–70, 483
    overcapacity, 311, 330, 482
Martin, Trayvon, 431, 438, 442
mass shootings, 454–60
mass surveillance, 382–84, 394–401, 407,
    415–17, 484
Massachusetts, 14–15, 40, 90, 108
Mayer, Jane, 178, 181, 195–96, 241, 493
McCain, John, 187, 198–202, 217
McDermott, Jim, 379
McDonald, Laquan, 439
media, xxi, 201, 218, 250, 371, 344
    Abu Ghraib in, 166–69, 173
    and Afghanistan withdrawal, 464–65

and American myths, 20, 36–37
and antiwar movement, 337
criticism of George W. Bush, 354,
    359–62, 367–68
Iraq War debate in, 345–70, 380
megacities, 286, 295
memorials, 110–11, 117, 125–28, 227–28,
    442
mental health, 69–70, 72–73, 75, 239,
    454–55
Mexico, 19, 308, 310–13, 325, 329, 486
    Mexico City, 286, 295
Military Commissions Act (2006), 187,
    423–24
Miller, Judith, 356–57, 359, 370
Miller, Todd, 313
Minority Report, 91
Minuteman Project, 301–5, 308–9
Mishra, Pankaj, 290–91
Missouri, 339, 438–444
Mohammed, Khalid Sheikh (KSM),
    39–40, 226–27
Monster.com, 97
mosques, 129, 131, 142–43, 145, 157, 425
Mubarak, Hosni, 218, 315–16, 328
Mueller, Robert, 140
Murdoch, Milena, 127–28
Murdoch, Paul, 127–28
Muslim Americans, xxiv, xxvi, 486
    after September 11, xxix, 128–44,
        155–59, 164–65
    surveillance of, 157–59, 400, 476
Muslim Student Associations (MSAs), 157
mythologies, 73, 78, 208, 338, 447, 487
    American, 132, 196, 302, 494–95
    and Chris Kyle, 66–67
    of Daniel Boone, 28–31
    frontier, 31, 46, 63, 97, 302
    of hunter, 28, 31, 36, 46
    and Native Americans, 11, 13, 16,
        27–28, 66
    and September 11, 32, 36–37, 371

National Football League (NFL), 80,
    83–85, 108–9
National Guard, xxi, 83, 443, 448, 490,
    492
nationalism, 82, 149, 239, 261, 324, 496
Native Americans, 11–15, 27–31, 126, 132,
    193, 277

nativism, 215, 306, 323–24
NATO, 83, 318–19, 468
Navy SEALs, 47, 56–57, 66, 231, 233–34,
    240–41
NBC, 4, 8, 10, 337
    Meet the Press, 36, 161, 356
    Nightly News, 345
    Today, 4
neoconservatism, 49, 51, 208–9, 315, 366,
    377
neoliberalism, 311
Netanyahu, Benjamin, 474–75
Netherlands, 271–74, 276, 278
New Atheism, 208–12, 354
New Jersey, 6, 27, 40, 125–26
New Orleans, Louisiana, 80–83, 108,
    421–22
New Republic, The, 350, 363, 365
NewsHour with Jim Lehrer, 345
Newsweek, 36–37, 350, 358
New York (magazine), 177
New York City, 5–8, 16, 113, 117–18,
    271–72, 382–3
    fire department (FDNY), 20, 23, 81
    Zuccotti Park, 130–31, 161, 339, 431–34,
        436, 438
New Yorker, The, 93, 241–42, 349, 351–52,
    362–63
New York Post, 350, 465
New York Review of Books, The, 368
New York Times, The, 58–59, 346–47,
    355–57, 359–62, 370, 379
New York Times Magazine, The, 37, 268
9/11 Commission, 80, 312, 388
Nolan, Christopher, 42–44, 437, 457
Noonan, Peggy, 367
North American Free Trade Agreement
    (NAFTA), 310–11
Nowak, Manfred, 424
nuclear weapons, 345, 355–59, 468,
    477

Obama, Barack, 37, 197, 212–18, 226–27,
    229, 317, 326
    and accountability, 426–31
    and Arab Spring, 316–20
    and drone strikes, xxii, 77–78, 129,
        219–21
    and immigration, 317, 325–27
    and Libya, 370–71
    and mass surveillance program, 224–26,
        398–99
    and Osama bin Laden, 230–31
    and Syrian civil war, 321–22, 326
    and troop levels in Afghanistan, xxii,
        220, 222–24, 239, 460
    and 2008 election, 198–202, 217, 493
    and war on terror, 493–94
Obama, Michelle, 428
Ocasio-Cortez, Alexandria, 339
Occupy! An OWS-Inspired Gazette, 433
Occupy Wall Street, 44, 216, 328–29,
    336–40, 431–38
    demands of, 450, 491
Oklahoma, 39, 110
Okun, Arthur, 267
One World Trade Center, 111–14, 117
outsourcing, 44, 284, 287, 310–11,
    469

Paik, A. Naomi, 310–11
Pakistan, 39, 77, 155, 218
    and drone strikes, 220–21, 243,
        426
Palestine, 24, 157, 217–18, 476, 497–98
    conflict with Israel, 49, 288, 473–81
Palin, Sarah, 201, 318
Passion of the Christ, The, 177–78
Patai, Raphael, 188–89
Pataki, George, 111, 113, 126, 152, 154
PATRIOT Act, 133–34, 385
patriotism, 195, 215, 225, 363, 496
    and consumerism, 98–100, 278
    and militarism, 78, 177
    after September 11, 37, 51, 97, 107, 199,
        351
    and U.S. troops, 64, 71
Paulson, Hank, Jr., 200
Pax, Salam, 247
Pennsylvania, 16, 26, 28, 127–28
    Philadelphia, 434, 446, 448
Pentagon, 8–9, 16, 24, 26–27, 36, 132
    memorial, 125, 127
    See also U.S. Department of Defense
Peters, Ralph, 293–99, 490
Philippines, 193, 195, 286, 374
Piestewa, Lori, 66
Plame, Valerie, 356–57, 427
Plotz, David, 367
Poindexter, John, 392–94

police, 83, 339–40, 434–50, 484, 487, 490
  Iraqi, 251–52, 259
  New York Police Department (NYPD), 113–14, 116
poverty, 298, 311, 335, 340, 446, 449
  and terrorism, 289–90
  urban, 286, 499
Powell, Colin, 47, 357–59
Priest, Dana, 401–4
prison abuses, 167–73, 178–86, 191, 194–97, 211
prisoners of war (POWs), 64, 66, 181, 423
privacy, 405, 411–13, 436
  and U.S. surveillance program, 224–26, 383, 393, 397, 400
protests, 157–58, 161, 431–33, 452, 466, 489–91
  Iraq War, 241, 336, 338–39, 345, 431
  over Palestine-Israel conflict, 476, 497–98
  See also Arab Spring; Black Lives Matter (BLM); Occupy Wall Street
public space, 117–20, 404–5, 438, 489
  and teenagers, 407–9, 413–15
Putin, Vladimir, 467–68, 481

racism, xxv–xxvi, 188–89, 197, 299, 313, 451
  and September 11, 128–31, 202
  and war on terror, 212, 216, 219, 229–30, 450
radio, 245, 352–54
Rather, Dan, 173, 179
Rattner, Steven, 358
Rauf, Feisal Abdul, 227–29
Raven, Charlotte, 365
Rawls, Alec, 128
Rees, David, 366
refugees, xxvi, 294, 323–24, 326, 487, 496
Republican Party, xxvi, 199, 306, 308, 415, 429, 485–86
Rice, Tamir, 439
Ricks, Thomas, 246, 348, 380
Ridge, Tom, 80
Riverbend, 247, 251–52, 254, 258–59
Roosevelt, Teddy, 82, 234
Rowlandson, Mary, 14–16, 67, 132

Rumsfeld, Donald, 26, 47—49, 51–52, 57, 356, 378
  and Iraq war, 161–62, 424
Russia, 269, 321, 467–68, 481, 486

Safire, William, 393
Saleh, Ali Abdullah, 315–16
Sanders, Bernie, 337, 449, 497
Sandy Hook Elementary School, 454, 459
Saudi Arabia, 40, 162–63, 315, 321, 477, 480–81
Saw, 176–78
Schambelan, Elizabeth, 191–92, 194
Schumer, Chuck, 194–96
Secret Service, 83–85
secular stagnation, 283–84, 286
semiconductor industry, 471–72
September 11, 2001, attacks, xxv, 79, 185, 231, 263, 465
  hijackers of, 128, 162, 306, 425, 477
  media coverage of, 3–10, 16–20, 24–27, 33–36, 40–41
Shah, Tarik, 146–50
Shapira, Harel, 303–5
Silicon Valley, 53, 332, 383, 405–6, 411
  and national security, 386, 388–89, 392, 395–97, 416
Silverstein, Larry, 110–11, 114
Simcox, Chris, 301–2
Singer, P. W., 55–56
Slate, 367
Sleeper Cell, 205
Slotkin, Richard, 13, 28, 193–95
Smith, Walter I., 192–93
Snowden, Edward, 224–25, 382, 384, 399, 427
social media, 346, 348, 353, 406–13
  and protests, 328, 432, 443
Somalia, 77, 221, 293, 375
Sontag, Susan, 289, 349–53, 365, 374
Soviet Union, 155, 202, 243, 257, 430
Spencer, Robert, 324
Stalin, Joseph, 211–12
Standing Rock, 489–90, 492
Stephanopoulos, George, 41, 424
Steve Madden, 99–100
suicide bombers, 39, 85, 204, 293, 326–27, 463
  and mass shootings, 454, 456–57

Sullivan, Andrew, 350, 364–66, 379, 468
Super Bowl, 83–85, 96–99, 107–9
superheroes, 44–47, 59–62
Supreme Court, 187, 216, 368, 375–76
surplus population, 286–88, 292–94, 299,
    310, 314, 477–78
    in U.S., 407, 439–40
surveillance, 117, 388, 393–94, 451, 466,
    493
    under Barack Obama, 224–26
    of Muslim and Arab Americans, 141,
        157–59, 400
    in public spaces, 119–20, 404–5, 407,
        411–12, 414
    and Silicon Valley, 391–92, 395–96, 407,
        414, 416
    technology, 52, 54
    and transparency, 427
Syria, 49, 319, 371, 375, 464, 475
    civil war in, 315–16, 320–22
    and Islamic State, 327
    refugees of, 322–24, 326

Taiwan, 471–72
Talent, James, 187
Taliban, xx, 38, 54–55, 163, 221
    in Kabul, xxii, 129, 223–24, 463–64
Tancredo, Tom, 308
Tapper, Jake, 385
Taylor, Astra, 437
Tea Party, 44, 227
tech bubble (2000), 53, 98, 330–33
technology industry, 389–90, 395–96,
    482–83
    and military, 52–56, 72, 297, 386, 388,
        392
teenagers, 407–15
television, 173–78, 205, 207–8
Terán, Manuel "Tortuguita," 491
Texas, 130, 205, 309, 325, 383
Thiel, Peter, 392
Tillman, Pat, 62–64, 66–67
Titanpointe, 382–83
Tocqueville, Alexis de, 343–45
Torres, Saeed "Shariff," 146–49
torture, 181–87, 188–89, 194–97, 423, 428,
    451, 493
    ban of, 216, 219, 226, 253
    criticism of, 191, 208
    in movies, 173–74, 176–78

Torture Memos, 183, 220, 423,
    428
transparency, xxiv, 93, 115, 224, 255,
    426–27
Transportation Security Administration
    (TSA), 88–95
Trillin, Calvin, 93–94
Trump, Donald, 134, 371, 380, 427–29,
    462–65, 479
    and Black Lives Matter, 449
    and China, 469, 471–72
    and "fake news," 346, 348
    and "Muslim ban," 323
    and elections, xxiii–xxiv, 418–20, 475,
        477
Tunisia, 315–16, 323–24
Turkey, 321, 375
24 (TV drama), xxvi, 174–78, 185,
    206–7
Twin Towers, 8, 23, 36, 43, 125, 172
    bombing (1993), 113
    replacing, 110–12, 126
Twitter, 328, 346, 406, 412–13, 437

Ukraine, 269, 467–69, 486
undocumented migrants, 306, 309–11,
    325–26
unemployment, 98, 266–67, 285–87, 294,
    299, 327
    and housing crisis, 335–36
United Nations (U.N.), 83, 287, 318, 424,
    426, 474
    and Colin Powell, 357–59
    Security Council, 150, 319, 371
Updike, John, 206
U.S. Border Patrol, 302, 307, 309,
    312
U.S. Customs and Border Protection
    (CBP), 307–9, 312–14
U.S. Department of Defense, xix, xxi, 54,
    60, 187, 401–3
    and Silicon Valley, 392
    1033 Program, 444, 490
U.S. Department of Homeland Security,
    307, 312, 388, 435–36
U.S. Federal Reserve, 99–100, 253, 329–31,
    333, 434
U.S. Green Berets, 47, 57, 78, 222
U.S. Immigration and Customs Enforce-
    ment (ICE), 308–9, 312, 325

U.S. Immigration and Naturalization
    Service, 306–7
U.S. Marines, 56, 81, 421, 444
U.S. military, 47–48, 50, 51–64, 72–75,
    187, 297–99
  and Abu Ghraib, 166–73, 178–82, 191,
    195–97
  spending, 262, 280, 452, 484
U.S. National Security Agency (NSA),
    224–25, 392, 407, 417
  and mass surveillance, 382–84, 394–401,
    415–16
U.S. Special Forces, xxi, 47, 62–64, 69, 183,
    297
  accountability of, 428–29
  in Afghanistan, 51, 54
  news coverage of, 56–59

veterans, 66, 69–73, 75, 129, 239, 281
  on border patrol, 308
  and Minuteman Project, 302–4
Vietnam War, 48, 67, 193, 195, 338,
    465–66
  and shame, 51, 69–70
vigilantism, 45, 129, 131, 302–4, 308–10
Vines, Jerry, 189–90

Wall Street Journal, The, 19–20, 362, 374
Walter Reed National Military Medical
    Center, 70–72
war crimes, xxix, 422, 424, 426–27, 474
Warnecke, John Carl, 381
Warner, John, 34
wars of aggression, xxix, 428, 467–68
war on terror, 11–13, 101, 129, 142,
    161–66, 262
  criticisms of, 132, 164–65
  as different, 47—48, 187–88, 193
  end of, 464, 467
  failure of, 239–40
  and fantasies, 61, 64, 73–75, 297
  reasons for, 268, 284, 288–289, 291–93
  rebranding, 220, 226
  and religious war, 190–91
War Powers Resolution, 372–73, 466, 484
Washington, D.C., 40, 118, 125, 127, 383,
    395–96
  protests in, 161, 345, 446–48

Washington, Harold, 214–15
Washington Post, The, 37, 70, 167, 220,
    348, 419–20
weapons of mass destruction (WMDs),
    145, 161, 239, 355—59, 361,
    363
Webster, William, 34
Weil, Simone, 461
Weinstein, Harvey, 432
West Point, 191–92, 194
Where Is Raed? (Salam), 247
whistleblowing, 224, 382, 399,
    427
White, Don, 73–75
white supremacy, 110, 130, 446
Whittington, Harry, 420–21
Wieseltier, Leon, 363
Willeford, Pam, 420
Wilson, Darren, 438, 440, 442–43
wiretaps, 388, 394–95, 398
women, 13–16, 27–28, 31, 37, 101–2, 218,
    431–32
World Bank, 275, 311
World Trade Center, 6–7, 21, 55, 210,
    263
  and Cordoba House, 227–29
  as public space, 117, 120
  rebuilt, 111–12, 115–17
World War I, 56, 482
World War II, 64, 67, 81, 99–100, 275,
    482
Wounded Knee, 490
Wuterich, Frank, 421

Yahoo, 390, 396
Yemen, xxviii, 299, 315, 425, 486,
    374–75
  drone strikes in, xxii, 77, 221, 243, 426,
    475
Yglesias, Matthew, 364, 366, 369, 452–53
Yoo, John, 393, 395, 429
  and Torture Memos, 181, 183, 186, 220,
    423, 428
YouTube, 328, 396

Zakaria, Fareed, 371
Zimmerman, George, 431, 438
Zuckerberg, Mark, 411

ABOUT THE AUTHOR

Richard Beck is a writer at *n+1* and the author of *We Believe the Children: A Moral Panic in the 1980s.* He lives in New York City.